**Patricia Unterman's
Food Lover's Guide to San Francisco**

PATRICIA UNTERMAN'S

Food Lover's Guide to San Francisco

2ND EDITION

PHOTOGRAPHS BY BARBARA LUCAS

CHRONICLE BOOKS
SAN FRANCISCO

FOR TIM AND HARRY

Text copyright © 1997 by Patricia Unterman.
Photographs copyright © 1995 by Barbara Lucas.
All rights reserved. No part of this book may be reproduced in any form without written permission from the publisher.

Printed in the United States of America.

ISBN 0-8118-1723-7

Library of Congress Cataloging-in-Publication Data available.

Cover design: Margery Cantor & Michael Carabetta
Text design & composition: Margery Cantor
Cover illustration: John Mattos
Maps: Ellen McElhinny

Distributed in Canada by Raincoast Books, 8680 Cambie Street, Vancouver, B.C. V6P 6M9

10 9 8 7 6 5 4 3 2 1

Chronicle Books
85 Second Street
San Francisco, CA 94105

Web Site: www.chronbooks.com

ACKNOWLEDGMENTS

This book is the product of over twenty years of reviewing restaurants, shopping, and cooking in the Bay Area with maniacal passion. Many, many, many thanks go to Tim Savinar, who trouped with me everywhere, and to Harry Savinar, who grew up in restaurants.

Niloufer Ichaporia King gleefully trekked through every ethnic market and neighborhood with me and graciously contributed endless time and knowledge. Anne Haskell, my former cooking partner at Hayes Street Grill, collected and worked wonders on many of the recipes. Special thanks to Laurie MacKenzie, an expert on the Mission and Latin American culinary arts; Yoko Tahara, my guide to Japantown; Yanek and Mary Chiu for my Chinese cultural education during hundreds of meals in Chinese restaurants here and abroad; Bruce Cost for his unfailing generosity and expertise on San Francisco's Chinatown; Lin and Kien Nguyen for Vietnamese shopping and eating; Gordon Wing for his help with Oakland's Chinatown; Stephen Singer, Bruce Cass, Pam Heminway-Wilder, and Denise Lurton Moulle for their expertise on wine and wineshops; Tim Savinar for his intimate knowledge of bars (though his list would have been different); Barbara Mendelsohn for her insight into Pacific Heights and everything else in life; and Howard Karel and Sue Moore for their willingness to go anywhere, anytime. Special appreciation to Alice Waters for advice, teachings, a lot of great meals together, and a higher vision. Thanks to Paul Johnson and Andy Powning for making the fish and produce charts; Bobbie Lucas for her upbeat energy and images; to Laura Shapiro for advice on writing and a trip to India; Wendy Lesser for help with the introduction; cartographer Ellen McElhinny for her handsome maps and great good nature; and big thanks to Paula Tevis, the best editor and assistant a writer could have.

Special thanks go the kitchen crew at the Hayes Street Grill for their unfailing support and generosity over the years, and to my partner Dick Sander, whose humanity and sense of fun teach me to keep things in perspective.

—Patricia Unterman
February 1997

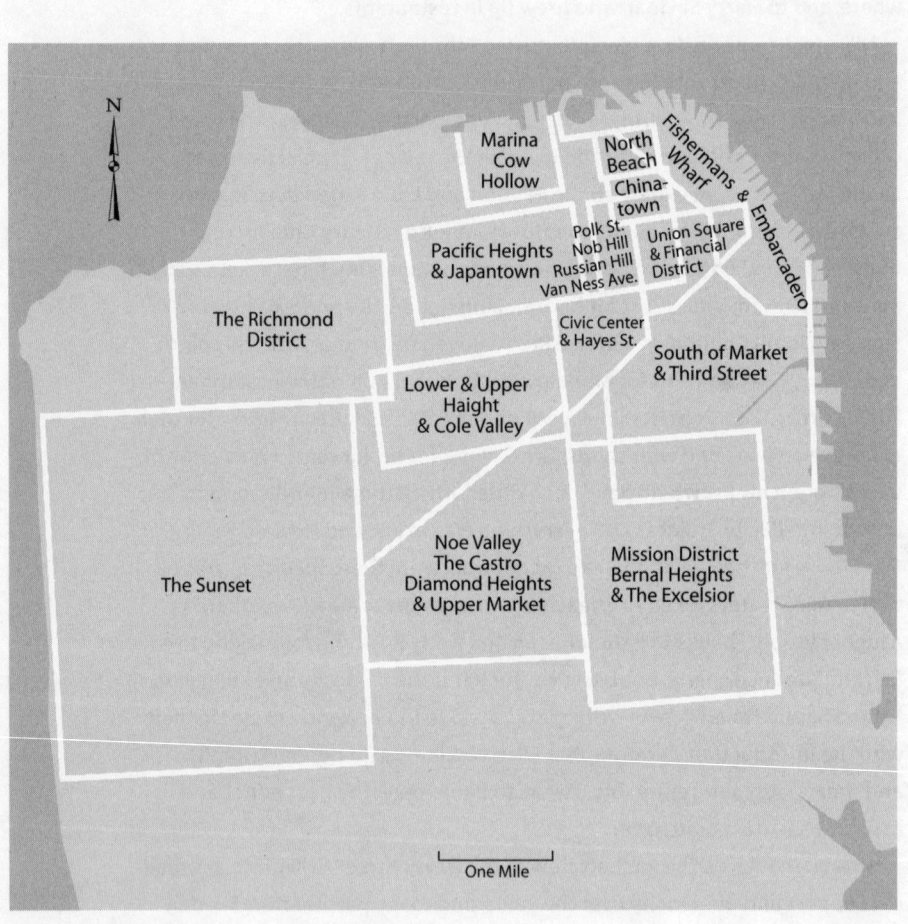

CONTENTS

Introduction 9

About the Categories 13

Seasonal Fish Chart 20

Seasonal Produce Chart 25

The Neighborhoods

   Chinatown   **31**

   Civic Center & Hayes Valley   **63**

   Embarcadero & Fisherman's Wharf   **89**

   Financial District & Union Square   **119**

   Lower & Upper Haight, Cole Valley   **159**

   The Marina & Cow Hollow   **181**

   The Mission District, Bernal Heights & the Excelsior   **205**

   Noe Valley, the Castro, Diamond Heights & Upper Market   **243**

   North Beach   **263**

   Pacific Heights & Japantown   **301**

   Polk Street, Nob Hill, Russian Hill & Van Ness Avenue   **335**

   The Richmond District   **363**

   South of Market & Third Street   **393**

   The Sunset District   **421**

Out of Town   **451**

   The East Bay   **457**

   Marin County   **501**

   The Wine Country of Napa & Sonoma   **525**

Restaurant Indexes

    Restaurants   553

    Cuisine   555

    Price   558

    Food Service at Counter or Bar   560

    Food Service after 10 p.m.   561

    Breakfast or Weekend Brunch   561

    Outdoor Seating   562

    Child-friendly   562

    Banquet Room   563

    Of Historic Interest   563

Specialty Indexes

    Bakeries/Pastries   564

    Bars   564

    Cafes   565

    Cheese   565

    Coffee   565

    Cookware and Books   565

    Delicatessens/Take-Out   566

    Ethnic Markets   566

    Fish   566

    Ice Cream/Chocolates   567

    Markets   567

    Meat and Poultry   567

    Produce   567

    Wines and Spirits   568

    Recipes   568

    Sidebars   568

Alphabetical Index   569

INTRODUCTION

The *Food Lover's Guide to San Francisco* was written both for visitors and for residents who want to explore the culinary landscape of their own city. Anyone who loves to travel knows the value of a guidebook that dovetails with his or her own passions and sensibilities. An intuitive writer can open up a seemingly impenetrable place and foster a deeper level of understanding and pleasure. Some travelers I know argue that arriving cold in a new place, completely open to any adventure, is provocative, but this argument does not convince me. If we travel to expand our senses and broaden our minds, then setting off unprepared and untutored lessens the scope of our experience. I like to know in advance where to find the qualitative best—especially when it comes to my personal passion, food—and I'm willing to go to the ends of the earth for a taste of the extraordinary.

These thoughts ran through my mind as I was sitting outside a small but famous coffeehouse in Rome called St. Eustachio, drinking the best caffè latte in the world. What if I had gone to Rome and missed this coffee? It wouldn't have been a disaster (you don't know what you haven't tasted), but I shudder to think about it. I went to St. Eustachio on the advice of an émigré Roman whose taste I trust, and whom I interrogated before I left home. As a result, my sense memory of Rome has been changed forever. I went to this cafe every morning and had not one, but two of these coffees, and I can still taste them, so strong, so rich, so sweet, so fragrant. Now I have a new standard by which I judge every other coffee, for better or worse.

For the last twenty years I have been developing my sense of taste as a restaurant critic (fifteen years at the *San Francisco Chronicle* and at magazines before that), and as a cook both at home and in San Francisco at the Hayes Street Grill. But what I really am is an eater, someone who loves food of every kind, but with an almost obsessive discrimination. Such openness combined with unrelenting critical consciousness seems like a paradox; being a connoisseur suggests a narrowing of taste. But eating something gorgeous, humble or high as it may be, floods me with pleasure. Looking for sensuous food has been an unending quest. I admit it: I eat, therefore I am. Sounds frivolous (I can hear Descartes turning over in his grave), but by extension, I taste, I buy, I cook, I feed, I nourish to enrich the lives of the people around me and, taking this line a step farther, I support the causes that nourish every human being. As far as I can see, the better the eating, the happier the person, if even for a moment. My idea of a better world pretty much hinges on wanting all people to have a good meal when they are hungry.

Since I am an enthusiastic user of guidebooks myself, I thought I would contribute to the genre from my own little piece of the earth, San Francisco and environs, and pattern it after a book that has been the source of hundreds of wonderful eating experiences for me, Patricia Wells's *The Food Lover's Guide to Paris* (Workman). Reading that guidebook and plotting a course from it sends a thrill down my spine, second to actually being in Paris. Wells writes about not only restaurants in every neighborhood, but bakeries, cheese stores, butchers, open markets, and the whole complicated tree of French culinary life, with an intelligent, personal, sensual voice. I can only hope to come close.

I am not sure I could have written a similar survey of San Francisco, or any American city (except New York), ten years ago because there simply wasn't that much to write about. Our Bay Area culinary resources have grown over the three decades I have been surveying them, however, and now I firmly believe that Northern California represents the most exciting and energetic food system in America—indeed, one that is equal to any in the world.

While Paris, Rome, and Hong Kong may be meccas for great eating, San Francisco has become a culinary crossroads where ethnic cooks and ingredients, especially from Asia, enrich our own indigenous products and cooking style. The mild Northern California climate supports an enormous variety of fruits, vegetables, and herbs. Our location on the edge of the Pacific assures a supply of fresh seafood. The cool fog and protected hills and valleys make for promising wine country. But even more interesting has been the development of artisan producers, some of whom have learned from European techniques, others who use traditional American methods to get a superior product. We have a vital organic farming movement here, not only in produce but in meat, poultry, and dairy, and an efficient distribution system that delivers these foods to consumers. Furthermore, the Bay Area has become a large enough market to support importation from all over the world. The products we don't make ourselves we fly in. This bounty attracts an ever more sophisticated food community and an influx of people who come here to eat, work, and live within it. San Franciscans never cry about coming home from a trip. They have too many pleasures right here.

A NOTE ABOUT THE SECOND EDITION

When Chronicle Books called about updating the *Food Lover's Guide* a mere two years after I turned in the first manuscript, I thought they were jumping the gun. First of all, the original book had been a monumental piece of work and I was just recovering. Secondly, I had started reviewing restaurants again for the *San Francisco Examiner* and writing columns about local ingredients for their Wednesday food section. Also, I had begun publishing my own newsletter, *Unterman on Food,* a bimonthly compilation of my current writings on eating in the Bay Area and beyond (see the last page of this book). So I felt the topic was pretty much covered, at least for my most diligent readers.

But then I started thumbing through the book. Quite a few places had closed while a new crop of interesting new places had opened. Of course I had chronicled many of them in the *Examiner*, but there were others that I thought serious eaters should know about. Before I knew it, I was deep into revisiting and revising, walking the neighborhoods and marveling at the mouthwatering diversity of our Bay Area dining out scene. So here are my latest finds, evaluations, and a set of neighborhood maps that I hope will be helpful for visitors, all in the spirit of encouraging people to eat well as often as they can.

—San Francisco, 1997

ABOUT THE CATEGORIES

Even I was surprised by the ethnic diversity of the city as I started marching through the market streets of each neighborhood. The discovery of new ingredients (new at least to me), made me want to cook with them, and many meals were inspired by finds from my wanderings. Hence the recipes along the side of the pages. Also along the side are tidbits of information that relate to the neighborhoods or to products.

The book is divided into chapters that explore loosely drawn neighborhoods in the city plus some important centers of good eating outside the city. While not every one of the following categories is represented in every chapter, the restaurants always are, because they, more than any other culinary institution, excite our desire to explore.

RESTAURANTS

Each chapter starts with a very personal selection of restaurants that I have enjoyed over the years for one reason or another. Sometimes a restaurant is included because it makes one dish I adore, or because it provides a useful service to its neighborhood, or because it feels good to be sitting in it. A very few have been included because of the importance of their role in the city's dining-out consciousness (though not necessarily mine), and I felt I had to say a few words about them. You'll just have to read the entries. Unlike Zagat and newspaper reviews, I am not providing a rating service. The very fact that a restaurant appears in the book means that it is interesting and the entries tell why. After fifteen years of assigning stars and thereby pigeonholing restaurants against my inclinations, these writings come from the heart. Something has grabbed me in all of these places.

There are so many restaurants in the city now that you almost don't need to reserve in advance, especially if you go at a slightly off hour. The weekends can be tougher at the most popular dinner houses, but unlike many European restaurants that will not seat you without a booking, whether they're full or not, San Francisco restaurants want to find you a table. Even without reservations, it never hurts to drop by if you can be flexible. Some parties don't show up for their tables, maddening and discourteous behavior though it is, which allows the maître d' to fit you in. The American appetite tends to be spontaneous (unlike that of Europeans, who all eat at certain hours), and many restaurants cater to this free-spirited dining by serving at the bar, cocktail tables, and counters. You can get a good taste of expensive restaurants without spending an arm and a leg by ordering a glass of wine and a few appetizers from a perch at the bar. This impromptu seating also works nicely if you are eating alone. In San Francisco's competitive atmosphere, restaurants want only to accommodate.

CAFES

You can always get something to eat in coffeehouses in San Francisco, but the food service is usually informal, requiring you to order at a counter. Some cafes put out stunning snacks, sandwiches, and light fare, but the draw of cafes is that you can sit, think, talk, write, or read over a beautifully made cup of coffee.

BARS

What are these doing in a food lover's guide? Ask my husband, who considers an ice-cold martini or a perfectly balanced margarita swirled in ice and served "up" as important sustenance. Many bars do serve food, but they are included in this category for their pub identities—their buzz—not their kitchens.

DELICATESSENS/TAKE-OUT

With more and more members of the household working, and little time left for shopping and cooking, a good delicatessen can be a godsend. Semi-prepared food requiring a minimum of last-minute cooking can greatly improve a meal served at home. The best delicatessens, no matter what their ethnic origins, prepare or import foods that are difficult to make at home, even if you had the time. How many of us have the equipment or patience to air-dry Peking duck, cold-smoke salmon, or make fresh sausages? Delicatessens also sell food to eat on the spot, though usually there are no places in the stores to sit.

BAKERIES/PASTRIES

Does the tremendous proliferation of bread bakers relate somehow to the demise of the pastry shop? Are people turning away from cake to eat bread? I think so, as evidenced by the scores of different kinds of fresh breads delivered to stores from bakeries all over the Bay Area, many of which have their own retail outlets. Of course, San Francisco has had a long tradition as the sourdough bread capital, and few artifacts represent San Francisco to the world as vividly as a crusty, chewy loaf. Several historic sourdough bakeries crank out thousands of fresh loaves every morning, having bought up many of the smaller operations, so those left remain vital.

Pastry shops, on the other hand, struggle. Perhaps because restaurants have such strong pastry kitchens, people eat their desserts out and don't buy them for home. Pastries are so labor-intensive and perishable that shops almost can't charge enough to stay in business and put out a good product.

ICE CREAM/CHOCOLATES

The ice cream parlor is disappearing like the pastry shop, and even simple ice cream scooperies seem to be diminishing. There are no great ones like Bertillon in Paris or Vivoli in Florence. San Franciscans buy their ice cream in the supermarkets and eat it at home. We have some wonderful local chocolate makers, though these, too, are under siege. The one-item specialty store depends so much on location, and location can be so expensive, that running a specialized operation becomes a precarious balancing act. Chocolates can be found in gourmet food halls in department stores and other outlets, allowing the chocolatiers to expand their production.

MARKETS

I have seen Russians cry at the bounty in American supermarkets. They cannot believe that so much food can be under one roof, waiting to be piled into carts. As convenient and tempting as supermarkets may be, I find that I shop in them less and less. I turn to specialty stores, Chinatown stores, and farmers' markets for fresh food, and try to use paper products and disposable goods as little as possible. To meet the challenge, the supermarkets try to be all things to all people. They have large deli counters, cheese sections, and their own bakeries. But too often the quality level is so low that the food is not worth buying even at the cheapest prices. The rock-hard warehoused fruit in towering pyramids in the produce department is tasteless, and the shelves are filled with over-packaged processed food, often quite expensive, that almost is not really food at all. The good general markets included in this book make an effort to carry better fresh food and more of it than the gigantic chains. They often have independent butchers and carry some organic produce and meats. They take daily deliveries from local bread bakeries and local dairies, and feature goods from small producers.

ETHNIC MARKETS

Many of the items I buy at ethnic markets are essential for my general pantry, necessary to the eclectic cooking style so many of us have developed over years of travel and ethnic eating. Visits to these markets are as close as you can get to a trip to another country, and a pastime that I find stimulating. Seeing the juxtaposition of ingredients and figuring out what to do with them puts me in a mood to cook. Ethnic markets often have a deli component that makes them invaluable if you've decided to cook an exotic meal and you don't quite know how to prepare everything.

PRODUCE

If any kind of shopping has blossomed over the last five years, it has been produce. Invigorated by the influx of Cantonese, then Vietnamese immigrants who buy, grow, and sell a huge variety of vegetables and herbs, and by the increasing demand for organic produce, availability and quality improves every year. People get turned on to fabulous tomatoes or sautéed pea shoots in restaurants and want to get their hands on them. Organic produce has moved from natural foods stores (still the major outlet for them) into general produce stores and even onto some supermarket shelves. Farmers' markets have proliferated so that almost every local community has one. Our growing season is year round, so even winter markets have wonderful things. As our diet shifts toward eating more fruits, vegetables, and grains, farmers and retailers are rising to the occasion, bringing greater and greater variety to the market.

MEAT AND POULTRY

The personalized butcher counter is making a comeback even as people turn to eating less meat. When they do, they want smaller and fussier cuts for use in recipes in which the meat is not the main ingredient. Organic beef and small farm–raised pork and lamb are more and more in demand. Everyone has gone chicken crazy, and the production of these birds has become specialized with the popularity of more flavorful, relatively free-range birds at a peak. Cooks are discovering quail, poussin, squab, pheasant, and other smaller birds, and the best shops are carrying them. Chinatown has always sold more flavorful chickens and birds of every sort, but specialty poultry is nudging red meat over to the side in butcher cases.

FISH

Even though people are eating more and more fish in restaurants, they don't cook it at home. I don't know which comes first, the paucity of good fish markets or the lack of retail demand, but finding pristine fish remains a challenge. Chinese fish markets are an excellent source for fresh fish, but you have to know what you're doing. The smell emanating from the fish departments in supermarkets is enough to make you walk by quickly, and very few butchers know how to buy and handle fish and shellfish. The fact is that there are only two or three non-Asian fish markets in the whole Bay Area that I trust.

CHEESE

Cheese is everywhere but great cheese almost nowhere. Like every small specialty shop, the independent cheese store faces the two-headed dragon of perishability and small purchases. Though some supermarkets have huge cheese sections, the cheese suffers from mass buying and indifferent handling, the same way produce does. We have one great cheese store in the Bay Area and a lot of places like delicatessens and natural foods stores where you dependably can find a favorite cheese.

WINE AND SPIRITS

The small, personally run wineshop is under siege from discounters, just the way the independent bookstores are from huge chains. The market for high-end wines seems to be softening as a generation of collectors in their late forties and fifties realize that they have to start drinking up if they are to outlive their cellars, and potential young buyers seem to be in love with beer. Even so, we have some famous, groundbreaking importers in the Bay Area with some retail outlets for their interesting wines, and the abundant supply of excellent West Coast wines keeps wine shelves full everywhere. As this book is geared toward the qualitative, I include the wineshops where the service, understanding, and knowledge of wine lead patrons to unusual and well-made bottles from all over the world.

COOKWARE AND BOOKS

Cookware chain stores and small cookware shops are everywhere in the Bay Area, but my favorites are Asian, stocked to the rafters with handsome crockery and elegant cooking utensils for a song. Every Asian market street has one or two "Kitchen Friends," and I have stocked my cupboard at them with a bazaar's worth of unmatched pieces, all of which miraculously seem to go together as needed. As for cookbooks, the best ones hold up over time, making used cookbook sections in bookstores a valuable resource. The Bay Area's best independent bookstores often have a broad selection of both new and used books, although the two bookstores that were dedicated to cookbooks alone have closed, alas.

INDEXES

By using the indexes you can scan quickly all the recommended bakeries, butchers, coffeehouses, and so forth in the individual subject listings. Restaurants are cross-referenced alphabetically by nationality and by price, among other groupings. But my main impetus was to explore the city neighborhood by neighborhood, so that if you found yourself in a certain part of town you'd immediately know where the good food is.

My companion and guide during much of the research, food anthropologist Niloufer Ichaporia King, told me that when she visits her eighty-two-year-old mother in Bombay, her greatest pleasure is starting a walk in the middle of the city and wending her way outwards through layers of neighborhood, observing, tasting, smelling, buying this and that as she goes. I have done that with this city on a spontaneous basis over the years, one spot leading to another, but with this book my research became more methodical. People who like to visit parks, monuments, and museums to get a feel for a city have the Michelin Guide. For those of us who learn about culture through food, this book should be of some help.

FISH AND SHELLFISH

	JAN	FEB	MAR
Angler (Monkfish) (East Coast)	x	x	
Cabezon, Rockfish, Lingcod (local)	x	x	x
Catfish (aquaculture)	x	x	x
True cod (East Coast, Alaska)	x	x	x
Flounder, Petrale (local)	x	x	x
Pacific halibut (local, hook & line)			
Northern halibut (Alaska, Canada, East Coast)	x	x	x
Mahi-mahi (both hemispheres)	x	x	x
True snappers (opaka, onaga, Gulf snapper)			
Salmon (local)			
King salmon (Alaskan)	x	x	x
Sand dabs, rex sole (local)	x	x	x
White sea bass (Channel Islands)			
Swordfish (California)			
Swordfish (Hawaiian)	x	x	x
Trout (aquaculture)	x	x	x

AVAILABLE IN THE BAY AREA

APR	MAY	JUNE	JULY	AUG	SEPT	OCT	NOV	DEC
							x	x
x	x	x	x	x	x	x	x	x
x	x	x	x	x	x	x	x	x
							x	x
							x	x
		x	x	x	x	x		
x	x	x	x	x	x	x	x	x
		x	x	x	x			x
		x	x	x	x	x	x	
	x	x	x	x	x			
								x
x	x	x			x	x	x	x
		x	x	x	x			
				x	x	x		
							x	x
x	x	x	x	x	x	x	x	x

FISH AND SHELLFISH

	JAN	FEB	MAR
Tuna (both hemispheres)	X	X	X
Spearfish, ono (Hawaii)	X	X	X
Opah (local)			
Dungeness crab (local)	X	X	X
Blue crab (East Coast)	X	X	X
Lobster (East Coast)			
Mussels (Northeast)	X	X	X
Oysters	X	X	X
Scallops (East Coast)	X	X	X
Spot shrimp (Santa Barbara)	X	X	X
White shrimp (Florida, North Carolina)			
Squid (Monterey)			
Squid (San Pedro)	X	X	X
Manila clams (Pacific Northwest)	X	X	X
Spiny lobster (Pacific)	X		
Crawfish (Louisiana, Oregon)			

APR	MAY	JUNE	JULY	AUG	SEPT	OCT	NOV	DEC
			x	x	x	x	x	x
						x	x	x
				x	x	x		
x	x						x	x
x	x	x	x	x	x	x	x	x
				x	x	x	x	x
x					x	x	x	x
x					x	x	x	x
					x	x	x	x
						x	x	x
x	x	x	x	x	x	x	x	
	x	x	x	x	x	x	x	x
x								
x	x				x	x	x	x
							x	x
x	x	x	x	x	x	x		

(from Paul Johnson, The Monterey Fish Company)

SEASONAL PRODUCE CHART

A MONTHLY LISTING OF FRUITS AND VEGETABLES

This list focuses on California-grown produce at its best, which is at the beginning of its growing season, although many items are available over a period of months or year round. Everything listed here should be available at farmers' markets or in good produce stores. Please note that growing areas do change from year to year, though the towns listed in parentheses have been primary sources for particular crops over the past several years. An asterisk indicates a personal favorite.

JANUARY

Arugula, mizuna, baby red mustard (Bolinas)
Savoy cabbage (Pescadero)
Baby bok choy, Napa cabbage, Lemongrass (Fresno)
Baby turnips, White Rose and red Irish potatoes,
    Bloomsdale spinach (Clovis)
Purple cauliflower, (Esparto)
Seville oranges (Porterville)
Meyer lemons, allspice tangerines, Page and Kinnow
    mandarins, Lavender Gem tangerines (Fallbrook)
Mooro blood oranges, kumquats (San Diego)

FEBRUARY

Carrots, turnips, fennel, leeks, gold, red, and Chiogga
    beets (Watsonville)
Green garlic (Santa Cruz, Bolinas, Guinda)
Choy sum, baby gai choy, gai lan (Gilroy)
Yellowfoot mushrooms (north and central California coast)
Chandler strawberries* (Santa Maria)

Rangpur limes (Santa Cruz)
Pomelos, Minneola tangelos* (Fallbrook)

MARCH

Baby lettuces, mâche, pain du sucre chicory, lavender and chive blossoms (Watsonville, Sonoma)
Treviso radicchio, Catalognia chicory (Guinda)
Young escarole, red and green chard (Pescadero)
Flambeau and Easter Egg radishes, salad Savoy (Santa Maria)
Dandelion greens (Bolinas, Watsonville)
Mustard greens (Capay)
Sorrel (Escondito, Guinda)
Navel oranges (Livermore)
Star Ruby grapefruit, Fortune and Dancy tangerines (Fallbrook)
Rhubarb, hothouse grown (Oregon, Washington state)

APRIL

Asparagus* (Delta)
English shelling peas,* sugar snap peas (Half Moon Bay)
New-crop Haas avocados* (Southern California)
Spring bulbing onions with tops, snow peas (Fresno)
Fiddlehead ferns, morel mushrooms (Pacific Northwest)
Japanese cucumbers, scented and opal basils (Watsonville)
Fava beans (Stockton)
Baby summer squashes, baby corn, baby Japanese eggplant (Selma, Vista)
Chervil, red Russian kale (Pescadero)
Meyer lemons (Fallbrook, Santa Cruz)

MAY

Young yellow wax, Blue Lake, haricots verts (Vista)
Red onions, green almonds, loquats, Thai basil (Fresno)
New-crop creamer,* Bintji, yellow Finn, ruby crescent potatoes (Guinda)
Summer squash, red and gold zucchini, crookneck, sunburst, pattypan (Fresno, Santa Rosa)

Tartarian, Rainier, Bing* cherries (Suisun, Santa Clara,
    Gilroy, Smith Flat)
Royal Blenheim apricots* (Winters, Brentwood)
Cantaloupe (Imperial Valley)
Valencia oranges (Fallbrook)
Local field-grown rhubarb (Pescadero)
Red and black currants (Sebastapol)

JUNE

Early Girl tomatoes* (Coachella)
Sweet 100 and Sungold cherry tomatoes (Capay, Winters)
German fingerling and red potatoes, pickling cucumbers
    (Bolinas, Fresno)
Baby Blue Lake beans* (Palo Alto)
Romano beans (Fresno)
Walla Walla onions (Washington)
Sea beans, or pousse pied, a seashore succulent (Oregon)
Red and white fraises du bois, red and gold raspberries
    (Watsonville)
Ollalieberries (Stockton, Fresno)
Boysenberries, loganberries (Winters, Palo Alto)
Montmorency sour pie cherries (Smith Flat, Placerville)
Santa Rosa plums,* Firebrite* and White Snow Queen
    nectarines, peaches, including Red Haven, Babcock,
    Regina, and Early O'Henry* varieties (Brentwood, Fresno)
Green Perlette seedless grapes (Delano)
Yellow and red watermelon (Imperial Valley)

JULY

White, yellow and bicolored* corn (Brentwood)
Heirloom tomatoes, including Golden Jubilee, Yellow Taxi,
    Brandywine, Green Zebra, Marvel Stripe, Great White,
    Purple Calabash and yellow and red plum and pear
    cherry tomatoes (Capay, Palo Alto, Winters, Davenport,
    Healdsburg)
New-crop red Italian garlic* (Pescadero)
Long beans, Armenian,* Jordanian, and lemon cucumbers
    (Capay, Stockton)

SEASONAL PRODUCE

Jacobs Cattle, Lima,* speckled butter, fresh cranberry* and
French horticultural shelling beans, Black-eyed and
Crowder peas, okra (Fresno, Watsonville)
Garlic chives, summer savory (Pescadero, Bolinas)
Plums, including Wickson, elephant heart, Satsuma,* and
Mariposa varieties (Placerville, Vacaville, Santa Rosa)
Red and green Thompson seedless grapes, Champagne
grapes (Fresno)
Wild blackberries* (Sonoma)
Italian butter pears (Walnut Grove)
Asian pears (Brentwood, Sebastopol, Guinda)
Melons, including Charentais, Sharlyn,* Crenshaw,
ambrosia,* pink and green honeydew (Guinda, Fallbrook,
Brentwood)
Gravenstein apples* (Sebastopol)
Blueberries* (Oregon)

AUGUST

Chanterelles* (Oregeon)
Peppers and chilies, including red, green, gold, and yellow
bell, jalapeño, serrano, long hot sweets, cubanelle,
Aconcagua, corno di toro,* Gypsy, cheesecake,* and lipstick
pimientos (Stockton, Winters, Fresno)
Red torpedo onions (Capay, Stockton)
Globe, Chinese, and Japanese eggplant (Fresno)
Figs: black Mission,* Kadota, Adriatic, and brown Turkey
(Stockton, Maywood, Chico)
Bartlett pears (Lakeport)
Italian and French* prune plums (Vacaville)
French butter pears* (Walnut Grove)
Concord, Italian Muscat grapes (Fresno)
MacIntosh, Mutsu, Jonathan apples (Sebastopol, Capay)

SEPTEMBER

Pumpkins, including Sugar pie, Baby Bear, White
Cheesequake, French Red; winter squash, including
delicata, sweet dumpling, red kuri, buttercup, butternut,
acorn, blue Hubbard, banana, hokaido (California)
Red* and white* Belgian endive (Santa Rosa)

Brussels sprouts (Pescadero, Half Moon Bay)
Tomatillos (Capay, Stockton)
Red, gold, and white pearl onions (Central California)
Chestnuts (Northern and Central California)
Cape gooseberries (Graton)
Pineapple quince (Stockton, Santa Rosa, Reedly)
Granny Smith, Rhode Island Greening, Ozark, Hawaiian
   Gold, Rome Beauty, Orange Cox pippin, Royal Gala,* and
   Fuji* apples (Smith Flat, Sebastopol, Capay, Redding)
Huckleberries* (Oregon, Northern California)
Seckel, Comice, and Bosc pears (Northern and Central
   California)
Pomegranates (Dinuba, Stockton, Woodland)
Medjool and khadrawi dates (Walnut Grove, Coachella)
Varietal grapes including Chardonnay, Pinot Noir,
   Sauvignon Blanc, Gamay Beaujolais, Zinfandel (Napa)

OCTOBER

Small loose artichokes,* fennel (Watsonville)
Many greens including red and green* chard, spinach,
   collard, kale (Central Coast)
Celery root (Fremont, Watsonville)
Cauliflower and broccoli, including Venetian, purple, and
Romanesque varieties, leeks (Central Coastal Areas)
Broccoli Rabe* (Salinas, King City)
Russet, purple Peruvian, yellow Finn, and Yukon gold*
   potatoes (Washington, Oregon)
Garnett and Jewell yams, sweet potatoes, Japanese sweet
   potatoes (Livingston)
Black trumpet, porcini and matsutake mushrooms (Pacific
   Northwest)
Gourds, decorative corn (Stockton)
Fuyu and Hachiya persimmons (Aptos, Santa Cruz,
   Santa Rosa)
New-crop Mission and Non-pareil almonds (Guinda)
New-crop walnuts (Hartley)
Cranberries (Michigan, Massachusetts)
Passionfruit* (Carpenteria)
Golden Delicious, Spitzenberg, and Sierra Beauty apples
   (Philo, Sebastopol)

Crab and lady apples (Placerville, Hairston)
Sapote, feijoa (Fallbrook)

NOVEMBER

Cardoon (Salinas)
Curly endive or frisée (Santa Rosa, Watsonville)
Baby turnip greens or rapine (Santa Maria)
Parsnips (Lamont)
Jerusalem artichokes (Watsonville)
Turnips and rutabagas (Fresno)
Uncured Manzanilla olives (Central Coast)
Late-harvest Granny Smith apples (Smith Flat)
Winter Nellis pears (Reedly)
Pepino melons (Graton, Santa Maria)
Fairchild tangerines (Coachella)
Orlando tangerines (Orosi, Fallbrook)
Kumquats (Thermal)

DECEMBER

Hedgehog mushrooms (Central Coast)
Green, red, and Dutch Flat cabbage (Central Califonria)
Black Spanish radishes, carrots (Watsonville
Beets (Oxnard)
Red Russian kale* (Pescadero)
Mixed winter braising greens, including chard, tat soi, kale, and mustard (Central California)
Dried shelling beans including cannellini, cranberry, tongue of fire, flageolet, French horticultural, and scarlet runner (Central California)
Wreaths and garlands of cedar, redwood, noble fir, juniper, and mistletoe (Pacific Northwest)
Blood oranges (Porterville, San Diego)
Satsuma mandarins*, oro blanco (a pomelo-grapefruit hybrid), pomelo (Orosi, Fallbrook)
Limequats (San Diego)
Fresh Barhi dates (Indio)
Kiwi (Chico)

—Compiled by Andy Powning, Greenleaf Produce

Chinatown

CHINATOWN

Restaurants:
1. Dol Ho 35
2. Gold Mountain 36
3. Hing Lung 37
4. House of Nanking 38
5. Imperial Palace 40
6. J & J 41
7. Lichee Garden 42
8. Oriental Pearl 44
9. Pearl City 45
10. R & G Lounge 46

Cafes:
11. Imperial Tea Court 47

Bars:
12. Li-Po 48

Delicatessens/Take-Out:
13. Janmae Guey 48
14. New Hong Kong Noodle Company 49

Bakeries/Pastries:
15. ABC Bakery Cafe 49
16. Eastern Bakery 51
17. Mee Heong Pastry Company 51
18. Mee Mee Bakery 52

Ethnic Markets:
19. May Wah Shopping Center 52
20. Metro 52

Produce:
21. Kum Luen 54
22. Sunny Food Mart (formerly Wo Soon) 54
23. Sun Tong Lee Inc. 54

Meat and Poultry:
24. Kwong Jow Sausage Company 55
25. Man Sung 55
26. Ming Kee Game Birds 56
27. New Hop Yick Meat 57

Fish:
28. Dragon Market 58
29. New Lee Sang Fish Market 59
30. San Francisco Hong Kong Market 60

Cookware and Books:
31. Chong Imports 60
32. Ginn Wall 61
33. Tai Yick Trading Company 61

RESTAURANTS

DOL HO

Dol Ho is one of my favorite places to stop for a bite of lunch during a Chinatown shopping trip. Even though Dol Ho is small, very informal, and seemingly chaotic, you don't feel out of place having a single plate of sparkling fresh *har gow* (shrimp dumplings) or crisp, lacy-crusted taro dumplings with creamy interiors. Plenty of people do. The complete lack of amenities combined with the freshness and high quality of the food only make the place more treasured among the cognoscenti. A single dim sum cart barely negotiates a parlor-sized room crammed with ancient black linoleum tables. Lunchers snatch up the dumplings, the chicken feet, the turnip cakes; the cart returns to the kitchen and everyone waits for the next load of tidbits.

Look for any of the shark's fin dumplings, so named because of the crimped edge that runs across the top of the noodle wrapper (not because of a shark's fin filling). Depending on the season, they will be filled with lovely combinations like pea sprouts with shrimp. Saucy tofu skin-wrapped pork and vegetable rolls, three large ones to an order, are a meal by themselves. Flat, chewy rice flour dumplings filled with garlicky Chinese chives and shrimp are a specialty here. Dol Ho's steamed rice noodle rolls are another. They are meltingly tender and velvety, stuffed with barbecued pork, or shrimp aromatic with fresh cilantro. These must be ordered from a waitress and will arrive the table hot and delectable.

808 Pacific Avenue (between Stockton and Powell), San Francisco
Tel: 392-2828
Open daily 7 a.m. to 5 p.m.
Price: Inexpensive
Cash only

I've never been able to figure out the system at this crazy little place. Some things must be ordered from a waitress. Some things come out of the kitchen on the carts. Others are distributed from a counter by a front window that's stacked with gigantic bamboo steamers from which to-go orders are dispensed. The selection from all three stations differs depending on the day and hour.

Though the much-worn carpeted floor can look messy and the dining room seems a bit out of control (the women working it barely have time to clear the tables and get the food out), the kitchen keeps sending out mouth-watering little plates. Because the place is so small, the food is cooked to order. Nothing hangs around, which makes this just the kind of place where you want to eat dim sum.

GOLD MOUNTAIN

644 Broadway (between Columbus and Stockton), San Francisco
Tel: 296-7733
Open Monday through Friday for lunch 10:30 a.m. to 3 p.m., weekends 8 a.m. to 3 p.m.; dinner nightly 5 to 9:30 p.m.
Price: Inexpensive
Credit cards: AE, MC, V

Though Gold Mountain at capacity roars like a coal mine in full operation, the food rolling out of the kitchen is nothing short of pure gold. Noise ricochets around the dining room as hundreds of people slurp down bowls of noodles or devour little plates of dim sum with many cups of tea. In the evening, full meals are served, cooked in the upstairs dining room kitchen and brought down. Located in the modern multistory Ocean City building, Gold Mountain uses both its second- and third-story dining rooms for huge Chinese banquets, a venue to consider if you're getting married. The food can be exceptional—Gold Mountain and the superb R & G Lounge are owned by the same people—depending on how much you want to spend.

A dizzying variety of dim sum, noodles, and soup flows out of the kitchen. An armada of carts negotiating a sea of tables ferries treasures like pleated dumplings filled with Yunan ham, shrimp, and vegetables decorated with minced carrot; translucent half-moons filled with shrimp, black mushrooms, and greens; and curly-edged dumplings filled with pungent Chinese chives and shrimp. Some of the carts have propane-fueled griddles for heating pot stickers or thick rice noodles studded with barbecued pork. Soup carts divided into four compartments distribute bowls of steaming *congee* (rice porridge) flavored with salt pork and thousand-year-old egg. Sticky rice topped with sweet Chinese sausage comes in glass bowls that are overturned on your plate to form a perfect mound. From the dessert carts come tiny egg custard tartlets with crusts that melt in your mouth.

In addition to the food wheeled to your table, you can order soup and noodles from the kitchen. Rice wine–cured chicken vermicelli in soup brings good chicken stock and white noodles with a huge portion of thick-sliced velvety chicken that you dip in a fresh ginger and green chili puree. When you can get a beautiful, clean, satisfying lunch like this in less than five minutes, it confirms that the Asian notion of fast food far outstrips ours.

In the evening, when a full menu goes into effect and the carts are garaged, the dining rooms become less like a train station and more like a restaurant, but I love Gold Mountain at its busiest. A river of people come and go, turning this teahouse into a crossroads of Chinatown life.

HING LUNG

Very Cantonese and unique to San Francisco, Hing Lung turns out thousands of bowls of white rice porridge called *congee*, or sometimes *juk*. It is kept hot in a gigantic sunken vat at one side of a wildly active glassed-in kitchen at the entrance to the restaurant. You can watch the porridge being ladled out into saucepans and brought to a rolling boil, at which time it is poured over finely shredded ingredients waiting in deep serving bowls, cooking them instantaneously. Cilantro, ginger, and green onions are a given, along with such things as "sliced hard head," a troutlike fish and my favorite, though not always available. (One time, on a takeout order, Hing Lung substituted chicken on me. Oh, the disadvantages of being Caucasian!) First-timers feel confident with Sampam porridge seasoned with bits of shrimp, fish, lettuce, and peanuts, but the cognoscenti go for the sweetest, most velvety pork liver, kidney, tripe, and meatballs in Hing Lung's famous pork giblet porridge. I wouldn't try this dish in very many places, but when my surgeon/Chinese dining guru was gobbling his up, I snatched a few bites. The pork giblets were impeccable—like silken foie gras.

674 Broadway (at Stockton), San Francisco
Tel: 398-8838
Open daily 8 a.m. to 1 a.m.
Price: Inexpensive
Credit cards: MC, V

The long oblong doughnuts you see on every table, translated as "fried bread," are yeasty, airy, crisp, and unsweetened. People tear them up and throw them into the *congee* or, better still, into bowls of lightly sweetened or salted warm soy milk. The doughnuts also come warm, wrapped in a sheet of rice noodles, cut into sections, sprinkled with sesame seeds and a gingery soy sauce. Wonderful!

The other specialty, pearly rice noodles, is made from a thin batter poured onto an oiled canvas in a rectangular steamer. Bits of that amazingly sweet pork liver, barbecued pork, and shrimp, just to name a few foods, are cooked right into them. The sheets are then folded over, cut with a scissors, and sauced with a mixture of soy, ginger, and peanut oil.

Hing Lung is a madhouse on weekends, but the turnover in the large, cheery, utilitarian dining room is rapid, the wait never too long. People from all segments of San Francisco's Chinese community come here. The owner of my Telegraph Hill cleaners, a city vice-mayor, my most elegant Pacific Heights friends, their Hong Kong nanny, and all the Chinatown chefs getting off the late shift rub elbows at Hing Lung.

I can see why. *Congee* is a restorative. Hot, soothing to the stomach, easy to eat, Hing Lung's superior version is as good for breakfast as it is at midnight, though the place turns out hundreds of bowls for lunch as well. *Congee* is not served after 3 p.m., when Hing Lung switches to its miraculously cheap and generous dinner menu. The *congee* returns to the menu late in the evening, ready to get people home with a full, but not heavy, stomach.

HOUSE OF NANKING

919 Kearny Street (between Jackson and Columbus), San Francisco
Tel: 421-1429
Open Monday through Friday 11 a.m. to 10 p.m., Saturday noon to 10 p.m., Sunday 4 to 10 p.m.
Price: Inexpensive
No credit cards

Peter Fang and his wife Lily personally have operated this hole-in-the-wall from the day it opened. The lines out the door have only gotten longer, even though the tiny restaurant doubled in size by moving into a storefront next door. Now there are two cramped dining rooms, mirror images of each other, crammed with nine or so tiny tables each and a counter with a dozen stools. Lily seats people so close to each other that they have to mind their elbows and hold onto their plates when tables are moved to allow others to get up and sit down. But you're so hungry by the time you get a seat, and, I suppose, psychologically primed for the experience, that everyone goes for it, grumpily or not. For some, the difficult conditions become part of the reason for eating here. I have also noticed that once the unusual, tasty, vaguely Shanghaiesque food starts coming out, people forget their discomfort, start joking with the strangers next to them, and leave the cafe happy, especially when they see how low the check is.

Peter Fang's cooking is nothing if not original. His primary goal is to keep prices about as cheap as they can be, and his next is to please the palates of the mostly young, Caucasian crowd that loves the place. Western broccoli, not Chinese broccoli, white mushrooms, not shiitakes, and enough garlic to satisfy a Sicilian have been incorporated into the style. However, since the restaurant is so amazingly small, with all the cooking, prepping, and dishwashing done right in front of the counters, there is absolutely no place to store anything. So shopping is done sometimes two or three times a day in Chinatown, where a savvy buyer can find the highest possible quality-to-price ratio.

What Peter Fang does under these conditions, frankly, is phenomenal. Each week or so he comes up with a new idea that is communicated to regulars by word of mouth. Most recently it was a platter of ethereal chicken dumplings wrapped in wonton skins, topped with dry-fried onions, chopped fresh Bing cherries, ground peanuts, and a light, clean, gingery sauce. I prefer to order dishes that use less-expensive ingredients here and forgo such creations as scallops stir-fried with thin slices of sweet potato, banana, and snow peas and sprinkled with toasted sesame seeds, which might have succeeded with better scallops (and have been twice as expensive). However, the regular menu is made up of successful dishes that do work on a shoestring budget, such as Shanghai dumplings made with raw bread dough, fried, then steamed and stuffed with vegetables. I like the tender chicken breast slices sautéed with long slices of zucchini and a resonant sauce made with Tsing-tao beer. For starters, crisp deep-fried pancakes stuffed with shrimp and vegetables napped in a salsalike mix of diced cucumber, green onions, and peanuts get a meal off to a good start. I also like the clear

Nanking fish soup seasoned with lots of coarsely ground black pepper. It wakes up the palate without filling up the stomach. Vegetable dishes like rich Szechuan-style eggplant, simmered in a spicy brown sauce and tossed with broccoli flowerets and snow peas, are as substantial as a main course. Ice-cold Chinese beer is plunked down on the table without glasses and tastes all the better for it.

I have to admire Peter and Lily for expanding their operation in a way that maintains the spirit of the place, because the House of Nanking magic depends on all its quirks. They have freshened the doubled space enormously by tiling the walls, hanging schoolhouse lamps, installing new sheet metal around the kitchen, and lining both miniscule dining rooms with the framed accolades that the restaurant has won over the years. These much-needed improvements don't ruin the grunge look at all. In fact, you feel that at the current nonstop level of business they have only stemmed the tide of wear, tear, and grime for the moment, keeping House of Nanking just a little ahead of its most authentic and beloved state of encrustation. But what this amazing success boils down to is Peter Fang's gentle, generous spirit and sense of fun. This little place deserves those lines out the door. It has earned its cult status.

IMPERIAL PALACE

919 Grant Avenue (between Washington and Jackson), San Francisco
Tel: 982-8889
Open Monday through Friday 10 a.m. to 10 p.m., Saturday and Sunday 9 a.m. to 10 p.m.
Price: Inexpensive
Credit cards: AE, D, MC, V

When the marvelous Lichee Garden (see page 42) burned down and took three years to reopen, some of its cooks and managers went off to other operations. This influence is recognizable at Imperial Palace, where people order magnificent crispy chickens, plates of sparkling fresh steamed greens, and platters of fillet of pork with Chinese sweet rice vinegar, which have the pedigree of the Lichee Garden versions. But Imperial Palace has a personality of its own, inherited in part from its former identity as the fanciest restaurant in Chinatown. Vestiges of its former swank remain in richly carpeted and paneled dining rooms decorated with Ching Dynasty paintings and late-nineteenth-century plates and vases. With its chic little bar in the front, perfect for a pre-dinner martini, and about half the number of tables that currently are jammed in the dining rooms, you can see how Imperial Palace once worked as an elegant Chinatown hideaway. In its current incarnation prices are incredibly reasonable and service can be dismissive, but there is some very good eating to be done.

From the Chinese menu order velvety slices of black cod, crisply pan-fried and seasoned with a relishlike mince of Chinese black beans, fresh chilies, garlic, and ginger. Insist that the waiter bring you the soup of the day, always a rich double chicken and pork broth with chicken feet and pork meat at the bottom. The mustard greens with threads of Yunan ham are lovely, especially with a crispy chicken. Preserved vegetable with fried bean curd brings golden brown tofu in a haunting sauce of pickled greens and hot red chilies.

At lunch, during the frantically busy dim sum service, people order from menus because there's no space in the dining room for carts. The dim sum chef is from the estimable Fook Yuen on the Peninsula. Some of his unique and tasty creations include spicy pork and peanut dumplings; a pan-fried curly-edged dumpling filled with shrimp and Chinese chives; plates of deep-fried black cod strips; glutinous rice–flour puffs stuffed with sweet-and-sour ground pork; and juicy pork dumplings wrapped in fried bread dough. *Yee min*, noodles first fried, then braised with Chinese chives and enoki mushrooms, take on an astoundingly tender texture, and noodle pillows topped with stir-fried meats and vegetables are perfectly crisp and greaseless.

The only drawback here, beside the roaringly loud dining rooms, is the difficulty of eliciting the best dishes from the waiters if you don't speak Cantonese.

J & J

When two different acpuaintances whose taste I respect recommended J & J in a single week, I knew I had to get there. Now I drop in all the time for tea lunch. The dining room full of large round tables (with a few rectangles for smaller parties) has utilitarian but comfortable appointments and a cadre of dim sum servers who carry trays of different selections. The moderate size of the restaurant allows for a wide

615 Jackson Street
(at Kearny),
San Francisco
Tel: 981-7308
Open daily for lunch 9 a.m. to 2:30 p.m.; dinner 5:30 to 10 p.m.
Price: Inexpensive
Credit Cards: AE, MC, V

range of dim sum made in small enough batches so they arrive at your table hot and fresh. I've had veritable feasts at J & J for less than $8 a person—and that's stuffing myself at the end when a new dumpling passes by that I just have to try.

I suggest a little restraint because you want to save yourself for some of the stars, such as the translucent wheat starch dumplings with light fillings that feature pea sprouts or Chinese chives. Two or three different dim sum may come from a single tray bearer, each in its own steamer. Hold out for shark's fin–shaped dumplings filled with coriander, garlic chives, peanuts, and pork; or the fabulous meaty shark's fin dumplings filled only with sweet, gently seasoned pork. Green Chinese chive and shrimp dumplings are round, delicate, and dreamy. The *har gow* (shrimp dumplings) pass the freshness and sweetness test with flying colors.

There are fabulous lacy-skinned deep-fried taro dumplings (a must), excellent sticky rice in lotus leaf packages, and deep-fried sesame balls filled with red bean paste, a favorite sweet dim sum. I love the peculiar chewy/airy dough. Egg custard tartlets with lard-rich crusts come out of the kitchen still warm. All and all, J & J delivers a consistently delicious tea lunch in a pleasant, well serviced dining room.

LICHEE GARDEN

1416 Powell Street (between Broadway and Vallejo), San Francisco
Tel: 397-2290
Open daily
7 a.m. to 9:30 p.m.
Price: Inexpensive
Credit cards: MC, V

Lichee Garden earned a reputation as the city's premier home-style Cantonese dinner house when it opened seventeen years ago, becoming the forerunner of the new generation of upscale Hong Kong–style restaurants like Flower Lounge. Early on it offered high-quality ingredients in a comfortable, though not formal, environment. As a result, Lichee Garden appeals to middle-class Chinese families and practically everyone else who lives nearby in North Beach, Telegraph Hill, and Russian Hill. They come in for meals of glistening spareribs, crispy chicken, radiant green vegetables, and creamy tofu cakes in thin gravy—the Chinese equivalent of meat and potatoes (or in the case of San Francisco, pasta and salad). Lichee Garden also has taken on the role of the Chinatown family club, with birthday, anniversary, marriage, and New Year's parties all celebrated here.

Much of the popularity of Lichee Garden can be attributed to the soulful cooking of chef-owner Chak Siu, who has been with Lichee Garden since it first opened. His wife Annie Siu is the maître d'. Everything that comes out of his kitchen has the heartiness, the savoriness, of food you could eat every day. He is famous for his crispy-skinned chicken and the house special pork spareribs, thin slices with bones lightly battered, deep-fried, and tossed in a piquant sweet-and-sour sauce. I adore them. From a list of amazingly cheap dishes written in Chinese (you'll have to ask for a translation) comes a huge platter of fried tofu, bone-in chunks of satiny black cod, and wilted iceberg lettuce seasoned with pickled greens, a dish you pile onto rice and slurp up, bowl after bowl. Pan-fried noodles here have the much-prized "taste of the wok" (for 50¢ extra), which turns chicken-and-black-mushroom chow mein into a crispy pillow slathered with chicken, baby bok choy, and mushrooms. The noodles cook so hot and fast that they caramelize slightly, skirting the edge of burning in the way that barbecue does, taking on a special flavor that only comes from the fire. The wonton soup is also a dream, boasting rich, clean stock and noodles stuffed with sweet-flavored shrimp and pork. The new dim sum lunch service is excellent and ridiculously cheap. I don't know how these highly competitive Chinatown restaurants can do it, but Lichee Garden's dumplings boast the sweetness of fresh shrimp and other high-quality ingredients.

The spacious dining room has the aura of a resonant old Hong Kong cafe with wooden chairs and wainscoting, a celadon-green carpet, and lots of small square tables interspersed with large round ones—the perfect configuration for a restaurant that accommodates two cultures with single-minded integrity.

ORIENTAL PEARL

760 Clay Street (at Grant)
San Francisco
Tel: 433-1817
Open daily for lunch
11 a.m. to 3 p.m.;
dinner 5 to 9:30 p.m.
Price: Inexpensive
Credit cards: AE, DC, MC, V

Unlike many Chinatown restaurants where low price is the most important consideration, Oriental Pearl's goal is to offer a civilized dining experience as well as authentic food for a still-reasonable tariff. When out-of-town visitors want a top-notch dinner spot in the heart of Chinatown, I always send them here, as do many well-informed concierges. I tell my guests to start with a house special chicken meat ball—one for each person at the table—a delicate bundle wrapped in a gossamer pancake made only of egg whites, tied with a Chinese chive. Inside is an ethereal forcemeat of finely chopped chicken, shrimp, black mushrooms, fresh water chestnuts, and Virginia ham. Another must is a dish called *pei pa* tofu, spicy golden-fried dumplings of bean curd in a lush, hot sweet-and-sour sauce. Tofu soup brings a peppery broth spiked with toasted garlic and cilantro leaves, an exciting background for lots of sweet, fresh shrimp. *Chiu Chow*, marinated duck braised with aromatic Chinese spices and served with a dipping sauce of vinegar and red chilies, reminds me of a duck stew, but don't expect the crisp skin of Chinese roasted duck. However, the spectacular spicy braised prawns, first battered and deep-fried, then sauced in a hot, chili-flecked sweet-and-sour syrup on a cloud of crackling fried rice noodles is all about crunchiness. Even simple vegetables like slightly bitter mustard greens taste different here, set off by tiny slivers of Virginia ham. The crisp-tender stalks refresh the palate at the end of the meal, almost like a sip of strong black tea. If you have room, order a plate of Oriental Pearl's elegant chow mein, made with the thinnest noodles quickly and cleanly tossed with slivers of chicken breast, shiitakes, green onion, and bean sprouts—a stellar preparation of an often pedestrian dish.

People travel across the city for a glass pie plate of Oriental Pearl's "house special noodles" (*yee min*), which are first deep-fried, then braised with Chinese chives and enoki mushrooms so that they achieve a miraculously soft, silky, yet elastic texture. It's hard to stop eating them.

This comparatively small Chinatown restaurant also puts out an accomplished tea lunch, which is ordered from a menu rather than being brought around on carts. This means that each item will emerge fresh and hot from the kitchen, though the tea lunch draw of immediate gratification is lost. The impeccably fresh shrimp and pork dumplings in all their various forms are certainly worth a wait. Be sure to try the scallop and shrimp dumplings, the rustic taro-leaf packets filled with sticky rice and pork, the fantastically crisp taro balls, and the cigar-shaped egg rolls of exceptional crunch. Finish with crisp thin pancakes filled with red bean paste.

PEARL CITY

A spot for very inexpensive, rustic dim sum in huge portions, this teahouse is almost unapproachable on the weekends, although unrelenting competition in price and quality from other dim sum houses in Chinatown have somewhat diminished the crowds during the week.

641 Jackson Street (between Kearny and Grant),
San Francisco
Tel: 398-8383
Open daily 8 a.m. to 10 p.m.
Price: Inexpensive
Credit cards: AE, D, MC, V

Some of my favorites here are sticky rice–stuffed lotus-leaf packets, more moist and savory than most; vegetarian rolls wrapped in crisp deep-fried tofu skin; and coarsely chopped *sui mai*, which are noodle-wrapped cylinders of pork and shrimp barely bound together. The best dumplings come in translucent wheat-gluten wrappers filled with chopped greens, garlic chives, and a little bit of pork. They have a delightful fresh flavor. Little accommodation is made for non-Chinese speakers here, but the authentic food at fantastic prices allows adventurous choosers to shrug off any unexplained surprises. The women bearing the trays and carts want only to lighten their loads.

R & G LOUNGE

The food at the R & G Lounge is excitingly good, and its small, upstairs dining room lined with Japanese screens provides a tasteful and comfortable place to eat. This has become my favorite Chinatown dinner house.

631 Kearny Street (between Sacramento and Clay),
San Francisco
Tel: 982-7877
Open daily
11 a.m. to 9:30 p.m.
Price: Moderate
Credit cards: AE, MC, V

Start with a specialty like salt-and-pepper-fried whole shrimp, so crisp and lightly battered in the proper balance of Sichuan pepper and sea salt that you devour the thin shells and head meat along with the bodies. Or get live spot shrimp from the tank cooked two ways—the heads salt-and-pepper roasted, the bodies steamed—to appreciate their exquisite freshness. Flounder gets a two-way treatment, too. The tiny dorsal bones are salt-and-pepper fried and taste like the best potato chips, while the fillets are steamed with vegetables. I am partial to the whole steamed flounder slathered in ginger, green onions, threads of pork, and shiitakes—one of the best preparations of this local fish I have tasted. I love oxtails so much that I ask for them in the upstairs dining room, though they are beloved downstairs in the cheaper, more casual adjunct of R & G. Gently aromatic with star anise, they cook in a clay pot with iceberg lettuce leaves, onions, and a sauce that is absolutely luscious over rice.

We coaxed the best dish of the year from our loquacious waiter, Raymond (who wore a name tag engraved with a happy face), by asking him what vegetables he had. He ran them down—asparagus, spinach, bok choy, Chinese broccoli—finally mentioning *yin choy*, a spinachlike leaf with a purple center called amaranth, or Chinese spinach. He suggested we have it cooked with two kinds of egg: salted and thousand-year-old. Well, I'm telling you Caucasians, it was a destination dish. The eggs added richness and texture to the amazingly tasty, juicy greens. Don't be put off by the exotic ingredients: Order this dish. For dessert, Raymond insisted on bringing us cool, barely sweetened coconut pudding, really a tender gelatin, scattered with red beans, ending the meal brilliantly.

On a recent visit in celebration of a birthday (I called ahead to arrange a banquet for ten of us), the kitchen came up with a stunning, battered, deep-fried whole crab that caused everyone to rake the shells with their teeth before pulling out the sweet meat; and an unusual Chinese "hash" of salted fish and pork flattened into a pancake and crisply fried. Strong in both flavor and aroma, it provided counterpoint to platters of clean, impeccable Chinese broccoli and pea sprouts and juicy roasted chicken.

The owners of R & G make a point of traveling to Hong Kong for ideas, although upon returning from their last trip they complained about the astronomical prices, even for dim sum. "You eat much better in San Francisco," Kinson Wong told me. One reason we do is because of his R & G Lounge.

CAFES

IMPERIAL TEA COURT

Every time I enter this serene haven in the form of a traditional Chinese teahouse I wonder why I don't come here more often. I spend a tranquil half hour or so sipping small cups of refreshing and invigorating tea and walk out a new person. Everything about this teahouse works against daily stress and soothes a person back into civilized existence. I don't know why this place has such a strong effect on me, because I am not a tea drinker or even someone who likes to linger in coffeehouses, but the minute I sit down at one of the Tea Court's antique square tables and the tea master takes a look at my face and suggests a certain brew, I know that my life will improve.

Most recently he suggested a light herbal tea called "silver needle," aptly named for its soft, furry pointed leaves, with two (not three, not one) chrysanthemum flowers in the pot. He set a kettle of water to simmer on a special heater at the table and, when the water reached the right temperature, which he could tell from its sound in the pot, he half filled the tea pot, then poured out the first brewing of tea, then rebrewed and finally served us our first cup. We continued to add water to the pot to drink four more small covered cups of tea. Time flew by, and I felt as if I had just taken a small vacation.

On other occasions I have had strong espressolike tea in thimble-sized cups, and medium-bodied *pu-erh* (po nay) tea after lunch across the street at Lichee Garden. Each infusion gets a different pot, a different cup, and undergoes a different brewing process. You can learn as much as you want from the eager teachers in the shop, or you can just enjoy your tea. The people who run this charming cafe are friendly and sensitive to their customers' desires.

1411 Powell Street (between Broadway and Vallejo), San Francisco
Tel: 788-6080
Open daily
11 a.m. to 6:30 p.m.
Credit cards: AE, MC, V

The room evokes old China. Dark, polished wood tables and shelving, jade-green Chinese silk insets in the burnished maple walls, a marble floor, wooden lanterns, and a beautiful antique tea counter look like they were all airlifted from some pre-Revolution Shanghai teahouse. If you're in the neighborhood drop by and see what it was like to be a mandarin.

BARS

LI-PO

916 Grant Avenue
(at Washington),
San Francisco
Tel: 982-0072
Open daily 2 p.m. to 2 a.m.
No credit cards

Like its sister street-level bars nearby, Bow Bow and Buddha, Li-Po was a historic haunt for seamen visiting the Barbary Coast. With a golden Buddha enshrined in a cave behind the bar, and an entrance that looks like it leads to a temple, Li-Po still provides an atmospheric haven. The women bartenders are welcoming and pleasant, but tough. You pay for each drink as it's served. Although the liquor and beer selection is generally unexceptional, the bar does stock a number of good Cognacs, brandy, and Scotch whisky.

DELICATESSENS/TAKE-OUT

JANMAE GUEY

1222 Stockton Street
(between Broadway
and Pacific),
San Francisco
Tel: 433-3981
Open daily
8:30 a.m. to 6:30 p.m.
No credit cards

You can buy glistening barbecued ducks, pork ribs, slabs of pork, and chickens at any number of places in Chinatown where you see them hanging in the windows, dripping onto steam-table trays of prepared foods. Janmae Guey is one of the oldest and most well established of the barbecue houses, with a brisk turnover. I take my duck home, cleaved through the bones by the counterman, and serve it with mango salad and rice. Other people eat their roast pig on the premises with a bowl of noodles and soup in the tiny dining room. You can catch a glimpse of whole pink pigs, hanging downstairs, waiting to be roasted.

NEW HONG KONG NOODLE COMPANY

For want of a better category, I put the Hong Kong Noodle Company here. This small shops sells only noodles: fresh, long, and of every width, in one-pound packages. These are tender egg noodles that cook up in boiling water in about a minute—ready to be stir-fried with meat and vegetables, served cold in peanut sauce, or put into soups. If you want the freshest Chinese noodles, pick them up here. Wonton skins fill the other half of the refrigerated case. They come in rounds for *sui mai* (a dim sum) and pot stickers, and squares for wontons and dumplings. The thickness of the skins determines their use: thin for deep-frying, medium for wontons in soup, thick for pot stickers. There are also packages of egg-roll skins. The noodle dough here is smooth and elastic, easy to separate, but always tender, with good flavor. Just seeing the stacks and stacks of skins inspires me to make wontons or dumplings, everyone's favorite food. The skins are so versatile, they can be filled with cheese to make Russian *vareniki* or with meat for *pelmeni*; layered with onions and deep-fried to make northern Chinese green onion cakes; or stuffed with all sorts of different ingredients for egg rolls. The only other item sold at this shop are eggs by the flat, which seems a bit odd since the eggs have already gone into the noodles.

874 Pacific Avenue (between Stockton and Powell), San Francisco
Tel: 433-1886
Open Monday through Saturday 8 a.m. to 5 p.m.
No credit cards

BAKERIES/PASTRIES

ABC BAKERY CAFE

In Chinatown, kids eat hot dogs baked into steamed white Chinese buns. They get them at ABC along with both savory and sweet Chinese cookies. I am partial to ABC's winter melon cakes, yellow glazed cookies of flaky pastry filled with sweetened, jellylike winter melon. Like most Chinese baked goods,

1085 Stockton Street (between Washington and Jackson), San Francisco
Tel: 981-0685
Open daily 7 a.m. to 7 p.m.
No credit cards

SHOPPING IN CHINATOWN

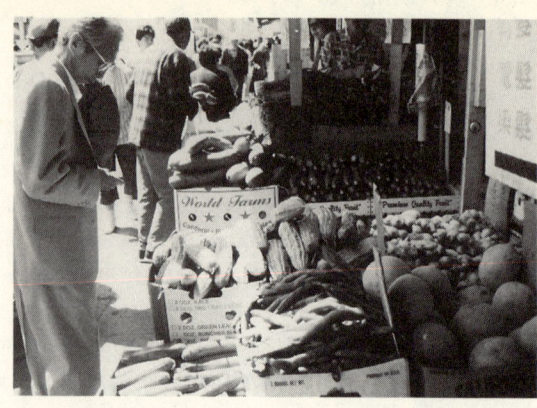

The market streets of Chinatown rival Hong Kong's in their frenzy, smells, and crowds. Chinatown can seem daunting to the uninitiated shopper, but there is no more exciting area in which to buy food in the city. You can find excellent raw materials here in the way of fish, poultry, shellfish, pork, and vegetables for any style of cooking, and of course anything you might need for the Asian pantry. The great shopping blocks are between Broadway and Pacific on Grant Avenue, and Broadway to Washington on Stockton Street, with growing activity on Powell. A scattering of good Chinese markets have jumped over Broadway into North Beach, as have a number of good Cantonese restaurants. Broadway itself between Stockton and Columbus offers a number of stores selling produce and groceries. You don't hear much English, although almost everyone does speak it, and the shops and stores want only to move their merchandise, so don't be shy about asking for what you want. The prices can be very good, but it takes a keen eye to find the best things. One store can have tables of beautiful baby bok choy and moldy water chestnuts. Another will have piles of tiny pea shoots, yet another mangoes and apricots. One of the fish markets will have local rockfish still gasping for breath; another, exquisite live spot prawns swimming in a tank. At first you think the same things are being sold everywhere, but certain places have special things, and those things seem to move around from place to place. I approach shopping in Chinatown the same way I do at a farmers' market: I go with empty baskets and cloth bags slung across my shoulder and an open mind instead of a specific shopping list. That way I can walk around and pick up the best things available at six different stores. Once you start shopping this way, you will find it boring to shop in the supermarket where everything is available whether in season or not, and where the emphasis is on packaged, not fresh, living foods.

they are not too sweet, but still satisfy a sweet tooth. Try the crisp cookies topped with crumbled Chinese sausage, an acquired taste for Westerners, but one not too difficult to like immediately. Eggy custard tarts also boast good, delicate pastry crusts, the hallmark of this beloved neighborhood bakery.

EASTERN BAKERY

A picture of President Clinton with the owners of Eastern Bakery graces the walls behind the counter of this destination for traditional Chinese moon cakes, the varieties of which stand in parade in the front window. These are dense pastries filled with hard-boiled egg yolks and sweetmeats, eaten at holidays. I am partial to Eastern's crisp, crumbly almond-egg cookies, as well as the old Chinatown look of this place in an ancient brick building with a tiled facade and an ornamental roof over the front door.

720 Grant Avenue (between Clay and Sacramento),
San Francisco
Tel: 392-4497
Open daily 8 a.m. to 7 p.m.
No credit cards

MEE HEONG PASTRY COMPANY

Lots of busy Chinese bakeries are sprinkled throughout Chinatown, most of them full of people eating the lightly sweetened, egg-rich Chinese pastries and drinking tea, but I like this bare little place because of their 35¢ sponge cakes, each wrapped in a piece of parchment. These individual airy, free-form cakes with puffy tops are so light and tender they practically dissolve on your tongue. They can be soaked and served with macerated fruit or served plain with tea and fresh lichees or mango. While the selection of pastries at Mee Heong remains small, they have a distinctive handmade, not machine-made, quality. In fact, you can see the baker in the back at all hours of the day, cutting and shaping pieces of dough on a large wooden table.

1343 Powell (between Broadway and Pacific),
San Francisco
Tel: 781-3266
Open Tuesday through Friday 7 a.m. to 6 p.m.,
Saturday and Sunday 8 a.m. to 6 p.m.
No credit cards

MEE MEE BAKERY

1328 Stockton Street
(between Broadway
and Vallejo),
San Francisco
Tel: 362-3204
Open Monday through
Saturday 8 a.m. to 6 p.m.
No credit cards

Not only are the fortune cookies baked here fresh, crisp, and delicious, but they can hold your very own messages. As you can imagine, the potential for fun cannot be overstated. Even if you settle for precomposed fortunes, the big bags of cookies make for an inexpensive and much-appreciated present for kids. For adults who might enjoy a bag of cookies with risqué messages, Mee Mee always has them on hand.

ETHNIC MARKETS

MAY WAH SHOPPING CENTER

1230 Stockton Street
(between Broadway
and Pacific),
San Francisco
Tel: 433-3095
Open daily
8 a.m. to 6:30 p.m.
No credit cards

Compared to the complete and expansive May Wah on Irving, the Chinatown May Wah seems cramped, but it still carries an enormous variety of fresh foodstuffs and groceries. Shoppers will always find good-quality walnuts and pecans, pickled greens in crocks, garlic shoots, and thick flat-stemmed Chinese chives in the produce section along with all the Southeast Asian herbs, since the May Wah company is owned by a Vietnamese family. This store happens to be one of the few places anywhere in the city to find clear-eyed fresh sardines and mackerel, a red-fleshed fish not typically used in Cantonese cooking. Slices of Smithfield ham and exotics like frozen river fish from China are among the hundreds of items that May Wah stocks. You could spend hours just wandering down the aisles marveling at the culinary diversity.

METRO

641 Broadway (between
Grant and Stockton),
San Francisco
Tel: 982-1874
Open daily
9:30 a.m. to 6 p.m.
No credit cards

A Shanghai grocery like Metro is a foreign store in Cantonese Chinatown. The neatly arranged Metro shelves are filled with northern ingredients like the salty dried Smithfield hams from Virginia used in many Shanghai dishes; all sorts of Chinese seaweed; salted and cured bamboo shoots in beautiful reed and leaf packages; jars of sweet fermented-rice pud-

May Wah piles its elegant purple-and-green-leafed Chinese spinach, or amaranth, on sidewalk tables to attract buyers. A huge bunch costs $1.29 and will easily serve four. This cooking technique works for big bunches of long-stemmed watercress, pea shoots, or regular spinach as well, although you don't need to cook these vegetables as long.

In a large wok or casserole with a cover over high heat, heat the oil. Add the garlic, ginger, salt, and chili flakes, if using. Cook over high heat until the garlic just starts to color, about 1 minute. Then add the amaranth. Toss the leaves in the aromatics and add 1/2 cup water. Cover. Lower heat to medium and cook for 5 minutes.

Check the pot or wok for water. If completely dry, add 1/4 cup more. Cook 5 minutes longer. Taste for tenderness and serve.

Serves 4

BRAISED AMARANTH

1 tablespoon vegetable oil

2 garlic cloves, minced

1 tablespoon minced peeled fresh ginger

1 teaspoon kosher salt

1/2 teaspoon dried red chili flakes (optional)

1 large bunch of amaranth, stemmed and washed, but not dried

1/2 to 3/4 cup water

---

ding in the refrigerator case; jasmine and short-grain rice; jars of Lan Chu brand sauces from Taiwan; and excellent peanut oils. Panther brand oil, sold in yellow gallon tins, is absolutely clean in flavor and superb for deep-frying since it has such a high flash point. Many Western as well as Chinese restaurants use this oil for their fryers. A whole section of Metro is devoted to Chinese *Shaoxing*, or rice wines, and liqueurs. One of the most surprising is *kuei hau chen*, a lightly sweet and haunting wine made from grapes infused with osmanthus (a relative of jasmine), which reminds me of Sauternes. It is lovely chilled and served as an aperitif—especially at $5 a bottle—or instead of vermouth in an icy vodka martini as Bruce Cost does at his Berkeley restaurant, Ginger Island. Aged rice wines, the oldest continually made wine, taste like sherry and come in handsome celadon jugs. At Metro you can find all the jarred, bottled, or cured ingredients you need to prepare practically any Chinese recipe, in one of the most pleasant shopping environments in Chinatown. The merchandise in this spacious store is organized logically, and friendly clerks (most of whom happen to be older women) will be happy to help you find anything you might need.

PRODUCE

KUM LUEN

1265 Stockton Street
(between Broadway
and Pacific),
San Francisco
Tel: 989-4668
Open daily
7:30 a.m. to 5:30 p.m.
No credit cards

The same woman owns both Kum Luen and another, slightly higher-quality produce store with outdoor tables directly across the street on the southwest corner of Stockton and Broadway. Western fruits like apricots and peaches, always several varieties of mangoes, bunches of the striking purple-leafed amaranth (a Chinese spinachlike vegetable; see previous page for a fabulous preparation of it), asparagus, Chinese chives and chive flowers, and whatever else is in season at good prices will be placed closest to the sidewalk, just as in Hong Kong. When expensive fresh lichees are in season in the early summer, Kum Luen will have them.

SUNNY FOOD MART (FORMERLY WO SOON)

1210 Stockton Street
(between Broadway
and Pacific),
San Francisco
Tel: 989-2350
Open daily
7:30 a.m. to 7 p.m.
No credit cards

This old Chinatown produce store lures buyers from the steady stream of foot traffic on Stockton with open-air tables piled with Bing cherries in season and the prettiest baby bok choy. This shop specializes in winter melon, sold by the chunk, that lovely huge white-fleshed melon that tastes so good in rich chicken broth. Mangoes at the best Chinatown prices and net bags of fresh lichees, worth every cent of their $7-per-pound price, always catch my eye. Leafy greens like big bundles of watercress and thick-stemmed mustard greens always look good here. If you need watercress, Chinatown produce stores have the best and biggest bunches for the cheapest prices. The Chinese sauté it like spinach, so buyers expect the bundles to be huge.

SUN TONG LEE INC.

Stockton and Vallejo Streets,
San Francisco
Tel: 989-0937
Open daily
8 a.m. to 6:30 p.m.
No credit cards

This grand corner market on the North Beach side of Stockton lays its most tempting produce outside on tables in front and along the sides of the store, protected by a red and yellow canopy. If you see piles of tiny purple amaranth leaves, huge bunches of watercress, or some hard green mangoes, you'd better grab them because an hour later they might be gone. The water chestnuts are plump and fresh, and there is always a table of special seasonal fruit of fairly good quality at loss leader prices—like Santa Rosa plums, oranges, or white peaches. I am attracted by Sun Tong; it's always busy, the produce looks appealing, and the lightning-fast clerks behind the registers smile. Inside, the store is stocked with Chinese dry goods of all sorts, including candies, cookies, and everything you need for red-cooked pork: rock crystal sugar, star anise, dark and light soy sauce, tangerine peel, rice wine. The sheer volume and variety of the inventory gives the store its color.

MEAT AND POULTRY

KWONG JOW SAUSAGE COMPANY

On one side of this specialty store hang long, skinny Chinese sausages and slabs of sugar-cured Chinese bacon (cook it with fresh fava beans or in sticky rice) dangling from strings; on the other is a refrigerated case of good-looking fresh pork, including hard-to-find spareribs and slabs of fresh bacon—just what you need to make luscious red-cooked pork (see recipe, page 57). When you walk into this immaculate shop, the smell of rice wine and curing pork makes you want to get cooking.

1157 Grant (between Broadway and Pacific), San Francisco
Tel: 397-2562
Open daily 9 a.m. to 5 p.m.
Credit cards: AE, MC, V

MAN SUNG

Basically a wholesaler with a tiny retail storefront, Man Sung only displays a few of the poultry items it sells. But this is the place to go for fresh chickens and chicken parts. Chinese shoppers insist on free-range chickens, and they bought them long before the Caucasian market caught on. These hormone-free chickens are raised for flavor and tend to be lean, but oh so tasty. Be sure to specify Petaluma chickens at Man Sung; they are specially raised by the Petaluma Poultry

1116 Grant Avenue (between Broadway and Pacific), San Francisco
Tel: 982-5918
Open daily
7 a.m. to 5:45 p.m.
No credit cards

Company for the Chinatown market. Take home a whole bird complete with head and feet, appendages that greatly enrich a stock. Birds with head and feet attached are called Buddhist chickens and may be sold because of an exemption granted by the U.S. Department of Agriculture, which otherwise requires that they be removed. Since these Buddhist chickens are bled, a method of killing required by Jewish law, they are also sold in kosher butcher shops.

Man Sung also sells Pekin ducks from Reichardt duck farm in Petaluma. These ducks do not have huge breasts, so they roast up quickly and stay moist, especially when bathed in an aromatic Asian marinade.

The California history of the Pekin duck, a mallard crossbred in China thousands of years ago, began in 1880 when a Yankee clipper ship, on its way to the East Coast from China by way of South America, docked in San Francisco. Somehow a dozen Pekin ducks in its cargo disappeared and ended up at a small poultry farm in the middle of the city. In 1901 Otto H. Reichardt bought the stock and moved the operation to Petaluma, where the duck farm, still in the family, raises over a million ducks a year, supplying most of the West Coast.

MING KEE GAME BIRDS

1122 Grant Avenue
(between Broadway
and Pacific),
San Francisco
Tel: 391-8287
Open Monday through
Saturday 8 a.m. to 6 p.m.,
Sunday until 5 p.m.
No credit cards

The word must have gotten out about Ming Kee, because there are signs in the window that ask tourists not to take pictures of the fluffy live hens, quail, squab, and partridges crowded into cages behind the counter. Chinatown women come to the ordering window, point at a handsome brown hen, and watch as the clerk grabs the bird by its feet, pops it into a heavy brown paper bag with holes in it, staples it shut, and puts it into a thin plastic bag for carrying. The shoppers walk off with the live birds, just as if they were carrying bags from the supermarket. Some French cooks I know tell me it's no big deal to kill a chicken, bleed it and pluck it, fry the blood (*sanguette*), and use every part of the bird in cooking, but I can't imagine doing it myself.

For the faint of heart, freshly butchered birds, vacuum packed in plastic, fill a small refrigerated case in the store. Expensive black-skinned chickens used for restorative broths

RED-BRAISED WHOLE PORK SHOULDER

This opulent braised pork has been a favorite dish of mine since Bruce Cost cooked it for my birthday once, surrounding the meat with baby bok choy. The recipe, from Bruce Cost's *Asian Ingredients* (William Morrow, 1988), is not difficult to make and the pork fills the kitchen with the most exotic aromas. You can buy all the dry ingredients you need at any of the Chinese markets listed in the book, and the pork at any of the Chinese meat counters.

In a large pot, bring the water to a boil and add the pork. When it comes to a boil again, skim off any foam and reduce heat to medium. Add the wine and cook, partially covered, for 20 minutes.

Add the star anise, cinnamon stick, garlic, ginger, tangerine peel, chilies, and green onion and cook for another 20 minutes.

Add the soy sauce, sugar crystals, and salt, and continue to cook, turning the meat occasionally, for another 2 to 3 hours. The rind and fat should be very soft when the pork is done.

Remove the pork from the liquid and keep warm. Strain the sauce into a large skillet and, over high heat, reduce to a syrup. This may take 15 minutes or longer.

When the sauce is the consistency of thin syrup, put the pork in the center of a large platter and pour the sauce over the meat. Eat with lots of rice and a green vegetable.

Serves 10 to 12

---

3 to 4 quarts water
One 5- to 7-pound pork
    shoulder, with bone and rind
3/4 cup Shaoxing wine
    (Chinese rice wine)
6 star anise pods
One 3-inch cinnamon stick
8 garlic cloves, smashed
Fresh ginger cut into 10 thin slices
2 or 3 pieces dried tangerine peel
2 dried red chilies
1 whole green onion
1 1/3 cups soy sauce
6 Chinese rock sugar crystals,
    each about 1-inch square
1 tablespoon kosher salt

(surprisingly their feathers are pure white) and superb quail and squab can be found here. In the spring, game-bird eggs are available, a rare delicacy, especially squab eggs that sell for $50 a dozen.

NEW HOP YICK MEAT

You can identify this shop by the crisp-fried pork rinds in the window. While New Hop Yick mostly sells wholesale, the retail counter displays a sample of its wares: nice-looking market steaks at $5.79 a pound, freshly ground beef, veal, an unending supply of hard-to-find, never-frozen pork ribs, and fresh pork

1145 Grant Avenue (between
Broadway and Pacific),
San Francisco
Tel: 989-0247
Open daily 8 a.m. to 5:45 p.m.
No credit cards

of every cut. If you're produce shopping in Chinatown and want to make a Western meal with meat, Hop Yick is Chinatown's most complete meat market. On the other side of the store, crisp freshly rendered pork rinds smell so good that you have to have a nibble, the potato chips of pork products.

FISH

DRAGON MARKET

1145 Stockton Street
(between Jackson
and Pacific),
San Francisco
Tel: 433-0403
Open daily
8:30 a.m. to 5:30 p.m.
No credit cards

This premier fish store in Chinatown gives off a breath of the sea when you walk by it, luring you in by displaying its freshest fish on tables of ice at the front, open to the sidewalk. The other day huge Monterey spot shrimp with bright orange roe caught my eye. Not only was the price a fraction of what it would be if you ordered these delicacies at Hawthorne Lane or Chez Panisse, they were sparkling fresh. If brilliant blue crabs are in, they will be wiggling around in boxes on the street. I always return to this market after a perusal of several others to buy bright red local rock cod, about two pounds each, with clear glassy eyes, blood-red gills, and firm flesh. You tear off a plastic bag and use it as a glove to pick up your fish by the gills (the slits by the head). A genial counterman weighs it, then scales, guts, and takes out the gills, leaving you with a beautiful whole cleaned fish. I preheat the oven to 450°F, put the whole fish seasoned with salt and pepper in a pan, fill the cavity with sliced fennel, lemon slices, sprigs of rosemary or Chinese aromatics like ginger and green onions, cover it with a piece of aluminum foil, cuts slits in the foil, and bake it for about twenty minutes. The fish comes out of the oven moist and firm, with the glorious chewiness that comes only with the freshest of fish cooked whole this way. These rockfish make an easy and very spectacular meal.

The Dragon Market carries red-fleshed fish like mackerel, not often seen in Cantonese markets, along with salmon, tiny pomfret, and yellow China cod. Price is keyed to quality. The cleaned and beheaded sand dabs on sale will be flabby. The fresh whole sand dabs at three times the price will be excellent. For selection and quality I head here; I have come to expect something rarely seen and wonderful. My visits here have inspired many a meal.

NEW LEE SANG FISH MARKET

Fish markets seem to come and go, and you have to make the rounds of a number of them to find the treasures. New Lee Sang currently has a source for the freshly caught whole rockfish so beloved by the Cantonese community. When these local rock cod have just been pulled from the water they have a firm, chewy texture much prized by lovers of truly fresh fish. Tables of whole fish stiff from rigor mortis, some still gasping, have been sighted here first thing in the

1207 Stockton Street
(between Broadway and Pacific),
San Francisco
Tel: 989-4336
Open daily 8 a.m. to 6 p.m.
No credit cards

WHOLE SALT-ROASTED FISH

Jean-Pierre Moullé, the downstairs chef at Chez Panisse, is a hunter, gatherer, and fisher, both on the water and under it. He knows how to cook everything from the sea, including seaweed. One day at his house he cooked a white sea bass in rock salt and it was the most succulent fish I ever tasted. Here is his recipe. It works for any whole fish with scales, such as a small salmon, sea bass, or local snapper. I used a beautiful green-skinned lingcod, and this method of cooking made it taste extraordinary. The fish is so delicious, moist, and aromatic, it needs no sauce, though you could put extra-virgin olive oil infused with lemon zest on the table.

One 3- to 4-pound whole lingcod, snapper, or sea bass, cleaned and with scales left on
6 to 8 fresh herb sprigs such as parsley, thyme, oregano, rosemary
10 pounds coarse rock salt

Preheat the oven to 500° F. Stuff the inside of the fish with the herbs.

Choose a baking pan just large enough to hold the fish. Cover the bottom with a 1-inch layer of rock salt. Lay the fish on top and cover the entire fish with more salt. The fish should be completely mounded with the rock salt. Depending on the size of the fish, bake for 20 to 30 minutes. (My lingcod was 3 1/2 pounds and I cooked it for 25 minutes.)

Remove from the oven and let rest for 10 minutes. Break the salt crust. Gently remove the fish from the pan. Lift off the skin. It should peel very easily. Serve the whole fish at the table. Be careful to brush off all the grains of salt.

Serves 4

morning. These whole fish are more expensive than the fillets of local snapper sold everywhere from Fisherman's Wharf to Safeway, but less expensive than live fish netted from tanks. The difference in flavor and texture of just-killed fish may not be to everyone's taste, but once you start appreciating the firmness and sweetness of the flesh, you can't go back. I started ordering live rockfish in Chinese restaurants with Chinese friends and have become an addict, so I always look for the fish with the stiffest bodies and the glassiest eyes. New Lee Sang also regularly carries fresh shrimp.

SAN FRANCISCO HONG KONG MARKET

1136–38 Grant Avenue (between Broadway and Pacific), San Francisco
Tel: 986-8410
Open daily 8 a.m. to 6 p.m.
No credit cards

You shop for fish in Chinatown just like you shop for vegetables, by popping in a bunch of shops to see what looks best. A perusal of this fish market with a cement floor and the fish laid out on metal tables covered with crushed ice might net you clear-eyed whole rockfish, farmed sea bass, pomfret, all sorts of whole local flatfish (flounder, sand dabs, rex sole), conch in the shell, live frogs, and huge abalone.

COOKWARE AND BOOKS

CHONG IMPORTS

838 Grant Avenue, Empress of China building basement (between Clay and Washington), San Francisco
Tel: 982-1432
Open Monday through Thursday 10 a.m. to 8 p.m., Friday and Saturday until 9 p.m., Sunday noon to 8 p.m.
Credit cards: MC, V

A huge space filled with all sorts of rare but mostly very affordable treasures makes the trip downstairs worthwhile. I never fail to find something irresistible—black and red hardbound notebooks for $1.50, handsome celadon dishes for cheap, pretty and utilitarian bamboo steamers. Chong also has elegant antique Chinese bowls in the shape of fruits—quinces and melons—at $450 each, and teapots in the shape of pigs with thimble-sized cups for $15. Lotus-shaped teapots with lotus seeds rattling in the tops, packets of Chinese vegetable seeds, and a lot of Chinese tableware make up a small fraction of the stock. Regular Chinatown shoppers drop by just to see what might have come in—like large and very inexpensive glass jars for pickling, and large and small clay pots with covers, one of the finest stewing vessels in any culture.

GINN WALL

This Chinese hardware store is filled with Chinese cooking essentials, from woks of all sizes to the utensils used to cook in them. Cleavers and knives, huge stockpots and steamers, marble mortars and pestles—the building blocks of an Asian kitchen—are all here at nontourist prices. A section of paperback Chinese cookbooks at the front of the store, including Shirley Fong-Torres's instructive guide to Chinatown, will inspire you to start cooking. But you don't have to be a Chinese cook to use a wok.

1016 Grant Avenue
(between Jackson
and Pacific),
San Francisco
Tel: 982-6307
Open Monday through
Saturday 10 a.m. to 6 p.m.
(closed Thursdays),
Sunday until 5 p.m.
Credit cards: MC, V

The wok's versatility as a cooking tool makes it an excellent and inexpensive addition to any kitchen. I steam vegetables, fish (on a glass pie plate), and tamales in mine on top of a beautiful and inexpensive bamboo basket insert. I also use the wok for deep-frying. Its efficient shape makes a small amount of oil go a long way. The oil heats quickly and recovers its temperature after food is dropped in it, which makes deep frying easy. Try frying fresh corn chips or whole sand dabs in it. Heat a couple of inches of olive oil in the wok until a piece of bread dropped into the oil turns golden. Dip the sand dabs in buttermilk, then in seasoned flour. Carefully slide them into the oil and cook until brown and crispy, about four minutes, depending on the thickness of the fish. Cook just a couple at a time so that the oil surrounds each fish and they do not touch. I serve one of these hot, crisp fish with a little green salad as a first course.

TAI YICK TRADING COMPANY

I'm a pushover for celadon, that mysterious gray-green color the bay becomes on certain overcast days. At Tai Yick, a store packed to the rafters with Chinese pottery and porcelain, you can buy a whole set of celadon plates, cups, saucers, and flat bowls at Crate and Barrel prices, though you may have to

1400 Powell Street (at
Broadway), San Francisco
Tel: 986-0961
Open daily
9:30 a.m. to 6:30 p.m.
Credit cards: AE, MC, V

sort through piles of dishes in a cluttered corner to find them. Celadon china always looks elegant and is particularly beautiful with fish or dark green vegetables served on it—colors you might find in the sea. Fresh fruit on celadon also is stunning. Deep Chinese soup bowls in all sorts of ornate patterns are stacked next to simple blue-and-white china decorated with cheerful brush-painted fish. Dark brown, glazed terra-cotta casseroles for all of $4.50 are suitable for both serving and cooking in the oven or even on top of the stove. You can bake potato gratins in them or heat up stews, and handsomely present them on the table where they will stay hot. Several sizes come with glazed covers. Finally, for fans of cracked-glaze porcelain, Tai Yick has all sorts of vases and planters, some huge, in mustardy yellow and celadon green.

Civic Center & Hayes Valley

CIVIC CENTER & HAYES VALLEY

Restaurants:
1. Carta   67
2. Hayes Street Grill   69
3. Millennium   70
4. Pacific Restaurant—Thai-Binh-Duong No. 2   72
5. Stars   74
6. Suppenküche   75
7. Vicolo Pizzeria   76
8. Vivande Ristorante   77
9. Zuni Cafe   78

Cafes:
10. Caffè Trinity   80
11. Momi Toby's Revolution Cafe   80
12. Spuntino   81

Delicatessens/Take-Out:
13. Ba Le   82
14. Saigon Sandwich Cafe   83

Bakeries/Pastries:
15. Alfred Schilling   83

Ice Cream/Chocolates:
16. Nuts About You   84

Ethnic Markets:
17. New Chiu Fong Company   85

Produce:
18. Civic Center Farmers' Market   86
17. New Chiu Fong Company   86

Cookware and Books:
19. A Clean Well-Lighted Place for Books   87
20. Richard Hilkert, Bookseller   88

RESTAURANTS

CARTA

Rob Zaborny, chef/owner of this small, smart cafe with big windows that look out to Market Street's monumental palm trees and vintage streetcars, is an internationalist who has a real knack for re-creating the spicy, ethnic dishes he's tasted during his travels all over the world. Every month he completely changes the menu, moving on to a different country and a new set of dishes. His culinary explorations at Carta (originally taken with co-owner Maureen McGarry, who left recently) have covered all shores of the Mediterranean, Oaxaca, Russia, India, and Greece, one of my favorites.

Here's a sample of the gorgeous dishes Carta turned out during Greek month: a stunning smooth white bean soup laced with roasted peppers; crunchy, deep-fried calamari; fingers of deep-fried okra and eggplant on a bed of wild greens with *skordalia* sauce (a garlicky emulsion); miniature Greek meatballs in a tomato sauce fragrant with herbs; mini–salt cod cakes with chicory salad and tomato-olive relish; tiny mussels sprinkled with feta in an oregano-scented tomato broth; and grilled baby leeks scattered with pistachios and fresh goat cheese. Just recalling these little dishes makes my mouth water.

Large plates featured a classic lamb moussaka, clean, light yet savory, showing a non-Greek restraint with olive oil; juicy pork and vegetable skewers; a lemon-marinated roasted poussin with a semolina-crusted spinach turnover; and nicely grilled tuna with an artichoke gratin.

1772 Market Street (between Octavia and Gough),
San Francisco
Tel: 863-3516
Open for lunch
Tuesday through Friday
noon to 3 p.m.;
dinner Tuesday through
Sunday 6 to 11 p.m.;
Sunday brunch
10 a.m. to 3 p.m.
Price: Moderate
Credit Cards: AE, DC, MC, V

No one expects Greek desserts to be great, except perhaps for baklava, but from pastry chef Laurie Mackenzie (another internationalist and an expert on Latin American cuisines) came an exquisite honey walnut cake soaked in tangerine syrup, and aromatic rice pudding infused with spices accompanied with Paula Wolfert's semolina almond cookies from her Eastern Mediterranean cookbook.

A tremendous amount of research goes into each menu. Cookbooks are consulted, recipes reconfigured. The excitement of the culinary journey infects both the cooks and the diners. How stimulating for a kitchen to be able to work with new ingredients and techniques each month! But how difficult. The specters of inconsistency and inauthenticity always hover.

What unifies the experience of eating at Carta from one month to the next is the versatile menu format that offers many small, tapaslike plates and just four or five carefully considered large plates. This allows for so much variety in ingredients and technique that a satisfying meal can be pieced together no matter what the cuisine.

CRAB, ENDIVE, AND RADICCHIO SLAW

1 tablespoon sherry vinegar
1 tablespoon minced shallots
1/2 teaspoon kosher salt
Freshly ground black pepper to taste
3 tablespoons olive oil
2 medium heads Belgian endive
1 small head radicchio
1 1/2 cups (8 ounces) fresh crabmeat
1/4 cup minced fresh chives
1 tablespoon fresh lemon juice

At Hayes Street Grill, we use fresh-picked blue crab for this salad, which can be purchased at Monterey Fish Market (see page 490). During local Dungeness crab season, cook a live crab yourself and pick out its meat to use in this recipe, making it extra special.

In a small bowl, combine the vinegar, shallots, salt, and pepper. Whisk in the olive oil. Set aside.

Separate the endive leaves, stack them, and cut them into thin strips with a sharp knife. Core the radicchio and cut it into thin strips as above.

In a large bowl, combine the crab, endive, radicchio, and chives. Toss with the lemon juice, then toss with the vinaigrette and serve.

Serves 4 as a side dish

Actually, the food stays amazingly consistent considering the huge shifts in the pantry as the menu moves from country to country. San Francisco has developed such a cosmopolitan market that authentic ingredients—and often typical local wines—are readily available. The cooks are clever at adapting seasonal produce to their needs, as well as fish, poultry, and meats. If the dishes aren't exactly the same as you might find in a home in Marrakesh or a taverna in Athens, the spirit of them comes very, very close to the real thing. Finally, Rob Zaborny's cooking always has soul, depth, conviction. He's an eater and a traveler, and in Carta he's found a way to bring everyone along.

HAYES STREET GRILL

320 Hayes Street (between Gough and Franklin), San Francisco
Tel: 863-5545
Price: Moderate
Open for lunch Monday through Friday 11:30 a.m. to 2 p.m.; dinner Monday through Thursday 5 to 9:30 p.m., Friday and Saturday until 10:30 p.m., Sunday until 8:30 p.m.
Credit cards: AE, DC, MC, V

I must be completely up front about this eighteen-year-old fish house across the street from the Performing Arts Center, because I am an owner and kitchen presence there. Instead of trying to give my own place a qualitative description, I will tell you what we do each day from the point of view of a chef.

The first thing in the morning, the grill chef has a chat with the fish man (Paul Johnson of Monterey Fish) to find out what looks good that day, and we base our daily menu on this. The Hayes Street kitchen is divided into three areas: a pantry or salad station, the mesquite grill, and a sauté station. We divide what we order among the three, so that big meaty fish like wild Alaskan king salmon or buttery swordfish come off the grill, while pan-fried Hama Hama oysters, petrale sole with chanterelles, or braised sea bass with artichokes are under the sauté chef's jurisdiction. The grilled fish comes with a pile of french fries cooked in peanut oil, our trademark, and a choice of at least four sauces and salsas. From the salad station comes our signature fresh crab "slaw" or a Mexican-style scallop cocktail with warm corn chips. The whole menu benefits from the stunning array of seasonal produce we get directly from the farm of an ex-employee (Pomponio Creek) as well as Greenleaf Produce, an organic produce broker. Collaboratively the cooks figure out what dishes to make to create a balanced and tempting menu. We use an international mix of recipes with the unifying theme of fish and seafood. Above every other consideration, we want the freshness and pristine quality of the fish and the produce to speak for itself. Though preparations may be Thai, French, Italian, American, or Mexican, they are always simple, allowing the ingredients to shine.

We opened the Grill because there simply wasn't a good place to eat before the opera, ballet, or symphony. My partners and I wanted such a place ourselves, so we created a restaurant that cooks unfussy food, casual enough to serve before a performance, but substantial and tasty enough to be a main event. We drew inspiration from old San Francisco grills like Tadich and Jack's, which have always featured local ingredients in straightforward presentations, but we took the grill concept a step farther by seeking out more sophisticated ingredients and cooking them in a modern style.

The Hayes Street Grill's walls are covered with autographed photos of the artists who use the restaurant as their club. We used to have bentwood chairs and worn wooden floors, but we remodeled and installed banquettes, chairs with upholstered seats, and carpeting, making the restaurant less noisy. The original brass coat hooks along the walls remain, as does our founding philosophy of cooking only the food we would serve at home to our families—dressed up a little—with a religious dedication to wholesomeness.

MILLENNIUM

246 McAllister Street
(between Larkin and Hyde),
San Francisco
Tel: 487-9800
Open for lunch Tuesday
through Friday
11:30 a.m. to 2:30 p.m.;
dinner Tuesday through
Sunday 5 to 9:30 p.m.
Price: Moderate
Credit cards: MC, V

Vegan restaurants are not a rarity in San Francisco now, but none are as sophisticated or as much fun as Millennium. This restaurant looks and feels like a French bistro until you open the menu and see a dish like Breaded Pan-Sautéed Seitan Medallions. Then you know you're in California.

Vegans eat only fruit and vegetables, and even avoid animal products like eggs, butter, and yogurt. Vegetable oils are used sparingly, as is sugar. Protein comes from soy products like tofu and tempeh, seitan (a chewy brown substance made from whole wheat flour), and of course combinations of

SCONES WITH DRIED SOUR CHERRIES

This scone recipe from Rob Zaborny at Carta is a winner: easy to make and delectable. You can purchase dried sour Michigan cherries at Nuts About You (page 84). Dried Michigan cherries are plumper and moister than the Washington State variety.

Preheat the oven to 400° F. In a large bowl, sift together the flour and baking powder. Add the salt, 3 tablespoons of the sugar, and combine.

Add the dried cherries and the cream. Mix with an electric mixer fitted with a paddle attachment on low speed for 30 seconds. Otherwise, hand mix with a fork, then knead on a floured board for about 1 minute.

Form the dough into 2 rounds, 6 inches across. Score the tops with a knife into 6 pie-shaped pieces. Brush with butter and sprinkle each round with 1 teaspoon sugar.

Bake on an ungreased baking pan until the tops are golden brown, about 30 minutes. Serve warm with unsalted butter.

Makes 12 scones

Note: The dough can be assembled up to 8 hours in advance and kept refrigerated. Allow the dough to come to room temperature before baking.

2 cups all-purpose flour
2 teaspoons baking powder
1/4 teaspoon salt
3 tablespoons plus 2 teaspoons sugar
2/3 cup dried sour Michigan cherries
1 cup heavy whipping cream
1 teaspoon butter, melted

---

vegetables, nuts, and grains. The kitchen does a pretty good job of turning out appetizing food using such a restricted palette of ingredients. Some dishes work; some don't. But by the end of a meal practically everyone leaves satisfied and feeling good. The food sits lightly on the stomach.

Meals begin with warm house-made whole-wheat baguettes and garlicky tofu spread. Starters include some fine salads, such as the Green Gulch butterball, which brings together seasonal fruits with big soft leaves of butter lettuce in a sparkling oil-free citrus-mint vinaigrette. One would be happy to get a salad like this in any restaurant. Warm spinach salad with mushrooms, red onions, and smoked tofu in a balsamic and extra-virgin olive oil vinaigrette falls into this category, too. A grilled Portobello mushroom is particularly satisfying in a Moroccan vinaigrette, meaty and bright. Stay away from the filo-wrapped dishes. Without butter between the layers, the dough becomes sodden and pasty.

Main courses can be hit or miss. One night you might get a delicious pasta with broccoli, roasted new potatoes, olives, and a lovely tomato sauce. On another, the kitchen throws in so many ingredients, the pasta turns into a sludge. A polenta torte with ricotta-like tofu layers works wonderfully; a muddy-flavored Corsican risotto does not. One can rely on the advice of waiters here. They are charmers—young, eager to please, well informed—and they don't get tired of answering the same questions over and over again. On two different occasions they steered me to good dishes and some delicious wines that went nicely with the food.

The restaurant inhabits two long descending rooms on the ground floor of the Abigail Hotel. A black-and-white checkered tile floor, comfy banquettes, French windows that look out to a garden, and a handsome wooden wine bar give Millennium a Parisian air.

After a clean, organic vegan meal and a few glasses of wine, you can repair upstairs to a room in the hotel on a Full Moon Aphrodisiac Night—almost for the cost of dinner. It's a great deal and you'll have the energy to take advantage of it.

PACIFIC RESTAURANT— THAI-BINH-DUONG NO. 2

**337 Jones Street
(between Ellis and Eddy),
San Francisco
Tel: 928-4022
Open Wednesday
through Monday
10:30 a.m. to 4:30 p.m.
Price: Inexpensive
No credit cards**

Although Pacific Restaurant No. 1 on Larkin is closer to the Civic Center, the No. 2 branch is worth a special trip. Rarely have I been to any restaurant that cooks with such integrity and care, and we are not talking about an upscale place, but a modest little noodle house that serves mostly noodles in soup (called *pho* and pronounced "faw") in a transitional neighborhood where many Vietnamese families live. *Pho* depends on good beef broth, but at most *pho* houses the broth derives much of its flavor from MSG. At Pacific, the broth is a dream, full of beefy character without a speck of fat. If you order No. 10, a huge bowl of clear soup with paper-thin slices of both well-cooked and rare beef (well cooked being tongue, rare being steaklike cuts) and thin white rice noodles, you will be getting *pho* at its best. With the hot soup comes a plate of bean sprouts, lime wedges, minty Thai basil, and cilantro, which you tear up and push down into the bowl. The Vietnamese friend who took me to Pacific sprinkled bottled red chili sauce into his soup, but I couldn't bear to muddy these pure flavors. This is a soup I could eat every day and never tire of it.

The other kind of dish at Pacific teams the hot and savory with the cold and salady, another example of the genius of Vietnamese cuisine. Try the supremely crisp Vietnamese spring roll called *cha gio*, wrapped in crackling layers of deep-fried rice paper and stuffed with a luscious minced pork and vegetable filling. You place a piece of hot roll in a perfect butter lettuce leaf, add some torn-up cilantro and mint, a tangle of cold rice noodles, add a slice of hot green chili if you like, wrap it up, and dip it into Pacific's clear sweet-and-sour dipping sauce. It's literally sensational. Or for a similar and even more interesting experience try No. 31, in which you get a little bowl of thinly sliced grilled pork tenderloin, fresh bacon, and tiny meatballs in a clear sauce with a haunting, garlic-enriched aroma. You put pieces of the pork in lettuce leaves with the fresh herbs and cold rice noodles and use the sauce as the moistener—another dish that makes my mouth water as I write about it. This dish comes on a woven bamboo tray, the pork in a glass bowl topped with tissue-thin slices of radish and carrot, the white noodles mounded next to the green herbs and lettuces.

You may have some reservations about the neighborhood, but during the day, the only time that Pacific 2 is open, the streets are full of Vietnamese families (as is the immaculate restaurant), and the sidewalks are clean and unthreatening. This central part of the city has been transformed by the energy and culture of Vietnamese émigrés, as evidenced by this amazing little place. At $3.50 or $4 a meal you can start saving for a trip to Saigon, where the same dish costs 40¢.

STARS

555 Golden Gate Avenue
(between Van Ness
and Polk),
San Francisco
Tel: 861-7827
Price: Expensive
Open for lunch Monday
through Friday 11:30 a.m. to
1:30 p.m.; dinner Sunday
through Thursday 5:30 p.m.
to midnight, Friday and
Saturday until 2 a.m.
Credit cards: AE, DC, MC, V

After the theater one night I spent two hours at the fascinating bar at Stars. This social crossroads, which some wags have likened to the Moscow train station where the peasants mingle with the bourgeoisie, stretches down one side of the roaring restaurant, requiring at least four lightning-fast bartenders just to service it. We were able to snag two stools at the end of the bar because we knew the people vacating. The place was packed. Both elevated dining areas were completely full, as was a sea of cocktail tables and every stool along the counters. A piano player was holding forth in the din, and the scene was no less lively when we left after midnight.

Stars is the city's premier eating and drinking institution. Chef-owner Jeremiah Tower knows how to throw a *soigné* party every night, and everyone wants an invitation. You can secure one by calling well in advance for a prime-time dinner reservation, or by dropping by and waiting for some seats to materialize. I am now at the point of preferring the bar, because it's more fun, and because a full course dinner can be hit or miss. But at the bar you can order any dish on the regular menu plus any dish on the bar menu; the suave bartenders might even honor your presence with an extra splash of Veuve Cliquot—if you spend enough—and it's there you have the best view of the shifting crowd made up of locals, tourists, politicians, socialites, restaurateurs, Peninsulites celebrating their birthdays, and bon vivants out on the town.

There's a sophisticated European ethos at Stars, though the restaurant is foremost a personal statement of Tower's, an amalgam of New World and Old World style. The look crosses a booming Parisian brasserie with a museum of Jeremiah memorabilia. Tower claims to have invented "California cuisine," and the energy emanating from the bar is fueled by the thousands of American-style cocktails downed in its environs, but French people and Italians feel at home at Stars. Tower intuitively understands how to satisfy everyone's food fantasies: for the hungry, short ribs, lamb shanks, and steaks teamed with crisp potato gratins, hearty ragouts of vegetables, and long-simmered white beans; for the demure, warm oysters in briny butter sauce, salmon slathered in wild mushrooms, or elegant lobster with two different dressings. Tower makes everything opulent by doubling up on sauce. Almost every dish has a *jus* and a mayonnaise, or a butter sauce and a salsa. But there are always simpler things like deep-fried vegetable threads, house-smoked salmon, ice-cold oysters, caviar, and plates of green salad. From the most lavish to the almost austere, the menu anticipates a world of preferences. Though beloved pastry chef Emily Luchetti has left, the desserts still strike a clever balance—the Stars style dresses up homey American favorites in Chanel suits.

Tower staffs the dining room with such pros (most of whom have been there for years), that they make everyone feel like a star. You end up spending more than you ever expected, seduced by opportunities to buy $25 glasses of wine, rare half bottles of Sauternes, and ancient Armagnacs, but you leave happy because you've had a glittering night out. And we need at least one restaurant in town where you can eat a hamburger at midnight with a bottle of Latour. Jeremiah Tower, one of the world's great restaurateurs, leaves no amenity unexplored.

SUPPENKÜCHE

Small, interesting shops have been opening in the Hayes Valley for a number of years, but especially in the last several after a portion of the earthquake-damaged freeway looming overhead between Gough and Laguna was finally carted away. What was once an alien neighborhood, a bit dicey for potential buyers of arty clothing and off-beat treasures, now basks in the sun of gentrification. These blocks of Hayes Street have become inviting.

Oddly enough, the most exciting culinary development in the area has been a German beer house and restaurant called Suppenküche, a lively, inexpensive place that serves superb German beers and simple German food on unfinished pine tables in a vaulted dining hall. We don't have good German restaurants in San Francisco, and the Western Addition would be the last place you would expect to find one. Yet from the moment it opened, Suppenküche has attracted a young crowd that appreciates beer and substantial, reasonably priced food. The spare, functional decor fits right into a minimally funded urban lifestyle, and sure enough, it has

601 Hayes Street
(at Laguna),
San Francisco
Tel: 252-9289
Open for dinner nightly
5 to 10 p.m.; weekend
brunch 10 a.m. to 3 p.m.
Price: Inexpensive
Credit cards: AE, MC, V

become the rage among a certain set to tuck into a plate of braised cabbage and bratwurst. The food is so good that people are coming from all parts of the city to eat here.

Thomas Klausmann, a Bavarian home cook, started the restaurant and runs the kitchen along with an experienced staff. The menu sticks to the traditional, though the cooking seems lighter, fresher, and more seasonal than a lot of German restaurant cooking I have tasted. Fresh pea soup comes out peppery and true flavored; the bread basket boasts moist sprouted-wheat bread and a German rye with a crackling crust; sauerkraut with sausages is resonant with bacon and sweet spices, a far cry from the stuff in cans. The oft-appearing mashed potatoes have a fork-mashed texture and a magical balance of butter, nutmeg, and milk. The mustard is hot, grainy, and delicious.

One of the most wonderful daily specials, from a chalked list that enlarges the small core menu, is an oxtail stew served with the tender noodle-dumplings called spaetzle. Others, like huge, soft veal meatballs in a caper cream sauce and a dreamy German-style chicken à la king served on noodles with big chunks of amazingly velvety chicken, represent the highest form of comfort food, especially with steins of cold, crisp, sparkly German lager.

The small place gets noisy as the large tables fill up, often with several different parties, and the beer bar in the middle of the room gets full. The waitresses handle it all with finesse and humor, endlessly describing and recommending dishes for the first timers. In every way this little soup kitchen knows how to please. It's a marvelous example of grassroots urban redevelopment.

VICOLO PIZZERIA

150 Ivy Alley (between Hayes and Grove, off Franklin Street), San Francisco
Tel: 863-2382

Once again I have to come clean. Vicolo (which is the Italian word for alley) is an operation we set up in a corrugated steel shed behind the Hayes Street Grill to serve the overflow pre-performance crowd as well as people who want a fresh, inexpensive lunch or dinner in the Civic Center neighborhood. To that end, Vicolo has expanded its menu somewhat to include house-made lasagnes, Italian sandwiches on house-made focaccia, and a greater variety of salads. Vicolo does not take reservations and the high-ceilinged room can get noisy during the pre-performance crush. Otherwise, the space is a comfortable hideaway. People order at the counter, find their own tables, and eat Italian vegetable salads or house-made soup while they wait for their pizza. The pizzas come by the slice or whole, in black cast-iron pans with torn-off sheets of waxed butcher paper as plates. The crisp cornmeal crust is sturdy enough to act as a shell for substantial fillings made with high-quality ingredients: whole-milk mozzarella, imported Italian cheeses, fresh and dried wild mushrooms, house-made sausage.

One interesting property of Vicolo pizza is that it can be successfully finished off at home. The half-baked pies cook in twelve to fifteen minutes in a preheated hot (425° F) oven. The half-baked pizzas also freeze well and go right into the oven from the freezer. The crust stays nice and crisp and the rich fillings retain their flavor and texture, whether eaten at home or at the restaurant. Vicolo has been voted best pizzeria in *Focus* magazine and *Bay Guardian* readers' polls year after year.

Open Monday through Thursday 5 to 9:30 p.m., Friday and Saturday until 11:30 p.m., Sunday noon to 9:30 p.m.
Price: Inexpensive
Credit cards: MC, V

VIVANDE RISTORANTE

Vivande at Opera Plaza is Carlo and Lisa Middione's dream come true, a handsome, warm, elegant trattoria/ristorante two blocks away from the Performing Arts Center. Carlo has always wanted a full-scale restaurant where he could serve his impeccable pastas and simple, quintessentially Italian antipasti and main courses. Lisa, an opera and classical music buff, loves the proximity to the city's performing arts halls. The restaurant has a comfortable bar with small tables for impromptu dining and an expansive dining room with a more intimate alcove for serious eating. The room is dominated by a long open kitchen where much of the food is prepared. It's hard to believe that this welcoming open space was once the austere, multiroomed restaurant Modesto Lanzone. The atmosphere has been radically transformed.

The food served at Vivande derives its authenticity from ingredients, including the many fine imports that Vivande

Opera Plaza,
670 Golden Gate Avenue (between Van Ness and Franklin),
San Francisco
Tel: 673-9245
Open Monday through Thursday 11:30 a.m. to 10 p.m., Friday and Saturday to 11:30 p.m.
Price: Expensive
Credit Cards: AE, MC, V

Porte Via on Fillmore sells, and traditional cooking equipment, like Vivande's wood-burning oven and wood grill. Yet, Carlo has developed a personal style that defines his cooking. He likes simplicity. He wants you to taste the raw materials. The silken texture of his house-made pasta becomes as important as the sauce.

At a recent meal before the symphony, I was inspired by Carlo's warm octopus salad—just tender octopus, red onion, and celery in lemon juice and extra virgin olive oil—each ingredient in perfect balance, a stunning little dish. I liked noodles richly coated in cream and cheese, and a marvelous antipasto of calamari stuffed with anchovies, garlic, and parsley served hot off the grill. We drank a soft Umbrian red from Marco Caprai, Sagrantino dei Montefalco 1994, at an amazingly reasonable price. But there was not time for dessert. Our order got confused—drinks arrived after wine, we didn't get the braised artichokes we ordered, and the main courses were brought in waves. We had to pull our own coats out of the closet and dash out the door in order to get to the symphony on time. I am sure that the Vivande staff will become more adept at handling the pre-performance seating, but from now on, I'm going to eat there after 8 p.m., when the time allows for a civilized Italian experience. You can really have one here in this temple of Italian gastronomy. Carlo Middione knows how to get his hands on the right stuff.

ZUNI CAFE

1658 Market Street (between Franklin and Gough), San Francisco
Tel: 552-2522
Open Tuesday through Saturday for breakfast 7:30 to 11 a.m.; lunch 11:30 a.m. to 6 p.m.; dinner 6 p.m. to midnight; Sunday brunch 11 a.m. to 6 p.m., dinner 6 to 11 p.m.
Price: Moderate
Credit cards: AE, MC, V

Despite its Southwest name (a holdover from its opening concept over eighteen years ago, when every dish was laced with cumin), Zuni Cafe is the most European restaurant/cafe/bar in the city, not just because of the style of the food but because of its function within the community. The place has grown organically over the years into a social crossroads, a meeting spot, a place that has become indispensable if you want a late-night hamburger, an early-morning coffee and roll, a baguette sandwich in the afternoon, or a sophisticated full meal. Zuni works on every level.

The most important development occurred when the restaurant doubled in size by annexing a neighboring triangular space between Market Street and an alley. In this sunny, glass-fronted room, Zuni installed the much-frequented copper-topped bar and indoor and outdoor cafe tables. Upstairs and deeper into the restaurant, a labyrinth of rooms with shelflike built-in banquettes and odd-shaped tables make up the dining areas. In the bar you can get casual food and pizzas from the wood-fired oven, as well as any conceivable drink, be it fresh-lime margaritas or glasses of Condrieu (a rare, flowery, but very dry white Rhône wine).

It was chef Judy Rogers who put Zuni on the national culinary map. She fell into cooking when she lived with the famous Troisgros family in France as an exchange student, and later spent a term at Chez Panisse. She worked with Marion Cunningham to create an American menu at the Union Hotel in Benicia. When she couldn't find the financing to open her own place in Berkeley, she ended up at Zuni as a partner. The match was made in heaven.

Her menus bring together the cooking of southwest France and most of Italy in her own peculiar and winning way. The restaurant's signature dishes come from the brick wood-burning oven in the center of one dining room. Roast chicken for two on a warm bread salad moistened with cooking juices and lightened with arugula has become a San Francisco classic. Her *fritto misto*, a changing array of vegetables, whole little fish, and paper-thin slices of lemon, emerges from the fryer irresistibly crisp. A starter of salt-cured anchovies and thinly sliced celery in olive oil remains my pick if I am not having oysters instead, usually a variety of pristine West Coast mollusks opened to order and presented on a stand holding a tray of crushed ice with brown bread and butter below. Long-braised meats like osso buco or lamb shanks appear regularly, and Rogers is never afraid to offer tripe or salt cod. Another innovation started by Rogers pairs a certain cheese with a fresh or dried fruit, the combination of which becomes a revelation. House-made ice creams and ices and biscotti dependably satisfy the sweet tooth. The menus are always so varied that no matter what the state of your appetite you will find something to eat and drink. So people just drop by, knowing that they will run into someone and that they will get something good. Rogers's genius is that she meets the eclectic needs of San Francisco with such unique personal style.

CAFES

CAFFÈ TRINITY

**1145 Market Street
(between Seventh and Eighth Streets),
San Francisco
Tel: 864-3333
Open Monday through Friday 6 a.m. to 4 p.m.
No credit cards**

This tiny jewel can be considered a gift to the city from developer Angelo Sangiacomo, whose office building it graces. No expense was spared in adorning this light-filled room with opulent materials—handcrafted mahogany woodwork, marble tables and counters, hand-painted panels of native American animals depicted in the style of seventeenth-century European naturalists, and crystal light fixtures. Sitting in this baroque parlor, pondering the street people across the way at United Nation's Plaza, makes you feel like a character in a novel by Charles Dickens.

Everything prepared by the young Italian couple who run the cafe is simple and tasty, like a salad of Roma tomatoes, red onions, and capers with tuna, or a cup of minestrone with honest, long-cooked flavor. The proscuitto, mascarpone, and radicchio sandwich on focaccia is moist and delicious. Good coffee made from Mr. Espresso beans is a pleasure to be enjoyed slowly while basking in the richness of the surroundings.

MOMI TOBY'S REVOLUTION CAFE

**528 Laguna Street (between Hayes and Fell),
San Francisco
Tel: 626-1508
Open Sunday through Thursday 7:30 a.m. to 10 p.m., Friday and Saturday 8 a.m. to 11 p.m.
No credit cards**

Noteworthy for its peaceful ambiance, Momi Toby's light-filled corner space has dark wood-framed windows and window seats, weathered wooden floors, and a handsome marble-topped coffee bar with Victorian slatted-wood shelving behind it. The whispery, soothing tones of gamelan music engulf you when you walk in the door. The coffee is competent and served in handleless pottery cups. If you are in the neighborhood, this cafe offers a sanctuary for reading or writing.

SPUNTINO

What a great location this cafe has, kitty-corner from the Veterans Building, across the street from City Hall, and a block away from the Opera House, with huge windows that look out onto Van Ness Avenue! The room is spacious and very Italian, with black metal chairs and tables, a long marble counter that snakes along the walls, and shelves filled with jars of artichokes, olives, tins of olive oil, and a rainbow of Torani syrups. Noise bounces off all the hard surfaces, including a veneered cement floor, and the sun pours through expansive west-facing windows in hot waves in the afternoon. People order at the counter, and what you don't carry to the table yourself is magically brought to you later. Spuntino offers an unusually full Italian menu for a self-service cafe, and bakes biscotti, breads, and pastry on the premises, but I don't consider this a serious place to eat. The food is competent yet not fully realized, so you end up being tempted without being satisfied. A white bean puree, for example, arrives completely unseasoned, with slices of soft white bread; capellini with fresh tomatoes and basil tastes mostly of the huge hunks of unpeeled, old-tasting tomatoes. The best bets here are the thin-crusted pizzas from the wood-burning oven, crisp and fun to eat, and excellent coffee made with Mr. Espresso beans. I see lots of caffè latte walk out the door in paper containers. I should add that two ten-year-olds loved Spuntino on my last visit and told me to recommend it as a kids' restaurant. They liked the white bread, which they dipped into the white bean soup, and ate the capellini after pushing aside the tomato hunks. They raved about the pizza. The people who work there couldn't be nicer, and the food comes out pretty fast—a kid's dream.

524 Van Ness Avenue
(between Golden Gate and McAllister),
San Francisco
Tel: 861-7772
Open Monday through Saturday 7 a.m. to 8 p.m.,
Sunday 10 a.m. to 7 p.m.
Credit cards: AE, MC, V

DELICATESSENS/TAKE-OUT

BA LE

511 Jones
(between Geary
and O'Farrell),
San Francisco
Tel: 474-7270
Open daily 6 a.m. to 6 p.m.
No credit cards

This branch of a wildly successful San Jose Vietnamese delicatessen specializes in ready-to-eat colorful cold and hot foods packaged to go, or to be eaten at tables on one side of the store. The cold foods, tightly wrapped in clear plastic, tempt with their sparkly combinations of flavor and texture. In one, three large salady spring rolls filled with rice, whole shrimp, and fresh herbs come with a little cup of piquant brown dipping sauce. Another, my favorite, displays soft fresh rice noodles stuffed with finely minced pork and black mushrooms next to several slices of Vietnamese mild white pork sausage (like French *boudin blanc*), on a bed of more wide rice noodles, herbs, shredded carrots and lettuce, slices of hot fresh chili, and sweet-and-sour dipping sauce. What a refreshing meal these neatly packed Vietnamese foods make!

For the home cook, Vietnamese white sausage or pâté, still warm from poaching, wrapped in banana leaves or foil, can provide the centerpiece of a meal. The most delicious of them all is a skinny banana leaf–wrapped tube fragrant with garlic. With rice noodles, dipping sauce, salad greens, and fresh herbs (purchased at a nearby Vietnamese grocery), you can put together a fantastic meal.

The hot dishes come off a steam table at the front, though skewers of spicy beef and pork are kept at room temperature during the lunch hour and taste better that way. For dessert, check out the refrigerator at the front filled with a rainbow of puddings and tapiocas. The firm coconut-milk pudding with hunks of banana and beautiful pearls of tapioca, topped with chopped peanuts, is universally appealing. One disappointment was a watery salad of green papaya and carrot threads that was probably defrosted. However, everything else I've eaten has been exceptionally fresh. Ba Le is a hit in the neighborhood, and the food turns over fast.

SAIGON SANDWICH CAFE

The immaculate Saigon Sandwich Cafe, which has been turning out delicious Vietnamese sandwiches for ten years, reminds me of snack stalls in the student quarter of Paris, except that the sandwiches are much better. Instead of *saucisson sec*, Saigon fills its French baguettes with five-spice chicken, roast pork, or Vietnamese meatballs, then kisses them with a sweet, hot, and sour dipping sauce, shredded carrots, sprigs of cilantro, and hot green chilies. The result is juicy, savory, exotic sandwiches that soon become addictive. My favorite is the warm meatball sandwich, which tastes like a sparkling Sloppy Joe. Long, generously filled sandwiches cost around $2, an amazing buy.

The shop has almost a cult following of Civic Center employees, cab drivers, delivery men, and SoMa types as well as the Vietnamese community that lives nearby. Many drop in for a glass of aromatic Vietnamese iced coffee creamy with sweetened condensed milk. The pleasant people who work behind the counter are efficient and eager to please. When I call ahead for sandwiches for meetings and the like, they are ready exactly at the assigned time, not before and not after. The Saigon Cafe knows the importance of freshness.

560 Larkin Street (at Eddy),
San Francisco
Tel: 474-5698
Open Monday through Saturday 7 a.m. to 4:30 p.m., Sunday 7:30 a.m. to 4:30 p.m.
No credit cards

BAKERIES/PASTRIES

ALFRED SCHILLING

Walking by the tall, open French doors of this canopied red-brick building next to Flax (the great art supplies store), you see cases of sharp-edged chocolate pyramids, elegant molded chocolates, and truffles. On top of the counter are trays of miniature tarts, brioches, and almond croissants. When you look deeper into the space you notice a huge open kitchen set up for major production. Next to it, though separated by a

1695 Market Street
(at Valencia),
San Francisco
Tel: 431-8447
Open Sunday and Monday 7 a.m. to 7 p.m., Tuesday through Saturday until 10 p.m.
Credit cards: MC, V

partition, is a cafe with rococo furnishings and a menu to match. I've never been able to work up any appetite for beet salad with beet granita and goat cheese dressing or chocolate pasta with chocolate sauce and spring vegetables, even though they may be perfectly fine dishes, but I am attracted to the European-style outdoor cafe tables. There you can sit with a coffee and an individual tart topped with a poached half pear with stem, anchored and filled with a mortar of ground nuts, sugar, and butter; or a miniature pumpkin tart alive with candied ginger. French pastry aficionados will be drawn to a refrigerated case of elegant, many-layered confections that strike a balance between candy and cake. You can place a hotel-sized order or just eat a sweet roll at Alfred Schilling. He caters to the institution and the individual.

ICE CREAM/CHOCOLATES

NUTS ABOUT YOU

325 Hayes Street (between Franklin and Gough), San Francisco
Tel: 864-6887
Open Monday through Saturday 10 a.m. to 7:45 p.m.,
Credit cards: AE, MC, V

When I was a young girl living in Chicago taking ballet lessons, my mother took me to see touring ballet companies at the Opera House. The part of the ritual I liked the best was the stop at a little candy and nut store before the performance to buy a bagful of turtles and chocolate-covered nuts to munch during intermission. (I guess that's why I became a food maven instead of a ballet dancer.) So it was with great delight that I watched the opening of Nuts About You, a tiny shop across the street from Davies Hall, with many glass jars filled with nuts of every sort, candies made with nuts, and chocolates in a sparkling glass counter. Every season, owner Bonnie Boren discovers a new sensation, such as toasted almonds glazed in the thinnest layer of buttery toffee, or a miniature chocolate truffle that seems to dissolve into pure fragrance. Gift baskets and boxes full of delectable treasures can be assembled and sent, whimsically wrapped and tied. But the real thrill of having this shop right by the Performing Arts Center is stopping there before a performance and choosing your own favorite treats to stimulate your senses during intermission.

ETHNIC MARKETS

NEW CHIU FONG COMPANY

The most complete Vietnamese market in the city, New Chiu Fong has everything from four-inch-thick chopping blocks made out of slices of tree trunk to imported dried Thai snapper. Fresh rice noodles are by the meat counter, and dried noodles of every conceivable kind, from rice threads to Chinese-style egg noodles, fill up their own aisle. Many are used in the Northern Vietnamese soup called *pho*, an amazingly restorative and refreshing soup that combines handfuls of fresh herbs and hot chilies with noodles, beef, and broth. In the meat counter, strips of fat-marbled beef, precut for *pho* and satays, streamline the preparation of these dishes. Every part of the pig and large fresh stewing chickens are piled high, while shelves of fish sauce, soy sauce, and hot chili pastes await the home cook. The freezer sections of ethnic markets are always worth a look because they hold useful ingredients like banana leaves for wrapping fresh sausage and rice, or *pandan* leaf, which you rarely see fresh.

But the produce section here is the draw, with its boxes of fresh Vietnamese herbs, some with the most delectable perfumes. Of particular interest for creative cooks is the fresh cumin leaf (*cá nâú chua rau om*), which smells like the seed but more complex; the minty, pointy-leafed Thai basil, wonderful in seafood stews with coconut milk; and an herb that looks like flat Italian parsley (*bò xaò cân*), but tastes like a

724 Ellis Street (between Larkin and Polk), San Francisco
Tel: 776-7151
Open daily
8:30 a.m. to 6:30 p.m.
No credit cards

cross between celery and parsnip, used for beef cookery in Vietnamese kitchens. There are big, flat, purple-tinted leaves (*rau kinh gioi*) that have a shiso-like, or chrysanthemum flavor, and aromatic elongated greens with pointy edges (*rau ngò gai*) that are used as salad or accompaniment to *pho* or savory grilled meats. And these are but a few. Many of the herbs are raised in Hawaii and flown in, so prices are not cheap, but at New Chiu Fong they arrive in excellent condition, fresh and aromatic. Since the prices and names of the herbs are not posted in English, the best way to find the flavors that interest you is to taste.

PRODUCE

CIVIC CENTER FARMERS' MARKET

**United Nations Plaza
(at Fulton Street)
San Francisco
Open Wednesday
7 a.m. to 5:30 p.m. and
Sunday 7 a.m. to 5 p.m.**

This heart-of-the-city farmers' market truly serves the local pedestrian community, especially since parking in the area can be a problem. You can find metered spaces on the other side of Market Street, which limits your shopping to whatever you can carry for several long blocks. As an expression of a market self-molded to serve a specific community, the Civic Center stalls are heavy on fresh and inexpensive Asian vegetables like long beans, the wonderful purple-leafed Asian spinach called amaranth, Asian mushrooms, bok choys, Vietnamese herbs, lemongrass, and cooking essentials like

carrots and onions. As at every vital farmers' market there will be seasonal surprises, like a stall full of the most fragrant tangerines, thin-skinned Rangpoor limes, or new-crop walnuts. Whenever I want dates to serve with mint tea, I go to the Civic Center date man. He has barhi and medjhool, large and small, sweet and sticky, creamy and juicy, which goes to show that when you need a good date in this town, remember the Civic Center. Just kidding. The beauty of this market is that you can buy fresh food at such cheap prices that a large family can be fed for a week at about half of what it would cost at the supermarket—and the quality will be far superior.

NEW CHIU FONG COMPANY

724 Ellis Street (between Larkin and Polk),
San Francisco
Tel: 776-7151
Open daily 8:30 a.m. to 6:30 p.m.
No credit cards
See listing, page 85.

COOKWARE AND BOOKS

A CLEAN WELL-LIGHTED PLACE FOR BOOKS

For other location, see page 523.

The most complete bookstore in San Francisco, A Clean Well-Lighted Place for Books has a well-chosen cookbook section as well as an extensive travel section with much food writing in it. The literature section carries many classic books on food and eating as well. The clerks will help you hunt down anything in the store or out. Authors visit frequently and sign their masterpieces, and if you are a contributor to City Arts and Lectures, a series of talks by authors the profits of which go to Friends of the Public Library, you get a 15 percent discount at the store. Clean Well-Lighted is community spirited and service oriented but, more important, if you want it, they'll probably have it.

601 Van Ness Avenue
(between Golden Gate and Turk),
San Francisco
Tel: 441-6670
Open Sunday through Thursday 10 a.m. to 11 p.m., Friday and Saturday until midnight
Credit cards: AE, MC, V

RICHARD HILKERT, BOOKSELLER

333 Hayes Street
(between Gough
and Franklin),
San Francisco
Tel/Fax: 863-3339
Open weekdays 9 a.m. to 5
p.m., Saturday and most
Sundays 11 a.m. to 5 p.m.
Credit cards: AE, MC, V

The one-man bookshop, in which every volume, new or used, reflects the sensibility of the owner, succeeds or fails on taste. Richard Hilkert has a quirky and iconoclastic take on what's interesting, and I am always curious to see which cooking and food books will make it into his long front window. He likes Europe; he likes photographs and high-quality production; he likes local authors; he likes personal expression; but his eccentricity keeps him open to civilization in the broadest sense. He knows a good treasure when he sees one, so it always behooves you to scan the used-book corner. The careful selection of books at Richard's store makes you think about each book on its own merits, a way of looking at books that disappears at supermarket bookstores.

Embarcadero & Fisherman's Wharf

EMBARCADERO & FISHERMAN'S WHARF

Restaurants:
1. Boulevard   93
2. Eagle Cafe   94
3. The Fog City Diner   95
4. Gaylord of India   96
5. Happy Valley   97
6. Harbor Village   98
7. Il Fornaio   99
8. One Market Restaurant   100
9. Pastis   101
10. Splendido   102
11. Tokyo Sukiyaki   103
12. Wu Kong   107

Cafes:
13. Pier 40 Roastery   108

Bars:
14. Gordon Biersch Brewing Company   109
15. Harry Denton's   109
16. Pier 23 Cafe   110

Delicatessens/Take-Out
17. Arabi   110

Bakeries/Pastries:
18. Bagel King   111
19. Boudin Sourdough Bakery and Cafe   111

Ice Cream/Chocolates:
20. See's Candies   112

Produce:
21. Ferry Plaza Farmers' Market   112

Cookware and Books:
22. Cost Plus Imports   115
23. Williams-Sonoma   117

RESTAURANTS

BOULEVARD

This much-heralded collaboration between hometown hero, chef Nancy Oakes, who made her reputation at a tiny dining room connected to a sports bar in the avenues, and superstar restaurant designer Pat Kuleto has caused such a stir that after two years of operation it still takes weeks to get a prime-time reservation. Everyone wants one of the 120 seats in this fantasy French bistro in the turn-of-the-century Audiffred building across the Embarcadero from the bay, especially now that the view has been liberated from earthquake construction.

One fall evening, two of us walked in early without a reservation and snagged two counter seats neatly enclosed by a marble carrel with a close-up view of the pastry station. We studied the menu and watched the dishes being constructed on the open cooking line. Fun. Oakes's plates are huge, creative, and colorful, with lots of different things going on in them, not always to best advantage. We began with a lovely, straight-ahead crab bisque, full of crab flavor undimmed by cream, and a pretty, molded crab salad muddied by orange-scented mayonnaise. Next came a gargantuan maple-cured pork chop, pink, thick, and juicy, with a divine sauté of chard and bacon, topped with cold fried onion rings and a barely warm, doughy apple cake seasoned with sage. A moist fillet of salmon came with great mashed potatoes and a decadent pool of mustard seed beurre blanc. Thin green beans and onions worked nicely with everything on the plate. For

One Mission Street
(at Steuart),
San Francisco
Tel: 543-6084
Open Monday through
Friday for lunch 11:30 a.m.
to 2:00 p.m., bistro menu
2:30 to 5:15 p.m.;
dinner Sunday through
Wednesday 5:30 p.m.
to 9:30 p.m., Thursday
through Saturday
until 10:30 p.m.,
Price: Expensive
Credit cards: AE, CB, DC, D,
MC, V

dessert we waited a long time for a tall, cold apple tart tatin with tough crust, ice cream, and a very sweet caramel-raspberry sauce. A molasses-sweetened gingerbread did come hot with melting honey ice cream, a boozy bourbon sauce, raspberry syrup, and bananas over the top. That's just what some of the plates are like here—over the top.

But you don't reserve here unless you really want to eat, and I feel like I'm nitpicking when I complain about too much stuff on the plates. Boulevard is an upscale, important-night-out kind of dinner house in the vernacular of California-American cuisine. The dishes, both as they read on the menu and arrive at the table, are meant to wow diners not with exquisiteness but with ebullience, imagination, and the chef's drive to please. Oakes is nothing if not generous, and she uses every conceivable combination of ingredients and cooking technique to extract oohs and ahhs from her adoring public. Boulevard is a big hit and Oakes has hit her stride. Her sensibility is very much present in all the dishes, which get better—more consistent, more confident—every time I eat here.

EAGLE CAFE

**Head of Pier 39,
Second Floor,
San Francisco
Tel: 433-3689
Open daily
7:30 a.m. to 3 p.m.
Price: Inexpensive
Credit cards: MC, V**

This funky, historic workingman's bar and cafe upstairs at Pier 39 is a real piece of old San Francisco, not an amusement park re-creation. The Eagle began serving breakfast and lunch in 1920 across the street from the pier in what is now a parking lot. When Pier 39 plans were approved, the Eagle was given landmark status and somehow moved unaltered to its current home. It's a bit of a shock walking off the touristy pier into this ancient place with its whitewashed wood-slat ceiling and walls, worn linoleum floors and linoleum tables, a bar tattooed with hundreds of initials and names, and a menu so out of date it seems like a relic, but with a timeless view of the bay framed by the ancient wooden windows.

The best meal at Eagle is breakfast, specifically a crisp thin circle of finely ground corned beef hash with two perfectly fried eggs. The hash browns are no treat, and the toast, either supermarket whole wheat or foamy white, is saved by a brush with melted butter. The pancakes are airy and good; the meat loaf is the best way to go at lunch. Drinks such as Bloody Marys are about half the price of those served at the other pier places, and the ambiance is much more interesting.

THE FOG CITY DINER

This groundbreaking restaurant (it was the first upscale diner in the country) designed by Pat Kuleto has expanded, adding a long narrow dining room that looks out onto the Embarcadero. The seats of choice, however, are still the roomy booths in the front, which you can get if you eat early. Fog City tends to get busy around 7:30, leaving the earlier dinner hours approachable for locals. The tourists take over later.

1300 Battery Street (at the Embarcadero), San Francisco
Tel: 982-2000
Open Sunday through Thursday 11:30 a.m. to 11 p.m., Friday and Saturday until midnight
Price: Moderate
Credit cards: DC, D, MC, V

To my mind, Fog City represents the best Pat Kuleto design of all. He took a wood-framed shack and turned it into a glamorous dining-carlike dining room with luxurious wooden booths each by a big window, dark wood paneling, a counter with stools, and a long bar that's always crowded. The streamlined metal exterior reminds me of sleek passenger trains with light glowing inside. Whenever you pass it, day or night, you want to stop in because it looks like everyone is having such a good time.

The menu has changed very little over the years, with daily specials adding variety, but to this day I order the same things: grilled pasilla peppers stuffed with goat cheese accompanied with a chunky avocado salsa, and a salad of pretty greens tossed with caramelized walnuts, aged goat cheese, and, most recently, peaches. The salads are perfectly dressed, the lettuces of proud California pedigree. At the opposite end of the food chain, Fog City's hamburgers with skinny fries and house-made catsup are always a temptation. The thick onion rings are never greasy though monolithic; you have to like crunchy batter to appreciate them. Sometimes the pot roast with a horseradish–potato pancake isn't cooked quite enough and is tough; and sometimes the tomatoes in a salad with green beans in a Dijon vinaigrette really don't taste like they've just been plucked from the garden as it says on the menu. A single order of warm chocolate banana bread pudding with rum caramel sauce will give everyone at the table a sweet send-off at the end of the meal. For the most part, the food here is peppy and fun, but don't go here for a serious dining experience.

GAYLORD OF INDIA

Ghiradelli Square,
900 Northpoint (at Larkin),
San Francisco
Tel: 771-8822
Open daily for lunch
noon to 2 p.m.,
dinner 5 to 11 p.m.
Price: expensive
Credit cards: AE, CB, DC, D, MC, V

Far and away, this is the best Indian restaurant in San Francisco. In fact, it may be the only restaurant where you can get dependably fresh, lively Indian cooking. All the other places in town seem to lose their chefs or their energy and end up sending out bland, rewarmed, mediocre food. Not so at the elegant third-floor Gaylord, with its romantic view of the bay, white tablecloths, posh interior, and waiters in uniform. When you walk into the dining room, the luscious smell of spices and roasting foods lets you know you're in for some real eating.

You can begin with roasted *papadums* (spicy lentil wafers) and greaseless, deep-fried vegetable *pakoras* (fritters), always made with an interesting variety of vegetables. The chutneys, green and tamarind, are freshly made. Tandoori-roasted items like lamb chops and chicken are juicy and aromatic, served on hot metal plates with sizzling onions, though the tandoori-roasted chunks of sea bass tend to be a bit dry. The vegetable dishes actually have individual character. You can taste the fresh ginger, cilantro, and freshly ground toasted spices. The spinach with white cheese is still bright green; the cauliflower and potatoes are cooked through but keep their textures and flavor. And the desserts, like hard-to-find *ras malai*, delicate white cheese balls poached in syrup and served in cream, and *kulfi*, real Indian pistachio ice cream made from boiled-down milk, are always a delight here.

There are two drawbacks, however. Every time I've been to Gaylord the service tends to disintegrate toward the end of the meal. The waiter disappears just when you want him, even when the restaurant doesn't seem that busy. The other problem is the high price of eating here if you order a la carte. A few vegetable curries and a tandoori item, some *nan* (tandoori-baked bread), *raita* (yogurt and cucumbers), and rice, with a bottle of wine from a serviceable list, always seems to run to $40 a person. If you order the set *thali* plates you get a lot of different dishes, though not necessarily the ones you want, for a lesser price ($16 to $25 a person), and the portions are huge. You either have to go all vegetarian or all tandoori, with only the most popular dishes included. Some of us hold the notion that vegetarian Indian food should be cheap because the ingredients are inexpensive, but to prepare any Indian dish well is labor-intensive. The food at Gaylord is so consistently bright and the appointments so civilized that I always feel a meal here is worth the price.

HAPPY VALLEY

This useful restaurant specializes in Mongolian hot pot service, fun when a group is going out to dinner. A pot of boiling broth is set on a burner in the middle of the table and platters of thinly sliced raw ingredients, beautifully arranged, are brought to the table along with spicy and mild dipping sauces, a beaten raw egg, and four kinds of ground dumpling pastes. You use chopsticks and mesh baskets on bamboo handles to cook the beef, crab, scallops, geoduck clam, shrimp, black cod, tofu, Chinese greens, and fresh herbs, and spoons to make little balls of squid, pork, beef, and fish pastes, pulling them out when they float to the top. At the end of the meal you drink the flavorful broth the food was cooked in. All guests at the table get to choose the tidbits they like, cook them as long as they like, and eat as much as they want. This style of dining proves to be light but satisfying, since there's very little fat in either the cooking method or most of the ingredients. Leave it to the twelfth-century Mongolians to invent the ideal modern diet.

Levi's Plaza, 1255 Battery Street (at Greenwich), San Francisco
Tel: 399-9393
Open for lunch Monday through Friday
10 a.m. to 3 p.m.;
dinner nightly 5 to 10 p.m.
Price: Moderate
Credit cards: AE, D, MC, V

HARBOR VILLAGE

4 Embarcadero Center
(between Clay and Drumm),
San Francisco
Tel: 781-8833
Open Monday through Friday
for lunch 11 a.m. to 2:30 p.m.,
Saturday 10:30 a.m. to
2:30 p.m., Sunday 10 a.m. to
2:30 p.m.; dinner nightly
5:30 to 9:30 p.m.
Price: Moderate
Credit cards: AE, DC, MC, V

This large, bustling branch of a Hong Kong restaurant chain mounts one of the best dim sum services in the city—and there are quite a few now. The variety of dim sum seems never ending and the quality is invariably high. With a view of the bay from the glassed-in room on Halladie Plaza, the tony, well-appointed dining rooms really do feel like Hong Kong. Women in starched white uniforms push carts silently over the carpeting offering bona fide delicacies. This is one of the few places that makes *shaolin bao,* twisted dumplings filled with shrimp, cabbage, black mushrooms, and an unexpected gush of flavorful stock, which is put into the dumpling as a gelatin but turns to liquid when the dumpling is steamed. Beautiful shrimp pearl balls, coated in opalescent rice, are filled with chopped shrimp barely bound together with a little egg. Elegant slices of cured pork shank rest on a bed of orange soybeans, waiting for a splash of Chinese vinegar from the server. Tender octopus flecked with hot red chilies and served with a mild green wasabi dipping sauce is one of the most delicious items here. Pork dumplings surprise you with the crunch of peanuts, dried shrimp, and Chinese celery. The measure of every teahouse, *har gow* (shrimp dumplings), meet the highest standards of dim sum cookery: The shrimp are naturally sweet and juicy, and the portion in each dumpling is large.

At night the dim sum carts are garaged and a long dinner menu goes into effect. The dishes, many of them inventive in a cross-cultural, Hong Kong style, are refined and attractively presented. I've had lots of intriguing preparations here, including some excellent lobster and whole fish and a signature chicken salad with fresh fruit that weaves together many different ingredients. Light, flavorful noodle dishes, made here with the thinnest strands of pasta, are a satisfying way to end a meal full of delicacies.

IL FORNAIO

I walked down to Il Fornaio the other day for lunch, expecting the usual multiunit, lowest-common-denominator Italian cooking, and ended up with one of the most stunning meals I've had in the city. The Il Fornaio at Levi's Plaza, part of an expanding chain that extends up and down the Pacific coast, is the flagship, even if the first Il Fornaio restaurant opened in a shopping center in Marin County. Not only is the cooking at a higher level at the Levi's Il Fornaio, but the space is more lyrical. A large patio filled with tables and umbrellas could be on a piazza in Italy, while a high-ceilinged interior, magnificently decorated with marble, hand-painted wall murals, terra-cotta, wrought iron, and majolica, with soaring arched windows that look out to the plaza, could be a trattoria in Milan. As in Italy, elegant materials do not mean formality; they signify the need for endurance because of constant use. People do use this Il Fornaio nonstop in all sorts of ways: as a cafe in the morning for coffee, as a take-out *panini* shop, as a bakery, and, of course, as a *ristorante*.

My great Il Fornaio meal began with *trippa alla milanese*. Now there aren't many restaurants I trust with tripe, so I looked the waiter straight in the eye and asked if I should order it. He gave me the go-ahead, and I was brought a flat metal bowl of a wonderful, rustic souplike stew with red beans, tripe, cabbage, and potatoes that melted together in the most profound way. It was the kind of dish you travel to a small Italian village to eat. After that, anything the kitchen put out would have been fine and much of it was, including a perfectly grilled piece of fresh Chilean sea bass with rosemary-scented roast potatoes and some buttery spinach, and a lively *penne all'amatriciana*, pasta tubes tossed with tomatoes, pancetta, onions, and pecorino cheese. A molded terrine of eggplant and goat cheese I used to like here has lost its sparkle, arriving as separate piles of ingredients. However, considering the huge size of the menu, which offers everything from pastas and pizzas baked in the wood-burning oven, grilled and rotisserie-cooked foods, pastas, antipasti,

Levi's Plaza, 1265 Battery Street (between Greenwich and Union),
San Francisco
Tel: 986-0100
Open Monday through Thursday 7 a.m. to 11 p.m., Friday until midnight, Saturday 8 a.m. to midnight, Sunday 8 a.m. to 11 p.m.; weekend brunch
9 a.m. to 2 p.m.
Price: Moderate
Credit cards: AE, DC, MC, V

plus an occasional authentic Italian dish or two like that *trippa*, Il Fornaio does a workmanlike job. With clever ordering you can have an Italian meal found nowhere else, especially during the monthly special menus from different regions in Italy. I've netted a great artichoke soup and some delicious, rarely found regional wines. Il Fornaio in San Francisco has the size, staff, and clientele to reach a little higher than the other units, and it gets much praise from omnivorous and adventurous eaters like me when it does.

ONE MARKET RESTAURANT

1 Market Street
(at Steuart),
San Francisco
Tel: 777-5577
Open Monday through
Friday for lunch 11:30 a.m.
to 2 p.m.; dinner
Monday through Friday
5:30 to 9:30 p.m.,
Saturday 5 to 10 p.m.,
Price: Expensive
Credit cards: AE, DC, MC, V

One Market, in the heart of the ever south-drifting Financial District, is celebrity chef Brad Ogden's most urbane venue. It offers a sweeping, sleek glass and granite dining room with power booths, a barroom with separate menu, and private dining rooms that open out onto the soaring atrium of One Market Plaza. Ogden is a great cook, but in a huge operation like this you have to delegate, especially since the Ogden empire has grown so much over the last couple of years. He and his partner Michael Dellar have opened two Lark Creek Cafes, one in Walnut Creek, the other in San Mateo, with others planned, and of course the original Lark Creek Inn has to be tended. So, Ogden has put George Morrone, former chef at Aqua, in charge at One Market.

I think the food has improved since the restaurant opened several years ago in that the dishes have become more focused and straightforward without gratuitous digression, a style that defines real American cooking. At lunch, which is always busy in this neighborhood of new office towers, people tuck into plates of delicious meat loaf with creamy pureed red potatoes and green beans. They start with a hearty "Greek" salad, a pile of romaine lushly tossed with feta, olives, and wedges of tomato, or a bowl of spicy, velvety winter squash soup. A vegetarian plate pleases meat eaters too, with a huge wedge of flavorful vegetable-filled quiche accompanied with a Caesar salad in a radicchio cup. Sounds weird, but it works. Beef Stroganoff turned out to be beef goulash, topped with sliced gherkins on a bed of coarse house-made noodles that were stuck together in a lump. This kind of preparation mistake by the kitchen happens here. You might find a big chunk of bolted romaine stem in a salad; a ravioli garnish can be tough. The scale of the operation takes its toll on the food, but in small ways. The general quality remains high.

Desserts are very fancy, decorated with many curlicues of caramelized sugar and wafer-thin leaves of pastry, but somehow the meticulous pastry kitchen sends them out perfectly dressed. I like a thin, baked-to-order apple tart, the apples barely done yet lovely, topped with a melting scoop of ice cream.

One Market prides itself on its professionalism and sophistication in its role as a big, urban restaurant. It offers every amenity—anything you want to drink, large dishes, small dishes, and a stunning interior that reminds me of the Four Seasons in New York. The design takes advantage of One Market's location with huge windows that look out to the Embarcadero, the bay, Justin Herman Plaza (the broad tree-lined end of Market Street where, in fact, a farmers' market mushrooms on Tuesdays), and tall surrounding buildings. I love the bar where you can eat oysters on the half shell, fabulous miniature hamburgers, and green chile-laced fried calamari. One Market suits Financial District business needs brilliantly. It radiates a sense of place.

PASTIS

Gerald Hirigoyen of Fringale fame has opened a second very French bistro on the north side of town. His new Pastis is a dreamy little place with wooden banquettes, a bar, a cool wall mural, and jazz playing in the background. People really like to hang out there. The intimate scale, the light, the chairs, the butcher paper–covered tables, the service, the simple menu, the affordable wine list, and the spirit of the place make them happy. Pastis feels very much like the "baby bistros" of Paris, reasonably priced small restaurants opened by fancy starred chefs who want to see a full, lively dining room for once. Like these new Parisian mainstays, Pastis is a bread-and-butter kind of operation where people really can eat every day.

I, and a lot of others, am partial to the oxtail *rouille*, a molded cake of shredded oxtail with a piquant ravigote sauce and a little green salad on the side. I could eat the spinach salad with lardons of bacon, sieved egg, and a delicious sherry

1015 Battery Street
(between Union
and Green),
San Francisco
Tel: 391-2555
Open for lunch Monday
through Friday 11:30 a.m.
to 3 p.m.; dinner Monday
through Saturday
5:30 to 10:30 p.m.
Price: Moderate
Credit Cards: AE, MC, V

vinaigrette every time, though what I really like are the generous slices of foie gras sautéed quickly in a lovely sauce made with *verjus*—tart grape juice. At $15 a serving, it's a buy.

Hirigoyen has appointed Isabelle Alexandre as chef here and I like her direct, unfussy cooking. Her pink tenderloin of lamb on a bed of thyme-seasoned white beans moistened with garlicky juices is a sensational dish. The salmis of squab marinated in red wine and surrounded by baby carrots, onions, and turnips in a dark, voluptuous sauce appeals to rare meat lovers like me. Any dish with crisp, soft, matchstick-thin *pommes frites* (french fries) is worth ordering.

And don't pass up dessert. Try the buttery pastry "package" filled with bananas and drizzled with chocolate sauce, or a caramel-meringue parfait. You'll have room, because portions here are moderate in size just like they are in France. You end up eating a civilized amount of food with wine as a complement. The two go together at Pastis in a way that makes both taste better.

This is, after all, a French restaurant. Everything flows from a strong, unified vision. Charming surroundings, good value, friendly and professional service, all the amenities as the French have defined them, add up to pure pleasure. You get a lot for your money here while you eat in style—authentic, simple French style—maybe the best restaurant style of all. It was the French, after all, who invented the restaurant.

SPLENDIDO

Four Embarcadero Center
(between Clay and Drumm),
San Francisco
Tel: 986-3222
Open Monday through
Friday for lunch 11:30 a.m. to
2:30 p.m.; bar menu served
2:30 to 5:30 p.m.; dinner
nightly 5:30 to 9:30 p.m.
Price: Moderate
Credit cards: AE, DC, MC, V

Aptly named, this dramatic restaurant boasts a flamboyant Mediterranean decor sprung from the imagination of designer Pat Kuleto. In typical Kuleto style, different areas of the sprawling room are demarcated by fantasy stage settings, all within a theme. A brick wine cellar entryway turns into a rustic wood-beamed bar-cave, which segues into a canvas-canopied garden area by windows that look out to the Ferry Building. And these are but three of the whimsically decorated areas. A huge and handsome open kitchen with a counter dominates the back portion of the restaurant, and as you walk through the podium level of Embarcadero Four, your eye is caught by a working pastry kitchen visible through a large window. A full-scale Bill Kimpton production, Splendido's goal is to offer something for everyone, not just in the style of decor, but in food and drink as well, for a good price.

Anything that comes from the oven shines at Splendido, starting with delicious house-baked Italian breads served with fruity olive oil and balsamic vinegar (for some reason), and including thin-crust pizzas, almost crackerish around the edges but tender in the middle. My favorite is topped with mozzarella and fresh tomato slices. A salad of good young lettuces, a decent pasta-and-white-bean soup, a plate of spinach- and ricotta-stuffed ravioli with brown butter and sage are good bets here. Main courses and more complicated pastas tend to be overwrought, full of unnecessary ingredients and kind of silly. However, anything from that open pastry kitchen will be lovely, especially a pomegranate and tangerine granita that looks like a glass full of jewels, and the most luscious *profiteroles* in town. The warm chocolate sauce on top of crisp cream puffs filled with unctuous vanilla ice cream is a triumph.

As in most of the Kimco restaurants (like the Italian-themed Kuleto's or Postrio), the energy buzz is almost tangible, a commodity. More is better in these restaurant productions, and restraint is not important to the concept.

TOKYO SUKIYAKI

When out-of-town friends come to San Francisco they head straight for Fisherman's Wharf. "We're just like the locals," they tell us with a wink. "We know those barking sea lions by name." As a local who lives a short walk from the wharf, I would shrug and let them go by themselves—until I rediscovered Tokyo Sukiyaki, an elegant Japanese restaurant I first visited twenty years ago. I will never forget the meal I had there. It was my first brush with real Japanese cooking. Little did I know then that I was getting a taste of what would become today's San Francisco, a city that belongs to the Pacific Rim as much as to the United States.

Climbing a flight of handsome stairs (an elevator stands open nearby) to the second-floor restaurant does not prepare you for the change in tone. In a matter of seconds you

225 Jefferson Street
(at Taylor),
San Francisco
Tel: 775-9030
Open Monday through
Friday 4 to 11 p.m.,
Saturday and Sunday
11:30 a.m. to 11 p.m.
Price: Moderate
Credit cards: AE, DC, MC, V

move from the carny bustle of wax museums and T-shirt shops to the peace of classical Japanese tatami rooms. In fact, Tokyo Sukiyaki has both Western and Japanese seating and English and Japanese menus. Both are accessible to everyone. The Western-style tables and chairs are next to large picture windows that gives diners a bird's-eye view of the wharf, while the tatami rooms, enclosed in rice paper and bamboo screens, are secluded. Beautiful woodwork, a stunning array of pottery, and waitresses in traditional Japanese kimonos give Tokyo Sukiyaki a timeless upscale look. Actually, the simple and classy decor reminds me of restaurants in midtown Manhattan.

The food is not as sophisticated as the look, though the featured dish, beef sukiyaki, is absolutely delicious. An electric burner in a wooden box is brought to the table with a shallow cast-iron pan. The waitress throws a cube of beef suet into the pan, and when it begins to melt she judiciously throws in petal-thin slices of beef, vegetables, and noodles arranged like a flower on a platter. She moistens the pan with sake and soy sauce, which cook down to form an intense caramelized sauce. You are given a clay bowl with a raw egg, into which you dip the hot foods. The foods are so hot, the egg coats them and cooks instantly, smoothing and enriching the intense flavors, a wonderful culinary transformation that occurs with each bite.

Foods cooked in broth at the table, in a service called *shabu-shabu* (a name that mimics the sound of foods being swished through liquid), represent a very clean way to eat, if not one as tasty as the sukiyaki. From the Japanese menu, which is written in English as well, I have had an excellent whole salt-broiled flounder, filleted and presented on a rectangular ceramic plate. It goes well with a small bowl of cold spinach topped with bonito flakes. Another refreshing starter brings a bowl of cold tofu cubes in a bath of ice and water. You fish out the cubes with a little gold strainer and slip them into a gingery soy sauce, the whole procedure quintessentially Japanese and delightful.

Undistinguished sake is the one surprising lapse at this rather elegant restaurant, but considering all the other civilized amenities here, Tokyo Sukiyaki is a valuable destination in the middle of San Francisco's most popular tourist area.

TAKING ADVANTAGE OF THE BAY: WHERE TO EAT WITH THE BEST VIEW

When people ask me for suggestions of restaurants with views, two yacht companies currently offering meal cruises on the bay come up over and over again. Though a bit pricy, the beauty outside their expansive picture windows makes a ride on them worthwhile. During the day, and at night as the sun sets, being on the water in these big, comfortable, smooth-riding ships can be very romantic, and you get to see the land from a perspective that makes you appreciate the geographical richness of the Bay Area more.

From a food perspective, I like the Sunday brunch cruise on the *San Francisco Spirit*, a Pacific Marine yacht that boards near Pier 39 (tel: 546-2700). The spacious, modern, handsomely appointed boat puts on a generous buffet with miraculously decent poached eggs on English muffins coated in a light, creamy hollandaise, delicious with juicy baked ham sliced to order by a chef on the serving line. The rest of the buffet consists of fruit salad, good, creamy potato salad, wilted spinach and other salads, some quite tasty, and the usual bad commercial bread and pastries. A fine Spanish sparkling wine is liberally poured. While sailing during the day may not be as romantic as at night, you see so much more. Sailboats whiz past your table; pelicans slowly soar by. A protected part of the deck lets you view everything from outside. The price ($40 for adults, $20 for children, tax and tip included) and duration (11:30 a.m. to 1:30 p.m.) feels just about right. The alternative is a Hornblower dinner cruise (tel: 788-8866, $58 to $73 per person), leaving from Pier 33 at 7 p.m. and returning at 10:30 p.m. The *California Hornblower* is one of the most majestic boats plying the bay. A white wooden structure encircled by rows of large square windows, the *Hornblower* looks a little like a tiered Victorian wedding cake. Inside, the carpeted salons are dimly lit by art deco wall sconces and candles, letting the windows frame breathtaking views of sparkling city lights. The service is formal and very friendly. Unfortunately, the food is the least satisfying part of the experience. You can taste all the corners that have been cut in the ingredients, and the execution is of the nondescript hotel variety. But there is dancing to a three-piece combo, and the drinks are not unreasonably priced. You can get a bottle of Kendall-Jackson Chardonnay, for example, for $18, and even if you don't eat very much, you leave the boat enchanted.

A STRATEGY FOR VISITING FISHERMAN'S WHARF

Who can resist going down to a waterfront, where monstrous sea lions bark and lounge on the piers, where you can hop on a ferry to Sausalito or Tiburon—or visit a wax museum? That's the problem with the wharf; it has turned into a kitschy tourist attraction with a plethora of T-shirt shops and boardwalk-candy emporia. The working part of the wharf, where San Francisco's fishing boats dock with their hauls of crab and salmon, is getting smaller and smaller as fishing is being regulated to protect diminishing supplies and the real estate gets more and more valuable. There are a number of long-established wharf restaurants that charge a pretty penny for indifferent food; you are paying for location when you eat at them. Then there are the sidewalk seafood bars and crab pots that stretch along the wharf, owned by a variety of different families. These are your best bets for getting a feel of the old working-man's wharf, when people really bought their live crabs and fresh-caught salmon there. Ideally, you can buy a whole live crab and ask that it be cooked to order in one of the huge, steaming, pressurized crab pots. The cooks will crack it for you, and with a glass or two of icy cold California Chardonnay you can have one of the nicest meals in the world. But all too often the crab has been frozen or overcooked, or cooked and then frozen. I've had every kind. You'll never get anything spoiled (the wharf smells only of appetizing fresh seafood), but you never really know what you're getting unless you see the crabs wiggling in crates. Most of the operations sell identical items: crab-salad sandwiches, shrimp cocktails, cold half lobsters, picked Dungeness crab, and tiny bay shrimp cocktails. If I had to choose one stand over another, I like the looks of Nick's; I like the funky old-wharf feeling of the street-level dining rooms of A. Sabella & La Torre; and I have actually witnessed the guys at Alioto's stand cook the crabs and crack them to order.

WU KONG

A large, modern Chinese restaurant in the Rincon Annex, Wu Kong specializes in Shanghai dishes and, in particular, Shanghai-style dim sum. The long menu can seem daunting to the uninitiated, but by seeking out Shanghai dishes, diners can have an exciting regional eating experience.

I especially love Shanghai-style appetizers like vegetable goose, a Taoist monk's dish of fried bean curd wrapped around a savory mushroom stuffing that when sliced actually looks like breast of crispy goose. Drunken squab marinated in rice wine, served cold, is refreshing, boozy, and velvet fleshed. The jellyfish salad is astonishingly crisp-tender in a tasty sesame dressing scented with lacy sprigs of Chinese parsley. Deep-fried eel, crunchy all the way through in a subtle sweet-and-sour sauce, is a must-order—even if you have doubts about eel.

Tea lunch items such as special Shanghai baby dumplings delicately stuffed with ground pork and clear broth, or steamed baby vegetable dumplings filled with Chinese greens and fruity winter melon in season, sparkle. As evidenced by the crispy eel preparation, Wu Kong's kitchen knows how to deep fry. Try yellowfish fritters, speckled with threads of seaweed. They melt in your mouth. If they are available, stir-fried blue crabs are worth the trouble it takes to get at their lovely meat. Shanghai-style onion cakes, little balls of flaky pastry dotted with sesame seeds and filled with green onions, are smashing. A bowl of chicken noodle soup, so common, yet so wonderful here, deserves a nod. The broth is the pure essence of chicken, and the little cubes of breast meat stay marvelously tender. Lest you think that the Chinese do not eat dessert, try Wu Kong's deep-fried clouds of beaten egg white with a little red bean paste at the center, deep-fried bean curd pancakes, or pan-fried Seven Treasures Rice. All are something to look forward to at the end of a tea lunch.

I think it is entirely possible to take some wrong turns when ordering a meal here, especially during the busy Financial District lunch hour. You can end up with some uninspired dishes made with canned or frozen ingredients. But weekend tea lunch or a banquet ordered and discussed

One Rincon Center (at Spear and Mission), San Francisco
Tel: 957-9300
Open for lunch daily 11 a.m. to 2:30 p.m.; dinner nightly 5:30 to 9:30 p.m.
Price: Moderate
Credit cards: AE, DC, MC, V

ahead will offer a rare culinary adventure. The large restaurant is nicely appointed, and service is attentively professional for banquets and efficient at all other times.

CAFES

PIER 40 ROASTERY

Pier 40, The Embarcadero
at Townsend Street,
San Francisco
Tel: 495-3815
Open daily 7 a.m. to 6 p.m.
Credit Cards: AE, DC, MC, V

The coffee, made from house-roasted beans, is delicious; the Central American–inspired breakfasts fresh and lively; the location, sublimely San Franciscan. You can sit at an outdoor table a foot from the water and bask in the morning sun. The wind relents on this particular shore of the bay, a stretch of the mild "Riviera" micro-climate. Indoors, this airy warehouse-like space is pleasant, too. The perfume of roasting coffee scents the air.

You order at the counter and your food is brought to you. A clean version of huevos rancheros, impeccably fried eggs with black beans, tortillas, and a pile of pristine fresh tomato salsa with *crema*, vies with house-made corned beef hash with poached eggs as my favorite. The lunch preparations

---

EATING ON PIER 39

I had a terrific sandwich the other day from a stand at the beginning of Pier 39, called BBQ Salmon on Sourdough, which pretty much sums up what it serves. For $4.75 you get a nice-sized piece of fresh salmon grilled to order (ask for it to be pink in the center if you don't want it to be dry and overcooked) and served on a crusty sourdough roll with lettuce, tomato, red onion, tartar sauce laced with fresh dill, and a fresh lemon wedge. When you eat it all together, with a squeeze of lemon, it makes for a very creditable lunch.

Farther down the pier is the Pier Market and Seafood Restaurant, which also makes grilled salmon sandwiches on a softer bread that has been deep-fried. Better is a fresh, savory salmon burger on a regular bun with tartar sauce and all the trimmings. You can get most of the typical wharf offerings here, including a cold half lobster with tartar sauce and cocktail sauce for $10.95.

don't have the sparkle of the breakfast dishes, but the location of this cafe is a real treasure. You can really sit here on the dock of the bay—drinking first-rate coffee.

BARS

GORDON BIERSCH BREWING COMPANY

This large, high-tech brew pub may be the most popular bar in town, even though it doesn't serve hard liquor. Every day downtown workers spill out into the street in front of the brewery, unable to get inside the jammed space. This has become the premier heterosexual meeting spot among those people young enough to prefer hearty beer to any other kind of drink. The place is so noisy and crowded that it's hard to see how anyone could possibly carry on a flirtatious conversation, though the upstairs dining area provides some respite.

2 Harrison Street
(at the Embarcadero),
San Francisco
Tel: 243-8246
Open Sunday through
Thursday 11 a.m.
to midnight, Friday and
Saturday until 1 a.m.
Credit cards: AE, D, MC, V

HARRY DENTON'S

Ebullient Harry Denton, often on the premises, creates the party at his bar, restaurant, and dance place just south of the Financial District. Everyone flocks here after work for a drink, a bite, and some jazz at the bar. A menu of substantial, stylish pub food is prepared at lunch and dinner. By ten o'clock, the back dining room, with a view of the bay, is cleared of tables and turns into a disco. Denton has the touch. Amidst the madhouse of people drinking, eating, and dancing, everything runs smoothly, professionally, in good spirits. From the moment it opened, Denton's has been wildly popular as a place to go for a good time.

161 Steuart Street
(between Howard
and Mission),
San Francisco
Tel: 882-1333
Open Monday through
Friday 8 a.m. to 2 a.m.,
Saturday and Sunday
8 a.m. to 2 a.m.
Credit cards: AE, D, MC, V

PIER 23 CAFE

Pier 23 (on the Embarcadero at Front Street), San Francisco
Tel: 362-5125
Open Sunday through Thursday 11:30 a.m. to 12:30 a.m., Friday and Saturday to 2 a.m.; Sunday brunch 11:30 a.m. to 3 p.m.
Credit cards: MC, V

One of the finest locations in town for a bar, this resonant old longshoreman's shack sits just yards from the bay on the water side of the Embarcadero. Patrons warming stools at the copper bar have a direct view of Treasure Island and sailing vessels just beyond a concrete pier. When the weather is warm, tables go out on the pier so you can eat and drink inches from the water. The place revs into high gear at night when live salsa, R & B, and jazz bands perform. Its excellent weekend brunch has become a San Francisco tradition. The best dish to order on the regular menu is the meat loaf with mashed potatoes in Cajun gravy. Owned by local character Flicka McGurrin, who hangs her expressive oil paintings on the walls between the stuffed marlins and sailfish, Pier 23 offers the best neighborhood ambiance of any bar on the Embarcadero.

DELICATESSENS/TAKE-OUT

ARABI

One Rincon Center
101 Spear Street (at Mission), San Francisco
Tel: 243-8575
Open Monday through Friday 7 a.m. to 2:30 p.m.
No credit cards

This Palestinian food stand, the star of the Rincon Center food court, dishes up spicy, garlicky food that tastes home cooked. The *mezze*—bulgur wheat salad, roasted eggplant puree, chickpea puree, dolmas, tomato and cucumber salad, marinated squashes in yogurt—have such depth of flavor, brightness, and balance that you can't stop dipping your pita bread into them. The pita filled with felafel sparkles; each bite is gloriously rich, juicy, and spicy. Chicken kabobs made velvety by a lemony marinade seem to melt in your mouth. Also try the *mujadara*, a deeply seasoned stew of rice and lentils topped with caramelized onions. Of course you have to eat all this wonderful food on paper and plastic in the noisy, crowded atrium, where the smells of cigarette smoke and spicy food waft through the air, but frankly, this environment does evoke North African markets, where you probably wouldn't find food as good as this.

BAKERIES/PASTRIES

BAGEL KING

The onion bagel won me over. Instead of acrid burned bits stuck to the top and bottom, caramelized onion is incorporated into the dough, which is properly boiled, then baked. These are real bagels: chewy, flavorful, dense. They can be ordered with all sorts of cream cheese spreads and some inappropriate fillings as well. But the bagels themselves are top-notch, a blessing for anyone in the neighborhood who want to eat them at the office or bring them home after work.

70 Mission Street
(between Steuart and Spear),
San Francisco
Tel: 278-9502
Open Monday through Friday 5:45 a.m. to 4 p.m., Saturday and Sunday 7:30 a.m. to 2:30 p.m.
No credit cards

BOUDIN SOURDOUGH BAKERY AND CAFE

When I'm down on the wharf I always stop at this Boudin outlet to buy one of their 1½-pound sourdough rounds. This particular kind of San Francisco sourdough has a tenderer crust, a softer but more dense interior, and less sourness than the equally famous Parisian loaf. The breads at this original bakery site are always very fresh because of the volume. For $11.50 you can get six loaves in a travel box, ready to check onto airline baggage. You also can buy a small round, walk up to the wharf to buy crab cocktails and a pound of shrimp in the shell, stroll down to a less crowded spot on a pier by the water, and have the quintessential San Francisco wharf picnic.

156 Jefferson Street
(between Taylor and Mason),
San Francisco
Tel: 928-1849
Open daily
7:30 a.m. to 8 p.m.
Credit cards: AE, MC, V

ICE CREAM/CHOCOLATES

SEE'S CANDIES

Three Embarcadero Center (at Drumm),
San Francisco
Tel: 391-1622
Open weekdays 10 a.m. to 7 p.m.,
Saturday until 5 p.m., Sunday noon to 5 p.m.
No credit cards
See listing, page 386.

PRODUCE

FERRY PLAZA FARMERS' MARKET

On the Embarcadero in front of the Ferry Building at Market Street
Open Saturdays around 8:30 a.m. to 2 p.m.

Serious food shoppers are fiercely loyal to their own farmers' market, the one they go to religiously every time it happens, the one where they have their favorite farmers, their favorite tomatoes, their favorite flowers. Well, mine is the Ferry Plaza Farmers' Market, a relatively new market started by organic-produce activist Sibella Krause. The Embarcadero market has taken such firm root in the community that after operating only one season it decided to stay open year round. The shoppers wouldn't let it close.

The trip to the market with empty baskets and canvas bags has become a Saturday ritual for thousands of San Franciscans who probably never shopped at a farmers' market before. At first they may have been stunned by the prices, which are high, because most of the produce sold at this market is organic. But once they tasted an organic peach or tomato, picked ripe, carefully packed, and brought to market that morning, they couldn't go back to the flavorless commercial kind. The taste of this organic produce is incomparable, and when you think about the time, effort, and expense of the farmers, paying more for it does not seem out of line. Though supermarket produce may be half the price of the organic produce sold at the market, it's not worth eating if it tastes like cardboard. More and more people, skeptical at first, are being won over. They come regularly to the market, buy more, taste more, learn about the importance of sustainable agriculture, and are feeding themselves and their families much the better for it.

This market is more than a produce depot, though one would be hard pressed to find a better seasonal gathering of locally grown fruits and vegetables. There is an egg vendor with free-range organic eggs of every size and color, including exquisite-tasting little pullet eggs; a mushroom stand with domestic brown Italian, oyster, Portobello, and shiitake mushrooms, to name just a few; a farmhouse goat cheese producer, Redwood Hill Goat Dairy; an organic cow's milk and butter producer, Straus Family Dairy; a fine producer of sheep's milk cheeses and lamb, Bellweather Farms; Bud Hoffman with his beautiful quail, squab, free-range chickens, rabbit, pheasant, and smoked game birds; Paul Johnson from Monterey Fish with salmon, crabs, mussels, rockfish, yellowfin tuna, and whatever else has come in that day; David Gingrass with his unsurpassed salami, pepperoni, and liverwurst; Acme Bread from Berkeley; the Downtown Bakery and Creamery from Healdsburg; flower vendors, orchid vendors, rose specialists; and the most dedicated, talented array of farmers anywhere. If you just come down once and take a few tastes you'll be hooked. Everyone will think that your cooking has improved, and it will when you start using these flavor-packed ingredients. You'll be inspired to cook more often, to try new things, to taste in a way you never have before.

On top of all the beautiful food, there is an ongoing shop-with-the-chef program, in which local chefs walk around the market assembling a basket of ingredients, demonstrate how they would use them, and then raffle off the basket. Every top chef in the city has made the tour, coming up with some extraordinary menus. For the little ones, there is a nearly free hands-on cooking class every Saturday at 10 a.m., which

JARDINIÈRE

6 slices good-quality thick-sliced bacon, cut into 1-inch pieces
2 tablespoons olive oil
1/4 cup flour
6 cups chicken broth
2 bay leaves
2 tablespoons minced garlic, plus 2 plump garlic cloves
1 bunch Italian (flat-leaf) parsley, leaves coarsely chopped and stems reserved
2 teaspoons minced fresh thyme (about 6 sprigs), plus 4 whole sprigs
2 teaspoons kosher salt
Freshly ground pepper
15 new potatoes, cut in half or quarters or left whole depending on size
2 onions, cut into quarters
2 bunches small leeks, trimmed to 4 inches
2 bunches small carrots, each about 3 inches long
1 pound green beans (Blue Lakes, Romanos, Kentucky Wonder, or tiny French haricots verts, or a combination), stem ends trimmed
2 pounds fava beans
2 pounds English peas, shelled
Up to 1 cup water as needed

Anne Haskell, my former partner at Hayes Street Grill and a great French home cook, makes this luscious vegetable stew in spring when English peas and favas come to market. Except for the potatoes, carrots, green beans, peas, and onions, which are crucial, the recipe is quite flexible. Fava beans and leeks are nice additions, as are asparagus, sugar snap peas, and green garlic. In April, May, and June, the vegetables are the most tender and sweet.

In a heavy pot large enough to hold all the cooked vegetables, cook the bacon in the olive oil until crisp. Remove the bacon pieces to a plate.

In the remaining fat, cook and stir the flour until golden, about 5 minutes. Add the chicken broth. Bring to a boil, then lower heat to a simmer. Add the bay leaves, minced garlic, the parsley stems tied with 4 sprigs of thyme, the kosher salt, and 20 turns of a peppermill.

Add the potatoes and cook until they are about half done, 10 to 15 minutes. Add the onions, leeks, and carrots and cook 10 minutes longer. If the potatoes are done at this point (a paring knife pierces them easily), remove them.

Add the green beans and continue to cook until they are crisp-tender. Taste and adjust the seasoning. Return the potatoes, if you removed them. The stew may be cooked several hours ahead at this point.

Shell the fava beans, then remove the skins by blanching the beans in boiling water for 30 seconds and popping out the bright green fava inside the thick gray-green skin.

Ten minutes before serving, bring the jardinière to a bare simmer. Add a little water if it looks dry, and add the peas, fava beans, minced thyme, 2 tablespoons of the chopped parsley, and the garlic cloves. Stir gently and cook for 10 minutes.

Stir in the reserved bacon and serve in soup plates with good bread. Sprinkle with fresh parsley.

Serves 4 to 6

gives young children a taste of some of the nicest things in the market; and once a month, at the height of tomato season or stone-fruit season or melon season, the Ferry Plaza Farmers' Market sponsors comparative tastings of many different varietals, and local restaurants set up booths where they cook seasonal bites—like grilled corn with spicy chili butter, grilled salmon sandwiches with tomatoes, or grilled asparagus tossed with Parmesan and olive oil.

The feeling here is different from that at any other farmers' market. Although there are few bargains to be found, you can get your hands on the highest-quality produce in the Bay Area for prices under what you would pay at specialty stores, if you could find like quality. That's the big advantage of shopping at a farmers' market: you get the produce in perfect condition, fresh picked, and full of flavor and nutrition. Many of us are unable (or unwilling) to buy the latest consumer luxuries, but why not try a perfect peach? The pleasure it gives ranks as high as practically anything I can think of. For about $1, why not take the plunge?

COOKWARE AND BOOKS

COST PLUS IMPORTS

The prices used to be fantastic at this gigantic warehouse of imported goods ranging from foodstuffs to dishes, cotton goods to baskets. I once shopped here for platters and serving bowls, but the prices rose and the pieces weren't as attractive as those I could find at Crate and Barrel for the same price. But there are always bargains, especially in Asian dishware and handwoven baskets. Cost Plus has one of the largest collection of baskets anywhere, and I have discovered, along with every caterer in town, that flat-woven rimmed baskets in different-sized circles are good for serving foods like cheese, fruit, bread, cookies, and raw vegetables. Baskets are light, unbreakable, and easy to transport. Just by wandering through the aisles at Cost Plus, you'll get some good ideas for presenting food in them.

2552 Taylor Street
(between Bay
and Northpoint),
San Francisco
Tel: 928-6200
Open daily 9 a.m. to 9 p.m.
Credit cards: MC, V

QUAIL STUFFED WITH PANCETTA AND SAGE LEAVES

6 quail, bone-in
6 thin slices pancetta
17 large sage leaves (about 1 bunch)
1/3 cup plus 2 tablespoons olive oil
2 teaspoons minced garlic
1 tablespoon butter
1 cup dry white wine
Kosher salt and freshly ground pepper to taste
1/2 cup water

You can buy superb quail from Bud Hoffman's poultry table at the Ferry Plaza Farmers' Market. He also has rabbit, poussin, pheasant, duck, fabulous chicken, and some smoked birds as well. You can get pancetta, which is unsmoked, cured, and rolled Italian bacon, at any Italian delicatessen mentioned in this book. Serve these quail with polenta, and be sure to use your fingers when you eat them to get all the meat off the tiny legs. This failsafe recipe came to me from Anne Haskell, adapted from *Marcella's Italian Kitchen* by Marcella Hazan.

Rinse the quail and pat them dry with paper towels. Stuff 1 slice of pancetta and 2 sage leaves into each cavity.

In a bowl large enough to hold the quail, combine 1/3 cup of the olive oil, the garlic, and the remaining 5 sage leaves. Add the quail, stir them gently in the marinade, cover, and refrigerate for at least 2, and up to 24, hours.

In a skillet just large enough to hold the quail on their sides, melt the butter and 2 tablespoons olive oil over medium-high heat. Brown the quail well on all sides, 4 to 5 minutes. Pour off the fat. Add the white wine, salt, and pepper. Let the wine bubble for 1 minute. Turn the quail and lower the heat until the sauce is just simmering. Cover the skillet with the lid slightly askew and cook, turning the quail every 20 minutes, until cooked through and tender, depending on the size of the birds, about 45 to 60 minutes (insert a knife in the breast at the bone; the flesh should not be pink). Transfer the quail to a warmed dish or serving platter. Turn the heat to high. When the pan juices are boiling, add the water and let the mixture bubble for 30 seconds. The juices will thicken slightly. Pour over the quail and serve.

Serves 3 to 4

WILLIAMS-SONOMA

Two Embarcadero Center (between Front and Sacramento),
San Francisco
Tel: 421-2033
Open weekdays 10 a.m. to 7 p.m.,
Saturday until 6 p.m., Sunday noon to 5 p.m.
Credit cards: AE, D, MC, V
See listing, page 157.

Financial District & Union Square

FINANCIAL DISTRICT & UNION SQUARE

Restaurants:
1. Alfred's Steak House   123
2. Anjou   124
3. Aqua   124
4. Armani Cafe   126
5. Burma's House   127
6. Café Claude   127
7. Campton Place   128
8. Cypress Club   129
9. Fleur de Lys   130
10. Le Central   131
11. MacArthur Park   131
12. Masa's   132
13. Original Joe's   133
14. Pacific   134
15. Palio d'Asti   135
16. Postrio   136
17. Rotunda at Neiman-Marcus   136
18. Rubicon   137
19. Rumpus   139
20. Sam's Grill   139
21. Sanraku Four Seasons   140
22. Scala's Bistro   141
23. Sears Fine Foods   142
24. Sol y Luna Restaurante   142
25. Tadich Grill   143
26. Vertigo   144
27. Yank Sing   145

Cafes:
28. Café de la Presse   146
29. Palio Paninoteca   146

Bars:
30. Bix   147
31. Harry Denton's Starlight Room   148
32. Red Room   148

Delicatessens/Take-Out:
33. Blondie's Pizza   149
34. Macy's Cellar   149
17. Neiman-Marcus Epicure   150
35. Specialty's Cafe and Bakery   150
27. Yank Sing   151

Ice Cream/Chocolates:
36. Candy Jar   152
37. Morrow's Nut House   152
38. See's Candies   153
39. Teuscher Chocolates of Switzerland   153

Wines and Spirits:
40. London Wine Bar   154

Cookware and Books:
41. Crate and Barrel   154
34. Macy's Cellar   155
42. Sur La Table   156
43. Williams-Sonoma   157

RESTAURANTS

ALFRED'S STEAK HOUSE

Alfred's, one of San Francisco's oldest restaurants, reassures us that the old-fashioned steak house, especially a clubby, traditional one with Italian overtones, can live on in a city overtaken by salad and pasta. At Alfred's the cocktails will be forthcoming, the service professional, and the amenities traditional: heavy white linen, booths, big tables, large upholstered chairs. If you want comfort and a luscious piece of dry-aged beef, you can count on this restaurant. It is the same today as when I first ate there eighteen years ago, and probably when it first opened over sixty years ago.

Although the menu offers a number of Italian dishes, everyone knows to stick to the steaks. The T-bone and the Alfred's Steak, which is a bone-in New York, are exemplary by today's standards: full of flavor and tender. The Porterhouse is magnificent on both sides of the bone. I have not eaten better beef anywhere in town. Expert grilling over mesquite means that your meat will be cooked to exact specification without acrid burn marks or a cold center. The grillers at Alfred's know how to control the fire. With these steaks come sweet-fleshed baked Idaho potatoes, properly soft, dry, and light textured, with real, not imitation, fixings.

Everything else on the menu can be hit or miss. The Caesar salad, made at tableside, varies with the mood of the waiter. The house green salad with a ton of blue cheese has a sugary sweet, mayonnaise-based dressing. Believe me, a foray into

659 Merchant Street,
San Francisco
Tel: 781-7058
Open for lunch Thursday
11:30 a.m. to 2:30 p.m.;
dinner Sunday through
Thursday 5:30 to 9:30 p.m.,
Friday and Saturday
5:30 to 10 p.m.
Price: Expensive
Credit cards: AE, MC, V

the Italian section (the antipasto is OK) only underscores that Alfred's remains first and foremost an excellent steak house. In this era of chain operations, Alfred's stands out as an individual—crusty, aging, smoky, masculine—and just where you want to go if you're hungry for red meat.

ANJOU

44 Campton Place (between Sutter and Post, Stockton and Grant), San Francisco
Tel: 392-5373
Open for lunch Tuesday through Saturday 11:30 a.m. to 2:30 p.m.; dinner 5:30 to 10 p.m.
Price: Moderate
Credit cards: AE, D, DC, MC, V

This cozy, very French bistro around the corner from Campton Place used to be called Janot's, but besides the name, nothing has changed since one partner, Chef Pierre Morin, bought out the other, Jacques Janot. This is still a haven for delicious, classic bistro fare such as calf's liver with bacon and onions, and the sweetest, creamiest chicken liver sauté you'll ever run across. A warm spinach salad with bacon topped by a juicy grilled quail, and a house-made seafood sausage on warm cabbage salad in a vinegary butter sauce are other signature dishes. One of my favorites is a warm duck-leg *confit* surrounded by a wreath of endive and watercress in a tart dressing. Typical of the well-prepared bistro dishes are tender, juicy rib lamb chops on a bed of delicately minted fresh *flageolets*, and a thin steak topped with a rosette of herb-shallot butter and accompanied with good *pommes frites* and French-cut green beans. Who could ask for anything more? The desserts may have fallen down a bit, but if Morin's hazelnut napoleon is available, give it a try. When it's fresh, it's a masterpiece. Prices are still amazingly reasonable, and eating at the tiny pushed-together cafe tables on two levels in this brick-walled dining room, softened by a floral canopy, feels very Parisian.

AQUA

252 California Street (between Battery and Front), San Francisco
Tel: 956-9662
Open for lunch Monday through Friday 11:30 a.m. to 2:15 p.m.;

Though founding chef George Morrone has left Aqua (to become executive chef down the street at One Market), his sous chef for three and a half years, Michael Minna, has carried on in much the same style and spirit, a combination of French (via New York) formality with the imaginative eclecticism of California. Aqua is an elegant seafood restaurant inspired in tone by the great Le Bernardin in New York. It has garnered a reputation for sophisticated, first-class service. Once you're known there your treatment becomes personal, completely tailored to your most minute preferences. Even if you're not known and are throwing an expense account party for business purposes, as many do here, the service is so professional and smooth you never have to worry about making the right impression.

dinner Monday through Saturday
5:30 to 10:30 p.m.
Price: Expensive
Credit cards: AE, DC, MC, V

The fact is, Aqua is one of the few dining rooms in the city that offers this degree of comfort and luxury. Conveniently located right next to Tadich Grill in the Financial District, with big plate-glass windows looking out to California Street and the cable car line, the interior, carpeted and draped in the palest shades of peach and decorated with gargantuan flower arrangements on sculpted pedestals, is indeed a civilized place to dine. While most other rooms in town lean more to the bustling bistro mode, Aqua's heavily linened tables and upholstered armchairs are spaced for comfort. The scale is grander here, yet completely contemporary. People are expected to eat a leisurely full-course meal with wine, and indeed, the complicated plates take some time coming out of the kitchen.

Some dishes are a revelation, like a pairing of rare tuna with foie gras that is absolutely stunning, as odd as the combination sounds. It must have been inspired by the flavor of *maguro*, the belly meat of tuna, which does taste like foie gras. A savory black mussel soufflé has become another constant on the menu, deservedly so. And diners can indulge in full out culinary luxury—a parfait of Russian ossetra caviar molded on top of a crisp potato cake with layers of crème fraîche and chopped egg, or a whole roasted foie gras with fruit garnish and glaze that actually ends up tasting like very delicate calf's liver. (I like my foie gras barely warmed through.) One night during Aqua's fifth anniversary celebration, the kitchen prepared a gorgeous, full-flavored consommé of wild mushrooms with sweet little bay scallops and a roasted Maine lobster with meat juice, a combination that Minna likes. The fish dishes can get elaborate with strong, reduced sauces and fussy presentation, which detracts from their purity, especially when first-rate ingredients are being used. At Le Bernardin, which is solidly founded in French technique, you are awed by the beauty of the ingredient first and then by the art of the preparation. The cooking at Aqua is jazzier than that, and people eat here for the total experience as opposed to paying homage at a temple of exquisite foods from the sea.

ARMANI CAFE

One Grant Avenue (between O'Farrell and Stockton), San Francisco
Tel: 677-9010
Open Monday through Saturday 10 a.m. to 4:30 p.m., Sunday noon to 4:30 p.m.
Price: Moderate
Credit cards: AE, D, MC, V

The Armani Cafe consists of a large oval island of counters and stools in the middle of an imposing former bank building now filled with Armani suits. Sidewalk tables are put out during good weather and are always full. Like the shoes, purses, toiletries, and other accoutrements of the Armani lifestyle, the cafe is an extension of Armani taste. In fact, it was reported during the opening that the king himself designed the menu and cafe. Peculiarly enough, lunch here does have a European graciousness, even if you have to sit on your coat at the counter and drop your bags on the floor. An elegantly suited maître d' seats you, and if you have to wait, he'll track you down among the blouses.

The best dish on the small menu is the pizza Ortolano, a thin, chewy crust paved with Fontina, chopped arugula, and radicchio drizzled with truffle oil. The bitter lettuces turn fruity as they melt into the fine imported cheese. A salad of artichokes, shaved Parmesan and baby greens with any of the pizzas and a glass of Italian Merlot make for one of the best downtown lunches. The pastas are OK, but don't sparkle; the antipasto misto is a mishmash. Desserts, however, are worth ordering. I am partial to an espresso granita parfait—icy coffee crystals layered with sweetened whipped cream. The warm chocolate soufflé cake served in a little white dish topped with hazelnut ice cream oozes in a very seductive way. Espresso is top-notch. When the tables and green metal chairs are arranged outside along Grant Avenue and O'Farrell Street, they become some of the most prized seats in town.

BURMA'S HOUSE

A Burmese meal can be a roller coaster of hot, sweet, and sour sensations, and Burma's House is a good place to hop on for the ride. Though the large menu looks daunting at first, it can be decoded by referring to small color photographs of selected dishes. The best and most typical plates to order are the Burmese salads, spectacular mélanges of spicy toasted ingredients individually arranged on a plate in little piles and mixed together at the table by the waiter with a squeeze of lime. The ginger salad epitomizes the genre, with tiny threads of fresh young ginger, toasted coconut, lentils and yellow split peas, fried garlic chips, fresh green chilies, and toasted sesame seeds. It's worth a visit to this restaurant just for this or their mango salad, made of finely julienned strips of green and ripe mangos, cucumber, chilies, and onion topped with deep-fried onion threads. It really is lovely. There are many Chinese-style stir fries and some strong-flavored stews, my favorite being fork-tender pork, potato, and onions in a classic yellow Burmese curry, served with rice cooked in coconut milk and scattered with fried onion threads. The decor here is nondescript, and the service can run hot or cold depending on your waiter, but when you're in the mood for something very spicy, completely exotic, and like nothing you've ever tasted before, head for Burma's House.

720 Post Street (between Jones and Leavenworth), San Francisco
Tel: 775-1156
Open daily
11:30 a.m. to 10 p.m.
Price: Inexpensive
Credit cards: MC, V

CAFÉ CLAUDE

This is one of my favorite lunch places in the city because it captures so well the spirit of the cafes I love in Paris. In fact, all the furnishings came from a small bar and *tabac* in the eleventh arrondisement that was about to be torn down. Café Claude's owner saved most of the interior intact and had it shipped to San Francisco, so the small, hidden-away space is full of vintage fifties French cafe chairs, banquettes, and tables, a bona fide zinc bar, and old cinema posters. The food and wines are typical: the delicious, crusty grilled-cheese sandwiches called *croque monsieur*, with a cheesy béchamel

7 Claude Lane (off Bush between Grant and Kearny), San Francisco
Tel: 392-3505
Open Monday through Friday 8 a.m. to 10 p.m., Saturday 10 a.m. to midnight
Price: Inexpensive
Credit cards: AE, D, MC, V

broiled on top of the sandwich and smoky Black Forest ham inside; green salad in a simple vinaigrette; *assiettes*, or plates of charcuterie, or smoked trout with vegetable salads; an authentic *salade niçoise;* and French-style sandwiches on buttered very fresh baguettes with thin slices of *saucisson sec* or ham inside. To wash all this down, glasses of inexpensive Rhône, Beaujolais, and Mâcon Blanc are sold by the glass, just as in France. The coffee is strong, and the waiters are French, young, and cute.

CAMPTON PLACE

340 Stockton Street
(between Post and Sutter),
San Francisco
Tel: 781-5555
Open for breakfast Monday through Friday 7 to 10:30 a.m., Saturday 8 to 11 a.m., Sunday brunch 10 a.m. to 2 p.m.; for lunch Monday through Friday 11:30 a.m. to 2 p.m., Saturday noon to 2 p.m.; dinner Monday through Thursday 6 to 10 p.m., Friday and Saturday 5:30 to 10:30 p.m., Sunday 6 to 9:30 p.m.
Price: Expensive
Credit cards: AE, DC, MC, V

It takes dedication from the top down to personalize a hotel restaurant, but the succession of dynasties at small, luxurious Campton Place have remained committed over the years. The current chef, Todd Humphries, formerly of Lespinasse in New York, took about a year to settle in, but now he is turning out his own refined and interesting food. His creations weave together a lot of ingredients—tiny diced vegetables, fragrant herbs, stocks and natural juices, exotic aromatics and spices—but Humphries controls the whole symphony. He uses seasonal ingredients as a focus.

In the spring you will find crunchy soft-shell crabs atop a luscious dab of creamed corn; or juicy squab on a bed of roasted corn, chanterelles, and green garlic moistened with foie gras, garnished with quail leg *confit*, served with nice cleansing spinach. It's a great dish. Or there might be roasted lobster sliced onto a sweet corn and rice risotto. Try a fantasy dish mundanely called tuna tartar (you'll be surprised and delighted) or the meltingly tender braised beef short ribs, deboned, with mashed potatoes and truffle sauce. Desserts can be iffy depending on when they were baked—I've had superb, fresh ones, particularly at lunch, and tired ones at dinner. Lunch dishes can be hit or miss. The lunch menu is a potpourri of unrelated dishes lacking in focus, but I wouldn't turn down a lunch invitation, especially preceded by a cocktail in the sophisticated little barroom.

From the moment it opened in 1983 with Brad Ogden as chef, Campton Place set out to create an environment of substantial, intelligent luxury. The dining room is small and quiet with soft banquettes, antique chairs, thick carpeting. Service runs deep. I've been greeted and waited upon by a lot of women here over the years—unusual in a high-end restuarant—and they are real pros. They know the menu, the wine list, and what you need before you want it. I've always felt personally cared for in this dining room.

Campton Place's opulent if pricy breakfast service is always fun, offering freshly baked breakfast breads, sweet rolls, and corn sticks, and gentle twists on such brunch classics as poached eggs with a delicate butter sauce on housemade English muffins; smoked salmon omelets; and a breakfast hash made of unexpected ingredients, such as chicken, turkey, or vegetables.

CYPRESS CLUB

Stop by this amazing-looking restaurant and bar just to see the opulent decor: a 1930s supper club gone wild. Huge nipple-shaped blown-glass light fixtures hang from a ceiling of enormous blimplike protrubances, glamorously enameled. Gigantic urn-shaped pillars, pounded copper archways, curved inlaid wood-paneled walls, a running wall mural of Northern California scenes that encircles the room, multicolored wooden floors, stone mosaic floors, overstuffed velvet booths and chairs, and a magnificent cast-bronze front door create an almost surrealistic baroque grandeur. Many people, in very chic costume, like to stop by the bar for a drink to check each other out. Others plumb the eclectic menu for a meal. The most interesting dishes feature game, inventively prepared and very good. An important wine list of new and old bottles await pairing with dishes that lend themselves to drinking serious red wine. Intelligent, sophisticated, very professional front-of-the-house man John Cunin is a principal here and has set up a first-class dining room staff that is knowledgeable about wine. However, the bartenders, for whatever reason, don't seem to uphold the same rigorous performance standards. Perhaps the spirits drinkers don't demand it.

500 Jackson Street
(between Columbus
and Montgomery),
San Francisco
Tel: 296-8555
Open daily 4:30 to 10:30 p.m.
Price: Expensive
Credit cards: AE, CB, DC, MC, V

FLEUR DE LYS

777 Sutter Street (between Taylor and Jones), San Francisco
Tel: 673-7779
Open Monday through Thursday 6 to 9:30 p.m., Friday and Saturday 5:30 to 10:30 p.m.
Price: Expensive
Credit cards: AE, DC, MC, V

Chef Hubert Keller put Fleur de Lys back on the map of important restaurants in the city when he took over this Michael Taylor–designed dining room in partnership with Maurice Rouas over a decade ago, and it has been full ever since. This is one of the most romantic-looking restaurants in the city, with the main dining area actually inside a Provençal floral print tent. One side of this draped tent is mirrored so cleverly it gives the illusion you're in a room twice as large. Little shaded lamps protrude from the material giving this soft structure an intimate glow. In the center of the room, under the peak of the tent, a towering exotic flower arrangement rises up out of the sea of tables to meet a huge wrought-iron chandelier.

Keller's cooking is equally pretty. He starts you out with charming little bites—a morsel of foie gras and chanterelles in a miniature cast-iron skillet; a tiny, savory wedge of Alsatian potato and onion cake; a bite of cauliflower puree topped with caviar and flanked with tiny purple potato chips. And then the meal unfolds with colorful, multifaceted dishes that almost always include a luxury ingredient, sometimes two or three. A thick slice of seared foie gras takes on new dimension from a sauce larded with smoked duck breast. Pink and juicy lamb chops have a crunchy coating that adds both texture and flavor. On his famous four-course, $52 vegetarian menu, Keller came up one evening with two really satisfying creations: a ragout of wild mushrooms with house-made shell pasta that mirrored the texture of the mushrooms; and a braise of celery hearts in a tomatoey Provençal sauce with niçoise olives. As an omnivore, I appreciated eating such a clean but voluptuous meal.

Partner Maurice Rouas works the dining room, telling jokes on himself, and Keller and his beautiful pastry-chef wife Chantal come out at the end of the evening to pay their regards to their fans. Fleur de Lys is run like a family restaurant, the way many starred restaurants in France are. The owners do the lion's share of the work themselves and take pleasure and pride in doing it. They set the tone. Fleur de Lys, though certainly expensive, fancy, and French, is not stuffy or pretentious. It's a place for a celebratory meal and a good time.

LE CENTRAL

What the food lacks in brilliance at Le Central, San Francisco's most authentic French brasserie, it makes up for in dependability and the exact replication of a beloved French form. The tiny crowded-together tables covered with butcher paper, the menu written in grease pencil on the mirrors, the celebrity lunchers like Mayor Willie Brown and pals strategically seated at tables in the front windows all give Le Central its cachet. When you're at the zinc bar sipping a Pernod, you can easily imagine yourself in Paris, and when you're at table, you'll be eating just what you might in the City of Light.

Start with a butterleaf salad with walnuts in a mustardy vinaigrette, tender braised leeks, or celery root rémoulade. Continue with roast chicken with watercress, a grilled tomato half, and *pommes frites*. My favorite dish here is the *boudin noir*, blood sausage from master *charcutiers* Marcel and Henri. The fat black aromatic sausages are sautéed to the bursting point, with lots of caramelized onions. The restaurant often has poached skate wing with capers in a vinegary butter sauce and prepares it perfectly. The desserts are brought in from Tarts, among others, who do a fine job on their buttery crusts and rich fillings, and the house Chardonnay comes from Chalone, a California winery inspired by the great wine makers of Burgandy. So all a diner's needs are met in a thoroughly French way.

453 Bush Street (between Grant and Kearny),
San Francisco
Tel: 391-2233
Open Monday through Saturday 11:30 a.m to 10:30 p.m.
Price: Moderate
Credit cards: AE, DC, MC, V

MACARTHUR PARK

For twenty-five years now MacArthur Park has been slowly smoking the best baby back ribs in town: moist, crisp, tangy, with a nicely balanced sweet-and-sour barbecue sauce served on the side. Half and whole slabs come with piles of skinny french fries and excellent coleslaw in a creamy, horseradish-spiked dressing. Other signature dishes include a tangle of deep-fried onion strings and, to my mind, a rather blandly dressed, if very popular, Cobb salad. Hearty American dishes like pork chops, juicy hamburgers, and sautéed calf's liver

607 Front Street (at Jackson),
San Francisco
Tel: 398-5700
Open for lunch Monday through Friday 11:30 a.m. to 3:30 p.m.; dinner Monday through Thursday 5 to 10 p.m., Friday and Saturday until 11 p.m., Sunday 4:30 to 10 p.m.
Price: Moderate
Credit cards: AE, CB, DC, MC, V

with bacon and onions are your best bets. The endless red-brick building was once a Barbary Coast produce district warehouse. I like the glassed-in front dining room that looks out to the greenery of Jackson Square, away from a long bar that gets lots of noisy play after work.

MASA'S

Hotel Vintage Court
648 Bush Street (between Powell and Stockton), San Francisco
Tel: 989-7154
Open Tuesday through Saturday at 6 p.m.; last seating at 9:30 p.m.
Price: Expensive
Credit cards: AE, DC, D, MC, V

Julian Serrano's cooking is what I dream about when I want a three-star French meal. He's the only chef in the Bay Area who has taken on the challenge with absolute conviction and unfaltering standards. You have nothing to worry about here. From the moment you walk in the door, the restaurant falls into action, playing its role as dispenser of the highest form of culinary art.

Serrano is a purist. He starts by finding superior raw materials, from *haricots verts* to imported cheeses, from lobster, scallops, and wild ocean fish to game birds, foie gras, and lamb. He bases his dishes around the beautiful ingredients and makes a dish only if he is inspired by what he gets. His suppliers know not to send him anything that is not extraordinary, because price is not an object. When he conceives a dish, it uses the magic of classical French technique without ever taking a short cut. You can taste the dedication in his cooking. The stocks are fresh and full of flavor, so there never has to be over-reduction, over-salting, or intrusive seasoning. The vegetables, so tiny, yet always ripe and full of sweetness, are handled gently. The birds are marinated in fine wines; the cooking of them is brief but just enough; the outcome brilliant. You don't have to muddle over what to order here because every dish will deliver a little shock of surprise at its deliciousness. Some of my favorites over the years have been a ragout of vegetables, foie gras, and black truffles served in a deep, covered bowl so that when the top is removed at the table, the fragrance of truffles wafts up. It's a glorious dish. Ask for it in the winter. Another dazzling first course brings a napoleon of alternating potato and lobster slices in a sharp, saffron-scented vinaigrette, topped with a beehive of deep-fried leek threads. The whole composition seems to melt together with each bite in a miraculous way. The roast squab, served in its own juice, is rivaled only by Alice Waters's at Chez Panisse. I always have to have it. Lamb is velvety and moist under a coating of herb-scented bread crumbs. Tiny onion tarts, corn custards, and exquisite vegetables are chosen to accompany, but the star of each dish is always the main ingredient.

You can order a la carte, or you can pretty much make up your own prix-fixe meal at two different levels, or you may leave the decisions to the kitchen. No matter which way you go, you should discuss the meal with the sommelier who will match each course with a completely eclectic and fascinating selection of wines, glass by glass if you want, that might range from Sercial Madeira to local small producers to great Sauternes. My feeling is that you should walk into Masa's willing to spend $150 a person, just the way you do in a three-star in France (actually, you would probably spend half again as much in Paris), and put yourself in the hands of the staff, expense be damned—unless you know what you love. I am always tortured by the choice of ordering just two of my favorite dishes with a great bottle of wine, and finishing with the best cheeses in the city, or trying new combinations of food and wine that always prove to be a revelation. Either avenue leads to heaven.

One problem for some people is the way the reservations are booked, either early, between 6 or 6:30, or late, starting at 9, because the kitchen does not want a full dining room of people all ordering at the same time. When you taste the beauty of this cooking, with every single dish started practically from scratch and cooked to order, you'll understand why.

ORIGINAL JOE'S

Once you've tasted one of Original Joe's famous three-quarter-pound hamburger steaks formed from coarsely ground beef, coated in chopped onions, and cooked medium rare on the griddle, you'll brave the neighborhood to eat here. This restaurant has been cranking out quintessential Joe's type food for over a half century: inexpensive, plentiful, of amazingly high quality. It's a cuisine based on beef (which the kitchen butchers itself from sides), sourdough bread, precooked pasta in meat sauce, fresh, if much-cooked, vegetables,

144 Taylor Street (between Eddy and Turk), San Francisco
Tel: 775-4877
Open daily 10:30 a.m. to 12:30 a.m.
Price: Inexpensive
Credit cards: DC, MC, V

and some daily long-cooked braised dishes. The way the bread is handled, for example—hollowed out, buttered, and grilled for hamburgers; sliced and bakery fresh with lots of pats of cold salted butter for the tables; pressed and griddled for gigantic ham and cheese sandwiches—teaches you something about the practical wisdom of San Francisco's culinary past. Once you've made it to the front door (there are attended parking lots directly next door and across the street) on one of the diciest blocks in the Tenderloin, you can sit in one of the commodious ancient booths or grab a seat at the counter in front of the cooking line. Some people like to hide away in the dark, smoky barroom with booths. Original Joe's feeds a lot of older neighborhood residents every day. They order one of the reasonably priced dishes, eat a third of it, and take the rest home to have for dinner and breakfast the next day. To tell you the truth, that's what I do, too. I'm addicted to that cold hamburger steak.

PACIFIC

Pan Pacific Hotel
500 Post Street (at Mason),
San Francisco
Tel: 771-8600
Open for breakfast Monday through Friday 6:30 to 11 a.m., Saturday 7 to 10 a.m., weekend brunch 10 a.m. to 2:30 p.m; lunch Monday through Saturday 11:30 a.m. to 2:30 p.m.; dinner Sunday through Thursday 5:30 to 9:30 p.m., Friday and Saturday until 10 p.m.
Price: Moderate
Credit cards: AE, DC, MC, V

The airy mezzanine dining room, with a view up to the atrium ceiling and through big windows that look out to Post Street, offers a generous, nicely prepared California menu at both lunch and dinner, noteworthy for its use of good vegetables and other fine local ingredients. Former Masa chef Takayoshi Kawai has put together an appealing seasonal menu that may be a little too ambitious for the kitchen to execute perfectly. I have been disappointed by lobster and fish dishes, but have loved pan-seared scallops in a melting Provençal tomato and eggplant gratin; perfectly grilled squab with baby vegetables and a white truffle-scented risotto; and a beautiful herb-stuffed chicken breast surrounded by a wreath of miniature vegetables. Desserts tend to be too fancy. The prix-fixe menu, which features many of the best dishes, is a terrific bargain at $29 and a fine option for pre-theater dining. Lunch, also very reasonable considering the level of luxury and service, features less elaborate preparations. It's always fun to eat here and savvy San Franciscans use Pacific regularly when they rendezvous downtown or in the Theater District. The restaurant has achieved an identity of its own even though it is located in the Pan Pacific Hotel.

PALIO D'ASTI

The energy behind this alluring modern Italian restaurant, now open only for weekday lunch, comes from Gianni Fassio, whose family owned the original Blue Fox a block away. In a complete break from family tradition, he insists upon serving the dishes he ate in Italy during his years as an international accountant there. This means house-baked Italian breads and bread sticks; a whole range of tasty antipasti; house-made pastas with rustic, long-cooked game sauces, or delicate ravioli filled with Fontina and toasted almonds tossed with spinach and truffle oil; huge grilled veal chops; and braised rabbit. Polenta is preferred over potatoes; a raw, fresh tomato sauce with arugula replaces humdrum cooked tomato sauce; and the desserts are really Italian and quite wonderful, such as a whole roasted peach filled with mascarpone and sprinkled with amaretto cookie crumbs. The large restaurant admirably makes practically everything they serve on the premises, including pasta and focaccias, which they supply to their *paninoteca* (Italian sandwich shop) and cafe around the corner on Montgomery Street (see Cafes, page 146).

The theme of the Palio, Siena's fabled bareback horserace that takes place in the central *piazza* two times a year, is manifested in colorful banners hanging from the ceiling. The expansive modern concrete and glass space is broken up by three glassed-in display kitchens, a smart bar, and comfortable upholstered booths and linen-covered tables.

Palio has adapted itself to the needs of its neighborhood, offering both a reasonable, quickly served lunch, or a more leisurely, luxurious one, depending on the parameters of your expense account. When ridiculously expensive white truffles come to town, or fresh porcini, or very rare, aged balsamic vinegar, you can depend on Palio to have them. Fassio sees his restaurant as an outpost of Italian culture, and everyone benefits.

640 Sacramento Street
(between Montgomery and Kearny),
San Francisco
Tel: 395-9800
Open for lunch Monday through Friday 11:30 a.m. to 2:30 p.m.
Price: Moderate
Credit cards: AE, CB, DC, D, MC, V

POSTRIO

545 Post Street (between Taylor and Mason), San Francisco
Tel: 776-7825
Open for breakfast Monday through Friday 7 to 10 a.m., brunch Saturday and Sunday 9 a.m. to 2 p.m.; lunch Monday through Friday 11:30 a.m. to 2 p.m.; dinner Sunday through Wednesday 5:30 to 10 p.m., Thursday through Saturday until 10:30 p.m.; upstairs cafe open 11 a.m. to midnight
Price: Expensive
Credit cards: AE, DC, D, MC, V

The two great originating chefs, Annie and David Gingrass, left to open their own restaurant, Hawthorne Lane (see page 401), and the eclectic, flamboyant California food has not been the same though service continues to be as impeccable and intelligent as always. On two visits I tasted most of the menu. A number of the old dishes remain, but they don't sparkle. Muddled, illogical combinations, over-the-top seasoning, and general lack of restraint characterize the new offerings. This change in the performance of the kitchen has in no way dampened the popularity of this restaurant, however.

The expansive Pat Kuleto–designed dining room, with a completely open kitchen, practically roars. The restaurant starts at street level with an always-packed bar with its own wood-burning pizza oven and menu, then lowers a level to a mezzanine that is a bit quieter for dining, then cascades down a dramatic staircase into the main dining hall. That staircase has provided an entrance for many a costume, many a celebrity, many an indiscreet pairing. Postrio is fun in that way. It's always full because Prescott Hotel guests get preferential reservations. You have to call way in advance to get a prime-time table, but regulars sneak in. When anyone glamorous comes to town from Los Angeles they always hit the Puck restaurant. For locals, its location near Union Square makes it a natural for a pre-theater dinner or a downtown lunch. The scene has become the draw.

ROTUNDA AT NEIMAN-MARCUS

150 Stockton Street (at Geary), San Francisco
Tel: 362-4777
Open daily 11 a.m. to 5 p.m.
Price: Moderate
Credit cards: AE, NM

The Rotunda at Neiman-Marcus is a light-filled haven of comfort, peace, and civilization high atop the atrium on the fourth floor. The service is downright coddling, as are the big, soft, fabric-covered booths under the original stained glass ceiling from the old City of Paris department store. If shopping makes you wilt, as it does me, the material world slips away when you are seated in your luxurious rotunda perch high above the costume jewelry, the cosmetics, and the shoes.

First thing, you are brought a demitasse of hot, fortifying chicken broth with a tiny pastry crescent, then a hot popover and whipped raspberry butter. After these, the Rotunda can do no wrong. Start with a generous plate of mild sugar-cured smoked salmon, which comes with a tiny salad. Splurge on the lobster club ($17.95). The design of the double decker sandwich is exactly right: thin triangles of soft, toasted brioche, bacon, tomato, avocado, and a generous layer of sliced lobster—though the lobster should really be cooked to order, or at least that day considering the price. You can pick up each neat quarter and bite through it easily. For dessert there is my favorite, the pecan ball, a frozen sphere of pecan-coated vanilla ice cream napped with a fabulous, buttery caramel sauce. During lunch, a glamorous model works her way around the terrace in a nonthreatening outfit, chatting pleasantly at each table. You can tell that she doesn't eat many pecan balls.

I am a fan of the Rotunda's tea service, which starts at 2:30 p.m. For $10.95 a person you are brought two tiers of freshly made finger sandwiches, lovely, crumbly cream scones with raisins, and cookies and sweets. The water could be hotter in the teapots, there could be more savory sandwiches and less sweets, but I am delighted by the freshness and simplicity of service. The Rotunda is the last of the great department store lunch rooms—like the Walnut Room in Marshall Field's in Chicago. May its sweet, generous spirit and comfort live on!

RUBICON

Rubicon, the San Francisco outpost of Manhattan restaurant wizard Drew Nieporent, with backing from local celebs like Francis Ford Coppola (who bottles a blended red wine called Rubicon from his Napa Valley vineyard and winery), is a restaurant built around a wine guru. Professor, lover, master of wine, Larry Stone has put together a deep and personal wine list that he deconstructs for any table that shows an interest. Though not cheap by any means, the list is so broad and interesting that Stone can plumb it for a wine that will titillate the palate and suit the pocketbook while making your meal taste even better. The other night I saw him presenting bottle after bottle of expensive-looking red to a large table of handsome people headed by Robin Williams, who kept

558 Sacramento Street (between Sansome and Montgomery), San Francisco
Tel: 434-4100
Open for lunch Monday through Friday 11:30 a.m. to 2:30 p.m.; dinner Monday through Thursday 5:30 to 10:30 p.m., Friday and Saturday until 11 p.m.
Price: Expensive
Credit cards: AE, DC, MC, V

nodding his head. On my other side, wine writer Robert Finnegan went into deep consultation with Stone over the list. Stone keeps up-to-the-minute on every release, practically worldwide, and colleagues pick his brain. An academic (philosophy) turned wine-nut, he attacks his field with passion and an infallible nose and palate. He once told me that 40 percent of sales at Rubicon come from wine, an astounding figure considering that the fine dining standard runs about 20 percent. Wine groupies come to Rubicon to pay homage.

He works with a terrific kitchen started by Traci Des Jardins, who as of this writing plans to leave to open up her own place. A young, intelligent chef, she has mastered the unique Northern California food market (just as Stone has mastered the wine market) and refined her cooking style during the two plus years Rubicon has been opened. Incorporating all the most interesting vegetables seasonally available (one spring menu was sprinkled with favas, fresh peas, chanterelles, asparagus, spring onions, leeks, bitter greens, rhubarb, fennel, radishes, Portobello mushrooms, and Jerusalem artichokes; a recent fall menu offered cardoon, brussels sprouts, parsnips, salsify, porcini, figs and persimmons), the cooks work them into dishes using traditional European techniques. You never have to suffer piles of undercooked cardoon or greens here. And true to her New Orleans roots, Des Jardin's kitchen does not fear rich sauces, fried foods, or creamy gratins. A side dish of sweet, perfectly cooked brussels sprouts in buttery mustard seed–flecked sauce made me want to eat here more often, as did perfectly handled seared foie gras; duck confit salad with cracklings; crispy-skinned fish; long cooked short ribs; roasted chicken with surprising character; rich, baked-to-order desserts. This is not eclectic, California winging-it cooking, but California-inspired French/New York cooking that boasts depth over style. The food here really goes with wine, and at Rubicon the combination of the two can be a revelation. Just remember to bring an extra credit card.

Drew Nieporent originally made his reputation on two downtown Manhattan warehouse conversions—Montrachet and the Tribeca Grill—and physically Rubicon reminds me of the latter with its location in an earthquake-proofed redbrick firehouse in the heart of the Financial District. While the downstairs with its small bar, cozy tables, and booths draws on of the natural charm of the old building, the larger upstairs dining room feels a bit faceless, an open space with earthquake bracing. Try to snag a table on the first floor, though in either location you'll eat and drink well.

RUMPUS

What a fine, honest, exuberant restaurant this is! The food is always fresh and lively and the prices amazingly reasonable. Rumpus is well worth seeking out in its hidden-away location at the intersection of two downtown alleys—Campton Place and Tillman Place, off Grant Avenue between Sutter and Post. It offers two sophisticated narrow dining rooms with banquettes; a long narrow bar where you can eat, and a menu of San Francisco favorites like Caesar salad; a signature crab ravioli full of fresh Dungeness crabmeat; salmon stuffed with leeks on a bed of pearl pasta risotto; pan-roasted chicken of velvety texture on luscious mashed potatoes; long-cooked lamb shanks in a simple broth with root vegetables; good pastas; and house-made ice cream. On top of all this, the atmosphere is fun and casual, not the least bit stuffy. The wait staff brings high energy, disarming friendliness, and professionalism to the job. Perhaps because the owners ran the West Beach Cafe in Venice (one of my favorite Los Angeles spots), they chose people to work here who have Southern California sunniness. Well it works. Rumpus pleases on all fronts. Locals regard it as their special find, especially the picky Nob Hill clique who appreciate good value and treatment.

One Tillman Place
(off Grant Avenue between Sutter and Post),
San Francisco
Tel: 421-2300
Open for lunch Monday through Saturday
11:30 a.m. to 2:30 p.m.;
dinner Sunday through Thursday 5:30 to 10 p.m.,
Friday and Saturday until 11 p.m.
Price: Moderate
Credit cards: AE, DC, MC, V

SAM'S GRILL

I include historic Sam's because I love the way it looks. The ancient wood-paneled dining room, the private cubicles with buzzers to summon the waiters, the solid-looking facade broken only by a small rectangular window covered with blinds, conjure up the old days in San Francisco when Financial District office buildings emptied every day at lunchtime and people sat down to real noontime meals.

374 Bush Street (at Kearny),
San Francisco
Tel: 421-0594
Open Monday through Friday 11 a.m. to 9 p.m.
Price: Moderate
Credit cards: AE, DC, MC, V

Sam's was one of the most popular, masculine, no-nonsense grill rooms, and actually, it still is. Order only local fish like sand dabs, petrale, and salmon. Have a seafood salad or cold asparagus with mustard sauce, and a few slices of sourdough. Have a cocktail or a bottle of wine and there you are. Don't stray much farther than this. The restaurant closes early and the liveliest time is at lunch.

SANRAKU FOUR SEASONS

704 Sutter Street (at Taylor),
San Francisco
Tel: 771-0803
Open Monday through Friday 11 a.m. to 10 p.m.,
Saturday and Sunday 4 to 10 p.m.
Price: Moderate
Credit cards: AE, D, MC, V

A new adjunct to an excellent, inexpensive Japanese restaurant that has been open for over eighteen years (called Sanraku), the Four Seasons puts on imaginative and delicious *kaiseki* meals Monday through Saturday nights from 6 to 10 p.m. in a special dining room next door. The *kaiseki* dinners must be reserved ahead, at which time the menu can be discussed with their young chef, Hiro Hattori. He might suggest a whole fish or crab, an all-seafood menu, or a vegetarian menu, all within the *kaiseki* (or formal Japanese meal) framework. Simply left to his own devices, he will put out one of the most exquisite, lush, varied Japanese repasts you will ever taste. Sanraku Four Seasons is a rare opportunity to taste a new kind of Japanese cooking, some of it gently influenced by the West, in a completely traditional form.

The linen-covered Western-style tables in a peaceful gray and beige dining room are set only with red lacquer place mats and a pair of black wooden chopsticks. A few intriguing brush paintings of geometric shapes and a ceramic pot are the only decorations in the room: The food and its presentation on elegant pottery appropriate to the form of each dish creates the aesthetic. The eight-course dinner always consists of *zensai* (appetizer), *suimono* (soup), *sashimi* (raw fish), *kuchinaoshi* (which translates to "a little break"), *agemono* (fried dish), *yakimono* (broiled dish), rice and pickles with miso soup on a tray, then dessert. Even with this progression, delineated in a typed-out menu, the meal comes as a surprise.

The appetizer arrives in three tiny bowls, each with a sparkling fish or vegetable salad. Next might come a seafood soup in a clay bowl, scented with shiitakes and capped with a delicate egg custard; or clear broth in a tiny teapot with a lilliputian saucer from which to drink it. The sashimi course always turns out to be an East-West creation served on a large round plate: slices of raw tuna and halibut perhaps flanked by a salad of red and green seaweeds and tiny Western lettuces in a delicious soy and rice wine vinegar dressing. The "little break" might bring a unique pair of sushi wrapped in grilled eggplant, or an emerald-green avocado with pieces of sweet eel inside. The fried course brings tempura; one evening the pieces looked as if they were encased in tiny pearls. At this point in the *kaiseki* meal, light eaters might call it quits, but how could they pass up a small piece of butter-tender fillet of beef with *ponzu* sauce? With the meat, a tray of rice bowls, pickles, and steaming miso broth is brought. Somehow, as full as you are, eating these foods cleanses and refreshes the palate for dessert. The last course will be light and cool, perhaps a poached pear in honey syrup or a small dish of green tea ice cream marbleized with a gorgeous dark green tea sauce and served in a turquoise ceramic square. Cold Otokoyama sake served in wineglasses goes wonderfully with the meal.

These *kaiseki* meals offer all the lyricism and art of Japanese cooking along with a certain kind of Western exuberance. Though each course is elegant, they add up to generous, almost hearty meals. Unlike some other *kaiseki* meals I have had at twice the price in a nearby hotel, the focus is on freshness and flavor, not garnish, and the presentations seem organic to the food. Chef Hattori shows a deep understanding of the poetry of his cuisine while still addressing the appetite.

SCALA'S BISTRO

I love the wood-fired pizzas here with thin crusts and interesting toppings. Pastas can be wonderful, too. The chef-owners know how to balance a pasta sauce in authentic Italian style—with restraint. *Frittos*, piles of perfectly deep-fried matchsticks of zucchini or calamari, are a treat, and prices in this loud, always crowded, cleverly decorated trattoria are affordable. Run by Donna and Giovanni Scala, who also operate the popular Bistro Don Giovanni on Highway 29 in Napa, Scala's Bistro represents the best of the big, bustling downtown hotel restaurants. I recommend it for families with kids.

Sir Francis Drake Hotel
432 Powell Street (between Post and Sutter),
San Francisco
Tel: 395-8555
Open Monday through Saturday 7 a.m. to midnight, Sunday 8 a.m. to midnight
Price: Moderate
Credit cards: AE, D, DC, MC, V

SEARS FINE FOODS

439 Powell Street (between Post and Sutter), San Francisco
Tel: 986-1160
Open daily 6:30 a.m. to 3:30 p.m.
Price: Inexpensive
No credit cards

This beloved downtown breakfast and lunch spot remains one of the best places in the city for an old-fashioned American breakfast. Always start with a huge fresh-fruit cup of high-quality fruit marinated in fresh orange juice, a must order here. If you're a one-fruit person, you can get bowls of berries in season, orange slices, juicy melons, papaya, or a large baked Rome Beauty apple served with cream. Then move on to Sears's "famous 18 Swedish pancakes," six baby stacks of airy pancakes the size and thickness of half dollars that have real character; or Sears's crisp dark-brown waffles with tender eggy interiors; or French toast made of well-soaked sourdough bread served with a small cup of Sears' own strawberry preserves, really a barely sweetened compote. The Canadian bacon truly is "the best obtainable anywhere" as the menu boasts, and the smoked country sausage, made especially for Sears and served in crisp patties, is excellent, too. At lunch, after an egg salad sandwich or a BLT, have fresh strawberry shortcake or a fresh-fruit deep-dish pie that comes in a glass cereal bowl filled to the top. If anyone staying around Union Square asks you to meet them for breakfast, do yourself a favor and suggest Sears. It's also a big favorite with kids.

SOL Y LUNA RESTAURANTE

475 Sacramento Street (between Battery and Sansome), San Francisco
Tel: 296-8696 (info 296-8191)
Open for lunch Monday through Friday 11:30 a.m. to 2:30 p.m.; dinner Monday through Saturday 5:30 to 10 p.m.; music Tuesday through Sunday nights
Price: Moderate
Credit cards: AE, DC, MC, V

The electrifying energy behind this New World tapas restaurant comes from the modern cultural crosscurrents at play in the Bay Area. The decor is unrelentingly austere, a multilevel cement and metal landscape that could be in Milan, Madrid, or Mexico City. The sprightly menu of tapas and paellas draws not only from Spain, but from all over Latin America. And the crowd, especially starting about nine at night, is as exotic as you can find in San Francisco. When a hot Latin band plays, the lower dining area is cleared of tables and dancing takes over. Tango, samba, and salsa aficionados of all ages, many of whom have worked out suave routines, perform, fueled by one of the tastiest drinks in the city, Rio-style *caipirinha* made with Brazilian *cachaca*, fresh lime, and sugar. They are dynamite!

Before the dancing begins there is much good eating to do. Some of my favorites on the long tapas menu are the simplest dishes like fried, creamy-textured purple potato slices with fiery Spanish-style aïoli, or a plate of exquisite, smoky serrano ham with manchego cheese, a dab of sweet pepper salsa, and some warm flat bread. House-made chorizo sausage comes on a tasty bed of black beans, and crisp cod cakes called *buñuelos de bacalao* are lifted by the delicious house salsa. The gazpacho is excellent, though not served with the traditional Spanish garnishes. Don't forget to order a plate of tiny marinated, organic Spanish olives.

Spanish purists may be shocked by the eclecticism of the tapas and the nontraditional presentation of dishes like paella, but the food works on its own terms. This is one place where you can ask your waiter for recommendations. They not only know most of the dishes well, but are eager to send out the kitchen's favorites of the moment. The staff here is first-rate: professional, enthusiastic, polite, and knowledgeable. They contribute to everyone's good time.

TADICH GRILL

A Yugoslavian family has run this historic fish house since the turn of the century, grilling fresh fish over mesquite charcoal and cranking out a fascinating menu printed daily all these years in offset type. The menus themselves are souvenirs, documents of culinary history, full of dinosaurs such as lobster Newberg, halibut Florentine, and deviled crab. The best way to proceed is to ask your crusty waiter what fish has come in fresh that day and order it simply charcoal-grilled or pan-fried. What a pleasure it is to hang your coat on a brass hook at Tadich's, grab a seat at the long, oval wooden counter, and dig into a fresh seafood salad slathered with an excellent Louie sauce, and a plate of buttery "griddled" sand dabs or rex sole served with Tadich's gigantic fried potatoes. The rex sole, which are small, flavorful local fish, are also delicious charcoal grilled, eaten with mounds of Tadich's unique and addictive tartar sauce thickened with sieved potato. The waiters will quickly fillet them for you, an old-fashioned luxury. Creamed spinach, sautéed spinach, thick clam chowder, and

240 California Street
(between Front and Battery),
San Francisco
Tel: 391-2373
Open Monday through
Friday 11 a.m. to 9:30 p.m.,
Saturday 11:30 a.m.
to 9:30 p.m.
Price: Moderate
Credit cards: MC, V

poached salmon with chopped egg sauce are other Tadich favorites. The wine list is simple and cheap—most people still have cocktails here. For dessert, there are huge baked Rome Beauty apples and rice custard pudding, which work perfectly after the straightforward meals.

The wonderful-looking dining room is paneled in ancient dark wood, with compartments that enclose small linen-covered tables and bentwood chairs. The original pressed-plaster ceiling, a white-tiled floor, and a busy wooden counter with wooden chairs that swivel on pedestals set the scene for a timeless experience, especially since most of the uniformed waiters have been there forever. There's always a crowd at the door having a drink at the small bar and waiting for one of the not-so-plentiful tables. However, if you don't want to wait, you can usually get a seat immediately at the counter, where the stools turn over quickly and the regulars are gracious about moving over to accommodate a pair who want to sit together.

VERTIGO

Transamerica Pyramid
600 Montgomery Street
(entrance on Clay between Montgomery and Sansome),
San Francisco
Tel: 433-7250
Open for lunch Monday through Friday 11:30 a.m. to 2:30 p.m.; dinner Monday through Thursday 5:30 to 10 p.m., Friday and Saturday until 10:30 p.m.
Price: Moderate
Credit cards: AE, DC, MC, V

This dramatic restaurant, seemingly built into the monumental pilings of the city's most distinctive office tower, offers theatrical East-West fare from chef Jeff Inahara. Some of the combinations this kitchen comes up with can be delightful when the exotic ingredients enhance each other, as in a very odd-sounding dish listed as sweetwater prawns with basil mashed potatoes and rock shrimp bolognese. (I grimaced when a friend ordered it, but it turned out to be the tastiest dish of the evening.) Sometimes the ingredients seem unrelated, brought together by the imagination of the chef without much culinary logic.

The menu features lots of fish and seafood, and the plates always look pretty. The highly professional management at Vertigo provides anything you might want by way of wine, cocktails, bar food, desserts, and service. You cannot go wrong by arranging a business lunch or dinner in this sophisticated restaurant. Vertigo has been set up to inspire confidence, not dizziness, in its well-heeled patrons and eating here makes you feel very Pacific Rim.

YANK SING

Seen through big plate-glass windows, Yank Sing looks like the typical modern, upscale Financial District restaurant, until the carts laden with exotic Chinese delicacies wheel into the picture. Then you know you're looking into a different culinary territory entirely. Yank Sing is one of the best dim sum houses in the city. The variety seems never ending, and every piece is meticulously made from high-quality ingredients: the sweetest-tasting shellfish, the freshest Chinese herbs and vegetables, the cleanest frying oil. The kitchen shows particular strength in everyone's favorite part of the dim sum meal, dumplings. The translucent shrimp-stuffed *har gow* boast pristine shrimp. The liberal use of black mushrooms adds a wild, meaty flavor to vegetarian dumplings seasoned with pickled turnip and to chicken dumplings with bamboo shoots. The pork-filled *sui mai* are savory and toothsome; the dumplings filled with pea shoots and black mushrooms absolutely sublime. In addition to these, you will see at least twenty other tempting little plates or bamboo steamers of food being wheeled by, including extraordinarily crisp, lacy, deep-fried taro balls with creamy taro and pork interiors; deep-fried crab fingers; and rich deep-fried shrimp toasts. Henry Chan, the gracious owner of Yank Sing, has always tried to set his dim sum house apart by experimenting with the form. He started serving individual portions of Peking duck with soft white buns, plum sauce, and green onions; a Japanese-inspired tidbit of deep-fried fresh water chestnut, bacon, and green onion on a toothpick; and stunning little plates of fiery, strongly sauced Chinese eggplant, all firsts for dim sum houses. From a small menu of noodle dishes, try tender noodles with Chinese chives and tiny enoki mushrooms, a taste and texture sensation and a great way to end a dim sum meal. For dessert nab a saucer of flaky-crusted egg custard tarts while they are still warm from the oven. Yank Sing does them better than anyone else.

In addition to the comfortable surroundings and all the lovely food, the staff at Yank Sing shows particular graciousness and efficiency. You are quickly recognized as a regular and guided to special dishes. First-timers are treated patiently

427 Battery Street (between Clay and Washington), San Francisco
Tel: 362-1640
Open Monday through Friday 11 a.m. to 3 p.m., weekends 10 a.m. to 4 p.m.
Price: Moderate
Credit cards: AE, CB, DC, MC, V

and always given a bit of help if they need it. A dim sum specialist—no other meals are served—Yank Sing takes a great interest in teaching about, refining, and expanding the service. Equal numbers of Chinese and Westerners fill the dining rooms, and at Yank Sing, everyone is equally pleased.

CAFES

CAFÉ DE LA PRESSE

352 Grant Avenue (at Bush),
San Francisco
Tel: 398-2680
Open daily 7 a.m. to 11 p.m.
Credit cards: AE, MC, V

Sitting at one of the outdoor tables hugging the building at Grant and Bush across from the entrance to Chinatown makes you part of the international tourist circuit that flows by this very corner. I like to dive in, if even for an hour, at Café de la Presse, which is next to the groovily decorated Triton Hotel (check out the lobby). The cafe not only serves a decent *salade niçoise* and a generous prosciutto and melon plate with a good baguette, but it also houses one of the best international newspaper and magazine stands in the city, so you can buy your *Herald Tribune* and pretend you're an American in Paris, or your *Le Monde* and pretend you're French. Two drawbacks: the waiters are sweet-natured but incompetent, and the Rhône and Beaujolais taste identical, as if they were bought at a French supermarket, a bit of authenticity I could do without.

PALIO PANINOTECA

505 Montgomery Street
(between Sacramento
and Commercial),
San Francisco
Tel: 362-6900
Open Monday through
Friday 7 a.m. to 4 p.m.
Credit cards: AE, MC, V

For other locations, see pages 410 and 437.

Just like the sandwich shops you see everywhere in Italy, this *paninoteca* has a case of pre-made sandwiches ready and waiting, which you can buy by the half or whole. Owned and operated by Gianni Fassio of Palio d'Asti around the corner, Palio Paninoteca uses ingredients and concepts that are authentically Italian and sophisticated, down to the cleverly designed wrapping. I take the tomatoes out of the prosciutto and mascarpone sandwich on a soft focaccia bun. Who needs the distraction when such fine proscuitto nestles within? The Nostromo—tuna, capers, red onions, gherkins, diced red pepper, and radicchio, all finely chopped and blended together on soft white Italian bread with a crunchy crust—gets my vote as the best tuna sandwich in town, even without mayonnaise! It's really delicious. So is the espresso. You really feel as if you've stepped into a shop in Milan.

BARS

BIX

Doug Biederbeck, the genial host-owner (along with Real Restaurants partners) of Bix, has made this *soigné*, intimate restaurant and bar hidden away in an alley off Jackson Square into one of the most happening venues in San Francisco. He is a true boulevardier, a man about town who knows what's going on in every spot in the city because he makes the rounds. He throws a sophisticated affair himself every night in his resplendent art deco quarters with a collagelike mural over the bar, an intimate mezzanine for diners, and a jazz trio holding forth on the main floor. Everyone stops by Bix when they're having a night on the town. It's also a popular Financial District lunch spot, especially when the stock market is heading straight up and bottles of Champagne are popping. The small menu has its strengths and weaknesses, but I have always liked a crisp chicken hash; an updated Waldorf salad with apples, walnuts, and blue cheese; and some crunchy potato-leek pancakes with smoked salmon. For dessert, the kitchen makes old-fashioned bananas Foster, bananas heated in butter, brown sugar, and rum, served with vanilla ice cream, a dessert that comes as close to being an after-dinner drink as it possibly can.

56 Gold Street (off Montgomery, between Pacific and Jackson), San Francisco
Tel: 433-6300
Open Monday through Thursday 11:30 a.m. to 11 p.m., Friday and Saturday until midnight, Sunday 6 to 10 p.m.
Credit cards: AE, D, DC, MC, V

HARRY DENTON'S STARLIGHT ROOM

450 Powell Street (atop the
Sir Francis Drake Hotel
between Post and Sutter),
San Francisco
Tel: 395-8595
Open daily 4:30 p.m. to 2 a.m.
Credit cards: AE, MC, V

Bon vivant Harry Denton knows what it takes to throw a party every night. On the 21st floor of the Sir Francis Drake, now a Kimpton Hotel, Denton has a venue with wraparound views, a small dance floor, a DJ booth, and yards and yards of red drapery. Small round tables draped in white tablecloths fill every nook and cranny. The room is furnished with couches and chairs; plush, intimate booths; and tall, slender cocktail waitresses in long, clinging black satin. The best booze—Appleton Jamaican rum, Basil Hayden bourbon—is poured in special house drinks, most of which cost $7.50. Bar food is inexpensive and ample, like a huge bowl of marinated olives and pickled peppers with breadsticks for $2. Caviar is practically sold at cost, $25 an ounce for ossetra, $45 for beluga. Out of towners, i.e. anyone who does not live in San Francisco proper, love this room. It has become a must for a night on the town. San Francisco residents prefer grittier places.

RED ROOM

827 Sutter Street (between
Jones and Leavenworth),
San Francisco
Tel: 346-7666
Open daily 5 p.m. to 2 a.m.
Credit cards: MC, V

Now this is a typical San Francisco bar—small, retro, really red, very smoky. Every surface is red except for the sexy bartendresses who dress in black, have black hair, wear black lipstick and show plenty of décolletage. You can sit on red stools at the curved red bar or on red banquettes at red vinyl tables. Drinks at $6 are well made and generously poured. Located in the Commodore Hotel, which is owned by hip young hotel entrepreneur Chip Connolly, the successful Red Room will no doubt be replicated in a number of his other establishments.

DELICATESSENS/TAKE-OUT

BLONDIE'S PIZZA

See listing, page 473.

Big, thick, floppy slices of pizza, slathered with cheese, tomato sauce, and pepperoni move out the door so fast at this sidewalk pizzeria that the pizza makers can barely keep up. You will always find a hot slice of pizza ready to go, usually two or three different kinds if you don't want to wait for that special slice. Blondie's makes likable fast-food pizza: One slice fills you up, it's not too oily, and the price is right.

63 Powell Street (between Ellis and Market),
San Francisco
Tel: 982-6168
Open Monday through Friday 9:30 a.m. to 9 p.m.,
Saturday 11 a.m. to 9 p.m.,
Sunday 11 a.m. to 8 p.m.
No credit cards

MACY'S CELLAR

This veritable food hall does a huge business as a quick meal stop. People choose goodies from three tiers of prepared salads of every sort, particularly Asian and Italian noodle salads, cold chicken, piroshkis from House of Piroshki, eggplant lasagne, some good-looking pre-made "wreath sandwiches" sliced off an egg bread circle, and Wolfgang Puck frozen pizzas heated to order in a pizza oven. Concessions include a frozen-yogurt bar, a full Boudin Cafe and bread counter, and a Tom's cookie stand, where the smell of warm cookies draws people like magnets. Many square feet of chocolates fill up one side, ranging from Godiva to Macy's own oversized versions of turtles and honeycombs. A small and pricy California wine department seemingly is there for show, along with cheese and sausage stations that offer nothing out of the ordinary.

Union Square
(Stockton and O'Farrell),
San Francisco
Tel: 397-3333
Open Monday through Saturday 10 a.m. to 8 p.m.,
Sunday 11 a.m. to 7 p.m.
Credit cards: AE, MC, V

NEIMAN-MARCUS EPICURE

150 Stockton Street
(at Geary), fourth floor,
San Francisco
Tel: 362-3900
Open Monday, Thursday,
Friday 10 a.m. to 8 p.m.,
Tuesday and Wednesday
until 6 p.m., Saturday until
7 p.m., Sunday noon to 6 p.m.
Credit cards: AE, NM

The unique draw here is a counter devoted to Petrossian caviar and smoked salmon at lofty prices. (See California Sunshine, page 418, or Polarica, page 241.) When Petrossian had a monopoly on Russian caviar, perhaps these products were worth the extra expense, but now other importers are setting up their own caviar stations and bringing in a fine product. My philosophy is when you eat caviar you want enough to really taste it—I mean an ounce per person at least, which makes Petrossian ridiculously expensive. Of course, if price is no object, just give Neiman a call and they'll send it right out. A small California and European wine department is pricy; the breads come from Bakers of Paris; the cheese is not special, and the pâtés are not particularly vibrant.

SPECIALTY'S CAFE AND BAKERY

312 Kearny Street (between
Bush and Pine),
San Francisco
Tel: 788-2254 (for daily specials call 896-2253)

22 Battery Street,
San Francisco
Tel: 398-4691
Open Monday through
Friday 6 a.m. to 6 p.m.
No credit cards

For other location, see page 411.

Americans love sandwiches, but they are particular about what belongs in them and what doesn't. Our sandwiches have more filling than bread, unlike the meager slice of prosciutto or dry sausage that gets buried in an Italian or French baguette. We want nothing of the Danish open-face variety. The English may have invented the sandwich, but their dry, skinny version spread with margarine gives sandwiches a bad name. To Americans, the sandwich is a meal you can hold in your hand. The best ones have to be juicy, rich, texturally varied, a little spicy, and almost impossible to bite through.

Specialty's, a nine-year-old sandwich company with three locations, understands the American sandwich and is a favorite with the office set. The success of its concept revolves around hot, soft just-baked breads used in forty different sandwich combinations. Each has a multitude of ingredients, and the effect in the best matchups is symphonic: The whole is greater than the individually undistinguished parts.

One of my favorites is No. 11, the Italian, a conglomeration of paper-thin slices of salami, bologna, mortadella, Swiss, mild peppers, provolone, and the basic setup of lettuce, tomato, pickles, onions, and black pepper, with mayonnaise and spicy brown mustard on potato–poppy seed bread. All these bland American-style cold cuts add up to a savory submarine-style sandwich with a charm of its own. Another hands-down favorite with everyone is No. 25, the Vegetarian, the classic California combo of avocado, cheese, mushrooms, and ranch dressing. In addition to the sandwiches, a large variety of warm, puffy, gigantic sweet and savory pastries are baked each hour, including huge coiled buns of white bread slathered with great amounts of Cheddar cheese and sliced pickled jalapeño peppers. The outlets are well-staffed counter operations, and the lines that invariably form at 11:30 a.m. move quickly and efficiently. These operations cleverly take the quickly made lunchtime sandwich to a higher level of freshness and appeal.

YANK SING

This great downtown dim sum house (see page 145) has a separate counter next door to the restaurant where you can order boxes of dim sum to go. A large variety of dumplings are kept hot in steamers, ready to be packed up, or you can order dim sum off a large menu, which are sent from the kitchen as they are cooked. Special sampler boxes posted above the counter are also quickly assembled. If you want to throw a dim sum party, Yank Sing's crack catering department will either deliver the food hot to your door, or set up woks and steamers on site and serve as well. For an amazingly reasonable price, you can impress a group with some of the tastiest and most interesting food this side of Hong Kong.

427 Battery Street (between Clay and Washington), San Francisco
Tel: 362-1640
Open Monday through Friday 11 a.m. to 3 p.m., Saturday and Sunday 10 a.m. to 4 p.m.
Credit cards: AE, CB, DC, MC, V

ICE CREAM/CHOCOLATES

CANDY JAR

210 Grant Avenue
(between Post and Sutter),
San Francisco
Tel: 391-5508
Open Monday through
Saturday 9 a.m. to 6 p.m.
Credit cards: AE, MC, V

The glass counter of this small candy store displays house-made bonbon-sized truffles and imported Godiva chocolates, but everyone I know drops in when they're downtown to refill their own candy jars with hard candies from all over the world, sold by the pound. Jars and jars of them line one wall, allowing you to put together your own mix. The best of them all is a hard, chewy toffee with a whole toasted hazelnut inside—don't be led off the track by the Irish hazelnut toffees that look almost identical, but are not nearly as good. OK, everyone has his or her own favorites, but I know you'll back me up on these toffees, which as of this writing are out of stock. Complain to the manager.

MORROW'S NUT HOUSE

111 Geary Street (between
Grant and Stockton),
San Francisco
Tel: 362-7969
Open Monday through
Saturday
9:45 a.m. to 5:45 p.m.,
Credit cards: MC, V

I challenge you to walk by this tiny nut shop without stopping in to buy at least one-quarter pound. The irresistible aroma of roasting (actually deep-fried) nuts wafts out the always-open door and practically pulls you inside. The nuts are of the highest quality: huge, fresh, and whole. The cashews are the size of a child's thumb, and the pecans, an adult toe. Almonds, Brazil nuts, and hazelnuts all look even plumper glistening with nut oil. Morrow's keeps roasting all day, so the nuts are always warm when you get them, but never stale or rancid. A box, even a small bag, of these fresh, fragrant mixed nuts makes just about the best gift I know.

SEE'S CANDIES

542 Market Street (at Sansome),
San Francisco
Tel: 362-1593
Open Monday through Friday 9 a.m. to 6:30 p.m.

846 Market Street (between Powell and Stockton),
San Francisco
Tel: 434-2771
Open Monday through Saturday 9 a.m. to 7 p.m.,
Sunday 10:30 a.m. to 6 p.m.
No credit cards
See listing, page 386.

TEUSCHER CHOCOLATES OF SWITZERLAND

These ridiculously expensive chocolates are so rich that one—well, maybe two—will satisfy your chocolate craving for a week—well, make that three days. The Champagne truffles, little milk chocolate balls of the most buttery, velvety texture with a swatch of Champagne cream in the center and a dusting of sugar on the exterior, are what bring most people into this tiny store. I've tried a number of the other chocolates with nuts, marzipan, and different flavors, neatly arranged in formation like tiny soldiers, but those Champagne truffles always seem to be worth the expense. You can buy them by the piece or in small gift boxes. Around each holiday, Teuscher makes children's packages, but I would never waste these chocolates on kids. Save them for yourself.

255 Grant Avenue
(at Sutter),
San Francisco
Tel: 398-2700
Open Monday through
Saturday 10 a.m. to 6 p.m.,
Sunday noon to 5 p.m.
Credit cards: AE, D, MC, V

WINE AND SPIRITS

LONDON WINE BAR

415 Sansome Street
(at Sacramento),
San Francisco
Tel: 788-4811
Open Monday through
Friday 11:30 a.m. to 9 p.m.
Credit cards: AE, D, MC, V

Fifteen to twenty California wines and five or so French ones are poured by the glass at this clubby, wood-paneled, British-style wine bar and store, in addition to pours from interesting magnums and jeroboams of older California wines. Half bottles of white Burgundy, glasses of port and sherry, and a veritable wine cellar of bottles await tasting. What a perfect way to decide what to buy! While the English-publike food is serviceable at best, the wine-tasting opportunities are first rate, and owner Gary Locke's picks for the bar and special sales on wines by the case are worth noting. The dual roles of retail store and tasting room work together to help people find the wines they like.

COOKWARE AND BOOKS

CRATE AND BARREL

125 Grant Avenue
(at Geary and Post),
San Francisco
Tel: 986-4000
Open Monday through
Friday 10 a.m. to 7 p.m.,
Saturday until 6 p.m.,
Sunday 11 a.m. to 5 p.m.
Credit cards: AE, D, MC, V

A good place to find simple, handsome dishware and glasses that will wear well and not cost a fortune, Crate and Barrel prides itself on uncovering these bargains from all over the world. About ten years ago I found some delicate, classic U-shaped hand-blown wineglasses with the thinnest stems and rims, just the right size for white wines and most reds. I bought two dozen and have tried to replace them ever since, but Crate and Barrel discontinued them. So my advice to you is, if you find a plate or a glass that you really like, buy enough of them because you probably won't get a second chance.

MACY'S CELLAR

I always think I can find just the small appliance I need at Macy's, but actually this seemingly large department only stocks one or two brands of items like juicers, toasters, or blenders, often not the one I'm trying to replace. The new model either does more than I want or not quite what I want, but maybe that's the complaint of someone who distrusts gadgets. However, I have found that getting service in this department is no easy matter, so I can't even be persuaded that the model they have in stock is really better.

The extensive pots and pans department at Macy's is another matter. It carries all levels of cooking equipment, from old-fashioned copper-bottomed stainless-steel Revere Ware to the latest generation of space-age, nonstick, non-scratch cooking-surface pans, stopping along the way to pay homage to Le Creuset's heavy enameled cooking pots. To my mind, some pieces from each line serve a cook better than monolithic matching sets. Many people ask my advice on what kind of pans they should buy, but unless I move in with them for a week to see how they cook, an answer is impossible. In my kitchen I couldn't live without a heavy nonstick saucepan with a glass cover for heating milk for coffee, which I bought at Macy's six years ago for $75. Since I use it every single day it was a terrific investment, amortized over the years. I have a nesting set of copper saucepans, a few cast-iron skillets, a few copper sauté pans, a heavy aluminum restaurant-style skillet, a pressure cooker, a large covered stockpot, a big Le Creuset covered casserole, and that's about it—except for a wok from Chinatown that I use all the time.

The casual dishware department harbors some charming painted dishes in five-piece place settings for four (around $100). The glassware selection is weak, but you can find treasures among the French white and painted serving dishes that fill one section. Many of them were on sale the last time I dropped by.

Union Square
(Stockton and O'Farrell),
San Francisco
Tel: 397-3333
Open Monday through
Saturday 10 a.m. to 8 p.m.,
Sunday 11 a.m. to 7 p.m.
Credit cards: AE, MC, V

SUR LA TABLE

77 Maiden Lane (between Grant and Kearny), San Francisco
Tel: 732-7900
Open Monday through Saturday 10 a.m. to 6 p.m.
Credit cards: AE, D, MC, V

For other location, see page 500.

I thought that the Bay Area did not need another cookware store when Sur La Table opened its first store in Berkeley. Then I started sifting through the merchandise. Sure enough, I found things that I didn't know I needed that were unique to this chain—a charming square platter hand-painted with olive branches at a very attractive price ($19); a huge wooden salad bowl actually big enough to toss a salad for six or eight ($89); and one of the largest collections of cookbooks (over 700 titles I was told). Sur La Table caters to serious cooks. If a recipe calls for a certain cake pan or mold, or you want to make cookies in the shape of sheep, or you need any basic kitchen tool or appliance, I would head here first. There are levels of tools at different prices and different styles of the same tool. As a peripatetic cook, I appreciate the depth of the merchandise in these stores. Everyone who has waited on me has been an absolute saint—patient, friendly, and knowledgeable. This really is a store for cooks as opposed to homemakers, though the latter will find much here, too.

WILLIAMS-SONOMA

For other locations, see pages 117, 203, 450 and 524.

The Post Street location has the biggest selection of merchandise of all the stores, from high-quality pots and pans in copper and high-tech materials to cookbooks, kitchen gadgets, and olive oil. If you're looking for the hard-to-find cooking item, like crème brûlée irons, or paella pans along with the rice, this is the place to look first. The prices are not cheap, but the cookware, small appliances, and utensils carried here have the store's backing, which includes the huge mail-order business and all the branches. The buyers do their research; they read *Consumer Reports* and have enough buying power to make a manufacturer improve a product. So the one toaster they carry has been chosen for a reason, winning the competition for quality and price, though quality is the more important factor.

I have always found the clerks to be extremely helpful. If an item is out of stock they will try to find it for you at another store, and they know their own inventories. They'll tell you exactly why Williams-Sonoma carries a specific item, and they're usually so convincing that you buy one. I've never been let down, and that includes the time I impulsively bought a bread machine for my husband who had yearned for one with every Williams-Sonoma catalog. It really works, if you like soft, airy bread with crisp crusts, and the smell of the warm loaf in the morning is better than an alarm clock. You also can find some handsome dishes and glasses for a moderate sum, and if you are tantalized by catalogues, Williams-Sonoma regularly sends out a thick one full of many items that you didn't know you needed until you saw them there, such as nonstick corn-stick molds in the shape of little ears of corn.

150 Post Street (between Grant and Kearny),
San Francisco
Tel: 362-6904
Open Monday through Saturday 9:30 a.m. to 7 p.m.,
Sunday 11 a.m. to 6 p.m.

865 Market Street
(at Fifth Street in the San Francisco Centre),
San Francisco
Tel: 546-0171
Open Monday through Saturday 9:30 a.m. to 8 p.m.,
Sunday 11 a.m. to 6 p.m.
Credit cards: AE, MC, V

RAISED WAFFLES

2 cups milk
1/2 cup (1 stick) butter, cut into chunks
1 teaspoon salt
1 teaspoon sugar
ckage active dry yeast
1/2 cup warm (105° to 115°F) water
2 cups all-purpose flour
2 eggs
1/4 teaspoon baking soda

This classic waffle recipe from an early Fanny Farmer cookbook makes the lightest, crispest, most flavorful waffles I know. I found it in Marion Cunningham's The Breakfast Book, which I use constantly. If there was ever a reason to buy a waffle iron, this recipe is it. The waffle irons sold today have teflon coatings so that the waffles never stick and always come out golden brown.

Put the milk, butter, salt, and sugar in a small saucepan. Gently warm over low heat until the butter is almost melted. Remove from heat and let cool to lukewarm.

In a large bowl, dissolve the yeast in the warm water. Add the milk mixture, then whisk in the flour, until the batter is smooth and creamy. Cover with plastic wrap and let stand 6 to 12 hours at room temperature.

The next morning, or just before cooking, whisk the eggs and baking soda. The batter will be thin.

Pour about 1/2 to 3/4 cup of batter into a very hot waffle iron. Bake until the waffles are golden and crisp, about 5 minutes.

Makes about 8 waffles

Lower & Upper Haight, Cole Valley

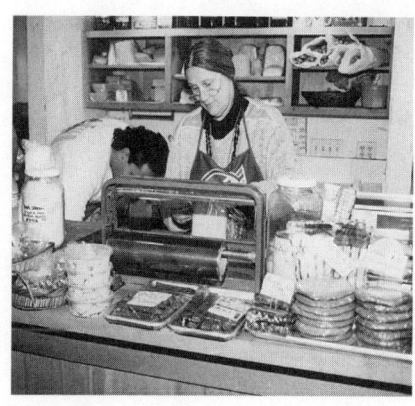

LOWER & UPPER HAIGHT, COLE VALLEY

Restaurants:
- ❶ Cha Cha Cha 163
- ❷ Eos 164
- ❸ Ganges Vegetarian Restaurant 1653
- ❹ Hama-ko 166
- ❺ Taqueria El Balazo 167
- ❻ Thep Phanom 167
- ❼ Ya, Halla from Nadia 168

Cafes:
- ❽ Bean There 169
- ❾ One World Cafe 170

Bars:
- ❿ DeLuxe 170
- ⓫ Kezar Bar and Restaurant 171
- ⓬ Noc Noc 171
- ⓭ Toronado 172

Delicatessens/Take-Out:
- ⓮ Brother-in-Law's Barbeque No. 2 172
- ⓯ Real Food Company 173

Ice Cream/Chocolates:
- ⓰ Gelato Classico 173

Coffee:
- ⓱ Spinelli Coffee Company 173

Markets:
- ⓲ Ashbury Market 174
- ⓳ Falletti's Finer Foods 175
- ⓳ Plaza Foods 175

Produce:
- ⓯ Real Food Company 176

Meat and Poultry:
- ⓳ Enrico's 178
- ⓳ United Fish and Poultry 178

Cheese:
- ⓴ Country Cheese 179
- ㉑ Say Cheese 179

Wines and Spirits:
- ⓲ Ashbury Market 180

Cookware and Books:
- ㉒ Cookin' 180

RESTAURANTS

CHA CHA CHA

The vibrancy of this popular Haight Street institution has not diminished over the years, even with Cha Cha Cha's expansion to a larger space on the corner. If anything, this Caribbean tapas spot is hotter than ever. With Cuban rhythm bands blaring on the sound system and fetishy folk art leaping off the black brick walls, the place always buzzes. Next door, but connected to the dining room, people both eat and drink at a very hip bar made of marble and pressed sheet metal in Cha Cha Cha's original tiny space.

They come here for tapas, huge plates of tender fried calamari or deep-fried new potatoes, golden and crisp, dressed with a dollop of dried-chili-infused aïoli. From the daily specials board might come a large fillet of trout, spicily breaded Cajun-style and pan-fried, served with grilled asparagus and a capery rémoulade—a surprisingly stylish dish for the venue. Platters of excellent black beans, yellow rice with green olives, and seared flank steak or roast leg of pork make for a dreamy meal if you're hungry. Everything on these Cuban-inspired plates is delicious. More tapas, like fried plantains with black beans and sour cream; whole mushroom caps sautéed with sherry, garlic, and olive oil; or a good warm spinach salad with bacon and mushrooms, draw on Spain and Latin America with a bit of California thrown in. The mix works, especially when washed down with pitchers of fruity but not too sweet sangría.

1801 Haight Street
(at Schrader),
San Francisco
Tel: 386-5758 or 386-7670
Open for lunch daily 11:30 a.m. to 4 p.m.; dinner Monday through Thursday 5 to 11 p.m., Friday, Saturday, and Sunday until 11:30 p.m.; brunch Sunday 10:30 a.m. to 4 p.m.
Price: Inexpensive
Credit cards: MC, V

The cooking is eclectic, but not confused or fussy. The unifying theme is spiciness, and each buoyant dish stays true to its ethnic origin. A Cuban dish tastes Cuban; a Cajun dish, Cajun.

This restaurant was made for the Haight; it's an extension of the energy on the street. It projects just enough funk to make neighborhood customers feel comfortable, yet the core of the operation is professional and pretty sophisticated. It has become one of the best neighborhood spots around—so good, in fact, that people come to Cha Cha Cha from all over the city. The loud and colorful dining rooms also happen to be a terrific place to take kids: They can eat a little or a lot (everyone gets a small empty plate and helps him- or herself) and drink their own version of sangría: exotic fruit juices in ice-filled glasses.

EOS

901 Cole Street (at Carl),
San Francisco
Tel: 566-3063
Open Monday through Wednesday 5:30 to 11 p.m.,
Thursday to Saturday 5:30 to midnight,
Sunday 5 to 10 p.m.
Price: Moderate
Credit cards: AE, MC, V

An energy field surrounds this once quiet neighborhood corner since Eos moved in. Who would have thought that a restaurant serving theatrical East-West creations with a mind-boggling collection of wines would take hold at this funky Cole Valley crossroads? But it has.

There are two parts to Eos: a wine bar with more than forty wines by the glass, a wine list of tremendous depth and originality, and an ambitious schedule of wine tastings with wine makers; and a loud, happening restaurant where you can order any of the wines from the wine bar along with large and small plates of wild-looking Euro-Asian food. If you can find a seat in the wine bar, you can eat there, too. The combination of dramatic Asian-accented food and limitless wine choice is exciting—even if the two don't go together.

I like all the starters that bring something meticulously deep fried, such as crispy rock shrimp cakes with a mayonnaise-like spicy ginger aïoli and a radicchio cup full of little dressed lettuces. A clay pot of clams steamed in sake and lemongrass, garnished with whiskbrooms of lemongrass and knotted long beans; a signature and aptly named dish called Tuna Tower; voluptuous, moist, Moorish marinated chicken breast on pearl couscous; or an intensely smoky duck breast served with fruit chutney have all been delicious, if challenging, dishes to match with wine.

The wine-knowledgeable wait staff must be used to people throwing up their hands in confusion when they read both the exotic menu and the huge wine list. So the waiters step right in and suggest. You can follow their advice with confidence to get the best out of this restaurant. On the other hand, wine buffs will be ecstatic to see all sorts of rarities available at small markups.

Chef Arnold Wong and wine manager Debbie Zachareas both worked at the Wong family's famous Ashbury Market where they became skilled at buying and tasting wines, cheeses, and produce. Eos offers ten different cheeses to accompany wine. There are no less than twenty dessert wines by the glass to go with fine desserts like Bananamisu—whole caramelized bananas—or pastry-wrapped pears. And there might be $36 glasses of rare Burgundy, but the question remains, Should you drink such a wine with a green papaya spring roll? I can't answer that question. I wasn't about to try.

GANGES VEGETARIAN RESTAURANT

At this modest restaurant in a converted Victorian residence, Malvi Doshi, a cookbook author and cooking teacher, serves aromatic, strikingly different Indian dishes. She runs the place practically singlehandedly, so her menus are small. The fixed-price vegetarian meals always start with *papadums* and little plastic cups of *raita* (yogurt and cucumbers) followed by vegetable *pakoras* (or fritters) and pyramid-shaped *samosas* stuffed with cooked vegetables accompanied with lively tamarind-raisin and bright green chili-and-cilantro chutneys. The main part of the meal brings dal (an aromatic, soupy lentil stew) and several curries, perhaps a delicious, classic mixture of bright green spinach and white cheese or an unusual combination of dried beans, sweet potato, and zucchini. These vegetable dishes are cooked to order so they retain their texture and bright color, singing of roasted cumin, cloves, and coriander. One of my favorites is Doshi's baked bananas stuffed with finely chopped fresh coconut, cilantro, and green chilies. Call ahead to make sure it's on the

775 Frederick Street
(at Arguello),
San Francisco
Tel: 661-7290
Open Tuesday through
Saturday 5 to 9:30 p.m.
Price: Inexpensive
Credit cards: MC, V

menu. *Chapatis* and saffron rice, hot carrot pickles, and a hot red-chili sauce complete these home-cooked meals.

Dessert is a high point. Ms. Doshi makes her own *kulfi*, a dense Indian ice cream scented with cardamom, and her *ras mali*, a delicate white cheese ball poached in syrup and served in cream, is stellar. Hot mugs of *chai*, Darjeeling tea boiled with milk, pepper, cloves, and honey, is so sweet and spicy it can substitute for dessert, but why not have both? The prices here would make a mendicant happy.

The cozy, almost impromptu dining room offers both Western seating at wooden tables and chairs and low seating on carpets with cushions. A sitar player often perches in the bay window seat. Everyone feels like a dinner guest in Ms. Doshi's home.

HAMA-KO

108-B Carl Street (at Cole),
San Francisco
Tel: 753-6808
Open Tuesday through
Sunday 6 to 10 p.m.
Price: Moderate
Credit cards: MC, V

It's a well-kept secret that you can get some of the best sushi in town at this practically invisible little restaurant, especially if you call ahead and order a special meal from sushi-chef and owner Ted Kashiyama. He goes to Pier 33 everyday, specifically to Paul Johnson's Monterey Fish stall, to find scallops, live Dungeness crab, and shrimp. He has his sources for *hamachi* (yellowtail), sea urchin roe, and *mirugai* (giant clam), which is practically still moving when he cuts it. For a modest sum patrons can order a plate of mixed sushi from a small menu, but for a stunning meal let Mr. Kashiyama compose a series of hot and cold courses that are simple, exquisite, and unique. He might begin with a few perfect oysters on the half shell and end with a whole Dungeness crab cooked Japanese style, with delicacies like sushi and sashimi of *toro* (tuna belly) and real, fresh *hamachi* along the way. Call ahead to order these meals and reserve a space; otherwise you can walk in and hope to find a seat at the tiny sushi bar or at one of the few tables. Mr. Kashiyama's wife handles the floor with unflagging Japanese graciousness, but if more than two or three parties come in at the same time she does not quicken her methodical pace in bringing drinks, meticulously setting places, and taking orders. Service for her is like a stately dance that will not brook syncopation. Yet when she's with you, you bask in her attention.

TAQUERIA EL BALAZO

In a leveling transformation typical of the Haight, the arty, slightly upscale Ozone space, which was started by a Star's Cafe alum, has become a very popular taqueria where people can eat a lot for cheap. A tasty chicken mole goes into burritos and tacos with amazing grace. One wouldn't think that chicken in an aromatic sauce deepened by bitter chocolate would work with guacamole, rice, beans, and salsa in a burrito, but it does. The *carnitas* (pork slowly cooked in its own fat) is fresh, moist, and buttery, delicious in soft tacos sprinkled with extra chopped onions and cilantro, which are set out on the counter. Grateful Dead references (roses, skulls, and dishes named after certain group members) abound in the colorful, folk-art-filled dining room that surround the bustling counter. The food here reaches the best Mission District standards: Freshness is key, nothing sits around, and good combinations can be put together with a bit of experimentation. The flavors are authentic, although an awful lot of salt is used in practically everything.

1654 Haight Street
(between Clayton and Cole),
San Francisco
Tel: 864-8608
Open daily
10:30 a.m. to 11 p.m.
Price: Inexpensive
No credit cards

THEP PHANOM

Although Thai restaurants abound in San Francisco, it is not because they are cooking for a Thai community. The ethnic Thai population (as opposed to Vietnamese or Cambodian, for example) is small in the Bay Area. Thai restaurants cook for Westerners, so the trick is to find a restaurant that will prepare dishes authentically. The excitement of Thai cooking lies in the explosiveness of the seasoning (hot being dominant), and in the sweet, sour, fermented, and aromatic flavors in every dish. The best of the Thai restaurants use fresh ingredients, grind their own pastes for curries, and keep their dishes incendiary. That's why many aficionados consider Thep Phanom one of their favorite Thai restaurants. The kitchen doesn't make concessions. When they warn that a dish is hot, be prepared!

400 Waller (at Fillmore),
San Francisco
Tel: 431-2526
Open nightly
5:30 to 10:30 p.m.
Price: Inexpensive
Credit cards: AE, MC, V

The calamari salad is divine, juxtaposing tender squid with hot chilies, cool lettuces, fresh cilantro, and lime juice. A lot of the appetizers and salads balance similar ingredients, and I love them all whether they are made with minced chicken or duck in the *larb* preparations or with strips of spongy fish cake. The deep-fried dishes here stand out, especially the quail on lettuce with a peanut sauce. Rubbed with dry spices, the plain quail are so flavorful and moist that dipping them is unnecessary. Angel wings—fried chicken wings stuffed with glass noodles—may be the most ordered and delicious dish at the restaurant. If you love chilies, try one of the fiery stir fries from a special section of the menu. Once you get used to the level of hotness you realize how deep the flavors go in these dishes. They are the most characteristically Thai, *but* you must be able to tolerate hot, hot seasoning. More delicate coconut-milk curries, red or yellow from the particular spice paste used, are well represented on the menu. Deep-fried bananas with coconut ice cream end the meal on a cool note.

Besides the good cooking, Thep Phanom impresses with a pleasant, low-lit dining room decorated with elegant Thai artifacts. Lacy gold-trimmed place mats soften the glass-covered tabletops. The waiters and slim, elegant hostesses in Thai dress know how keep the dining room hopping. The place is always full, but somehow the wait is never long.

YA, HALLA FROM NADIA

494 Haight Street
(at Fillmore Street),
San Francisco
Tel: 522-1509
Open daily
11 a.m. to 10:30 p.m.
Price: Inexpensive
Credit cards: MC, V

Nadia Musleh and Hany Abuelrouf cook from their hearts at this earthy Middle Eastern cafe, Ya, Halla (which means "welcome" in Arabic). Consider their *mezze* menu, the array of appetizers that start a Middle Eastern meal. There are all sorts of surprises here, waiting to be ordered, such as squares of grilled mild cheese sprinkled with mint; deep-fried cracked wheat fritters stuffed with ground lamb, pine nuts, and fragrant spices; dreamy stuffed tomatoes; and big, brown fava beans in lemon, olive oil, and garlic. There's a meal. Even the usual stuff, smoky pureed eggplant, bulgur wheat and parsley salad, and warm dolmas sparkle. With a table full of these dishes, a basket of fresh pita bread, and icy bottles of Almeza beer from Lebanon, you feast for a very small sum. Or order a main course like my beloved *kefta* (spicy ground lamb kabobs) served with hummus (chickpea and sesame paste), pine nut–studded rice pilaf, and an Arabic salad of chopped tomato, cucumber, and onions, preceded by a plate of fantastic house-made pickles with feta cheese and olives. All of this delicious food comes for $7.

The cafe is a family-run affair and you get a personal welcome the minute you step through the door. The enticing open kitchen displays bowls of orange, brown, red, and yellow spices on glass shelves, and a spit of slowly roasting lamb for *shawerma* (pita sandwiches). Diners feel comfortable lingering over baklava and demitasses of thick Arabic coffee in the cheerful yellow dining room with wooden banquettes, lots of cushions, and Middle Eastern music playing in the background.

CAFES

BEAN THERE

Good light makes a good cafe, something that Hemingway knew. Bean There, a classy newcomer to the Lower Haight neighborhood, not only has wonderful natural light that pours in through tall windows, but a choice location on a residential corner lined with sycamores facing a block of refurbished Victorians. Chairs play an important role and the handsome ones here, made of heavy bamboo with ladder backs, beckon. A painted cement slab floor, wooden bench-like banquettes, and sponged ochre-colored walls give the room airy warmth. Background music has been carefully chosen; local newspapers and the *New York Times* are sold at the counter; and best of all, the espresso is rich and unburnt and the short latte is in perfect proportion. A large selection of teas are also featured. This cafe merits a trip across town; it transcends its neighborhood while being completely a part of it.

201 Steiner Street (at Waller),
San Francisco
Tel: 255-8855
Open Monday through
Friday 7 a.m. to 10 p.m.,
Saturday and Sunday
8 a.m. to 10 p.m.
No credit cards

ONE WORLD CAFE

1799 McAllister (at Baker),
San Francisco
Tel: 776-9358
Open Monday through
Friday 6 a.m. to 10 p.m.,
Saturday and Sunday
7 a.m. to 10 p.m.
No credit cards

The One World Cafe is hidden away on a broad, sunny, avenuelike street in a residential section of the Western Addition, a location you would only happen on by accident if you didn't live in the neighborhood. Yet a lot of people know about this cool little spot, another inventive expression of what constitutes a vital cafe. Coltrane plays at just the right level in a room painted in the brightest yellows, turquoises, and oranges. The menu is health-foody, with vegetarian sandwiches and salads based on nice greens. The espresso is worth a detour, and the sunny room gives off universally good vibes.

BARS

DELUXE

1511 Haight Street
(at Ashbury),
San Francisco
Tel: 552-6949
Open Monday through
Friday 4 p.m. to 2 a.m.,
Saturday 3 p.m. to 2 a.m.,
Sunday 2 p.m. to 2 a.m.
No credit cards

When a jazz combo plays on Fridays, Saturdays, and Sundays, it might cost you $4 or $5 to get in the door. At other times, the jazz comes from the sound system and admission to this suave, retro bar is free. The DeLuxe is one of my favorite bars in the city, not only for the mix of people who hang there, some of whom slick back their hair and make vintage clothing look like Armani, but because the drinks are so good. Bartenders make first-rate fresh-lime margaritas with just the right balance of sweet and sour so that the salt on the rim of the glass becomes part of the thrill. Ron de Barolito rum, so rich in flavor it reminds me of butterscotch, blossoms in a warmed brandy snifter. Dry, ice-cold martinis come in chilled V-shaped glasses, the very embodiment of sophistication. The scene is elevated enough so that people who like to dress feel appreciated. Yet there's nothing snobby about the DeLuxe. Old and young, matronly and hip, casual and dressy—everyone looks good here, and after a perfect drink or two everyone feels pretty good too.

KEZAR BAR & RESTAURANT

A cozy neighborhood sports bar that was opened by the people who owned the long-defunct Ironwood across the street, the Kezar offers a comfortable barroom with two video monitors and an adjoining dining room. The food here is terrific, just what you want when you belly up to a bar. There are spicy garlic peanuts and warm, thick corn chips with delicious tomato salsa. The hamburgers are juicy and full of flavor. More elaborate dishes turn out to be surprisingly good; Greek-style spinach salad, pot roast, and seafood chowder have been standouts. Anchor Wheat beer is on tap and drinks are generously poured. Good spirit pervades: Fellow patrons are friendly, the staff accommodating. Kezar fulfills every requirement of a fine neighborhood pub.

900 Cole Street (at Carl),
San Francisco
Tel: 681-7678
Open Sunday through Thursday 5 to 10 p.m., Friday and Saturday until 11 p.m.
Credit cards: AE, D, MC, V

NOC NOC

Its singular Flintstones-meets-high-tech interior has been lifted by others, but Noc Noc created the original Iron Age–hippie-pad look, augmented by a few glowing video screens without vertical hold and collaged surfaces embedded with bottle openers. Its patronage has gone through stages: super-counterculture hip and exclusive; then druggie and nodding out in the crannies; and currently, youngish and bohemian from the neighborhood. Beer is the thing—from microbreweries up and down the West Coast to German lagers and ales, all on tap. Tucher lager, a crisp, sweet, scintillating German beer served in a tall pilsener glass with a lemon slice perched on the rim, makes for universally good drinking.

557 Haight Street (between Fillmore and Steiner),
San Francisco
Tel: 861-5811
Open daily 5 p.m. to 2 a.m.
No credit cards

TORONADO

547 Haight Street (between Fillmore and Steiner), San Francisco
Tel: 863-2276
Open daily 11:30 a.m. to 2 a.m.
No credit cards

This has become the choice hangout in the lower Haight: a safe place in a dicey neighborhood. Toronado is mobbed on the weekends by people who arrive in cabs and do not look as if they live anywhere nearby, perhaps because it is a dead ringer for a collegiate bar with traditional wood wainscoting and green walls. The list of beers goes on and on—from raspberry wheat to Boont Amber from the Anderson Valley to Guinness Stout, all on tap—and there is enough light in this bar to see the differences in brew color. The bartenders know the brews and describe them well.

DELICATESSENS/TAKE-OUT

BROTHER-IN-LAW'S BARBEQUE NO. 2

705 Divisadero (at Grove), San Francisco
Tel: 931-7427
Open Tuesday through Thursday 11 a.m. to midnight, Friday and Saturday until 2 a.m., Sunday 11 a.m. to 8 p.m.
Credit cards: DC, MC, V

Brother-in-Law's gets crowded late and on the weekends, and sometimes the line can move very slowly. As you wait by the counter engulfed in the mouthwatering aromas of cooking meat, you can barely restrain yourself, especially if you've spent the prior part of the evening drinking. Too often have I prematurely torn open the sturdy cartons, which really do keep the food hot until you get it home, and coated the car with barbecue sauce. Brother-in-Law's short ends are worth the mess. These are the chopped-off tops or chine bone of the pork rib—thick, stubby, meaty bones laced with fat that melts as the ribs smoke, bathing them in flavor. The regular pork ribs are excellent too, but don't have quite the succulence of those short ends. Think about ordering brisket here—crusty, moist, and full of smoky flavor. Baked beans are sweet and intensely smoky from slow cooking in the barbecue oven. Very sweet corn bread is still preferable to commercial white. Brother-in-Law's medium-hot barbecue sauce does it for me; the hot is incendiary.

REAL FOOD COMPANY

1023 Stanyan Street (between Carl and Frederick),
San Francisco
Tel: 564-1117
Open daily 9 a.m. to 8:30 p.m.
Credit cards: MC, V
See listing, page 176.

ICE CREAM/CHOCOLATES

GELATO CLASSICO

201 Parnassus Avenue (at Stanyan),
San Francisco
Tel: 566-9696
Open Sunday through Thursday noon to 10:30 p.m.,
Friday and Saturday until 11:15 p.m.
No credit cards
See listing, page 295.

COFFEE

SPINELLI COFFEE COMPANY

For other locations, see pages 256, 322, 358, 442, and 520.

Very much in the Peet's mold, Spinelli believes in dark roasting, daily delivery of freshly roasted beans, and intense brewing. In fact, the founders of the intentionally small chain were acolytes of Mr. Peet's in Berkeley and escapees from the corporate-minded Starbucks headquartered in Seattle. Like Peet's, the personnel at each store takes a proprietary interest in the quality of the coffee and the education of

919 Cole Street (at Carl),
San Francisco
Tel: 753-2287
Open Monday through
Friday 6:30 a.m. to 9 p.m.,
Saturday and Sunday
7:30 a.m. to 9 p.m.
Credit cards: MC, V

its patrons. The Cole Street branch stands out for its pleasant, efficient, enlightened service and consistent brews. In a part of town where counterculture cool outweighs service in many places, earnest Spinelli stands out as an oasis of civilization.

MARKETS

ASHBURY MARKET

205 Frederick Street
(at Ashbury),
San Francisco
Tel: 566-3134
Open Monday through
Saturday 9 a.m. to 9 p.m.,
Sunday until 3 p.m.
Credit cards: AE, MC, V

Wilfred Wong, the ebullient wine writer, California county fair wine judge, and general ubiquitous presence on the wine scene, put the Ashbury Market on the map by gathering together an eccentric but very good selection of California wines and choice wines from France for his family's grocery. Though he no longer works at the Ashbury Market (a bit of a family disagreement), the wine collection still fills a whole back room on closely placed shelves that almost reach the ceiling. A committee of three wine buyers who trained with Wilfred are continuing on, maintaining the Ashbury Market as a neighborhood resource for the likes of Forman Cabernet or Au Bon Climat wines.

It's unusual to find a corner grocery store that carries Acme bread, organic chips, and snacks like the incomparable Newman's Own Pretzels, some organic vegetables, super-high-butterfat Plugra butter (covered in plastic wrap by the store to stay fresh), Straus Family Dairy milk, Hobbs bacon, Gerhard sausages, Rocky free-range chickens, and ground turkey. All of these items are finds a few blocks off Haight Street. Pails of flowers outside the rustic wood-trimmed market signal the upscale goodies within, from cat food to imported pasta. Though the wines are by no means discounted, specials signs can lead the way to some decent buys. The checkout clerks are nice and loquacious, and the wine people in the back will be happy to schmooze about any bottle.

FALLETTI'S FINER FOODS

Formerly a Petrini's, Falletti's gets high marks for carrying freshly baked breads from Acme, Semifreddi, Grace, and Tassajara among others; Dande's shrimp chips (very tasty if you like this variety of snack); Castle Creamery cream-topped milk and chocolate milk in glass quart bottles; sharp New York Cheddars from the Marin Cheese Company; the superlative Columbus-brand anchovies; and a huge variety of upscale packaged cookies. The snack and chip buyer is discriminating. I found the only "diet" chip I've ever liked here: Michael Season's lightly salted potato chips, with 40 percent less fat (6 grams versus 10 grams of fat per 1-ounce serving). A lively wine section next to a well-chosen fruit juice section that offers lots of tropical fruit nectars strikes me as a smart way to arrange a store: Put all the drinks in one area so you don't forget to buy something for the kids when you're mulling over wine. The produce is commercial but complete, with berries usually featured.

1750 Fulton (at Masonic; Plaza Foods), San Francisco
Tel: 567-0976
Open Monday through Saturday 9 a.m. to 8 p.m., Sunday 9:30 a.m. to 7 p.m.
Credit cards: D, MC, V

PLAZA FOODS

Under one roof at this older, venerable city shopping center, food lovers will find a high-quality grocery store and an excellent meat market, a so-so fish but a good poultry market, and a serviceable delicatessen, liquor store, and outpost of Just Desserts.

Corner of Fulton and Masonic, San Francisco
Open Monday through Saturday 9 a.m. to 8 p.m., Sunday 9:30 a.m. to 7 p.m.

PRODUCE

REAL FOOD COMPANY

1023 Stanyan Street
(between Carl
and Frederick),
San Francisco
Tel: 564-2800
Open daily
9 a.m. to 8:30 p.m.
Credit cards: MC, V

For other locations, see pages 173, 259, and 358.

The Real Food group of natural foods stores made organic produce accessible in San Francisco. Kimball Allen, the owner of the stores, fell into his successful chain by accident. He owned some property that he needed to lease and ended up opening a profitable natural foods chain by letting independent managers run the stores. He prefers being a club owner and jazz impresario (see Kimball's East, page 472).

Though a centralized produce department now buys for all the Real Foods stores, produce cognoscenti still consider these health food outlets to be some of the best sources for organic fruits and vegetables in the city. The buyers have established long-term connections with local organic farmers and all the stores make a point of labeling produce by farm and growing practice. Prices can be astronomical for produce that might be

FRESH PEAS

The Real Food Company is one of the few places to find good local English peas during their short season in spring before it gets too hot. Some of the best peas grow in the cooler finger valleys off Half Moon Bay and San Gregorio Beach. When I think about what it takes to bring fresh peas to market, I marvel that it ever happens at all. The peas must be picked at just the right moment before they mature and get starchy, but when they are large enough to make up more than a spoonful after they're shelled. As so often happens, some peas in a batch may be too large and others small and sweet in the same harvest, so picking must be done judiciously with consistency in mind. The picked peas must be cooled immediately and delivered to market quickly so they keep their sugar. (Peas lose up to 40 percent of their sugar in six hours at room temperature.) At the store the same rules apply. The peas must be kept cool and sold fast. Each moment warming on the display shelves and sitting in the coolers in the back detracts from their charm. Too many times I have come away from a market with peas that tasted pretty good when I bought them but changed overnight in the refrigerator. When you take the time to shell fresh peas at home you want them to be worth the effort, and the trip from field to the plate is a long one, fraught with pitfalls. Next to careful buying at a farmers' market, the Stanyan Real Foods produce section has offered the highest probability in town for securing sweet peas.

slightly out of season or fragile, like berries, but seasonal organic vegetables are affordable and usually much tastier than cheaper, commercially grown produce. At the Stanyan store, a whole room is devoted to carefully stored and groomed fruits and vegetables. I like the respectful handling here, the informative labeling, and the wide variety. I always find something unusual that can inspire a dinner.

FRESH PEAS WITH SHALLOTS

2 tablespoons butter

2 large shallots, minced

3 pounds fresh peas
   in the pod, shelled
   (about 2 1/2 cups shelled peas)

1 teaspoon kosher salt

Freshly ground pepper

1/2 cup water

Melt the butter in a large skillet over medium heat. Add the shallots and cook until soft. Add the peas, salt, pepper, and water. Stir, bring to a boil, then cover and cook over high heat until the peas are sweet and tender but not mushy, about 3 to 5 minutes, depending on the size of the peas. If they are still hard after 5 minutes, add a little more water, if necessary, and cook 2 minutes longer. Most of the liquid should be gone when the peas are ready.

Variation At the last moment, you may add finely chiffonnaded fresh mint leaves or 1/2 teaspoon minced fresh thyme or chervil. For a wonderful treat, cook peas in this way with chanterelle mushrooms, adding 1 tablespoon olive oil to the butter and continuing on in the same manner with shallots, then chanterelles, then peas, using less water, depending on the moisture in the mushrooms.

Serves 4

MEAT AND POULTRY

ENRICO'S

Fulton and Masonic
(Plaza Foods),
San Francisco
Tel: 346-7934
Open Monday through
Saturday 9 a.m. to 8 p.m.,
Sunday 9:30 a.m. to 7 p.m.
Credit cards: MC, V

This meat counter looks appealing with its neat trays of nicely displayed, freshly cut meat. Showing particular strength in lamb and veal, Enrico's often has veal chops with kidneys still attached; small lamb shanks; meaty racks of lamb trimmed of excessive fat; thick-sliced bacon; hard-to-find fresh country pork ribs; and cured meats used for cooking, like smoked ham hocks. The most attractive cuts of beef here are short ribs, oxtails, tongue, and beef knuckle for stock. Butchers cut and trim to order. Lots of them work behind the counter, so your number comes up quickly. Though there are other Enrico's meat counters in the city, this is one of the best, a fine resource for that fresh, unusual cut of meat.

UNITED FISH AND POULTRY

Fulton and Masonic
(Plaza Foods),
San Francisco
Tel: 567-3855
Open Monday through
Saturday 9 a.m. to 8 p.m.,
Sunday 9:30 a.m. to 7 p.m.
Credit cards: CB, DC, MC, V

I would not buy fish here, but the high-quality chickens come from Fulton Valley at excellent prices and you can get as many of any part as you need; wings, breasts, thighs, legs, or gizzards. Whole chickens abound, and large Rocky free-range roasters are also part of the roster. All cuts of fresh turkey can be found here, including separately ground dark and white turkey meat, breasts, half birds, and small whole birds. Sometimes I have seen fresh rabbit, but use your common sense. If something looks old, don't buy it, or ask for another piece. One would hope that food retailers would groom their cases, but in some instances the line between fresh and what can pass for fresh becomes fuzzy, especially when it's been a slow week.

CHEESE

COUNTRY CHEESE

People like to shop here for large hunks of cheese at wholesale prices, like Reggiano Parmesan at $6.99 per pound—at least a dollar a pound cheaper than most other stores. Extra sharp Cheddars from Vermont and New York, sweet butter in bulk for $1.99 a pound, and huge wedges of Saint-André for $7.99 per pound can make party purchases less expensive. The nuts in bulk could be fresher. The dry goods in bins, like basmati rice for 69¢ per pound, dried beans of all sorts, and popcorn, are the building blocks of dishes that can feed large groups.

415 Divisadero Street
(between Oak and Fell),
San Francisco
Tel: 621-8130
Open Monday through
Saturday 10 a.m. to 7 p.m.
Credit cards: MC, V

SAY CHEESE

One of the better-stocked cheese stores in the city, Say Cheese carries hard-to-find cheeses on a regular basis. Try the Mona Lisa aged Gouda (pronounced "how-da" by the purists), a buttery, nutty semi-hard cheese that merits a trip across town. Say Cheese will have the seasonal Brin d'Amour, an evocative, mild, but complex Corsican sheep's milk cheese rolled in wild herbs that charms cheese-lovers. On the more mundane level, two-year-old Vermont Cheddar is always available, as is English clotted cream (divine on scones if you can get it fresh enough), a large selection of imported English cheeses, and rarities such as a superior brand of bagel chips (Burns & Ricker from Paterson, New Jersey), and buttery madeleines. Good imported and local cured meats and sausages are made into sandwiches on the premises on Semifreddi baguettes, or sliced and wrapped to go. Because Say Cheese does carry a large inventory of cheeses, you might want to ask for tastes just to make sure your selection is in good condition.

856 Cole Street (between
Frederick and Carl),
San Francisco
Tel: 665-5020
Open Monday through
Thursday 10 a.m. to 7 p.m.,
Friday and Saturday
until 8 p.m.,
Sunday until 5 p.m.
Credit cards: MC, V

WINES AND SPIRITS

ASHBURY MARKET

See listing, page 174.

COOKWARE AND BOOKS

COOKIN'

339 Divisadero Street
(between Oak and Page),
San Francisco
Tel: 861-1854
Open Tuesday through
Saturday noon to 6:30 p.m.,
Sunday 1 to 5 p.m.
Credit cards: MC, V

In a town of dueling cookware giants (Sur La Table, Crate and Barrel, Williams-Sonoma), Cookin's unique and ever-changing collection of old cooking utensils, dishes, and glassware stimulates my culinary imagination. Gazing at a collection of butter molds, tartlet pans, and fragile unmatched teacups, I contemplate serving a tea. Porcelain egg coddlers, small delicate glasses, tin molds, tarnished copper pieces in unusual shapes, Fiestaware, bundt pans, madeleine tins, cookie cutters, Christmas things, Easter things—the odd, rare, and common—have all been sorted through for intrinsic beauty, utility, and good condition. Often you can find the very item you are looking for at Cookin' when it maddeningly has been discontinued or changed in the name of improvement at the other stores, like long, wooden-handled potato mashers, or plain, rectangular spatulas. Like the old-fashioned card catalog they have removed from the New Main Library, I find this store indispensable for finding what I really need.

The Marina & Cow Hollow

THE MARINA & COW HOLLOW

Restaurants:
1. Betelnut   185
2. Bistro Aix   186
3. Cafe Marimba   187
4. E'Angelo   189
5. Greens   190
6. Marina Central   191
7. Pane e Vino   191
8. PlumpJack Cafe   192
9. Zinzino   193

Cafes:
10. Bugatti's Espresso Cafe   194

Bars:
11. Balboa Cafe   194
12. Bus Stop   195
13. The Paragon   195
14. Perry's   195

Delicatessens/Take-Out:
15. Lucca   196
16. Rosti   197
17. World Wrapps   197

Bakeries/Pastries:
18. Just Desserts   198
19. La Nouvelle Pâtisserie   199

Coffee:
20. Peet's Coffee and Tea   199

Markets:
21. Marina Super   201

Wines and Spirits:
22. California Wine Merchant   202

Cookware and Books:
23. Fredericksen's Hardware   202
24. Williams-Sonoma   203

RESTAURANTS

BETELNUT

I was much taken by this wildly popular *peiju-wu*, or Asian beer house, when it first opened a year ago. Cecilia Chiang, veteran restaurateur and former owner of the Mandarin in Ghirardelli Square, put together the menu of spicy, pan-Asian dishes and watched over it like a mother hen. She has since left the operation to the management of the Real Restaurants group, who own Fog City Diner, Bix, and other popular restaurants, and the cooking has become more inconsistent. But I am addicted to some of the dishes, like a fiery, intensely salty stir-fry of tiny sun-dried anchovies, hot chiles, sliced garlic, scallions, and peanuts that absolutely requires large draughts of cold, house rice beer (and a full commitment from whomever you happen to be eating this with, because no one will want to be within ten feet after a little plate of it).

The intriguing menu offers dishes from Singapore, Thailand, Japan, Malaysia, Indonesia, Hong Kong, Shanghai, Canton, Taiwan, Vietnam, and Korea—each with its own distinctive pantry of flavors. This is not California-style crossover cooking, but true renditions of dishes from many different parts of the Far East. The noodles, dumplings, curries, and soups; the tea duck, pickles, deep-fried squid, and seafood; and small plates of vegetables are all served in a stunning collection of hand-thrown bowls and plates. The unifying concept is that all the dishes go with beer—or sake, or Trader Vic–style cocktails, or tea, or Chinese sherrylike plum wine, or maybe even Western wine, though the last is a long shot.

2030 Union Street (between Webster and Buchanan),
San Francisco
Tel: 929-8855
Open Sunday through Thursday 11:30 a.m. to 11 p.m., Friday and Saturday until midnight
Price: Moderate
Credit cards: D, DC, MC, V

Betelnut is as much a bar as it is a restaurant. The look of the bar was inspired by the Long Bar in Singapore's Raffles Hotel. The ever-packed dining areas arranged around an open kitchen are noisy, fun, and exciting. True to all Real Restaurants operations, Betelnut is witty in its details. A whole Asian world of food and drink has been packaged for you to explore. Though I'm a culinary purist, I find the wrapping here to be pretty irresistible.

BISTRO AIX

**3340 Steiner Street
(between Lombard
and Chestnut),
San Francisco
Tel: 202-0100
Open Monday through
Thursday 6 to 10 p.m., Friday
and Saturday until 11 p.m.,
Sunday 5:30 to 9:30 p.m.
Price: Moderate
Credit cards: AE, MC, V**

Bistros come and go but this one will stay—if the chef-owner of this small, wonderful place doesn't exhaust himself cooking. His exceptional roast chicken with crusty skin and juicy flesh served with superb, buttery mashed potatoes and fantastic, almost caramelized ratatouille, for all of $10.50, is one reason why people come back here again and again. This is a dish I could eat practically every day. The light flavorful broth in an onion soup lets the sweetness of onions shine through, a single cheesy crouton adding salt and savoriness. A thin paillard of halibut, seared quickly and topped with a ton of delicious mango salsa on a bed of couscous, strikes a surprisingly delicious balance. Though done all over town in one variation or another, a salad of grilled pears, goat cheese, and walnuts with wintry greens has straightforward rustic charm here. You can tell that this cook tastes his food and knows exactly what flavors and textures he wants in each dish. The cooking glows with hominess and good culinary sense.

The small dining area, wedged in around an open kitchen with a few counter seats, can get noisy and crowded. Luckily a clean, modern decor does not add clutter, though a cranked-up sound system seems superfluous. Seating is almost doubled by a pleasant outdoor patio with heat lamps that toast you on one side. Still, many prefer sitting in the romantically lit, open-air patio because they can hear each other talk. Frankly, when the food is so good and so reasonable—and that describes a small, well-chosen wine list as well—I am happy in any seat I can find.

CAFE MARIMBA

Some people confronted by a three-legged stone mortar filled with grilled pork and onions don't know what to do, especially when they are expecting platters of soft, saucy Mexican food finished off under a broiler. At Cafe Marimba, one of the few authentic, full-scale Mexican restaurants in the United States, they learn how to tuck the luscious morsels of pork into small, soft corn tortillas, just off the griddle, and spoon on some hot, smoky chipotle salsa. The taste of such regional, made-from-scratch Mexican food is sublime and unexpected; very earthy but punctuated by explosive flavors.

A meal could start with a platter of Cafe Marimba's sparkling snapper ceviche, consisting of big chunks of tomato, onion, and local rockfish in a vibrant lime and chili marinade. Delicious little quesadillas filled with squash blossoms and fresh white cheese; rock shrimp enchiladas in a creamy avocado sauce; or a whole fried snapper, crisp under a blanket of dried red pasilla chilies cut into rings and lime, are but some of the dishes inspired by originating chef Reed Hearon's travels through regional Mexico. Hearon has since left the Cafe Marimba kitchen, but partner Louise Clement and her crew continue to explore the rich and varied cuisine. Clement, well traveled in Mexico herself, sent her chef to Mexican cooking guru Rick Bayless's intensive class at Greystone, the Culinary Institute of America's campus in the Napa Valley.

Since Cafe Marimba's menu is divided into small and large dishes, with most plates served family style, diners end up sharing and tasting lots of the new and sometimes exotic dishes without making a major commitment.

Lest one of the pleasures of eating Mexican be ignored, drinks here get special attention. Fresh fruit juice combos like strawberry-lemonade or pineapple-ginger *agua fresca* especially please kids (who love many of the tacos and quesadillas), while fresh-lime margaritas, kept intentionally tart, do fine with the adults. Smooth tequilas from small producers are a revelation—and may cause a few as well.

2317 Chestnut Street (between Scott and Divisadero), San Francisco
Tel: 776 1506
Open Monday 5:30 to 10:30 p.m., Tuesday through Saturday 10:30 a.m. to 10:30 p.m.
Price: Moderate
Credit cards: AE, MC, V

WATERMELON AND PINEAPPLE-GINGER AGUAS FRESCAS

The delicious fresh fruit drinks at Cafe Marimba come in many flavors depending upon the season. Once you've made one, you can easily make any of them. The key is a simple syrup of sugar and water, which can be purchased or made at home. Similar aguas frescas are ladled from huge glass jars on the counters of taquerias all over the Mission. In the Mission you find exotic flavors like Jamaica, or red hibiscus flower, pruney tamarind, and almost always a wonderful cantaloupe. Cafe Marimba adds extra ingredients to theirs, such as vanilla bean and lemon to their strawberry agua fresca, or mint to the mango blend. When the fruit drinks are spiked with dark rum, as they often are at Cafe Marimba, they turn into batidas.

WATERMELON AGUA FRESCA

4 cups watermelon flesh, seeded (about 2 pounds whole watermelon)
1 cup simple syrup (recipe follows)
2 3/4 cups water

Cut the watermelon flesh into small chunks. Blend for 10 seconds in a blender or food processor. The mixture should be chunky. Put in a pitcher and stir in the simple syrup and water. Let stand for 1 or 2 hours. Serve over ice. Best drunk the same day.

Makes about 2 quarts

PINEAPPLE-GINGER AGUA FRESCA

1 ripe medium pineapple
1 tablespoon grated peeled ginger (about one 1 1/2-inch piece)
1 1/4 cups simple syrup (recipe follows)
3 cups water

Peel the pineapple and remove the eyes. Core and cut into small chunks. Blend in a blender or food processor for about 25 seconds. The mixture will be pulpy. Put the pureed fruit in a pitcher. Add the ginger and simple syrup. Let stand for 1 or 2 hours, stirring occasionally. Add the water and serve over ice.

Makes about 2 quarts

SIMPLE SYRUP

1 cup water
1 1/4 cups sugar

Mix the ingredients together in a medium saucepan. Boil for 1 minute, cover, and chill thoroughly. Refrigerated syrup keeps indefinitely.

Makes 1 cup

E'ANGELO

2234 Chestnut Street
(between Pierce and Scott),
San Francisco
Tel: 567-6164
Open Tuesday through
Sunday 5 to 11 p.m.
Price: Moderate
No credit cards

Seated at one of E'Angelo's tiny tables, my nine-year-old and I were horrified to see the host push the table next to us even closer and seat a dad with two young children. This was our grown-up night out, and we did not want two little kids right on top of us. The host thought he was being cute by sticking all the kids and parents together, but that's life at this eighteen-year-old Marina institution. Just be happy you get a seat at all at this popular restaurant, whose dining room is mostly taken up by a partially open kitchen.

In all the years I have been eating here the menu has not changed, but why should it when the traditional house-made pastas are timeless? E'Angelo made them from scratch long before the Italian food frenzy swept the nation. The luscious green lasagne made with the most tender spinach noodles layered with tons of Fontina, mozzarella, and a signature dried porcini and chicken liver meat sauce is both refined and rustic. The kitchen is famous for a delicate eggplant parmigiana that melts in your mouth. The small pizzas with crisp, paper-thin crusts and the simplest of toppings, like tomato sauce, mozzarella, and mushrooms, are among the best in town. Ricotta- and spinach-filled ravioli, and soft, tender gnocchi napped in tomato sauce are both classics. A crisp, old-fashioned iceberg lettuce salad, briskly dressed in vinegar and oil and topped with a few anchovies, seems retro in this age of arugula, but it always hits the spot. Although in some respects closer to the old school of Italian-American eateries, E'Angelo continues to satisfy because it executes the basics: a silken noodle dough and a resonant meat sauce.

GREENS

**Fort Mason, Building A
(Buchanan at
Marina Boulevard),
San Francisco
Tel: 771-6222
Open for lunch Tuesday
through Saturday
11:30 a.m. to 2 p.m.;
dinner Monday through
Friday 5:30 to 9:30 p.m.;
prix fixe dinner
Saturday 6 to 9:30 p.m.;
Sunday brunch
10 a.m. to 2 p.m.
Price: Moderate
Credit cards: MC, V**

When Deborah Madison, the original chef at this vegetarian restaurant started by the Zen Center, put together her first menus, people could not believe how intriguing and satisfying a meatless meal could be. She developed a whole new style of vegetarian cuisine that looked to France and the Mediterranean for flavors, and local farms and producers for pristine ingredients. Her five-course prix-fixe dinners became legendary for their imagination and elegance—a far cry from the hippie health-food genre that had taken hold in California in the 1960s.

Madison moved to Santa Fe, but her recipes are available to everyone in *The Greens Cookbook* and *The Savory Way* (Bantam). Greens has flourished under the guidance of Annie Somerville, an author in her own right (*Field of Greens*, Bantam), who has kept the standards high and the menus lively. You will find Greens classics like a Bloomsdale spinach salad tossed with creamy feta, croutons, and threads of red onion in a gorgeous dressing fragrant with mint, sherry vinegar, and warmed olive oil; or the best tofu sandwich in the world, made with smoky charcoal-grilled tofu with horseradish mayonnaise on Tassajara potato bread. There might be airy vegetable pancakes enriched with ricotta and Gruyère, served with a piquant tomato-sherry sauce and a dab of crème fraîche; or a house-made pasta with chanterelles, leeks, and Parmesan. The range is stunning and the food always tasty. The restaurant uses only the highest-quality ingredients, from olive oil to nuts.

Greatly improved over the years is the service, which used to be performed, more or less, by Zen students. Now the service is brisk and professional. Another big plus, in addition to the lovely view of the Marina and the airy, art-filled dining room, is a list of eight unusual wine specials, offered by the glass or bottle, that go wonderfully with the food. Just inside the front door of the restaurant there is a handy to-go outlet that sells Tassajara breads and pastries along with soups, sandwiches, and pastries made on the premises.

MARINA CENTRAL

Owner Doyle Moon, a veteran of the San Francisco restaurant business (Stars, Balboa Cafe), has chosen a comfy crossover concept for his new Marina Central. He hired chef Tony Gulisano to update the big San Francisco–style Joe's menu with some lighter California and Italian creations. Now practically everyone can be happy in this bustling bar and restaurant committed to staying open long hours.

Though the food was inconsistent during the opening months, you can look forward to a whole spit-roasted local snapper sauced simply and piquantly with garlic, lime, and parsley, especially with a side order of Marina Central's curried-vegetable fried jasmine rice, an invention so tasty it must be ordered as a side. Braised veal shanks; fried petrale sole with chanterelles; tender, egg-battered abalone (a rare treat); and an antipasto platter have all been fine. The idea behind the menu is to cover all the bases in a no-nonsense way, so Marina Central offers everything from Niman-Schell hamburgers to a stunning pomegranate and orange granita—covering pastas, roasts, grills, salads, pizzetta, and a lot of side vegetables and starches along the way.

The interior of the large, clubby restaurant, with a long bar on one side and an open kitchen on another, was hand-built by Moon himself, who obviously favors lots of dark wood, generous booths, comfortable tables and chairs, and a high ceiling. He has achieved an uncanny hybrid of his former venues. Men, in particular, like it here.

2001 Chestnut (at Fillmore),
San Francisco
Tel: 673-2222
Open Monday 11:30 a.m. to 9:30 p.m., Tuesday through Thursday until 11 p.m., Friday and Saturday until midnight, Sunday 10:30 a.m. to 9:30 p.m.
Price: Moderate
Credit cards: AE, DC, MC, V

PANE E VINO

Pane e Vino was one of the first restaurants in San Francisco to cook real Northern Italian using first-rate imported ingredients. Simple, authentic dishes like arugula salad; bread and tomato soup; juicy, thick veal chops; a whole striped bass grilled with fennel; lamb stew over soft white polenta; a sparkling warm salad of cuttlefish, mussels, green beans, and black olives rotate on and off of a menu mostly dedicated to pastas. On a recent visit, however, several of the formerly impeccable pastas were ruined by way too much raw-tasting garlic.

3011 Steiner Street
(between Union and Filbert),
San Francisco
Tel: 346-2111
Open for lunch Monday through Thursday 11:30 a.m. to 2 p.m.; dinner Sunday through Thursday 5 to 10 p.m., Friday and Saturday 11:30 a.m. to 10:30 p.m.
Price: Moderate
Credit cards: AE, MC, V

Two small rustic dining rooms with terra-cotta floors and beamed ceilings are separated by a tiled open kitchen, cordoned off with counters that display attractive antipasti. The high noise level counterbalances intimately close tables, so you really can't eavesdrop on the local Pacific Heights politicos, doctors, and lawyers who consider Pane e Vino their club. They have come to appreciate the sophisticated Italian wine list and the insouciant but efficient young Italian waiters. You must book well ahead at dinner to secure a table.

PLUMPJACK CAFE

3127 Fillmore Street
(between Greenwich
and Filbert),
San Francisco
Tel: 563-4755
Open for lunch Monday
through Friday
11:30 a.m. to 2 p.m.,
dinner Monday through
Saturday 5:30 to 10:30 p.m.
Price: Moderate
Credit cards: AE, MC, V

Following in the footsteps of the PlumpJack wine store down the street, which sells popular wines at affordable prices, the PlumpJack Cafe offers a Mediterranean-California menu at similarly friendly tariffs. The current chef, Maria Helm, has turned the restaurant into a first-rate neighborhood spot with her meticulous, yet surprisingly voluptuous cooking. Though she's not breaking any new culinary ground with her delicate, well-balanced pastas, flaky Fontina and chanterelles tarts, or flavorful seared pork medallions with dried fruit sauce served in a flat bowl of buttery orzo, her versions of them have personality and elegant simplicity. I particularly like the bright green salads that play a contrasting role on many a plate.

This is a small, sophisticated Pacific Heights hangout (named for an opera written by Gordon Getty, the father of one of the owners) with a beige, gray, and silver color scheme, irregularly shaped wood and metal chairs, and banquettes upholstered in metallic silver. An abstract crossed-sword motif suggests things medieval. An internal window looks across a walkway to a large Buddha in an Asian antiques shop, providing a serendipitous bit of decor, while a completely separate and hidden private dining room in the back stands ready to host society bachelor parties. Service is top-notch.

What is extraordinary about PlumpJack is its wine prices, which are a few dollars above retail and many dollars below what most restaurants charge. You can drink Randall

Grahm's bracing Ca'del Solo "Il Pescatore" for $12 or his Bonny Doon Syrah for $30, both retail prices; or soft, fruity PlumpJack cabernet for $4 a glass. The whole package—food, wine, prices, appointments and service—cannot be beat any place in town, but as my dining companion pointed out, profit may not be a motive here. Lucky us.

ZINZINO

Since its opening, Zinzino has been struggling for a physical identity. Located in an odd, ground-level space with a garden patio in the back, Zinzino doesn't feel like either a full-scale restaurant or a self-service pizzeria. A confusing outdoor/indoor decor doesn't help. The restaurant started off as an order-at-the-counter place, but the sophisticated menu really called for table service, which has been instituted. The surprisingly delicious Italian food here warrants at least this level of amenity.

Start with a clean and refreshing shaved fennel salad, or a long-cooked Tuscan minestrone. Most people come here for thin-crust pizzas baked in the wood-fired oven with fresh, bright-flavored toppings. One of my favorites, thinly sliced eggplant sprinkled with herbed bread crumbs and mozzarella, is transformed by a squeeze of lemon. Who would have thought? Lamb shanks are fall-off-the-bone tender, yet still retain plenty of natural character, though spaghetti in meat sauce cooked in a parchment package with huge meatballs succumbs to an overzealous use of herbs. For dessert, try an apple baked in the wood-fired oven—a brilliant idea—served with ice cream and caramel sauce. I don't like to drink wine from Zinzino's thick tumblers, and I have never felt comfortable at any Zinzino table, where I seem to be either in a cold draft or a heat wave from the oven. But true to the contradictory nature of this place, service by sweet, enthusiastic wait people charms. I really like Zinzino for its food and service—but I can't get my husband to go there because he can't get over the way the place feels.

2355 Chestnut Street
(between Divisadero and Scott),
San Francisco
Tel: 346-6623
Open Monday through Thursday 5:30 to 10 p.m.,
Friday until 11 p.m.,
Saturday 5 to 11 p.m.,
Sunday 4 to 9:30 p.m.
Price: Moderate
Credit cards: MC, V

CAFES

BUGATTI'S ESPRESSO CAFE

3001 Webster Street
(at Filbert),
San Francisco
Tel: 922-4888
Open Monday through
Thursday 7 a.m. to 6 p.m.,
Saturday and Sunday
7:30 a.m. to 6 p.m.
Credit cards: MC, V

Located on a sunny corner on a residential street one block off Fillmore, Bugatti's brings a whiff of authentic North Beach to this preppy part of town. Indeed, the cafe uses Caffé Roma beans to prepare its well-made espresso and cappuccino, though one of the more popular drinks, the Depth Charger, a cup of brewed coffee spiked with a shot of espresso, would never be made in North Beach. (In a properly brewed cup of coffee, espresso would be superfluous.) When Bugatti's was about to open in 1982, the neighborhood put up a fuss, but now it's become a beloved fixture with full outdoor tables on sunny days and the expansively windowed interior well populated with typical cafe dwellers. The people behind the counter have better dispositions than most cafe workers.

BARS

BALBOA CAFE

3199 Fillmore Street
(between Greenwich
and Filbert),
San Francisco
Tel: 921-3944
Open daily
11 a.m. to 10 p.m.;
Sunday brunch
11 a.m. to 4 p.m.
Credit cards: AE, MC, V

As one point of the "Bermuda triangle," a Cow Hollow intersection with bars at each of three corners, the Balboa attracts crowds of aging fraternity and sorority types, now well into their thirties. The expansive windows let passersby view the party and decide whether they want to join it. During the day, the clubby, light-filled interior makes for a pleasant setting for lunch—and that first martini—especially now that it has been bought by the PlumpJack conglomerate. The food has improved under the supervision of Maria Helm, and the Balboa continues to be a popular lunch spot with the Pacific Heights social crowd. Now, at last, they are getting their hamburgers and Caesar salads decently prepared.

BUS STOP

Though single heterosexuals consider the Cow Hollow/Marina area their playground, everyone likes to hang out at Bus Stop, an endearing neighborhood saloon that has been open continuously since 1900. People of all ages watch games on easily visible video screens with impeccable reception, shoot pool at two tables, or gaze at the passing parade on Union street. The bar prides itself on its popularly priced "super well" drinks ($3.75), made with such high-quality liquors as Dewar's White Label, Bombay Sapphire, Smirnoff Vodka, Cuervo Especial, Ron Bacardi Superior, Jack Daniels, and Seagram's VO. Drinks are generously poured and correctly mixed. The good-natured bartenders happily serve both regulars and drop-ins. On top of all this, you might be able to get your car washed on the street outside the bar by a curbside detailer while you watch a game.

1901 Union Street (at Laguna), San Francisco
Tel: 567-6905
Open daily 10 a.m. to 2 a.m.
No credit cards

THE PARAGON

The twenty-year-olds migrate here after work and stay late into the night. Opened by a group of young San Franciscans from old families, the Paragon quickly became the place to be seen for the young, straight, and eligible. A clubby muraled back room has been dedicated to dining. While the kitchen has had its ups and downs, the hamburger and grilled tuna sandwich are dependable and go well with beer, the Paragon's most popular drink.

3251 Scott Street (between Lombard and Chestnut), San Francisco
Tel: 922-2456
Open daily 4 p.m. to 2 a.m.;
Dinner 5:30 to 10 p.m.
Credit cards: AE, MC, V

PERRY'S

Perry Butler practically started the singles bar movement in the sixties at his eponymously named watering hole. Now many of his patrons, a couple of marriages later, will admit to pushing forty (well, late forties), but the spirit of the place remains convivial and fun. As much a spot for a blue cheese salad and a good hamburger with cottage fries as a bar, Perry's continues to serve classic pub food in congenial surroundings.

1944 Union Street (between Laguna and Buchanan), San Francisco
Tel: 922-9022
Open Monday through Saturday 9 a.m. to midnight, Sunday until 11 p.m.
Credit cards: AE, MC, V

DELICATESSENS/TAKE-OUT

LUCCA

2120 Chestnut Street
(between Steiner
and Pierce),
San Francisco
Tel: 921-7873
Open Monday 10 a.m. to
6:30 p.m., Tuesday through
Friday 9 a.m. to 6:30 p.m.,
Saturday and Sunday
until 6 p.m.
No credit cards

Food lovers from all over the city migrate to the well-stocked Lucca delicatessen for two house specialties: superb celery-scented bolognese sauce sold by the pint, and tender hand-rolled spinach-and-ricotta ravioli sold by the box. With either of these items in your shopping bag, you have the foundations for a gorgeous meal.

Opened in 1929 by Mike Bosco, a man with a great recipe, and two partners, Lucca supplied Nob Hill hotels with ravioli. Now his son, Eddie, and two grown grandchildren, Linda and Paul, carry on the tradition, thank goodness.

Around lunchtime, a line forms in front of the long counter stocked with always-fresh foods (nothing sits around at Lucca) for made-to-order Italian sandwiches on Italian rolls and wedges of Lucca's famous spinach frittata. Rotisserie chickens; irresistible marinated vegetable salad rife with beans, artichokes, and chunks of avocado; Acme bread; Italian cheeses; an excellent nutty Emmenthal; imported olive oils and pastas; anchovies in salt; and house-made minestrone sold by the pint mean that customers never walk out the door with only one item.

ROSTI

I approached this branch of a Tuscan take-out chain started in Los Angeles with skepticism, but I was pleasantly surprised by the signature chicken cooked under a brick on a griddle called *pollo al mattone*. Judiciously seasoned with garlic and rosemary, and not cooked too far in advance, the flattened chicken halves stay moist under a crisp, charred skin. The beauty of this operation is that you can walk in anytime, pick up warm half chickens (for $7.50) that come with crusty rosemary-roasted potatoes, buy a few antipasti ($2.75 to $3.75), and you've got yourself a decent meal without waiting. You can also eat on the premises at cafe tables. For pre-prepared, packed-to-order food of considerable variety and good basic quality, Rosti should be welcomed to the northland.

2060 Chestnut Street
(between Fillmore and Steiner),
San Francisco
Tel: 929-9300
Open daily
11:30 a.m. to 10:30 p.m.
Credit cards: AE, MC, V

WORLD WRAPPS

This tiny shop on Chestnut Street is where the wrap craze started. Chef Aaron Novoshen invented a recipe for putting a whole ethnic meal into a gigantic tortilla. When I first discovered this place, I was on a diet, and I couldn't believe how tasty and satisfying the 99 percent fat-free (though high carb) Roasted Veggie Wrapp was; it is a luscious ragout of zucchini, squashes, peppers, Japanese eggplant, rice, well-seasoned soupy black beans, and balsamic tomato salsa rolled into a huge tortilla. Soon abandoning my diet, I fell in love with all the Asian wraps, like the popular Thai chicken, an absolutely stunning combination of hot, grilled chicken, jasmine rice, gingery slaw, cucumbers, red onion, and peanut sauce rolled into a bright green spinach tortilla. I also love the teriyaki chicken, the Peking duck, and the vegetarian Mandarin Stir-Fry Wrapp. For $5 to $6, you get a meal that satisfies you all day. For some reason, people drink fruit smoothies with these complex creations when a cold beer or glass of mineral water would work better. Luckily, the fruit drinks here more resemble the aquas frescas you see on the counters of Mission District taquerias, (where you can also get wonderful burritos).

2257 Chestnut Street
(between Scott and Pierce),
San Francisco
Tel: 563-9727
Open daily 11 a.m. to 11 p.m.
No credit cards

World Wrapps should be eaten immediately. Their charm—vivid flavor—comes from the technique of cooking key elements to order. They really don't hold all that well for very long.

BAKERIES/PASTRIES

JUST DESSERTS

3735 Buchanan Street (at Marina), San Francisco
Tel: 922-8675
Open Monday through Wednesday 7 a.m. to 9 p.m., Thursday and Friday until 11 p.m., Saturday and Sunday 8 a.m. to 11 p.m.
Credit cards: MC, V

Elliot Hoffman started this chain of American-style dessert cafes in 1974 on the strength of a cheesecake recipe. This store, across the street from the mammoth Marina Safeway where relationships blossom among the salad greens, and next door to a popular gym, causes particular anguish to those who work on their bodies. A hefty wedge of Just Dessert's moist devil's food cake with fudge frosting can obliterate the effects of a good workout. And, despite their healthful ring, the classic carrot cake with cream cheese frosting, homey lemon-buttermilk cake, and banana bread made with sour cream and walnuts cannot be considered diet fare. Just Desserts bakes everything from scratch, using whole butter and wholesome products, and delivers to its cafes every morning. Freshness is key here.

In 1992 Just Desserts bought the Tassajara Bread Bakery from the Zen Center and expanded distribution of Tassajara's hearty American breads to supermarkets like Safeway. When the two operations were combined in a large facility in the Bay View/Hunters Point neighborhood, Hoffman was instrumental in securing an adjacent empty lot for the Garden Project, a program started by the San Francisco County Sheriff's Department. Now, inmates and ex-cons grow fresh vegetables for soup kitchens all over the city. The bakery also uses some of the produce nurtured next door in the urban garden.

LA NOUVELLE PÂTISSERIE

The croissant, in all its flaky, buttery glory, brings me regularly to this French pastry shop. I take mine home, but many eat the croissants at small cafe tables in the shop, accompanied with decent café au lait. The cases here are full of colorful fruit tarts and handsome French pastries in generally fresh condition. A favorite item, especially among the French customers, is the bamboo, a crisp puff pastry sandwich filled with raspberry jam. Airy baguettes, just like the ones sold on Paris street corners, are also available.

2184 Union Street (between Webster and Fillmore),
San Francisco
Tel: 931-7655
Open Monday through Thursday 6:30 a.m. to 8 p.m., Friday and Saturday until 11 p.m.,
Sunday 8 a.m. to 7 p.m.
No credit cards

COFFEE

PEET'S COFFEE AND TEA

For other locations see pages 322, 358, 442, 495, and 520.

Widely considered to be the Cadillac of coffee stores, Peet's has set the standard for coffee-bean buying and roasting throughout the country. If you are a true coffee drinker, you will love the intensity and individual character of Peet's carefully roasted beans. Each store, the most famous being the original location at the corner of Walnut and Vine in Berkeley, brews coffee every thirty minutes, throwing out any leftovers. When you buy a pound of beans, you get a free cup—and what a cup it is! You will never taste coffee with as much flavor and depth.

There are many reasons for the heady richness of Peet's brews. Selective buying from known producers all over the world; daily roasting of each type of bean to exact degrees of toastiness; diligent tasting of coffee made with the newly roasted beans; and daily delivery of the beans to the stores all contribute to the coffee's brilliant flavor.

Although the list of different coffees can seem daunting to the uninitiated, the company has published an extremely helpful booklet describing each one, with recommendations from the head roaster and buyer. It sheds light on the difference in flavor between coffees from different regions of

2156 Chestnut Street
(between Pierce and Steiner),
San Francisco
Tel: 931-8302
Open Monday through Friday 6:30 a.m. to 7 p.m., Saturday and Sunday 7:30 a.m. to 6 p.m.
Credit cards: D, MC, V

the world, lists the components of Peet's blends, and describes the effects of different degrees of roasting. The booklet is free and available at all Peet's stores. Of course, the only way to understand the differences in flavor is to taste the coffees side by side. Peet's personnel are willing to set up coffee tastings for their customers. Take them up on it and come to your own conclusions.

In addition to coffee beans, Peet's offers a variety of teas, coffee- and tea-brewing equipment from all over the world, and a mail-order service.

A COFFEE TASTING

Jim Reynolds, the head coffee roaster and buyer for Peet's, invited me to a coffee tasting at the Emeryville headquarters. He set out three flights of short glasses, each with an inch of coarsely ground coffee at the bottom. He poured water that had cooled down a few minutes from the boiling point into each glass and then stirred. We waited to taste until the coffee cooled to warm.

Armed with a brass spittoon and a rounded soup spoon, we began by noisily slurping up, actually drawing in through the teeth, each coffee. We swished each spoonful around our tongues, smelled it in the back of our mouths, chewed it, and spit it into the receptacle. Very distinct characteristics of each coffee became clear.

Coffees from the Americas—Guatemala, Costa Rica, and Panama—define, to my mind, what we dream of in a cup of coffee. They are full-bodied, balanced, unquirky, aromatic, rich. Guatemala is Jim Reynold's favorite of all the coffees. I preferred the slightly fuller cup from Costa Rican beans. Lightest of the three was Panama coffee, with flowery overtones. Peet's House Blend and Blend 101 are made entirely from Latin American coffee beans.

The African coffees—Kenya, Ethiopian, and Arabian Mocha Sanani—have a spiciness and pronounced acidity. The rare Arabian Mocha Sanani, because it is harvested and dried so primitively, has a syrupy, fermented quality to it. We smelled a slight petroleum quality in the Ethiopian, which comes from a treatment to the burlap sacks, a practice that Reynolds is trying to change. Coffees from the Pacific—New Guinea, Sumatra, and Sulawesi—have distinctive herbal and earthy qualities. Given the characteristics of the different coffees, you begin to understand the advantages of blends like Peet's Top Blend, which combines coffees from the Pacific and Latin America, or the famous Major Dickason's, whose regional makeup remains a secret. Each bean has something to say.

Peet's generally roasts darker than most other companies. However, two blends, Italian roast and the really dark French roast, get even longer roastings. Very dark roasting produces a cup with less body, but with an intense flavor and smoky overtone that stand up to milk and sugar, good for morning latte or café au lait. After the coffee tasting, I started enjoying coffee in a new way. What was a generic flavor blossomed with complexity and nuance. Here was a food I have every morning and I had never explored its possibilities. An hour at a Peet's tasting could improve the quality of your daily life significantly.

MARKETS

MARINA SUPER

With Patricia Wells's cookbook *Trattoria* in hand, I walked into the Marina Super, next door to Cafe Marimba, one day after lunch. This market, along with its independent butcher, Puccini Meats, has been supplying the Italian community of the Marina with all the ingredients needed to cook dishes just like the ones in any classic Italian cookbook. I picked up a free-range chicken, pancetta, and some very lean ground sirloin. Rather nice vine-ripened tomatoes, for mid-October, and beautiful red peppers were piled outside on produce tables. Plump heads of garlic, huge bunches of Italian parsley, fresh thyme, and oregano are regularly available. Though the market does not buy organic produce, they always have the best commercially available representatives of whatever may be in season. You never see bad green beans here when good ones are available. Organic canned tomato products earn their own display shelf. Berkeley Farms dairy products are stocked, although not extra-rich milk for those who prefer it with espresso. Baskets of dried beans, ranging from gigantic borlotti to tiny white beans, call out to be made into a Tuscan soup. A whole rack of fresh breads from Semifreddi completes the family meal. Although very much a neighborhood market, this can be one of the most useful stops in the city for Italian-American shopping.

2323 Chestnut Street (between Scott and Divisadero), San Francisco
Tel: 346-7470
Open Monday through Saturday 8 a.m. to 9 p.m., Sunday until 8 p.m.
Credit cards: CB, DC, MC, V

WINES AND SPIRITS

CALIFORNIA WINE MERCHANT

3237 Pierce Street
(between Lombard
and Chestnut),
San Francisco
Tel: 567-0646
Open Monday through
Saturday 11 a.m. to 7 p.m.,
Sunday noon to 5 p.m.
Credit cards: MC, V

Hard-to-find California wines line the walls of this tiny twenty-one-year-old shop guarded by a huge golden retriever snoring away at the front door. The elegance of a shop that does one thing well cannot be underestimated. Only high-quality California and a few Oregon wines tasted and chosen by the owner, Gregory O'Flynn, get a slot in the floor-to-ceiling wooden racks. Small production wines like Terrace Zinfandel or impossible-to-find Stony Hill Chardonnay or the elegant Shafer Merlot can all be found here at fair-market prices. Since the wine selections have been so carefully edited, shopping here will expand your knowledge of the most exciting California wines. The shop will ship.

COOKWARE AND BOOKS

FREDERICKSEN'S HARDWARE

3029 Fillmore Street
(between Union
and Filbert),
San Francisco
Tel: 292-2950
Open Monday through
Saturday 9 a.m. to 6 p.m.,
Sunday 10 a.m. to 5 p.m.
Credit cards: MC, V

Hardware stores don't get better than this. Not only does Fredericksen's stock every conceivable item you might need for your house and kitchen, but the service is so good that you will be steered to exactly the right thing. One third of this packed store is dedicated to kitchen and housewares, and the level of sophistication is high. This is the place to find kitchen timers, food mills, springform pans, juicers, coffee grinders, good basic lines of pots and pans, glass baking dishes, graters: all the building blocks of a practical, old-fashioned kitchen and then some. Fredericksen's will always have the innovation on the traditional item if it is really an improvement, but it does not carry frivolous gadgets. I love the integrity of this store, the dependability, the completeness. I'm willing to pay a bit more here because I know they will have what I need and I won't have to waste time driving around town.

WILLIAMS-SONOMA

2000 Chestnut Street (at Fillmore),
San Francisco
Tel: 929-2520
Open Monday through Saturday 10 a.m. to 8 p.m.,
Sunday 11 a.m. to 6 p.m.
Credit cards: AE, MC, V
See listing, page 157.

The Mission District, Bernal Heights & the Excelsior

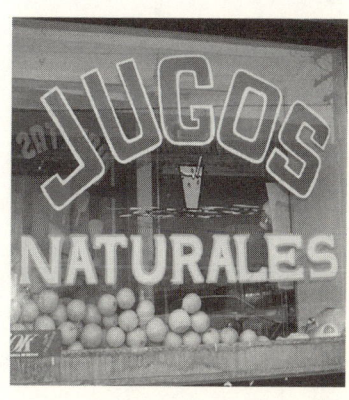

THE MISSION DISTRICT, BERNAL HEIGHTS & THE EXCELSIOR

Restaurants:
1. Angkor Borei 209
2. Bruno's 210
3. Burger Joint 211
4. El Balazito 211
5. Esperpento 212
6. Fina Estampa 213
7. The Flying Saucer 214
8. La Movida 216
9. La Santaneca 216
10. La Taqueria 217
11. Liberty Cafe 218
12. Los Jarritos 218
13. Mom Is Cooking 219
14. Pancho Villa Taqueria 220
15. Slanted Door 221
16. Ti Couz Crêperie 222
17. Timo's 222
18. Val 21 223
19. Woodward's Garden 224

Cafes:
20. Cafe Istanbul 225
21. Radio Valencia 226

Bars:
22. Dalva 226
23. Elbo Room 226

Delicatessens/Take-Out:
24. Hungarian Sausage Factory 227
25. La Palma Mexicatessen 227
26. Lucca Ravioli Company 229

Bakeries/Pastries:
27. La Reyna Bakery and Coffee Shop 231
28. Panaderia La Mexicana 231

Ice Cream/Chocolates:
29. Latin Freeze 232
30. Mitchell's Ice Cream 233
31. St. Francis Fountain and Candy Store 233

Ethnic Markets:
32. Bombay Bazaar 234
33. Casa Lucas Market 235
34. Greek American Food Imports 235
25. La Palma Mexicatessen 236
35. Samiramis Imports 236

Produce:
36. Alemany Farmers' Market 236
37. Barrasa Market 237
33. Casa Lucas Market 237
38. La Hacienda Market 238
39. 23rd and Mission Produce 239

Meat and Poultry:
40. La Gallinita 239
41. The Lucky Pork Store 240
42. Mission Market Fish and Poultry 240
42. Mission Market Meat Department 240
43. Polarica 241

Fish:
42. Mission Market Fish and Poultry 242

RESTAURANTS

ANGKOR BOREI

This neighborhood Cambodian restaurant, decorated with handsome Khmer artifacts, turns out intricate dishes with surprising finesse. The dishes here are characterized by a ravishing tapestry of flavors, textures, and colors. Like intricate Khmer carvings, Cambodian food is composed of many tiny, exquisite elements like a mosaic, such as cold white noodles, julienned cucumbers, bean sprouts, basil, red chilies, and carrots, all in separate piles that come together with a fragrant coconut milk dipping sauce; delicate Cambodian spring rolls with moist multi-vegetable fillings; or crisp Cambodian omeletlike crepes folded over a juicy, crunchy filling of vegetables, herbs, and nuts.

I love the curries at Angkor Borei, particularly a fiery green one aromatic with Thai basil and lemongrass served on Japanese eggplant and big chunks of white fish. A milder red curry with many deep layers of flavor enhances tender sautéed shrimp on a bed of bright green spinach. The charcoal broiling shows equal skill: Marinated chicken or beef skewers come with delicious vinegared vegetables—the perfect accompaniment. Even the rice, served from a covered silver tureen, has a marvelous, nutty flavor and chewy texture.

Artfully presented and complex, yet immediately delicious, this Cambodian food enchants everyone—even those trying Cambodian cooking for the first time. This so-called neighborhood spot would be a find anywhere in the world.

3471 Mission Street
(between Cortland and 30th Street),
San Francisco
Tel: 550-8417
Open for lunch Monday through Saturday
11 a.m. to 3 p.m.;
dinner Monday through Thursday 5 to 10 p.m.,
Friday and Saturday until 10:30 p.m.,
Sunday 4 to 10:30 p.m.
Price: Inexpensive
Credit cards: AE, D, MC, V

BRUNO'S

2389 Mission Street
(between 19th
and 20th Streets),
San Francisco
Tel: 550-7455
Open Tuesday through
Thursday 6:30 to 11 p.m.,
Friday and Saturday
until midnight
Price: Moderate
Credit cards: MC, V

Those who remember the old Bruno's on Mission, one of the funkier Joe's-style restaurants, will be amazed by this tony incarnation. At first glance, the new Bruno's looks like the old one until you notice how pristine everything is. The current owners decided to reopen with every detail of the original fifties decor intact, achieving a swank supper club look straight out of a "Rat Pack" movie. Though Bruno's has created a hot club scene with live music and bartendresses showing lots of décolletage in vintage cocktail dresses, I'm taken by dinner where patrons are sequestered in oversized red vinyl booths in a separate dining room.

Chef James Ormsby, a veteran of such diverse kitchens as The Flying Saucer and Lark Creek Inn, has put together a small, interesting, manageable menu that takes advantage of seasonal produce and fine local ingredients in a sophisticated, personal way. I love his braised meats—oxtails, short ribs, lamb shanks—because they remind me of the old Bruno's though at a cooking level raised about 100 percent. He has a special way with soups, understanding that a great soup starts with a beautiful broth. His salads of elegant little lettuces incorporate unusual things like fried chickpeas and a citrus vinaigrette. Desserts are somehow old-fashioned and current at the same time—warm apple huckleberry crisp, huge portions of house-made sorbets wreathed in fresh fruit. Just like everything else about the operation, the wine list is full of the hippest bottles, mostly from California.

This kind of full-scale operation in the middle of what had become an abandoned block of Mission Street represents a major breakthrough in the neighborhood. Bruno's has drawn inspiration from the old place while reinventing itself with youthful energy. The combination is very San Francisco and a whole lot of fun.

BURGER JOINT

Owned by the Val 21 people, the cheerfully decorated, immaculate Burger Joint does what it does perfectly. The organic Niman-Schell hamburgers are cooked exactly to specification over a charcoal grill. They go on delicately crusty buns with decent tomato slices, red onion, and romaine on the side. I go for a pile of grilled onions for 50 cents additional. All condiments are meticulously maintained on each table. The largish fries, with peel still on, stay crisp due to frying in hot, clean-flavored oil. Finally, thick old-fashioned milk shakes made with Double Rainbow ice cream are so big they last through the hamburger eating and finish off this classic American meal as dessert.

807 Valencia Street
(between 18th
and 19th Streets),
San Francisco
Tel: 824-3494
Open daily 11 a.m. to 11 p.m.
Price: Inexpensive
No credit cards

EL BALAZITO

Fondly called the "car wash taqueria," El Balazito dispenses exquisitely simple and authentic tacos from a permanent stand on a self-service car cleaning lot. Beyond the obvious convenience of being able to shampoo your vehicle and get a sublime taco at the same place, you will get much pleasure from the purity and uniqueness of El Balazito's food. Everyone comes here for tacos filled with a delicious braise of cactus with tomatoes and onions piled into two soft mini-tortillas topped with salsa fresca and cilantro. The *huachinango* taco, just grilled rockfish and salsa, and the buttery tongue tacos define what tacos should be. El Balazito's outdoor counter and stools let you watch the progress of shampooers as you lick your fingers and decide if you want another round.

2560 Marin
(at the junction of Cesar
Chavez and Bayshore),
San Francisco
Tel: 824-6684
Open Monday through
Saturday 9 a.m. to 5 p.m.
Price: Very inexpensive
No credit cards

ESPERPENTO

3295 22nd Street (between Valencia and Mission), San Francisco
Tel: 282-8867
Open for lunch Monday through Saturday 11 a.m. to 3 p.m.; for dinner Monday through Thursday 5 to 10 p.m., Fridays and Saturdays until 11 p.m., Sunday noon to 10 p.m.
Price: Inexpensive
No credit cards

Started by a group of young Spaniards with more creativity than capital, this small, funky tapas-and-paella cafe will appeal to anyone who has eaten in Spain or in Berkeley in the seventies, or has dreamed of opening her or his own restaurant. A lot has been done with paint in the airy, high-ceilinged storefront decorated in a vaguely surrealistic, Dalí-esque theme. (Not finding *Esperpento* in my Spanish-English dictionary, I learned from a waiter that it means "weird.")

From the moment it opened, Esperpento proved to be a hit in the neighborhood. Good, inexpensive food had a lot to do with it, but people find Esperpento's bohemian authenticity endearing. The rough edges that give Esperpento character also can cause inconsistencies in food and service, but this seems like a fair price for a taste of the real thing.

The tapas really do conjure up memories of Spain. Usually served at room temperature, a *tortilla de patatas*, a cake of potatoes and onions held together with eggs, comes out of the kitchen warm and heavenly here. Garlicky mushrooms are sautéed until all their juices evaporate and their flavors intensify. *Escalivada* is a marvelous mixture of roasted eggplant and peppers seasoned with vinegar. Delicious, creamy chicken croquettes; oven-roasted clams; shrimp drenched in garlic, olive oil, and hot red chilies; and crisp fried squid all can be terrific if you hit Esperpento on the right night. Besides tapas, the main attraction is paella, authentically served in a searing-hot cast-iron pan set right on the table. This luscious rendition, with shellfish, chicken, and pork peeking through a blanket of moist saffron rice, is worth a few scars.

Spanish wines, like the gratifyingly full, drinkable, yet inexpensive Torres Sangre de Toro or Cornonas, are intrinsic to a meal here, as are glasses of *amontillado* or *fino* sherry. For dessert, *crema Catalana* with a burnt sugar crust or thick rice pudding scented with lemon zest, along with a *cafe cortado*, a demitasse of espresso cut with warm milk, make for a buoyant ending.

ESCALIVADA

This is a popular Spanish tapa served at Esperpento.

2 medium eggplants, unpeeled
About 2 tablespoons kosher salt
2 tablespoons olive oil
3 red bell peppers
1 3/4 tablespoons red wine vinegar
1 large garlic clove, minced
4 1/2 tablespoons extra-virgin olive oil, plus oil for coating pepper

Preheat oven to 350° F. Cut the eggplants in half lengthwise, sprinkle with salt, and lay cut-side down on paper towels for 30 minutes. Dry the eggplant and rub it all over with 1 tablespoon of the oil and 1 tablespoon of the salt, and place cut-side down in a baking pan. Rub the whole red peppers with oil and 1/2 tablespoon salt and add to the baking pan. Bake until tender, about 1 hour.

Remove the cooked vegetables from the oven, place in a bowl, and cover with plastic wrap for 15 minutes.

With your fingers, remove the skin and seeds from the peppers and peel the eggplants. Slice each vegetable lengthwise into 1/2-inch-thick slices. Lay the slices on a platter.

Whisk together the remaining 1/2 teaspoon salt, the vinegar, and garlic. Whisk in the remaining 3 1/2 tablespoons olive oil. Pour the vinaigrette over the vegetables and mix gently. Marinate at room temperature. Serve within a few hours of roasting.

Serves 4 to 6 as a first course

FINA ESTAMPA

Although Gus Shinzato might look more like a sushi chef, one taste of his *parihuela de mariscos* makes it clear that he is a masterful Peruvian cook. A third-generation Peruvian, now living in the United States, he opened Fina Estampa with his wife Tamie Takaesu, a Japanese-born Peruvian who runs the dining room. They serve spectacularly delicious food in a comfortable, if modest, Mission Street storefront, the kind of place that puts glass over the tablecloths.

Before I started eating at Fina Estampa, Peruvian food meant boiled potatoes and skewered beef heart (very tasty, actually). But after several visits here, I discovered that the breadth of the cuisine parallels the spectacular geography of the country. From seaside towns come opulent seafood

2374 Mission Street
(between 19th and 20th Streets),
San Francisco
Tel: 824-4437
Open for lunch Tuesday through Thursday
11:30 a.m. to 3:30 p.m.,
dinner 5 to 9 p.m.;
Friday through Sunday
11:30 a.m. to 9 p.m.
Price: Inexpensive
Credit cards: MC, V

soups like *parihuela*, a deep bowl full of shrimp, squid, mussels, clams, and rockfish in a tomato broth resonant with dried chilies. Another seafood triumph, *jalea de pescado*, brings a gigantic fish fry served with *salsa criolla* (marinated onions and tomatoes) and a fiery dark green salsa called *ají*. The frying is impeccable. A huge, moist seafood paella has remarkable depth of flavor. Since both San Francisco and Peru share the Pacific coast, the fresh local catch here works particularly well in many of the seafood dishes.

From the mountains come potatoes: orange, yellow, purple, white. Fina Estampa includes them in one of the best ceviches in town, a revelatory combination. Chef Shinzato serves them traditionally, *a la huancaina*, in a pungent cheese sauce as an appetizer, or rubs them with red spice paste and deep-fries them as an accompaniment to skewers of marinated beef heart.

Wonderful, crisp, deep-fried bone-in chunks of chicken called *chicharrón de pollo* come with a bowl of fresh lime juice and chilies and a pile of *salsa criolla*. A luscious dish called *bisteck a la pobre*, a small, tender grilled steak served on a slice of toast that soaks up all the juices, is piled with sautéed onions and tomatoes, a deep-fried banana, and crowned by a fried egg. *Ají panca*, grilled chicken rubbed with a red spice paste, has the texture of velvet. Both Peruvian beer and Chilean and Spanish red wine enhance the food. Don't be put off by the Mission District custom of putting out margarine with soft white bread; the plates to come will be dazzling.

THE FLYING SAUCER

1000 Guerrero Street (at 22nd Street), San Francisco
Tel: 641-9955
Open Tuesday through Saturday 6 to 10 p.m.
Price: Moderate
Credit cards: AE, MC, V

This fanciful, eccentric, extremely personal bistro of chef Albert Tordjman's has doubled in size, and the flamboyant plates coming out of the now glassed-in display kitchen seem to have done the same. What started out as a rough-edged Mission District hideaway has turned into a more comfortable, more controlled dining experience. However, the cooking continues to beam in from outer space—a territory in chef Tordjman's head.

French training sets his eclecticism apart from that of more amateurish endeavors. His mastery of technique adds the gloss of refinement and allows him to incorporate exotic flavors in sauces, vinaigrettes, and marinades with a high level of sophistication. What differentiates the Flying Saucer from a downtown restaurant like Postrio, also from the California-eclectic school, is its still-small scale and remaining ragged edges, but more significantly, Tordjman's imagination. This chef's creations, whether you like to eat this way or not, have a highly designed look and strong flavors. This is not watered-down cooking. Tordjman is an artist with an uncompromising vision.

The main ingredient of a dish is merely an excuse to fill a plate with vegetables, potatoes, sauces, greens, herbs, noodles —a world of food. The portions are gigantic. A starter could be a slice of an absolutely classic terrine of foie gras with a sharply dressed salad and a buttery slice of grilled brioche; or an exotic seafood *empanada* of soft cornmeal flanked by greens, a jícama-chayote salad, and searingly hot jalapeños stuffed with smoked salmon. Asian flavors are often paired with fish, as in a Japanese-style hunk of salmon served in a flat bowl with soba noodles, shiitake mushrooms, and asparagus. Crisp duck *confit*, with a sprig of thyme growing out of a leg, gets a cylinder of cabbage with red and green layers laced strongly with fennel seed, roasted potatoes, and carrots, all in an aromatic broth. Lots of molded shapes, vegetables fashioned with cookie cutters, and sprigs of fresh herbs are used to architecturally construct the plates. As a fellow food writer noted, all the sous chefs in town eat here to get ideas.

The Saucer has expanded into the next storefront, thereby adding a bar and six or eight more unlinened tables of different sizes and composition. This means no more waiting outside, although those with later reservations should not expect to be seated immediately. Even though the chefs work nonstop behind their glass wall, the plates are so complicated that it is no surprise that service backs up.

LA MOVIDA

3228 16th Street (between
Guerrero and Dolores),
San Francisco
Tel: 552-3889
Open Wednesday and
Thursday 6 to 11 p.m.,
Friday and Saturday
5:30 to 11 p.m.,
Sunday until 10 p.m.
Price: Moderate
Credit cards: MC, V

The specialty at La Movida is paella, that tricky Spanish rice dish tinted with saffron and studded with vegetables, seafood, chorizo, and chicken. To make a good one, as the kitchen does at La Movida, you need the right ingredients. La Movida has the jump on essentials because one of its three owners is the West Coast importer of fine Spanish products: L'Estornell organic olive oil, organic olives, short-grained Alcazaba rice, Spanish vinegars, and pure saffron. The kitchen makes the most of its advantage, turning out three kinds of paella—vegetarian, seafood, and a combo with seafood, chicken, and chorizo—as well as a daily changing selection of tapas. The tapa of *setas* is gorgeous if available, a luscious sauté of velvety, garlicky wild mushrooms. And be sure to order a saucer of small, marinated arbequina olives. The *escalivada* with goat cheese makes for a fine starter if you don't order the vegetarian paella, which uses the same vegetables. All the salads boast tasty vinaigrettes made with fruity Spanish olive oil. For dessert, La Movida makes its own ice creams and ices, which can be mixed and matched with exotic coffee or vanilla sauces.

The long narrow dining room, mostly filled by a handsome bar with many stools where people both drink and eat, has been wittily furnished using steel and sheet metal and warm, bright colors, a sophisticated, modern Spanish look that somehow feels as if it belongs in the Mission. La Movida, which refers to the political and cultural revolution that took place in Spain twenty years ago with the death of Franco, has become part of the Mission District renaissance.

LA SANTANECA

3781 Mission Street
(near Richland),
San Francisco
Tel: 648-1034
Open daily
10:30 a.m to midnight
Price: Very inexpensive
No credit cards

My Latin American food experts sent me to La Santaneca for Salvadorean food, and thanks to them I discovered a whole new cuisine. At this modest, immaculate storefront in Bernal Heights, I started with *pupusas*—thick, handmade, griddled tortillas stuffed with a paste of very rich, very savory, deep-fried pork rind called *chicharrón*. *Pupusas* are served with an oregano-scented cole slaw and a delicious, mildly hot, cooked tomato salsa, both clean and bracing. I moved on to a lively, full-flavored shrimp soup with vegetables and a hard-boiled egg simmered in it. The Salvadorean-style tamale has an almost custardlike *masa* (corn meal dough) and a pork and potato filling that melts in your mouth, wonderful with La Santaneca's salsa. Fried plantains with beans and sour cream are a favorite, but I also like a plantain dessert fritter called an *empanada*, sprinkled with sugar. No beer and wine here, but try a *guayabana*, a frothy tropical smoothie, delicate and refreshing. Many families in the neighborhood use La Santaneca for take-out meals. The prices are incredibly cheap and the cooking is meticulous.

LA TAQUERIA

One of the most long-lived (since 1975) and meticulous taquerias in the Mission, La Taqueria earned its reputation through cleanliness, freshness, and efficiency. This family taqueria sports an attractive Mission-style arched facade, adobe walls decorated with a vibrant folk mural, and a dining room full of rustic wooden tables with leather stools. Jars of excellent green and red salsa sit on each immaculate table.

2889 Mission Street
(between 24th and 25th Streets), San Francisco
Tel: 285-7117
Open Monday through Saturday 11 a.m. to 9 p.m., Sunday 11 a.m. to 8 p.m.
Price: Inexpensive
No credit cards

Although a list of typical and well-prepared fillings for burritos and tacos is posted on the wall above the tiled kitchen, La Taqueria's soft, moist, savory, miraculously greaseless *carnitas* (pork slowly cooked in its own fat) deserves special attention. Prepared every day, this rich pork shines brightest in tacos made with two soft, warm corn tortillas and a little salsa. Shredded chicken simmered with tomatoes and chilies, and aromatically spicy chorizo sausage that has been crumbled and fried, also make for exceptional tacos. This friendly taqueria ranks high on my list of favorites because it fulfills its simple menu perfectly, day after day, year after year.

LIBERTY CAFE

410 Cortland Avenue
(between Bennington
and Wool),
San Francisco
Tel: 695-8777
Open for lunch Tuesday
through Friday
11:30 a.m. to 3 p.m.;
dinner Tuesday through
Thursday 5:30 to 9 p.m.,
Friday and Saturday until
9:30 p.m.; brunch Saturday
9:30 a.m. to 2:30 p.m.,
Sunday 10 a.m. to 2 p.m.
Price: Moderate
Credit cards: AE, MC, V

If I were to invent my dream around-the-corner cafe, it would be very much like this cozy little place in Bernal Heights, a touchstone for skillful home-style cooking and friendly atmosphere. Moderate prices; organic produce; meats and poultry from small local producers; warm house-baked breads, rolls and desserts; a menu that works for omnivores, vegetarians, and children; and the unpretentious good spirit of the place add up to a constant stream of customers. People wait outside on benches with a glass of wine or stroll the cute little neighborhood until their table is ready. Others stand by the small service bar in the middle of the room, trying not to stare at the diners tucking into their warm frisée salads (the best in town) or big bowls of country-style soup.

Since the chef-owner is a baker, the menu always offers a luscious, flaky-crusted chicken potpie as well wonderful dessert pies. But Liberty's hearty, multifaceted plates of pork chops with creamy white beans, soft polenta, and winter squash; or sliced duck breasts on lentils with baby mustard greens and creamed cabbage take you to more sophisticated culinary territory. What I love about Liberty is that the bright, home-cooked quality of the dishes never diminishes no matter how creative the combination.

LOS JARRITOS

901 South Van Ness Avenue
(at 20th Street),
San Francisco
Tel: 648-8383
Open daily 8 a.m. to 10 p.m.
Price: Inexpensive
Credit cards: MC, V

While good taquerias abound in the Mission, the sit-down Mexican restaurants are surprisingly similar and uninspired. One of my favorites, Los Jarritos, distinguishes itself by its colorful, folk-art-filled dining room and tasty *chilaquiles*, the current dish of choice in the Mission among those who have partied too hard the night before. *Chilaquiles* are stale tortillas that are fried and then cooked in a sauce, often with other ingredients. At Los Jarritos, the tortillas are fried with eggs, white cheese, and pickled jalapeños, then braised in a lot of piquant ranchera sauce. A huge portion comes with mashed red beans seasoned with lard and Spanish rice.

Mission families drift in all afternoon for delicious eggs scrambled with cactus and onions, and served with beans, rice, and excellent made-to-order tortillas hot from the *comal*. These tortillas are puffy and lighter in texture than any you have tasted from a package. If you are a tortilla fan, you owe it to yourself to try them. They are especially good with huevos rancheros, two perfectly poached eggs in ranchera sauce topped with melted cheese (ask them to go light on the cheese or the eggs get buried and overcooked).

Jarritos are small clay cups. Strings of them hang all over the immaculate dining room next to shelves of old-fashioned smiling clay piggy banks. A resonant wooden floor and old Formica and aluminum tables with bright blue and red tops add warmth and cheer to this folksy little restaurant.

MOM IS COOKING

When I first heard that Mom Is Cooking had moved a few doors from its original crusty spot, I was worried that this Excelsior District destination for authentic Mexican home cooking might be going upscale. But the best of all possible things happened: Mom moved to larger quarters with more seating and a bigger kitchen, which means no more unbearably long waits either to get a table or to get your food. In the move she acquired a liquor license, which adds good margaritas to the drink possibilities, and chef-mom Abigail Murillo has not changed her cooking or prices at all. The food is as vibrant, earthy, and cheap as ever, the surroundings just as funky. You could be sitting in a neighborhood restaurant in an out-of-the-way district of Mexico City.

For the uninitiated, the menu may seem long and disorganized, handwritten on seven or eight pages enclosed in plastic, but you almost can't go wrong. Take the first item on the menu, *boquitos*, warm tortilla chips individually layered with melted cheese, guacamole, mashed beans, crema (Mexican sour cream), and salsa. You can taste each ingredient separately, yet every bite is a complete trip through Mexican cuisine. This same integrity of flavor makes items such as crisp-shelled tacos, soft *flautas*, and airy tamales feel like exciting new dishes.

1166 Geneva Avenue
(at Naples),
San Francisco
Tel: 586-7000
Open daily noon to 10 p.m.
Price: Inexpensive
No credit cards

More unusual preparations expand the horizons of Mexican restaurant cooking, like *huevos con chorizo*, scrambled eggs with delicate, greaseless, house-made sausage crumbled into them, served with beautiful plump red beans; or a *carnitas* plate with buttery, long-cooked pork as a centerpiece to an array of salsas, black beans, Spanish rice, oregano-scented cabbage salad, and chunky guacamole; or a spectacular quesadilla filled with whole grilled shrimp and tangy Mexican cheese. At Mom Is Cooking, you can play it safe or explore and reap equal rewards.

PANCHO VILLA TAQUERIA

3071 16th Street (between Mission and Valencia), San Francisco
Tel: 864-8840
Open daily
10 am to midnight
Price: Inexpensive
No credit cards

When you bite into one of Pancho Villa's monumental burritos, you know why a line always extends past the front door. Though you may have to wait, the endless turnover means that all the components of the various tacos, burritos, and dinner plates have been prepared very recently. This freshness makes the earthy Mexican food sparkle.

The Mission District favorite is the *carne asada* special, a huge flour tortilla lined with melted white cheese and filled with about a pound of Spanish rice, red beans, thinly sliced grilled steak, guacamole, and fresh salsa. All these elements work together in some magical way to make a completely satisfying rolled-up meal. If you eat a Pancho Villa burrito for lunch, don't plan on dinner. *Carnitas*, pork slowly cooked in its own fat, also makes stunning burritos or soft tacos with beans and salsa.

On the lighter side, try a grilled-shrimp burrito with black beans, or a satisfying vegetarian burrito that features firm cubes of tofu in a red ranchera sauce. Besides the tortilla dishes, Pancho Villa puts out some gorgeous-looking platters of butterflied garlic prawns, or hot, spicy prawns griddled with whole dried *chiles de árbol*, all cooked to order. Be sure to get a side order of grilled green onions to go with the shrimp.

Ladled from huge glass jars afloat with strawberries, cantaloupe, or seeded watermelon and ice, Pancho Villa's *aguas frescas* alone merit a visit, especially on a warm afternoon when the kids want something quick to eat and refreshing to drink.

SLANTED DOOR

The Slanted Door has catapulted authentic ethnic cooking into the forefront of the hip restaurant world, incorporating the stylishness of the modern San Francisco bistro with an authentic Vietnamese kitchen. The combination is irresistible, and a line tends to form outside the restaurant almost every evening.

Even if you don't have a reservation, the meal you'll get is worth the wait. Young chef-owner Charles Phan has put together a changing menu of Vietnamese favorites that not only sparkle with freshness and bright flavor but take on new cachet by being served on a stunning mix of Japanese and Western china. Chopsticks, silverware, glassware, plates, tea service, napkins—everything that lands on the table has chic, as does the food itself, which naturally juxtaposes the raw and the cooked, crisp and tender, cold and hot, clean and rich, which characterizes Vietnamese cooking. This cuisine is particularly appealing to salad-and-vegetable-loving Californians.

At Slanted Door you will find traditional crisp, fried shrimp and pork rolls, which you wrap in lettuce leaves with sprigs of mint and dunk into sweet, hot dipping sauce; and unusual steamed vegetarian dumplings topped with fried shallots. There is the refreshing green papaya salad, juicy and very finely shredded; and a superb watercress and shrimp soup served in a deep pottery bowl full of clear, elegant chicken broth. Don't miss the velvet-textured five-spice chicken, or a fried whole pompano served with a hot gingery dipping sauce, jasmine rice, and pickled, julienned carrots.

In keeping with the hip decor and presentation, the Slanted Door invented a wine list that groups wines by characteristics—"floral and soft," "crisp n' dry," "aromatic and rich." This helps you choose among little-known wines imported from all over the world that are especially well matched with the food.

The choices offered in fine Western restaurants—housemade desserts (especially tropical ice creams and ices); wine; beer; herbal, green, and black teas; espresso; service by course—only seems natural for Vietnamese dining. Indeed the kind of dishes coming out of Slanted Door's open kitchen has inspired many a Cal-Asian dinner house. How rewarding that the real cuisine delights the most!

584 Valencia Street
(at 17th Street),
San Francisco
Tel: 861-8032
Open for lunch Tuesday through Sunday
11:30 to 3:30 p.m.;
dinner 5:30 to 10 p.m.
Price: Inexpensive
Credit Cards: MC, V

TI COUZ CRÊPERIE

3108 16th Street (between Guerrero and Valencia), San Francisco
Tel: 252-7373
Open Monday through Friday 11 a.m. to 11 p.m.,
Saturday 10 a.m. to 11 p.m.,
Sunday 10 a.m. to 10 p.m.
Price: Inexpensive
Credit cards: MC, V

A real *crêperie* like you might find in Brittany, Ti Couz turns out thin, irresistible pancakes, filled with everything from ratatouille to ice cream and chocolate sauce. As a cheap, satisfying meal, you can't beat them. In fact, so many people were banging at the doors at Ti Couz's tiny dining room that the *crêperie* has doubled in size. Happily, only the seating has expanded; the menu remains the same.

For me, the simplest crepe is the most sublime, and I can barely walk past Ti Couz without sitting down at the counter where the crepes are made for a hot buckwheat crepe spread just with softened butter and sprinkled with sugar. My new favorite, however, has become a crepe spread with almond butter. The Gruyère and cheese crepe topped with an egg is completely satisfying as a main course.

The authenticity of this place comes from owner Sylvie Le Mer, who keeps Ti Couz doing just what it does best. A green salad, sometimes a charcuterie plate, and a soup are the only other dishes offered. The crepes come off the griddle tender but crisp and buttery on the outside. I hate to order them with too much stuff because the pancakes themselves are the treat.

Mildly alcoholic French cider on tap comes in whole and half carafes with pottery bowls instead of glasses, a quaint service that only makes the crepes taste that much better. The small wooden tables and chairs, wood floors, French country china cabinets, and blue and white color scheme add to the authenticity of this Mission District *crêperie*.

TIMO'S

842 Valencia Street (between 19th and 20th Streets), San Francisco
Tel: 647-0558
Open Sunday through Thursday 5 to 10:30 p.m., Friday and Saturday until 11:30 p.m.
Price: Moderate
Credit cards: AE, MC, V

Carlos and Theresa Corredor took over this funky Mission District bar and turned it into a hot spot with their delicious, creative tapas. One fantastic little plate of savory food after another emerges like some kind of miracle from an immaculate kitchen. Crusty roasted new potatoes, the diameter of a quarter, are dabbed with the velvety house-made garlic mayonnaise called *aïoli*. Big firm mushrooms, hot off the grill, are tossed in finely chopped garlic and parsley, as delicious as they are simple. Bright green Catalan spinach with pine nuts, raisins, and bits of dried apricot refreshes the palate. Timo's continues to prepares a superior version of a very typical Spanish dish, salt cod and potato cake, creatively pairing it with a lively cilantro-mint salsa. The chef takes a detour to neighboring southwest France with his crispy leg of duck *confit* surrounded by tender baby turnips. However, the last time I ordered Timo's legendary Potato Decadence, a cake of Yukon Gold potatoes, chanterelles, and lobster mushrooms dusted with fresh marjoram, it had become soggy, dominated by chewy dried porcini.

Since the couple recently opened a second place in Ghirardelli Square, the food at the original Timo's has not been as breathtakingly exciting, but I'd still rather go to Timo's in the Mission than most other places in town. I love the wine list with plenty of Spanish and California red wine by the glass, and the variety of tapas on the menu—the simplest of which are still prepared perfectly and authentically. The colorfully painted rooms of this former bar remind me of Beat coffeehouses, complete with a live guitarist who plays Spanish melodies instead of folk songs.

VAL 21

More means better for the kitchen at Val 21, a lively and much-loved Mission restaurant that opened originally as a juice bar. The plates created here have more color, more ingredients, more flavors, just plain more going on than most others—though the trend these days in San Francisco's newest uptown restaurants seems to be a similar piling on of stuff. At Val 21, a multicultural representation of seasonings and ingredients throw a powwow in each dish, but meeting together does not mean that all the parties will get along. In Val 21's case, sometimes they do and sometimes they don't.

The mélange of ingredients might transcend their diversity in a wonderful starter of crisp filo pastry stuffed with a savory, aromatic ground chicken filling, served with a fig chutney. They end up losing their identities in a spicy hot ragout of many different wild mushrooms lavished on deep-fried Gorgonzola-polenta fingers. True-flavored passion fruit and coconut sorbets in an elegant tulip-shaped Florentine

995 Valencia Street (at 21st Street), San Francisco
Tel: 821-6622
Open for dinner Sunday through Thursday 5:30 to 10 p.m., Friday and Saturday until 11 p.m.; Saturday and Sunday for brunch 10 a.m. to 1:30 p.m.
Price: Moderate
Credit Cards: MC, V

cookie charm, while a warm, soft chocolate pudding-cake in a berry sauce hits you over the head with obtuse flavors. However, if you are eating out with a vegetarian, Val 21 is a godsend, because it is one of the few restaurants in town that wholeheartedly creates satisfying and stylish nonmeat dishes.

The small dining room is filled with original hand-crafted furnishings, round wooden tables with bright green tops, a blonde-wood floor, and a smart curved bar with matching stools. The service is enthusiastic, and the wine list offers some carefully chosen California bottles like a balanced Ferrari-Carano Fumé Blanc that goes exceptionally well with the wild mix of flavors.

WOODWARD'S GARDEN

1700 Mission Street
(at Duboce),
San Francisco
Tel: 621-7122
Open Wednesday through
Sunday 6 to 10 p.m.
Price: Moderate
Credit cards: MC, V

This tiny place epitomizes the "let's start our own restaurant" impulse, although the four young partners running it know exactly what they are doing. Far from being a beginner experience, a meal at Woodward's Garden represents the height of civility with the added charm of a hidden location and proudly modest surroundings.

The food, cooked by Dana Tommasino and Margie Conard, veterans of Greens and Postrio respectively, is fresh and seductive, a unique composite of the styles of the two mother-ship restaurants. The minuscule kitchen dictates a small menu, but everything coming from it sparkles. A typical winter menu might include a salad with jewel-like segments of blood orange and grapefruit; a deeply flavored vegetable saffron risotto; ravioli stuffed with potato and black truffle; a satiny, tender duck breast on a bed of fava beans, greens, and other winter vegetables in a delicate vinaigrette; and a silken fillet of salmon on a bed of couscous slathered with an assertive tamarind sauce. The meal might end with a simple but gossamer dessert such as a Meyer lemon pot de crème with buttery cookies. The completely eccentric and wonderful wine list offers the opportunity to drink such oddities as smooth and spicy Portuguese red wines. For food and wine of this caliber, one would expect to pay twice the price anyplace else.

This restaurant's diminutive size, minimalist decor, and obscure location only add to its appeal. Nestled near a freeway overpass where Mission and Duboce meet, Woodward's Garden is the only piece left of the entry facade to a famous amusement park and garden that entertained San Franciscans from 1866 to 1892—hence the name of the restaurant. You can barely tell that a restaurant is inside the lace-curtained windows. The small room is about equally divided between tables and open kitchen, with a dark wooden counter and stools demarcating the two functions. Banquettes and white-linen-covered tables, thin, elegant glassware, pretty flowered plates, a very hip, austere room painted white, all help create the cachet of a Paris *boîte*. Everything about this little place is first class and civilized, including the quiet, intelligent service by one of the partners, who unobtrusively makes you feel like a guest at her dinner party.

CAFES

CAFE ISTANBUL

After a night of carousing in the Mission, stop by Cafe Istanbul for a soothing pot of tea. Sit in the carpeted nook near the front window at low, pounded-brass tray tables, or at Western-style tables and chairs under a tented ceiling. Try a mixture of mint and black tea called *damas,* or *chai,* an Indian-style Darjeeling spiced with cinnamon and cardamom, smoothed by milk. Or drink a tiny cup of muddy Turkish coffee. On Wednesdays at 8:30 and 9:30 p.m. you can catch the belly dancers, exotic Mission District–style performers with tattoos and many pierced body parts. They never fail to draw a crowd inside or, peering through the front window of the cafe, outside.

525 Valencia Street
(at 16th Street),
San Francisco
Tel: 863-8854
Open Sunday through
Thursday noon to 11 p.m.,
Friday and Saturday
until midnight
No credit cards

RADIO VALENCIA

1199 Valencia Street
(at 23rd Street),
San Francisco
Tel: 826-1199
Open Monday and Tuesday
5 p.m. to midnight,
Wednesday through Sunday
noon to midnight
Credit cards: MC, V;
$15 minimum

Though many funky, if comfy, cafes now dot the Mission, most of them serve burnt coffee and are used more as bohemian hangouts than places for a good cup. Radio Valencia is the exception, probably because it is as much an eating place as a cafe. Though its many neighborhood patrons spend lots of time seated at wooden tables in the green-and-yellow-painted corner storefront with loud and eclectic music always playing, they also appreciate its integrity when it comes to food and drink. The emphasis is on nicely turned-out focaccia sandwiches, salads, soups, and chili made with healthful ingredients. I was sad to see the brunch service discontinued, but the cafe now hosts progressive live music three nights a week.

BARS

DALVA

3121 16th Street
(at Valencia),
San Francisco
Tel: 252-7740
Open Saturday through
Thursday 4 p.m. to 2 a.m.,
Friday 2 p.m. to 2 a.m.
No credit cards

Next door to the Roxie Theater, Dalva offers a tonier atmosphere than most Mission District bars, mostly brought about by its sponged, coral-colored walls. Späten and Bass ale, among others on tap, sangría, some women bartenders in tight T-shirts, and nightly DJs who seem to specialize in the 1970s keep the action lively. The bar comfortably fills up early and buzzes throughout the night.

ELBO ROOM

647 Valencia Street (between
17th and 18th Streets),
San Francisco
Tel: 552-7788
Open daily 5 p.m. to 2 a.m.
No credit cards

Appropriately named, this bar gets so packed with a young crowd that you can barely elbow your way to the bar for a draft beer. Formerly a lesbian bar called Amelia's, the Elbo Room has become the Mission District hot spot for heterosexual singles in their twenties. A $3 cover charge gets you upstairs for dancing orchestrated by a changing lineup of DJs and live bands.

DELICATESSENS/TAKE-OUT

HUNGARIAN SAUSAGE FACTORY

The smell of garlic is so strong it nearly pushes you over when you walk into this tiny deli and restaurant in two connected Victorian storefronts on Bernal Height's main shopping street. In one light-filled, lace-curtained room are cushion-covered wooden benches, handsome varnished tables, and a piano. Jars of fresh flowers sit on all the tables, including a few on the sidewalk basking in the sun. People order at the deli case and then sit down or take their food to go. The whole system is fairly impromptu, at least during the day when all the ordering is done at the deli counter. Though a very small repertoire of Hungarian specialties is made here, they are all homemade-tasting and delicious, particularly the garlicky Hungarian sausages, which come fresh, smoked or cured, hot or mild. The hot are barely so and enhanced by long-simmered sauerkraut, a huge pickle, and soft egg bread on the Sausage Plate. The stuffed cabbage is also soul-satisfying with as much rice as ground pork in the savory filling. For dessert have a warm crepe (*palacsinta*) with butter and sugar.

The deli augments its own sausages with imported goods from Hungary, including hams, dry sausages, paprika, fruit syrups, and soft, fruity Hungarian red wines that go wonderfully with the food and cost all of $10.50 a bottle. You can drop in for some house-baked Hungarian pastries like a fine, barely sweetened Hungarian cheesecake—two layers of yeast dough with a thick layer of farmer's cheese in between—and some of the best espresso in the city, served in a small glass, just the way I like it.

419 Cortland Avenue
(between Bennington and Wool),
San Francisco
Tel: 648-2847
Open Tuesday through Thursday 10 a.m. to 9 p.m.,
Friday and Saturday until 10 p.m.,
Sunday 10 a.m. to 9 p.m.
Credit cards: MC, V

LA PALMA MEXICATESSEN

Serious lovers of tortillas make regular pilgrimages to La Palma, a "Mexicatessen" and small tortilla factory, where thick tortillas are hand-patted Central American style, or thinly pressed Mexican style, or fried into the best thick chips in town. La Palma also sells fresh masa dough by the pound for tamales or homemade tortillas. The masa has no preservatives

2884 24th Street (at Florida),
San Francisco
Tel: 647-1500
Open Monday through Saturday 8 a.m. to 6 p.m.,
Sunday until 5 p.m.
Credit cards: MC, V

TAMALES IN THE MISSION, WITH A MURAL DETOUR

The differences between tamales from different parts of Latin America will take you by surprise. Although all of them are based on corn *masa*, dried corn softened with a lime solution then stone ground, what happens to the *masa* next creates the contrasts. You can start at Barrasa Market at Mission and 24th Street, where three or four kinds of tamales are kept warm in a steamer at the perpetually busy counter. The Mexican tamales wrapped in corn husks have a dense, almost cakey texture with a monochromatic filling of stewed pork or chicken, but the *nacatamales* from Nicaragua are a revelation. Wrapped in foil and thin white paper, the *nacatamales* look like fat baked potatoes. Girdled with a banana leaf, which infuses the tamale with a gentle herbal flavor, the *masa* inside has a soft, light texture from being precooked in broth.

The ample filling brings together delicious stewed pork, sliced potatoes, green chilies, tomatoes, *chicharróns* (crisped pork rind), huge capers, hard-cooked egg, and rice. The balance of filling to tasty *masa* is almost one to one, so you feel like you are eating a satisfying casserole.

In Salvadorean tamales, the *masa* has been cooked until it almost turns into a custard, and the generous filling is usually one ingredient, such as chicken stewed in a dried-chili sauce with rice. A banana leaf wrapping inside the paper lends this most delicate of tamales its flavor.

La Palma Mexicatessen on 24th Street and Florida also makes an array of tamales to try, and on your walk down 24th Street, the Mission's finest market street, you will encounter a living gallery of folk murals in as many styles as tamales. When you get to Balmy Alley on the south side of 24th between Treat and Harrison, take a right and walk down one side and up the other. The alley must have been named for its micro-climate, which is amazingly warm and sunny even within a part of the city that is famous for its tropical temperatures. All the tall wooden fences and garage doors that line the alley have been painted by Latin American artists, some depicting Central American solidarity, others the culture of daily life, all sophisticated and original executions. The tradition of Diego Rivera lives on! Along 24th Street itself, the walls of churches, apartment buildings, and stores provide more canvasses for the buoyant paintings. A map to the murals in the Mission can be purchased for 50¢ at Galeria de la Raza on 24th and Bryant Streets. While you're mapping out your route, you can restore yourself with a new set of tamales at La Palma.

in it. Each day a new batch of corn is ground and fresh tortillas are made. A world of difference exists between reheated packaged corn tortillas, even those hot from La Palma's griddle, and ones that are shaped, cooked, and eaten immediately. Just as yeast, flour, and water act a hundred different ways in the hands of bakers, lime-softened ground corn and water can deliver many subtle pleasures depending on how it is handled.

A glimpse into the back of La Palma, where a group of women stand around patting out tortillas from hills of *masa* and slapping them onto a rectangular griddle, will whet your appetite for Mexican food. Hunger can be satisfied on the spot from the counter at the back, which sells tacos and burritos or prepared fillings to go. If you want to cook at home, La Palma is the place to buy your basic ingredients. Bags of freshly ground dried chilies of different varieties (California, New Mexico, pasilla, ancho), fresh *epazote* and other Mexican spices, freshly made *chicharróns*, which are Mexican cracklings, fried-to-order tortillas for tostadas in any size you like, and all sorts of canned and jarred Mexican products fill the immaculate shelves. La Palma renders its own lard, which is ever so much more flavorful than the preserved bricks on supermarket shelves. The lard is sold by the quart from the refrigerator case. If you happen to see little bags of La Palma's potato chips, which are fried in clean vegetable oil, grab them. You will never taste a more satisfying chip. To wash them down, try a glass of *jamaica*, a refreshing red iced tea made from hibiscus flowers. Every time I go to La Palma, I come away with a new Latin American food—either for eating right there or for cooking.

LUCCA RAVIOLI COMPANY

At one time the Mission was home to a large Italian community, and this sixty-three-year-old Italian delicatessen is one of the last vestiges of it. Lucca still has a huge neighborhood following, because everyone likes their reasonably priced house-made ravioli, tortellini, and sauces. The volume of sales is so large that meat-and-chard-filled ravioli are actually prepared every hour; more perishable cheese-filled ravioli

1100 Valencia Street
(at 22nd Street),
San Francisco
Tel: 647-5581
Open Monday through
Saturday 9 a.m. to 6 p.m.
Credit cards: AE, MC, V

are always frozen, although they cook up well. Chewy house-made spinach tortellini and plain meat-filled tortellini, displayed in beautiful wooden boxes in the refrigerator case along with many different kinds of fresh noodles, offer other mealtime alternatives. A sweet dried-mushroom-infused tomato sauce and an excellent pesto—one of the best I have ever come across—complete the package. The freshness of the pesto, especially in regard to the garlic, makes a world of difference. The fast turnover at Lucca ensures a bright-flavored sauce.

Certain cheeses like the *grana padano* (a less-aged Parmesan-type cheese that Lucca imports itself), aged jack, and house-imported double cream Brie are offered at excellent prices. So are wines. In fact, Lucca Ravioli Company has the best selection of Italian bottles in the $6 to $7 range I have seen in the city. The loquacious ravioli chef, Mike Feno, will steer you to the best bottles, using the huge map of Italy on the ceiling to show you where the wines come from. This store's dedication to good value makes it a shopping destination for olive oils, dried pasta, olives, and all things imported from Italy.

BAKERIES/PASTRIES

LA REYNA BAKERY AND COFFEE SHOP

Along with the typical range of *pan dulce* and soft white Mexican rolls called *bolillos*, this bakery offers something unique: fresh handmade white-flour tortillas, which are a rare find. The bakery usually prepares them on Tuesdays or Thursdays, but not dependably. The only way to be sure to get some is to call ahead. They have no preservatives in them unlike the ubiquitous packaged ones.

3114 24th Street (at Folsom Street), San Francisco
Tel: 647-6502
Open Monday through Friday 7:30 a.m. to 7 p.m., weekends 8 a.m. to 7 p.m.
No credit cards

PANADERIA LA MEXICANA

At Mexican bakeries scattered up and down 24th Street, you will encounter shelves of largish, bunlike pastries, all pretty much made out of the same dough, but shaped, glazed, or sugared differently. There are crocodiles, conch shells, rocks, ears, turtles, and shoes, all made of the soft, airy, pleasant pastry called *pan dulce*, or Mexican sweet bread. Among aficionados, Emilio Valle, the former baker at Panaderia La Mexicana, is considered the reigning master of the *pan dulce*. His shapes were the most whimsical, and I can attest to their freshness and lightness. The baker still turns them out. A cinnamon-and-sugar-dusted *concha* with a cup of Mexican chocolate makes for a morning treat. *Pan dulce* delivers the tactile pleasure of a doughnut but without all the oil, because these pastries are baked.

At a *panaderia* you do not wait to be served, but grab a tray and tongs from the counter and choose your own pastries, which are then counted and bagged. A dollar will buy you a bagful. Besides the *conchas*, I also pick up sugared sticks of *pan de yema*, which are filled with a layer of sweetened egg

2804 24th Street (at York), San Francisco
Tel: 648-2633
Open Thursday through Tuesday 6 a.m. to 8 p.m.
Wednesday until 7 p.m.
No credit cards

yolk; crisp pretzel-shaped cookies sprinkled with rock sugar; and mild spice cookies. Not rich, these cookies boast crumbly texture and gentle flavor.

ICE CREAM/CHOCOLATES

LATIN FREEZE

3338 24th Street
(at Mission Street),
San Francisco
Tel: 282-5033
Open daily 10 a.m. to 6 p.m.
No credit cards

From this tiny shop comes a rainbow of fresh fruit *paletas*, or frozen fruit bars, that taste just like the exotic and familiar fruits from which they are made. Any fruit flavor that you have ever dreamed of, and then some, find their way into Latin Freeze *paletas*. The watermelon bars have chunks of fruit and seeds; the cantaloupe bars have big pieces of pulp. I love the coconut, a red tangy bar called *jamaica* made from dried hibiscus flowers, the pruney tamarind, and the most strawberry-flavored strawberry. All are made without artificial flavorings. At 55¢ and 85¢ respectively for small and large bars, they constitute yet another reason for spending time in the Mission. The *paletas* are also vended from carts up and down 24th Street on the busiest weekend shopping days.

MITCHELL'S ICE CREAM

Although a bulletproof window with sliding panels might seem more appropriate at a bank than an ice cream shop, Mitchell's is a friendly and crowded place—and they do serve ice cream late into the night, which accounts for the safety features. All the ice creams are made on the premises to old-fashioned, light, but creamy specifications, unlike the super-dense ice creams that have become the vogue. This texture allows more delicate, exotic flavors like *buko* (young coconut), avocado, or *ube* (purple yamlike taro) to come through. Personally, I am a big fan of *buko* cones. The tropical Philippine flavors are part of a long and changing list that includes a distinctive Mexican chocolate, a pallid mango, and fresh peach in the summer. The clerks will give you tastes of any flavor before you decide. This ice cream shop also makes ice cream cakes for special occasions, sodas, shakes, and sundaes. Fruit-flavored ice slushes are also popular.

688 San Jose Avenue
(at 29th Street),
San Francisco
Tel: 648-2300
Open daily 11 a.m. to 11 p.m.
No credit cards

ST. FRANCIS FOUNTAIN AND CANDY STORE

Before the genre dies, you owe it to your kids to take them to the St. Francis for an authentic American fountain and sandwich shop experience. No Disneyland replica this, the St. Francis Fountain was founded in 1918 by the Christakes family, who still make their own ice cream, syrups and fruit toppings, peanut brittle, heavenly hash with house-made marshmallows, and all the other chocolate candies in their counter. They also make their own mayonnaise, which ennobles such sandwich classics as egg salad and tuna salad served open face on slices of sourdough. I adore their grilled ham and cheese prepared just the way I remember: pressed into the grill so the toast ends up thin, crisp, and buttery, the American cheese completely melted, and the thin, thin slices of real baked ham hot. A pile of thin pickle slices makes for the perfect accompaniment. Soup does not come from a can

2801 24th Street (at York),
San Francisco
Tel: 826-4200
Open Monday through
Friday 9 a.m. to 9 p.m.,
weekends 11:30 a.m.
to 8 p.m.
Credit cards: MC, V

here, but from real stock with real vegetables. A slightly thickened beef barley or minestrone brings back the memory of made-from-scratch American soups. Another reason I love this place is for its old-fashioned strawberry sodas served in tall, thick parfait glasses and made with chunky strawberry syrup, soda water, two large scoops of ice cream, and real whipped cream. What heaven! Unlike chain coffee shops, the food at St. Francis is made from real ingredients. The difference is rewarding.

The shop, which was remodeled after World War II, has wooden booths, a counter with stools, linoleum floors, and art deco light fixtures. As much as the food and ambiance are preserved in time, so are the prices. The other night two of us had a cup of beef barley soup, a grilled ham and cheese, a strawberry soda, and a small hot fudge sundae and got a check for $11.50. I felt so guilty I had to spend another six dollars on candy and a quart of hand-packed ice cream to take home.

ETHNIC MARKETS

BOMBAY BAZAAR

548 Valencia Street (between 16th and 17th Streets), San Francisco
Tel: 621-1717
Open Tuesday through Sunday
10 a.m. to 7 p.m.
No credit cards

The most complete Indian dry goods store in San Francisco, Bombay Bazaar is a large, neatly arranged store with bins of bulk spices, flours, dals—all the myriad ingredients of Indian cuisine. A few fresh items like ginger root, occasionally Kaffir lime leaves, and fresh *kari* leaves, show up. Avoid the sweets. You can find good buys on basmati rice, in sacks ranging from five to forty pounds, and Darjeeling tea. I am drawn to the many shelves of shiny stainless-steel *thali* plates and saucers, covered jars and canisters, both smart and traditional at the same time. They can be adapted to many Western uses. Indian cookware, such as heavy cast-iron woks with sturdy pounded-steel handles (the Chinese wok came from India) and all sorts of stainless-steel skillets and saucepans come at excellent prices. For cooking vessels of similar quality you pay more at Macy's.

CASA LUCAS MARKET

See Produce, page 237.

A full range of Mexican ingredients, canned, fresh, dried, and frozen, including cheeses, chorizo, spices, herbs, tons of dried chilies—anything you might need for a Diana Kennedy recipe.

GREEK AMERICAN FOOD IMPORTS

Anyone who has been to Greece knows that you can throw together one of the best picnics in the world from salty green and black olives, mild and pungent sheep's milk cheeses, cucumbers, tomatoes, radishes, bread, olive oil, and Greek honey. All these ingredients (minus the bread and produce) can be gathered at Greek American Food Imports, a headquarters for important items in the Mediterranean pantry. Solon, a Greek extra-virgin olive oil, this store's best-seller, has a buttery olive flavor without being as rich as the super-expensive Italian oils. The beauty of Solon is its mildness and balance. You can use it liberally in vinaigrettes, mayonnaise, and for cooking without overpowering the dish or your pocketbook. Olympia Extra Virgin has about the same level of pungency but a higher degree of pepperiness. Both are extraordinary buys.

Their imported Greek barrel feta will make you rethink the complexity of this crumbly white cheese, and *manouri*, a Greek cream cheese, has a tantalizing, if subtle, sheepy edge. Fragrant olive-oil soaps for $1 a bar sell for $3.50 at other stores. Glorious Greek honey and preserves made from rose petals, grapes, or bitter oranges fill the shelves. The only disappointments in this food shop full of treasures are forgettable Greek pastries imported from Cleveland for some reason.

223 Valencia Street
(between 14th Street and Duboce),
San Francisco
Tel: 864-0978
Open Tuesday through Friday 9:30 a.m. to 6 p.m., Saturday until 5 p.m., Sunday 10 a.m. to 1 p.m. (closed on Sunday during the summer)
Credit cards: MC, V

LA PALMA MEXICATESSEN

See Delicatessens/Take-Out, page 227.

The place for *masa*, or ground-corn dough, in all its forms, as well as many prepared items like lard and chips.

SAMIRAMIS IMPORTS

**2990 Mission Street
(at 26th Street),
San Francisco
Tel: 824-6555
Open Monday through
Saturday 10 a.m. to 6 p.m.
Credit cards: AE, D, MC, V**

A long-established store that caters to Middle Eastern ethnic needs, Samiramis's shelves are piled with everything from videos in Arabic to North African cooking equipment like *couscoussiers*. At least five different kinds of imported couscous are sold in bulk or in packages, along with the Cortas brand of pomegranate molasses, nuts, dried fruits, spices, and olive oils. In the refrigerator section is thick, creamy, deliciously sour Persian-style yogurt, Armenian string cheese, fetas from everywhere, and Mexican *queso fresco*, a mild, crumbly whole-milk cheese that also tastes good sprinkled on Mediterranean dishes. The emphasis, though, is not so much on fresh foods, but on the imported Middle Eastern groceries, spices, and grains necessary to stock a pantry.

PRODUCE MARKETS

ALEMANY FARMERS' MARKET

**Alemany at Crescent
(parallel to highway 280),
San Francisco
Saturdays from first light
through the afternoon**

This is the oldest farmers' market in the Bay Area, started by pear farmers in 1943 who had extra fruit to sell. In 1945 it moved into two long parallel cement structures divided into stalls. So many farmers come today that they spill out on the ends into the rather chaotic parking lot, setting up their own booths. This is the great multiethnic market in the city, with a dazzling array of Asian greens, exotic bird eggs (quail, duck, turkey), unusual citrus, melons, flowers, and tons of local stuff at the peak of the season. If you want the rare find, you have to get there before 8 a.m. If you're looking for great prices on farm fresh produce, go late when the farmers are trying to unload. Each week brings something new. This market keeps unfolding with every season and every year as farmers experiment with different crops.

BARRASA MARKET
(FORMERLY CASA FELIX)

The produce is stacked outside on wooden tables underneath an awning, and the small, dark interior is crammed with Latin American products. There's barely a place to wait in front of the three-cash-register counter, where up to six different kinds of tamales are dispensed along with such delicacies as the best *alfahores* in the Mission. *Alfahores* are elegant sandwich cookies—two thin Mexican butter cookies dusted with powdered sugar and filled with *cajeta*, a rich buttery caramel made with goat's milk—only the best cookie in town. On the produce shelves you are apt to find unrancid fresh coconuts and other hard-to-find ingredients in good shape. La Raza always seems to draw crowds of neighborhood housewives out shopping with their babies.

2840 Mission Street
(between 24th
and 25th Streets),
San Francisco
Tel: 824-4474
Open daily 8 a.m. to 7 p.m.
No credit cards

CASA LUCAS MARKET

The lines can be long at this popular and complete Latin American market with tables of plantains, jícama, and citrus outside its perpetually open doors. There are no carts, so shoppers fill up numerous plastic baskets with young coconuts, tomatillos, fresh and dried chilies in bulk, packets of Latin American herbs, frozen fruit purees for *liquados*, vinegars, capers at good prices, huge purple olives in brine from Peru, cut-up cleaned fresh cactus (*nopal*), *piloncillo* (cakes of moist, molasses-rich brown sugar), three kinds of chorizo, powder mixes for Mexican drinks, and Mexican cheeses. Customers line the baskets up on the wooden floor by the check-out counters and push the train forward with their feet. If you cannot find what you need at Casa Lucas, it is probably out of season or unavailable anyplace else.

2934 24th Street (between
Alabama and Florida),
San Francisco
Tel: 826-4334
Open daily 7 a.m. to 7 p.m.
No credit cards

LA HACIENDA MARKET

3100 16th Street
(at Valencia),
San Francisco
Tel: 431-8445
Open daily 8 a.m. to 9 p.m.
Credit cards: MC, V

This former branch of Casa Lucas, now under Palestinian ownership, still provides a wide range of Latin American produce and grocery items. From the north part of the city, La Hacienda is the closest outpost for warm packaged tortillas and fresh Mexican cheeses in bulk, kept in a refrigerated case. The excellent *queso fresco* here has a soft, crumbly texture, not gelatinous, and a gentle tang. Stronger *queso cotijo* and smoked and aged Mexican cheeses along with Mexican jack are sold in large quantities, so they are always fresh. Many markets in the Mission dispense *queso fresco* from an unrefrigerated counter, madness when it comes to such a fresh, delicate cheese. At La Hacienda, and at Casa Lucas on 24th Street, the bulk cheeses are always refrigerated.

AVOCADO QUESADILLAS

1/2 cup (2 ounces) coarsely grated queso chataleño
1/2 cup (2 ounces) coarsely grated queso cotija
1 cup (4 ounces) coarsely grated Monterey jack cheese
1 serrano chili, seeded and minced
1/4 cup minced fresh cilantro
2 green onions, minced
4 teaspoons vegetable oil
4 flour tortillas
2 ripe avocados, peeled, pitted, and diced
1 large tomato, seeded and diced
Kosher salt to taste

La Hacienda Market has the best selection of Mexican cheeses in bulk at their refrigerated front counter, and you can get all the other ingredients for these quesadillas there, too. Of course, everyone has his or her favorite cheese combo—I like to use half sharp cheddar and half mozzarella. When we serve these quesadillas at the Hayes Street Grill, we add a small amount of grilled tuna or shrimp and reduce the amount of avocado, or omit it altogether.

In a small bowl, combine the *quesa chataleño*, *queso cotija*, and Monterey jack cheese. In another small bowl, combine the chili, cilantro, and green onions.

In a 10-inch skillet over medium heat, heat 1 teaspoon of the oil until it spreads over the surface of the pan. Add a flour tortilla. Cook on one side for 30 seconds, then turn over. Reduce heat to medium-low.

Sprinkle over the tortilla one fourth of each of the cheeses and the chili mixture, avocado, and tomato, and add a pinch of kosher salt. Cover the skillet and cook until the cheese is melted and begins to bubble, about 5 minutes. Then, with a spatula, fold the tortilla in half to form a semi-circle and remove it from the skillet to a warmed plate or serving platter. Place in a preheated 250° F oven and repeat with the remaining tortillas. Serve immediately.

Serves 4

23RD AND MISSION PRODUCE

This neatly stocked Latin American produce store knows how to entice shoppers. During the winter when people are hungry for fruit, the market stacks up huge piles of sweet, juicy yellow mangoes with blushing red cheeks and sells them for a dollar each when they are at least half again as much anyplace else.

Always in perfect condition, the fruit is either ripe or within several days of ripening. Sometimes flat green organic mangoes from Haiti with deep orange flesh are available, or fifteen perfect mangoes by the case for twelve to thirteen dollars. I happen to be crazy about mangoes, and nothing pleases me more than the thought of having my own case at home to eat as they ripen. The other drawing card of this market are Haas avocados, always in good shape and 25 cents less per piece than anyplace else, and well-priced limes and lemons. The produce buyer for the store knows what he is doing. Most of the produce here turns over quickly and looks fresh and handsome.

2700 Mission Street
(at 23rd Street),
San Francisco
Tel: 285-7955
Open Monday through Saturday 7:30 a.m. to 6:30 p.m., Sunday until 5 p.m.
No credit cards

MEAT AND POULTRY

LA GALLINITA

You can tell what this tiny, always packed butcher shop specializes in by the aroma of fried pork wafting out the front door and down the street. On a table at the back of this dark little place are two stainless-steel pans of crisp, warm *chicharróns*, freshly rendered pork cracklings, which Salvadorans use in their *pupusas* and on salads, but many people buy them by the bag for snacks. You pick out your own crispy pieces with tongs and put them in a white bag. I know most people don't eat bags of pork fat these days, but one melting

2989 24th Street
(at Harrison),
San Francisco
Tel: 826-8880
Open daily 7 a.m. to 6 p.m.
Credit cards: MC, V

bite is not enough. You have to have another. Besides the *chicharróns,* people buy butterflied flank steak for *carne asada* and bags of chicken parts for soup. Fresh blood sausage moves quickly from the counter when it is available, and sometimes super-hot plump red chilies are sold by the piece. Though the principles of modern marketing have passed this dark hole of a shop by, there are many treasures to be mined.

THE LUCKY PORK STORE

2659 Mission Street
(between 22nd
and 23rd Streets),
San Francisco
Tel: 285-3611 or 550-9016
Open Monday through
Saturday 9 a.m. to 7 p.m.,
Sunday until 6 p.m.
No credit cards

This large and very inexpensive Chinese-run butcher shop housed in a market specializes in pig. Whole heads, snouts, ears, tongues, feet, shins, fat back, ribs, tripe, liver—almost every conceivable part of the animal—are surrealistically piled in the long glass refrigerated counter. More usual cuts like pork butt, loin, and shoulder, good-looking beef short ribs, oxtails, and other cuts of beef that take to long cooking are all abundant, fresh, and low in price. This butcher shop will find you whole suckling pigs and *cabrito* (young goat) for major Mexican barbecues. When you think of more unusual cuts of animals, think Lucky.

MISSION MARKET MEAT DEPARTMENT & MISSION MARKET FISH AND POULTRY

2590 Mission Street
(at 22nd),
San Francisco

Meat Department: 282-1030
Open Monday through
Saturday 9 a.m. to 6 p.m.
No credit cards

Fish & Poultry: 282-3331
Open Monday through
Saturday 8:30 a.m. to 6 p.m.
Credit cards: MC, V

What a surprise to find excellent meat, poultry, and fish counters in a multistalled market building off Mission Street. The counters are located at the back of the building, past the gift shop, the taqueria, the sweet shop, and a serviceable produce-grocery shop. Among the treasures to be found in the immaculate refrigerated counters are Harris beef, thick slices of beef shin for stock or succulent stew, beautiful-looking oxtails and short ribs, Rocky free-range chickens, sparkling fresh salmon, freshly ground turkey meat, and fresh, not frozen, turkeys, whole and in parts, fresh chicken gizzards and backs, and rabbits. Strolling by the counters and just seeing what is available makes you want to get cooking. Here are the building blocks you never see for good stocks—poultry and beef—and the cuts you need for the savory stews you crave. Shopping in the Mission on a Saturday comes very close to being in the middle of a sprawling Latin American mercado.

POLARICA

Polarica imports game, meats, and specialty products from all over the world and sells them both wholesale and retail, delivered and on site, for the same price. Home cooks can visit the attractive storefront warehouse or call ahead to order something specific. This is the place where many cooks go for one of my favorite birds, the rich-flavored, dark-fleshed guinea fowl (roast or grill the breasts, braise the legs, and serve with long-cooked cabbage), as well as fresh pheasant. The fresh California-grown rabbits have no off flavors, and the vacuum-packed fresh lamb from Australia in all cuts is some of the best available. Fresh venison from New Zealand and duck, whole and in parts, from the Grimaud duck farm are always in stock. Both Hudson Valley foie gras and our local Sonoma foie gras, and smoked salmon from Norway and Scotland at half the price you find them in delicatessens (Polarica will sell the salmon in small quantities if you wish) are but a few of the items available and listed on a detailed product list that will be mailed to you if you call. Polarica is also a source for fresh black truffles and all sorts of fresh wild mushrooms. Russian and American caviars are also sold at competitive prices.

Finally, if the urge to eat emu or eland overtakes you, Polarica has them. This outfit, which also has an office in Manhattan, prides itself on finding sources for every conceivable kind of domestically raised game, world wide. In fact, if you're looking for any rare or exotic ingredient you might want to check here first.

107 Quint Street
(near Third Street
and Cesar Chavez),
San Francisco
Tel: 647-1300
Open Monday through
Friday 9 a.m. to 5 p.m.
Credit cards: AE, MC, V

FISH

MISSION MARKET FISH AND POULTRY

See Meat and Poultry, page 240.

Noe Valley, the Castro, Diamond Heights & Upper Market

NOE VALLEY, THE CASTRO, DIAMOND HEIGHTS & UPPER MARKET

Restaurants:
1. Bacco   247
2. Firefly   248
3. Mecca   249
4. Pozole   250

Cafes:
5. Cafe Flore   251
6. Orbit Room Cafe   252

Bakeries/Pastries:
7. Bakers of Paris   253
8. Noe Valley Bakery   253
9. Sweet Inspiration   254

Ice Cream/Chocolates:
10. Joseph Schmidt Confections   255

Coffee:
11. Spinelli Coffee Company   256

Markets:
12. Tower Market   256

Produce:
13. Harvest Ranch Market   258
14. Mikeytom   258
15. Real Food Company   259

Meat and Poultry:
12. Viglizzo's Meats   259

Cheese:
16. 24th Street Cheese Company   259

Wines and Spirits:
17. Caruso's   260
18. Castro Village Wine Company   261

Cookware and Books:
19. Cliff's Hardware   261
20. Echo   261
21. Lehr's German Specialties   262

RESTAURANTS

BACCO

The 24th Street corridor in Noe Valley has been notoriously bereft of good neighborhood restaurants, especially considering that the community has become more sophisticated about food over the years. Tastes in Noe Valley have been moving from hippie health food to European-inspired home cooking. Young professionals, lured by the somewhat-affordable houses in the area, cut their culinary teeth on bistros and trattorias in France and Italy before their kids came along. This group is used to eating out in restaurants, yet they don't want to spend a fortune. So when Bacco a modern, Northern Italian–style trattoria, opened on Diamond Street, the bravos echoed throughout the neighborhood. At last there was a place where people could get a plate of well-made pasta, interesting antipasti, and decent Italian wines at a fairly comfortable price.

The brightly lit, cheerful orange dining rooms of this perpetually full restaurant beckon passersby, although a reservation will save you a wait. The small linen- and butcher paper–covered tables turn over at a leisurely pace. The food is similar to that served in a number of small Italian places around town—Alto Adige, Ideale, Milano—fresh, lively, tasty; just what you want to eat on a casual night out.

Start with the terrine of eggplant, peppers, and goat cheese, quite elegantly molded together but rustically flavorful, served with a green salad. Move on to giant ravioli

737 Diamond Street
(at 24th Street),
San Francisco
Tel: 282-4969
Open nightly 5:30 to 10 p.m.
Price: Moderate
Credit Cards: MC, V

filled with chard and ricotta, drizzled with brown butter and crisp leaves of fried sage. What makes them so lovely is their thin, tender noodle wrappers. For Italian broccoli lovers (those who like the slightly bitter flavor) Bacco makes a wonderful bowl of *orechietti*, ear-shaped pasta, tossed with anchovies, garlic, red chili flakes, and perfectly cooked broccoli rabe, a classic combination.

Simple things like grilled Italian sausages with polenta are dressed up with a tomato and olive puree and accompanied with a favorite Italian vegetable, chard stems. (The green parts, which cook at a different rate, are used in other dishes.) Even desserts, often neglected in small restaurants, get full attention from the kitchen here. One night our meal ended triumphantly with a luscious chocolate pudding cake moistened with hazelnut custard and garnished with strawberries, a real culinary event for 24th Street.

FIREFLY

4288 24th Street
(near Douglass),
San Francisco
Tel: 821-7652
Open Tuesday through
Sunday 5:30 to 10 p.m.
Price: Moderate
Credit Cards: AE, MC, V

When a restaurant puts out baskets of costly Acme *levain*, you know it is out to please. Though I had my doubts about Firefly, where the cooking by ex-Embarko chef Brad Levy falls into the California-eclectic school, his good sense keeps the food appealing. One meal might bring dishes from all over the world, but they are unified by Levy's sensibility. In an affordable neighborhood restaurant, the energy and thought behind the creative menu deservedly causes a stir.

A good way to start is with scallop and shrimp pot stickers, densely filled with a chunky mousse of sweet-flavored shellfish nicely set off with black pepper and served with chopsticks, which adds to the pleasure of eating them. A lemony Caesar salad with huge croutons is also popular and good. Items like Thai salmon cakes apply ethnic forms to Western ingredients. Unlike the spongy fish cakes served in Southeast Asia, these were dense and gingery, presented on a bed of room-temperature wilted spinach. They made for a very substantial starter. Firefly presumes that people will be sharing the first courses, so all the wooden tables are already set with blue and white print plates. Main courses are generous as well and span the globe. A moist, perfectly grilled chicken breast crowned a plate of black beans, lemony chayote squash still crisp, and a chunky avocado salsa that was sweet and citrusy. The chef likes to season with both sugar and lemon, but not offensively.

If any sort of fruit shortcake is on the dessert menu, order it. The crisp, sweet, salty, crumbly shortcakes are so tasty they stand on their own.

The neighborhood atmosphere of the Firefly make it all the more charming. Two small dining rooms, one with a wine bar where people can eat, share the space with a tiny open kitchen. The do-it-yourself decor has homegrown style yet the service is amazingly professional. You can tell that the people behind this restaurant have had experience. The Firefly is not of the "Oh, let's start a restaurant because we cook so well for our friends" ilk. Rather, it reflects a lot of current restaurant-industry trends that have been downscaled to work in a modestly capitalized operation. The combination is particularly winning—and it's happening all over San Francisco and the East Bay. A food-loving city full of chefs-in-training reaps the benefits of their coming of age.

MECCA

2029 Market (between Dolores and 14th Street), San Francisco
Tel: 621-7000
Open nightly 6 p.m. to midnight, Sunday until 11 p.m.
Price: Moderate
Credit cards: AE, D, MC, V

The opening last year of this hot restaurant, bar, and club on Market Street signals a rebirth of fun in the Castro, and people from all over the city are coming in droves to join the party. The campy interior, designed around a huge central bar outlined by a track of fluorescent lights that change color every five seconds, is cavernous, painted black and darkly lit—shades of the seventies disco clubs. Try to reserve a table in a cordoned-off dining nook somewhat protected from the bar and club activity if you want to eat.

A versatile menu put together by Rubicon alumnus Lynn Sheehan offers large platters of crispy calamari, roasted whole Eastern snapper from the wood-burning oven, pizzas, chicken *tagine*, delicious sautéed skate wing, and all sorts of appealing dishes inspired by the most popular menus around town. Desserts can be wonderful. I still dream about a small, warm macadamia–brown butter cake with caramelized bananas, pineapple, passion fruit, and a coconut sorbet.

As much a bar as a restaurant, Mecca stocks fine *grappas*, cognacs, and ports, and an extensive, mostly California wine list organized by varietal. Practically every wine maker is identified, so if you just wanted to drink wines made by women, you could do it and compare them to the same varietals made by men. Fun. The bartenders, by the way, mix excellent cocktails, even if they do call them by silly names.

You can eat and drink memorably, dance, take in some cabaret, meet someone new, meet someone old, or just hang out at Mecca, a crossroads for the gay and straight communities united by the shared impulse to have the best possible time.

POZOLE

2337 Market Street
(between Noe
and 17th Streets),
San Francisco
Tel: 626-2666
Open Monday through
Thursday 4 to 10 p.m.,
Friday and Saturday
noon to midnight,
Sunday noon to 11 p.m.
Price: Inexpensive
No credit cards

Eating styled-out Mexican street food in a gallery of jauntily dressed skeletons and romantically inscribed tombstones may seem an unlikely pastime, but Jesse Acevedo, the creative force behind Pozole, makes it work. Pozole is the most interesting taqueria in the city both for food and surroundings. Unrelentingly casual—you can order at a counter or get table service—and very reasonable in price, the experience nevertheless is upscale: The beautifully presented food comes on carefully chosen pottery, the decoration is more folk art than artifice, and the combinations of flavors will broaden your notion of Mexican cooking. Acevedo draws on a far-reaching market basket of authentic ingredients, and he puts together his burritos and tacos, soups and appetizers with many regional references. Lately he has expanded to include Caribbean and Latin American flavors, the fruits and hot, hot chili sauces of Creole islands, and the fish soups of Peru and Ecuador. Yet the overall style of the food at Pozole mostly reflects Acevedo's personal culinary imagination.

Nearly half of the dishes on the current menu are purposely low in fat, and there are seven vegetarian items. *Pollo sin grassa* (which means "without fat"), for example, is a satisfying pinto bean stew with a skinless chicken breast sparked by chopped onions, cilantro, and tomato, served with white rice and a cooked-to-order corn tortilla. The seafood bisque has tremendous flavor while staying lean. On the vegetarian front are satisfying Cuban quesadillas filled with roasted garlic, roasted peppers, and mushrooms, served with fried bananas, black beans, and rice. Old favorites like fish tacos on handmade tortillas; rich crab quesadillas; grilled beef burritos; chicken mole with apricots, cumin, and grated chocolate; Oaxacan tamales stuffed with bananas and raisins, topped with mango salsa; and burritos filled with pork stewed in an achiote-orange-tequila-spiked broth keep Pozole's customers loyal. The sangría, beers, and Mexican fresh fruit drinks make a meal here even more fun. What all this adds up to is a brilliant, well-run fast-food restaurant that draws on the best of traditional, ethnic, and avant-garde culinary ideas in a highly personal way. Instead of compromising to meet the demands of a fat-conscious vegetarian market, Pozole has simply invented a series of exciting new dishes that stand on their own. People who eat there will not be joining those Day-of-the-Dead skeletons anytime soon.

CAFES

CAFE FLORE

Call me ridiculous, but the stretch of upperish Market Street from Van Ness to Castro reminds me of the boulevard Montparnasse, Paris's broad, traffic-filled thoroughfare lined with historic cafes (La Coupole, Le Dome, Le Select . . .) and movie houses. Our slanting Market Street has two great triangular cafes, Zuni and Cafe Flore, as well as a row of huge, majestic palm trees on the median in the middle of the street. While Cafe Flore does not come close to having the panache of a French cafe, it possesses a certain *je ne sais quoi* that makes it a gathering place. Its outdoor tables on a patio decorated with Cinzano umbrellas and protected from the wind by glass screens are always full, and the red-and-blue-tiled indoor tables turn over constantly. Although the Flore still looks like the gas station it once was, its interior has taken on the patina of age and use. The corrugated-iron roof, the

2298 Market (at Noe),
San Francisco
Tel: 621-8579
Open daily
7:30 a.m to 11:30 p.m.
Price: Inexpensive
No credit cards

exposed wooden structural bracing, the long Victorian counter where people order their coffees and health-foodish sandwiches and salads (ample and inexpensive), and the wisteria vines all feel organic to the neighborhood. The hundreds of people who come and go at Cafe Flore create the ambiance and energy of the place, just as they do at Parisian cafes. The difference is that even cosmopolitan Paris has never seen the likes of a Market Street crowd at practically any time of day or night. By the way, the counterpeople willingly make excellent Graffeo espresso, which they will pour into a small glass with an equal amount of steamed milk (called an Africano)—the current rage.

ORBIT ROOM CAFE

1900 Market Street (at Laguna), San Francisco
Tel: 252-9525
Open Monday through Thursday 7:30 a.m. to midnight, Friday until 2 a.m., Saturday 8 a.m. to 2 a.m., Sunday 8 a.m. to midnight
Price: Inexpensive
No credit cards

Years ago this lofty corner spot was an Uncle Gaylord's ice cream parlor. Its current identity as a hip, rather elegantly designed cafe during the day and bar at night does justice to its soaring quarters. Daylight pours in through art deco–framed two-story windows onto a pressed-metal ceiling, streaky golden walls, varnished distressed concrete floors, and sculptural cone-shaped tables made out of marbleized plaster. Art deco–inspired light sconces glow handsomely on wooden pillars. The space draws you in from the street and keeps you there with classical music (during the day), excellent Mr. Espresso coffee from the coffee bar, and the likes of Späten, Sierra Nevada pale ale, Blackthorn cider, and Golden

Bear lager on tap at a second bar in the middle of the room. Tables placed outside soak up the sun and provide a choice place to have a coffee while doing your laundry at the handy laundromat next door. The staff here is competent, cool-looking, but friendly; the patrons have that urbane lower-Haight aura. All told, the Orbit Room gives off great vibes.

BAKERIES/PASTRIES

BAKERS OF PARIS

For other location see page 439.

When you break into a Bakers of Paris baguette, lightly crusted and soft inside, you could be starting a meal in Paris. These long, skinny, lightweight breads are exactly what are served in every neighborhood bistro and sold in every corner *boulangerie*. They can be used for sandwiches, for spreading with butter and jam, and for sopping up sauce—all noble purposes. Bakers of Paris baguettes, like Parisian baguettes, are best eaten the same day they are bought. The bakery also makes buttery raisin rolls, decent croissants, and pain au chocolate, a bun made of croissant pastry filled with chocolate.

3989 24th Street (at Noe),
San Francisco
Tel: 863-8725
Open daily 7 a.m. to 6 p.m.
No credit cards

NOE VALLEY BAKERY

This vital, relatively new bakery has taken hold in the neighborhood, but it thrives because of a citywide demand for its focaccia, morning rolls, and breads. Many cafes and sandwich shops incorporate Noe Valley Bakery's baked goods into their own menus (Palio Paninoteca for one). And every Saturday a long line forms in front of the Noe Valley Bakery booth at the Ferry Plaza Farmers' Market.

Having met at the oven of Il Fornaio, the couple who started the Noe Valley Bakery thought they would make their mark by specializing in dense breads laden with fresh and dried fruits. Now their most popular (and my favorite) items include a soft-centered, crusty Italian-style white bread, buttery

4073 24th Street (between Castro and Noe),
San Francisco
Tel: 550-1405
Open Monday through Friday 7 a.m. to 7 p.m., weekends 8 a.m. to 6 p.m.
Credit cards: MC, V

almond croissants, cinnamon twists, and crisp breadsticks. Poppyseed cakes and pound cakes are sold by the slice or whole cake. Fresh fruit pies are reasonably priced at $12. The bakery turns out old-fashioned treats—chocolate eclairs, large macaroons dipped in chocolate or plain, frosted tea cakes—and modern passions—focaccia with toppings, Italian breads, and fruit breads, which really reflect the divided tastes of the neighborhood. A mix of people stream into the attractive shop, piled with a breathtaking variety of freshly baked things, and seem to know exactly what they want. I find it impossible to buy just one item here. Luckily, Noe Valley Bakery's bread stays fresh for several days—and the buttery pastries heat up well.

SWEET INSPIRATION

2239 Market Street (between Sanchez and Noe), San Francisco
Tel: 621-8664
Open Monday through Thursday 7 a.m. to 11:30 p.m., Friday until 12:30 a.m., Saturday 8 a.m. to 11:30 p.m., Sunday 8 a.m. to 11:30 p.m.
No credit cards

Old-fashioned whipped-cream cakes made with up-to-the-minute ingredients fill the refrigerated cases of this large dessert cafe/bakery. Albeit with a modern twist, the cakes remind me of the bakery goods my mother used to bring home from the French Swiss Pastry Shop on the north side of Chicago. Our favorite was made of layers of soft yellow cake, sweetened whipped cream, and lots of fresh strawberries. At Sweet Inspiration, airy yellow layers are paved with whipped cream, candied ginger, and thin sheets of chocolate in a jelly-roll configuration—to my mind the nicest of this genre of cakes made here—or whipped cream and shredded coconut between layers of cake soaked with rum. At the rather chilly-feeling cafe you can have a large slice of cake with coffee or a pot of tea, or you can take pastries home. The wholesale bakery sells to Kuleto's, Macy's, and Spinelli coffee stores, among others.

ICE CREAM/CHOCOLATES

JOSEPH SCHMIDT CONFECTIONS

For thirteen years now, Joseph Schmidt has been working his chocolate artistry at this colorful shop filled with seasonal specialties. In the spring, expect lovable Easter bunnies of the richest Belgian chocolate; for Mother's Day, long, thin boxes covered with hydrangeas holding a dozen miniature truffles, Joseph Schmidt's signature confection. Truffles may have catapulted him to fame, but his sculptural talent has kept him there. If Schmidt were not working in chocolate, he might have made a career in stone. His large chocolate bowls and vases with ragged, pointed edges, marbled with white and mint chocolate, serve as Baccarat-like containers for more chocolates or even flowers made out of chocolate. San Franciscans order these dramatic bowls for parties and special events. A new confection, thin round disks of chocolate about two inches in diameter with soft fillings like caramel, coconut cream, or nougat, each disk painted with a colorful and delicate abstract design, now fill one whole case. Rich truffles with flavored fondant interiors fill another. I personally cannot resist the chocolate nut bark and the huge, flat turtles with pecans, buttery caramel, and carapaces of light or dark chocolate, the best of their genre. Schmidt also makes a changing array of small traditional chocolates filled with nuts, creams, and jellies.

While Schmidt chocolates are carried at Neiman-Marcus, Macy's, Confetti, Saks Fifth Avenue, and in special batches at Williams-Sonoma, a trip to the store can net some unique treasures. Schmidt is nothing if not whimsical, and who knows what he might make that day? His wife manages and grooms the shop with passion, for she is a lover of chocolate as well. She runs up and down Telegraph Hill every morning just so she can keep tasting.

3489 16th Street
(at Sanchez),
San Francisco
Tel: 861-8682
Open Monday through
Saturday 10 a.m. to 6:30 p.m.
Credit cards: MC, V

COFFEE

SPINELLI COFFEE COMPANY

3966 24th Street (between Noe and Sanchez),
San Francisco
Tel. 550-7416
Open Monday through Friday 6:30 a.m. to 10 p.m.,
weekends 7 a.m. to 10 p.m.

504 Castro Street (at 18th Street),
San Francisco
Tel: 241-9447
Open Monday through Thursday 6:30 a.m. to 9 p.m.,
Friday until 10 p.m., Saturday 7 a.m. to 10 p.m.,
Sunday 7 a.m. to 9 p.m.
Credit cards: MC, V
See listing, page 173.

MARKETS

TOWER MARKET

635 Portola Drive
(at Terracita),
San Francisco
Tel: 664-1600
Open Monday
through Saturday
8 a.m. to 8:30 p.m.,
Sunday until 8 p.m.
Credit Cards: AE, D, MC, V

In this part of town, Tower Market looms as the best resource for high-quality ingredients under one roof. A medium-sized store, intelligently stocked, it draws a large patronage from St. Francis Wood and West Portal to Glen Park. The produce department always has seasonal treasures such as small, fat stalks of rhubarb in the spring, and year-round organic produce such as thick bunches of spinach. The independently owned deli section is a source for prosciutto from Parma as well as German-style cured meats. Viglizzo's Meats has been operating since 1915 and they have kept current with free-range chickens, freshly ground turkey, Harris beef, and butchers who will cut and grind to order. The dairy section is a source for Plugra brand butter, which has twice the butterfat of regular butter and the full, sweet flavor of European butters. Sold in half pounds that cost as much as a full pound of other butter, Plugra turns morning toast into the best dish of the day. Also available in this section are glass quarts of Straus Family Dairy organic milk, a new product from Western Marin from cows that are not treated with hormones and only eat organic grains. You have to shake the bottles before you pour to dislodge the cream off the top, and the sweet, delicately grassy flavor of this milk will make you take notice of what you're drinking for the first time (if you're under forty-five).

PECAN TARTLETS

I learned this recipe for miniature tartlets from my mother when I was a child. They melt in your mouth. All the ingredients can be purchased at any grocery store. The miniature muffin pans can be found at Frederickson's Hardware (page 202), and at cookware stores.

3 ounces cream cheese

1/2 cup (1 stick) butter at room temperature, plus 2 tablespoons butter for filling

1 cup all-purpose flour

1 egg

3/4 cup packed brown sugar

1 teaspoon vanilla extract

2/3 cup pecans, coarsely chopped

Preheat the oven to 350° F. Butter two mini muffin tins (each cup about 1 inch in diameter), carefully coating the bottom and sides.

In a food processor fitted with a steel blade, or by hand, blend together the cream cheese, 1/2 cup butter, and flour to make a smooth uniform dough. Divide into 24 equal pieces. With your thumb, press the dough into the molds, covering bottom and sides. In a small bowl, blend the egg, brown sugar, remaining 2 tablespoons of butter, and vanilla until smooth.

Layer half the pecans in the dough cups. Using a teaspoon, fill the molds two-thirds full with the brown sugar mixture. Top with the remaining pecans.

Bake until the dough is golden and the nuts toasted, about 30 to 35 minutes. Run a knife around the edges to loosen the tartlets and unmold them. Let cool on a wire rack. These are best eaten the same day.

Makes twenty-four 1-inch tartlets

PRODUCE

HARVEST RANCH MARKET

2285 Market
(between 16th
Street and Noe)
San Francisco
Tel: 626-0805
Open daily 9 a.m. to 11 p.m.
Credit cards: AE, MC, V

Really more a spontaneous cafe than a market, this flashy natural foods store has turned into a Market Street hot spot. Day and night customers come in to cruise the salad bar, filling up clear plastic containers with legume and pasta salads, tofu, and the usual salad-bar vegetable assortment with curry dressings. Fast-moving items include giant sushi rolls about the size of a fist, coated with sesame seeds, pinwheeled with seaweed, and filled with asparagus, cucumber, and *surimi*, imitation crab. Dipped into soy sauce and wasabi they make for a destination snack or light meal. The sushi, like all the other foods on the salad bar, cost $2.49 per pound and weigh out to about $1 a piece. Two will fill you up. Their best trait is their freshness; they move so fast new trays are constantly brought out. People eat outside on impromptu benches made of wood beams and metal crates. For shoppers, the store carries all sorts of bread, including Acme and Grace Baking Company loaves, and a limited selection of organic produce. The usual natural foods store bulk nuts, cheeses, yogurt, chips, and granola are sexily displayed.

MIKEYTOM

1747 Church Street (at Day),
San Francisco
Tel: 826-5757
Open Monday
through Saturday
7 a.m. to 9 p.m.,
Sunday 8 a.m. to 8 p.m.
Credit cards: MC, V

The residents from Mikeytom's outer Noe Valley neighborhood rejoiced when this modern, brightly lit, organic produce and natural foods store opened. While the selection is small, the fruits and vegetables look inviting, nicely set out in baskets. The small heads of lettuce are particularly beautiful here. Breads from the Metropolis bakery in Emeryville, and Clover and Straus Family dairy products are good to have in any neighborhood market, along with buckets of fresh flowers. Some marble tables have been placed outside for those who want to have a coffee made at the coffee bar inside.

REAL FOOD COMPANY

See listing, page 176.

The highlight of this branch is a refrigerated room for all the items sold in bulk. Turnover is pretty quick at most Real Food stores, but I always worry about the freshness of nuts, flours, grains—anything that loses nutritional value or can change in flavor when stored too long. Keeping these foods cool extends their life.

3939 24th Street (between Noe and Sanchez), San Francisco
Tel: 282-9500
Open daily 9 a.m. to 8 p.m.
Credit cards: MC, V

MEAT AND POULTRY

VIGLIZZO'S MEATS

See Tower Market listing, page 256.

CHEESE

24TH STREET CHEESE COMPANY

There are only a handful of noteworthy cheese shops in the Bay Area, and this is one of them. You can taste anything, and the range is extensive. You might find some tangy Pyrenees goat milk cheese set out on the counter, a lusciously runny rice flour-coated teleme (very fresh in flavor, but it must be eaten quickly), a whole table of Cheddars or a *pavé d'affinois*, a small cube of soft cheese encased in rind. Half the price of the *pavé d'affinois* from Paris's Androuët sold at The Cheese Board in Berkeley or at Real Food on Polk Street, 24th Street's brand, unfortunately, does not deliver the same pleasure. When I discussed this with the counterman, he said that Androuët cheeses were simply too expensive for his clientele. This store may be price-conscious, but the staff is meticulous in keeping and cutting the cheeses.

3893 24th Street (at Sanchez), San Francisco
Tel: 821-6658
Open Monday through Friday 10 a.m. to 7 p.m., Saturday until 6 p.m., Sunday 10 a.m. to 5 p.m.
Credit cards: MC, V

All the merchandise looks appealing and fresh displayed on wooden counters, casks, and shelves. A worn wooden floor only adds atmosphere. A long-time ingredient resource in Noe Valley, this cheese store also carries Molinari salami, lots of olives, crackers, Acme bread, bread sticks, and wine—practically anything you might need for an Italian lunch.

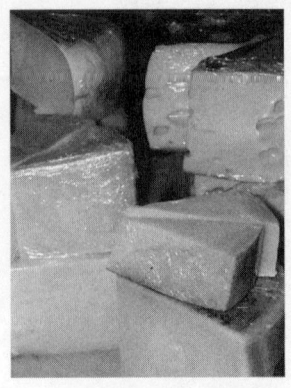

WINE AND LIQUOR SHOPS

CARUSO'S

4011 24th Street (at Noe),
San Francisco
Tel: 282-3841
Open daily 10 a.m. to 9 p.m.
Credit cards: AE, D, MC, V

When you can walk into a wine store and come away with a bag full of surprisingly delicious bottles for under $10 each, you know you have struck gold. The owners of Caruso's specialize in reasonably priced imports, and I must say that they have come up with some extraordinary wines for the price. The inventory changes often so you have to depend on their recommendations, but recently they sent me home with a soft, full, remarkably tasty red from Corbières that went smashingly with Indian food, and a Portuguese red of such distinction that it could have sold for twice as much with a different label. If you want to stock up on these kinds of everyday wines, Caruso's is well worth a trip from across town. The store also carries aged rums from Nicaragua, Haiti, and Martinique, single-malt Scotches, and limoncello, a lemon-infused spirit from the Amalfi coast that is all the rage in Northern Italy. The two owners are perpetually on a search for a moderately priced Sauterne.

CASTRO VILLAGE WINE COMPANY

The neatly displayed wines in this twenty-one-year-old pioneering shop all come from California. Though the selection is not as deep or interesting as at the California Wine Merchant in the Marina, the gracious clerks will spend as much time as you like trying to fit you with the best bottle for the occasion. This is a spot to find some of the most elegant California Cabernets and French-style blends.

4121 19th Street (between Castro and Collingwood), San Francisco
Tel: 864-4411
Open Monday through Thursday 11 a.m. to 7 p.m., Friday and Saturday until 8 p.m., Sunday noon to 7 p.m.
Credit cards: AE, MC, V

COOKWARE AND BOOKS

CLIFF'S HARDWARE

Cliff's Hardware has a huge housewares section featuring coffee and espresso makers, Trident knives, peppermills, water filters, old-fashioned wooden ice cream makers, cast-iron skillets in hard-to-find shapes and sizes, as well as a wide range of the ever-popular Revere Ware pots and pans (stainless steel with copper bottoms): the bread and butter of outfitting a kitchen. To meet the entertainment needs of its immediate community, Cliff's stocks coolers from small to gigantic, barbecuing equipment including Webers, fire starters, charcoal, wood chips, and many outdoor serving accessories that you never knew you needed until you saw them. Though prices are not cheap, the convenience of shopping in a neighborhood counts for a lot.

479 Castro Street (at 18th Street), San Francisco
Tel: 431-5365
Open Monday through Saturday 9:30 a.m. to 8 p.m.
Credit cards: AE, CB, MC, V

ECHO

This refined garden and housewares store on a block of 24th Street closer to Mission than Castro with a refreshingly clean esthetic, gets better and better every time I visit. Stocked with only wonderful things—huge solid-colored cotton napkins, floral print tablecloths, beeswax candles, terra-cotta pots in beautiful shapes for plants, pounded

3775 24th Street (between Church and Dolores), San Francisco
Tel: 282-3330
Open Monday through Friday 11 a.m. to 7 p.m.,

Saturday 10 a.m. to 6 p.m., Sunday noon to 5 p.m.
Credit cards: AE, MC, V

metal bowls, pot racks, lyrical ceramic platters and pitchers —each item is displayed so you can understand its beauty. Prices are refreshingly reasonable, a confirmation that taste, design, and context can mean more than cost.

LEHR'S GERMAN SPECIALTIES

1581 Church Street (at 28th Street),
San Francisco
Tel: 282-6803
Open Monday through Saturday 10 a.m. to 6 p.m., Sunday noon to 6 p.m.
Credit cards: MC, V

A German cultural-necessities store, Lehr's carries everything from German cleaning supplies to liverwurst. The inventory includes some handsome two-toned horsehair brushes with wooden handles for sweeping up crumbs, and tubes of concentrated traveling detergent for $7.95 each. (I was tempted to buy one for my husband who does a wash every day on the road, even though he packs a full complement of underwear.) A large assortment of German baking pans ranges from miniature to party size. I was drawn to some patterned springform bundt pans. You can find old-fashioned potato ricers and handy spaetzle makers, which solves the mystery of how these tiny noodle dumplings are made. The gadget is just a large-holed grater with a slide over it that pushes the dough through. Often seeing the right instrument to make a dish inspires me to cook it. Several long aisles are dedicated to candy and chocolates including Lindt and liquor-filled Asbach Uralt, a favorite among those who like a shot of brandy with their sweet. Elaborate beer steins fill the front window. The pretty woman with a sexy German accent behind the counter will be happy to show them to you as she hums along to Aretha Franklin on the radio.

North Beach

NORTH BEACH

Restaurants:
1. Cafe Jacqueline   267
2. Cho-Cho   268
3. Enrico's Sidewalk Cafe   268
4. Helmand   270
5. The House   271
6. Il Pollaio   271
7. Julius' Castle   272
8. La Felce   272
9. Little Joe's   273
10. Lo Coco's   274
11. L'Osteria del Forno   275
12. Moose's   276
13. Mo's   278
14. Ristorante Ideale   278
15. Rose Pistola   279
16. San Francisco Art Institute Cafe   280
17. Tommaso's   281
18. Zax   282

Cafes:
19. Caffè Freddy's   283
20. Caffè Greco   284
21. Caffè Roma Coffee Roasting Company   285
22. Caffè Trieste   285
23. Mario's Bohemian Cigar Store   285

Bars:
24. Gino and Carlo's   287
25. The Saloon   287
26. Savoy Tivoli   287
27. Specs'   287
28. Tosca   288
29. Vesuvio   288

Delicatessens/Take-Out:
30. Florence Italian Deli and Ravioli Factory   289
31. Golden Boy   289
32. Molinari   290
33. North Beach Pizza   290
34. Panelli Brothers   292
35. Prudente & Company   292

Bakeries/Pastries:
36. Danilo   293
37. Liguria   294
38. Stella   294
39. Victoria   295

Ice Cream/Chocolates:
40. Gelato Classico   295

Markets:
41. The Nature Stop   296
42. Rossi Market   296

Meat and Poultry:
43. Little City   297

Wines and Spirits:
44. Coit Liquors   297

Cookware and Books:
45. Biordi   298
46. Columbus Cutlery   299
47. Figoni Hardware   299

RESTAURANTS

CAFE JACQUELINE

Jacqueline Margulis, the sole owner and chef at this very French neighborhood bistro, is the queen of the soufflé. In fact, that's pretty much all she has been serving for the last fifteen years: tall, airy, crusty-topped, aromatic soufflés with sensuous, creamy interiors. The alluring aromas of baking cheese and garlic and the warmth from the ovens enfold you as you walk in the door of this small restaurant, its steamy front windows framed in lace curtains. Each white-linen-covered table sports a fresh rose, heavy silverware, thin wineglasses, and huge napkins. High ceilings, worn wooden floors, original wainscoting, and shaded wall sconces bring back visions of pre-Earthquake San Francisco. Both the cooking and the surroundings at Jacqueline are timeless.

1454 Grant Avenue
(between Union and Green),
San Francisco
Tel: 981-5565
Open Wednesday through
Sunday 5:30 to 11 p.m.
Price: Moderate
Credit cards:
 AE, CB, DC, D, MC, V

You start with a salad of butter lettuce or watercress dressed in a traditional mustard vinaigrette. Baskets of warm, crusty baguettes with sweet butter tide you over until your soufflé finally emerges from the kitchen. In the winter I make a special visit for Jacqueline's magnificent black truffle soufflé made from eggs that have been stored with the truffles (so the truffles' aroma permeates the shells), Gruyère, and lots of slivered fresh truffles. The $50 soufflé, plenty for two and fine for three, becomes affordable when shared and worth every penny. Her wild mushroom soufflés, textured with roughly chopped morels, boletes, and chanterelles ($30), are also worth a detour. Less lavish, but very savory, are her prosciutto and domestic mushroom, and garlicky broccoli and cheese soufflés, which cost around $20.

Whatever you order remember to specify that you want your soufflé runny in the middle. Otherwise, they come baked all the way through and lose their charm. For some reason Jacqueline thinks that Americans want them cooked airy and dry.

If you ever go out for dessert, come here for a spectacular chocolate soufflé. Jacqueline uses tons of dark, rich chocolate, turning the center into a creamy, intense chocolate pudding. It's one of the best chocolate desserts in the city.

CHO-CHO

1020 Kearny Street (between Pacific and Broadway), San Francisco
Tel: 397-3066
Open for lunch Monday through Friday 11:45 a.m. to 2 p.m.; dinner Monday through Saturday 5:45 to 10 p.m.
Price: Moderate
Credit cards: AE, MC, V

This fixture on the edge of the Financial District has been serving impeccable *tempura* from a *tempura* bar, sukiyaki in the upstairs dining room, and *shabu-shabu* in the downstairs dining room for as long as I can remember. Built to look like a Japanese country inn, the upstairs room has heavy, rough-hewn wooden tables with griddles inset in the middle. The surrounding benches are softened with cushions in Japanese cotton. Blue and white banners and ancient baskets decorate the walls. Groups can spend an evening up here in relative privacy, sizzling their meal on the griddle and chatting away. Downstairs, there are burners instead of griddles for the broth-based *shabu-shabu*. Many people stop in after work for a martini or a jar of sake and some lacy *tempura* cooked piece by piece by the chef behind the *tempura* bar, waiting to hear what you want next: an oyster mushroom, a *Chihuahuas* leaf, the delicate tail of a small sole, a strip of pasilla pepper. Cho-Cho is one of the those places that has not changed a bit since it opened decades ago, and is the better for it.

ENRICO'S SIDEWALK CAFE

504 Broadway (at Kearny), San Francisco
Tel: 982-6223
Open Sunday through Thursday noon to 11 p.m.,

Everyone in the city eventually gravitates to Enrico's, the raffish, historic cafe on Broadway with prime outdoor seating, now owned by Rick Hackett, Meredith Melville, and Mark McLeod, formerly of Oliveto, Chez Panisse, and Bay Wolf, respectively. They pumped a lot of money into the kitchen and the decor, making the inside as exciting as the outside patio, and they raised the quality of the menu, bar, and wine list at least 100 percent. Now Enrico's stands on its own as a top-notch restaurant as well as a coffeehouse, bar, and live-music venue.

At lunch at a table outside you'll undoubtedly see some of the old crowd of pols, writers, lawyers, and North Beach denizens munching on golden-crusted pizzas, Tuscan soups, al dente spaghetti with seafood, and Caesar salads. In the afternoon the coffeehouse crowd drops by for excellent espresso and imaginative desserts: ice creams and *sorbetti* made with seasonal fruits; a luscious tiramisù layered in a goblet; melt-in-your-mouth black satin fudge cake; banana-rum crème brûlée.

At dinner chef Hackett comes up with all sorts of lively turns on traditional dishes, like a soup of all sorts of fresh beans and vegetables topped with grilled salmon and drizzled with a pesto of basil, garlic, and olive oil; a duck breast with sour cherry sauce served over mashed potatoes and wilted spinach; or grilled sea bass with a spicy Mexican tomato sauce and sautéed sweet corn.

At all hours people order from Hackett's innovative tapas menu, a world beat selection of very imaginative small dishes that turn traditional tapas on end. The latest crop includes a crab brandade, tuna tartar, bruschetta with smoked salmon and cucumber marmalade, crispy fried oysters with aïoli, braised Catalan-style tripe, and more. I've sampled lots of them and have always been intrigued and delighted. Hackett has the ability to make odd-sounding combinations work. The less adventuresome can always fall back on Enrico's juicy Niman-Schell hamburgers on focaccia with fries and house-made condiments.

Some of the best modern music ensembles on the West Coast play here nightly without a cover charge. Everyone loves this San Francisco venue and wants to support it. The bar stays open until 2 a.m. every night, and many's the time I've dropped in for an espresso or a glass of Cognac on the way home from a night out and wished that I'd spent my whole evening there.

Friday and Saturday until midnight; bar until 2 a.m. every night
Price: Moderate
Credit cards: AE, D, MC, V

HELMAND

430 Broadway (between
Kearny and Montgomery),
San Francisco
Tel: 362-0641
Open Sunday through
Thursday
5:30 to 10 p.m.,
Friday and Saturday
until 11 p.m.
Price: Inexpensive
Credit cards: AE, MC, V

The Bay Area boasts so many different ethnic restaurants that it's hard to get excited about one more, but Helmand, a formally appointed Afghan dinner house, rises above exoticism to take its place as one of the best restaurants in San Francisco of any nationality. Afghan cooking draws on Persian, Indian, and Middle Eastern flavors, but the food at Helmand is immediately appealing to Western palates. Start with *aushak,* large, tender ravioli filled with sautéed leeks and topped with a mild, buttery meat sauce, served on a bed of yogurt speckled with fresh mint; or *kaddo borawni,* pumpkin that has been deep-fried, roasted, then sauced with garlic-scented yogurt, achieving a melting texture. Another permutation on pasta, a dish called *mantwo,* fills house-made noodles with braised onions and chopped beef, topping them with a delicious sauce of carrots and slightly al dente yellow split peas. All these appetizers are so yummy you want to make a meal out of them alone—until you taste the soups at Helmand, which are served in huge bowls with just a ladleful at the bottom. Try *aush,* a liquid version of addictive ravioli-like *aushak.* Here, thin noodles come in a minted yogurt soup drizzled with the buttery meat sauce. Another warm yogurt soup, *mashawa,* is thick with legumes—mung beans, chickpeas, black-eyed peas—and chunks of beef, a meal in itself.

Several excellent main courses feature lamb in different cuts accompanied with light, airy rice pilaf seasoned with cumin seed and cinnamon. Try *koufta callow,* large soft meatballs in hot cinnamon-scented tomato sauce, or *dwopiaza,* medium-rare lamb kabobs sauced with vinegared onions and yellow split peas on a square of flat bread that soaks up all the juices.

Desserts may seem the most exotic dishes of all, but a cardamom-scented basmati rice pudding, or *burfee,* an ice cream made from reduced milk and served in a sundae glass filled with frozen clotted cream, are well worth trying.

The long, narrow dining room is decorated with polished antique cabinets with glass doors displaying bowls of colorful ground spices and Afghan artifacts. The brick walls, carpeting, soft light, and tablecloths give the room a dressy look belying the amazingly inexpensive prices. The intelligent and attentive service would be welcome in restaurants that charge three times as much.

THE HOUSE

This is the original restaurant of a young husband-and-wife team, Angela and Larry Tse. With its success, they have opened a larger and more dramatic House in the Sunset. The casual North Beach outpost continues to turn out light, colorful, fresh preparations that combine Asian and Western ingredients and techniques with an underlying dedication to freshness—daily shopping in nearby Chinatown for beautiful fish and good-looking produce with some stops at non-ethnic produce markets as well. The food is seriously good. Try the house Caesar salad in a creamy, not too strong dressing that lends itself to the little bits of warm grilled tuna tossed in it, or a Chinese chicken salad of shredded vegetables and juicy hot chicken breast.

The room feels a bit austere in its modernity, especially in contrast to the resonant North Beach spots around it, but this House begins to feel like home when you dig into the clean, tasty food, reasonable enough in price to eat every day.

1230 Grant Avenue
(near Columbus),
San Francisco
Tel: 986-8612
Open for lunch Tuesday
through Saturday 11:30 a.m.
to 3 p.m.; dinner Tuesday
through Thursday 5:30 to
10 p.m., Friday and
Saturday until 11 p.m.
Price: Moderate
Credit cards: AE, MC, V

IL POLLAIO

One of my favorite neighborhood hangouts, Il Pollaio does one thing and does it perfectly: chicken. Small chickens with large bones are lightly marinated and grilled over hot rocks, and always come off the fire clean-flavored, juicy, and hot. Silver-haired Jose, the Argentine-Italian owner-griller, never cooks in advance. Served with a mixed salad of crisp, shredded cabbage, carrots, shell beans, and chopped lettuce in a tangy Italian dressing, the half-chicken combo always satisfies. The few other items on the menu, tasty Italian sausage made especially for Il Pollaio; a satiny, cold, marinated eggplant antipasto; and fortifying house-made lentil, split pea, or minestrone soups, one offered each day, are also impeccable. The pleasant little dining room, always full,

555 Columbus Avenue
(between Union and Green),
San Francisco
Tel: 362-7727
Open Monday through
Saturday 11:30 a.m. to 9 p.m.
Price: Inexpensive
Credit cards: MC, V

looks onto the passing parade on Columbus Avenue, and smiling Jose knows practically every nontourist who walks in or by the door. Much Italian is spoken here over many bottles of wine.

You can call ahead for take-out or be buoyed by the cheerful scene in this popular spot while you eat. Everyone in North Beach considers Il Pollaio an essential resource.

JULIUS' CASTLE

1541 Montgomery Street (at Union), San Francisco
Tel: 392-2222
Open daily 5 to 10 p.m.
Price: Expensive
Credit cards: AE, DC, MC, V

This romantic restaurant, hidden away on Telegraph Hill, has been given a gentle face-lift by owner Jeffrey Pollock and a new menu. In its newly polished incarnation with a fashionable open kitchen discreetly tucked away at the back of the larger of two resplendent Victorian dining rooms (so as not to obscure the sweeping views of the bay), people dine on delicious main-course lobster salads, roasted sea bass in a horseradish crust on a big mound of mashed potatoes, elegant veal carpaccio, and tuna tartar on toasts with celery root salad. Some of the meat dishes, though generous to a fault, arrive at the table tepid and juiceless, as if they've been held. The wine list is long and pricey; the service first rate. The main reason to go here is for the view, the romantic setting, and the sense of place. Besides the vegetarian Greens at Fort Mason, Julius' Castle is your best bet for fine dining with a view in San Francisco.

LA FELCE

1570 Stockton Street (at Union), San Francisco
Tel: 392-8321
Open for lunch weekdays (except Tuesday) 11:30 a.m. to 2 p.m.; dinner Wednesday through Monday 5:30 to 10 p.m.
Price: Inexpensive
Credit cards: AE, DC, MC, V

At one time, North Beach was considered a mecca for family-style dining in the city, as it was full of restaurants that served copious antipasti of sliced meats and canned beans, tureens of good minestrone, pasta in various forms in tomato sauce, then big platters of sliced meat or roast chicken followed by neon green and pink spumoni. Though their number—and quality—has diminished, La Felce, which opened in 1974, continues on in fine form, pretty much serving this classic fare with interesting variations. The soup might be a full-bodied chicken stock laced with hundreds of white dots of pasta into which you sprinkle grated Parmesan. A meaty baked lasagne might be the pasta of the night, and chicken cacciatore, in a lively sauce made with tomatoes, mushrooms, green peppers, and onions that have cooked down to a puree, the star main course. An a la carte salad Macedonia, a platter of sliced tomatoes layered with transparently thin onion slices, anchovies, and fresh parsley in an excellent vinaigrette, is worth sharing. Though the menu will sound familiar, a broader range of entrees to choose from is offered and the food is alive, prepared with fresh ingredients and a sure hand. I like the white tablecloths and cheery ambiance of the dining room, a departure from the utilitarian linoleum decor of many North Beach family-style restaurants.

LITTLE JOE'S

About thirteen years ago, Little Joe's moved from its cramped quarters around the corner on Columbus to its current mural-festooned dining hall on Broadway. Despite the fall of several venerable businesses nearby, Little Joe's has been going strong ever since. Little Joe's belongs to the colorful San Francisco genre of eateries characterized by noisy, flame-throwing, open cooking lines cranking out huge plates of North Beach/Italian food for cheap, which has assured this dining hall a place in every guidebook as well as in the hearts of thrifty Bay Area diners. Besides getting a lot to eat for the price, people love Little Joe's raffish spirit and family-style atmosphere. Be prepared to share a long table with other groups.

523 Broadway (between Columbus and Kearny), San Francisco
Tel: 433-4343
Open Monday through Thursday 11 a.m. to 10:30 p.m., Friday and Saturday until 11 p.m., Sunday noon to 10:30 p.m.
Price: Inexpensive
Credit Cards: AE MC, V

The regulars know to order chicken livers and onion sauté (be sure to order them pink) in red wine and tomato sauce; calamari sauté finished off with a great deal of garlic, white wine, and tomato sauce; and Little Joe's famous *caciucco*, a fish stew of squid, snapper, clams, and mussels in a broth of red wine, tomatoes, and lots of garlic—well, you get the idea. Garlic, wine, and tomato sauce are the holy trinity here. True aficionados grab a counter seat for platters of beef tongue in a piquant, relishlike green sauce, or order the daily special, usually many slices of roast veal in a brown gravy. With your entree you get a huge portion of fresh cauliflower, zucchini, carrots, and chard, or sides of precooked spaghetti in a muddy meat sauce. For a slight surcharge, the accompaniment can be heavy ravioli stuffed with something akin to library paste. Bottles of decent Chianti at excellent prices will greatly enhance the meal if you can somehow catch the eye of a gum-chewing, T-shirted waitress to order some. They like to keep it simple by bringing carafes of dirt-cheap house red and white. (Service is hardly a high point.) However, piles of just-baked and delivered San Francisco sourdough and butter are liberally supplied. People come here for the refreshing grittiness of the place anyway.

LO COCO'S

510 Union Street (between Grant and Stockton), San Francisco
Tel: 296-9151
Open Tuesday through Thursday 5 to 10 p.m., Friday and Saturday until 11 p.m., Sunday 4 to 10 p.m.
Price: Moderate
Credit Cards: MC, V

The eponymously named Lo Coco's is one of the few pizza and pasta places in North Beach that serves authentic Sicilian food. The chef-owner, Giovanni Lo Coco, a true Sicilian, is not shy about putting some of his island's most soulful dishes on the menu. This is the place to order *mezza zita alla Norma*, tubes of hard durum-wheat pasta imported from Italy, tossed with tomatoes, eggplant velvety with olive oil, and lots of garlic: the very essence of Sicily. For those who have acquired the taste, the famous Sicilian *pasta con sarde* is made much the same way it has been for the past thousand years. The combination of saffron-infused curly spaghetti tossed with sardines, anchovies, licoricey fennel tops, pine nuts, currants, and bread crumbs resonates all the way from the Middle Ages. More familiar is Lo Coco's version of spaghetti with meatballs, in this case pasta tubes in a tasty Naples-style tomato sauce with two large, soft, fine-textured meatballs studded with currants and toasted pine nuts.

Demonstrating his versatility, Lo Coco makes two Tuscan pastas with equal finesse: capellini with fresh tomato sauce and lots of nutty arugula; and the classic capellini dressed only with toasted garlic, olive oil, and lots of freshly ground black pepper.

His individual pizzas are distinctive for their rich, almost flaky crusts. The Neapolitan, paved with paper-thin slices of mushroom, is my favorite. The pepperoni pizza comes scattered with green onions, an inspired touch. Whatever topping you order, the thin, yeasty crusts are a main attraction. Starters include a couple of unique salads: *insalata emancipata*, which somehow brings together currants, blue cheese, pecans, olives, and romaine and a simple vinaigrette to good effect; and a large platter of arugula, endive, radicchio, and fennel scattered with tiny black olives. The classic presentation of ripe melon and prosciutto is always appealing during melon season. Save room for lovely house-made cannoli filled with ricotta sweetened with bits of the preserved dark cherries called *amarone*. These wonderful imported cherries in liqueur also turn vanilla ice cream into a fantastic Italian sundae. The small Italian wine list is a bit pricey, but the bottles are interesting and include several refreshing wines from Sicily.

Customers can see the small open kitchen from the red brick dining room, which has terra-cotta floors and front windows that slide open completely. On warm North Beach evenings, you feel like you are eating on the Mediterranean, especially since some of the waiters don't speak English.

L'OSTERIA DEL FORNO

This little hole-in-the-wall serves authentic and tasty food by keeping its menu tiny and specializing in dishes from the brick-lined oven. The two Italian women who own L'Osteria have attracted a wildly loyal and appreciative following, including my kid Harry, and his parents never complain when he gets his way on this one. We do wrestle over the fingers of crunchy, thin focaccia for which L'Osteria is famous, brought warm from the oven in little baskets during the meal, until Harry moves on to a slice of very thin-crusted pizza, nicely coated with melted mozzarella, good tomato sauce, and tiny balls of Italian sausage. It's also my favorite thin-crust pizza and sometimes the boy has to protect it from being nibbled away by you-know-who. We start with a couple of antipasti: roasted onions sprinkled with bread crumbs; roasted red peppers in olive oil; tissue-thin *speck* (Italian smoked ham); or *bresaola* with arugula salad and another favorite, canned tuna and white bean salad (see recipe, page 277), a version superior to any I've tasted. I always get a plate of paper-thin sliced roast pork cooked in milk, a traditional method that forms the sublime brown curds that are scattered over the meat. The pork comes with roasted sweet and white potatoes lightly seasoned with herbs—a dish that must be served in heaven. Each day brings one pasta, like house-

519 Columbus Avenue (between Green and Union), San Francisco
Tel: 982-1124
Open Wednesday through Monday 11:30 a.m. to 10 p.m.
Price: Inexpensive
No credit cards

made green ravioli, tender and light, stuffed with ricotta and sauced in a sprightly marinara; or a ramekin of baked rigatoni in a luscious slightly creamy beef and tomato sauce. The women at L'Osteria make one of the best cups of espresso in town—comparable to Caffè Greco's—so I always end with one, then another tiny cup of coffee (very full-flavored, aromatic, almost syrupy, without a hint of bitterness) served with a *biscotto*. A choice of three or four Italian wines, all inexpensive, by the glass or bottle, completes the experience. (I wish there were a few more interesting bottles.) Only eight tables have been squeezed into the tiny storefront, with several stuck into alcoves by the front windows. Every six months or so the women upgrade a bit—paint the walls, improve the lighting, change the color of the tablecloths under the glass-topped tables—but prices stay amazingly low, and everyone understands that any change in scale could ruin the magic.

MOOSE'S

1652 Stockton Street
(between Union and
Filbert), San Francisco
Tel: 989-7800
Open Monday through
Thursday 11:30 a.m. to
11 p.m., Friday and
Saturday until midnight,
Sunday 9:30 a.m. to 11 p.m.;
Sunday brunch
9:30 a.m. to 3 p.m.
Price: Moderate
Credit cards: AE, DC, MC, V

Publican Ed Moose, the beloved former owner of the Washington Square Bar and Grill across the park, has figured out how to provide everything any self-respecting North Beach schmoozer could want: a lively bar with two video monitors tuned to timely sporting events; friendly bartenders with impressive memories (once you order a special drink or even ask for something the bar doesn't stock, it will be there the next time you come in); a big, open, grand cafe-style dining room with front windows that open on the park; a jazz combo in the evenings; and a menu of stylish California bistro dishes. Since opening three years ago, Moose's has run through a number of chefs, but each has been conscientious about using fresh ingredients and turning out handsome, generous plates at decent prices. A contingent of old-timers will only order the thick Mooseburger, but you can also get the likes of porcini carpaccio with preserved Meyer lemon vinaigrette, grilled salmon on a bed of sliced celery root in a lobster broth, or Ed's famous gigantic veal chop with seasonal accompaniments. The food under current chef Fabrice Canelle, a Frenchman, can get a bit complicated—

INSALATA RUSTICA L'OSTERIA

This is the best canned tuna salad you'll ever taste. You can get canned cannellini beans at any Italian delicatessen. Fresh shell beans make this preparation superb, and cooked dried cannellini beans are also wonderful, but if you want something fast and really good, use canned. The ratio of beans to tuna is about equal.

Drain the canned cannellini beans, if using. Rinse and drain well, again. Drain the tuna. In a serving bowl, combine the beans and tuna. Add the celery, oregano, and onion.

In a bowl, mix the balsamic vinegar with the salt and pepper. Whisk in the olive oil. Pour over the beans and tuna and mix gently. Taste for salt.

Serve with Italian bread.

Serves 4 as an appetizer

One 20-ounce can cannellini beans, or 2 cups cooked cannellini beans
One 6-ounce can tuna, packed in water
1/2 cup chopped celery
1/2 teaspoon minced fresh oregano
1/2 cup thinly sliced red onion
2 tablespoons balsamic vinegar
1/2 teaspoon kosher salt
Freshly ground pepper to taste
7 tablespoons olive oil (L'Osteria uses Fortuna extra-virgin)

ingredients tend to be piled on—but the unifying theme of heartiness keeps the menu on track for a popular watering hole like this. I was particularly taken by dessert on a recent visit, a baked pear on top of a warm crouton of filo pastry subtly layered with Cambazola, a creamy blue cheese. I devoured it with a glass of Tria Late Harvest Carneros Pinot Noir 1994, an obscure (at least to me) red dessert wine that the menu recommended to go with the pear. The matchup was a lovely surprise.

Everyone who walks through the front door, whether they're part of the regular crowd or not, gets personal treatment. The attitude on the floor and at the door couldn't be more genuine, welcoming, friendly, infecting the entire restaurant with high spirits. People always have hung out at Ed Moose's place to drink and have a good time, but now they go there to eat as well.

MO'S

**1322 Grant Avenue
(between Vallejo and Green),
San Francisco
Tel: 788-3779
Open Monday through
Friday 11 a.m. to 10:30 p.m.,
weekends 9 a.m. to 11 p.m.
Price: Inexpensive
Credit Cards: MC, V**

You can see the grill man scooping up big handfuls of bright red freshly ground beef, gently forming them into patties, and placing them just so on a round revolving grill. All this happens in the front window of this immaculately clean and orderly hamburger joint strategically located within stumbling distance of Grant Avenue's premier saloons. I like Mo's meticulously prepared hamburgers on their unique soft-crusty buns smeared with mustardy house-made mayonnaise, any time of day. The crisp, skinny fries; thick milk shakes made the old-fashioned way in tall silver containers; and the spicy grilled chicken kabobs tucked into pita bread and seasoned with big spoonfuls of roughly chopped tomatoes, onions, and cilantro make Mo's a destination even if you're not in North Beach. The one drawback is the chilly decor, an attempt at high-tech design. The white tile, chrome, and black Formica under stark lighting give the small room all the warmth of a gym locker room. However, the counter seats with a view of the slim, efficient cook and his grill are just fine.

RISTORANTE IDEALE

**1309 Grant Avenue
(at Vallejo),
San Francisco
Tel: 391-4129
Open Tuesday through
Thursday 5:30 to 10:30 p.m.,
Friday and Saturday until
11 p.m., Sunday 5 to 10 p.m.
Price: Moderate
Credit cards: D, MC, V**

I like the Roman vibes in this North Beach Italian restaurant, very different from the old-fashioned Italian-American joints that line Columbus and your stomach with too much bitter garlic and canned tomato sauce. At Ideale, the regular-menu pastas take a thrilling, al dente, undersauced stance and come up sparkling. The daily specials, like luscious house-made ravioli filled with ricotta and spinach in a fresh tomato sauce aromatic with basil; or tender fettuccine in a creamy tomato sauce with big chunks of fresh lobster tail, demonstrate a subtler side of noodle cookery. I always order an antipasto of warm grilled vegetables, which includes my favorites, grilled radicchio and endive; and a satisfying classic version of carpaccio, scattered with shaved Parmesan, capers, arugula, and extra-virgin olive oil and lemon. The *arrosto misto*, a platter of succulent rosemary-perfumed grilled rabbit, a tiny lamb chop, and slices of pork loin with roasted potatoes and vegetables represents the star main course. For dessert, have shaved espresso ice with whipped cream or a coffee ice-cream cake. Ideale knows that to stay ideal the menu has to be small and controllable.

Ideale's location on one of the most picturesque blocks of Grant Street gives it added cachet. The double storefront has red tile floors, high ceilings, walls covered with wine racks, paintings, and mosaics; a spare, modern atmosphere with bohemian overtones. The Italian waiters and maître d' charm the pants off you when things are going well and lose it completely if the restaurant gets too busy.

ROSE PISTOLA

532 Columbus Avenue
(between Union and Green),
San Francisco
Tel: 399-0499
Open Sunday through Thursday 5:30 p.m. to midnight, Friday and Saturday until 1 a.m.
Price: Moderate
Credit cards: AE, MC, V

Reed Hearon, the wunderkind of San Francisco restauranting, severed working relationships with both LuLu and Cafe Marimba to concentrate on his own projects, the most noteworthy of which is the ebullient Rose Pistola. The restaurant stretches from Columbus Avenue to Stockton and uses every square inch of space, starting with outdoor tables under amazingly efficient heaters; a white-tiled bar area with tables; an open kitchen with wood-burning ovens, rotisseries, and grills; and two cordoned-off dining areas. The dining room on Stockton Street, tucked away under earthquake bracing, feels the most private. The place is perpetually packed for lunch and dinner, cocktails, and late-night snacks. Hearon's signature is to provide all levels of service with European style.

I personally use Rose Pistola as an Italian tapas bar because I love all the authentic antipasti served in small portions for a small price—things like cured swordfish; shaved artichokes with Parmesan; plates of fresh green fava beans in season with pecorino cheese; grilled sweet rabbit liver wrapped in pancetta on rosemary skewers; wood-oven-baked *farinata* (a pizza made of chickpea flour, topped with olives, sage leaves, and caramelized onions); a tender octopus salad. The bartenders have never failed on my favorite Harry's Bar cocktail (Punt e Mes and gin chilled in a martini shaker and strained into a martini glass), and the wine list offers a wealth of Italian and California bottles.

At a table I might move on to a buoyant cioppino made with fresh tomatoes and fish stock; some grilled quail; or a Florentine-style steak on the bone. And who can resist fried cream for dessert? This gives you a small idea of what Rose Pistola might be serving each day. I love the casual, family-style presentations, the unadorned plates, the incredible value. No one in town more inventively explores regional Italian cooking, the result of ardent traveling and research by Hearon. When I walk by Rose Pistola, I almost always find an excuse to drop in.

SAN FRANCISCO ART INSTITUTE CAFE

800 Chestnut Street
(at Jones),
San Francisco
Tel: 749-4567
Open Monday through
Thursday 8 a.m. to 9 p.m.,
Friday until 5 p.m., Saturday
9 a.m. to 2 p.m. Call ahead, as
hours vary during the year.
Price: Inexpensive
No credit cards

Looking for a great $5 lunch with one of the best views in San Francisco? Check out this funky cafe in a cement courtyard inhabited by outré art students, and take advantage of the wholesome cooking of Peter Stanwood, a first-rate cook with experience in well-known restaurants. The cafe offers two hot lunch specials each day, homey baked goods still warm from the oven, nicely dressed fresh salads, and thick made-to-order sandwiches. The portions are so large and prices so cheap that no art students starve around this institute.

The setting of the cafe comes as a spectacular surprise. You enter off Chestnut Street and walk through a tiled courtyard with a fountain. Emotive student art hangs in the arcade surrounding the courtyard and in public galleries to the left. Past these is a large, open plaza with expansive views of the bay and oversized concrete tables and benches. You forget about the utilitarian indoor seating when you gaze through glass walls at the grand vista.

I eat at the cafe often, but I bring my own plate and silverware for perfectly cooked sunny-side up eggs, bacon, crusty hash browns made from real potatoes, good coffee, and toasted bagels with cream cheese. (I can't eat eggs on paper plates with plastic utensils.) For lunch there may be a big blob of soft polenta covered with a southwestern black bean and vegetable stew or a meatball sandwich on Bread Workshop baguettes overflowing with sautéed red and green peppers, onions, and tomato sauce. Spicy red beans and rice, based on an old New Orleans recipe from photography teacher Pirkle Jones, or tasty Italian meatballs and spaghetti are perpetual favorites. The cafe makes hearty minestrone and excellent white bean and escarole soup.

The house bakers produce crumbly, plate-sized scones, chewy oatmeal-butterscotch bars, and large chocolate chip–peanut butter cookies that give Mrs. Field a run for her money, and the coffee cakes are most satisfying. Though the operation is casual, almost to the point of sloppiness, all the food tastes really good.

TOMMASO'S

Time stops when you step down into Tommaso's cavelike dining room with partitioned-off tables along the walls and a long communal table stretching down the middle of the dimly lit room. Nothing has changed in this pizzeria for decades, but that's the way the lines of people waiting to get in like it. They're enticed by the luscious smell of pizza baking in a wood-fired oven. Well before everyone else was cooking in wood-burning ovens, Tommaso's was turning out crisp, sweet, chewy-crusted pizzas scented with smoke and layered with copious amounts of whole-milk mozzarella. The aroma of the vegetarian pizza blanketed with green pepper, onions, fresh mushrooms, and olives really gets to me, though my all-time favorite is the super-deluxe pizza with mushrooms, peppers, ham, and Tommaso's allspice-scented Italian sausage. Ask them to hold the anchovies, which are too strong on this pizza (and I'm an anchovy lover). Tommaso's also makes a massive calzone stuffed with ricotta, mozzarella, prosciutto, and a special spice mixture, which all melt together in a happy way inside a crisp folded-over crust. For starters, order plates of peeled peppers, crisp whole green beans, and trees of broccoli all lightly dressed in lemon juice and olive oil. Though most people go for pizza, don't overlook an airy lasagne baked in the wood-fired oven. At prime meal hours expect a wait. Reservations are not taken.

1042 Kearny Street
(at Broadway),
San Francisco
Tel: 398-9696
Open Tuesday through
Saturday 5 to 10:45 p.m.,
Sunday 4 to 9:45 p.m.
Price: Inexpensive
Credit cards: MC, V

ZAX

2330 Taylor Street
(near Columbus),
San Francisco
Tel: 563-6266
Open Tuesday through
Saturday 5:30 to 10 p.m.
Price: Moderate
Credit cards: MC, V

A restaurant in a hidden-away location can be both a blessing and a curse. In the case of Zax, a small, handsome dining room lost behind an apartment building construction site on a part of Taylor near the cable car turn-around, the charm of discovery may not outweigh the disadvantages. If more people found the place they would be sitting down to dinner. Zax is one of the nicest new developments in North Beach and, in fact, the city, for diners who like sophisticated, ingredient-inspired dishes of a California-Mediterranean style at prices well below restaurants of similar quality.

The first courses and salads are absolutely stunning, as evidenced by a plate of romaine leaves scattered with anchovies, lemon, garlic, and romano cheese; a crusty, airy, goat-cheese soufflé with an apple, celery, and fennel salad; and a simple and beautiful pile of tiny field greens with caramelized walnuts. Main courses pair fresh fish like salmon, tuna, or sturgeon with lots of seasonal vegetables, vinaigrettes instead of sauces, and imaginative starches. A free-range chicken breast comes with morels and a potato pancake made of thin potato sticks. A chewy Niman-Schell flatiron steak is dressed up with spicy onion rings and sautéed spring greens. The menu of six starters, six main courses, and a handful of desserts changes monthly, drawing its energy from the fantastic variety of produce in the Bay Area. If you're a vegetable and salad lover you will rejoice at the way they are woven into the cooking at Zax.

The clean-lined, comfortable dining room with banquettes, a bar where single diners like to sit, and a revolving exhibit of photographs and paintings makes for a very hip scene. The staff and the two chef-partners who own the restaurant, veterans of a number of excellent San Francisco kitchens, want only to make customers feel at home; well served but relaxed. With such clean and stylish food at moderate prices Zax can be a place for a special night out or a regular spot, and is guaranteed by me to satisfy at either level.

CAFES

CAFFÈ FREDDY'S

Over the years Freddy's has become more of an eating place than a coffeehouse, albeit without a seriously equipped kitchen, but the casual food has a logic of its own dictated by the available cooking methods. The small countertop pizza oven, the kind used in cafes all over North Beach, allows for little pizzas with good prebaked crusts topped with interesting combinations like pancetta, new potatoes, mozzarella, hard-cooked egg slices, and spinach leaves (my favorite). Warm open-face sandwiches made on slices of polenta work nicely too, especially one topped with melted mozzarella, tomatoes, and an aromatic pesto accompanied with a crisp mélange of sliced cucumber and radishes in a red-wine vinaigrette. All the salads and vegetable antipasti use fresh seasonal produce and lively vinaigrettes. Well-made coffee, fresh cookies, and pastries brought in daily offer sustenance anytime in two sunny rooms, one filled with roomy booths, the other with small tables and a counter with stools. Oil paintings by David Bruce, the owner, decorate the walls, while the expansive plate-glass windows frame an urban composition of their own: a view of Lombard, Columbus, and crisscrossing cable cars.

901 Columbus Avenue
(at Lombard),
San Francisco
Tel: 922-0151
Open Tuesday through
Friday 11:30 a.m. to 10 p.m.,
Saturday and Sunday
10 a.m. to 10 p.m.
Credit cards: MC, V

CAFFÈ GRECO

423 Columbus Avenue
(between Vallejo and Green),
San Francisco
Tel: 397-6261
Open daily 7 a.m. to 11 p.m.
No credit cards

I live on Telegraph Hill because I like the European amenities of North Beach, and the place I walk down to the most is Caffè Greco, owned by Hanna Suleiman, who happens to be Lebanese. His coffee, made from Illy Espresso beans on a machine kept as finely tuned as a concert grand, has the depth, aroma, and body of the best coffee in Italy. Yes, Caffè Greco does offer the option of low-fat milk for its cappuccino and latte, and the portion of espresso does exceed the thimbleful of ambrosia you get in Italy, but Greco's coffee is always delicious. I particularly like a mixture of espresso and hot milk served in a little glass, which has been called at various times the Algerian or the Africano, stronger than a latte and without the bland foam of a cappuccino.

The smallish cafe has large sliding windows facing Columbus and a few tables on the street. The floor is so tightly packed with chairs and tables that you have to plot out a path before you make a move—especially with several cups of coffee in hand. You order at one end of a counter that holds baskets of fresh croissants and raisin rolls. A refrigerated glass section displays truffle cakes from the great Pasticeria Rulli (see page 512) and an exceptional house-made tiramisù from a special family recipe. Focaccia sandwiches accompanied with pickled Italian vegetables and a variety of antipasti are also available, but it is at prime coffee hours that the cafe is the fullest—in the morning, the afternoon, and late evening. The crowd is completely mixed—young, old, local, tourist, Asian, European—everyone who appreciates a great cup of coffee in a clean, well-lighted place.

CAFFÈ ROMA COFFEE ROASTING COMPANY

For other location, see page 410.

One of my favorite spots to sip a strong, creamy espresso is on the sunny bench in front of Caffè Roma Coffee Roasting Company, a coffee roastery and cafe run by the Caffè Roma people. Both the beans to take home and the espresso made in the cafe have extraordinary character and richness. Only coffee and a few biscotti are served here, but the coffee is so good that many folks regularly stop by for a quick shot.

526 Columbus Avenue
(between Green and Union),
San Francisco
Tel: 296-7942
Open Monday through Thursday 7 a.m. to 6 p.m., Friday and Saturday 8 a.m. to midnight, Sunday 8 a.m. to 10 p.m.
Credit cards: MC, V

CAFFÈ TRIESTE

I had a delicious, strong, creamy, not-bitter espresso here the other day and it took me by surprise. Consistency has not been a strong point at Trieste, though its scruffy regulars would wrestle me to the ground over this one. There may be new attention to coffee quality—certainly Trieste has stepped up its marketing of house-roasted coffee beans to restaurants and consumers. On the weekend afternoons when live opera singers hold forth, you can't get near the place. During the week, Trieste is the home of vestigial and nouveau beatniks who eye everyone who orders a cup of coffee as a potential soul mate. If you're in the mood, you can talk all afternoon.

601 Vallejo Street
(at Grant),
San Francisco
Tel: 392-6739
Open daily 6:30 a.m. to midnight
No credit cards

MARIO'S BOHEMIAN CIGAR STORE

People gravitate from all over town to little Mario's to eat delicious warm focaccia sandwiches straight from the miniature Baker's Pride pizza oven. They also come to drink coffee expertly made from Graffeo beans, or to drink a cold imported beer or a glass of wine. Seating is so close at this sardine can of a cafe that you cannot help but exchange a few words with the person next to you. I always find Mario's to be an exceptionally friendly, low-key spot. The people who frequent it tend to like eating, which means that attitude does not take precedence over humanity.

566 Columbus Avenue
(at Union),
San Francisco
Tel: 362-0536
Open Monday through Saturday 10 a.m. to midnight, Sunday until 11 p.m.
No credit cards

Mario's actually was a cigar store at one time, though Mario, Liliana, and son Paul Crismani have been running it for the last eighteen of its seventy-plus years as a coffeehouse with a counter and six or so tables. Windows that look across the street to Washington Square slide open on warm days, letting a breeze into the almost claustrophobic interior lined with photographs of beloved patrons.

Mario's luscious sandwiches are made on soft, olive oil–rich focaccia from nearby Liguria and Danilo bakeries, with rich, savory fillings like tender house-made meatballs in a buttery tomato sauce spiked with thinly sliced onions. Both the chicken and eggplant sandwiches use crisp, breaded cutlets, which are slipped into the focaccia with just the right amount of tomato sauce and melted mozzarella. On the lighter side, try a warm open-face tuna salad sandwich with melted cheese and onions, the best tuna melt in the world. A tumbler of Chianti with them does a world of good for the digestion. These are the kind of sandwiches that stay with you all day.

BARS

GINO AND CARLO'S

Just a bar with a couple of television sets, Gino and Carlo's belongs to the North Beach old-timers who have staked out a stool and like cheap booze, friendly talk, and no constraints on their habits, like smoking.

548 Green Street (between Columbus and Grant), San Francisco
Tel: 421-0896
Open daily 6 a.m. to 2 a.m.
No credit cards

THE SALOON

Junkies and ex-cons prefer the Saloon during the day; at night when local R & B bands play, passersby and everyone in the neighborhood stop in for a drink and a dance, pulled in by the music and the nostalgic beery, smoky Saloon breath that pours out the front door. Started in 1861, the Saloon's ancient bar and funky walls have seen it all.

1232 Grant Avenue (at Fresno near Vallejo), San Francisco
Tel: 989-7666
Open daily noon to 2 a.m.
No credit cards

SAVOY TIVOLI

The other great outdoor venue in North Beach along with Enrico's, Savoy Tivoli's patio attracts a young, cruising crowd that congregates on Grant Avenue every evening, leaving the Savoy's spacious indoor bar and cafe empty even on the coldest nights. The roar from the patio rivals the noise coming out of the biker bars down the street. People who hang here check out each other, plus everyone else who walks by on the narrow street.

1434 Grant Avenue (between Green and Union), San Francisco
Tel: 362-7023
Open Tuesday through Thursday 5 p.m. to 2 a.m., Friday through Sunday 3 p.m. to 2 a.m.
No credit cards

SPECS'

Artists, photographers, and merchant marines hang out at this historic seaman's bar with a worn wooden interior that looks like the hold of a ship. On any drinking tour of North Beach, Specs' is a required stop.

12 Saroyan Alley (off Columbus between Broadway and Pacific), San Francisco
Tel: 421-4112
Open weekdays 4:30 p.m. to 2 a.m., weekends 5:00 p.m. to 2 a.m.
No credit cards

TOSCA

242 Columbus Avenue
(between Pacific
and Broadway),
San Francisco
Tel: 391-1244
Open 5 p.m. to 2 a.m.
No credit cards

Jeannette Etheredge, proprietor of this beloved, seventy-eight-year-old North Beach bar, knows every ballet dancer, movie star, and filmmaker in this town and many others all over the world, and when any of them are in her neighborhood they drop by Tosca. The long bar, vaulted front windows, and antique espresso machine are just half the picture. Beyond lies a large room filled with booths and tables, plus another back room with a pool table where luminaries tend to hang out with their entourages, the setting for hundreds of arty, impromptu parties. Even if you're a nobody, you might enjoy a special house cappuccino served in a glass and composed of hot espresso, steamed milk, sugar, and brandy, guaranteed to warm you up on a cold summer night. A jukebox filled with arias competes with the pounding bass from a dance club in the same building.

VESUVIO

255 Columbus Avenue
(between Pacific
and Broadway),
San Francisco
Tel: 362-3370
Open daily 6 a.m. to 2 a.m.
No credit cards

This original beatnik bar next to City Lights bookstore has remained true to its founding spirit year after year. The walls are like a work in progress, full of scribblings, ever-changing photographs, and pieces of art. The upstairs mezzanine overlooking the historic conjunction of Columbus Avenue and Jack Kerouac Alley affords a choice view of North Beach shenanigans, and if you insist, the bartender will flick on a slide show that pays homage to James Joyce.

DELICATESSENS/TAKE-OUT

FLORENCE ITALIAN DELI AND RAVIOLI FACTORY

This deli stocks the essentials of the Italian larder at excellent prices, like three-liter tins of clean, neutral Fortuna Fontana Italian olive oil for cooking (the one with the colorful tiger on the front) and large cans of imported tomatoes. A case of *baccala*—salt cod—and a bin of polenta sit next to each other, suggesting some good winter fare. Beautiful olives, especially the green varieties, the superior oil-packed Columbus anchovies, and a good selection of Italian cheeses are located on the marble counter. Florence carries Reggiano and the even more aged, crumbly Parmesan called *rocca*. Try the runny local teleme with a rice flour crust. Florence has the best. Although this deli manufactures veal- and spinach-filled ravioli and sells them to many well-known restaurants around town, the best are made at Lucca on Chestnut.

1412 Stockton Street (at Vallejo), San Francisco
Tel: 421-6170
Open Monday through Saturday 7 a.m. to 6 p.m., Sunday 9 a.m. to 3 p.m.
Credit cards: AE, MC, V

GOLDEN BOY

They put the big sheet pans of hot, fragrant pizza right at nose level in the open front window, so when you walk by the smell practically grabs you. How can anyone resist eating a slice of pizza that has just come out of the oven? Golden Boy makes its pizzas on soft, olive oil–rich focaccia dough and slathers them with lots of stuff, so that one piled-up square slice makes a satisfying meal. I am partial to the vegetarian, heavily layered with the thinnest slices of zucchini, fresh tomato, olives, onions, and mushrooms, then drizzled with pesto, but if I don't want to wait for a reheat (and Golden Boy slices do reheat well in the countertop oven), I go for the pizza still warm from its first cooking, whatever it may be. I usually walk down the street eating the slice, trying not to dribble on my shirt, but for the more civilized, there is a high counter and stools plus a few boothlike tables in the back. Only pizza and beer, wine and espresso are sold here, and that's why the pizza stays so delicious, slice by slice, year after year.

542 Green Street (between Columbus and Grant), San Francisco
Tel: 982-9738
Open Sunday through Thursday 11:30 a.m. to 11:30 p.m., Friday and Saturday until 1:30 a.m.
No credit cards

MOLINARI

373 Columbus Avenue (at Vallejo), San Francisco
Tel: 421-2337
Open Monday through Friday 8 a.m. to 5:30 p.m., Saturday 7:30 a.m. to 5:30 p.m.
Credit cards: MC, V

The front window of this popular Italian deli is a mosaic made of tightly fitted-together imported tins, jars, and boxes of olive oil, biscotti, anchovies, olives, artichokes, peppers, pasta, polenta, and tomatoes. Just walking by makes my mouth water. Inside, the small, narrow store is similarly packed to the rafters with foodstuffs. Many a great sandwich has been composed around Molinari's spectacular, hot, red pepper–flecked salami. Behind the counter, Italian pickled peppers, marinated artichokes, mushrooms, red peppers, olives of every sort—all the stuff you need to construct a dream sandwich—await selection. Fresh mozzarella from Ferrante in Walnut Creek and imported buffalo milk mozzarella sit next to each other not far from handy two-ounce tins of Columbus anchovies. I like the frittata here, a cold cheese, spinach, and bread-crumb cake held together with eggs. The fresh sausages are excellent, vying with Prudente as the best in North Beach. The sweet Italian with fennel, which cooks up slightly pink in color, is out of this world and so are the tiny pure pork breakfast links. Any pantry ingredients called for in any Italian recipe, including imported Italian cheeses in good condition, can be found here.

NORTH BEACH PIZZA

1499 Grant Avenue (at Union) and 1310 Grant (at Vallejo), San Francisco
Tel: (both stores) 433-2444
Open Monday through Thursday 11 a.m. to 1 a.m., Friday and Saturday until 3 a.m., Sunday noon to 11 p.m.
Credit cards: AE, DC, D, MC, V

I mention the two North Beach Pizza parlors not so much for their sometimes soggy, extremely cheesy, often indifferently put together pizzas, but for the fact that they have an amazingly efficient call-in and delivery system that gets your pizza to your door hot and within forty-five minutes. North Beach pizza is a hundred times better than the chain-style pizzas, and this independent operation has figured out how to beat the chains at their own game.

A lot of people do love this thick, rich pizza and often line up outside the Union and Grant corner door to wait for a booth. (The branch down the block near Green stays full, but isn't as wildly popular.) When made well, the vegetarian pizza has a pleasant balance of savory and fresh vegetables that melt in the oven into pillows of cheese. So much cheese is piled on the pepperoni that it gets lost underneath.

Leo Rossi would cure his own pancetta with lots of sweet aromatic spices, such as allspice and cloves. His pancetta recipe is still used at Prudente and it really adds character to any dish. You can buy excellent rabbits from Bud Hoffman at the Ferry Plaza Farmers' Market on Saturdays (page 112) or Polarica, a wholesale-retail operation south of Market (page 241). This recipe comes from a Roman friend who made it for me when he was living in San Francisco. You should cook it a day before you want to serve it; the improvement is miraculous. This rabbit stew is delicious with polenta or flat noodles.

In a bowl large enough to hold the rabbit pieces, combine the marinade ingredients. Add the rabbits, cover, and refrigerate for at least 24 hours.

Drain the rabbit pieces, reserving the marinade, and pat them dry with paper towels.

In a large skillet over medium heat, heat 2 tablespoons olive oil and brown 2 or 3 pieces of rabbit. Discard the oil after browning and repeat with the remaining rabbit until all the pieces have been browned in fresh oil. Put the rabbit pieces in a bowl and reserve the pan juices to add to the sauce.

Put the remaining 2 tablespoons olive oil in a large, heavy pot or Dutch oven and cook the pancetta until it starts to color, about 5 minutes. Add the celery, carrots, and onions and cook over medium heat for 10 minutes. Add the tomatoes, rabbit, and reserved marinade and juices. Cover and simmer on top of the stove for 1 hour. Check the thinner pieces and remove if tender. Continue to cook the legs another 15 minutes, if necessary.

In a colander with a large bowl underneath, drain the rabbit and vegetables. Place the sauce back in the pot, spoon off the surface fat, bring to a boil, and cook to reduce by one third. Let cool. Add the rabbit and vegetables to the pot. Cover and refrigerate overnight.

Gently reheat and serve the next day, accompanied with pasta or polenta.

Serves 8

STEPHANO'S BRAISED RABBIT, ITALIAN STYLE

Marinade

1/4 cup olive oil

1 bottle decent dry red wine such as Chianti, Zinfandel, or Merlot

10 cloves

10 garlic cloves, minced

30 turns of a pepper grinder

1 cup green olives, pitted and chopped

Stew

2 rabbits cut into 8 pieces

5 to 8 tablespoons olive oil for browning, plus 2 tablespoons

1 cup diced pancetta (about 8 ounces or three 1/4-inch slices)

1 1/2 cups diced celery (about two large stalks)

2 cups diced peeled carrots (about three medium)

2 cups chopped onions (about two medium)

Two 28-ounce cans peeled Italian (plum) tomatoes, drained and roughly chopped

However, it takes only a few slices to fill you up, which is just what prompts all those young, hungry, budget-minded kids to cool their heels on the sidewalk.

PANELLI BROTHERS

1419 Stockton Street
(between Vallejo
and Card Alley),
San Francisco
Tel: 421-2541
Open Monday through
Saturday 7:30 a.m.
to 5:30 p.m., Sunday
8:30 a.m. to 2:30 p.m.
Credit cards: MC, V

I have gotten such fruity, buttery, nutty, tissue-thin slices of imported prosciutto from Parma at Panelli, I always buy it here. Panelli stocks the usual Italian staples, but shows particular strength as a *salumeria*, a place that sells a wide range of Italian-cured meats like *coppa*, a prosciutto-like cured pork roll; and *soppressata*, a peppery, coarsely ground salami. A large part of their operation is devoted to making sandwiches on soft Italian rolls from the freshly sliced meats, and the friendly deli men behind the counter show no end of patience and cheerfulness while you compose your masterpiece on the spot.

PRUDENTE & COMPANY

1462 Grant Avenue
(at Union),
San Francisco
Tel: 421-0757
Open Monday through
Saturday 9 a.m. to 7 p.m.,
Sunday until 5 p.m.
Credit cards: MC, V;
$15 minimum

Generous Leo Rossi, the oversized man who used to run this North Beach nexus of house-cured Italian pork and restaurant gossip, has retired but not before he taught the current owner some of his secrets. Though his house-cured prosciutto is no longer available, Prudente continues to use his recipe for curing pancetta, unsmoked bacon rolled with aromatic spices. Leo's pancetta is the key ingredient in many important dishes around town (see recipe for rabbit on page 291). The skin from the pancetta is parboiled and ground into a superb *coteghino*, a huge tied sausage used for cooking white beans, or as part of *bollito misto*. Prudente also makes Leo's Marsala-scented dried sausages, which are draped over a wood dowel in the side window next to burlap sacks of the largest white beans you'll ever see, grown and dried by a cousin of Leo's and of limited supply. Grab a pound or two when you see them. Prudente's coarsely ground fresh sausages—sweet Sicilian with fennel; hot, red pepper–laced

Calabrese; and my favorite, the garlicky Toscano—have an authentic, rustic, homemade quality about them. The dried Monterey jack coated in black pepper, and the oozy, rice flour–coated teleme, two of our oldest and most delightful Northern California cheeses, beckon from atop the long meat counter.

You never know what you'll find in or on the long glass counter to eat on the spot. Leo's ex-wife invented a mascarpone torta, terrines of Italian cream cheese layered with pesto, figs, or caviar, and the store still sells a lot of them. The little Cariani dry *salametti* hanging from hooks behind the counter can make the centerpiece of a picnic, and you can buy everything else you need right there—either separately or in made-to-order sandwiches.

BAKERIES/PASTRIES

DANILO

Bakeries that look just like Danilo are found all over Italy, with shelves full of hard Italian biscotti, hard toast for seafood soups, and crumbly Italian cookies. In back of the cookie counter are wooden shelves of baked breads, the most notable being the yeasted Italian corn bread, so popular that Danilo has started to bake it every day. (It's excellent toasted, buttered, and slathered with caviar.) Rounds of focaccia scattered with coarse salt and rosemary, green onions, or tomato sauce have a soft, olive-oily texture that appeals to kids. The grandmotherly Italian women behind the counter have a soft spot for children and often hand them a crisp, yard-long bread stick. I have never walked into Danilo without seeing an elderly man or woman peacefully sitting in the chair by the open door, carrying on a running conversation with the counter ladies and anyone else who walks in the door.

516 Green Street
(at Bannam),
San Francisco
Tel: 989-1806
Open daily
6:30 a.m. to 6:30 p.m.
No credit cards

LIGURIA

1700 Stockton Street (at Filbert), San Francisco
Tel: 421-3786
Open Monday through Friday 8 a.m. to 4 p.m. (earlier if sold out), Saturday 7 a.m. to 4 p.m., Sunday 7 a.m. until noon
No credit cards

A focaccia store kitty-corner from Washington Square, Liguria sells plain, tomato, or green onion–topped focaccia in big flat sheets, which they cut in half, wrap in waxed paper, and tie with string. If you don't get there before 11 a.m., there's a good chance that your focaccia of choice will be sold out. Not only does everyone in the neighborhood stop by for a square, but Liguria wholesales to lots of cafes who use the focaccia for warm sandwiches. PlumpJack, the restaurant off Union Street, came on the idea of using the tomato focaccia as a bun for hamburgers, thereby internalizing the catsup. Try it. It really works. Early in the morning you can smell the baking dough and see the golden sheets coming out of the huge brick ovens in the back. The singleness of purpose and the perfect consistency of their product make Liguria part of many people's regular North Beach ritual.

STELLA

446 Columbus Avenue (between Green and Vallejo), San Francisco
Tel: 986-2914
Open daily at 7:30 a.m.; closes Sunday and Monday at 6 p.m., Tuesday through Thursday 7 p.m., Friday 11 p.m., and Saturday midnight.
No credit cards

This tiny bakery specializes in *sacripantina*, an Italian cake made with soft, yellow layers soaked with Marsala, then filled and frosted with airy zabaglione enriched with whipped cream. Twenty years ago these molded cakes—juicy, boozy, and light, with a pleasant sherrylike flavor—used to be served in every Italian restaurant in town. Now, of course, restaurants have their own pastry departments, but they would do well to create a cake as good. I much prefer the original Stella *sacripantina* to some of the flavored ones that have slipped into the repertory since the bakery has taken to preparing single servings in clear plastic cups. Recently, one of these was soaked in orange liqueur, an unexpected and not welcome surprise. Be sure to ask for the original Marsala cake and buy a whole one rather than an individual serving if you want the proportions to be right. The whole cakes, which must be refrigerated, come in several sizes, the smallest quite workable for an intimate dinner party.

VICTORIA

Each bakery in North Beach has made its reputation on a certain cake. At Victoria, it's the St. Honore, a festive white-frosted cake rimmed with miniature custard-filled cream puffs. Inside, layers of crunchy Italian "leaf" pastry, custard, and rum-soaked cake make each sweet bite an adventure. Generations of families have celebrated special occasions with the St. Honore, which can be ordered ahead in many different sizes. The other specialties at Victoria are their molded refrigerator cakes: the *zuccotto*, a bright-red mound soaked in cherry liqueur with custard; my favorite, the Fantasia, a tasty conglomeration of soft cake, mocha cream, and shaved chocolate; and a cheesy tiramisù. All the cakes now come in single-serving sizes so you can try them before you commit to a larger cake. I also like the powdered sugar–dusted cornmeal pound cake, much lighter than a regular pound cake with a hint of grit. Sliced and toasted, buttered and spread with jam, or as a vehicle for macerated berries and whipped cream, the simple cornmeal pound cake is nothing if not versatile. I can see it as a base for your own Italian cake of custard, fruit, and liqueur.

1362 Stockton Street (at Vallejo),
San Francisco
Tel: 781-2015
Open Monday through Saturday 7 a.m. to 6 p.m., Sunday 8 a.m. to 5 p.m.
Credit cards: MC, V

ICE CREAM/CHOCOLATES

GELATO CLASSICO

For other locations see pages 173 and 386.

Lots of Italian ice cream shops have opened and closed, but Gelato Classico (with two other locations) thrives because it's the best. The ice creams taste natural, and the tricky creamy, thick texture has always been consistently maintained through proper storing and handling. This ice cream is so soft, it gets shoveled into little cups. I cannot pass the shop without stopping in for a *coppa mista*, a lovely mixture of chocolate, pistachio, vanilla, and rum-flavored ice

576 Union Street (between Stockton and Grant),
San Francisco
Tel: 391-6667
Open Monday through Thursday 11 a.m. to 11 p.m., Friday through Sunday until midnight
No credit cards

creams all swirled together. The true tropical fruit flavors—coconut, banana, mango—have been the base for a tropical fruit sundae I make at home layered with fresh pineapple, kiwi, papayas, toasted nuts, coconut, and whipped cream. The guys behind the counter at the North Beach store deserve a medal for patience and generosity; they proffer endless tastes and have a particular affection for children.

MARKETS

THE NATURE STOP

1336 Grant Avenue
(between Vallejo and Green),
San Francisco
Tel: 398-3810
Open Monday through
Friday 9 a.m. to 10 p.m.,
Saturday and Sunday
10 a.m. to 9 p.m.
Credit cards: AE, D, MC, V

I have watched this roomy Grant Street natural foods store upgrade its inventory over the years so that now it carries a growing variety of organic fruits in season, like white peaches and nectarines, berries, and melons, along with commercial fruits and vegetables. Metropolis and Semifreddi breads are delivered daily, and the full complement of bulk nuts, seeds, and grains from Sun Ridge Farms fills up a portion of the store. A smoothie bar at the entrance takes advantage of the plentiful tropical fruit by offering such delights as fresh mango or papaya yogurt drinks, thinned by fresh orange juice, swirled in the blender to order.

ROSSI MARKET

627 Vallejo Street
(at Columbus),
San Francisco
Tel: 986-1068
Open Monday through
Saturday 8 a.m. to 9 p.m.,
Sunday 9 a.m. to 7 p.m.
Credit cards: MC, V

One of a dying breed of relatively small neighborhood grocery stores, Rossi's serves a useful role in North Beach as a place to buy Italian vegetables. Rossi's produce section, though commercial, will have broccoli rabe, arugula, bulbs of fennel, large and small artichokes, Italian parsley, chard, cardoons, and other seasonal vegetables in varying condition. Small, difficult-to-find glass bottles of Italian olive oil of all grades along with large tins, imported dried pasta, lots of pickled Italian peppers, and Berkeley Farms dairy products make Rossi a resource. In the newspaper rack in front of the store, the *South China Morning Post* shares space with *Corriere della Sera,* British, and German newspapers, democratically covering all the bases.

MEAT AND POULTRY

LITTLE CITY

This Italian butcher shop specializes in veal shanks, baby beef liver, veal breast, and other favored Italian cuts. The friendly butchers will order anything they don't have, as well as cut and grind on the spot. Carlo Togni, my Roman friend who lives near Precita Park, travels all the way across town to buy his meat here—and to have an espresso at Greco—because the butchers understand what he needs for his meat sauces and roasts. Excellent fat-marbled boneless chuck roasts are always available, along with fresh pork tenderloin and meaty country-style pork ribs for American cooks. Little City carries Petaluma Poultry Producers chickens, which have excellent flavor and texture.

1400 Stockton Street
(at Vallejo),
San Francisco
Tel: 986-2601
Open Monday through
Friday 8 a.m. to 6 p.m.,
Saturday until 5:30 p.m.,
Credit cards: MC, V

WINE AND LIQUORS

COIT LIQUORS

This vital neighborhood liquor store carries a far-ranging selection of wine carefully chosen for value and quality. When the new Beaujolais arrives in the fall, Coit always has the one from the best producer. If a California wine from a small grower gets some media attention, Coit will get it and mark it up the least. The spirits inventory is complete and

585 Columbus Avenue
(at Union),
San Francisco
Tel: 986-4036
Open daily 9 a.m.
to midnight
Credit cards: MC, V

sophisticated while still catering to mass tastes. Many locals buy their cigarettes and lottery tickets at Coit, but this independent store aims to please a wider audience with excellent prices on some classy wines, knowledgeable service, and enlightened buying.

COOKWARE AND BOOKS

BIORDI

412 Columbus Avenue
(at Vallejo),
San Francisco
Tel: 392-8096
Open Monday through
Saturday 9:30 a.m. to 6 p.m.
Credit cards: AE, CB, DC, MC, V

I used to think the hand-painted Italian pottery in the window of Biordi was pretty hokey until I looked deeper into the store. At first I was shocked by the high prices; then I saw a hand-painted pasta bowl in the most elaborate and imaginative geometric design, every inch covered with brilliant color. I could imagine pears in it, spaghetti, or a green salad. I bit the bullet and bought it, as expensive as it was, and haven't regretted the purchase since. I use that flat bowl all the time, and when food isn't in it, I set it in the middle of the dining-room table just to gaze on its peculiar rustic opulence. That piece of ceramic radiates humanity. You can feel the sensibility of the person who painted it. I must say that year after year, washing after washing, it has neither chipped nor faded. Since that time I have bought wedding presents and presents for myself at Biordi in the form of plates, cups, saucers, pitchers, and platters, all with different patterns, but all wonderful together. In this Italian-food-crazed time, a few Biordi pieces will make your Italian favorites look and taste better, I promise.

COLUMBUS CUTLERY

Every cook in town uses Columbus Cutlery. Packed into a tiny space are cooking knives of every size and shape from the foremost makers in the world at the fairest prices, as well as scissors, pocket knives, hunting knives, and any implement used for cutting. The sweet woman behind the counter of Columbus moves very deliberately, bringing out the samples and carefully looking up the prices. She does one thing at a time, but the shop has such an old world ethos about it, you hesitate to break into the ritual just to drop off your knives for sharpening. I did that the other day when I was parked in a red zone at the corner, sticking my card into my gray canvas knife case and pleading with her to have them sharpened by the following afternoon. I think it was OK, but I felt that I had breached custom.

The head sharpener is the counterwoman's husband, red of cheek and always with an army-style hat made out of a folded brown paper bag on his head. Over the years, this couple has hired extra sharpeners, so you can get your knives back quickly, crucial if you're a working chef. The sharpeners have been trained to take off as little of the metal as possible while still giving the blades a clean, razor-sharp edge; they never butcher your knives. The sharpening charge is reasonable, but one drawback is that the store is closed on Wednesdays. Plan accordingly.

358 Columbus Avenue
(between Vallejo and Grant),
San Francisco
Tel: 362-1342
Open weekdays except Wednesday 9:30 a.m. to 6 p.m., Saturday until 6 p.m.
Credit cards: AE, MC, V

FIGONI HARDWARE

I love this ancient hardware store with its beautiful worn wooden floors and high wooden shelves. One of Figoni's two storefronts is dedicated completely to Italian cookware, everything from pasta bowls to pasta makers to pasta pots. Pizza stones, ravioli-making equipment, a *mezzaluna* (a double-handled curved chopping tool that you rock back and forth to finely mince herbs and garlic), marble rolling pins, ornate glass bottles with stoppers for putting up

1351 Grant Avenue
(between Vallejo and Green),
San Francisco
Tel: 392-4765
Open daily except Wednesday and Sunday 8 a.m. to 5 p.m.
Credit cards: MC, V

flavored liqueurs or vinegars, copper zabaglione pans with wooden handles, painted water pitchers, old-fashioned food mills, knives, simple glassware, cast-iron crepe pans, and a whole rack of Italian vegetable seeds make up but a fraction of the merchandise, all of which takes on a timeless glow in this store. Italian cooking has come full circle. The Italian grandmothers who did it all by hand have been succeeded, not by their children, but by their grandchildren who want to learn the old ways, rebounding from their mothers who defected to convenience foods. Surprisingly, many of the faces in Figoni are younger—and many of them are Asian. More than one culture in the world understands the pleasures of homemade noodles.

Pacific Heights & Japantown

PACIFIC HEIGHTS & JAPANTOWN

Restaurants:
1. Alta Plaza   305
2. Cafe Kati   306
3. Ella's   307
4. Isuzu   308
5. Jackson Fillmore   308
6. Maki   309
7. The Meetinghouse   310
8. Mifune   311
9. Oritalia   312
10. Rosmarino   314
11. Sanppo   314

Cafes:
12. Tan Tan   316

Bars:
13. Jack's   317

Delicatessens/Take-Out:
14. Bryan's Quality Meats   318
15. Maruya Sushi   318
16. Vivande Porte Via   319

Bakeries/Pastries:
17. Le Chantilly   319
18. Pâtisserie Delanghe   320
19. Yamada Seika   321

Coffee:
20. Peet's Coffee and Tea   322
21. Spinelli Coffee Company   322

Markets:
22. Cal-Mart   322
23. Grand Central Market   324

Ethnic Markets:
24. Maruwa Foods Company   324
25. Super Koyama   325
26. Uoki Market   326

Meat and Poultry:
22. Antonelli's Meat, Fish, and Poultry in the Cal-Mart   326
14. Bryan's Quality Meats   327
23. Grand Central Market   328

Fish:
22. Antonelli's Meat, Fish, and Poultry in the Cal-Mart   329
14. Bryan's Quality Meats   329
24. Maruwa Foods Company   329
25. Super Koyama   329
26. Uoki Market   329

Cheese:
27. California Street Creamery   329

Wines and Spirits:
28. Wine Impression   330

Cookware and Books:
29. Books, Inc.   330
30. Fillamento   331
31. Forrest Jones   331
32. Homechef   331
33. Kinokuniya Bookstore   332
34. Mashiko Folkcraft   333
35. RH   333
36. Sanko Cooking Supply   334
37. Soko Hardware   334
38. Sue Fisher-King   334

RESTAURANTS

ALTA PLAZA

Chef Amey Shaw, who has cooked in and headed a number of notable kitchens in the Bay Area, has found her niche at this popular, mostly A-crowd gay bar and restaurant. The dining area, though up a small flight of stairs from the bar, can be hot, noisy, and smoky. But frankly, the food is worth any discomfort. With gracious service and a full wine list, you can regard Alta Plaza as a full-scale restaurant, and an excellent one at that.

Shaw's current menu at Alta Plaza shows off all her experience and her integrity about ingredients. I was completely charmed by a dish called Hawaiian ahi tartare, an original composition that subtly balances mirin (sweet Japanese rice wine), sesame, and soy; her white corn salad, a molded vegetable medley alive with southwestern flavors; and her richly dressed Caesar. Her interpretations of hearty barroom favorites—chicken and mashed potatoes wreathed in baby vegetables and pan sauce, bavette steak (a tender cut from the sirloin) with braised greens and salsa verde—could turn me into a pub crawler. Followed by house-made desserts and good coffee, Alta Plaza sends customers away happy—even if they don't drink.

2301 Fillmore (at Clay),
San Francisco
Tel: 922-1444
Open Sunday through
Thursday 5:30 to 10 p.m.,
Friday and Saturday
until 11 p.m.; Sunday
brunch 10 a.m. to 3 p.m.
Price: Moderate
Credit cards: AE, D, DC, MC, V

CAFE KATI

**1963 Sutter Street
(between Fillmore
and Webster),
San Francisco
Tel: 775-7313
Open Tuesday through
Sunday 5:30 to 10 p.m.
Price: Moderate
Credit cards: MC, V**

I resisted going to Cafe Kati for the longest time because I was afraid that chef Kirk Webber's highly stylized "blend of East and West" cuisines would not taste like food to me. But when I finally got there, I had one of the nicest evenings in my memory. The plates did attain new heights of visual whimsy in the tradition of San Francisco's Flying Saucer, and the menu did combine French and Southeast Asian flavors with the crossover aplomb of Wolfgang Puck's Chinois on Main, in Venice, California.

Cafe Kati is, above all, a personal statement. This long, narrow storefront with one charming tiny dining room in the front, an incredibly small kitchen, considering the elaborateness of the food, in the middle, and a somewhat larger back dining room could only support the efforts of a single chef with perhaps a couple of assistants. Webber runs it with his wife Tina and a small, dedicated professional staff who seem as enamored of the restaurant as its fanatically loyal customers are. I can see why it would be a pleasure to work here. Every time a new set of plates reach a table, diners cannot help gasping with delight.

The first dish that came my way won me over forever, a flat bowl of elegantly clear vegetable consommé tasting exactly like tomatoes. A delicious Caesar salad of richly dressed whole romaine leaves bundled together and standing on end had to be deconstructed in order to be eaten. A fabulous salad of whole spot shrimp deep-fried with head and dramatic tendrils attached were bound in crispy noodles, filled with a spicy Thai mousse, and accompanied with little lettuces, nests of beet, carrot, and daikon radish threads, and a lemongrass vinaigrette. Succulent nonfish sushi made with grilled shiitake mushrooms and sheets of toasty seaweed, and mango spring rolls flamboyantly garnished with vegetable threads and carved vegetables bring joy to the hearts of vegetarians. Cafe Kati must be a godsend to those who eat only plants. A wonderful meal could be made out of meatless starters.

For a main course, a clay pot of spot prawns in the most delectable, creamy, aromatic red Thai curry could be the center of my meal, though I would be hard put to pass up a velvety seared fillet of rock cod in a crisp mustard seed crust bathed in pink crayfish hollandaise.

The fantasy does not let up with desserts such as butterscotch pudding under a hive of spun sugar or a plate of warm, gooey chocolate cake splashed with three fruit purees and arranged on the plate like a Sam Francis canvas.

Of course, by the time you read this, the whole menu may be different. Webber likes to change his dishes with the seasons. However, the spirit will be the same, and I would be surprised if his patrons will let him take certain items off the menu.

ELLA'S

A sunny, charming corner cafe that puts out a delicious breakfast is a gift to a neighborhood. I know many people who live around the Jewish Community Center and Laurel Heights who could not start their day without stopping at Ella's. The delicious breakfasts are bolstered by excellent home-style baking and first-rate coffee, both American and Italian. Even the white bread is baked from scratch, and what a difference that makes when your poached eggs come on thick slices of yeasty, buttered, gently crisp white toast. Ella's moist banana-nut-cinnamon coffee cake; sticky buns thick with pecans and orange zest; and light, buttery sweet potato–raisin muffins capture the spirit of inventive American home cooking. The orange juice is freshly squeezed; the buttermilk pancakes are airy and flavorful, especially when drizzled with real maple syrup.

Ella's small lunch menu is also enlivened by home baking: The hamburgers come on buns still warm from the oven; a classic chicken potpie has a meltingly flaky top crust. Salads are prepared with proper conviction and lovely greens and sparkly dressings. The delicious warm spinach salad makes for a fine lunch, leaving room for a tall, judiciously sweetened slice of fresh apple pie. Ella's also serves an agreeable California-American dinner, strong on salads, vegetables, and homey baked things.

500 Presidio Avenue
(at California),
San Francisco
Tel: 441-5669
Open for breakfast Monday through Friday 7 a.m. to 11 a.m.; lunch 11:30 a.m. to 2:30 p.m.; dinner 5 to 9 p.m., Saturday and Sunday brunch 9 a.m. to 2 p.m.
Price: Inexpensive
Credit cards: AE, MC, V

ISUZU

1581 Webster Street (at Post), San Francisco
Tel: 922-2290
Open for lunch weekdays (except Tuesday) 11:30 a.m. to 2 p.m.; dinner Monday through Friday 5 to 10 p.m., Saturday noon to 9 p.m., Sunday 4 to 9 p.m.
Price: Inexpensive to moderate
Credit cards: MC, V

When you are in the mood for a meal of Japanese seafood served the way Japanese families would eat it, try Isuzu, a large, full-scale Japanese restaurant in the same block as the Kabuki movie theater. People always think of sashimi and sushi as the typical Japanese fish preparations, but the range of Japanese fish cooking is vast and wonderful. At Isuzu, you can sample many different techniques, and fish, by requesting the Japanese menu and asking your waiter what the specials are.

I cannot eat here without ordering the buttery broiled mackerel, either whole or in fillets, brushed with a teriyaki-type sauce that makes the meaty, oily fish delectable. A whole flounder deep-fried with its bones is another treat: the tiny dorsal bones get so crisp they taste like potato chips. Start with a strong miso soup of the day and an array of vegetables and salads, like a sparkling cucumber and octopus salad; a refreshing, cold, cooked spinach salad sprinkled with sesame seeds; and a crisp and vinegary seaweed salad. Whatever you order, don't pass up a salad made of burdock root, that long, skinny carrotlike vegetable you see in Japanese groceries. The Isuzu kitchen shows you how it should taste. All the little dishes go in the middle of the table and everyone shares. I love the way a table looks filled with pottery in different shapes holding small portions of clean and juicy food, setting up your palate for the rich, hot fish to follow.

Isuzu has a full bar, a sushi bar, and lots of tables in its high-ceilinged dining room. It has become a very popular spot, especially among Japanese, for its reasonable prices, high-quality food and presentation, yet casual setting.

JACKSON FILLMORE

2506 Fillmore (at Jackson Street), San Francisco
Tel: 346-5288
Open Monday 5:30 to 10 p.m.,

The first time I ate at Jackson Fillmore (about ten years ago) the service and seating policy aggravated me so much that it made me grumpy to be there. The tenor has changed at this ever-popular Pacific Heights trattoria, but reservations still are taken only for parties of three or more, and parties of one and two are assigned on a first-come first-served basis to seats at the counter. The counter seats turn over pretty fast, though, and the people at the door now are cordial and understanding. The casual counter eating suits the tasty, short order Italian cooking well. This is just the place to drop in for a plate of pasta and a glass of wine, and many, many people do.

The daily menu tempts with first courses like salt cod *crostini*, which are pleasant if too potatoey (and short on the salt cod), and a tasty, warm asparagus salad with prosciutto, radicchio, and toasted bread crumbs. From the regular menu comes the classic Jackson Fillmore dish, *radicchio al forno*, small wedges of radicchio wrapped in pancetta roasted crisp in the oven. Al dente pastas served in flat bowls like spaghetti *all'amatriciana*, in a copious, spicy tomato sauce with pancetta and onions, hit the spot. Three risottos are offered on the regular menu, but getting them out proves tricky for this busy kitchen. A risotto milanese one night—rice stirred with chicken broth, onion, and saffron—almost worked, but in such a simple dish, perfection, especially of texture, is imperative. Lots of veal, chicken, and fish dishes make up the rest of the long menu. For those of you who remember the great counter restaurant, Vanessi's on Broadway, Jackson Fillmore's menu almost seems like an updated version. The inspiration for much of the cooking on Fillmore Street comes from Italy, but the North Beach/Italian influence seems to have flowed right up Broadway to Pacific Heights. Jackson Fillmore, now a professionally run restaurant with many lively, fun-to-eat Italian dishes, has taken on the aura of an old-time San Francisco spot.

Tuesday through Thursday until 10:30 p.m., Friday and Saturday until 11 p.m., Sunday 5 to 10 p.m.
Price: Moderate
Credit cards: AE, MC, V

MAKI

A tiny (four small blonde-wood tables, five counter seats), very charming Japanese restaurant hides behind a cotton banner in a Japan Center hallway. Maki specializes in *wappa meshi*, rice cooked in a covered bamboo steamer topped with meats or fish. These delicious rice-based dishes are clean, filling, and savory all at the same time. My favorite, of course, is topped with sweetly glazed fillets of fresh water eel, a luxury. I like to order it as a dinner to get a lacquered tray full of pretty containers, each with its special food. Maki also features

Kunokuniya Building of the Japan Center, 1825 Post Street (between Fillmore and Webster), San Francisco
Tel: 921-5215
Open for lunch Tuesday through Sunday 11:30 a.m. to 2 p.m.; dinner 6 to 9 p.m.
Price: Moderate
Credit cards: MC, V

high-quality sakes, served cold in special decanters that allow an ice cube to cool the rice wine without actually touching it. With sake you can have appetizers like a pristine mixed sushi plate; mosaic-centered vegetarian sushi rolls; or an unctuous braise of yam, fresh bacon, and daikon that melts in your mouth. Elegant Mrs. Makaguchi, in refined kimono, presides over the dining room while her husband does the cooking. Her sense of style gives this little gem its sparkle.

THE MEETINGHOUSE

1701 Octavia (at Bush),
San Francisco
Tel: 922-6733
Open Wednesday through
Sunday 5:30 to 9:30 p.m.
Price: Moderate
Credit cards: AE, MC, V

The Meetinghouse is a small, stylish neighborhood restaurant that serves exceptional American food, much in the tradition of my other favorites, Zax, Woodward's Garden, and Liberty Cafe. The cooking goes well beyond typical neighborhood fare, yet it has a heartiness and hominess about it that makes you want to drop in anytime. A young couple, Joanna Karlinsky and Bryant Snell, both experienced professional cooks, set up their dream restaurant in a former Victorian apothecary (a space that once housed Robert and La Fiammeta). Hundreds of little drawers with green wooden knobs line the walls, and vases of seasonal flowers now fill the shelves. Large tables are spaciously placed in a square dining room with huge plate glass windows on two sides. It's a very welcoming place to eat house-pickled salmon with colorful beet, fennel, and cucumber salads, and house-baked rye bread; or airy rock shrimp and scallion johnnycakes served with watercress salad. Snell likes to cook meat, and his fork-tender braised pork butt with crispy skin, celery root–mashed potatoes and warm cabbage salad is my idea of heaven on a cold night. Pan-roasted chicken on a warm frisée and bacon salad flanked by thick fried potato batons is another. Karlinsky is the baker and her warm, moist, flavorful whole grain breads are reason enough to come to The Meetinghouse. For dessert she serves warm, fragrant gingerbread with lemon sauce, and rich chocolate layer cake with house-made coffee ice cream. A charming, efficient wait staff all know the well-composed American wine list (with a number of tenths) and can steer you to some interesting bottles.

Karlinsky herself likes being in the dining room, making you feel at home at this most personal of restaurants. I love the intimacy of The Meetinghouse and the fact that it is so professionally run—two different restaurant worlds do meet here, as well as friends over dinner.

MIFUNE

One of the most beloved small restaurants in Japantown, Mifune has been satisfying San Franciscans' yen for noodles for thirteen years, its thirty-one or so noodle offerings cast in realistic plastic gracing a glamorously lit front window. First-timers would do well to take a look, because service brooks few explanations. Noodle houses serve quickly; in fact, they really represent a superior version of fast-food outlets.

For under $5 at Mifune, you can get either house-made *udon*, which are thick white-flour noodles, or *soba*, thin buckwheat noodles in big bowls of hot, tasty soup topped with the likes of grilled beef and green onions or shrimp and vegetable tempura. True noodle lovers prefer them cold, as in the Mifune Special, a wooden boat with a cargo of white and brown noodles on deck, sprinkled with seaweed, hot shrimp and vegetable tempura on the prow, and a bowl of cold, gingery dipping sauce with green onions, wasabi, and grated daikon on the stern. You dip the noodles and tempura into your custom-made sauce.

Many of the noodle and rice dishes (there are several *donburis* available) are designed to give you protein in the form of seaweed, egg, or miso without meat, making this a good restaurant for vegetarians. Even if you're carnivorous try No. 3, *wakame udon*, thick white noodles with toasty seaweed, or No. 17, *udon* with mountain fern. Mifune also appeals to kids who always like noodles and don't want to wait for their food. You can be in and out in half an hour, but are never rushed. You can sit and sip tea all afternoon if you'd rather. I long have treasured Mifune as my haven of noodley comfort in the middle of the city.

Japan Center, 1737 Post Street (between Webster and Buchanan),
San Francisco
Tel: 922-0337
Open daily
11 a.m. to 9:30 p.m.
Price: Inexpensive
Credit cards: AE, DC, D, MC, V

ORITALIA

**1915 Fillmore Street
(between Bush and Pine),
San Francisco
Tel: 346-1333
Open daily 5 to 10 p.m.,
Friday and Saturday
until 10:30 p.m.
Price: Moderate
Credit cards: AE, DC, MC, V**

Chef Bruce Hill keeps coming up with stunning new creations at this stylish Euro/Asian bistro. The last time I parked myself at the bar (the wait for a table in this small restaurant on a Saturday night was too long and I didn't have a reservation), I had a terrific meal made up of small dishes, the most memorable being a carpaccio of halibut, barely heated through on a hot plate, strewn with fermented black beans, crispy pancetta, Asian silk squash, and minced tomatoes. I

SPECIALTY RESTAURANTS IN JAPANTOWN
THAT DO A GOOD JOB ON A SINGLE TYPE OF DISH

SAPPORO-YA (West Wing of the Japan Center, Post and Webster Streets, tel: 563-7400) is kitty-corner from Tan Tan, the dessert cafe. Sapporo-Ya stays open until midnight. People regularly drop by for a late-night bowl of Chinese-style ramen in broth or wok-fried noodles with meat and vegetables.

Two story IROHA (in the Japan Center mall, tel: 922-0321), owned by the Mifune people, is a good spot for inexpensive Japanese ramen noodles (as opposed to soba and udon) in soup.

AKASAKA (also in the Mall, tel: 921-5360) offers amazing $5.25 lunches that include almost every element of the Japanese meal including soup, pickle, rice, tempura, grilled meat or fish.

In the first building of the Japan Center on the second floor, KUI SHIN BO, a cozy traditional space handcrafted in wood, puts out fine sushi, sashimi, noodle dishes, and buttery grilled mackerel. But the standout is small, crisp *gyoza*, or Japanese pot stickers, presented in a diagonal line on a square dish.

OSAKAYA (next to Mifune in Japan Center) has earned a reputation around Japantown for its generous take-out *nigiri sushi* at $6 and *bento* boxes (really compartmentalized foil containers) of sushi, salad, and pickles at $6.50.

Everyone loves ISOBUNE (across the walkway from Mifune), for its amusement-park delivery of sushi on wooden boats, which circulate in a waterway around a long oval sushi bar. The sushi makers stand in the middle of the counter, cutting fish and slapping together rice. Diners pluck little plates off the boats as they sail by. At the end of the meal, the number and sizes of saucers at your place determine the check. You can always ask for specially made pieces from the sushi makers, something I like to do because you never know how long some sushi have been traveling.

know this sounds weird, and I hesitated before ordering it, but it was one of the most delicious dishes I've been served all year. I don't know how Hill stumbled on this divine convergence of particularly strong flavors, but the memory of them still inspires me. After this, I ate a garlicky flan on a generous bed of black trumpet mushrooms, but gave away three of the four mounds of tuna tartar on Asian pear slices and rice cake rounds—too much sesame oil. For dessert, how could I resist a Meyer lemon fantasy plate, four miniature lemon desserts highlighted by a hot beignet filled with Meyer lemon cream, and a fine Meyer lemon ice cream with pine nuts. In many ways, Oritalia lends itself to this kind of grazing. There are more small dishes on the menu than large, including crispy-fried spring rolls, pot stickers with imaginative fillings, noodles, and exotic salads. Chances are you'll end up tasting something you'll never forget.

A SMALL JAPANTOWN DETOUR

A whole row of original Victorian cottages still stands along one side of a miniature park on Cottage Row, a block-long street across from Yamada Seika (see page 321). These dwellings are the only remnants of the original Japanese neighborhood that was destroyed during the redevelopment of Japantown, according to Yoko Tahara, a personal friend and long-time resident of the neighborhood both before and after her family's deportation to relocation camps during World War II. Take a stroll down the brick pathway to get a closer look at the lovingly maintained cottages and gardens. This is one of the most charming secret streets in San Francisco.

ROSMARINO

3665 Sacramento Street
(between Locust
and Spruce),
San Francisco
Tel: 931-7710
Open Tuesday through
Saturday for lunch
11:30 a.m. to 2 p.m.;
dinner 5:30 to 10 p.m.;
Sunday brunch
10 a.m. to 2 p.m.
Price: Moderate
Credit cards: AE, DC, MC, V

Hidden away in a courtyard off Sacramento Street, Rosmarino has had to earn its clientele through word of mouth and it has. In fact, Rosmarino's opening about four years ago anticipated the small, upscale neighborhood-restaurant boom (Zax, Woodward's Garden, and in the East Bay Citron and Rivoli) that has greatly contributed to life in the city. If you live in Pacific Heights and want a sophisticated but simple meal made with fine ingredients, an interesting bottle of Italian wine, and civilized, if casual, service, you do not need to dress up and go downtown. Rosmarino is an outpost of civilization in the neighborhoods. Most recently, I devoured a lovely, pristine antipasto and then a seemingly simple-minded two-ingredient pasta like the ones served everywhere in Italy that taste so wonderful. In this case, hot al dente spaghetti was tossed with tons of freshly ground black pepper and grated imported pecorino cheese until it just melted. I could have eaten bowls of it. The oft-changing menu is mostly Italian, but takes advantage of fresh local ingredients, always adding up to light, clean, satisfying meals. The modern, carpeted, banquette-lined dining room is softly lit and comfortable. On sunny days and those rare warm nights, you can eat outside on wrought-iron tables and chairs in the courtyard. If I lived around upper Sacramento Street, Rosmarino would be my neighborhood hangout.

SANPPO

Japan Center, 1702 Post
Street (at Buchanan),
San Francisco
Tel: 346-3486
Open Tuesday through
Saturday 11:45 a.m.
to 9:50 p.m., Sunday
12:30 to 9:50 p.m.
Price: Inexpensive
Credit cards: MC, V

For twenty years I have been going to Sanppo for homey, country-style Japanese dishes served in a cozy, almost communal dining room from a tiny open kitchen. The food is always fresh, the soup stocks well balanced, the tempuras ethereal, the sushi and sashimi honest and clean. I love a dish here called *gyoza nabe*, a cast-iron pot of soup afloat with delicate Japanese pot stickers filled with finely ground pork, glass noodles, Japanese cabbage, and squares of bean curd. A

When you eat this kind of simple pasta in Italy, you can't believe how good it tastes. When I had a plate of it at Rosmarino, I was hooked forever on this restaurant. The key is to use high-quality butter, either Plugra (see Tower Market, page 256, or Ashbury Market, page 174), or Straus Family Dairy butter (see Ferry Plaza Farmers' Market, page 112, or Grand Central Market, page 324); pecorino, such as Locatelli brand from Florence Delicatessen (page 289); and imported pasta. Ross Brown of Rosmarino uses De Cecco brand spaghettini.

Bring a large pot of salted water to a boil and add the spaghettini. Bring the pot back to a boil and cook for 8 minutes. Drain the pasta thoroughly and pour it back into the pot. Add the butter and cheese and toss until the pasta is thoroughly coated. Grind in the pepper. Toss again. Check for salt, add if necessary, toss again, and serve.

Serves 4 to 6

SPAGHETTINI WITH PECORINO CHEESE

1 pound dried spaghettini
1/2 cup (1 stick) unsalted butter
1 1/2 cups (6 ounces) grated dried aged pecorino
30 turns of the pepper grinder set to coarse
Kosher salt to taste (optional)

little bowl of gingery soy sauce comes on the side for dipping. Indicative of skillful deep-frying, the always sweet, impeccable oysters have the lightest of batters and the crispiest exteriors. The grilled fillets of fresh-water eel, *unagi*, presented like jewels on a bed of rice in a covered lacquer box, have been of exceptional quality at Sanppo: rich, firm, and not muddy tasting. With lots of small appetizer plates to choose from, such as cold sesame spinach, cucumber, and octopus salad, or an East-West lettuce salad made with sweet-potato noodles, greens, and onions in a creamy dressing, you can share a full Japanese meal or just get one dish. Even if you have to sit with other parties at one of the larger, square wooden tables that look like old ship hatches, this intimate dining room always feels comfortable. Everyone who eats here, Eastern or Western, is united by appreciation of the tasty food.

CAFES

TAN TAN

Japan Center,
1825 Post Street (between
Webster and Laguna),
San Francisco
Tel: 346-6260
Open daily
10:30 a.m. to 7 p.m.
No credit cards

I highly recommend you visit this tiny Japanese dessert cafe off the skylit second-floor atrium of the Japan Center, right next to the gigantic Kunokuniya bookstore. The room is beautifully crafted with a bleached-wood counter and floors and five small blonde-wood tables. A tall window looks out to Geary Boulevard below. Western-style tarts and cakes are displayed in a refrigerated glass case, but the real treats are the Japanese desserts served on their own square lacquer trays with decorative and culinary accompaniments. A perfect *shiso* leaf holding a little pile of pickled ginger strings comes with a glass bowl of red beans in sugar syrup topped with tiny white rice dumplings that were first poached and then cooled in ice and water. Each Japanese dessert involves a labor-intensive procedure of being cooked and/or cooled, decorated, and assembled, tasks often performed by one young Japanese woman who goes through the motions as if dancing. She looks like she stepped out of a Chanel ad, with her glossy bobbed hair and flawless makeup.

The cold red beans with rice powder dumplings described above are called *shiratama* and are served with a ceramic mug of green tea, which really does complete the range of sensations in the dessert. I also like *tokoroten*, cubes of shimmering agar-agar, crystal-like cubes of gelatin with bits of strawberry, canned peach, and fruit juice for flavor and dots of red bean for color. It's very refreshing. Yoko Tahara, a resident of the neighborhood long before the Japan Center was built and a patron of Tan Tan, loves a hot red bean dessert called *zenzai*, with super-glutinous *mochi*, or sticky-rice-flour balls, all presented in a lacquer bowl. I found all the red bean desserts wonderfully satisfying after meals at nearby Japanese restaurants (like Kame Sushi, a good eight-seat sushi bar a few yards away run by an eccentric who only opens when he feels like it). The pleasure of Japanese sweets is subtle for the Westerner: You are not assaulted by sugar or butterfat, but really feel as if you have had dessert. For those who insist on something a little more sybaritic, a creamy, beautiful green-tea mousse topped with a dab of red beans and decorated with sliced strawberries offers a compromise between Eastern and occidental tastes.

Many people use Tan Tan as a tea- and coffeehouse for iced coffee, green tea, hot cappuccino, and green tea floats. If the indoor space gets too smoky, you can sit outside in the atrium at cafe tables and thumb through a Japanese or English magazine that you have just purchased at the bookstore next door.

BARS

JACK'S

When you ask Information for the telephone number of Jackson Fillmore the restaurant, you often get the number for Jack's instead. It might behoove you to stop by sometime, because Jack's is a blues bar with hot-looking young women bartenders with low-cut tops, shorts, and nice legs. The scene is loose and funky. You can dance to live blues bands on a small floor and work off some of the pasta you had down the street. Also, if you're going to a show at the revitalized historic Fillmore Auditorium, your stamped hand will admit you to Jack's.

1601 Fillmore Street
(at Geary),
San Francisco
Tel: 567-3227
Open daily 2 p.m. to 2 a.m.
No credit cards

DELICATESSENS/TAKE-OUT

BRYAN'S QUALITY MEATS

See Meat and Poultry, page 327.

MARUYA SUSHI

1904 Fillmore Street
(at Bush),
San Francisco
Tel: 921-2929
Open Monday through
Saturday 10:30 a.m. to 6 p.m.,
Sunday until 5 p.m.
No credit cards

On the face of it, sushi seems to be the perfect food to go. After all, it's supposed to be served at room temperature (though the fish is kept chilled before it is cut), and unlike salad, it doesn't wilt. But the fact is, held or refrigerated sushi loses its charm. The rice dries out and starts to separate and the delicate flavors of raw fish disappear. I always hesitate to buy prepackaged sushi in groceries because you don't know how long ago it was made. That's why tiny Maruya is such a find. All the delicate sushi is made to order, and only the delicious vegetarian selection, No. 9, which includes two kinds of nonfish sushi, is prepackaged, though usually the woman behind the counter only has one order available at any time. When that one is sold she prepares another. The four large pieces of pickle-and-vegetable-filled *maki* (a fat, seaweed-wrapped roll that is sliced into rounds), and three large balls of sushi rice sweetened just a bit and tossed with threads of seaweed, then wrapped in a thin crepe of egg, add up to a light, delicious, and satisfying meal. You can almost feel each slightly chewy grain on your tongue, yet each finger of rice holds together as if by magic. A pyramid of wasabi, a packet of soy sauce, and a mound of pickled ginger threads nestles into one corner of the package along with green plastic grass and wooden chopsticks. Other types of sushi can be ordered by the piece or off a small menu of combinations. If the order is large or even small, calling ahead is a good idea since everything is made to order. The tiny shop holds a kitchen so miniature that you know that everything is made from scratch each day. Since Maruya is dedicated to take-out, the full attention of the sushi chef can be lavished on your order, with no demanding customers eating at the sushi bar to distract her. When a shop can sustain itself at this level of specialization, you know it makes something people really want.

VIVANDE PORTE VIA

Carlo Middione's Italian culinary empire used to be headquartered at this bustling delicatessen-trattoria on Fillmore, until he opened a full-scale restaurant in Opera Plaza (see page 77). His Pacific Heights patrons still can eat both lunch and dinner at tiny pushed-together tables in the narrow, brick-walled dining area, really an extension of the kitchen. People also can take home a tempting selection of antipasti, Italian baked savories, the best Italian desserts in town, and shop for exquisite Italian ingredients and cookbooks (including Middione's growing opus). Vivande does catering of any size.

If you want to cook an Italian meal at home, Vivande presents a high-level resource. The purest, richest extra-virgin olive oils, rare aged balsamic vinegars, Arborio rice for risotto, dried and house-made fresh pasta, Reggiano Parmesan, a selection of other hard and soft Italian cheeses, prosciutto from Parma, and Middione's *biscotti di Prato* are but a few of the treasures here. You can buy prepared foods, such as roasted chickens from the open-flame rotisserie, whole onions slowly baked in balsamic vinegar, crusty walnut breads, and Italian tortas to incorporate into your own meals. Everything that Middione turns out reflects his sense of integrity and the ebullience with which he cooks and creates in his shiny open kitchen.

2125 Fillmore Street
(between Sacramento and California),
San Francisco
Tel: 346-4430
Open daily 10 a.m. to 10 p.m.
Credit cards: AE, DC, MC, V

BAKERIES/PASTRIES

LE CHANTILLY

This French pastry shop looks like a jewelry store, its gleaming glass cases filled with elaborately constructed and decorated cakes and petits fours. The cakes are so architectural that it's hard to believe they're made with eggs, butter, and flour. Are they food? In fact, they are brought in from Le Chantilly's bakery in Novato and their high butterfat content practically preserves them. The best cakes have a chocolate

2119 Fillmore Street
(between Sacramento and California),
San Francisco
Tel: 441-1500
Open Sunday through Thursday 10 a.m. to 7 p.m., Friday and Saturday until 9 p.m.
Credit cards: AE, MC, V

component, like a chocolate-encased pyramid filled with thin layers of chocolate cake and velvety chocolate mousse. The lighter, fruitier petits fours flavored with liqueurs tend to lose their sparkle. I was pulling for a tropical fruit number, but its overwhelming flavor was sugar. The hazelnut daquoise layered with meringue was competent if not thrilling—a description of most of the pastry here. Perhaps that's the price to be paid for such elegant-looking cakes. I do, however, like the small, hand-dipped chocolates very much. They are fresh, lively, and varied in filling and shape, employing nuts and creams as well as ganache. A tony gold box of these would go a long way in wooing someone over to your point of view.

PÂTISSERIE DELANGHE

1890 Fillmore Street (at Bush), San Francisco
Tel: 923-0711
Open Tuesday through Friday 7 a.m. to 6 p.m., Saturday 8 a.m. to 6 p.m., Sunday 8 a.m. to 2 p.m.
No credit cards

What wonderful, buttery French sweet rolls come out of the open kitchen of this one-man bakery run by Dominique Delanghe! They are filled with fresh strawberries, plums, or apricots and a bit of custard. His croissants taste like the real thing, flaky, buttery, handmade. Large *palmiers*, palm leaf–shaped cookies made of crisp, sugar-glazed puff pastry, dissolve on your tongue. Miniature éclairs, chocolate-covered madeleines, and meringue mushrooms make for charming after-dinner desserts with demitasses of coffee. M. Delanghe makes a small version of the classic French wedding pastry called *croquembouche*, a tower of little cream puffs filled with custard and held together with caramel. These towering constructions serve twelve or more, and each serving of the dismantled puffs can be made more festive by drizzling a homemade chocolate sauce over or under them. I can't walk by the shop, especially in the morning when the pastries are still warm from the oven, without stopping in for at least one cheese-filled roll with a cup of good coffee.

This is my recipe for the easiest and most luxurious dark chocolate sauce to ever moisten a cream puff.

In a saucepan over medium heat, melt the butter. Add the chocolate and melt, stirring constantly. Stir in the sugar until completely dissolved. Add the cream. Stir until incorporated and bring to a simmer for 1 minute. Serve hot or warm. This will keep in the refrigerator for a long time if tightly covered, and may be rewarmed or eaten cold like fudge.

Makes about 1 cup

CHOCOLATE SAUCE

4 tablespoons butter

3 ounces unsweetened baking chocolate

1 cup sugar

1 cup heavy (whipping) cream

YAMADA SEIKA

Japanese-baked sweets with red bean fillings may be an acquired taste, but the wonderful aromas at this bakery make you want to try them. While we were sampling the pastel green and pink sweets, a huge Mercedes sedan neatly parallel-parked in front of the shop and out glided a young woman in full kimono with traditionally piled hair and masklike make-up, holding leather-encased car keys. For a moment it felt like old Japan in the shop with its antique wooden cases. The Japanese woman ever so politely talked to the Japanese baker in his floury garb, who carefully wrapped the selected pastries in paper. Where did she come from? The Japanese consulate? A condominium on top of Nob Hill? Seeing her buy the Japanese sweets in her traditional garments put them in context. I can imagine how satisfying one perfect red bean-filled pastry would taste with frothy green tea. My own preference, completely uneducated and uncultivated, was for *fubiki*, oval sweets wrapped in delicate, barely sweetened white yeast dough with a generous filling of nutty red bean paste. The seasonal pink sweets actually have cherry blossoms in them and a barely detectable floral taste. For lovers of the chewy and sticky, the *mochi* (glutinous rice-flour squares covered with toasted soybean powder) will deliver a thrill.

1955 Sutter Street
(between Fillmore and Webster),
San Francisco
Tel: 922-3848
Open Tuesday through Saturday 9 a.m. to 6 p.m.,
Sunday until 5 p.m.
No credit cards

COFFEE

PEET'S COFFEE AND TEA

3419 California Street (between Spruce and Laurel),
San Francisco
Tel: 221-8506
Open Monday through Friday 6:30 a.m. to 7 p.m.,
Saturday and Sunday 7 a.m. to 6 p.m.
Credit cards: D, MC, V
See listing, page 199.

SPINELLI COFFEE COMPANY

2455 Fillmore Street (at Jackson),
San Francisco
Tel: 929-8808
Open Monday through Friday 6:30 a.m. to 9 p.m.,
Saturday 7 a.m. to 9 p.m., Sunday 7 a.m. to 6 p.m.
Credit cards: MC, V
See listing, page 173.

MARKETS

CAL-MART

3585 California Street
(at Spruce),
San Francisco
Tel: 751-3516
Open Monday through
Saturday 8 a.m. to 7:30 p.m.,
Sunday 9 a.m. to 6 p.m.
Credit cards: MC, V

A fine, versatile neighborhood grocery with a comprehensive produce section, Cal-Mart is further strengthened by Antonelli and Son's meat, fish and poultry counter, which has expanded into the space vacated by Bryan's Meats. While most of the produce is commercial, some organic and/or local specialty items like little Yukon Gold potatoes, small red creamer potatoes, Portobello mushrooms, brown field mushrooms, beautiful Flambeau radishes (pink and white oval

WARM BERRY COMPOTE

The Cal-Mart produce section features berries, usually commercial ones, but a number of different kinds. This fast, simple recipe, adapted from Jeremiah Tower's New American Classics (Harper and Row, 1986), turns any kind of berry into an opulent warm compote that tastes heavenly with vanilla ice cream.

In a large skillet dissolve the sugar in the water by stirring over medium heat. Bring to a boil. Add the lemon juice and berries and cook over medium heat for 2 to 3 minutes. Swirl in the butter until it melts. Remove from heat. Spoon into 4 shallow soup bowls and place scoops of vanilla ice cream in the center.

Serves 4

1/2 cup sugar
1/4 cup water
2 teaspoons fresh lemon juice
1 cup hulled fresh strawberries, halved
1 cup fresh blueberries, halved
1 cup fresh blackberries
4 tablespoons unsalted butter, cut into pieces
1 pint vanilla ice cream

shaped), and organic cherry tomatoes from del Cabo farms in Baja, California, represent but a small sample of what's available. Piles of seasonal stone fruit and a myriad of different berries look luscious, but are of varying quality: much better than warehoused, underripe supermarket stuff, but not as rewarding as organic produce from farmers' markets. The produce displays are groomed and well cared for, and I have to pat the produce buyer on the back for taking some risks by offering unusual items.

An active deli counter cranks out made-to-order sandwiches, rotisserie chickens, and prepared salads and entrees, while a bakery counter run by Sweet Things from Marin offers time-saving items like pints of fresh lemon curd and raspberry puree along with rich bar cookies and gooey cakes. All the major local bread bakeries deliver here daily, and all the upscale grocery standbys, like a full range of Häagen-Dazs ice cream products (a find at this level of completeness), make Cal-Mart a very useful independent grocery store.

GRAND CENTRAL MARKET

**2435 California Street
(between Fillmore
and Steiner),
San Francisco
Tel: 567-4902
Open daily 8 a.m. to 11 p.m.
Credit cards: MC, V**

This historic market, once the site of Bercut Meat Company (where Bryan Flannery of Bryan's Meats started out), still boasts a long meat counter featuring Superior lamb, Harris beef, and real butchers who will cut and grind to order. Across the aisle is an equally long fish and poultry counter that offers some special items, like turkey and chicken sausages from different makers, including chicken linguiça and spicy or mild Italian sausages made with turkey. Reichardt ducks and Fulton Valley broilers, Petaluma Poultry Company fryers (the same people who raise Rocky free-range chickens) and stewing hens fill the counter. Small hen turkeys and parts come from Ladino. I am not wild about the fish section, but nifty small wooden crates of salt cod at $8.99 per pound, a good price, inspired me to get out the *brandade* recipes.

The produce department is pedestrian, small, and commercial, but the dairy case is stocked with high-quality Marin Cheese Company packaged cheeses and Pavel's superior yogurt. Breads come from Acme, Grace, and Metropolis. A separately run delicatessen counter offers nothing out of the ordinary. The miniature shopping carts for small children bring great joy, and many a mom and dad shop here just to give their children the pleasure of using one.

ETHNIC MARKETS

MARUWA FOODS COMPANY

**1737 Post Street
(near Webster),
San Francisco
Tel: 563-1901
Open Monday through
Saturday 10 a.m. to 7 p.m.,
Sunday until 6 p.m.
Credit cards: MC, V**

Owned by Koreans, Maruwa epitomizes the modern Asian supermarket, which features lots of precooked convenience foods to take out. A quick look at the pickle section confirms the Korean influence. Kimchees of chili-spiked daikon and cabbage share refrigerator space with salted Japanese pickles. Farther along the refrigerated case, simple steamed daikon mixed with other Asian vegetables, wrapped in plastic on

Styrofoam boards, stands ready for immediate eating. Like Super Koyama, lots of fresh, pristine-looking fish have been cut and packaged for sashimi or marinated whole (but gutted and scaled of course) in sake lees or miso paste. Fish cakes in all shapes can be bought in bulk. The grocery aisles are stocked with Japanese ready-to-eat products: cereal, soft drinks (cold cans of Calipio Water), snacks, candy, as well as soup bases, rice, noodles, and other ingredients for assisted home cooking. For dessert, cartons of green tea or lichee ice cream beckon.

SUPER KOYAMA

The cognoscenti in Japantown shop at the relatively new and sparkling Super Koyama grocery, where the fish cut for sashimi, tightly wrapped in clear plastic, look opalescent. A trip to this market inspires you to serve your own Japanese meal at home since you can buy most of the components already prepared: seaweed salad in sesame oil with red chilies; octopus and cucumber salad; jellyfish salad; ready-made sushi; sliced fresh *hamachi* (yellowtail) and *toro* (the rare belly cut of tuna) for sashimi; all sorts of other ready-to-eat sliced raw fish. With Japanese beer of every kind and sake, you have the components of an impressive Japanese spread.

1790 Sutter Street
(at Buchanan),
San Francisco
Tel: 921-6529
Open Monday through
Saturday 9 a.m. to 7 p.m.,
Sunday 10 a.m. to 6 p.m.
Credit cards: MC, V

For slightly more ambitious cooks, paper-thin slices of beef for sukiyaki, capellini-thin baby eels, fish cakes, fresh tofu, and fresh roe of all kinds inspire you to get out a Japanese cookbook. All the makings for miso broth and bonito stock are here, along with a healthy-looking produce section, the nicest in Japantown, with fresh burdock root, baby turnips, *shiso* leaves, firm Japanese cucumbers, plump unblemished lotus root, mountain potatoes, and even tiny green plums for pickling. Whole fish, staring out at you with clear, glassy eyes from behind the immaculate sashimi counter, and fillets marinating in sake *kasu* (the lees of sake) or white miso paste stand ready to be broiled. Everything at Super Koyama looks so neat and pristine, from the vegetables to the fish, that you trust that even the marinated fish will be fresh.

UOKI MARKET

1656 Post Street (between Buchanan and Laguna), San Francisco
Tel: 921-0515
Open Monday through Saturday 9 a.m. to 6 p.m., Sunday 10 a.m. to 5:30 p.m.
No credit cards

The fish at the ever-busy Uoki Market fish counter is not prepackaged or precut, and often not precleaned. You have to wait for service at this counter, as you do in the Chinatown bustle, to get your allotment of small clams, fresh squid, fat tentacles of octopus, hunks of tuna, and whole salmon. The busy fish clerks will cut small pieces to order and the quality is generally high. The produce section is not as carefully weeded of old vegetables as at Super Koyama, and there is much less prepackaging of prepared ingredients. Instead, you scoop out your own pickled daikon from vats. Of course Uoki Market has whole aisles of jarred pickles in neon colors to put on rice, tea, soup mix, candy, big sacks of California short-grain rice for the larder, plus up-to-the-minute imports of Japanese breakfast cereal and snacks. By the checkout counter I couldn't resist buying a can of Pocari Sweat Refreshment Water just for its name. It tastes better than it sounds.

MEAT AND POULTRY

ANTONELLI'S MEAT, FISH, AND POULTRY IN THE CAL-MART

3585 California Street (between Laurel and Spruce), San Francisco
Tel: 752-7413
Open Monday through Saturday 8 a.m. to 7 p.m., Sunday 9 a.m. to 6 p.m.
Credit cards: MC, V

Antonelli's is the only source in the city for some of my favorite lamb, Bruce and Nancy Campbell's CK lamb from Healdsburg. Their lambs may be a bit larger than the Superior lambs from Dixon sold at many butcher shops in the city, but they have real character without ever being muttony. One evening I roasted CK and Superior racks of lamb next to each other; the CK lamb had a deeper flavor and more personality while being just as tender. The CK racks turned out to be a couple of dollars more expensive because the bones were larger, but this lamb earns its higher price.

The chicken counter features hormone-free though not free-range Fulton Valley chickens, which to my mind are some of the best commercial chickens on the market. They have character without any off flavors and they roast up like a dream. The small, fresh Fulton Valley turkey parts carried here are also delicious and an underused meat alternative. What could be better, or easier to cook, than golden-skinned roast turkey meat for dinner, with leftovers for sandwiches the next day?

Since Antonelli's started out as a fish and poultry seller, you can expect to find some seafood treasures, like jars of tiny Pacific oysters from Johnson's Oyster Company in Point Reyes or fresh whole sand dabs with clear eyes. Antonelli's still cuts halibut and salmon steaks, which actually grill up more evenly than fillets (which are also sold), though you have to contend with a few bones and skin. Antonelli's may not be as complete or up-to-the-minute as Bryan's down the block, but the strong poultry section and special lamb make it an invaluable resource.

BRYAN'S QUALITY MEATS

Bryan's operated the meat counter at the Cal-Mart for thirty years, but four years ago opened its own store a few doors away. Now Bryan's has become the best all-around butcher in the city. In addition to meat, the shop has separate counters for fish, poultry, and an ever-growing selection of attractive prepared foods. Although the fresh corn salad, old-fashioned potato salads, platters of roasted vegetables, and rotisserie-roasted organic chickens entice as you walk in the back door from the Laurel Village parking area, the beauty of the raw ingredients here inspires home cooking.

Bryan's dry-ages its own prime beef for four weeks. You can taste the pedigree in a Prime market steak ($12.99/pound, call for availability): fat-marbled, tender texture, and tons of flavor. The choice beef comes from Harris Ranch, which I have come to admire for its consistency and lively western flavor. Bryan's dry-ages its California lamb for two weeks as well, and the racks, completely trimmed of fat and with a plump loin, are marvelously juicy and refined in flavor. Fresh country-style pork ribs and pork roasts and chops make for another dinner alternative. Anyone who has run out of cooking ideas only needs to step into this shop.

3473 California Street
(between Spruce and Laurel),
San Francisco
Tel: 752-3430
Open Monday through Friday 8 a.m. to 7 p.m., Saturday until 6 p.m.
Credit cards: MC, V

Of course chicken and fish have become staples in a health-conscious diet and Bryan's has taken up the banner. Terry Flannery, the son of the founder, has put together the prettiest fish counter in town. He knows how to buy and who to buy from. I have seen salmon, tuna, striped bass, fresh day-boat scallops, fresh shrimp, delicious northern halibut, swordfish, local rockfish, and seasonal items like soft shell crabs and shad roe in pristine condition. He is not afraid to stock unusual fish like bright red whole bee-liners from the Gulf of Mexico, whose eyes were so bright one day they looked as if they had just been pulled in from the water. The seafood chowder, sold refrigerated by the pint, is one of the best I have tasted anywhere, and the notion of offering fresh mango salsa at the fish counter is inspired. Moving over to poultry, Bryan's carries poussin, or baby chicken. Pale-skinned and without fat, they cook up so moist, tender, and full of flavor. Ducks from Grimaud farm, local quail, and excellent, tender squab figuratively fly out the door. The freshest little rabbits I have seen in a market are displayed next to the game birds.

On top of all the choice raw materials, Terry Flannery knows where to get the best restaurant-quality cured and smoked items, like Hobbs' bacon and hams and Robert Morris's incomparable smoked salmon, trout, and sturgeon. He's got artisan breads, and a few crucial produce items like shallots, garlic, onions, lemons, and potatoes.

When you buy something of the highest quality, hand cut and perfectly fresh, you do not need a lot of it. Bryan's charges for the quality, but the pleasure of eating fine meat, fish, and poultry go a long way.

GRAND CENTRAL MARKET

See listing, page 324.

FISH

ANTONELLI'S MEAT, FISH, AND POULTRY IN THE CAL-MART

See Meat, page 326.

BRYAN'S QUALITY MEATS

See Meat, page 327.

MARUWA FOODS COMPANY

See Ethnic Markets, page 324.

SUPER KOYAMA

See Ethnic Markets, page 325.

UOKI MARKET

See Ethnic Markets, page 326.

CHEESE

CALIFORNIA STREET CREAMERY

An interesting if small collection of cheeses can be found at this tiny shop, some of the most alluring right out on the marble counter, such as ripe, bulging Chaumes; buttery, crumbly aged Gouda; a strong, creamy Taleggio from Italy; and some high-end triple-cream French imports. An assortment of breads, rolls, and pastries from different bakers are kept in the front window, and the small refrigerated case is stocked with an odd assortment of things like Casa Sanchez tomato salsa and house-made crème fraîche. People in the neighborhood depend on the Creamery for certain favorite specialty items like nonsupermarket cheeses and exotic crackers.

2413 California Street
(at Fillmore),
San Francisco
Tel: 929-8610
Open Monday through
Friday 7 a.m. to 6:45 p.m.,
Saturday 9 a.m. to 6:45 p.m.,
Sunday 9 a.m. to 6 p.m.
No credit cards

WINES AND SPIRITS

WINE IMPRESSION

**3461 California
(in Laurel Village),
San Francisco
Tel: 221-9463
Open Sunday 10 a.m. to
6 p.m., Monday through
Friday until 8 p.m., Saturday
9 a.m. to 8 p.m.
Credit cards: AE, D, MC, V**

My spirits expert (who happens to be my husband) says that Wine Impression carries the best and hardest to find booze no matter what the type: Chinaco Tequila; Booker's and Basil Hayden bourbons; herby, citrusy Veranda Gin made in Vermont; high-quality French and Italian vermouths; rye whiskey like Old Overholt; cognacs; Armagnacs, and single-malt Scotches, to name just a few of the bottles that attract the connoisseur of spirits. If you're a cocktail lover or like your liquor straight up, stock your cabinet here.

COOKWARE AND BOOKS

BOOKS, INC.

**3515 California Street
(at Locust),
San Francisco
Tel: 221-3666
Open Monday through
Friday 9 a.m. to 7 p.m.,
Saturday 10 a.m. to 7 p.m.,
Sunday 10 a.m. to 6 p.m.
Credit cards: AE, D, MC, V**

This smallish, but amazingly well-stocked bookstore has a cookbook remainder table, with interesting titles at 50 to 90 percent off retail price. The other day I saw Victoria Wise's classic *American Charcuterie* in a pretty paperback edition marked down to $2.88. Anyone who thumbs through a book like this will find timeless recipes from the woman who brought the French delicatessen to the United States when she ran Pig by the Tail in Berkeley. Next to the remainders, a whole table of new books at full price titillates the seemingly insatiable cookbook buyer. The repetition of subject matter in books stylishly devoted to one ingredient makes me wonder how many recipes anyone needs for potatoes, green salad, or chicken. Books, Inc.'s many shelves of cookbooks do contain an intelligently chosen inventory of classics, like all three of the Greens-inspired cookbooks, for example. For those who associate travel with food, the excellent travel section is stocked with an unusual number of food guides to different countries.

FILLAMENTO

A vibrant housewares store now with three levels of trendsetting merchandise, Fillamento has added extravagant upscale items to its stylish, yet affordable, inventory. Opulent Versace place settings at $500 each are displayed a few steps away from piles of large, serviceable cotton napkins from India that cost $4 apiece. If I were setting up an apartment on a budget I would turn to Fillamento for well-designed silverware, dishes, glasses, and table linens; and when ready to upgrade my china cabinet, I could return for some finer pieces. Through creative and daring buying, Fillamento has kept a step ahead of the big guys like Crate and Barrel and Williams-Sonoma, and now has taken on Gump's. Fillamento may not offer as many choices in every price range as these stores, but what ends up on the floor is both provocative and useful. And since it is a one-unit store, chances are you won't see your dishes and glasses on your next-door neighbor's table.

2185 Fillmore Street
(at Sacramento),
San Francisco
Tel: 931-2224
Open Monday through
Saturday 10 a.m. to 6 p.m.,
Sunday noon to 5 p.m.
Credit cards: AE, D, MC, V

FORREST JONES

This cleverly stocked housewares shop often has the very thing you've been looking for all over town, like a plain, heavy glass cake dome (without the plate) or large white rectangular platters at half off the original price, which I found there between Thanksgiving and Christmas one year. Baskets, tote bags, dish towels, Roger and Gallet soaps by the bar, sturdy glassware, and an ever-changing array of goods that households really need make Forrest Jones an invaluable resource, well worth checking out before or after you've shopped elsewhere.

3274 Sacramento Street
(between Presidio
and Lyon),
San Francisco
Tel: 567-2483
Open Monday through
Saturday 10 a.m. to 6 p.m.,
Sunday 11 a.m. to 5 p.m.
Credit cards: AE, MC, V

HOMECHEF

A complete collection of cooking utensils and some serving and tableware fill the shelves of this densely packed store. It seems to me that the most important tool in any kitchen is a decent knife that is heavy enough to keep an edge, yet many home kitchens overflow with doodads without a decent cutting tool to be found. Homechef does everyone a favor by

3525 California Street
(at Locust),
San Francisco
Tel: 668-3191
Open Monday through
Saturday 9:30 a.m. to 6 p.m.,
Sunday noon to 4:30 p.m.
Credit cards: AE, D, MC, V

putting both their special label collection of chefs' knives and a case of first-class imported knives from Solingen, Germany, front and center in the shop. Before people move on to the miniature tart pans and the food processors of every conceivable size, they ought to buy themselves one good knife. Having gotten that off my chest, I must say I was drawn to some brightly enameled charcuterie dishes in cheerful greens and blues. I was happy to see Donvier ice cream makers, an ingenious Japanese invention that only requires a home freezer and a minimum of arm power to quickly turn out fresh fruit ices and ice cream (so wonderful during the summer fruit season). If you're a pots-and-pans fan, the store carries the latest in nonstick technologies. Rolls of hard-to-find untreated cooking twine, wire fish holders for the grill, simple imported crystal wineglasses in classic shapes at $5 apiece, and tons of pure cotton dish towels make for good gifts for your own kitchen or someone else's. Homechef stocks the arcane and the necessary with an eye to finding the best examples in every genre.

KINOKUNIYA BOOKSTORE

Japan Center,
1581 Webster (between Post and Geary),
San Francisco
Tel: 567-7625
Open daily
10:30 a.m. to 7 p.m.
Credit cards: AE, MC, V

This spacious book emporium has racks full of Japanese food and housekeeping magazines written in Japanese, but also a large, interesting collection of Asian cookbooks in English. This is the place to find Chinese, Indian, Thai, Burmese, or Indonesian cookbooks in paper- and hardback, not to mention a superior collection of Japanese cookbooks, including Shizuo Tsuji's *Japanese Cooking: A Simple Art*, the definitive Japanese cookbook in English with a foreword by M. F. K. Fisher. Books on Japanese country cooking, on culinary artifacts of Japan illustrated with lively black and white photos, and an international survey of rice cookery are but a few of the gems to be mined. Kunokuniya has the best vegetarian and macrobiotic cookbook section in the city; the titles fill many shelves. The variety of meatless dishes in Asian cuisines stretches the imagination, and even the most exotic ingredients for many of the recipes can be found nearby. The cookbook aisle segues right into Asian massage and sexual instruction section, a juxtaposition I find salubrious.

MASHIKO FOLKCRAFT

The uncased displays in this intimate shop of antique Japanese tableware tempt you to pick things up for close examination, but the eagle-eyed store owner will scold you if he catches you. Nineteenth-century wooden buckets for $7,500 and small antique chests sit next to contemporary bamboo noodle trays. There are lyrical, handmade rice containers carved of cedar; hand-thrown tea mugs at $22; wooden water ladles for the garden fountain; and ladles made of bamboo for the Japanese tea ceremony. The shapes and sizes of the singularly glazed ceramics expand your idea of dinnerware. Many of the prices here have caught up to those at Gump's, but there are still bargains to be found. A visit to this small shop of exotic and beautiful things would certainly solve the problem of finding an exquisite house gift or wedding present for people with worldly taste.

Japan Center, 1581 Webster (between Post and Geary),
San Francisco
Tel: 346-0748
Open Wednesday through Monday 11 a.m. to 6 p.m., Sunday until 5 p.m.
Credit cards: AE, MC, V

R H

It's easy to miss this small, tasteful store around the corner from flashy Fillamento, but there are some beautiful, carefully chosen things here, like leaf-patterned plates in green or white, and simple, colorful Italian crockery. Large, finely woven cotton napkins from India at $7.50, stunning candle holders, and a small but interesting selection of cookbooks, most with photographs, represent some of the seductive merchandise scattered about the small shop. The owner's signature is on every piece, and he does not lead you astray. Though prices are solidly mid-range to expensive, the beauty and simplicity of the objects give them value. RH strikes me as a very hip and civilized spot to shop.

2506 Sacramento Street (at Fillmore),
San Francisco
Tel: 346-1460
Open Monday through Saturday 10 a.m. to 6 p.m., Sunday noon to 5 p.m.
Credit cards: MC, V

SANKO COOKING SUPPLY

1758 Buchanan Street
(at Sutter),
San Francisco
Tel: 922-8331
Open Monday through
Saturday 9:30 a.m. to 6 p.m.,
Sunday noon to 5 p.m.
Credit cards: AE, MC, V

Looking for an electric rice maker, a rectangular cast-iron skillet for making sweet Japanese omelets, a ginger grater, Japanese knives, ridged Japanese mortars, cast-iron sukiyaki pots, or any shape and size of ceramic dish and lacquered bowl? These and every other utensil or vessel you might need for Asian cooking and serving can be found here at reasonable prices.

SOKO HARDWARE

1698 Post Street
(at Buchanan),
San Francisco
Tel: 931-5510
Open Monday through
Saturday 9 a.m. to 5:30 p.m.
Credit cards: MC, V

My husband spotted a most attractive cracked-glaze Japanese vase in the window here nine years ago. It looked like something rare, but it cost $70. Now, anytime either of us walk by Soko Hardware, we dash in for a quick look at the ceramics on the main floor. You never know what treasure you might find. Downstairs, everything from child-sized chopsticks with Eggplant Club, Potato Club, and Turnip Club inscribed on them to gorgeous, heavy, $295 cast-iron miso *shiro* kettles with thick wooden tops are filed away someplace in the vast housewares department. I'm a sucker for this store. I love the tiny dishes the size of a half dollar, and the earthy, glazed rectangles of pottery that look as if their edges were torn and bent. I imagine putting together an elegant Japanese table with this pottery and salads, sushi, and sashimi bought at Super Koyama, but laying Super Hero chopsticks at each place. Upstairs, along with the Japanese carpentry tools and larger ceramics, a rack of Japanese seeds for burdock, cucumber, and *shiso* snags you on the way out.

SUE FISHER-KING

3067 Sacramento Street
(between Broderick
and Baker),
San Francisco
Tel: 922-7276
Open Monday to Saturday
10 a.m. to 6 p.m.
Credit cards: AE, MC, V

If you're looking for top-of-the-line imports like Italian tablecloths and napkins, or wonderful, over-sized French silverware with bone or wooden handles at the highest possible prices, Sue Fisher-King has an exclusive, personal selection. Her table of cookbooks is also worth a look for the quirkiness of what's there. I usually find something I didn't know I was looking for.

Polk Street, Nob Hill, Russian Hill & Van Ness Avenue

POLK STREEET, NOB HILL, RUSSIAN HILL & VAN NESS AVENUE

Restaurants:
1. Acquerello   339
2. Antica Trattoria   340
3. Charles–Nob Hill   341
4. Cordon Bleu   342
5. Golden Turtle   342
6. Harris'   343
7. House of Prime Rib   344
8. La Folie   344
9. Nob Hill Grille   345
10. Ritz-Carlton Dining Room   345
11. Swan Oyster Depot   347
12. Tai Chi   347
13. Vanessi's   348
14. Venticello   349
15. Zarzuela   350

Bars:
16. Johnny Love's   351
17. New Orleans Room in the Fairmont Hotel   351

Delicatessens/Take-Out:
18. Piccadilly Fish and Chips   352
19. Real Food Deli   352

Bakeries/Pastries:
20. Ahren's   354
21. The Bagelry   354
22. Bob's Donuts   355

Ice Cream/Chocolates:
23. Double Rainbow   355
24. Pure T   356
25. See's Candies   357
26. Swenson's   357

Coffee:
27. Freed, Teller & Freed   357
28. Peet's Coffee and Tea   358
29. Spinelli Coffee Company   358

Markets:
30. Real Food Company   358
31. Whole Foods   359

Produce:
30. Real Food Company   360

Meat and Poultry:
32. Quilici's Meats in the Polk & Vallejo Market   360
30. Real Food Company   360

Fish:
11. Swan Oyster Depot   361

Cheese:
33. Leonard's 2001   361

Wines and Spirits:
34. The Jug Shop   362

Cookware and Books:
35. City Discount   362

RESTAURANTS

ACQUERELLO

Chef Suzette Gresham and maître d'/Italian wine expert Giancarlo Paterlini have formed an inspired partnership at their jewel of a restaurant. They both believe in refinement and civility, and insist on the highest quality in performance and ingredients. A meal at Acquerello affords its patrons a moment of pure luxury, not necessarily of the elaborate or showy sort, but of the quiet, deeply satisfying sort—perhaps because the wrapping on the package is Italian rather than French.

The food is a little bit fancy, but held down to earth because of the Italian idiom. Gresham's house-made pastas have the texture of silk, yet her rustic sauces deliver the vitality of the countryside even though they're really quite refined. She uses fresh herbs like a fine oil painter, each small stroke adding dimension. Her antipasti are particularly inventive, as evidenced by a warm squab salad with chard sprinkled with extra-virgin olive oil and toasted pine nuts; or tomato slices spread with a paste of anchovies, capers, and cooked egg yolk. The main courses bring roasted quail stuffed with pancetta; a classic Florentine preparation of sole rolled around spinach; or beef fillet stuffed with prosciutto, Parmesan, and rosemary. Her cooking imagination is fertile, and she is not timid about trying new dishes, though always with the control of a dedicated professional chef. An ambitious program of special dinners, based around the wines of a certain region or celebrating a single ingredient like tomatoes,

1722 Sacramento Street
(between Polk
and Van Ness),
San Francisco
Tel: 567-5432
Open Tuesday through
Saturday 5:30 to 10:30 p.m.
Price: Expensive
Credit cards: AE, DC, D, MC, V

pasta, or seafood, is worth following because they represent excellent all-inclusive buys.

Equal to the pleasure of eating such lovely food is the experience of being in Giancarlo's watercolor-filled dining room. To my mind he has always been the best captain in the city. He knows how to make everyone feel like a million bucks—special, cared for, intelligent, sophisticated—by gently offering guidance, helping people get to the best his restaurant has to offer in just the way that will please them. His expertise on Italian wines, and his generosity in cracking open wonderful bottles to pour glasses that fit each course, expands the whole sensual landscape of the meal. The quiet, anticipatory service, the sparkle of the silver and glasses on the table, the unflagging attention to every detail, all speak to Paterlini's highly trained European sensibility, one that understands and appreciates the tradition of service. This unique restaurant maintains a loyal following of people who like to be treated well.

ANTICA TRATTORIA

2400 Polk (at Union),
San Francisco
Tel: 928-5797
Open Sunday, Tuesday through Thursday 5:30 to 10 p.m., Friday and Saturday until 11 p.m.
Price: Moderate
Credit cards: MC, V

I was first attracted to Antica by its spare, timeless, essentially Italian look. Everyone loves Antica's resonant dark-wood walls and floors. A distressed cream-colored paint job covers the ceiling from which hang stunning bowl-shaped light fixtures. Dark-wood banquettes run along two walls with brown wooden chairs pushed up to them. The rest of the decor consists of white linen–covered tables with white butcher paper. A partially open kitchen at the back and a maître d' stand at the front with flowers are the only other visual details. Being in this stark and rustic room makes you want to drink Italian wine and eat pasta.

The food matches the decor. A bare bones menu offers a handful of antipasti, pasta dishes, and main courses served in European-sized portions. For once, they aren't gigantic. If it's winter, start with a ramekin of braised leeks napped in *fonduta* (a white sauce of melted Fontina) infused with white truffle oil; or a plate of brussels sprouts in brown butter and capers. Have a flat bowl of whole wheat spaghetti tossed in a lot of deep-flavored bolognese sauce. A rosemary-scented seared chicken breast comes on a bed of saucy white beans and black cabbage presented on a small oval plate. Drink soft, fruity sangiovese or dolcetto. Prices for wine and food are wonderfully affordable. I like everything about Antica—its authenticity, restraint, simple presentation, no-nonsense Italian waiters, muted lighting, and international clientele. Somehow the folks behind it have come up with a concept that's so old, it feels new.

CHARLES–NOB HILL

The history of this posh, intimate restaurant, literally hidden away in a classy old apartment building on Nob Hill, goes way back. An evening at Le Club, its former incarnation, epitomized class, luxury, and the height of continental service—even if toward the end the food wasn't quite what it should have been.

Most recently, the owners of Aqua have taken over, renamed the restaurant Charles, and are successfully putting out an elegant, contemporary French-California menu with an emphasis on meat (in contrast to their fish restaurant downtown). Indeed, the best dish on the Charles menu is a Niman-Schell tenderloin steak strewn with amazing seared nuggets of marrow in a classic Bordelaise sauce, flanked by sweet little cipollini onions and a plump, fantastically delicious short rib ravioli. What a great plate! The fillet is full of flavor—a surprise considering a usually bland cut—and the sauce a triumph. A port sauce and tangerine marmalade that partners a thick lobe of scored foie gras also impressed me, though I thought that the intentional charring of the liver gave it an unwelcome bitter edge. Tasty French lamb chops, chestnut soup drizzled with white truffle oil, pretty desserts, a complete wine list with a number of good drinking, affordable bottles, and very gracious service ennobled my most recent visit. It's a romantic place and oh, so tiny. A clubby bar room separates the two parlor-sized dining rooms with a few lushly appointed tables pushed very close together. The closeness works here. The intimacy of the rooms and the secret Nob Hill location give Charles character. This is one restaurant that does not care to be casual or bistro-ish.

1250 Jones Street (at Clay), San Francisco
Tel: 771-5400
Open Tuesday through Thursday 5:30 to 10 p.m., Friday through Sunday until 10:30 p.m.
Price: Expensive
Credit cards: AE, DC, MC, V

CORDON BLEU

**1574 California Street
(near Polk),
San Francisco
Tel: 673-5637
Open for lunch Tuesday
through Saturday
11:30 a.m. to 2:30 p.m.;
dinner Tuesday through
Saturday 5 to 10 p.m.,
Sunday 4 to 10 p.m.
Price: Inexpensive
No credit cards**

The tiny Cordon Bleu, one of the city's first Vietnamese eateries, reminds me of food stalls in tropical Asia, where cooks set up their steamers and grills right on the street. I have eaten the best chicken of my life at a card table and folding chair on a Bangkok sidewalk; the Cordon Bleu uncannily replicates this experience. Though there is a front door and ceiling, the painted brick walls suggest food operations set up in a crevice between two buildings with a canopy overhead. Very little light filters into Cordon Bleu during the day; at night a few dim bulbs barely do the job. People squeeze onto stools at a counter in the front of a small stove and grill or sit at two tiny tables at the back. Every time the door opens a blast of cold air sweeps into the room.

This authentic atmosphere only makes the five-spice roast chicken, the house specialty, taste better. For an extremely small tariff you get a half chicken, aromatically marinated, and a pile of crunchy cabbage and carrot salad with a large dollop of rice moistened with a Vietnamese version of bolognese sauce. Only two other dishes are available: crisply deep-fried imperial rolls stuffed with ground shrimp, pork, and vegetables; and beef on skewers, both of which come with the sauced rice and salad. Whatever the combination, all these foods are wonderfully satisfying eaten together. While not as refined or authentic as the top Vietnamese places, Cordon Bleu has maintained a strong neighborhood following by turning out hearty plates of good chicken year after year.

GOLDEN TURTLE

**2211 Van Ness Avenue
(between Broadway and
Vallejo), San Francisco
Tel: 441-4419
Open Tuesday through
Sunday 5 to 10:30 p.m.
Price: Inexpensive
Credit cards: AE, MC, V**

A visit to the comfortable dining room of this first-class Vietnamese restaurant will net you one of the nicest meals in town for the most reasonable price. The small multilevel restaurant is decorated with wall murals hand-carved in wood, and light sconces made of gnarled tree branches. The tables are set with wineglasses and tablecloths. At first you think you've walked into a French restaurant—until the piles of exotic fresh herbs, cold noodles, and lettuces start coming. Many dishes at the Golden Turtle deliver the classic Vietnamese juxtaposition of hot and savory with cold and crisp, like hot, crisp crab-filled spring rolls, which you eat in lettuce leaves with sprigs of fresh mint, cilantro, cold white rice noodles, and a dip into a piquant sauce. Another brilliant combination brings five-spice roast chicken with golden skin and velvety, aromatic flesh, served on a bed of juicy Vietnamese vegetable slaw in a sparkly dressing—a dish I could eat every day. The menu offers one delight after another, like a whole fresh sea bass gently steamed, cleanly sauced, and topped with fresh herbs and ginger threads; or thinly sliced grilled beef marinated in lemongrass and served on a watercress salad. Quail, for which Vietnamese cooks have a special affection, are prepared in several different ways and all are worth ordering. The consistently meticulous preparation and high-quality ingredients insisted on in this kitchen make almost every dish a revelation. The graceful wait staff in long skirts or tunics and pants is well informed and efficient, and they know how to serve the wines on the small, but choice, wine list, which includes some French whites that go superbly with the food. Golden Turtle meals work as either satisfying, everyday fare or as special-occasion food. The beauty is that you can eat so well and so elegantly for a song.

HARRIS'

2100 Van Ness Avenue
(at Pacific),
San Francisco
Tel: 673-1888
Open Monday through Friday 6 to 10 p.m., Saturday and Sunday 5 to 10 p.m.
Price: Expensive
Credit cards: AE, D, MC, V

When dynamic Anne Harris, who married into the well-known cattle-raising clan, left the fold, she took over a famous, but defunct, city steak house called Grisson's and reopened it as Harris'. Her luxurious restaurant boasts king-sized upholstered booths, tall potted palms, a huge wall mural by Barnaby Conrad, and a clubby bar that serves pour-yourself martinis in miniature glass decanters resting in miniature ice buckets. Her delicious signature sweetbread pâté with fresh toast points makes an inspired accompaniment. The menu is steak-house simple and well executed: juicy grilled Harris Ranch steaks (my favorite is the Harris Steak, a New York with the featherbone left on), baked potatoes with butter, sour cream, and real bacon bits; excellent creamed spinach; and for starters, blue points on the half shell; a tasty Caesar with freshly made croutons; spinach salad with sieved eggs; and decent deep-fried zucchini. Wine drinkers can find a big California red with some age on it on the multipaged wine list. Overall, Anne Harris's place is the most satisfying steak house in the city. It has its role down cold and plays it like a trouper, night after night.

HOUSE OF PRIME RIB

1906 Van Ness Avenue (between Jackson and Washington), San Francisco
Tel: 885-4605
Open Monday through Thursday 5:30 to 10 p.m., Friday 5 to 10 p.m., Saturday 4:30 to 10 p.m., Sunday 4 to 10 p.m.
Price: Moderate
Credit cards: AE, DC, MC, V

A restaurant that serves slabs of rare roast beef (with a bone if you want, and I do) carved at tableside from huge silver carts should be protected like a national treasure. In this town, the House of Prime Rib practically has that designation since it's the last outpost for this kind of eating nearly anywhere. For one all-inclusive price you get a salad dressed at tableside in the famous spinning salad bowl—the waitress spins the bowl on a bed of ice as she pours pink dressing over chopped vegetables and then dishes it up on chilled plates with forks right out of the freezer—followed by roast beef, a baked potato, and Yorkshire pudding. You can decide if you're up to dessert. The old-fashioned windowless dining room with a large bar that is particularly active preprandially, thick carpeting, booths, and heavy linen is distinguished on the exterior by an arresting trompe l'oeil mural. Service is professional; the wine list improving; and the experience of dining there totally and wonderfully predictable. People who love prime rib don't want any surprises.

LA FOLIE

2316 Polk Street (between Union and Green), San Francisco
Tel: 776-5577
Open Monday through Saturday 5:30 to 10:30 p.m.
Price: Expensive
Credit cards: AE, DC, D, MC, V

Chef Roland Passot uses this charming, sky-blue dining room as his gallery for artistic plates of very inventive French-California cooking. He has a passion for decoration, and each plate is conceived for its visual effect, using sauces and purees in a rainbow of colors and a wild array of other ingredients to form his mosaics, architectural constructions, and strata. Passot loves luxurious ingredients—foie gras, lobster, caviar, and the like—and his ability to interweave them into multifaceted plates means that a little of them go a long way, keeping prices under control. The cheerful dining room has always been one of my favorites in the city, with fluffy white clouds painted on the blue ceiling, a copper-framed window that looks into the kitchen, and Roland's wife Jamie and sommelier brother George adding their warmth and generosity to the floor.

NOB HILL GRILLE

In a town blissfully short on franchise restaurants and fast-food chains, an independently owned coffee shop like the Nob Hill Grille fills a real need. It offers the inexpensive everyday food beloved by Americans, prepared with integrity and flair. Located across the street from St. Francis Hospital, the Grille is busy all day, cooking platters of eggs, top-notch home-fried potatoes (baked potatoes broken up and crushed against the griddle until they get brown and crusty), sausages, and crisp bacon. The No. 1 club sandwich is thick with real, moist roast turkey, and it comes with a tasty cucumber salad in cumin-scented dressing. Devotees of bacon, lettuce, and tomato sandwiches should make a pilgrimage here—the sandwich comes with a pile of carrot sticks, instead of french fries, and freshly cut coleslaw, a nice touch. Milk shakes, malts, and fresh lemonade highlight the drink card. The Nob Hill Grille understands what makes all these seemingly simple things taste so good and unfailingly executes them with high standards.

969 Hyde Street (at Pine),
San Francisco
Tel: 474-5985
Open daily 7 a.m. to 6 p.m.
Price: Inexpensive
No credit cards

RITZ-CARLTON DINING ROOM

Hotel dining rooms have traditionally earned a bad rap for over-priced luxury and fancy, but soulless institutional cooking, but the Dining Room at the Ritz Carlton is actually one of the best high-end restaurants in the city.

Run almost like an independent restaurant (except for the fact that it is subsidized by the hotel), the Dining Room and its dedicated team came up with an appealing format: various set-price meals ($45 for three courses, $52 for four, and $59 for a five-course tasting menu, with accompanying wines by the glass an extra $29) that allow diners to order as many

600 Stockton Street
(at California),
San Francisco
Tel: 296-7465
Open Monday through
Saturday 6 to 9:30 p.m.
Price: Expensive
Credit cards: AE, DC, D, MC, V

dishes as they want from any section of the menu—appetizers, fish dishes, meat and poultry dishes, desserts, plus a superior cheese cart option. If you feel like having two appetizers and a fish course, or a fish course as an appetizer and an appetizer as a main course, or two fish courses and a cheese course and dessert, the kitchen will adjust the portions to make the meal work.

The courses can be mixed and matched because they are stylistically related, especially now that Sylvain Portay, formerly of Le Cirque in New York, has taken over the helm from the inventive California chef Gary Danko, who put the Dining Room on the map. Portay's cooking, of course, is richer, creamier, more buttery, more reduced—in a word, French. His best dishes use classic ingredients in classic preparations, like a voluptuous Crayfish Veloute "Cappuccino," a shellfish soup deep in flavor enriched with a little cream, lightened by a froth of steamed milk, hence the name. I love every dish here that involves lobster, such as an exquisite salad or a huge three-tail main course serving of roasted Maine lobster bathed in a velvety coral sauce, showered with artichokes and chanterelles. I also come here for Portay's impeccable sweetbreads meunière, the best in town, and a warm shellfish salad with white beans accompanied with a pile of piquantly dressed arugula. Yes, you will find squab, foie gras, and fillet of beef, but whatever you order, save room for cheese. The born maître d'/manager Nick Peyton assembles and personally administers the best cheese cart in San Francisco. He combs the world for the most intriguing specimens, and tells you about them lovingly as if they were of his own making. He's clued in to the importance of ripeness—and because the cheese service gets so much play here, he is able to present cheeses at their peak.

Even after cheese you may want dessert. The pastry department comes up with lovely seasonal ones. In the fall, for example, you may find two small Seckel pears baked in crisp pastry. Chocolate soufflés are offered here (I think they should be oozier), and house-made ice creams and sorbets. Or, you can opt for a plate of tiny chocolates and cookies that arrive with coffee.

The Ritz-Carlton dining room is traditionally luxurious, appointed with soft heavy linens, elegant china, silver, and glassware, heavily draped tall French windows, and lots of polished wood and thick carpeting. You settle into large upholstered chairs at tables placed far enough apart for intimate conversation above the glissandos of a harpist. Trained in every detail by rigorous Nick Peyton, the bartenders make perfect martinis; the waiters know what goes into every dish; the sommelier administers a huge wine list of bottles and glasses in every price range, and loves to come up with just the right wines to suit your pocketbook and the dishes you're eating. This town's great food reputation does not come from our high-end restaurants. In fact, we have only a handful of interest. Nick Peyton and Sylvain Portay's Dining Room at the Ritz Carlton happens to be one of them.

SWAN OYSTER DEPOT

1517 Polk Street (between Sacramento and California),
San Francisco
Tel: 673-1101
Open Monday through Saturday 8 a.m. to 5:30 p.m.
Price: Moderate
No credit cards
See Fish Markets, page 361.

TAI CHI

Over the years this modest neighborhood spot, which prepares hot, spicy Hunan and Szechuan dishes, has grown in popularity so that during prime dinner hours you might face a wait. The draw, besides very cheap prices and a Western orientation (which means that the dining room and kitchen are set up to accommodate parties of two instead of large round tables of ten), is the saucy, incendiary northern food. When I get a yen for pot stickers I come here. I could eat a whole plate of these well-seasoned pork dumplings with thick but tender wrappers, dipped into vinegar and red chili oil. Any of the chili-marked hot dishes will be pretty good, like dry-fried long beans with pork, or the indulgent "Hunan-style" preparations in which chunks of boneless chicken or pork are thickly battered, crisply deep-fried, and

2031 Polk Street (between Broadway and Pacific), San Francisco
Tel: 441-6758
Open Monday through Thursday 11:30 a.m. to 10 p.m., Friday and Saturday until 10:30 p.m., Sunday 4 to 10 p.m.
Price: Inexpensive
Credit cards: AE, MC, V; $10 minimum

tossed in a copious amount of garlicky hot sweet-and-sour sauce, divine over rice. Hot-and-sour soup is also OK, but this is not the place to go to order seafood or even plates of simple vegetables. Bowls of spicy noodles are the draw, not to mention congenial waiters who are used to dealing with a mostly Western clientele.

VANESSI'S

1177 California Street
(at Jones),
San Francisco
Tel: 771-2422
Open for lunch Monday through Friday 11:30 a.m. to 4 p.m.; dinner Sunday through Thursday 4:30 to 10 p.m., Friday and Saturday until 11 p.m.
Price: Moderate
Credit Cards: AE, DC, MC, V

Those of us eating out in San Francisco during the seventies and eighties remember what an exciting scene the old Vanessi's on Broadway was. People gravitated there at all hours of the day and night for huge portions of short-order Italian-American cooking. The crowd came from every social strata, every profession, every age group. You had to pay the maître d' just to get into the place, even with a reservation. The tourists stood by and watched the regulars privateer their tables.

As often happens in the restaurant business, things changed quickly. Giovanni Leoni, Vanessi's chef, left to open his own fine place nearby called Buca Giovanni. Broadway became too seedy and the older clientele stopped coming. The employees went on strike, and gradually, the old Vanessi's lost its energy and closed. So in 1986 owner Bart Shea and his daughter Lorna opened a second Vanessi's on Nob Hill in the Gramercy Tower condominium complex across the street from Grace Cathedral. The new, spacious dining room feels just like the old Vanessi's with the trademark open kitchen, counter seating in front of it, and lots of burgundy vinyl booths, mirrors, and chandeliers. Subsidized parking right in the building brought the old-timers back, many of whom just walk over from their Nob Hill apartments.

As for the menu, it has been edited from its original long version. Some of it survives in all its old glory, while some of it just doesn't work. The Caesar tossed at tableside can be good or terrible depending on who makes it. However, Vanessi's classic spinach salad with lots of bacon and sliced mushrooms has been consistently good. Also dependable because of a lively house vinaigrette are hearts of romaine salad and tomato slices in season with onions and anchovies.

Spaghetti carbonara brings back fond memories of the original Vanessi's al dente pasta in a rich sauce of pancetta, shallots, cream, and egg yolk cooked by the hot noodles. The once beloved white clam sauce now seems thin and flavorless. Chicken sauté Vanessi, pieces of chicken sautéed with peppers, onions, parsley, garlic, and a little white wine, still satisfies. And for dessert, the warm, frothy, made-to-order zabaglione, overflowing its glass dish onto two ladyfingers, remains a lovely constant.

VENTICELLO

At Venticello, a chic trattoria hidden away in a valley between Nob Hill and Russian Hill, diners feel as if they are seated in a Tuscan country kitchen complete with enticing aromas emanating from the tiled oven in the middle of the room. Antique china cabinets, polished wooden floors, heavy wooden chairs, and rosy, mottled walls make the room look as if it had been airlifted from some ancient inn in Chianti. The tables, covered with linen and butcher paper, are decorated with little pots of fresh herbs. The windows from the lower dining room afford a glimpse of the Bay Bridge through the apartments across the street. Venticello is the kind of neighborhood secret that savvy tourists consider a trophy.

1257 Taylor Street
(at Washington),
San Francisco
Tel: 922-2545
Open daily 5:30 to 10 p.m.
Price: Moderate
Credit Cards: AE, D, DC, MC, V

The meals start with freshly baked loaves of whole-wheat bread and a saucer of black olives. Soft red and crisp white Italian wines are poured by the glass for reasonable prices. A lush antipasto brings grilled endive, zucchini, and Japanese eggplant, ripe tomatoes in season, fresh mozzarella, melon wrapped in prosciutto, and fabulous marinated shrimp on a bed of radicchio and Italian parsley. Every item on the plate shines. Grilled shrimp wrapped in pancetta make for another fine starter as do country vegetable soups. The thin-crusted pizzas from the wood-fired oven are delicious, especially the classic pizza Margherita, sublime with only tomato sauce, mozzarella, and basil.

House-made ravioli stuffed with spinach and ricotta, and wide noodles sauced in duck or rabbit ragout, are but some of the satisfying, often rustic pastas. The menu changes daily, but if you find a poussin (a baby chicken) roasted in the wood-fired oven with wild mushrooms, peppers, and garlic, served with mashed potatoes and arugula, order it. For dessert both tiramisù and *panna cotta*, "cooked cream" slathered with fresh berries, are lovely.

ZARZUELA

2000 Hyde Street (at Union), San Francisco
Tel: 346-0800
Open Monday through Saturday noon to 11 p.m.
Price: Moderate
Credit cards: D, MC, V

Finally, the highly visible corner location at Hyde and Union that used to be the Marcel and Henri charcuterie and butcher shop, then La Ferme Beaujolais, has found the perfect new identity: a Spanish restaurant that specializes in tapas and paella. The wine-cellarish back room, used as a cheese-ripening room in its former incarnation, lends itself to a Spanish *cava* motif, while the glass deli counters now showcase a tempting display of tapas. The small front room, with a terra-cotta tile and stone interior and big windows that look out to the cable car line, evokes the Mediterranean. I can't imagine a more suitable match of place and purpose.

The delicious food is as traditional as it can get—if you're eating on Spain's Costa del Sol. Start with, or make a meal of, tapas, little servings of hot and cold dishes that draw on the entire Spanish pantry. Try a plate of the paper-thin, cold, marinated grilled vegetables called *escalivada*, or a ramekin of hot, miniature, spicy chorizo sausages, served in a gravy that you'll want to sop up with pieces of good rosemary bread (one of the few I've ever cared for) or baguette, brought to the table with a saucer of olives. Or have a typical Spanish tapas plate of bread slathered with a puree of fresh tomatoes and garlic, thin slices of nutty serrano ham and slices of *manchego* cheese (a great all-around cooking and eating cheese that is becoming more and more appreciated in the Bay Area). If you don't make a meal of these excellent small plates, by all means have the paella, an absolutely stunning Spanish rice preparation that comes in an authentic flat cast-iron pan. The pearly, short-grained rice soaks up all the juices from impeccable shrimp, clams, mussels, bits of chicken, and a colorful scattering of fresh peas and red peppers, yet the dish is voluptuously moist and flavorful. Zarzuela makes one of the best versions I have tasted in this country.

You can have glasses of cold *fino* sherry with tapas or a bottle of light, fruity Spanish red wine, a number of which are on the wine list. It's amazing how wonderful these wines are with the food, made more so by their reasonable prices.

The whole experience is so nicely realized, and the tariff so affordable, that I predict people will be lined up in front of the tapas counters crying for little bites of food and sherry while they wait for a table. Currently the service is not organized to accommodate these requests, and that is my only criticism of this terrific new restaurant.

BARS

JOHNNY LOVE'S

This popular bar, favored by the airline industry, rises above being a mating scene during the dinner hour when a hearty, imaginative pub menu of hamburgers, deep-fried calamari, southwest-accented meat dishes, substantial salads, and the inevitable pasta flow out of the kitchen. It's best to come early, before the room turns into a dance club with live music, so you can talk over dinner.

1500 Broadway (at Polk),
San Francisco
Tel: 931-8021
Open daily 5 p.m. to 2 a.m.
Credit cards: AE, MC, V

NEW ORLEANS ROOM IN THE FAIRMONT HOTEL

Situated off the Fairmont's grand lobby, the New Orleans Room offers an intimate and civilized venue to take in jazz and veteran rhythm and blues headliners. The bartenders, who happen to be jazz fans, put out well-made drinks and bowls of fancy mixed nuts. There's a moderate cover charge and drinks are a bit pricy, but the room is perfect for a nightcap with some entertainment.

California and
Mason Streets,
San Francisco
Tel: 772-5259
Open daily 3 p.m. to 1 a.m.;
jazz Tuesday through
Saturday at 8 p.m.
Credit cards: AE, DC, D, MC, V

DELICATESSENS/TAKE-OUT

PICCADILLY FISH AND CHIPS

1348 Polk Street (at Pine),
San Francisco
Tel: 771-6477
Open daily
11 a.m. to 11 p.m.
No credit cards

When the urge to eat a big pile of fish and chips sprinkled with malt vinegar overtakes you, come to this immaculate little shop that does nothing but fry up fish and potatoes. The cod fillets come from Ireland; they're battered and deep-fried to order, staying moist inside a crunchy golden batter. The thick-cut potatoes are precooked to a creamy consistency, then barely browned in oil a second time. They stay limp and potatoey—just the way true fish-and-chips lovers like them. Though the oil in the gigantic fryer is kept very clean—you can see this—it does have its own special smell, which we neutral-oil fanatics have to get used to. My long-time dining-out companion (otherwise known as "Chicken Bucket" for his love of fried chicken), says that the oil is fine and that Piccadilly is the best fish and chips place this side of the Atlantic.

REAL FOOD DELI

2164 Polk Street
(at Vallejo),
San Francisco
Tel: 775-2805
Open daily
8 a.m. to 8 p.m.
Credit cards: D, MC, V

Ever since it opened, the Real Food Deli has increasingly taken on the role of a neighborhood cafe. Its few sidewalk tables are almost always full, and people drop by all afternoon for a cup of soup, a salad, or a sandwich. The deli cases are full of an international, natural foods array of dishes—Asian noodles, couscous salads, tofu, grilled vegetables—and house-baked goods. A large kitchen located a store away in the Real Food market supplies the deli with fresh and often inventive preparations, many of which use organic produce. People order at the counter and either take the food to go or find a seat.

BUTTERMILK BREAD

1 cup buttermilk
3 tablespoons sugar
2 1/2 teaspoons kosher salt
1/3 cup butter, cut into chunks
1 cup warm (105° to 115°F) water
1 package active dry yeast
5 3/4 cups unbleached all-purpose flour
1/4 teaspoon baking soda

The Real Food stores sell organic unbleached flour, stone-ground whole-wheat flour, yeast, wheat germ, oat bran, and every other conceivable flour in bulk for bread baking. This buttermilk bread has a light, firm texture and an amazingly full flavor; it's an old-fashioned white bread, great for toast. I found it in The Margaret Rudkin Pepperidge Farm Cookbook (Gosset & Dunlap, 1970), which has a number of excellent American bread recipes including a yeasted corn bread and a full-flavored wheat-germ bread. The volume is worth seeking out for these three recipes alone.

In a small saucepan over low heat, combine the buttermilk, sugar, salt, and butter and warm until the butter is almost melted. Remove from the heat and let cool to warm (105° to 115°F).

Pour the warm water into a large bowl. Sprinkle in the yeast and stir until it dissolves.

Add the warm milk mixture to the yeast mixture. Stir in 3 cups of the flour and the baking soda. Beat with a wooden spoon until smooth. Alternatively, use an electric mixer with the paddle attachment and beat until smooth.

Mix in the remaining 2 3/4 cups flour to make a dough that has a rough, dull appearance and is a bit sticky. Turn the dough out on a lightly floured board and knead until smooth and elastic, about 8 to 10 minutes. Or use the dough hook of the electric mixer and knead for 7 minutes.

Grease a large bowl with butter. Form the dough into a ball and put into the prepared bowl, turning the dough to lightly coat all sides with butter. Cover with a clean, damp cloth and let rise in a warm place free from drafts until doubled in bulk, about 1 hour.

Punch the dough down, turn it out on a lightly floured board, and let rest for 15 minutes.

Divide the dough in half. Shape into loaves and place in 2 buttered 9-by-5-inch bread pans. Cover and let rise in a warm place free from drafts until doubled in bulk, about 1 hour.

Preheat the oven to 375°F. Bake the dough until golden brown, about 35 minutes. When you turn out the loaves onto a rack, knock the bottom with your knuckle. The breads should make a hollow sound.

Makes two 9-by-5-inch loaves

BAKERIES/PASTRIES

AHREN'S

1946 Van Ness Avenue
(at Jackson),
San Francisco
Tel: 885-5060
Open daily
5:30 a.m. to 7 p.m.
No credit cards

An old-fashioned American-style bakery with a sit-down counter that dispenses thin coffee, white bread toast, well-made eggs, and coffee-shop sandwiches, Ahren's is a hold out for a certain kind of comfort food that is fast disappearing in this town. The doughnuts, especially the crisp holes, are very good, and baked goods like coffee cakes and rolls have a tender, not too rich, easy-to-eat quality about them without the off flavors of artificial ingredients. Ahren's baked goods are the models for the items coming out of supermarket bakeries these days, and frankly it pays to make a special trip for the real thing.

THE BAGELRY

2134 Polk Street (between
Vallejo and Broadway),
San Francisco
Tel: 441-3003
Open Monday, Tuesday,
Thursday through Saturday
6:30 a.m. to 6 p.m.,
Wednesday until noon,
Sunday until 4 p.m.
No credit cards

To my mind, The Bagelry makes the best bagels in the Bay Area. They are chewy, not soft and crumbly, and carry some weight. They have a good, deep flavor and toast up fragrantly. Unlike the "lite" bagels being sold everywhere—in supermarkets, natural foods stores, and bagel chains that use bagels for ham sandwiches—the one main purpose of a Bagelry bagel is as a landing for cream cheese and, on flush days, smoked salmon, both of which are sold prewrapped in a small refrigerator at the front of the bakery. The singleness of purpose at this store underscores how important the quality of their product is to them and their customers. In fact, if you don't get there early the egg bagels will be gone (they run out first) and several others, like poppy seed or onion, will be in short supply. The seedy bagel sticks have been attracting a following and will do if the bagels have run out. If you are a true bagel aficionado, the Bagelry merits a trip across town.

BOB'S DONUTS

There are doughnuts and there are doughnuts, and 90 percent of them are inedible. Bob's, a small doughnut shop that has been open for years, not only makes edible doughnuts, but delicious doughnuts. First of all, they are fresh. They're made in batches and turn over quickly because everyone in the north end of the city makes doughnut pilgrimages there. Secondly, they are perfectly fried in clean, neutral oil. Thirdly, they're made from scratch, just an old-fashioned conjunction of flour, yeast, eggs, and sugar, so they're free of artificial preservatives and off flavors. These doughnuts, crumbly or airy, iced, glazed, or sugared, sprinkled with cinnamon or plain, are never cloying, rancid, sticky, stale, or greasy. Since I am the only one who feels that doughnuts don't taste good with coffee (which makes them taste greasy, except for the milky chicory coffee at Café du Monde in New Orleans, which goes perfectly with their hot beignets), the serve-yourself Colombian coffee station at Bob's gets lots of action. The women behind the counter—efficient, intelligent, not overly friendly—know their regulars and have their doughnuts ready as the familiar faces walk through the door. Once you compare Bob's to other doughnuts, you'll buy them here.

1621 Polk Street (between Clay and Sacramento), San Francisco
Tel: 776-3141
Open 24 hours everyday
No credit cards

ICE CREAM/CHOCOLATES

DOUBLE RAINBOW

For other locations, see page 441.

Michael Sachar and Steve Fink, two guys from Brooklyn, started this local ice cream company on September 18, 1976, when they saw a double rainbow over San Francisco, an incredibly rare event in that dry time of the year. They took it as a lucky omen—two pots of gold—and started making their rich ice cream with a vengeance, opening their first store at Castro and Market. Currently, they distribute their products through Double Rainbow ice cream shops, many of

1653 Polk Street (between Sacramento and Clay), San Francisco
Tel: 775-3220
Open Sunday through Thursday 11 a.m. to 11 p.m., Friday and Saturday until midnight
No credit cards

which have taken on the role of neighborhood cafes, and in cartons at grocery stores. Their sweet eggy vanilla and strawberry, strong-flavored coffee and chocolate, and assorted flavors that come in and out of season have earned them many devoted followers, not the less for Double Rainbow's unceasing contributions to local causes and community celebrations. The vanilla malts and thick shakes have risen to classic status, but Double Rainbow keeps up with the times. Their low-fat strawberry frozen yogurt has such satisfyingly creamy texture and voluptuous flavor you would never guess it has only 5 percent fat. Fresh fruit ices, like an intense and true-flavored raspberry, have become a Double Rainbow signature. The Asian-style ice creams—lychee nut, green tea, and mango—have taken off in San Francisco, perhaps a reflection of Double Rainbow's enormous success in Hong Kong.

Every shop is independently owned and varies in size, menu, and appearance; the Double Rainbow on Polk Street is one of the busiest, with tables that spill out onto the sidewalk, suggesting the atmosphere of a European cafe.

PURE T

2238 Polk Street (between Vallejo and Green), San Francisco
Tel: 441-7878
Open daily
11:30 a.m. to 10 p.m.
No credit cards

I'm not sure yet if tea makes sense as an ice cream flavor, but this whole shop devotes itself to the art of combining the two. Passion fruit tea, jasmine tea, black and green teas, spicy Indian *chai*, and other infusions are the flavoring agents for a rather thin, milky ice cream served in cups with waferlike Japanese tea cakes. I shrugged at first taste, but by the end of a cup of different flavors, some had endeared themselves to me and become quite refreshing. On the face of it, the idea of tea and ice cream seems antithetical: tea is so clean, and its bouquet so delicate that mixing it with thick, rich textures and sugar undermines its best qualities. But there might be meals after which this tea-infused ice cream would work very well, especially paired with certain kinds of fruit or fruit compotes. The shop has a Zen air to it, with a small, well-designed counter and a few tables. It provides the most sympathetic context for tasting the ice creams.

SEE'S CANDIES

1519 Polk Street (between Sacramento and California),
San Francisco
Tel: 775-7049
Open Monday through Saturday 9 a.m. to 6 p.m.
No credit cards
See listing, page 386.

SWENSON'S

On the cable car corner of Hyde and Union, Swenson's has been making its own ice creams and scooping its generous cones for generations. The ice cream is old-fashioned, middle-of-the-road, all-American quality, not as rich as Double Rainbow or Häagen-Dazs, but creamier and of much higher quality than Baskin-Robbins. I like Swenson's low-fat ice creams, which still have a voluptuous texture and bright flavor, particularly the toasted almond, a personal favorite. In fact, I can barely taste the difference between the two. If I did, I certainly would opt for the creamier. Why waste calories by eating something that doesn't satisfy?

1999 Hyde Street (at Union),
San Francisco
Tel: 775-6818
Open daily
11:30 a.m. to 10 p.m.
No credit cards

COFFEE

FREED, TELLER & FREED

Opened in 1907, Freed, Teller & Freed set the standard for coffee and tea merchandising and still does with its daily-roasted coffee beans from Central America, Africa, and the Pacific, and a wide selection of teas. F, T & F roasts light, which allows you to make a double-strong brew without bitterness. The dark wood shelves are stocked with coffee makers of every conceivable shape and kind, including elegant glass vacuum pots, which run on candle power and can be set up at the dinner table. On the more modern front are a whole shelf of home espresso machines, which the shop services as well as sells. Freed, Teller & Freed has always been a proponent of,

1326 Polk Street (between Bush and Pine),
San Francisco
Tel: 673-0922
Open Monday through Friday 9:30 a.m. to 6 p.m.,
Saturday until 5 p.m.
Credit cards: MC, V

and educator about, the culture of coffee and tea drinking, a stance that the new higher end chains have taken as their own. When you walk into this handsome old store with its attractive merchandise displayed like works of art (exquisite demitasses for French roast; old-fashioned coffee makers), you know that this shop has history behind it. The clerks in coffee-colored lab coats know everything about coffee and will be happy to tell you as much as you want to hear.

PEET'S COFFEE AND TEA

2139 Polk Street (between Vallejo and Broadway),
San Francisco
Tel: 474-1871
Open Monday through Saturday 6:30 a.m. to 8 p.m.,
Sunday 7 a.m. to 7 p.m.
Credit cards: D, MC, V
See listing, page 199.

SPINELLI COFFEE COMPANY

2255 Polk Street (between Vallejo and Green),
San Francisco
Tel: 928-7793
Open Monday through Friday 6:30 a.m. to 9 p.m.,
Saturday 7 a.m. to 9 p.m., Sunday 7 a.m. to 8 p.m.
Credit cards: AE, MC, V
See listing, page 173.

MARKETS

REAL FOOD COMPANY

2140 Polk Street (between Vallejo and Broadway),
San Francisco
Tel: 673-7420
Open daily 9 a.m. to 9 p.m.
Credit cards: D, MC, V

For other locations, see pages 173, 176, and 259.

The Polk Street location is the most active branch of the Real Food Company and has become a full-service market over the years by installing a meat, fish, and poultry counter in the back of the store. As in the produce section, the emphasis is on natural and organic (Bradley Ranch beef, Fulton Valley Farms' chickens) and locally made sausages, many made of chicken, many from Bruce Aidells. A small fish section is not inspiring.

The major draw of Real Food is the wide range of organic produce at exorbitant prices. When it's good, it's very good and worth every penny. When it's disappointing—old perhaps—and you've paid an arm and a leg, you feel like murdering the management, but I go back because it's the only store in the northern part of the city that gives me some choice in buying organically. Early on this Real Food carried Acme bread, which now arrives fresh, and excellent Italian style breads from Metropolis Bakery in Emeryville. The store stocks much of what I like—extra-rich Clover Guernsey milk for caffè latte, Plugra butter, organic flours, organic nuts and dried fruits in bulk, fruit juices, Vitamin C in every form and hormone-free brown eggs—for which I am willing to pay the premium charged here.

WHOLE FOODS

The arrival of a branch of the Whole Foods chain to San Francisco was regarded by many as the second coming. Indeed, its prime location in the north end of the city, with its large size and parking lot, made it seem like a miracle. I have mixed feelings about it. As part of a publicly traded national company, Whole Foods buys bulk produce. Though a lot of it is organic, it tastes like the same kind of produce I find at Safeway, picked underripe for transport and warehousing, and lacking in character. (I myself prefer to buy organic and locally, something I do at the Ferry Plaza Farmers' Market and at the smaller, local operation of San Francisco Real Foods). I do like the freshness and variety at the extensive fish counter and the fact that there is a live butcher behind the well-tended meat counter. And the Whole Foods store in San Francisco is the only West Coast outlet for Major Farm sheeps' milk cheese from Vermont, maybe the best cheese produced in America.

1765 California Street
(at Franklin),
San Francisco
Tel: 674-0500
Open daily 9 a.m. to 10 p.m.
Credit cards: D, MC, V

PRODUCE

REAL FOOD COMPANY

See Markets, page 358.

MEAT AND POULTRY

QUILICI'S MEATS
IN THE POLK & VALLEJO MARKET

2150 Polk Street (between Vallejo and Broadway), San Francisco
Tel: 885-1134
Open weekdays 8:30 a.m. to 7 p.m., Saturday until 6 p.m., Sunday 10 a.m. to 6 p.m.
No credit cards

I go here to buy things like unsurpassed breakfast sausage links from Schwarz, seasoned with a little thyme and absolutely fresh, simple, and satisfying; and free-range chickens at less than Real Food prices. The butchers will cut and bone to your specification, grind pork and veal, and slice whatever cured or smoked meats you need for cooking. They're used to selling small amounts to the Russian Hill apartment dwellers nearby, and have patience for the pickiest requests.

REAL FOOD COMPANY

See Markets, page 358.

FISH

SWAN OYSTER DEPOT

This little store, half oyster bar with counter and stools, half fish market, has been the premier source for high-quality local fish for decades. I have had the most beautiful salmon, elegantly filleted, pristine, full of wild flavor from them, as well as good specimens of lingcod, local rockfish, local halibut; the biggest, sweetest Dungeness crabs cooked, cleaned, and cracked per request; as well as some eastern items like scallops and Swan's standby, blue point oysters. These mollusks are sweeter and milder than Pacific oysters. You can sit at the counter to eat them with an old-fashioned catsup-horseradish cocktail sauce, or take them home, but ask that they not to be rinsed in water after they are opened. Regulars sit down at the counter for slabs of velvety smoked salmon on buttered bread and Swan's good, not overly thickened clam chowder. The white tile walls, resonantly worn counter, and pleasant, oceany smell draw people who like their seafood chilled, unadorned, and in large quantity.

1517 Polk Street (between Sacramento and California), San Francisco
Tel: 673-1101
Open Monday through Saturday 8 a.m. to 5:30 p.m.
No credit cards

CHEESE

LEONARD'S 2001

Leonard Born, the proprietor of this relatively new store, is serious about cheese. He likes to turn his customers on to his favorites from all over the world, and he buys a wide and interesting selection. He seduces you with tastes so you often end up buying two or three more cheeses than you planned. The one problem is that all cheeses are cut and prewrapped so you can't get the size you want, especially under a half pound, a big mistake if Leonard wants his customers to expand their cheese repertoires. You really have to think twice about buying a huge hunk when you know you will only eat a small part of it. However, prices are excellent on popular cheeses like imported

2001 Polk Street (at Pacific), San Francisco
Tel: 921-2001
Open Monday through Saturday 9:30 a.m. to 7:30 p.m., Sunday 10 a.m. to 6 p.m.
Credit cards: D, MC, V

Italian Fontina, Parmesan, delicious *manchego* from Spain, and high-quality French cooking cheeses.

To go with the cheese, Leonard's carries Boudin and soft Bread Workshop baguettes, both excellent and refreshingly different choices, as well as the famous Bread Workshop half-baked pizza dough, a tender, thick round that bakes up crisp and golden when topped with cheese and brushed with olive oil. The large, light-filled corner store stocks grains, dried fruits, spices, and pastas in bulk and in packages, but the cheese is the draw, along with the enthusiastic service.

WINES AND SPIRITS

THE JUG SHOP

1567 Pacific (at Polk),
San Francisco
Tel: 885-2922
Open Monday through
Saturday 9 a.m. to 9 p.m.,
Sunday 9:30 a.m. to 7 p.m.
Credit cards: MC, V

This well-stocked liquor store is noteworthy for an extensive wine selection at good prices as well as a huge inventory of beers and spirits. Open since 1959, The Jug Shop has kept up with the times by installing a wine bar and offering personal service. If I'm buying cheese at Leonard's across the street, I always like to drop in to see what they have on special.

COOKWARE AND BOOKS

CITY DISCOUNT

2436 Polk Street (at Union),
San Francisco
Tel: 771-4649
Open Monday through
Saturday 10 a.m. to 6 p.m.,
Sunday 11 a.m. to 6 p.m.
Credit cards: AE, MC, V

You never know what you might find at this funny little cookware shop which stocks more and more stuff each month. You can depend on kitchen gadgets and utensils, pots and pans, but dishware and ramekins shift with the tides of restaurant-supply surplus. Large platters with Chinese motifs, heavy white china in all sizes, thick glasses, thin silverware—really everything you need to set up mismatched housekeeping—can be found here at reasonable prices, especially if you grab something on special.

The Richmond District

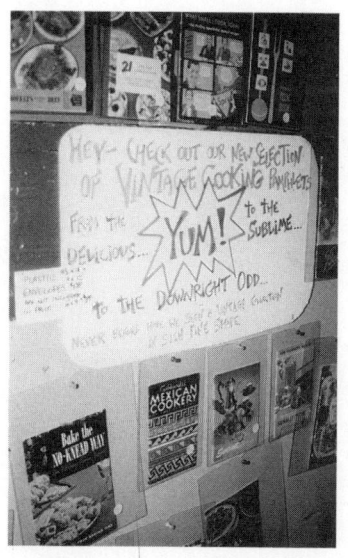

THE RICHMOND DISTRICT

Restaurants:
1. Alain Rondelli 367
2. Dragon House 368
3. Fountain Court 369
4. Hong Kong Flower Lounge 369
5. Hong Kong Villa 370
6. Jakarta 371
7. Kabuto 372
8. Katia, A Russian Tea Room 373
9. Kyung Bok Palace 374
10. Laghi 374
11. Mayflower 375
12. Straits Cafe 376
13. Taiwan 377
14. Ton Kiang 378
15. Ton Kiang Cafe 379

Cafes:
16. Sam and Henry's Cool Beans 380

Bars:
17. Pat O'Shea's Mad Hatter 381

Delicatessens/Take-Out:
18. Gastronom 382
19. Odessa Deli 382
20. Shenson's 383
21. Tip Toe Inn 383

Bakeries/Pastries:
22. House of Bagels 384
23. Moscow and Tbilisi Bakery 384
24. Schubert's 385

Ice Cream/Chocolates:
25. Gelato Classico 386
26. Joe's Ice Cream 386
27. See's Candies 386

Ethnic Markets:
28. Bangkok Grocery 387
29. Haig's Delicacies 387
30. New May Wah Supermarket 388

Produce:
31. Clement Produce 388
32. Village Market 389

Meat and Poultry:
33. New On Sang and San Francisco Chicken 390

Fish:
34. Seafood Center 390

Cheese:
35. Sixth Avenue Cheese Shop 391

Cookware and Books:
36. Green Apple Books 392
37. Kamei Household Wares 392

RESTAURANTS

ALAIN RONDELLI

Wunderchef Alain Rondelli redecorated his restaurant recently and sent out an announcement with a color picture of himself, bare shouldered, dressed as a Caravaggio boy. We all rushed over. Rondelli was in chef's whites. His long hair was pulled into a ponytail. His restaurant looked terrific, the bar and dining areas opened up to form one airy, modern room with banquettes, upholstered chairs, and fresh flowers everywhere. The Rondellian twist came in the place settings: glass plates on large round mirrors that reflect back the food, plus the underside of your face. Rondelli says that the image of the food in the mirror reminds us that food is art. He likes the way the mirror exposes his cooking. As a perfectionist he has nothing to hide.

126 Clement Street
(between Second and Third Avenues),
San Francisco
Tel: 387-0408
Open Tuesday through Sunday 5:30 to 10 p.m.
Price: Moderate
Credit cards: MC, V

He's right. His food is witty, pretty, and very delicious, especially hearty French dishes like beef short ribs on the bone braised in red wine served with big hunks of bacon, meltingly sweet carrots, and a potato puree. His pot au feu, lamb loin, tiny chops, breast and stunning lamb sausage poached in an oregano-scented broth with vegetables is dreamy.

Rondelli has a genius for bringing together unlikely combinations with subtlety and finesse. His calamari "martini" is one of these triumphs, even though it sounds contrived. Tender calamari rings are suspended in a barely gelled tomato water perfumed with mint and jalapeños. The waiter pours orange carrot juice on top of the martini at the table. You start eating it with a spoon and then drain every clean, bracing drop. Almost every dish brings a surprise. Foie gras is molded into the shape of a fig and stuffed with one. Ethereal gnocchi and rock shrimp come in a buttery lime sauce crunchy with toasted black mustard seeds, a culinary poem. Rondelli reinvents desserts like warm apple bread pudding using featherlight brioche, or accompanies poached pears with an almond sorbet.

What's so nice about Alain Rondelli is that you can afford to return often. Prices are amazingly reasonable for food so elegant, imaginative, and brilliantly executed. This policy of fair pricing extends to the honed wine list as well. A meal at Alain Rondelli does make you think about the relationship between food, sensuality, and art, especially since this chef lavishes you with all three.

DRAGON HOUSE

5344 Geary Blvd. (between 17th and 18th Avenues), San Francisco
Tel: 751-6545
Open for lunch daily 11 a.m. to 3 p.m.; dinner nightly 4 to 9:30 p.m.
Price: Inexpensive
Credit cards: MC, V

With only ten or twelve small tables, Dragon House still offers a huge menu, but everyone comes here for the Shanghai specialties. Unfortunately, many of these are listed only on the Chinese menu. Luckily, you have me to steer you to some of the best, like tofu skin with preserved mustard green and beans—salty, chewy, vegetarian, and delicious with rice. Lions Head, large meatballs glistening with brown gravy served with bright green spinach melt in your mouth. Begin with superb Shanghai dumplings called *shao lin bao*, juicy pork filled and served with Chinese vinegar with threads of fresh ginger. Jellyfish salad makes for a refreshing starter. It tastes like a chewy, sesame-scented pasta. Also try the soup with tofu, preserved mustard greens, and pork. It's both clean and fortifying.

On the English menu, you can't go wrong with mu shu vegetables or pork with pancakes and hosin sauce, or a clay pot of Chinese cabbage with vermicelli and pork. During crab season don't pass up a pristinely fresh Hunan-style crab coated in spicy black bean sauce. I love the red-cooked carp, pulled live from a freshwater tank, braised in a thick, sweet, salty gravy with tons of scallions that melt into the sauce. Every dish uses fresh ingredients, yet prices are astoundingly cheap. The waitresses, who have been there forever, are cheerful and friendly. They want you to get to the dishes you like. Just ask for the Shanghai specialties.

FOUNTAIN COURT

This Shanghai-style restaurant has a solid neighborhood following, but it really pulls everyone in for weekend dim sum. People order huge bowls of either gently sweet or lightly salty warm soy milk into which they tear bits of hot, unsweetened Chinese doughnuts. The salty version is particularly delicious, with bits of dried shrimp and pickled radish in it. Crisp, layered, green onion pancakes are also eaten with the soy milk soup. With an order of thick Shanghai noodles, stir-fried with vegetables and pork, you can feed the whole family a luscious lunch for well under $5 per person.

This restaurant will also prepare delicacies like braised soft-shell turtle, now available fresh in Chinatown, cooked with bamboo shoots and black mushrooms on an order-ahead basis. For less adventurous eaters, simple mu shu pork sets the standard for other versions.

Fountain Court is relatively small, clean, cheerfully decorated, and comfortable. Lots of light pours in through its large corner window, and you might spot celebrities like Amy Tan there. It's one of her favorite spots.

354 Clement Street
(at Fifth Avenue),
San Francisco
Tel: 668-1100
Open daily for lunch 11 a.m. to 3 p.m.; dinner 5 to 10 p.m.
Price: Inexpensive to moderate
Credit cards: AE, DC, MC, V

HONG KONG FLOWER LOUNGE

What a fine meal I had the other evening at the venerable Hong Kong Flower Lounge, Alice Wong's San Francisco outpost of her family's restaurants in Hong Kong. (There are two Hong Kong Flower Lounge restaurants on the Peninsula, both excellent.) The Flower Lounge was the first of the high-quality Hong Kong–style restaurants to open in the Bay Area ten years ago. The level of cooking, the quality of ingredients, the decor, and service all took a leap forward. Today, this restaurant continues to be first-rate, offering a large elegant menu with a number of signature dishes. It's always useful to

5322 Geary (at 17th Avenue),
San Francisco
Tel: 668-8998
Open Monday through Friday 11 a.m. to 2:30 p.m., weekends 10 a.m. to 2:30 p.m.; dinner nightly 5 to 9:30 p.m.
Price: Moderate
Credit cards

know these dishes, especially when confronted by a hundred items on a transliterated menu. So here are some of the San Francisco Hong Kong Flower Lounge specialties that I love:

Pei Pa Tofu, juicy, lightly curried tofu dumpling served with baby bok choy—a must-order. E-Fu Noodles with Chives, velvety, flat, fresh noodles with strands of Chinese chives and bean sprouts, one of the most delicate and delicious noodle dishes in any cuisine. Peking Duck served with steamed white buns. Smoked Black Cod or Wok-Charred Black Cod, both of buttery texture and strong flavor cut by a sweet Japanese-style marinade. Soup of the Day, always a simple but rich meat and chicken broth with boiled chicken feet and soup meat served in it. Minced Squab in Lettuce Cup, a savory chopped mixture of squab, water chestnuts, and aromatics, which you pile into lettuce leaves and eat like a taco. Mustard Greens Braised with Virginia Ham, always refreshing after a rich meal.

Of course this list could be expanded twice over, but it gives you an idea of the range of this kitchen. I like to put a table of eight or ten people together and order ahead so we can be served banquet style, course by course. Few non-Chinese meals compare in price, variety, or quality.

HONG KONG VILLA

2332 Clement Street
(between 24th and 25th Avenues),
San Francisco
Tel: 752-8833
Open daily for lunch
10:30 a.m. to 2:30 p.m.;
dinner 5 to 10 p.m.
Price: Moderate
Credit cards: MC, V

Hong Kong Villa has set itself apart for the sparkling flavor and freshness of its food. Although some of the dishes may not be as adventurous as the creations at some other Cantonese restaurants, Hong Kong Villa's dedication to high quality shines through. I never hesitate to go there for a vibrant seafood and vegetable meal. Currently the restaurant offers live shrimp from the tank for $12 per pound, large meaty crabs for $12 apiece, and lobsters for $20 apiece. These are great prices for live seafood.

The restaurant also excels at black cod dishes, velvety textured, dense, full of salubrious fish oil. Salt-baked black cod in chunks, dusted with fresh chilies and garlic or marinated and steamed in sweetened rice wine, are sublime. Whole fish steamed with ginger and green onions; crisp roast chicken;

and platters of tender pea shoots stir-fried with egg white and crabmeat are the building blocks of a stellar meal. I depend on Hong Kong Villa for its simple and beautiful Cantonese dishes and unusually helpful and gracious service. It's a valuable bread-and-butter Chinese dinner house for people who like fresh fish and vegetables.

JAKARTA

This relatively new Indonesian restaurant has a more extensive menu than we've seen before in the Bay Area as well as a whimsical decor. One room has high ceilings and a tall dracaena, a tree-sized palm with many tufts and aerial roots that uncannily mirrors an Indonesian landscape hung nearby. Another room has a low acoustic ceiling with the silhouettes of Balinese shadow puppets showing through translucent tiles. The airiness of the white walls and gleaming plate glass windows is contrasted by dark burgundy carpeting, chairs, tablecloths, and batik place mats under glass. A gallery's worth of shadow puppets, masks, miniature instruments, and figurines look stunning in the simple surroundings.

615 Balboa Street
(at Seventh Avenue),
San Francisco
Tel: 387-5225
Open Tuesday through
Sunday 5 to 10 p.m.
Price: Inexpensive
Credit Cards: AE, D, MC, V

Sitting down to a meal here can be a real culinary adventure. Start with *bakwan*, crunchy shrimp cakes studded with corn and bean sprouts laced with hot chilies. They are absolutely irresistible when dipped into mild, fruity chutney. *Cumi cumi isi*, squid stuffed with a pâtélike mixture of seafood, then deep-fried and cut into wedges, has a hot and haunting flavor, as does *otak otak*, a ground-fish pancake cooked in a banana leaf. *Soto ayam kudus*, a heap of chicken, bean sprouts, and rice noodles in a lightly curried broth, makes for a very substantial starter. The rest of the menu is divided into grills, vegetarian plates, fried dishes, and braised dishes in spicy sauces. A selection from several categories allows you to put together your own impromptu rice table.

Here are my favorites from each menu section, starting with the classic *sate ayam*, juicy chicken satay with two sauces; and grilled rockfish cooked on a banana leaf in a hot, red chili paste. The fish's texture stays moist and velvety. The spicy, saucy dishes are knockouts, like *gulai bantut*, fork-tender oxtails in a thin, aromatic coconut-milk sauce with a background of chili. A braised dish called *gundeg*, from the Javanese city of Jogjakarta, brings chunks of beef, a whole preserved egg, chicken, and jackfruit, which tastes like turnip, in a fruity, fragrant gravy. From the fried section I recommend the spicy-hot fried chicken in chili sauce called *ayam goreng balado*. It's greaseless, batterless, and explosively seasoned. The vegetarian dishes here, like the famous *gado-gado* in peanut sauce, are lifeless and bland, however.

For dessert try *kue dada susudara*, a caramelized mound of chewy coconut on a crepe, an exotic tropical thrill, and finish with thick Indonesian coffee served with the grounds still in it.

KABUTO

5116 Geary Boulevard
(between 15th and 16th Avenues),
San Francisco
Tel: 752-5652
Open Tuesday through Saturday 5:30 p.m. to 11 p.m.
Price: Moderate
Credit cards: MC, V

Sachio Kojima, the sushi chef-owner of beloved Kabuto, has the demeanor of a marathon athlete, a samurai wielding knives, a cowboy who never leaves the saddle. Yet he presides over his sushi bar like a mother hen who gauges the appetites and yearnings of the brood. He lets new customers order for themselves and then gives them a few things he thinks they'd like. For regulars, Sachio creates.

One evening he started the regulars with a little salad of marinated kelp, followed by a glazed pottery bowl arranged with two slices of monkfish on a pile of pickled onions and a *shiso* leaf. Then came a beautiful composition of sashimi with a gingery dipping sauce. Sushi of *toro*, the rich stomach meat of tuna, arrived, followed along with a contrastingly assertive mackerel sushi, then mild yellowtail sushi. From the kitchen emerged a red lacquered bowl with a broiled tofu dumpling, a fried potato dumpling, and a slice of seafood-stuffed squash. Then more sushi appeared, this time of sea urchin roe and of raw shrimp. A tiny pottery teapot of clear bonito stock enriched with bits of fish and vegetables refreshed the palate for a sushi of broiled freshwater eel and a final hand roll stuffed with mountain potato. The meal was a masterpiece, a progression of flavors and textures that made you appreciate every item more fully.

During your service Sachio keeps track of fifteen other diners, all of whom get different things. He makes his patrons feel like they have a private relationship with him. The sushi-bar customers get a bit of theater, just the right amount of food, and special attention. Of course the attraction of sitting in front of Sachio instead of at a table means that you might have to wait for a place. As it gets later, the sushi bar gets more crowded, turning into a hot spot in the late evenings when the scene gets really interesting. You might sit next to Japanese students, aging hippies, or characters that look like they play roles in *yakuza* sagas. What more could anyone want from a restaurant experience?

KATIA, A RUSSIAN TEA ROOM

600 Fifth Avenue (at Balboa), San Francisco
Tel: 668-9292
Open for lunch Tuesday through Sunday 11:30 a.m. to 2:30 p.m.; dinner Tuesday through Sunday 5 to 9 p.m., Friday and Saturday until 10 p.m.
Price: Inexpensive
Credit cards: AE, DC, D, MC, V

Katia Troosh prepares home-style Russian food with a light hand at her charming little restaurant—really the best Russian restaurant in the city. Start, of course, with *zakuski*, small plates of cold appetizers that always begin a formal Russian meal. Katia's include house-pickled cucumbers, marinated mushrooms, the most delicious chopped Russian salad called Vinaigrette, and garlicky eggplant caviar. Frankly, I could make a whole meal out of the chopped salad with thick slices of moist rye–whole wheat bread set out on the table.

Katia's blini are thin, crepelike, and slightly sour. The best. They come with sweet-and-sour pickled herring and smoked salmon. The beet borscht made me think of my grandmother. Main courses change often, but small meat-filled dumplings called *pelmeni* served in rich chicken broth with a dollop of sour cream are a mainstay. They should be. I adore the crisp chicken pancakes made of ground chicken breast. For dessert, look for crisp meringues topped with whipped cream and fresh fruit. They are lovely.

Service can be slow, but the food is so marvelous, the atmosphere so warm and friendly, that you don't care. This little family-run place has true Russian soul.

KYUNG BOK PALACE

**6314 Geary Boulevard
(at 27th Avenue),
San Francisco
Tel: 221-0685
Open daily for
lunch 11 a.m. to 3 p.m.;
dinner 5 to 10 p.m.
Price: Inexpensive
Credit cards: MC, V**

You can't complain if your short ribs are undercooked at this Korean phenom because you do the cooking yourself. You not only cook, you also gather your own ingredients from a central refrigerated counter well protected by sneeze guards. The hungry young crowd that lines up at the front door (you write your name on a yellow pad and wait until the next table opens up) pile their plates high with thinly sliced sesame-marinated pork and beef short ribs to take back to long tables outfitted with built-in lava-rock grills. Before the cooking begins, several trips need to be made to the buffet to set up your table with the myriad hot, spicy, garlicky pickles, kimchee, and salads, hot and cold, that make up Korean barbecue service. Nutty rice from a rice warmer and large curly lettuce leaves complete the picture.

Then the fun begins. You flip your meat onto the barbecue with tongs—smoke is drawn up by fans directly over each table—turn it a few times, cut it with a scissors when it's done, and wrap the pieces in the lettuce leaves with rice, pickles, and vegetables. What a divine way to eat! Hot, cold, spicy, juicy, savory, all adjusted just the way you like, a different taste sensation with each combination. The $6.99 lunch and $12.99 dinner price makes for an affordable party, and this way of eating is perfect for groups. Cold Korean beer is the drink of choice, and orange wedges from the buffet serve as the perfect conclusion.

LAGHI

**1801 Clement Street
(at 19th Avenue),
San Francisco
Tel: 386-6266
Open Tuesday through
Saturday 5 to 10 p.m.,
Sunday until 9 p.m.
Price: Moderate
Credit cards: AE, DC, MC, V**

Gino Laghi and his cooks run the Laghi kitchen as if *they* were having the party. The enthusiasm and love of cooking of this chef and his chef-waitress-wife transfer right into the food, which happens to be as good as it can get in San Francisco when you want an authentic Italian meal. Each evening the small typewritten menu changes, offering a handful of intriguing possibilities.

There might be a warm salad of radicchio and endive scattered with crisp bits of Laghi's house-cured pancetta; or a simple green salad in one of the tastiest balsamic vinaigrettes in town; or house-cured prosciutto with sweet ripe winter pears. A ramekin of baked lasagne features tender homemade noodles, a crumbly meat sauce, and old-fashioned béchamel, all delicately layered. I still dream about a risotto with red wine and fresh black truffles Gino offered one night. At Laghi I want to settle in for a complete Italian meal: an antipasti, a pasta, and then a main course like perfectly grilled loin lamb chops dressed with garlic, olive oil, and herbs, served with bread crumb–topped roasted eggplant and tomato. When the lamb chops or any meat dish comes out of Laghi's kitchen it is consummately Italian.

An imaginative, affordably priced Italian wine list offering almost everything by the glass as well as the bottle complements this cohesive dining experience. You eat and drink at Laghi exactly the same way you would at a small trattoria in Italy. The highest-quality raw ingredients and traditional, simple preparation give the dishes their beautiful depth and complexity. I love eating this way, and Laghi is one of the handful of restaurants in town that enables you to do so. The rewards for all the integrity and work it takes to keep a small personal place going at this high level must be mostly spiritual. For this good-natured dedication, the Laghis deserve a special kind of culinary sainthood.

MAYFLOWER

The Mayflower, a low-key, one-room family-style Cantonese restaurant, was opened by some ex–San Francisco Flower Lounge employees. It stands out from the pack because of its high standards for food and service. Their earthy clay pot and simple seafood dishes shine. Although parts of the menu read exactly like the one at nearby Flower Lounge, the execution is different. On the more complicated dishes, such as deep-fried sole with deep-fried bones, the kitchen can falter. The successes here come with family fare, like the freshest, crisp-skinned, succulent roast chicken; plates of sparkling fresh vegetables of the day; salt-baked shrimp in their shells

6255 Geary Boulevard
(at 27th Avenue),
San Francisco
Tel: 387-8338
Open for lunch Monday through Friday 11 a.m. to 2:30 p.m., Saturday and Sunday 10 a.m. to 2:30 p.m.; dinner nightly 5 to 9:30 p.m.
Price: Inexpensive to moderate
Credit cards: MC, V;
$20 minimum

or the signature shelled "crystal" shrimp; and the rich double chicken broth that usually comes as soup of the day. Both eggplant with hot sauce in a clay pot and thinly sliced beef short ribs with lots of black pepper explode with flavor. Small 1½-pound steamed rockfish are unsurpassed anywhere in the city, and the crabs seem more pristine and sweeter than any others in town.

Of course the place is mobbed and very noisy at 6 p.m., slowing down a bit by 8 p.m. on weeknights, the best time to go. General manager Vincent Chan's effusive personality draws regulars, and helpful service has always been a high point here once you get a seat. The waiters know the menu and make good suggestions, although regulars know to consult the one-page specials menu for such delicacies as salt-baked oysters or velvety textured squab in soy sauce with tender greens.

STRAITS CAFE

3300 Geary Boulevard (at Parker), San Francisco
Tel: 668-1783
Open Monday through Thursday 11:30 a.m. to 10 p.m., Friday and Saturday until 11 p.m.
Price: Moderate
Credit cards: AE, MC, V

If you find explosive Asian flavors and exotic tropical ingredients seductive, you must eat at Straits Cafe, a charming Singaporean restaurant operated by chef Chris Yeo. His peculiar Nonya cooking (a cross-ethnic style developed in Singapore) will sweep you off your feet. Yeo keeps the hot, sweet, sour, gingery, garlicky, perfumey, fermented riot of flavors in each preparation under strict control. Working with an intense palette in which balance is everything, he creates a quintessential tropical-crossroads cuisine: a unique mix of Malaysian, Chinese, Indian, and Burmese influences.

You may think you recognize some of the dishes on the menu, but even the most familiar will surprise you. Satays, skewers of juicy beef, are fragrant with layers of flavor from wet and dry *masalas* of spices and herbs. The unique peanut sauce served with them has its own spicing that somehow fits into the larger picture like a jigsaw puzzle. The presentation with chunks of cooling cucumber is simple and beautiful. An appetizer called *murtabak*, an Indian-style flat bread filled with minced beef, comes with a luscious coconut milk–curry dipping sauce and a pile of pickled red onions, a must-order dish. Spring rolls turn out to be a room-temperature crepe stuffed with slivered vegetables and pungent dried shrimp, each section topped with its own dab of plum sauce and a perfect cilantro leaf.

Angel hair noodles get an exquisite, if pungent, treatment in a hot and sour tamarind broth, topped with hard-cooked eggs and tender pink shrimp. Dark green long beans stay crisp, stir-fried with hot chilies, dried shrimp, and minced pork. How good this dish tastes with aromatic jasmine rice! A mild, creamy coconut milk–based chicken curry, in which the chicken retains its character, will please everyone. Although the desserts sound completely odd, they too are surprisingly delicious. One of my favorites, sago pudding, is a custard of large pearl tapioca in a heavenly palm sugar syrup.

Even the look of the restaurant conjures up tropical romance. The interior resembles a Singaporean street with columns transformed into palms, faux windows with wooden shutters and balconies high up on one wall, an internal sheet-metal roof, and wainscoting, ceiling fans, slatted doors, and vents. Straits Cafe does remind you of the all-night street food stalls of Singapore, but it also offers such Raffles Hotel fillips as Singapore slings and gin and tonics, along with vanilla bean sodas, sweetened iced tea, and coffee, wines, and beer. In every respect, Straits Cafe promises exotic fun and adventure at the foot of San Francisco's avenues.

TAIWAN

This small cafe specializes in superb dumplings and noodles and a wide range of spicy northern Chinese and Shanghai dishes. It's one of my favorite restaurants of any nationality. Once I started eating here I couldn't stop. I had to return every day to taste a few more things. The compact noodle and dumpling kitchen situated right in the front window lets you know how fresh these items are. Behind, a rosy little dining room with a skylight gets constant turnover. People come here for a bite or a full meal all day.

Start with hot-and-sour soup, bright, clean, and bracing. Then choose a *mu shi* dish, a stir fry of julienned vegetables, egg, and sparkling shrimp that you pile onto thin white pancakes. Smear them with bean sauce. I can't eat at Taiwan

445 Clement Street
(at Sixth Avenue),
San Francisco
Tel: 387-1789
Open Monday through
Thursday 11 a.m. to 10 p.m.,
Friday until midnight,
Saturday 10 a.m. to
midnight, Sunday 10 a.m.
to 10 p.m.
Price: Inexpensive
Credit cards: AE, MC, V; $15 minimum

without having at least one plate of gingery, pork-filled boiled dumplings (you get ten to an order) or shrimp, leek, and pork boiled dumplings, which have a lovely wild onion edge, or steamed vegetarian dumplings with that slightly grassy herbal flavor lovers of greens adore.

The noodles are also superb. Try the thick, chewy Shanghai noodles tossed with vegetables and slivers of pork; or the stunning mustard green and pork noodles bathed in a smoky broth. In braised beef "ligamen" noodles, gelatinous cuts of brisket add texture and buttery flavor to a beef broth.

Lest you think that you have to stick to noodles, try the luscious crispy chicken, a burnished bird with velvety meat in a rich brown sauce—great with a plate of perfectly cooked young bok choy. Unctuous red-cooked eggplant is sublime over rice, as are the addictively tasty dry-braised Chinese long beans.

Thirty years ago the island of Taiwan inherited uprooted northern chefs from Shanghai, Beijing, Hunan, Sichuan, and Shandong provinces, while many of the Cantonese master chefs emigrated to Hong Kong. Reflecting the northern influence on Taiwanese cooking, a special menu offers soulful cold-weather dishes with lots of tripe, pickled greens, and fish paste for the adventurous.

On top of all the exciting cooking, the obliging waiters will pace your meal so you don't get all your dishes at once. What's hard to believe is that these sensuous, spicy, well-served meals cost under $10 a person.

TON KIANG

5821 Geary Boulevard (at 22nd Avenue), San Francisco
Tel: 387-8273
Open Monday through Thursday 10:30 a.m. to 10 p.m., Friday until 10:30 p.m., Saturday, Sunday, and holidays 10 a.m. to 10:30 p.m.
Price: Inexpensive
Credit cards: MC, V

This new, two-story branch of Ton Kiang excels at dim sum, the freshest in town. At the bigger houses you never know how many rounds the dumplings have made before the carts pull up to your table. At small Ton Kiang, the dim sum arrive hot from the kitchen and the variety is astounding. You cannot eat fast enough to keep up with the stream of new temptations.

What surprises me is the quality of it all. Clean, lean, bright, fresh, Ton Kiang's dim sum taste homemade. Different delicate noodle-wrapped dumplings are filled with a stunning combination of scallops and shrimp or shrimp and pork or just very fresh, sweet shrimp, a sign of well-made dim sum. Look for deep-fried taro croquettes, the outside coated with crackling shredded taro threads, the inside filled with soft, creamy mashed taro. The Shanghai-style dumplings, filled with pork and Chinese chives, are wrapped in thinly rolled raw bread dough. They are fried on one side and then steamed to create a taste sensation. The miniature egg custards have shimmering fillings and warm, flaky crusts. For a change, try a plate of miniature doughnuts, soft and chewy with a rich egg-custard filling.

The first-floor dining room has more amenities than the incredibly low prices of its food would warrant. Painted pale rose with Chinese landscapes on the walls and patterned carpeting, the room comfortably seats parties of four at blonde-wood booths and larger groups in the center of the room at round tables. This branch of Ton Kiang is going for a more upscale Hong Kong crowd than the bustling cafe at Spruce.

TON KIANG CAFE

This Ton Kiang in the Inner Richmond serves as an all-day Chinese cafe frequented by a wide spectrum of San Franciscans ranging from cab drivers to nearby Pacific Heights families. Everyone comes to this friendly place for Hakka specialties like skinless salt-baked chicken served with two fabulous dipping sauces and flavorful clear chicken broth with Hakka-style beef or fish balls and emerald leaves of spinach.

3148 Geary Boulevard (at Spruce),
San Francisco
Tel: 752-4440
Open daily 11 a.m. to 10 p.m., weekends until 10:30 p.m.
Price: Inexpensive
Credit cards: MC, V

The Hakka people immigrated to Canton province several hundred years ago from northern China, retaining their own dialect, costume, and cuisine. Hence the chefs at Ton Kiang cook not only Hakka dishes but Cantonese and some northern Chinese dishes as well. The most characteristic are dark and dusky stews of pork or beef, full of dried and fermented ingredients—the soul food of China. Order one of these rich dishes to share, perhaps Hakka home-style braised pork cooked in a clay pot with tofu and lily stems; or bacon with dried mustard greens, big slabs of soft, fresh bacon in a slightly sweet gravy. Another of my favorites is tofu stuffed with ground pork braised in Hakka wine sauce with julienned vegetables. These items can be found on the one-page list of Hakka specialties on the front cover of the huge menu.

The restaurant is divided into two brightly lit dining rooms. At lunch the Formica tables are uncovered; at dinner Ton Kiang pulls out the tablecloths. The classic meal at either lunch or dinner includes the aforementioned salt-baked chicken, one rich Hakka clay pot dish, either fish ball or a terrific wonton soup made with the restaurant's signature broth, and a plate of very simple, always sparkling fresh vegetables like baby bok choy, young spinach, or Chinese broccoli. Steamed with a little stock, garlic, and oil, the vegetables are always refreshing and beautiful, a high point of the meal.

CAFES

SAM AND HENRY'S COOL BEANS

4342-A California Street
(at Sixth Avenue),
San Francisco
Tel: 750-1955
Open daily 7 a.m. to 8 p.m.
No credit cards

Painted blue like the summer sky, this miniscule coffeehouse has but four or five stools and a counter, with a few indoor tables newly added and a tiny table and a bench outside next to a metal newspaper rack with the local sheets and the daily *New York Times*. The two owners, Sam and Henry, make absolutely exquisite coffee: intense, rich, aromatic without any bitterness, on a par with what you get in Italy. At last they don't have to serve it in paper cups. With a mini expansion into a space next door, they now can wash dishes. They also offer first-rate House of Bagels bagels with cream cheese and a few nice sandwiches.

The Cool Beans guys never forget a face. They know practically everyone who hangs out in their shop and most of the patrons seem to know each other. Laid-back reggae seems to be the sound of choice, a background for talk and reading. People also buy their coffee beans here and pluck cookies from jars to munch. A funny assortment of photographs and containers of wrapped candy constitutes the decor, along with the whimsical paint job. Everyone who steps into Sam and Henry's knows that something special is happening here. If you love coffee, get over there and see for yourself.

BARS

PAT O'SHEA'S MAD HATTER

This rollicking neighborhood sports bar was catapulted to culinary fame when Nancy Oakes started cooking lunch here. No self-respecting, beer-guzzling football fan could believe he was eating and loving the likes of stuffed quail, grilled veal sweetbreads, and roasted monkfish with mussels, but Oakes put it out for the price of barroom hamburgers. Later on she opened L'Avenue in a tiny and charming spot next door. Most recently she launched the multimillion-dollar Boulevard with super-designer Pat Kuleto, and Pat O'Shea's food service floundered. Now, an apprentice of Oakes's has taken over the bar's kitchen and the food is back to being its imaginative best. And it's still a great bar, with many easily visible televisions mounted on the walls, new pool tables, and pints of draft beer for low prices.

3848 Geary Boulevard
(at Third Avenue),
San Francisco
Tel: 752-3148
Open Monday through Friday 11 a.m. to 2 a.m., weekends 9 a.m. to 2 a.m.
Credit cards: D, MC, V

DELICATESSENS/TAKE-OUT

GASTRONOM

5801 Geary Boulevard
(at 22nd Avenue),
San Francisco
Tel: 387-4211
Open daily 9 a.m. to 9 p.m.
Credit cards: MC, V

If you want to put on a Russian meal, call Gastronom. They'll put together a buffet of *zakuski* (Russian salads), smoked fish, stuffed fish, stuffed cabbage, piroshki, *pelmeni*—the works. Or, you can drop in to buy excellent Russian-style dairy products like quarts of pourable yogurt, a wonderful drink, farmers' cheese for blintzes, and whipped farmers' cheese for drizzling with perfumey Australian honey or preserved apricots from Gastronom's shelves. One advantage of shopping at Gastronom is that the women behind the counter speak English. Another is the selection of smoked fish, house-made cucumber and tomato pickles, and dairy products.

ODESSA DELI

5427 Geary Boulevard
(between 18th
and 19th Avenues),
San Francisco
Tel: 387-8314
Open daily 9 a.m. to 9 p.m.
Credit cards: AE, MC, V

English may not be spoken by the single clerk behind the counter, the line can get long, the wait is often ridiculous, but Odessa carries the largest selection of imported Russian candies, individually and colorfully wrapped. The small candies are mundane, artificially flavored fruit drops, but the larger $3.98 per pound candies can be delightful and a fantastic buy. Though there may be some surprises, like bubble gum–flavored chocolate inside the wrappers with a child's face on them, I have found that any wrapped in dark green will be dark chocolate–covered and have crisp, nutty toffee, or chocolate and toasted nut fillings. The dairy case offers flavorful Russian yogurts and fresh cheeses, but also half pounds of Schaller and Weber whipped butter, which has lots of character and spreads easily on black bread awaiting a blanket of smoked fish.

SHENSON'S

One of the few Jewish delis in the city, Shenson's does a good job preparing many Jewish specialties, such as relatively light, well-seasoned gefilte fish; dense, naturally sweet chopped liver; and house-pickled green tomatoes. The plump garlic sausages are absolutely delicious, better than the pedestrian skinny hot dogs. Items like satiny smoked sablefish and pickled herring are fresh and tasty. The corned beef and pastrami are as good as you can get in the city. Some patrons eat at one of the eight or so tables in front of the counter in a carpeted dining area decorated with shelves of matzoh and other packaged products, but no crusty waitresses take your order. You pick up the food yourself at the counter. While this is no Carnegie Deli, Shenson's does take care of the needs of San Franciscans who crave a nice piece of low calorie gefilte fish.

5120 Geary Boulevard
(at 15th Avenue),
San Francisco
Tel: 751-4699
Open daily
8 a.m. to 5:45 p.m.
Credit cards: AE, D, MC, V

TIP TOE INN

This whimsically decorated Russian delicatessen looks like a fairytale castle outside and in, with charming wall murals and the most attractive food displays of any of the Russian delis. Unlike the newcomers to the neighborhood, long-established Tip Toe prepares a wide range of Russian specialties and the best baked meat-filled piroshkis in town. When warmed in the oven, these shiny, golden-brown buns are exquisite, with crusty exteriors, tender, brioche-like interiors, and a savory filling of chopped beef, among several choices. They are available to eat on the premises or to take home. One could base a wonderful luncheon or tea around them. Other good things are house-cured pickles, pork-and-rice-stuffed cabbage rolls in a buttery tomato sauce, and thin blintzes coated in bread crumbs with a sweet cheese stuffing, which reheat in the oven quite well. Other Russian savory pastries take up a large section of the counter, particularly sheet pans of baked *pirog*, two layers of yeasty egg dough filled with meat, cabbage, or potato, cut into squares, and sold by the pound.

5423 Geary Boulevard
(between 18th and
19th Avenues),
San Francisco
Tel: 221-6422
Open Monday through
Saturday 9 a.m. to 7 p.m.
No credit cards

BAKERIES/PASTRIES

HOUSE OF BAGELS

5030 Geary Boulevard
(between 14th and
15th Avenues),
San Francisco
Tel: 752-6000
Open daily 6 a.m. to 6 p.m.
No credit cards

Bagel lovers from all over the city converge on this Jewish bakery for authentic, chewy, substantial bagels. I love them. The onion bagels are not coated with burned bits but rather a scattering of sweetly caramelized onion. The sesame bagel is judiciously sprinkled with the perfume of the Middle East. When you buy the bagels at the bakery they are always fresh, which allows a texturally correct bagel to be divinely chewy. The difference between a House of Bagels bagel and Noah's bagels, which seem to be taking over the world, is one of style. Noah's bagels are soft and bready: the Wonderbread of bagels. They do make for easy-to-eat bagel sandwiches, but bagel sandwiches are preparations with no basis in tradition (as are croissant sandwiches). Anyone even a little bit Jewish knows that you eat bagels open-face. If you covered the cream cheese, lox, tomato, cucumber and onion with another half bagel you really couldn't bite through it.

House of Bagels also makes an old-fashioned rye bread, a bit soft but full of flavor. The rye with seeds is laced with too many assertive caraway seeds; the plain rye is better. Other Jewish baked goods are available, such as corn rye and sweet rolls, but the bagel reigns supreme at this house.

MOSCOW AND TBILISI BAKERY

5540 Geary Boulevard
(between 19th and
20th Avenues),
San Francisco
Tel: 668-6959
Open daily 7 a.m. to 9 p.m.
No credit cards

The line never stops at this neighborhood crossroads for the Russian community. Very few words of either English or Russian are uttered by the sullen counter girls (they really are girls) who grab your delicious, amazingly light-textured black bread or tall, crusty-but-soft white (the rye is OK, but not as wonderful as these two loaves), and slap them into plastic bags. Both miraculously demonstrate that a bread can have character, flavor, and a real crust while still having a soft texture. These are breads even children will like. The one thing the girls do ask is if you want them sliced. I happen to like the heavy cherry and almond strudel, but the sweet rolls are too light and airy. The bakery really looks Russian: just a counter with bread, a man counting money, the actual ovens and bread tables visible through an open door. A community bulletin board outside the bakery will no doubt be helpful to you if you read Russian.

SCHUBERT'S

Among the mousse-cake set, Schubert's has been a hangout since 1911, but I like the old-fashioned coffee cakes, particularly a walnut–sour cream ring that tastes gloriously of sour cream. It is lighter and less sweet than most others of its ilk, but full of honest flavor, just like the simple sugar cookies. The bakery also carries luxurious Joseph Schmidt truffles (see page 255).

521 Clement Street
(between Sixth and Seventh Avenues),
San Francisco
Tel: 752-1580
Open Monday through Saturday 7 a.m. to 6 p.m., Sunday 9 a.m. to 5 p.m.
Credit cards: MC, V

ICE CREAM/CHOCOLATES

GELATO CLASSICO

750 Clement Street (at Ninth Avenue),
San Francisco
Tel: 751-1522
Open daily 10 a.m. to 10 p.m.
No credit cards

See listing, page 295.

JOE'S ICE CREAM

5351 Geary Boulevard
(at 18th Avenue),
San Francisco
Tel: 751-1950
Open Sunday through
Thursday 11 a.m. to 10 p.m.,
Friday and Saturday
until 11 p.m.
No credit cards

The home of the It's It, a chocolate-encased ice cream sandwich made with two oatmeal cookies, Joe's charms by staying so old-fashioned. All the ice cream is made on the premises and scooped to order. The wonderful milk shakes are constructed with a lot of ice cream, and blended with enough milk to make them drinkable. The young counterpeople couldn't be sweeter or more meticulous, and the place looks timeless and well used. There is a small sit-down counter with stools where you can get grilled sandwiches and fountain items, and a ledge with short stools in the window provides just the place to sip a shake and watch the activity at the Alexandria Theater across the street. Joe's also sells frozen chocolate-covered bananas, another old-fashioned classic. The only concession to modern trends comes in the form of Bud's frozen yogurt.

SEE'S CANDIES

754 Clement Street
(at Ninth Avenue),
San Francisco
Tel: 752-0953
Open Monday through
Saturday 10 a.m. to 6 p.m.,
Sunday 9 a.m. to 5 p.m.
No credit cards

For other locations see pages 112, 153, 357, and 441.

Everyone in San Francisco knows about See's peerless peanut brittle: crunchy, buttery, and liberally studded with fresh peanuts. You find yourself nibbling one piece after another until you're a quarter pound into a box. The brittle is as beloved and symbolic of San Francisco as Dungeness crab and sourdough bread and it travels a lot better. Hence the convenient stands at the San Francisco airport. The company was started by the See family in Los Angeles in 1921 and expanded to San Francisco in 1934.

Many treats present themselves in long glass cases in See's immaculate, white-tiled candy shops. The thrill of putting together a box of your favorites piece by piece—dark and light chocolate-covered nuts, turtles, the fabulous milk chocolate–covered English toffee rolled in chopped almonds (you can tell I'm a nuts and chews gal)—ranks with a walk across the Golden Gate Bridge on a sunny day. See's makes solid, middle-of-the-road, moderately priced, American-style chocolates of the highest order. Their candy is always fresh, and with every purchase, large or small, the buxom ladies in their white uniforms hand you a free chocolate.

ETHNIC MARKETS

BANGKOK GROCERY

This small grocery dedicated to Thai ingredients has ten-pound sacks of nutty, aromatic jasmine rice for $6 and small covered baskets for serving Thai sticky rice. At the counter are freshly made, albeit packaged, Thai snacks like chewy sago balls stuffed with savory sweet pork on a bed of lettuce leaves, whole chilies, and cilantro. They make a fine lunch to eat on the run.

3236 Geary Boulevard
(at Parker),
San Francisco
Tel: 221-5863
Open Monday through
Saturday 10 a.m. to 5 p.m.
No credit cards

HAIG'S DELICACIES

One of the oldest international food shops in the city, Haig's shelves are packed with jars and cans of exotic products from all over the globe. Patak brand Indian curry pastes, Indonesian ingredients, Middle Eastern and Armenian prepared foods, coffees, teas, Louisiana hot sauces, candy, spices —any sort of packaged food necessary to prepare a mind-boggling variety of ethnic dishes can be found here. The problem for Haig's is that many of these items now appear in stores either dedicated to one cuisine, like Indian markets, or in large Asian supermarkets. The ethnic population has caught up with Haig's and opened their own specialized

642 Clement Street
(between Seventh and
Eighth Avenues),
San Francisco
Tel: 752-6283
Open Monday through
Friday 9:30 a.m. to 6:30 p.m.,
Saturday 9 a.m. to 6 p.m.
Credit cards: MC, V

shops. It's wonderful to have a Haig's in the neighborhood, but serious shoppers need produce and other fresh ingredients. If the *kecap manis* (Indonesian soy sauce) is on the shelves of their vegetable market, they will buy it there.

NEW MAY WAH SUPERMARKET

547 Clement Street
(between Sixth and
Seventh Avenues),
San Francisco
Tel: 668-2583
Open daily 7 a.m. to 8 p.m.
Credit Cards: MC, V

Not nearly as exciting or large as the May Wah on Irving Street in the Sunset, this branch still covers most Asian cooking needs. Some meat, fish, and poultry has been frozen and sits defrosting in the refrigerated cases—a common sight on Clement Street—but much is fresh. You have to be observant. Such delicacies as live soft-shell turtles and live frogs are sold here. You can find fine produce like big bunches of very fresh watercress, plump mangoes, and young ginger, while other produce will be wilted. For Clement Street, New May Wah is as large and complete as any Asian grocery.

PRODUCE

CLEMENT PRODUCE

645 Clement Street
(between Seventh and
Eighth Avenues),
San Francisco
Tel: 221-4101
Open daily 7 a.m. to 8 p.m.
No credit cards

This long, narrow, bustling produce store does not carry unusual produce, but the prices are cheap. Sometimes there are piles of desirable things like blood oranges or Fuji apples that are especially inexpensive. Clement Produce is but one of many serviceable produce stores within five blocks or so on lower Clement. Each one might display one or two special items—mangoes, some good-looking pea shoots—at an excellent price to tempt people into the store, so on a serious shopping trip you might want to give them all a quick visit to grab the best things.

VILLAGE MARKET

This market deserves a trip across town. It has one of the prettiest, most inviting organic produce sections in the city. In front under an awning, wooden shelves of fruit and buckets of the most luscious flowers—in April, daffodils, tulips, and ranunculuses at excellent prices—make you want to fill your arms with them. Indoors, the old wooden floors are stacked with casually arranged displays of organic strawberries, white asparagus, organic bananas, spring greens, and del Cabo tomatoes (organically grown tomatoes from Baja California to get you through most of the winter). Other items of interest include organic jarred baby food, the excellent and hard-to-find sharp New York Cheddar from the Marin Cheese Company, Semifreddi breads, and all sorts of organic dried beans in burlap sacks. Only a couple of years old, the Village Market combines a commitment to healthful and organic foods with an aesthetic that makes you want to join up. Two wooden benches with cast-iron legs have been placed outside the store between large wooden flower boxes, and you are tempted to plop down and admire the beauty and color of nature's gifts, so appealingly offered. Not overly arranged or boutiquey, the Village Market helps you discover what you really want to eat.

4555 California Street
(at Eighth Avenue),
San Francisco
Tel: 221-0445
Open daily
7:30 a.m. to 7:30 p.m.
Credit cards: AE, MC, V

MEAT AND POULTRY

NEW ON SANG AND SAN FRANCISCO CHICKEN

617 Clement Street
(at Seventh Avenue),
San Francisco
Tel: 752-4100
Market open daily 8:30 a.m.
to 8:30 p.m.; rotisserie open
daily 11 a.m. to 9 p.m.
No credit cards

One address, but two operations in this Richmond District headquarters for chicken. In the New On Sang side you can get Chinese-style butchered chickens with head and feet, and partridges, pheasants, and ducks with all appendages attached. Nothing enriches a chicken stock more than gelatinous chicken feet. Duck wings and feet by the pound are also available. You find this impeccable poultry past the Chinese deli counter with hanging roast ducks and premade dishes kept warm on steam tables. A branch of the bustling On Sang Poultry Company on Stockton Street in Chinatown, New On Sang's raw birds can induce real culinary excitement if you're a cook.

Across the aisle from New On Sang, an Italian-style wood-fired rotisserie slowly turns behind a counter that demarcates the San Francisco Chicken shop. The chickens on the rotisserie have been marinated in lemon juice and rosemary, and though a bit overcooked, especially if they have been kept warm in a heated drawer, they do stay moist and boast a flavorful golden skin. They make for wholesome take-home meals.

FISH

SEAFOOD CENTER

831 Clement Street
(between Ninth and
Tenth Avenues),
San Francisco
Tel: 752-3496
Open Monday through
Saturday 9 a.m. to 6 p.m.,
Sunday until 5:30 p.m.
No credit cards

This fresh-smelling Chinese fish store features fillets of local snapper and petrale, whole sand dabs, rockfish, and pomfret, a small silvery fish that bakes and barbecues well. I have spotted skate wing, live sea bass, carp, catfish, crab, and lobsters. The beauty of whole flatfish, like sand dabs or rex sole, is that they cook quickly in the oven. Here's how. Preheat the oven to 400° F. Sprinkle the whole fish with chopped shallots, salt, pepper, a little white wine, and some olive oil or butter. Cook for about 5 minutes, depending on the thickness of the fish. You can test for doneness by sticking a knife in to the bone. If the fish is ready, the delicate meat will easily lift off, and you will have a delicious main course in no time at all.

CHEESE

SIXTH AVENUE CHEESE SHOP

A tiny shop filled with cheese, charcuterie, cold imported beer and ale, bottles of wine, and a small selection of necessary groceries like Sasso extra-virgin olive oil, French brown-sugar cubes, and fresh Semifreddi baguettes is always a welcome addition to a neighborhood. Being able to taste the cheese and get the size you want cut to order remains a civilized amenity. A few tiny tables covered in cheerful yellow-print oilcloth beckon those who want to eat their bread and cheese or a made-to-order sandwich on the spot with a bottle of wine plucked off the shelves.

311 Sixth Avenue (between Geary and Clement), San Francisco
Tel: 387-1436
Open Monday through Friday 10 a.m. to 6:30 p.m., Saturday until 5 p.m., Sunday 11 a.m. to 5 p.m.
Credit cards: MC, V

COOKWARE AND BOOKS

GREEN APPLE BOOKS

In the heart of the best food shopping section of Clement Street, Green Apple Books holds down the food literature front with one of the largest collections of new and used cookbooks in the city. Shelves and shelves of practically new volumes marked down to half price, plus many rarities (like Doris Muscatine's guide to San Francisco restaurants with recipes, published thirty years ago, a book many of us cut our culinary teeth on), make it difficult to leave the store without an armful of books. By thumbing through some of the treasures, such as a yellowing volume called *Southern Cooking* by

506 Clement Street
(at Sixth Avenue),
San Francisco
Tel: 387-2272
Open Sunday through Thursday 9:30 a.m. to 11 p.m., Friday and Saturday until midnight
Credit cards: MC, V

Mrs. S. R. Dull, a 1928 edition for $10, you might find a recipe for orange juice ("cut oranges in half . . .") or Foolish Pie. More-current works by the best food writers, including Betty Fussel's evocatively photographed *I Hear America Cooking* ($12) and Paul Prudhomme's volumes (which always stay timely if you like rich, spicy food), are well represented, which indicates that the store's cookbook buyers know what they're doing.

KAMEI HOUSEHOLD WARES

606 Clement Street
(at Seventh Avenue),
San Francisco
Tel: 666-3688
Open daily 9 a.m. to 7 p.m.
Credit cards: MC, V

Some stunning china for both serving and setting the table can be purchased for a song at the many Asian cookware stores in the city. At Kamei, Clement Street's entry, one finds Japanese bowls with intricate, speckled glazes, Chinese bowls in gorgeous shades of jade green, and all sorts of plates and platters in useful shapes and sizes. Heavy stone mortars and pestles at a fraction of the cost at tony houseware stores, and hard-to-find coconut graters, in both stool and portable configurations (the latter for all of $1.50), can be gleaned from the piled-high shelves. There might be seven-gallon calibrated plastic food containers with covers for home pickling, woks large and small, bamboo steamers, and a whole section of hanging car deodorizers, which lends Kamei the authentic aroma of Hong Kong.

South of Market & Third Street

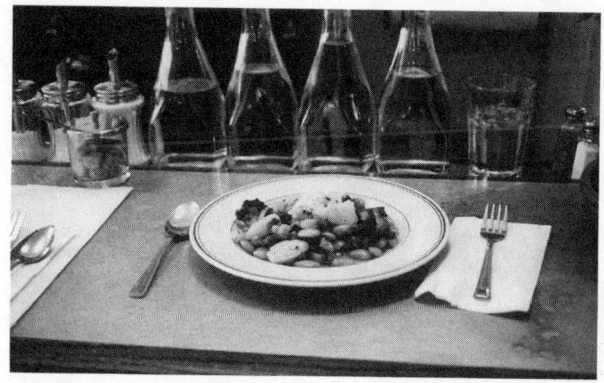

SOUTH OF MARKET & THIRD STREET

Restaurants:
1. Bizou 397
2. Fly Trap 398
3. 42 Degrees 399
4. Fringale 400
5. Hawthorne Lane 401
6. Kyo-Ya at the Sheraton Palace Hotel 402
7. LuLu 404
8. Moxie Bar and Restaurant 405
9. Ristorante Ecco 405
10. South Park Cafe 406
11. Thirsty Bear 407
12. Universal Cafe 407

Cafes:
13. Brain Wash Cafe 409
14. Caffè Centro 409
15. Caffè Roma Coffee Roasting Company 410
16. Palio Paninoteca 410
17. Specialty's Cafe and Bakery 411

Bars:
18. Caribbean Zone 411
19. Eleven 412
20. Hamburger Mary's 412
21. House of Shields 412
22. Infusion 413
23. Julie's Supper Club 413
24. The Ramp 413
25. Twenty Tank Brewery 414
26. Up and Down Club 414

Markets:
27. Rainbow Grocery 415
28. Trader Joe's 415

Produce:
27. Rainbow Grocery 416

Fish:
29. California Sunshine 418

Wines and Spirits:
30. K & L Wines 419
31. Wine House Limited 419

Cookware and Books:
32. Economy Restaurant Supply 420

RESTAURANTS

BIZOU

This small, terrific bistro boasts an unusually creative menu of Mediterranean-inspired dishes and a smart, resonant decor. The chef, Loretta Keller, a Stars veteran, and her husband Joseph Graham have put together a model restaurant and bar for the nineties: small, manageable, visually uncluttered, culinarily sophisticated, yet moderate in price. Bizou works because it is a unified statement, a completely realized vision anchored in a European tradition but free enough to draw on the New World eclecticism of California.

The menu derives its energy from a wood-burning oven in which all sorts of surprising things are cooked, such as sand dabs, our wonderful local flatfish served on the bone, or a ramekin of rich rigatoni baked with pancetta, ricotta, and tomato. Addictive thin-crusted pizzas emerge from the oven, topped perhaps with bitter broccoli rabe, smoky wood-roasted onions, and thin slices of pancetta. My favorite dishes here mine the French country repertoire, but imbue them with current style. *Chou farci* comes as a wedge of a round cake made of layers of Savoy cabbage, thinly sliced ham, and sliced apples in a sauce of crème fraîche enriched with the cooking juices. Keller's ethereal *brandade* of salt cod is one of the best versions to be found anywhere. The pastas tend to be untraditional, like chewy fresh pappardelle moistened with a hot, spicy tomato broth, onions cooked in the wood-fired oven, eggplant, and assertive feta. They work because the

598 Fourth Street
(at Brannan),
San Francisco
Tel: 543-2222
Open for lunch Monday
through Friday 11:30 a.m.
to 2:30 p.m.; dinner Monday
through Thursday 5:30 to
10 p.m., Friday and Saturday
until 10:30 p.m.
Price: Moderate
Credit cards: AE, MC, V

kitchen understands how to balance a dish of disparate ingredients, making a reason for them to come together.

True to form, the concise one-page wine list is culled from many small importers and introduces interesting bottles from lesser-known wine-growing regions of France and Italy. Cocktails are also available, and it is fun to have them at a small, handsome bar at the front of the restaurant with a signature Bizou flat bread, crisp and paper-thin, studded with olives, onions, and cheese.

Small white-linen-covered tables are pushed very close together, and the noise level can be high despite carpeting. The walls of the restaurant are painted a particularly delicious color of mustard yellow. Lots of light pours in through oversized square windows during the day, and soft light from hanging glass lamps adds a glow to the dining room at night. A lyrical flower arrangement on a buffet represents the only nonfunctional object in the room. I find the economy of space, of scale, of decor, as refreshing as the food.

FLY TRAP

606 Folsom Street
(at Second Street),
San Francisco
Tel: 243-0580
Open Monday through
Thursday 11:30 a.m. to
10 p.m., Friday and Saturday
5:30 to 10:30 p.m.;
call for Sunday hours
Price: Moderate
Credit cards: AE, DC, MC, V

The Fly Trap recreates a famous San Francisco restaurant that operated from the turn of the century until 1963 in various locations. Indeed, a glance at the Fly Trap's daily printed menu conjures up meals taken at Jack's, Sam's, Tadich, and the Old Poodle Dog; the bentwood chairs, wooden floors, butcher paper–covered tables, shaded wall sconces, and a tailored wooden bar all seem familiar and appealing.

The decor suits the menu, which offers lots of old-fashioned salads, chops, steaks, pastas, and grilled fish with a la carte accompaniments, a number of them very good. A spectacular celery Victor brings a gigantic half head of gently braised chilled celery, generously garnished with niçoise olives, anchovies, and slices of hard-cooked egg, all moistened with a mild French dressing. Perfection. The classic Caesar is enhanced with high-quality anchovies and big house-made croutons. One of my favorites, white salad, brings together hearts of palm, endive, and mushrooms in a sour-cream dressing topped with a round of goat cheese. A big plate of vinegary pickled herring served with mounds of sour cream and pickled red onion really makes old-timers happy, and me, too.

For a main course, two chicken dishes stand out: a wonderful old creation called chicken Raphael Weill, napped in sour cream with lots of mushrooms and big pieces of braised celery (ask for it if it's not on the menu); and coq au vin, chicken in a rich red-wine sauce full of bacon and mushrooms. The kitchen can come up with some lovely hand-formed tortellini stuffed with minced ham and sauced in cream and wild mushrooms; and perfect plates of steamed asparagus and broccoli in hollandaise. For dessert, have a chocolate sundae.

True to old San Francisco grill form, not all the dishes on the long menu are worth ordering, but the Fly Trap does evoke a beloved native restaurant style that is as much fun today as it was eighty years ago. Given the choice between a trendy SoMa statement and the updated Fly Trap, I'd buzz into the Trap any day.

42 DEGREES

Northern Spain, the Basque country, Provence, and Tuscany all happen to be on 42 degrees latitude. What a happy coincidence! Geography thus becomes the unifying theme at this striking warehouse district restaurant whose menu of small and large dishes sometimes reads better than it tastes. No matter. The space, next to the Esprit wholesale outlet and originally developed as a cafe for the clothing manufacturer, has enough cachet to carry a visit. On sunny days, the front of the restaurant is literally rolled up, turning 42 Degrees into a spacious outdoor cafe where people eat focaccia sandwiches, pizzas, and salads. At night, the restaurant becomes a hip, dimly lit clubhouse for graphic artists, multimedia types, and book publishers, who drink at the long bar, take in the live music, and nibble at small plates of food. Serious eaters should try to get a seat upstairs in the mezzanine, which has a view of the shipyards and bay, and stick to the main course dishes like Niman-Schell rib eye steak, sand dabs with lentils, braised chicken, and chocolate pots de creme for dessert.

235 16th Street
(just east of Third Street),
San Francisco
Tel: 777-5558
Open for lunch Monday through Friday 11:30 a.m. to 3 p.m.; dinner Wednesday through Saturday 6:30 to 11:30 p.m.
Price: Moderate
Credit cards: MC, V

FRINGALE

570 Fourth Street (between Brannan and Bryant), San Francisco
Tel: 543-0573
Open for lunch Monday through Friday 11:30 a.m. to 3 p.m., Dinner Monday through Saturday 5:30 to 10:30 p.m.
Price: Moderate
Credit cards: AE, MC, V

J'ai la fringale means "I'm starving" in colloquial French; it's what you utter when you're overtaken by a sudden hunger. If this condition should hit you, Gerald Hirigoyen's smart, casual little bistro, Fringale, provides the antidote. This French-Basque chef turns out an inventive repertoire of dishes that will satisfy deep hunger without taxing a shallow pocketbook.

Start right in with a frisée salad with bacon, croutons, and a poached egg tossed in a warm vinaigrette; or if you're really hungry, have the Fringale classic mashed-potato cake studded with shredded duck *confit* and walnuts, and sauced with a mild, savory vinaigrette. Tricky presentations that draw on classic French technique, such as a chilled terrine of lentils with a rosette of pink lamb tenderloin in the center, sauced in a shalloty mustardy rémoulade, are as delicious as they are stunning.

Hirigoyen has a fine touch with fish. His poached halibut drizzled with nutty brown butter served with a psychedelic puree of beets, a mound of buttery spinach, and a pile of green beans is dreamy. If monkfish is on the menu, swathed in a lively bordelaise sauce of shallots and red wine, don't pass it up. Of course a tasty steak *frites*, with a shalloty red wine butter and thin fries, is always a welcome sight at a good price, but so is a tender roast rack of lamb with the most lus-

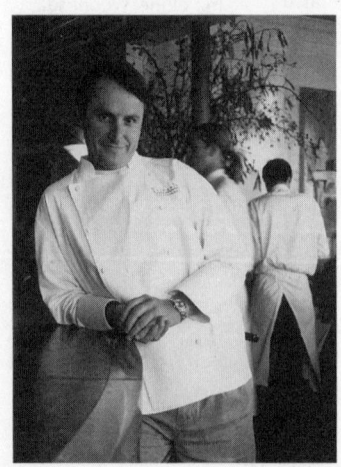

cious potato gratin and green beans tossed with fresh herbs, a plate made in heaven, for only a few dollars more.

Since Hirigoyen started his cooking career as a pastry chef, better save room for a crisp, warm apple tart with a puff pastry crust; or a Biarritz *rocher* of chocolate mousse on a crisp meringue surrounded with crème anglaise; or a palate-cleansing iced Armagnac and coffee parfait.

The cheerful interior has been done in beiges and shades of white with blond wood trim and an elegantly curved bar. Very small tables covered with linen and white paper are pushed close together in front of banquettes. The ambiance is 100 percent

French bistro. The waiters are mostly French and completely professional; the wine list reasonably priced and full of good little imported wines; the noise level high. From the moment Hirigoyen opened his bistro, it has been packed with discriminating diners who recognize a great bargain, trying to edge out the customers who are there for a great time. Be sure to call ahead, particularly for dinner.

HAWTHORNE LANE

A number of big, glittery restaurants have opened in the last couple of years in San Francisco, but none with the pedigree of Hawthorne Lane. Started by chefs Annie and David Gingrass, formerly of Postrio, Hawthorne Lane instantly became the most important restaurant in town—like Stars did a decade ago. Because of its scale, the myriad choices it offers, and the breathtakingly high standards applied to every detail of its operation, Hawthorne captured everyone's attention. Anything you want to eat or drink, including much you didn't even know you wanted until you tried it for the first time here, flows out of the bar, kitchen, and wine cellars just for you, and for the hundred people sitting around you. The owners like big concepts; they wanted a major restaurant, but have attacked the project from an individual diner's point of view. You are made to feel special here.

22 Hawthorne Street (off Howard between Second and Third Streets), San Francisco
Tel: 777-9979
Open for lunch Monday through Friday 11:30 a.m. to 2 p.m.; dinner Sunday through Thursday 5:30 to 10 p.m., Friday and Saturday until 10:30 p.m.
Price: Expensive
Credit cards: DC, D, MC, V

The couple chose the ground floor of the Crown Point Press building, a lyrical hidden space with expansive arched windows that look out to a quiet urban alley, to build their elegant barroom and dining room. The interior of little club lamps, red brick walls, Mondrianesque earthquake bracing, hanging lights in sculptural geometrical shapes, and stunning fine art prints somehow reminds me of the Four Seasons in New York, the classic modern American restaurant. Hawthorne Lane wears this kind of luxury easily.

The menu is completely original. You haven't seen the likes of it before. Start with sweet-fleshed Alaskan spot shrimp netted from an aquarium in the dining room. They're simply steamed and served with Asian dipping sauces. Or, you can have an iced platter of shellfish; grilled marinated anchovies with frisée salad; seared foie gras that melts in your mouth; or any seasonal delicacy that comes around, prepared in unexpected ways. A basket of American breads—eggy dinner rolls, herbed biscuits, soft peppery white bread, breadsticks sprinkled with coarse salt—is refilled the minute they're devoured.

Main courses are finely honed. I'll never forget a springtime dish of satiny Atlantic cod with a Provençal mélange of vegetables and herbs, and some fabulous raviolis stuffed with favas and roasted fennel. Meats are lovely here, rosy leg of lamb thinly sliced and juicy; poached fillet of beef, buttery and unusually flavorful. The accompaniments dazzle. Roast chicken comes with a miniature corn and cheddar spoonbread in its own little mold; boned quail perch on squares of scalloped potatoes topped with currants and crispy bread crumbs.

Of course there is a deep and original wine list, a spirits list, a port list. Desserts have become less fussy and more focused—how about hot beignets, as ephemeral as sighs, with a cherry salad? The well-trained, high-level service staff makes the monumental effort coalesce. All the details that give Hawthorne Lane its character, from having its very own street, to the little nut-coated truffles that come with coffee, accumulate layer upon layer to create a truly grand vision. This restaurant is fresh, exciting, and rewardingly substantial. It's the flower that California cuisine has produced in the nineties, and a spectacular hybrid it is.

KYO-YA AT THE SHERATON PALACE HOTEL

2 New Montgomery Street
(at Market),
San Francisco
Tel: 392-8600
Open for lunch Tuesday through Friday
11:30 a.m. to 2 p.m.;
dinner Tuesday through Saturday 6 to 10 p.m.
Prices: Sushi bar, expensive; restaurant, moderate
Credit cards: AE, DC, D, MC, V

A branch of a Japanese restaurant chain, Kyo-ya brings a higher level of ingredients and Japanese cooking technique to San Francisco. Far and away, it's the best sushi bar in town. To eat here, have about $75 in your pocket, then don't worry about the cost of each pair. You'll get some of the most exquisite sushi you have ever tasted, along with a couple of martinis or jars of sake. The most fabulous sushi at Kyo-ya are made with raw scallops flown in live from Boston in the shell, scooped out and sliced to order, and fresh *hamachi*, or yellowtail, which tastes completely different from the frozen served everywhere else. Also spectacular are the *toro* (at $16 a pair), tuna-belly meat not even available most places, which

Try these chicken burgers at home for your kids. Everyone likes them. Ground chicken can be found at most of the meat and poultry counters discussed in this book. This recipe is adapted from local chef Morgan Song.

In a large bowl, combine all the ingredients, except for the oil. Cover and chill the mixture for about 30 minutes. Divide the mixture into 4 patties. Warm the oil in a large skillet over medium heat. Sauté the patties on each side until done, about 5 minutes per side; they will be firm when pressed with your finger. Serve on hamburger rolls with hamburger fixings, or eat separately with a salad.

Serves 4

CHICKEN-VEGETABLE BURGER

1 pound ground chicken,
   preferably dark meat
1/4 medium red onion, finely diced
1/4 medium carrot, peeled, finely diced
1/4 zucchini, finely diced
3 fresh basil leaves, minced
1 teaspoon minced fresh garlic
2 tablespoons dried bread crumbs
1 teaspoon Worcestershire sauce
1/2 teaspoon kosher salt
10 turns of the pepper grinder
2 tablespoons vegetable oil

reminds me of a slab of butter; sea urchin roe that has a creaminess and nuttiness I've only experienced when I've pried them off the rocks myself; and delicacies like clean-flavored and refreshing Japanese red snapper. There are no fireworks, no inventions, nothing to distract the diner from the perfection of nature. The fish is framed by fingers of rice, each grain huge, fragrant, and chewy, barely adhering to the mass, seasoned with the most judicious application of hot wasabi. If you want to experience sushi at its best, a meal here is worth every penny.

The food is much less expensive in a series of small, luxurious, simply appointed dining rooms in the restaurant. In fact, many of the authentic dishes served here are tasty, unusual, and a terrific buy. A selection of sushi served at table will be much less expensive than at the sushi bar, but of a more mundane quality. Instead, try a whole crab, stir-fried with matsutake, enoki, and shiitake mushrooms enriched with egg, which all melts together into a fantastic sauce that you spoon over a bowl of chewy Japanese rice; or a butter-tender steak, sliced into thick pieces and brought sizzling to the table in a covered ceramic dish with two dipping sauces. In addition to these hearty dishes, a whole range of vibrant

Japanese salads and small dishes, soups, and rice porridges are artfully presented and carefully made. Service by waitresses in kimonos brings traditional graciousness to the dining room floor, where you hear as much Japanese spoken as English. This Tokyo-based restaurant, set up to accommodate Japanese visitors to San Francisco, is an emissary of the best of Japanese culture for those of us who live here.

L U L U

816 Folsom Street (between Fourth and Fifth Streets), San Francisco
Tel: 495-5775
Open for lunch daily 11:30 a.m. to 2:30 p.m.; dinner Sunday through Thursday 5:30 to 10:30 p.m., Friday and Saturday until 11:30 p.m., Sunday 5 to 10:30 p.m.
Price: Moderate
Credit cards: AE, MC, V

Flames leap high in a huge wood-burning rotisserie and fireplace at center stage in the cavernous dining room of LuLu, a brilliant restaurant concept created by chef Reed Hearon who left the daily operation in 1996. The new chef, Jody Denton, wisely has left the menu unchanged.; the food is still simple and delicious. LuLu starts out with first-rate raw materials and puts 90 percent of its effort into manipulating them over one open fire or another. Tasty thin-crusted pizzas and iron pans of mussels in the shell come out of the wood-burning oven. Juicy rotisserie chickens and pork loin are licked with smoke as they slowly turn in front of a roaring wood fire. They are served to be shared on large platters, accompanied with mashed potatoes enriched with olive oil, or roasted potatoes with arugula. From the grill, sweet-fleshed Alaskan spot prawns with roe, shell, and head should not be passed up when they are available; nor grilled asparagus dusted with shaved Parmesan. Except for the pastas, which somehow don't have the focus of the other dishes, the one-page daily printed menu is full of mouthwatering choices, large and small. I'm not the only one who thinks so, because the barnlike dining room has been packed from the moment it opened. The noise level is deafening. The fact that both the bar and most of the kitchen are in one room, along with a sea of small wooden tables packed close together, does not help matters. No one really cares, because the place has become a scene, attended as much for the action as the terrific, reasonably priced food. If you're an eater, the best time to arrive is for late lunch, when the dining room has emptied and the cooks have a moment to take a deep breath. You can order a bottle of an interesting French or Italian wine and linger over the rustic French desserts, which always include a warm, caramelized upside-down tart and house-made ice cream, and have a good cup of espresso.

MOXIE BAR AND RESTAURANT

Theater Artaud, the city's premier avant-garde theater space, has always needed a good bar and restaurant nearby and now they have one in Moxie, a witty, friendly Eastern European cafe with a South of Market sensibility. Located on two floors of an attractive, small redbrick building, Moxie has put together lively lunch and dinner menus that somehow lighten traditional Jewish and Eastern European cooking with California ingredients—delicious house-cured pastrami on Metropolis rye bread accompanied with a beautiful baby lettuce salad; fabulous potato pancakes topped with house-cured salmon and chive oil; house-made vegetable pickles and marinated olives served with iced vodka; brisket with leek fritters and a big dollop of mild horseradish cream on top. Have the "noshka" for dessert, a sublime construction of crisp filo pastry, dried fruit compote, and whipped cream. You'll be back for more of Moxie's cooking whether you're attending the theater or not. I'd drive across town for the airy matzoh ball in rich chicken broth and one of those superb pastrami sandwiches with baby lettuces. Oy!

2742 17th Street
(at Florida),
San Francisco
Tel: 863-4177
Open for lunch Monday through Friday 11:30 to 2:30; dinner Tuesday through Thursday 6 to 10 p.m., Friday and Saturday until midnight.
Price: Inexpensive
Credit cards: MC, V

RISTORANTE ECCO

The second venture in the neighborhood by the South Park Cafe people (see next page), Ristorante Ecco embodies breezy, sophisticated urbanity. Taking advantage of its location in the hidden enclave of South Park, one modern dining room looks out to the greenery through tall, clean-lined wood-framed windows. A stunning, arched barroom and cafe, hung with lithographed maps of Rome and clever, small black Italian light fixtures, draws a steady crowd of well-dressed people who just want a bite or a drink. The food here is ample and lively, though the one-page Italian menu does not break any new ground. A noteworthy aspect is the price column. If you are watching your pocketbook and still want

101 South Park (between Second and Third, Bryant and Brannan),
San Francisco
Tel: 495-3291
Open for lunch Monday through Friday
11:30 a.m. to 2:30 p.m.;
dinner Monday through Saturday 6 to 10 p.m.
Price: Moderate
Credit cards: AE, DC, MC, V

a stylish evening out, you can do well at Ecco. The other evening two of us sat at the beautiful bar. We had perfectly mixed cocktails, then a light meal of grilled radicchio in balsamic vinaigrette; buttery sautéed spinach with raisins and pine nuts; a superb soup of pureed root vegetables; and a whole-wheat spaghetti tossed with cauliflower, broccoli, olives and capers. It couldn't have been nicer and the whole tab came to $35. The wine list is as smart as the surroundings, with a handful of interesting American wines and a large, enticing selection of Italian bottles at excellent prices.

SOUTH PARK CAFE

108 South Park (between Second and Third, Bryant and Brannan), San Francisco
Tel: 495-7275
Open Monday through Friday 7:30 a.m. to 10 p.m., Saturday 6 to 10 p.m.
Price: Moderate
Credit cards: AE, MC, V

From the moment this charming, very French cafe and restaurant opened ten years ago, I wanted to be there. The design of the narrow room, with front windows that open completely onto the sidewalk, a copper bar, and painted wooden banquettes that stretch the length of the restaurant, is so simple, yet so perfectly done, that I felt I was sitting in a Left Bank bistro in Paris. The food here has had its ups and downs with partnership and chef changes, starting off terrific, faltering a bit, but now at its best ever under the direction of chef Ward Little. I have sat at the bar in the evening and eaten crispy *brandade* and potato cakes, savory quail salad, and juicy slices of roast pork loin with luxurious potato puree. At lunch you can have a perfect roast chicken with skinny *pommes frites,* or aromatic *boudin noir* sautéed with apples and surrounded by watercress, served by a French-speaking wait person. The wine list, augmented by many interesting, inexpensive glasses listed on a blackboard, only waits to be mined. The prices are gratifyingly moderate, and the casual bistro atmosphere allows you to order as much or as little as you like. The place gets very full during lunch with nearby designers and architects who vie for the few choice outdoor tables on the sidewalk, but the light is so good in this cafe that it doesn't matter where you sit. You'll be bathed in the warm glow of an authentic bistro.

THIRSTY BEAR

You wouldn't think that a gigantic, roaring brew-pub filled with hordes of twenty-something beer drinkers would offer authentic Basque and Catalan food, but it does. I, who will only drink a small glass of beer under duress, love to come here for the first-rate Spanish tapas prepared by chef Daniel Olivello. Thank goodness the open kitchen and tables for dining are sequestered at one end of the brick warehouse that houses the whole operation. There you can have a classic *tortilla de patatas*, (a thick wedge of thinly sliced potatoes, eggs, and onion) that I could eat every day; wonderful finger sandwiches of cured Spanish ham on soft crusty bread; *escalivada* (roasted peppers and onions with olive oil and vinegar); fried potatoes with spicy mayonnaise; and a casserole of shrimp sautéed with sliced garlic and chili flakes. They're all delicious. I drank amontillado, a medium-bodied sherry with my meal, but actually the lighter beers here do go well with the menu. I've had many a cold little glass of beer in Spain with my tapas. Though not as light as the beer in Spain, the Thirsty India Pale Ale here works rather well. Thirsty Bear covers all the bases, however. They not only offer appropriate, fairly priced wines, but a full bar. Take note of Thirsty Bear's long hours. This is one of the few places that serves late into the night, and tapas make for a perfect late-night snack or midafternoon meal.

661 Howard Street
(near Third Street),
San Francisco
Tel: 974-0905
Open for lunch Monday through Saturday 11:30 a.m. to 2:30 p.m.; dinner Sunday through Wednesday 5:30 to 10 p.m., tapas until 11 p.m., Thursday to Saturday until 10:30 p.m., tapas until 11:30 p.m.
Price: Moderate
Credit cards: AE, MC, V

UNIVERSAL CAFE

My heavy-equipment-mover friend Roger, who hangs out in funky bars with house bands, bowled me over the other day when he told me I had to have lunch at the Universal Cafe, "because it felt so cool to be there." A fabricator of objects for his own Potrero Hill fixer-upper, he appreciates the craftsmanship that has gone into converting a small wooden warehouse on an unexpectedly charming, semi-industrial South-of-Market block into a very hip cafe. Cement, cast aluminum, and maple veneer plywood have been used in witty ways. A bank of floor-to-ceiling windows with hefty-looking aluminum hardware opens entirely onto a quiet block dotted

2814 19th Street (between Florida and Bryant),
San Francisco
Tel: 821-4608
Open for lunch Tuesday through Sunday 11:30 a.m. to 2:30 p.m.; dinner Tuesday through Saturday 6 to 10 p.m., Sunday 5:30 to 9:30 p.m.; Sunday brunch 9 a.m. to 2:30 p.m.
Price: Inexpensive
Credit cards: AE, MC, V

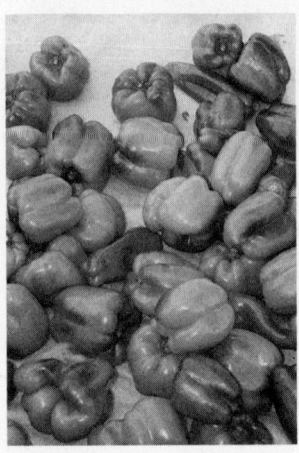

with trees. Smart aluminum and wood chairs and marble-topped tables from the workshop of South Park Fabricators Jeff and Larissa Sand somehow combine modernity with cafe tradition. Half the room is taken up by a long benchlike banquette with tables, the other by an open kitchen and counter dominated by a coffee roaster. All the excellent coffee served here, at Ristorante Ecco, and the South Park Cafe, has been roasted in it.

The connection between these stylish SoMa cafes comes as no surprise. They all share a common partner, Bob Voorhees. However, the menu at Universal is based on pizza dough and focaccia. The individual pizzas are particularly stunning, with light yet chewy crusts. One topped with caramelized onions, prosciutto, ricotta, and Fontina is a brilliant invention—through not one Italian purists would be likely to order. Don't miss it. The focaccia sandwich filled with roasted chicken and aïoli is another triumph. In a town where every second restaurant offers individual pizzas and focaccia sandwiches, the Universal has actually made its own mark with them. The sandwiches come with a pretty green salad, larger versions of which can be ordered with Gorgonzola and glazed walnuts or strips of moist grilled duck breast with mango. The Italian wines by the glass will not strain your pocketbook, and you should be sure to end with a creamy-topped espresso. All the details of the Universal Cafe please so much that I have to agree with Roger's unusual enthusiasm for a cafe that serves designer pizzas.

CAFES

BRAIN WASH CAFE

This cafe-laundromat kills two birds with one stone. One part of this eye-catching two-story glass building contains thirty-two state-of-the-art, heavy-duty computer-operated washers, twenty-four dryers, a wash-and-fold service, and a dry cleaner. Separated from the machinery by a diagonal glass wall is a self-service cafe with cement floors, clever metal chairs covered with epoxied collage, and a loud jukebox, giving it a Cafe Flore feel. Though most of the food is mediocre, with the exception of a tasty Chinese chicken salad in a light soy and walnut-oil dressing, you can fill yourself up with the likes of thick focaccia pizzas or baked apples. The scene is so weird and happening that it makes washing your dirty clothes an important social experience.

1122 Folsom Street
(between Seventh and Eighth Streets),
San Francisco
Tel: 861-3663
Open daily 7 a.m. to 11 p.m., Friday and Saturday until 1 a.m.
Credit cards: MC, V

CAFFÈ CENTRO

Caffè Centro's South Park location gives it its cachet. Outdoor tables on the sidewalk around the perimeter of the cafe bask in the ample sun in this protected good-weather belt in the middle of the city. Light floods in through usually open windows and seems to make the creamy-colored walls glow. Details in the design of the cafe, like a poured and painted floor that looks like a mosaic, bottle-glass light fixtures, tiny round metal tables that tend to wobble, and metal chairs, set

102 South Park Avenue
(between Second and Third, Bryant and Brannan),
San Francisco
Tel: 882-1500
Open Monday through Friday 7:30 a.m. to 6:30 p.m., Saturday 8 a.m. to 4:30 p.m.
Credit cards: AE, MC, V;
$10 minimum

the backdrop for lots of arty, expressively dressed young patrons. Caffè Centro offers the inexpensive alternative to Ristorante Ecco and South Park Cafe in the same neighborhood.

Warm sandwiches, like a delicious open-faced sandwich of roasted red peppers with melted Gruyère on toasted bread, star on the menu. Frittatas layered with all sorts of vegetables held together with garlic-scented custard are also good, as are the house-made soups. Unfortunate in a cafe, the coffee consistently has a bitter edge.

CAFFÈ ROMA COFFEE ROASTING COMPANY

885 Bryant Street (at Gilbert between Sixth and Seventh Streets),
San Francisco
Tel: 296-7662
Open Monday through Friday 6 a.m. to 5 p.m.
Credit cards: MC, V

See listing, page 285.

PALIO PANINOTECA

201 Mission Street (at Beale),
San Francisco
Tel: 979-0451
Open Monday through Friday 6:30 a.m. to 3:30 p.m.
Credit cards: AE, MC, V

53 Stevenson (between First and Second Streets),
San Francisco
Tel: 546-3141
Open Monday through Friday 6:30 a.m. to 4:30 p.m.
Credit cards: AE, MC, V

See listing, page 146.

SPECIALTY'S CAFE AND BAKERY

150 Spear Street (between Mission and Howard)
San Francisco
Tel: 978-9662
Open Monday through Friday 6 a.m. to 6 p.m.
No credit cards
See listing, page 150.

BARS

CARIBBEAN ZONE

55 Natoma Street (between First and Second, Howard and Mission), San Francisco
Tel: 541-9465
Open Monday through Thursday 11:30 a.m. to 10 p.m., Friday until 11 p.m., Saturday 5 p.m. to 2 a.m.
Credit cards: AE, MC, V

Trader Vic may have invented the tropical drink and island decor, but Caribbean Zone takes it to new, campy heights. This sheet-metal beach shack in an alley between parking lots is a jungle of plastic tropical plants and trees, complete with a waterfall tumbling over artificial rocks and a real airplane cabin as a cocktail lounge. Nothing is more fun than repairing down the aisle to an upholstered seat, with videos of passing clouds lighting up the windows, a large and expensive ($6.50) tropical drink in hand. Sex in the Jungle, a rum-spiked slush of guayabana pulp with plenty of nutmeg, or my favorite, Goomba Boomba, fresh bananas, lime, and rum blended with ice, will get you flying relatively fast. As you can imagine, the Caribbean Zone is a place where life can be zany and laid-back, but not necessarily the site for great eating. If you need something to counteract the effects of topical drinks, order the conch fritters or jerk chicken, rubbed in a lively spice mixture and grilled. They'll ground you enough for a second takeoff.

ELEVEN

374 Eleventh Street
(between Harrison
and Folsom),
San Francisco
Tel: 431-3337
Open Monday through
Thursday 6 to 11 p.m., Friday
and Saturday until midnight; bar open until 2 a.m.
Credit cards: AE, DC, MC, V

This lyrical, high-ceilinged space across the street from Slim's has had a number of different identities since it opened. All of them have been appealing, but the fickle nature of the South of Market crowd dictates a short life span for anything more ambitious than a watering hole or club. Such is the case with Eleven. Its handsome, dark-wood bar and SoMa location are now the draws, though the inexpensive Italian menu is certainly serviceable. The newest set of owners have added live music every night.

HAMBURGER MARY'S

1582 Folsom Street
(at 12th Street),
San Francisco
Tel: 626-1985
Open Monday through
Thursday 11:30 a.m. to 1 a.m.,
Friday until 2 a.m., Saturday
10 a.m. to 2 a.m., Sunday
10 a.m. to 2 a.m.
Credit cards: AE, D, MC, V

Everybody who hangs out at Hamburger Mary's looks like they're dressed up for a party, though most of the time the party is in their own head. A scene can't get much weirder or wackier, but even blatantly straight customers can feel at home here because some people come in that costume. The hamburgers have a health-food overlay. They come on soft whole wheat bread with sprouts, all the better to go with a bourbon and a smoke. The bizarre energy of the place has made it a famous and beloved South of Market landmark, which continually attracts new generations of weirdnesses.

HOUSE OF SHIELDS

39 New Montgomery Street
(between Market
and Mission),
San Francisco
Tel: 392-7732
Open Monday through
Friday 11 a.m. to 9 p.m.
Credit cards: AE, DC, MC, V

This historic bar, now under new, energetic management, serves hearty blue-collar fare to white-collar workers: stockbrokers and lawyers, South of Market small businesspeople and their employees. A piano plays in the ancient dark-wood barroom with white tile floors and brass rails. It's noisy and smoky, especially after work. The drinks are nothing special, but just what you'd expect at a resonant old San Francisco watering hole. A nice-looking young bartender, who has been there for ages, takes care of everyone with friendly conviction.

INFUSION

Infusion has become a popular hangout for the architects and designers who work around South Park. After several different identities and decors, the space has evolved into a comfortable, handsome bar with Mapplethorpe photographs of orchids on the walls and a shelf of large glass jars with spigots that hold the advertised infusions of vodka and fruit. People make special pilgrimages here for pineapple vodka and cranberry juice, a refreshing drink that tends to go down rather easily. Coconut, starfruit, pears, persimmons (gack!), huckleberries, and some disintegrating kiwi were hard at work infusing the night I was there. The food is actually quite good as evidenced by crispy cornmeal-breaded, fried calamari with jalapeño mayonnaise, which goes brilliantly with fruity vodka cocktails. The cute, friendly bartenders steer you to the best dishes and the most popular infused vodka drinks.

555 Second Street (between Bryant and Brannan), San Francisco
Tel: 543-2282
Open Monday through Friday 11:30 a.m. to 2 a.m., Saturday and Sunday 5 p.m. to 2 a.m.
Lunch Monday through Friday 11:30 a.m. to 5 p.m., dinner nightly 5 p.m. to 11 p.m., late menu Sunday through Thursday until midnight, Friday and Saturday until 1 a.m.
Credit cards: AE, DC, MC, V

JULIE'S SUPPER CLUB

Still a happening spot after a decade, Julie's serves updated American diner food with a spicy twist amid the din of a bar that attracts a young crowd. There's always a wait for a table during prime meal hours, and everyone seems to like it that way. Large groups tend to come here to celebrate special occasions.

1123 Folsom Street (between Seventh and Eighth Streets), San Francisco
Tel: 861-0707
Open Monday through Wednesday 5 p.m. to midnight, Thursday through Saturday 5 p.m. to 1:45 a.m.

THE RAMP

The Ramp's location, right next to a working shipyard with towering cranes and dry docks where massive ships are repaired in front of a small boat marina, tests your perspective after a few Bloody Marys or margaritas at the outdoor bar that looks straight into the harbor. Though the food is acceptable, eating it outdoors under an umbrella by all the activity on the water makes it taste much better, especially a breakfast of sunny-side up eggs and spicy Italian sausage. The Ramp is a must-stop for breakfast on the way to Giants'

855 China Basin (off Third Street at Mariposa), San Francisco
Tel: 621-2378
Open Sunday through Thursday 8 a.m. to 10 p.m., Friday and Saturday until 2 a.m.; closed during December and January
Credit cards: AE, MC, V

day games if you're coming from the city. You get to The Ramp by turning toward the bay on Mariposa from Third Street. To get to Candlestick, simply continue up Third until you see the Candlestick turnoV sign. (The Third Street route is the fastest and most hassle-free way to go.)

TWENTY TANK BREWERY

316 Eleventh Street
(at Folsom),
San Francisco
Tel: 255-9455
Open daily 11:30 to 1 a.m.
Credit cards: AE, DC, MC, V

A branch of a Seattle outfit that also owns Triple Rock Brewery in Berkeley, Twenty Tank is most beloved among serious followers of beer culture. They love the big, rich, distinctive beers brewed here, full of character without off-flavors. This is a grungy, feel-good place that serves thick-crusted pizzas as a sidelight to their beloved beers.

UP AND DOWN CLUB

1151 Folsom Street
(between Seventh
and Eighth Streets),
San Francisco
Tel: 626-2388
Open Monday through
Saturday 8 p.m. to 2 a.m.
Credit cards: AE, MC, V

Partially owned by model Christy Turlington, who hangs out here when she isn't on a shoot, the Up and Down Club is the bar of choice for local photographers, art students, budding designers, and people interested in style who like to be seen. Amenities include live music, dancing, and a fairly ambitious menu of vegetable-sensitive bar food. Even the bartenders, male and female, are cute.

MARKETS

RAINBOW GROCERY

Imagine my surprise at walking into the new Rainbow Grocery store on Folsom and seeing a clean, neat, well-organized, modern health-food supermarket that still had all the great local stuff in it. I used to grit my teeth whenever I sidestepped the street people to enter the old chaotic Mission Street store manned with surly co-op members. I don't know if the new, expansive quarters changed the attitude of the workers, but I had a very pleasant conversation with my pierced checkout person, who handed me a fresh bag in which to pack my groceries. I now make a special point of shopping at Rainbow. The array of foods is mind-boggling. Things you only see in small cellophane packages other places come in bulk, ready to be scooped out here—that includes seaweed of every color and shape, organic jasmine rice, Thai jasmine rice, basmati rice, beautiful dried beans in all hues and patterns, maple sugar, chestnut flour, spelt, masa harina, organic vegetable-flavored penne, organic linguine, and organic dried anchos. This eclectic list only skims the surface.

The large produce department looks terrific now. Everything is meticulously labeled as to origin, down to the bunches of herbs. Of particular note is produce bought directly from the farmer posted with "farmer direct" signs—like romaine and red butter lettuce from Dale Coke, dill and cilantro from Pomponio. You come pretty close to shopping in a farmers' market atmosphere here.

To compete with stores like Andronico's and Whole Foods, Rainbow has its own olive bar and a fine little cheese section with interesting selections that include lots of fresh goat cheeses, sheeps' milk ricotta, and rice flour teleme (not as good as the one at Florence Delicatessen in North Beach, see page 289). Top-of-the-line imported groceries like Capezzano extra virgin olive oil and Rustichella hard durum wheat

1745 Folsom Street
(at 13th Street),
San Francisco
Tel: 863-0621
Open Monday through
Saturday 9 a.m. to 9 p.m.,
Sunday 10 a.m. to 9 p.m.
Credit cards: D, MC, V

pasta made on ancient machines in Italy fill out your market basket and empty your pocketbook. If you want a Juicerator, you can buy it here, and your complete hippie needs as well —natural fragrant oils, soaps, candles, cosmetics, organic pet food, recycled paper products. Rainbow has taken itself into the next millennium, much to the surprise of everyone who got into fights at the grungy old store, and has reinvented itself as a whole foods superstore on the cutting edge. It's worth traveling across town to shop here.

TRADER JOE'S

555 Ninth Street
(at Brannan),
San Francisco
Tel: 863-1292
Open daily 9 a.m. to 9 p.m.
Credit cards: D, MC, V

I've never really found shopping at Trader Joe's to be very productive. Who wants giant tubs of frozen lasagne or mediocre snack chips? But the last time I was there I noticed ten-pound bars of Ghirardelli chocolate for $18.99, a $60 savings over purchase of the same bar at a Ghirardelli outlet. Amazing. I also bought a pound of fresh, new crop pecans, whole and perfect for just $3.89. I needed these things to make milk chocolate pecan clusters, this year's Christmas gift. Then I noticed huge bottles of Stolichnaya Vodka, my favorite, for practically half price, and liters of uncarbonated spring water for 99 cents. For certain odd items, some of which seem to shift on and off the shelves, you can't beat Trader Joe's. You just have to discover what they might be.

PRODUCE

RAINBOW GROCERY

See Markets, page 415.

MILK CHOCOLATE PECAN CLUSTERS

1 pound Ghirardelli milk chocolate
1/2 pound pecan halves
4 tablespoons salted butter
Pinch of kosher salt

This recipe is adapted from a session with Sydney Goldstein, who learned how to make them from Emma Jones.

Preheat oven to 375° F.

In the top of a double boiler, or in a large metal bowl placed over a pot of boiling water, melt the chocolate in the bowl.

Put the pecans in another bowl. Melt the butter in a saucepan. Pour the melted butter over the pecans. Add a pinch of salt. Toss. The pecans should taste buttery and a little salty. Spread the buttered pecans on a cookie sheet and roast them in the oven for 10 minutes until they become fragrant.

Stir the chocolate, making sure it is completely melted. Pour the hot, buttery pecans into the bowl of melted chocolate. Mix them together.

Spread waxed paper on a counter. Scoop out a teaspoon of the mixture containing 3 or 4 chocolate-covered pecans and drop onto the paper. Each candy will look different, the beauty of hand-dipped chocolates. Let set for 2 hours, after which the clusters will be ready to box or bag. Eat within a week or so. Their sparkle comes from their freshness.

FISH

CALIFORNIA SUNSHINE

144 King Street (between Second and Third Streets), San Francisco
Tel: 543-3007
Open Monday through Friday 8 a.m. to 5 p.m.
Credit cards: AE, MC, V

Mats and Dafne Engstrom have ascended the throne as the king and queen of American, eastern Russian, and Chinese caviars, having been in business now for twenty-one years. Their seven-ounce tins of Tsar Nicoulai (their trademark) ossetra, the medium-sized caviar with a nutty flavor that I like the most, offers the best price for the quality I have encountered. California Sunshine set up their own caviar-making operation in Russia once the market opened, and both quality and freshness are monitored. Buying caviar, of course, is a crapshoot, because every fish produces eggs of different quality. The ideal is to get it as fresh as possible, which is why buying new-crop caviar in the spring will net you the best flavor. Of course, most Americans want caviar around the winter holiday season, but once you've tasted the fresher eggs, you'll be tempted to have it earlier in the year. When I was in Soviet Georgia, just months before it declared its independence, we ate, with a spoon, small plates thickly paved with the most delectable, nutty, barely salted sturgeon eggs and washed it down with icy vodka. Now I serve caviar this way here, in California. Though the prices at California Sunshine have risen considerably during the last year, it is still the place to buy caviar for a special occasion. On a smaller budget, you can make a rather pretty and not too expensive presentation of caviar toasts using California Sunshine's crunchy, bright golden whitefish caviar, orange salmon roe, and black Russian sevruga. Though the wholesale outlet does not have a retail sales room per se, people are welcome to drop in if they are planning to buy.

WINES AND SPIRITS

K & L WINES

A parking lot makes it easy to shop at this small but fully stocked wineshop with most bottles displayed in wooden racks. An excellent Bordeaux selection at some surprising prices draws collectors here. In fact, on a recent visit I saw several elegant Bordeaux, like 1988 Domaine de Chevalier Blanc, on sale below cost. An eclectic selection of imported wines from Chile, Spain, and Australia entices cost-conscious buyers. K & L also sells fine spirits like *grappa* and double-malt Scotch. Nestled onto its shelves you will find at least one of the Gourmel Cognacs, a Cognac whose smoothness, delicacy, and finesse make the inevitable headache you get the next morning, when one taste has led to another, worth the pain.

768 Harrison Street (between Third and Fourth Streets), San Francisco
Tel: 896-1734
Open Monday through Friday 9 a.m. to 7 p.m., Saturday until 6 p.m., Sunday 11 a.m. to 5 p.m.
Credit cards: AE, MC, V

WINE HOUSE LIMITED

The yeasty smell of wooden wine crates greets you when you walk into this redbrick room with exposed beams and a cement floor. Stacks of these boxes full of Cru Bordeaux at decent prices—a 15 percent discount on two cases—call out to be examined. Many Bordeaux are available in hard-to-find half bottles. The Wine House also brings in the Robert Kacher selection of Burgundies, a favorite label of wine guru Robert Parker. The Wine House sells no liquor, and 90 percent of the eighteen-year-old wine store's bottles are imported, making the Wine House a real bottle shop, not just a room filled with very good wines. The people who work here care about wine and want to help you find great bottles. This is one of the few places of its kind left in the city, and is well worth a trip if only to visit a wine operation with old-style values.

535 Bryant Street (between Third and Fourth Streets), San Francisco
Tel: 495-8486
Open Monday through Friday 10 a.m. to 6 p.m., Saturday until 5 p.m.
Credit cards: D, MC, V

COOKWARE AND BOOKS

ECONOMY RESTAURANT SUPPLY

1200 Seventh Street
(at Irwin),
San Francisco
Tel: 626-5611
Open Monday through
Friday 8 a.m. to 5:30 p.m.,
Saturday 10 a.m. to 3 p.m.
Credit cards: AE, D, MC, V

All the restaurant people come here to buy supplies. There are rows and rows of restaurant-style aluminum skillets and pots, all sorts of large cooking utensils, cutting boards, knives, metal bowls: all the essentials for a production kitchen. I have outfitted many a home kitchen here as well, with basic, useful equipment. All the marked prices are 10 to 15 percent higher than the actual price, so remember to ask for a discount. Just tell them you're opening a restaurant, and thank your lucky stars that you really aren't.

The Sunset District

THE SUNSET DISTRICT

Restaurants:
1. Beach Chalet   425
2. Hana   426
3. House   427
4. Jeong Hyun Charcoal Barbecue House   427
5. Just Won Ton   429
6. Old Krakow   429
7. Ristorante Marcello   430
8. River Side Seafood Restaurant   431
9. San Tung & San Tung #2   432
10. Stoyanof   432
11. Win's   433
12. YaYa Cuisine   434

Cafes:
13. Cafe de Young   435
14. Jammin' Java Coffee House   436
15. Java Beach Cafe   437
16. Palio Paninoteca   437

Delicatessens/Take-Out:
17. Just Like Home   437
18. New Hai Ky   438
19. Sunrise Deli   438

Bakeries/Pastries:
20. Bakers of Paris   439
21. Shaharazad Bakery and Filo Specialists   439

Ice Cream/Chocolates:
22. Double Rainbow   441
23. See's Candies   441

Coffee:
24. Peet's Coffee and Tea   442
25. Spinelli Coffee Company   442

Markets:
26. Andronico's   442

Ethnic Markets:
27. Irving Seafood Market   444
28. May Wah   444
29. Twenty-Second and Irving Market   445

Produce:
29. Twenty-Second and Irving Market   446

Fish:
27. Irving Seafood Market   446
30. Yum Yum   447

Wines and Spirits:
31. Mr. Liquor   447

Cookware and Books:
32. Easy Money Discount Outlet   449
33. Kitchen Friend   449
34. Sunset Bookstore   450
35. Williams-Sonoma   450

RESTAURANTS

BEACH CHALET

What a location! The historic Willis Polk Building on the edge of the Pacific at one end of Golden Gate Park lay empty for years until a young Sunset couple finally won the lease from the city and re-opened it as a rollicking brew pub. Everyone had their eye on this fabulous two-story, colonnaded building. The eventual owner wrote a business plan for the property when he was a business student at San Francisco State. Then years later, he and his wife ended up developing the ground floor as a museum of Golden Gate Park memorabilia with restored wrap-around murals of San Francisco life in the 1930s, and the upper floor as a vast restaurant and bar with expansive views of the crashing Pacific. He hired a brewer from Colorado and a Square One–trained chef. Now the place serves one thousand meals a day and literally tanks of well-made, easy-to-drink beer.

The pub-food menu is fairly priced and reasonably well executed considering the volume. I particularly liked a platter of house-made sausages with rice and flavorful black beans, a dish that is pretty much foolproof from the kitchen's point of view. A mixed seafood and vegetable fry shows promise—scallops, shrimp, and mussels were fresh but a bit greasy as of this writing. A hot, spicy, made-to-order Cajun Seafood Gumbo makes up in exuberance what it lacks in finesse. All the food on the menu goes particularly well with beer, though the Beach Chalet offers a full bar and wine list.

1000 Great Highway
(between Lincoln
and Fulton),
San Francisco
Tel: 386-8439
Open Monday through
Wednesday 11:30 a.m.
to 10 p.m., Thursday
through Sunday
until midnight.
Price: Moderate
Credit cards: MC, V

The real draw is the magnificent natural setting and a San Francisco crowd that gives the place resonance, especially later in the evenings.

HANA

408 Irving Street (between Fifth and Sixth Avenues), San Francisco
Tel: 665-3952
Open Tuesday through Friday for lunch 11:30 a.m. to 2 p.m., dinner Tuesday through Saturday 5 to 9:30 p.m.
Price: Inexpensive
Credit Cards: MC, V

Hana started out as a closet-sized restaurant, but its tasty, hearty Japanese cooking, cheap prices, and residential location only a few blocks from the University of California Medical Center caused overflow business. The demand for something decent to eat in the neighborhood far exceeded the number of seats available, especially since people were coming from other parts of the city to eat at this little place. Happily, Hana expanded, making conditions much more comfortable. The enlarged dining room looks like an old Japanese inn with weathered wooden booths, thick wooden tables, and a beautiful deep blue and red paint job. The prices are still reasonable, and the Japanese mainstays on the menu just as delicious.

Although sushi is available at both a sushi bar and in the dining room, I prefer the cooked dishes. The kitchen has a way with chicken, like a breast with wing attached, basted in the lightest of teriyaki sauces and sprinkled with sesame seeds. The meat stays miraculously tender and juicy. The same extraordinary texture makes chicken *tonkatsu*, a battered and fried chicken cutlet, a standout. Frying is always nicely done at Hana. The fried oysters are barely coated in a crumbly batter and cooked in very hot oil until they are just firm. They melt in your mouth. *Gyoza*, Japanese pot stickers with a spicy pork filling in a crimped noodle wrapper, have an intense gingery flavor and a light texture. Hana is also famous for its *yosenabe*, a perfectly cooked stew of clams, shrimp, oysters, and vegetables in a ginger-scented broth. Portions are geared to Western appetites, and dinners include little plates of pickled cabbage, miso soup, and a lettuce salad, albeit with cellophane noodles and a delicate sweet-and-sour dressing. Service by a group of Japanese women in kimonos could not be friendlier or more efficient. They know most of their customers and will quickly get to know you.

HOUSE

With the recent opening of House, a stylish, minimally decorated Euro-Asian bistro, the once dowdy Sunset has its own glamour spot. House makes a strong, sophisticated statement with a tempting menu of pan-Asian appetizers, unusual main courses that feature underused varieties of fish, and a progressive wine list keyed to the difficult-to-match flavors in the cooking. Prices are very moderate for the level of dining. As a result, House became a surprise hit soon after it opened, drawing patrons from all over the city. This is remarkable considering how difficult it is to park around Golden Gate Park, but a meal here rewards the hassle.

I myself will circle Ninth Avenue for this restaurant's impeccably deep-fried green bean tempura and five-spice calamari, both with vibrant dipping sauces. Saucy satay chicken wings also have their following. But what I really love here are the thick hunks of Chilean sea bass and butterfish, both loaded with natural oil and silken of texture. They're marinated and served with flavorful jasmine rice and bright green long beans, making for well-balanced, satisfying plates. The smart, high-concept decor and handsome modern table appointments, ennobled by thin, elegant wine glasses, add cachet to the simple presentations of the food. House has both style and substance. To a growing audience for Cal-Asian food that is not complicated and overwrought, it's beginning to feel like home.

1269 Ninth Avenue
(between Irving
and Lincoln),
San Francisco
Tel: 682-3898
Open for lunch Tuesday
through Sunday 11:30 a.m.
to 3 p.m.; dinner Sunday and
Tuesday through Thursday
5:30 to 10 p.m., Friday and
Saturday until 11 p.m.
Price: Moderate
Credit cards: AE, MC, V

JEONG HYUN CHARCOAL BARBECUE HOUSE

Of all the Asian cuisines one can sample in San Francisco, Korean barbecue is the most familiar and the most exotic at the same time. Charcoal-grilled beef is the heart of the meal. These thin slices of short rib appeal to beef-loving Americans. But the rest of the meal, a table full of little bowls of hot, spicy, garlicky pickles and salads, some fermented and some fresh, tastes like nothing you would find in an American pantry. The combination of these assertive, juicy cold vegetables with savory hot meat makes for exciting eating,

2123 Irving Street (between
22nd and 23rd Avenues),
San Francisco
Tel: 665-0966
Open Monday through
Thursday 11 a.m. to
10 p.m., Friday and Saturday
until 10:30 p.m.,
Sunday 5 to 10 p.m.
Price: Inexpensive
Credit Cards: MC, V

especially when they are wrapped up together in a lettuce leaf so you get the flavors and textures of all of them in each bite.

Jeong Hyun does the whole service so well it has become a Sunset District destination with a broad cross-cultural clientele. There are two rows of roomy wooden booths. Each booth easily seats six people and has its own ventilation system, a hood and a fan descending from the high ceiling. If you elect to barbecue at the table, which is what everyone does, the waitress comes out with a large hibachi full of white-hot coals. The tables are big enough so you don't feel threatened by the fire and the fans are so strong—and loud—that they pull off all the heat and smoke. Then, platters of sesame oil–marinated beef and at least fifteen little bowls of vegetables, *kimchee*, tofu, and glass noodles, along with rice and curly leaf lettuce, are brought out. The meat, cut very thinly, cooks so fast you simply can't go wrong. A few flips with the tongs and it's ready.

Actually, the cooking done in the kitchen of the restaurant is worth a trip across the city. On being seated, fabulous toasted-rice tea and deep-fried mung bean pancakes appear; crisp, laced with green onions and with a delightfully creamy texture, they remind me of the best potato pancakes. The famous Korean steak tartar is done beautifully here, a mound of hand-shredded beef tossed with sesame oil, garlicky hot cabbage pickle, and minced onion, topped with a raw egg yolk and garnished with vinegared pears. For a less-beefy meal, try *jap chae*, a luscious stir fry of bean-thread noodles, bits of beef, peppers, mushrooms, and ribbons of egg in a delicately sweet, rich brown gravy. Nutty Korean rice stars in a preparation that comes in a hot stone pot, topped with spinach, seaweed, onions, shredded beef, and a raw egg yolk, which quickly cooks as you stir it into the rice. The crusty rice at the bottom is the prize. Boneless barbecued chicken, which arrives on a sizzling hot cast-iron plate, has a velvet texture.

Of course the central culinary experience of a tableful of tastes with grill-it-yourself beef is that each meal here feels like a feast. Yet, as is the genius of Asian style, you leave without feeling overfed.

JUST WON TON

This tiny place in a converted house in the Sunset devotes itself entirely to making wonton. The skins are gossamer thin, tender, and flavorful, the filling simple and sublime: roughly chopped sweet, impeccably fresh shrimp bound with just a little ground pork. The wontons come in soup with noodles, soup without noodles, with fish balls, roast duck, barbecued pork, spicy chicken, different cuts of beef, innards, and pigs' feet. For a small pittance you can get wonton soup with any of the above and extra wontons.

Also good are thick, white *chow fun* noodles made with rice flour, tossed with bright-green bok choy and bits of velvetized beef. Although this is primarily a noodle house, it is also known for two appetizers: vegetarian duck, made with ribbons of tofu skin wrapped around a filling of savory mushrooms, and something called a Chinese tamale, a gigantic mound of sticky rice with a center of braised Chinese sausage and taro paste. The beauty of a visit here is that you can take the wontons to go and serve them in your own rich chicken broth, a meal that pleases a lot of kids I know.

1241 Vicente Street
(between 23rd and 24th Avenues),
San Francisco
Tel: 681-2999
Open Tuesday through Sunday 11 a.m. to 10 p.m.
Price: Very inexpensive
Credit cards: MC, V;
$10 minimum

OLD KRAKOW

This cozy "Polish art cafe" in the mist and fog belt of the Sunset has soul. It's warm and comfy inside, even though dramatic Polish expressionist oil paintings stare down from the walls. As is true in all Eastern European kitchens, the delicious soups are a mainstay. Try the intense, creamy mushroom soup full of chopped mushrooms; or a thin, sweet beet borscht with meat-filled dumplings; or fortifying garlic soup with garlic croutons. Or start with strong cured herring with marinated onions, pickles, and peppers; or the tasty chopped potato and vegetable salad napped in mayonnaise; or sliced cucumbers with fresh dill and sour cream.

My favorite main course is a thickly breaded but crisp pork cutlet served with crispy fried potatoes, a double whammy. The *Bigos*, or hunter's stew of beef, pork, and sausage comes with smoky sauerkraut and mashed potatoes, a real comfort

385 West Portal Avenue
(near 15th Avenue),
San Francisco
Tel: 564-4848
Open Monday through Friday 5 to 10 p.m., weekends 10 a.m. to 10 p.m.
Price: Inexpensive
Credit cards: AE, MC, V

plate. Stuffed cabbage is a little bland here, smothered in tomato sauce, but still satisfying, while house-made Polish sausages (kielbasa) are very garlicky, moderated by the smoky sauerkraut and mashed potatoes. Glasses of Polish beer (the stronger, more hoppy Zywiec, or the light, crisp Okocim) add much to the meal. Don't miss the house-baked desserts, a tall multilayered apple cake with a crisp brioche crust, or a five-inch-tall farmers' cheese cake with raisins that is barely sweetened, both fine with tea or well-made coffee.

RISTORANTE MARCELLO

2100 Taraval
(at 31st Avenue),
San Francisco
Tel: 665-1430
Open Tuesday through
Saturday 5 to 10:30 p.m.,
Sunday 4 to 10 p.m.
Price: Moderate
Credit Cards: MC, V

The food, the customers, the look and feel of Ristorante Marcello take you back to another era when arugula, grilled radicchio, and balsamic vinegar hadn't entered the common culinary vocabulary and spaghetti with meat sauce held sway. To tell you the truth, this was not a bad time, and at Ristorante Marcello its best qualities have been preserved. This restaurant reminds me of the old Vanessi's on Broadway: It has the same raffish spirit and the same broad cooking style.

Furnished with red vinyl banquettes, padded wooden chairs, linen-covered tables pushed close together, and a long, active bar where people also eat, the room has that classic Italian dinner-house style. The waiters, in tuxes, know the menu and have a sense of humor. They don't coddle their customers but they serve efficiently.

This is the place to get a classic Caesar salad or hearts of romaine in a fabulous shalloty, mustardy, relishy, rémoulade-like vinaigrette. The spaghettini comes bathed in a celery-scented bolognese sauce with an authentically gravelly texture from finely chopped beef, chicken livers, and prosciutto. The house-made ravioli, moistened with a little bit of this sauce, are plump with well-seasoned ricotta. The tender green *panzotti*, large ravioli also filled with ricotta and spinach, are sauced with a clean-flavored tomato puree. Don't pass up the old-fashioned *cannelloni della casa*, made with hand-rolled dough and stuffed with finely chopped veal, spinach, and prosciutto, covered with a creamy tomato sauce. The spicy *spaghetti alla matriciana* juggles bacon, tomatoes, and onions masterfully.

People come to this restaurant for two main courses: *pollo ai ferri*, a flattened-on-the-grill half chicken with a superb satiny texture, and a gigantic veal chop, very tender but pink enough to have flavor. Try the rest of the menu at your own risk. The wine list is woefully short on good Italian or California red wines, but most people who eat here prefer their martinis and Manhattans anyway. When the place is packed on the weekends you can almost feel the specter of crusty old San Francisco North Beach hovering overhead.

RIVER SIDE SEAFOOD RESTAURANT

A chef and a manager from the well-regarded Fook Yuen on the Peninsula opened this neighborhood restaurant within the last year. The room is clean, comfortably appointed, and miraculously quiet due, perhaps, to low acoustic ceilings, and large groups of eight or ten can eat well here for a very reasonable sum. Value is much prized in the Sunset, and River Side aims to please.

Saucers of barely pickled cucumbers tide you over while you order your dinner off the handwritten list of specials clipped to the cover of an otherwise long menu. The list simplifies the entire process. Start with soup of the day, a magnificently rich and restorative chicken broth. Have Peking duck: Tuck the crackling skin into tender white buns smeared with plum sauce and green onions. Then eat the meat of the duck as a separate course, minced with crisp white rice noodles, which you eat rolled in lettuce leaves. The spicy pork ribs are hot, sweet, vinegary, and chewy, just the way they should be. The oxtails in wine sauce with carrots could have come out of a French kitchen. They are delicious over rice. The sake-marinated black cod, a large, thick hunk, defines the sensation of velvety and rich. The service is pleasant, the experience civilized. You pay more here than at bargain-driven places like Szechuan Taste, but the price is less than at many Richmond District restaurants for equally high quality.

1201 Vicente Street
(at 23rd Avenue),
San Francisco
Tel: 759-8828
Open daily for lunch 11 a.m. to 3 p.m.; dinner 5 to 10 p.m.
Price: Inexpensive
Credit Cards: MC, V

SAN TUNG

2240 Irving (between 23rd and 24th Avenues)
San Francisco
Tel: 661-4233
Open Tuesday through Sunday 11 a.m. to 9:30 p.m.
Price: Inexpensive
Credit cards: MC, V

SAN TUNG #2

1031 Irving Street (between 11th and 12th Avenues)
San Francisco
Tel: 242-0828
Open daily 11 a.m. to 9:30 p.m.
Price: Inexpensive
Credit cards: MC, V

I used to eat at the first San Tung, a hole-in-the-wall at 24th and Irving, until the bright new San Tung #2 opened, which is larger, more comfortable, and has somewhat easier parking. Most important of all, the northern-style noodles, dumplings, and soups have remained spectacularly good. People make a pilgrimage here for San Tung's famous shrimp and leek dumplings; juicy, garlicky from garlic chives (which the menu calls leeks), and they are addictive. Many people polish off a plate of twelve themselves. I have. But then I don't have room for San Tung's luscious little round pork dumplings vibrant with ginger. Steamed or fried pot stickers are also much ordered here. I also love the seaweed soup; jellyfish and cucumber salad; dry sautéed string beans flecked with bits of pickled mustard and crisp garlic; and of course, hand-pulled noodles. These are noodles so tender they practically melt in your mouth. They shine in a dish called Three Deluxe Spicy Sauce Noodles, a chili-flecked soup with seafood and vegetables. Kids like them slathered in a mild peanut sauce. Shantung (from which the name of the restaurant was transliterated) is a coastal province between Shanghai and Beijing that has its own distinctive cooking style, and the delicious handmade dumplings, noodles, and seafood soups prepared here are fine examples of it.

STOYANOF

1240 Ninth Avenue (between Irving and Lincoln), San Francisco
Tel: 664-3664
Open Tuesday through Saturday 10:30 a.m. to 9:30 p.m., Sunday 4:30 to 9:30 p.m.
Price: Inexpensive
Credit cards: (dinner only) AE, MC, V

This modern, light-filled neighborhood cafe run by two generations of Macedonians has become famous for its savory and sweet Greek pastries made by the elder Stoyanof. His *borek,* a hot turnover of the lightest, flakiest filo pastry imaginable, stuffed with a combination of Greek cheeses, is a masterpiece. So are the spinach-, lamb-, and feta-filled pastries. The many layers of filo in nut-filled baklava disappear on your tongue like snowflakes. A beautiful raspberry cake roll with homemade cream custard over a thin layer of sponge cake will tempt anyone to eat dessert. Seventy-three-year-old

Georgi Stoyanof also makes luscious *baba au rhum*, a crumbly rum-syrup-soaked brioche, and he offers gigantic slices of fresh apple strudel.

The emphasis here is on high-quality ingredients and simple preparation. Angel Stoyanof, Georgi's son, gets his seafood from Paul Johnson's Monterey Fish, which means that the swordfish brochettes strung with bay leaves and thin slices of lemon taste like butter. Sweet fresh shrimp get a classic Macedonian treatment with tomatoes, feta, and oregano. The *moussaka* served in a ramekin has a crusty cheese and béchamel topping blanketing layers of velvety eggplant and spicy ground beef instead of lamb. Georgi says his patrons prefer beef. They also love an appetizer called *saganaki*, a rectangle of tangy kasseri cheese dipped in egg and homemade bread crumbs and sautéed.

The uncovered tables are placed close together cafe style in a gaily painted spacious high-ceilinged room. Most of the kitchen is in the middle of the dining room. At lunch, it serves as a cafeteria counter; at night, waiters take over. The beauty of Stoyanof is that it elegantly meets the needs of the neighborhood by putting out fresh, honest, tasty food and keeping prices low.

WIN'S

3040 Taraval Street (between 40th and 41st Avenues),
San Francisco
Tel: 759-1818
Open Tuesday through Sunday 11 a.m. to 10 p.m.
Price: Inexpensive
Credit cards: MC, V;
$10 minimum

People come here to eat Chinese-style roast duck, especially at lunch when it is still hot and juicy from the ovens. The burnished skin crackles; the velvety brown flesh is infused with the perfume of the Chinese spices that have been rubbed into the meat before roasting. You can get these ducks and other good barbecued items like hunks of pork belly and Chinese spareribs to go, or you can eat them there over rice accompanied with steamed iceberg lettuce leaves, a luscious combination. Although many of the dishes on the amazingly long menu are not worth trying, there are some standouts: excellent, rustic pot stickers; crisp-skinned soy sauce chicken; stir-fried Chinese broccoli; and crisp, panfried Hong Kong–style chow mein noodles topped with lots of bok choy, Chinese broccoli, and chicken.

YAYA CUISINE

1220 Ninth Avenue
(at Lincoln),
San Francisco
Tel: 566-6966
Open Tuesday through Friday for lunch 11:30 a.m. to 2 p.m., dinner Tuesday through Thursday 5:30 to 9:30 p.m., Friday and Saturday until 10 p.m.
Price: Moderate
Credit cards: AE, MC, V

Chef Yahya Salih grew up near the ruins of Nineveh in northern Iraq. In his wittily decorated restaurant next to Golden Gate Park, he celebrates ancient flavors in dishes that generations of Iraqis ate in their mothers' kitchens. He applies modern cooking techniques to them, and the result is completely original and surprising food that looks quite beautiful.

Cardamom, cumin, pomegranate syrup, pickled mango, dried lime, sumac, tamarind, allspice, cinnamon, mint, cilantro, and basil weave their way throughout a meal, fragrant and assertive, yet always in balance. The layers of flavor remind me of Indian cooking, but the large portions, particularly of protein, seem lavishly Western. The abundant use of vegetables cooked lightly to keep their color and texture demonstrates the salubrious influence of California.

Golden roast baby chicken is stuffed with rice, raisins, and cashews surrounded by a wreath of brilliant vegetables and tender dried apricots. The vegetarian dolmas molded into a Cubist mosaic turn out to be whole vegetables stuffed with delectably moist bulgur spiked with chilies and surrounded by a yogurt-mint sauce. It's the best vegetarian dish in town. A dreamy *biriani* brings velvety chunks of lamb, basmati rice, and potatoes aromatic with onions, garlic, cumin, cinnamon, and sun-dried lime, heaped on a plate rimmed with creamy lemon sauce. Another lamb stew might be composed of thick slices of Japanese eggplant and squashes in a dark red sweet-and-sour pomegranate sauce that explodes with flavor.

The eclectic wines on the small list have been chosen carefully to work with this food. The Italian whites and soft, spicy California Zinfandels do the job admirably. Two dense little desserts also hit the spot after a meal of powerful flavors: pistachio baklava topped with shredded coconut, and a honey cake. Both are voluptuously surrounded by Iraqi-style clotted cream drizzled with date syrup.

The interior of this small restaurant somehow evokes the shapes, colors, and history of Mesopotamia, the ancient land between the Tigris and Eurphrates Rivers. In the middle of a detailed, sandy-hued mural of the walled city of Babylon, which decorates one full side of the dining room, is a tiny blue arch, the gateway into the city. When you walk into the restaurant a series of ceiling-high blue arches echo the painting. Dramatic blue-rimmed front windows and a tiled open kitchen frame a sand-colored dining room furnished with ziggurat-patterned banquettes and small linen-covered tables.

The service is accommodating and enthusiastic. Chef Yahya himself comes out of the kitchen frequently to talk with customers. His energy sets the tone for this modern crossroads of civilization south of Golden Gate Park.

CAFES

CAFE DE YOUNG

This indoor-outdoor cafe boasts one of the most charming garden settings in the Bay Area. Nestled in a protected courtyard basking in sunlight, the outdoor seating area is furnished with wrought-iron tables shaded with umbrellas around a small pool. The surrounding garden is particularly wonderful in the spring when the rhododendrons are in bloom. A Victorian arbor, landscaped and dotted with sculpture, serves as one enchanting wall.

The cafe is run by Rick O'Connell, a well-known chef and caterer in San Francisco. Her menu emphasizes fresh, colorful seasonal produce best shown off in excellent salads prepared at the moment behind a cafeteria counter where you

M. H. de Young Museum in
Golden Gate Park,
San Francisco
Tel: 752-0116
Open Wednesday through
Sunday 10 a.m. to 4 p.m.
Price: Inexpensive
Credit cards: MC, V

order. Items like warm goat cheese *crostini*, showered with a luscious tomato, cucumber, and red onion salad in a sparkly balsamic vinaigrette, are delivered to the table when they're ready. All the sandwiches are made to order and exceptionally tasty. A children's menu offers half sandwiches with cups of house-made soup. O'Connell understands quality and simplicity, and her dishes always make good culinary sense.

One drawback to using the de Young Cafe as a drop-in destination is the $5 admission charge you pay at the museum gate to get there. However, admission to the de Young is free from 10 a.m. to noon every Saturday and all day the first Wednesday of the month. And if you are a museum member, you can use this first-rate cafe in the park whenever you want without a surcharge.

JAMMIN' JAVA COFFEE HOUSE

1398 Judah Street
(at Ninth Avenue),
San Francisco
Tel: 566-JAVA
Open Monday through
Saturday 6 a.m. to midnight, Sunday 7 a.m.
to midnight
Price: Inexpensive
No credit cards

Typical of so many coffeehouses in the city outside of North Beach, where coffeehouses take their mission seriously, this popular corner cafe exudes grunge. From the uncleared tables to the overflowing lattes, Jammin' Java couldn't be more relaxed. This environment attracts a steady flow of young and middle-aged patrons from the neighborhood as well as students from the nearby University of California, San Francisco. The drawing card for food lovers is the steamed-milk drinks. The coffee makers ascribe to the more is better philosophy, so an espresso comes as a brimming-full demitasse of strong, rich coffee without the intensity or creaminess of the best espresso. However, this copious kind of espresso makes for a good latte. Eclectic and loud music, revolving art shows, and friendly, efficient counterpeople keep the scene hopping.

JAVA BEACH CAFE

A civilized little cafe at the end of the N-Judah streetcar line, Java Beach is a hangout for surfers, cyclists, and that peculiar kind of person who would live no place other than the edge of the ocean. The smell of the sea, the moist soft air, the beach stretching for miles just over an embankment, make a good cup of coffee taste even better. The juxtaposition of a cafe that turns out full-flavored, unbitter espresso and offers ten or so blends of brewed coffee (kept warm in thermoses on the counter) with laid-back beach life gives Java Beach its cachet. A brisk walk could be planned with a payoff at this welcoming cafe.

1396 La Playa Boulevard (at Judah),
San Francisco
Tel: 665-5282
Open daily 6 a.m. to 11 p.m.
Price: Inexpensive
No credit cards

PALIO PANINOTECA

500 Parnassus Avenue (UCSF Millberry Union),
San Francisco
Tel: 681-9925
Open Monday through Friday 7 a.m. to 5 p.m.
Credit cards: AE, MC, V
See listing, page 146.

DELICATESSENS

JUST LIKE HOME

A dining room with vinyl booths looms in the back of Just Like Home, but I rarely have seen anyone eat there. Most people take home the Middle Eastern standbys displayed in the refrigerated counter at the front of the store. I particularly like Just Like Home's garlicky *baba ganoush* (smoky eggplant puree) and a tasty, saffron-tinted potato salad. The green and black olives are both nice. Try some hot sauce made with roasted red sweet and hot peppers; it adds sparkle to everything. Although the pastries made on the premises look

1924 Irving Street (between 20th and 21st Avenues),
San Francisco
Tel: 681-3337
Open daily 11 a.m. to 9 p.m.
Credit cards: D, MC, V

tempting (filo-topped custard squares and honey cake), they have been rancid on occasion. Augment your meal with cucumbers and Persian yogurt bought at the Twenty-Second and Irving Market.

NEW HAI KY

2191 Irving Street
(at 23rd Avenue),
San Francisco
Tel: 731-9948
Open daily 8 a.m. to 10 p.m.
No credit cards

Although many people eat noodles and plates of Chinese roast duck over rice here, the main draw of this place for me is Chinese barbecue to go. Hai Ky makes several different kinds of roast and barbecue duck and pork, which stay moist and fresh from generally quick turnover. For a change, try the Roast Duck Chinese Guitar, in which the bird is splayed out (in a vaguely guitarlike shape) to take on extra-strong curing and deeper roasting. The guitar duck's skin and flesh is saltier, sweeter, and more aromatic of Chinese five spices than the regular roast duck, and the meat has an even more velvety texture.

SUNRISE DELI

2115 Irving Street
(at 22nd Avenue),
San Francisco
Tel: 664-8210
Open Monday through
Saturday 9 a.m. to 8 p.m.,
Sunday 10 a.m. to 6 p.m.
Credit cards: MC, V

A small, homey Middle Eastern deli, Sunrise stocks a variety of Middle Eastern cooking supplies, like fruity Lebanese extra-virgin olive oil, flat breads in several sizes, and huge sheets of whole-wheat flat bread. The pistachio Turkish delight, a very sweet jellylike dessert, is fresh here. Rich whole-milk Persian yogurt takes up a section of the deli case along with tabbouleh, hummus, *baba ganoush,* grape leaves—all the usual. The felafel are better eaten hot on the premises. People sit at a few round tables in the store while they nibble pita bread sandwiches constructed to order.

BAKERIES/PASTRIES

BAKERS OF PARIS

1101 Taraval Street (at 21st Avenue),
San Francisco
Tel: 863-8726
Open daily 7 a.m. to 6 p.m.
No credit cards

See listing, page 253.

SHAHARAZAD BAKERY AND FILO SPECIALISTS

Filo dough has many uses, especially for those of us who have trouble working with dough. You can buy a pound of tissue-thin filo sheets at Shaharazad and make a fresh fruit dessert wrapped in crisp pastry that will impress anyone. The freshly made filo at Shaharazad can be used like puff pastry, though you actually form the layers yourself by using multiple sheets of filo brushed with butter. Shaharazad also carries premade Greek and Middle Eastern desserts and turnovers, including sour cherry and apple turnovers made with filo, and heavenly finger baklava, called *burma*, which can be exceptionally crisp and light if you catch them at the right time. This is the only place in the city that makes its own filo dough and sells it fresh.

1586 Noriega Street
(between 22nd
and 23rd Avenues),
San Francisco
Tel: 661-1155
Open Monday through
Saturday 9 a.m. to 5 p.m.
No credit cards

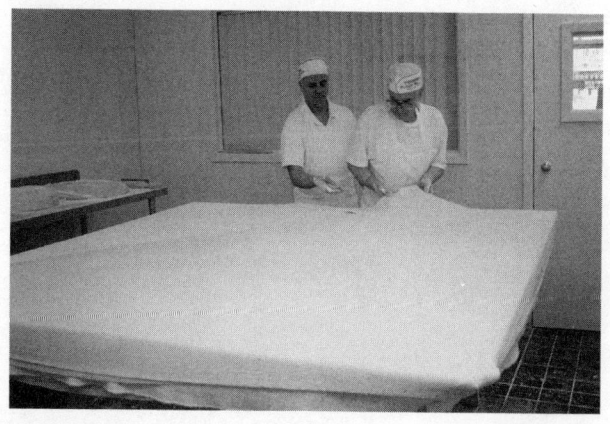

FILO-WRAPPED APPLE TART

4 tablespoons Calvados or dark rum

1/3 cup raisins

6 tart apples, peeled, cored, and cut into 1/8-inch slices

2 tablespoons plus 1/2 cup sugar

Juice of 1/2 lemon

12 sheets fresh or thawed frozen filo

1 cup (2 sticks) unsalted butter, melted

The fresh filo dough from Shaharazud Bakery is soft, luxurious, moist, and easy to use. It will keep in the refrigerator for five days. This is a luscious and dramatic-looking dessert, inspired by the Medieval Apple Tart from The Silver Palate Cookbook, but it should be served immediately to stay crisp. My friend John Chalik cooked it for me one evening, and I have been playing around with the recipe ever since.

Preheat the oven to 400°F.

Warm 2 tablespoons of the Calvados or rum in a small saucepan. Remove from heat and add the raisins.

In a mixing bowl, toss the apples with 2 tablespoons of the sugar and the lemon juice.

Unwrap the filo dough and cover it with a damp cloth. Using a pastry brush, lightly butter a 14-inch pizza pan or baking sheet. Lay 1 sheet of filo in the center of the pan, brush it with melted butter, and sprinkle it with 2 teaspoons of the sugar and 1/2 teaspoon of the rum or Calvados. Repeat this process with 5 more sheets of filo, laying each new sheet a one-quarter turn from the previous one to create a circle effect.

Combine the apples and raisins. Mound them onto the center of the dough in a pile about 6 inches in diameter. Brush the top with butter and sprinkle with 1 tablespoon of the sugar.

Cover the apple-raisin mixture with another sheet of filo, brush it with butter, sprinkle with 2 teaspoons of the sugar and 1/2 teaspoon of the Calvados or rum, and repeat the process with 5 more sheets of filo, placing each sheet a one-quarter turn from the previous one. Brush the topmost layer of the filo with butter but do not sugar or sprinkle it.

Gently turn the edges of the dough up to seal it. Brush any dry edges with butter. Bake in the middle of the oven until golden brown, about 30 to 40 minutes. Serve immediately.

Makes one 9- to 10-inch tart, serves 4 to 6

ICE CREAM/CHOCOLATES

DOUBLE RAINBOW

2116 Irving Street (at 22nd Avenue),
San Francisco
Tel: 665-3090
Open Monday through Thursday 11 a.m. to 10 p.m.,
Friday and Saturday until 11 p.m.,
Sunday 10 a.m. to 10 p.m.
No credit cards

68 West Portal Avenue (between Ulloa and Vicente),
San Francisco
Tel: 564-9412
Open Monday through Thursday 11 a.m. to 11 p.m.,
Friday and Saturday 11 a.m. to midnight,
Sunday noon to 10 p.m.
No credit cards
See listing, page 355.

SEE'S CANDIES

Stonestown Galleria, 19th Avenue (at Winston),
San Francisco
Tel: 731-1784
Open Monday through Saturday 10 a.m. to 9 p.m.,
Sunday 11 a.m. to 6 p.m.
No credit cards
See listing, page 386.

COFFEE

PEET'S COFFEE AND TEA

54 West Portal Avenue (between Ulloa and Vicente),
San Francisco
Tel: 731-0375
Open Monday through Friday 6:30 a.m. to 8 p.m.,
Saturday 7 a.m. to 8 p.m., Sunday 7 a.m. to 6 p.m.
Credit cards: D, MC, V
See listing, page 199.

SPINELLI COFFEE COMPANY

Lakeshore Plaza, 1509 Sloat Boulevard,
San Francisco
Tel: 665-9055
Open Monday through Friday 6:30 a.m. to 10 p.m.,
Saturday 7 a.m. to 10 p.m., Sunday 7 a.m. to 9 p.m.
Credit cards: MC, V
See listing, page 173.

MARKETS

ANDRONICO'S

1200 Irving Street
(at Funston),
San Francisco
Tel: 661-3220
Open daily 8 a.m. to 11 p.m.
Credit Cards: D, MC, V

The only San Francisco branch of Androncio's, an independently owned chain of grocery stores with four branches in Berkeley, is getting better and more focused since it opened three years ago. This huge, clean supermarket shows particular strength in unusual luxury cheeses in good eating condition. I've picked up some obscure, pre-wrapped treasures based on well-written descriptions and been delighted. I also have found fresh, not moldy, coconuts and organic bananas. Tempting aromas always waft from a large prepared-food counter with cafe seating. Some of the best features of the

NILOUFER'S TURKEY KABOBS

My Parsi friend Niloufer Ichaporia King makes these turkey kabobs all the time, and now I do too. I serve them with basmati rice, Persian yogurt purchased at the Twenty-Second and Irving Produce Market, cucumbers, and mango sliced and marinated in lime, salt, and red chili flakes. You can serve these kabobs with almost anything and they will disappear.

Soak the bread crumbs in the half-and-half. In a large bowl, combine all the rest of the ingredients, except the oil, with the soaked bread crumbs.

Heat a little oil in a large skillet and cook 1 teaspoon of the turkey mixture. Taste for salt and correct the seasoning if necessary.

Form the turkey mixture into patties about 2 inches in diameter and 1 inch thick. Heat 1 to 2 tablespoons vegetable oil in the skillet. Sauté the kabobs until they are crisp and brown on one side. Then turn and cook until firm to the touch, about 5 minutes. These kabobs are almost as good cold as they are hot.

Makes about 8 kabobs, serves 4

1/2 cup fresh bread crumbs
1/4 cup half-and-half or milk
1 pound ground turkey, preferably dark meat
1 1/2 inches ginger
1 teaspoon kosher salt
3 garlic cloves, minced
3 serrano chilies, seeded and minced
1/2 bunch cilantro, minced
1 egg
Vegetable oil for frying

market are an olive bar with eight different kinds that customers scoop into containers and bring to the checkout line. In the long deli case, salads and prepared foods (like four different kinds of lasagne to take home and warm up) cater to the family that does not have time to cook. You'll also find delicacies, such as smoked salmon sliced to order and real Italian proscuitto. In front of the deli case are breads from the best local bakers: Acme, Metropolis, and Semifreddi to name but a few. The meat department will cut to suit and has hard-to-find items like freshly ground turkey and chicken. Andronico's has brought Western grocery shopping to new heights in this part of town.

ETHNIC MARKETS

IRVING SEAFOOD MARKET

See Fish Markets, page 446.

MAY WAH

2201 Irving
(at 22nd Avenue),
San Francisco
Tel: 665-4755
Open daily 8 a.m. to 7 p.m.
Credit Cards: MC, V; $10 minimum

This is a terrific, all-around Asian market specializing in Chinese, Vietnamese, and Thai ingredients. Produce, fish, meat, dry goods, prepared foods—practically anything imaginable needed to cook these cuisines is available at May Wah. At the meat and fish counters you can get pork ground to order or any sort of cut, slices of Smithfield ham (dry, salted ham akin to Yunan ham), chickens, bones, chicken parts, and fresh shellfish, much of it still alive in tanks. Gorgeous silvery pomfrets, a small, tasty fish much used in Asia and convenient for home cooking, sell quickly here, as do local whole flatfish like rex sole and sand dabs. In the produce department you often find a multicultural mix of Asian items like beautiful fresh *shiso* leaves, lotus root, boxes of pickled Chinese greens, young ginger, and piles of lemongrass. There are whole aisles of Asian candies and cookies from all over the world that happen to appeal to the Asian palate. Sacks of rice—black, pink, white—are stacked into tall piles. At the front of the store near the cash registers are elegant taro leaf bundles bound with stems, filled with sticky rice to take home and steam. What lovely packaging for an age-old convenience food! Bins of cashews and macadamias share the same display with bins of tiny dried shrimp and fish. The abundance of things to buy, to try, to find out about, dazzles; underscoring how lucky San Franciscans are to have so many vital ethnic communities to support markets like this.

TWENTY-SECOND AND IRVING MARKET

*22nd Avenue and Irving,
San Francisco
Tel: 681-5212
Open Monday through Sunday 8 a.m. to 6 p.m.
No credit cards*

Only in the Sunset can a market with so many eddying cross-cultural currents thrive. The outer Sunset (19th Avenue toward the ocean) has become the place where immigrants from Russia, the Middle East, Eastern Europe, and Asia converge, and this store caters to everyone. In one small area of the refrigerator case for example, I sighted tofu, *queso fresco*, Armenian string cheese, Persian yogurt, Greek feta, and Danish cream cheese in glass jars. On the grocery shelves bottles of Cortas pomegranate syrup, Bulgarian jam, Calamata olives, Polish cookies, and pitted sour cherries sit next to each other in mind-boggling proximity. You think that you're in the Adriatic or Mediterranean section until you notice the boxes of Japanese soup base. Such variety, such turnover. No dust gathers on the jars.

The other great draw of the Twenty-Second and Irving Market is the produce section, full of fresh nut meats and seeds along with hard-to-find seasonal items like olives to cure at home, green almonds, pickling cucumbers, and other products most often found at farmers' markets. Maybe because rents are cheaper out in the Sunset, the markets can be large and variously stocked, and prices can be low, which encourages a large volume of shoppers. Fuji apples, a loss leader at practically every other store, cost 39 cents per pound here ($1.29 for extra-large ones at Andronico's, 29 cents for blemished ones in the Richmond). The Twenty-Second and Irving Market is one more reason to grant the three or so blocks on Irving between 21st and 24th the best-food-shopping award.

PRODUCE MARKETS

TWENTY-SECOND AND IRVING MARKET

See Ethnic Markets, page 445.

FISH

IRVING SEAFOOD MARKET

2130 Irving (between
22nd and 23rd Avenues),
San Francisco
Tel: 681-5000
Open daily 8:30 a.m.
to 7:00 p.m.
No credit cards

Smaller and less frenetic than the large May Wah across the street, this tidy market displays a wide variety of fresh fish and shellfish, pork and beef, and some good-looking produce as well as Asian groceries in a connecting storefront next door. Whole sparkly-eyed sand dabs, carp, tiny smelt, large and small trout, and rex sole glisten on tables of crushed ice. Tanks full of live crabs and lobster stand ready to be mined. Different varieties of shrimp are arranged like jewels behind a glass case. You don't have to be assertive to be waited on at the Irving Seafood Market. This smaller store is eager to serve, out to compete with the big guys across the street.

In addition to pristine fish, this market puts out some choice produce at the front of the store, which recently included (in April) tiny pea shoots, (delicious sautéed like spinach with garlic and ginger), exceptionally fresh lotus root, durian, whole winter melon sold by the hunk, Fuji apples, real green papayas (as opposed to underripe papayas), and ripe, flesh-heavy navel oranges. In the grocery section next door, look for bags of the spectacular, explosive, true-flavored ginger drops called Jae Jae Ginger Drops. Each clear amber candy gets its own wrapper, so you can carry them around to refresh your mouth any time.

YUM YUM

Western shoppers like Yum Yum, a branch of Nikko Fish on Third Street, for its neat refrigerated counter full of easy-to-handle filleted fish. However, the selection at nearby May Wah or Irving Seafood Market surpasses the one here. At Yum Yum you can buy local snapper fillets and other filleted fish without being growled at. If you need a salmon steak or two, Yum Yum has them. A sushi-to-go bar prepares sushi to order, a nice amenity at a fish store.

2181 Irving Street
(at 23rd Avenue),
San Francisco
Tel: 566-6433
Open daily
9:30 a.m. to 6:30 p.m.
No credit cards

WINE AND LIQUOR SHOPS

MR. LIQUOR

A friendly, sophisticated wineshop in the outer reaches of Parkside? Yes. Though Mr. Liquor also carries beer and liquor, this twenty-one-year-old operation knows how to put together a tasty selection of California, French, and a few Italian wines from the best importers (Kermit Lynch, Chambers and Chambers). Beautiful Champagnes and elegant Burgundies share the limited shelf space with hand-picked wines in the $6 to $15 range, some of which you can

250 Taraval Street
(at Funston),
San Francisco
Tel: 731-6222
Open Monday through
Saturday 8:30 a.m.
to 6:30 p.m., Sunday
10 a.m. to 5:30 p.m.
Credit cards: AE, MC, V

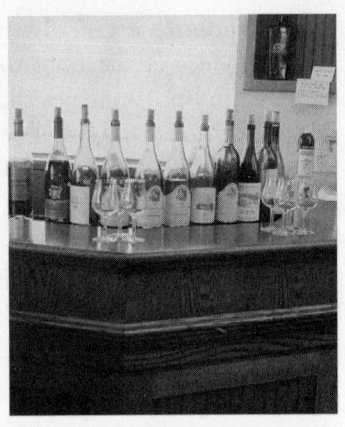

taste at a serve-yourself wine bar for 50 cents a pour. I recommend that you do so. Some of the least-expensive wines may not be worth the savings. The knowledgeable clerks are eager to guide you. They hold special vertical tastings every Saturday as part of their education program, and Mr. Liquor's monthly newsletter is both informative and literate. If you are a serious collector or just a drinker, Mr. Liquor is well worth a trip. The store also stocks hard-to-find single-malt Scotches and specialty bourbons, *grappas*, and imported stouts and ales.

COOKWARE AND BOOKS

EASY MONEY DISCOUNT OUTLET

When I walked into Easy Money in search of a notebook, the jumble of cheap merchandise made me discount this discount store. Then my eagle-eyed shopping expert spotted some large white oval and rectangular gratin dishes for about $3.99 each that cost six times as much anywhere else. The glaze on these had a few imperfections, but I had to put on my reading glasses to find them. I bought them all, debating over some fluted crème brûlée cups at three for a dollar, identical to some three times more expensive. Then the owner took me to the back to show me some rather elegant Champagne glasses he had, unfortunately stamped with a logo. No go. But who knows what other treasures might show up at Easy Money. If you're in the neighborhood, you should stop by.

2312 Irving (at 24th Avenue),
San Francisco
Tel: 731-3538
Open Monday through Saturday 9 a.m. to 7 p.m., Sunday 10 a.m. to 6 p.m.
Credit cards: AE, MC, V

KITCHEN FRIEND

Chinese and Japanese cookware and china fill the shelves of this well-organized store. A careful perusal will turn up treasures like a pair of deep Japanese bowls in an exquisite dark green, almost black glaze, or a heavy red clay charcoal brazier wrapped in aluminum with a carrying handle for somewhat-portable cooking (the brazier must weigh about thirty pounds). Rice cookers in all sizes fill up a long shelf, as do a variety of huge stainless steel steamers at excellent prices. A wall of kitchen gadgets and shelves of Western implements like wooden rolling pins and covered saucepans of different grades can be a boon to any budget-minded cook looking for the right tool.

2200 Irving (at 24th Avenue),
San Francisco
Tel: 564-3385
Open daily 9 a.m. to 7 p.m.
Credit cards: MC, V

SUNSET BOOKSTORE

2161 Irving Street
(between 23rd
and 24th Avenues),
San Francisco
Tel: 664-3644
Open Monday through
Saturday 9 a.m. to 9 p.m.,
Sunday 10 a.m. to 9 p.m.
Credit cards: AE, MC, V

Right in the thick of the best food-shopping district in the Sunset, a large section of used cookbooks waits to be mined. My shopping routine includes a stop at the Sunset Bookstore. On a recent visit I spotted the superb Paula Wolfert's *World of Food* (perfect for the neighborhood), a Diana Kennedy *Art of Mexican Cooking* (better for the Mission) and *The Pepperidge Farm Cookbook*, all in hardback and in almost pristine condition for about half the original price.

WILLIAMS-SONOMA

Stonestown Galleria, 19th Avenue (at Winston),
San Francisco
Tel: 681-5525
Open Monday through Saturday 10 a.m. to 9 p.m.,
Sunday 11 a.m. to 7 p.m.
Credit cards: AE, MC, V

See listing, page 157.

Out of Town

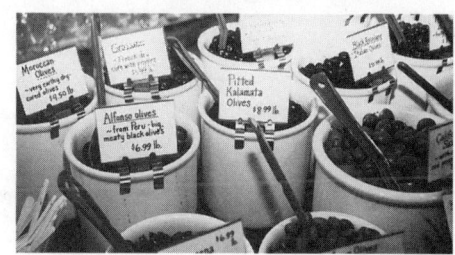

TOWNS INCLUDED

THE EAST BAY

Albany
Berkeley
Danville
Emeryville
Kensington
Oakland
Orinda

MARIN COUNTY

Corte Madera
Larkspur
Mill Valley
San Anselmo
San Rafael
Sausalito
Tiburon

**THE WINE COUNTRY
OF NAPA & SONOMA**

Calistoga
Healdsburg
Napa
Oakville
Sonoma
St. Helena
Rutherford
Yountville

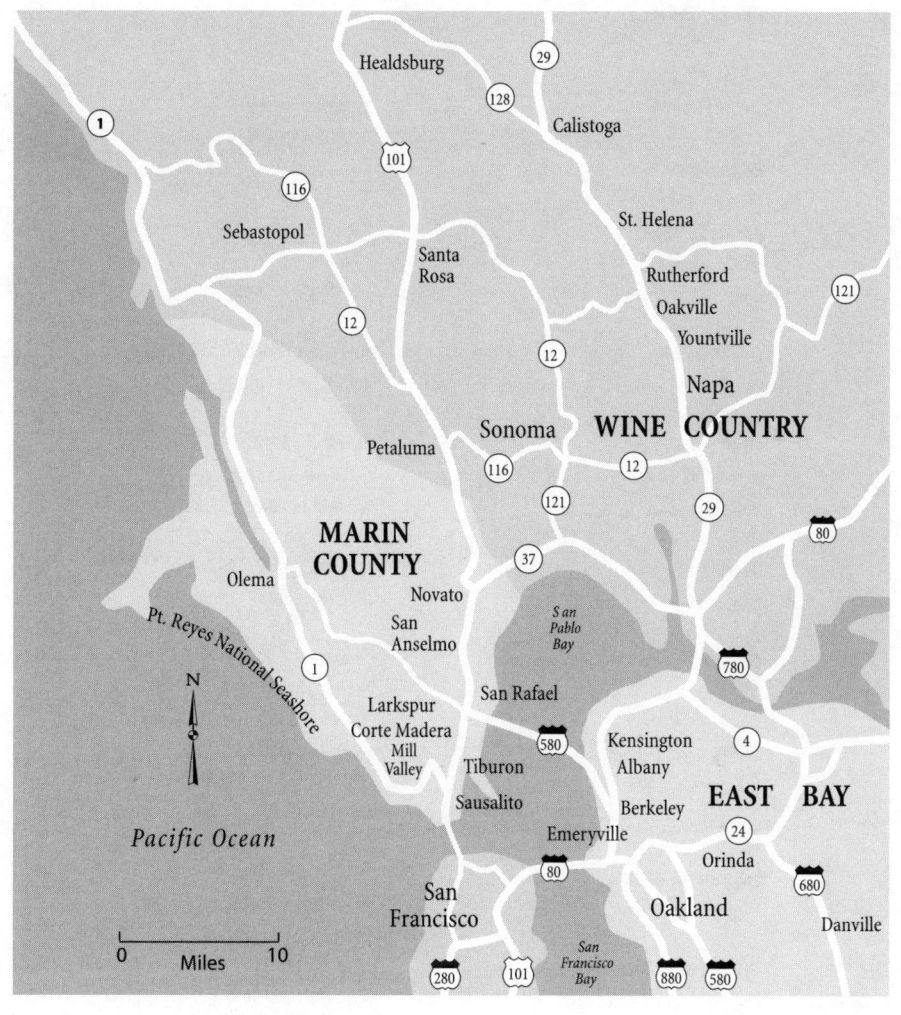

OUT OF TOWN

THE EAST BAY

Restaurants:
Ajanta 457
Bay Wolf 458
Bombay Cuisine 459
Brennan's Restaurant 459
Bridges 460
Cafe at Chez Panisse 461
Cafe Rouge 462
Casa Orinda 463
Chez Panisse 464
Citron 465
Hong Kong East Ocean 466
O Chamé 466
Oliveto 468
Picante Taqueria 469

Cafes:
Cafe at Oliveto 470
Cafe 817 470
Cafe Fanny 471
Caffè Strada 472

Bars:
Brennan's Restaurant 472
Kimball's East 472

Delicatessens/Take-Out:
Blondie's Pizza 473
Doug's Bar-B-Q 473
Made to Order 474
Market Hall Pasta Shop 475
Phoenix Pastaficio 475
Ultra Lucca 476
Vik's King of Chat 476
Yung Kee 477

Bakeries/Pastries:
Acme Bakery 477
Bread Workshop 478
The Cheese Board 478
Katrina Rozelle 479
La Farine 479
Semifreddi's 480

Ice Cream/Chocolates:
Yogurt Park 480

Ethnic Markets:
G. B. Ratto and Company 481
Milan International 481
New Saigon Supermarket 482
Oakland Market 483
Sam Yick 483

Produce:
Berkeley Bowl 484
Berkeley Farmers' Market 484
Market Hall Produce 485
Monterey Foods 485
Old Oakland Farmers' Market 486

Meat and Poultry:
Alan's Meats 486
Enzo 488
Magnani's Poultry 488
T & S Market 488
Taylor's Sausages 489
Ver Brugge Meats 489

Fish:
Berkeley Bowl Fish Market 490
Monterey Fish 490
Moura's Fish Market 491
New Basement Seafood Market 492
Rockridge Fish Market 492

Cheese:
The Cheese Board   492
J. Wiggins Cheese   494

Coffee:
Peet's Coffee and Tea   494

Wines and Spirits:
Kermit Lynch Wines   495
North Berkeley Wine Company   497
Odd Lots   497
Paul Marcus Wines   498
Vino   498

Cookware and Books:
Black Oak Books   499
Cody's   499
The Gardener   499
Sur La Table   500

MARIN COUNTY

Restaurants:
Bistro Alsacienne   501
Bubba's   502
Frantoio   503
Insalata's   504
Kasbah   505
Lark Creek Inn   506
Left Bank   508
Rice Table   510

Cafes:
Book Passage Cafe   512
Pasticceria Rulli   512

Bars:
Guaymas   514
Sam's   514

Delicatessens/Take-Out:
David's Produce/David's Taqueria   515
"Hamburgers"   515
Ultra Lucca   515

Bakeries/Pastries:
Pasticceria Rulli   516

Ice Cream/Chocolates:
Lyla's Chocolates   517
Pasticceria Rulli   517

Produce:
David's Produce/David's Taqueria   517
Marin County Farmers' Market   518

Cheese:
The Cheese Shop   519
Ultra Lucca   520

Coffee:
Pasticceria Rulli   520
Peet's Coffee and Tea   520
Spinelli Coffee Company   520

Wines and Spirits:
Marin Wine Cellar   521
Mill Valley Market   522

Cookware and Books:
A Clean Well-Lighted Place for Books   523
Book Passage   523
Homechef   524
Williams-Sonoma   524

455

THE WINE COUNTRY OF NAPA & SONOMA

Restaurants:
All Seasons Cafe and Wine Store 525
Babette's 525
Bistro Don Giovanni 527
Bistro Ralph 527
Brown Street Grill 528
Catahoula Restaurant and Saloon 528
Domaine Chandon 530
French Laundry 530
The General's Daughter 532
Greystone Restaurant 532
Madrona Manor 533
Mustards 533
Napa Valley Wine Train 534
Piatti 534
Pinot Blanc 535
Ravenous 535
Terra 536
Tomatina 537
Tra Vigne 537
Wappo Bar Bistro 538

Cafes:
Flying Goat Cafe 539

Bars:
Auberge du Soleil 539
Martin's John and Zeke's 539

Delicatessens/Take-Out:
Cantinetta at Tra Vigne 540
Oakville Grocery 540

Bakeries/Pastries:
Downtown Bakery and Creamery 541
Sciambra French Bakery 542

Ice Cream/Chocolates:
Downtown Bakery and Creamery 543

Markets:
Keller's Market 543
Palisades Market 543

Ethnic Markets:
La Luna Market 543

Produce:
Healdsburg Farmers' Market 544
Palisades Market 544
St. Helena Farmers' Market 546

Meat and Poultry:
Big John's Food Center 546
Keller's Market 547

Cheese:
Oakville Grocery 548
Vella Cheese Company 548

Wines and Spirits:
All Seasons Cafe and Wine Store 548
J. V. Warehouse 549
Oakville Grocery 549
St. Helena Wine Center 549
St. Helena Wine Merchants 550
Tip Top 550

The East Bay

RESTAURANTS

AJANTA

Laxman Moorjani, the owner of Ajanta, presides over his restaurant like a mother hen. He wants everyone to be pleased with his monthly changing menu of specials drawn from all the states in India. He sends out chatty, informative newsletters announcing the dishes and developments in the restaurant—who's gone back to India, who has returned. Once you've visited a couple of times, he knows what dishes you love and can usually conjure them out of the kitchen, even though they are not on the menu. Some of my favorites are chicken *Makhanwala*, a boneless breast in a velvety cream sauce; and the stunning chicken *tikka*, an appetizer of boneless tandoori chicken kabobs that are so juicy and tender that I always order them along with *aloo tiki*, crisp potato and onion patties served with chutney. I like many of the fresh okra dishes and the spectacular *badal jam*, thick creamy slices of eggplant topped with a garlicky tomato sauce and yogurt, a must-order. Mr. Moorjani and his staff gently remind you that Ajanta makes its own Indian desserts and that it would be a shame to miss them. He's right. The housemade *kulfi* (dense Indian ice cream), studded with pistachios, and *ras malai* (paneer cheese patties in yogurt sauce) are exceptional, and both the mango mousse and mango ice cream boast fresh fruit flavor.

1888 Solano Avenue,
Berkeley
Tel: 510-526-4373
Open for lunch daily
11:30 a.m. to 2:30 p.m.;
dinner Sunday through
Thursday 5:30 to 9:30 p.m.,
Friday and Saturday
until 10 p.m.
Price: Inexpensive
Credit cards: AE, DC, D, MC, V

BAY WOLF

3853 Piedmont Avenue,
Oakland
Tel: 510-655-6004
Open for lunch Monday
through Friday 11:30 a.m.
to 2 p.m.; dinner Monday
through Friday 6 to 9 p.m.,
Saturday and Sunday
5:30 to 9:30 p.m.
Price: Moderate
Credit cards: MC, V

Michael Wild, the intellectual, twinkly-eyed chef-partner of Bay Wolf, has been putting out a different seasonal menu every two weeks for over twenty years now. This East Bay institution is ensconced in a graciously converted house with a wide front porch for outdoor dining, two wood-paneled dining rooms with good modern art on the walls, and a pleasant little bar. The food has gotten better and better over the years, simpler rather than fussier, as it draws on a marketplace offering ever more naturally delicious ingredients and focuses more directly on Provençal- and Italian-inspired preparations. Bay Wolf has always had a style of its own: generous, homey, good on meats, great on wines, with a few mannerisms. Over the years the kitchen has been influenced by a number of its different chefs, but Francophile Wild has been a steadying constant, insisting on luscious dishes like roast chicken with chickpea flour crepes and grilled leeks; juicy leg of lamb with garlic custard; grilled northern halibut with roasted rosemary potatoes; and of course a duck dish with a fruit sauce, a Bay Wolf specialty. The starters might be a chilled shrimp salad in mustard vinaigrette with greens, or a yellow pepper stuffed with goat cheese. An apple *galette* with lavender honey, or a chocolate-ginger pot de crème might be dessert.

I went to a book party for a mutual friend of Michael's and mine, put on at Bay Wolf, and I don't think I have ever been served such nice food for a large group. After all these years, Bay Wolf still has conviction, energy, and integrity. So many people eat there regularly that they feel part of the extended Bay Wolf family, with much exchanging of books, talk about wine, and discussion of art. In many ways, Bay Wolf is the quintessential East Bay restaurant, and many of the neighborhood newcomers, such as Citron, have been inspired by it.

BOMBAY CUISINE

On a good day, a diner at this little Indian cafe might be served a brightly seasoned vegetarian *thali* plate, or all sorts of South Indian snacks like *vadas, dosas, idli,* and *uttapam,* as well as vegetable curries and wonderful *chapatis* and *parathas,* Indian breads cooked on a griddle. Bombay Cuisine does not have a tandoori oven, which means it is liberated from the omni-present Punjabi lamb-centered menus. The hard-to-find Indian snacks can be a real treat, like *dahi vada,* small, tender, fried balls of dal flour sauced in yogurt and served with pruney tamarind chutney; or *bataka vada,* deep-fried potato fritters served with cilantro-mint chutney. A fried chickpea *vada* flattened into a patty and laced with onion is particularly crisp and savory, a favorite of mine, especially with a white chutney made from dried coconut and chilies. *Dhokla,* airy steamed squares of chickpea flour, tastes like nutty, fragrant risen bread. The *raita,* yogurt mixed with onions and cucumber, is great on everything. Don't pass up the puffy bread called *puri,* worth ordering just for the warm wheaty breath they expel when you tear into them. Use the pieces to scoop up a vegetable curry. For dessert, *gulab jamun,* Indian doughnuts soaked in rose water–scented syrup, maintain their fluffy texture.

The small dining room is clean and pleasantly decorated. Service may not be a high point here, but when the food finally gets to the table it tastes freshly made and homey. You get the feeling that the cooks themselves get true satisfaction feeding an expatriate Indian community real tastes of home.

2006 Ninth Street,
Berkeley
Tel: 510-843-9601
Open for lunch Tuesday through Sunday 11:30 a.m. to 3 p.m.; dinner Tuesday through Sunday 5 to 9 p.m.
Price: Inexpensive
Credit cards: AE, MC, V

BRENNAN'S RESTAURANT

This beloved Berkeley hofbrau and bar has undergone a face-lift after thirty-five years, but the pensioners and students who depend on its first-rate cafeteria food for basic sustenance don't have to worry that the place is going upscale. A coat of bright Egyptian-green paint has been rolled over the old, amazingly drab institutional shade, and customers are dazzled by such modern turns as clear glass windows, perimeter lighting, wooden partitions with coat hooks, and two large new televisions for sporting events. Though

720 University Avenue,
Berkeley
Tel: 510-841-0960
Open every day 11 a.m. to 9:30 p.m.; bar open Sunday through Tuesday until midnight, Wednesday and Thursday until 1 a.m., Friday and Saturday until 2 a.m.

Price: Inexpensive
Credit cards: MC, V

Brennan's has taken on a publike cachet—well, kind of—prices have stayed the same. The blown-up photos of Mr. Brennan posing in front of prize steers at 4-H auctions still gaze down at customers tucking into their chewy roast beef sandwiches, French dipped, of course. And the same cast of characters—artists, sailors from the nearby marina, metalworkers, people off the dinner shift from restaurants around Berkeley—still stops by for late-night drinks. (Brennan's will always remain dear to me as the scene of a fistfight between my two drunken boyfriends many, many years ago.) The food on the cafeteria line still includes gigantic roast turkeys, whole briskets of corned beef, and massive top rounds of roast beef, thickly sliced to order and generously stacked onto French rolls, rye bread, or white. Excellent coleslaw in a creamy dressing and incendiary horseradish on the tables enhance all the sandwiches. Turkey plates with nicely seasoned bread stuffing, mashed potatoes, canned or frozen vegetable of choice, and gravy mean that hundreds can celebrate Thanksgiving every day. Some people make a point of going to Brennan's on Wednesdays for the smoked tongue plate with boiled potatoes and cabbage; others always get there early enough to grab the almost giraffe-size turkey necks while they last. One truly new development is the chicken rotisserie, the source for a juicy half-chicken plate, which has become the most popular to-go item. For cheap, substantial eats and a friendly bar, Brennan's is still the best.

BRIDGES

44 Church Street,
Danville
Tel: 510-820-7200
Open nightly 5:30 to 9:30 p.m.; lunch served Fridays 11:30 a.m. to 2 p.m.
Price: Moderate
Credit cards: AE, DC, MC, V

This stunning modern restaurant in the center of a bucolic suburban village provided the setting for some of the most hilarious scenes in Robin Williams's movie *Mrs. Doubtfire*, but beyond its big-screen stardom, Bridges has earned a reputation for an eclectic, well-executed East-West menu. The inspiration comes from the far corners of the world, with special attention focused on Japan, south Asia, and the Mediterranean. In fact, the dishes are so far flung you have to think about how to compose a palatable meal, matching up geographically compatible appetizers and main courses like a puzzle. You could start with a mildly spicy Thai beef salad with julienned vegetables and cellophane noodles and follow it with a ravishingly delicious Thai seafood stew in coconut-milk broth with shrimp toasts. Or, you might pair a Caesar salad with an orange- and star anise–scented smoked pork loin on top of wild rice and almonds. The desserts are Western and rich. The superb wine list draws together unusual wines from all over Europe and California, making it possible to find both bottles and half bottles to go with so many disparate flavors. Thoroughly professional service adds to the sophisticated attractions of this restaurant. Several generations of chefs have run the kitchen, but the overall tone and quality of the cooking stays high, always with a special nod toward vegetarian diners.

CAFE AT CHEZ PANISSE

Having trouble getting a table at dinner when the cafe will only take same day reservations Monday through Thursday before 6 or after 9 p.m.? Go for lunch at this world-famous cafe when you can make same-day reservations and have a three-course fixed-price lunch for around $17.50, which brings you the best of the daily menu for an affordable sum, especially when you consider the unsurpassed quality of everything that is served at this temple of beautiful ingredients. Still anchoring the menu are crusty pizzas, aromatic from the wood-fired brick oven, and the definitive green salad of the tastiest, tiniest lettuces with garlic croutons and a perfect vinaigrette. The rest of the menu changes with the seasons, but you can always count on something sublime and ingenuous, like toasts covered with wild mushrooms drizzled in fragrant olive oil and baked in the wood-fired oven; or LuLu Peyraud's Provençal-style grilled steak served in thin, juicy, rare slices topped with anchovy butter, a few bitter greens, and some roasted potatoes that taste better than any others. That's the thing about Chez Panisse. You get food here that you think you have tasted before—roasted peppers,

1517 Shattuck Avenue, Berkeley
Tel: 510-548-5049
Open for lunch Monday through Thursday 11:30 a.m. to 3 p.m., Friday and Saturday until 4 p.m.; dinner Monday through Thursday 5 to 10:30 p.m., Friday and Saturday until 11:30 p.m.
Price: Moderate
Credit cards: AE, DC, D, MC, V

tomatoes, melon, lamb chops, scallops—that take you by surprise: You never realized that they could taste like this. The key to serving such naturally delicious food goes way, way back to the growing, the picking, the collecting. Alan Tangren, who used to be a chef at Chez Panisse, now works full-time as a forager, discovering and commissioning ingredients; gathering, searching, encouraging farmers to raise certain species, and teaching everyone through the lusciousness of the stuff he finds about the importance of ecologically sound growing practices. Of course, the cooking itself certainly plays a large part, but letting the ingredients when they're at their peak dictate the menu has been the Chez Panisse breakthrough. I marvel at the presentations, so simple, yet so beautiful. Nothing is crowded onto the plates or fussy; the arrangements are naturally full of color and life. Eating here is always a pleasure. You feel nourished, refreshed, delighted, meal after meal, year after year. Not enough can be said about the influence of Alice Waters's vision and the enormous impact she has had on cooking and eating in America. If you're a believer, you might as well be nourished at the source.

CAFE ROUGE

1782 Fourth Street,
Berkeley
Tel: 510-525-1440
Open Monday 11:30 a.m. to 3 p.m., Tuesday through Thursday 11:30 a.m. to 10 p.m., Friday and Saturday until 11 p.m.
Price: Moderate
Credit cards: MC, V

Marsha McBride, the longtime kitchen manager at Zuni Cafe in San Francisco, and Kelsie Kerr, prized chef at Chez Panisse and Zuni, run this buoyant uptown bar and restaurant with natural ease and panache, bringing big city energy to Berkeley. They decided to concentrate on meat, and the way these women handle it, the seemingly heavy meat dishes are made light and palatable. They use sustainably raised products, mostly from Niman-Schell, and prepare them in all sorts of ways with simplicity and elegance. Eating anything here—pork chops with rutabaga-potato puree, braised leeks, and spiced prunes in natural juice; crisp-skinned rotisserie chicken; jewel-like salads of endive, persimmon, and pomegranate; house-made charcuterie—is pure pleasure. This is market cooking at its best, and quite appropriate to Cafe Rouge's market hall location. There's even a meat counter in the back by the open kitchen exclusively stocked with Niman-Schell products.

Cafe Rouge also fills a market niche by bringing a Zuni-style zinc bar to the East Bay, complete with oysters, a sophisticated wine list, and lots of well-made cocktails. The front of the restaurant opens completely onto a patio of tables and umbrellas, a fine spot for lunch. At night, the lighting softens the warehouselike interior so that it feels more intimate than it does during the day. The noise level can be high. People drop by for drinks and food throughout the day and into the evening, making Cafe Rouge a significant new addition to the Bay Area dining scene. A meal here is well worth a special trip.

CASA ORINDA

20 Bryant Way,
Orinda
Tel: 510-254-2981
Open nightly 4 to 10 p.m.,
Friday and Saturday
until 11 p.m.
Price: Moderate
Credit cards: AE, MC, V

I have a soft spot in my heart for this old-fashioned steak, prime rib, and fried-chicken house in Orinda with its long western bar, wonderfully warm service, and practically everything made from scratch. John Goyak, the second generation of his family to run this sixty-eight-year-old roadhouse with a racy past, called on some chef friends from Chez Panisse to help him update the menu. But he could only change a little of it without disappointing his regulars, thank goodness. No customer would tolerate giving up the hot cream biscuits with honey that go with Casa Orinda's southern-fried chicken. Casa Orinda actually uses the original Kentucky Fried Chicken cooking equipment and formulas, which they bought when the Colonel was selling his process door to door. The way the chicken comes out at Casa Orinda makes the greasy fast-food version seem pale. People buy tons of prime rib and steak and a delicious chicken cutlet breaded in fresh Acme bread crumbs and fried in clarified butter. The pastry department makes all sorts of fresh fruit pies and cobblers, and even old customers love a sparkling fresh lemon tart taught to the kitchen by Patty Curtan from Chez Panisse. There aren't many old-fashioned American restaurants left, and very few that are owned by individuals with integrity. Casa Orinda is one of them and you can tell the moment you walk in the door: People are happy to work here, the dining rooms are immaculate. and the food is comforting and tasty.

CHEZ PANISSE

1517 Shattuck Avenue,
Berkeley
Tel: 510-548-5525
Open Monday through
Saturday with seatings at
6, 6:15, 6:30, 8:30, 8:45,
9, and 9:15 p.m.
Price: Expensive
Credit cards: AE, DC, D, MC, V

The famous prix-fixe dinner that has been served for over two decades is now in the hands of two chefs: Christopher Lee in the first part of the week and Jean-Pierre Moullé in the latter. Lee comes up with inventive turns on rustic favorites for his three-course Monday meals, $38, such as an interesting pot au feu with duck *confit*, cabbage crepinette, and beef short ribs simmered in savory broth with winter vegetables served with caper sauce and coarse-grain mustard. His Tuesday and Wednesday dinners for $58 currently feature dishes from the new tome, *Chez Panisse Vegetables*. A recent winter offering included a green garlic and potato galette with garden salad, turnip soup with turnip green flan, grilled black sea bass with Barolo sauce, leeks, spinach, roasted fennel and celery root, ending with a caramelized banana gratin. Jean-Pierre Moullé's weekend menus at $68 begin with an aperitif, an elixir of white wine infused with fruit or herbs. The stunning meal I ate the other night continued with salads of Chino Ranch vegetables, shrimp beignets with fried leeks, the most succulent tiny lamb chops and loin in a fresh shell bean and chanterelle ragout, and for dessert a fresh berry soup with vanilla ice cream. Moullé, who is a fisherman and hunter, moves in the kitchen like a ballet dancer. He combines the highest technical ability with a love of beautiful ingredients, weaving truffles, foie gras, wild mushrooms, and caviar into his menus with elegant simplicity.

Once you eat at Chez Panisse you'll know how magically everything fits together; how superb the individual dishes are; how every detail from flowers to lighting to bread to wine service flows out of a single vision. I've praised this restaurant to the skies so many times that now all I want to say is that it continues on at the highest level; that no other restaurant in the world possesses its purity, and charm; that a meal here is worth every penny—even though it can really add up, what with tax and 15 percent service added right onto the bottom of the check—and that I'd rather eat here than anywhere else in the world.

CITRON

5484 College Avenue, Oakland
Tel: 510-653-5484
Open nightly 5:30 to 9:30 p.m.
Price: Moderate
Credit cards: MC, V

Chef Craig Thomas's ode to the neighborhood bistro has charmed the picky East Bay crowd in a way that I haven't seen since Chez Panisse opened its cafe years ago. Romantic yet low key, the small dining room glows with warmth. Someone got all the details down just right: the wicker chairs and banquettes, the little bar, the soft lighting, the tile floors, the casual large arrangements of flowers. The menu is small, interesting, nicely executed, and always delivers a couple of clever new twists on classic dishes. Generous portions and simple presentation complete the picture.

The first courses sound heavier than they are; they're really green salads accompanied with a tiny puff pastry filled with goat cheese or a few shreds of duck confit. These light starters work well with the substantial main courses: a smoky coq au vin served with polenta, flanked by sweet little turnips; a seafood couscous with *harissa* on the side. Real bistro fare featuring pork loin, duck breast, or thick fillets of fish on lentils is the order of the day. Desserts follow suit with a more American bent, like fresh fruit crisp with ice cream or crème brûlée (which has become an American dessert based on how often it appears on local dessert menus).

An elegant but reasonably priced international wine list plays a large role in the pleasure of meals taken here. Each bottle on the small list has won its place for versatility and character. Citron reminds me of one of my favorite restaurants in San Francisco, Woodward's Garden, in that it is very small, personal yet professional, and delivers outsized satisfaction for its scope.

HONG KONG EAST OCEAN

3199 Powell Street,
Emeryville
Tel: 510- 655-3388
Open for lunch Monday through Friday 11 a.m. to 2:30 p.m., Saturday and Sunday 10 a.m. to 2:30 p.m.; dinner nightly 5 to 9:30 p.m.
Price: Moderate
Credit cards: MC, V

I have had sparkling Cantonese food at this large, modern restaurant perched at water's edge with a sweeping view of the Bay Bridge and the city. The food has been delicious, inventive, and impeccably fresh both at dim sum lunch and full-scale dinner. That it is served in a comfortably appointed dining room on several levels, all looking out to an expanse of water, only makes the experience more fun, especially after a cocktail or glass of Champagne in the sunset-lit barroom. You should not eat dinner here without ordering a thick fillet of velvety black cod, smoked and marinated in sake lees, which slightly beats out a salt-baked version sprinkled with fried, minced chilies. If there are enough people at the table, order one of each. Marinated calamari with spicy sesame oil are crisply deep-fried and completely addictive; scallops, shrimp, and water chestnuts finely chopped and served in an iceberg lettuce–leaf cup makes for another amusing starter. Seafood, as in all the best Cantonese restaurants, is subtly handled. One of my favorite dishes here is a clay pot of pristine shellfish, glass noodles, and lots of Napa cabbage in a clean but luscious broth. Tea lunch brings many Cantonese classics as well as Shanghai-style dumplings, pan-fried and stuffed with a juicy pork filling. *Yee mien*—soft, wide, very fresh noodles—are barely sauced so their remarkable texture can be appreciated. I have attended several banquets for groups of ten, planned ahead with the manager, with stunning food and first-rate service. When people ask where they can eat seafood with a view of the bay, I send them to Hong Kong East Ocean.

O CHAMÉ

1830 Fourth Street,
Berkeley
Tel: 510-841-8783
Open for lunch Monday through Saturday 11:30 a.m. to 3 p.m.;

David Vardy, the chef-owner of this unique teahouse and restaurant, arrived at his culinary calling by studying t'ai chi in a monastery in Taiwan with a Taoist master. He sailed to Japan for further study, but became interested in *kaiseki* cooking and the tea ceremony instead. He returned to California with a Tokyo-born wife and opened the Daruma Tea Shop, where he baked tea cakes in such perfect traditional style that teahouses in Japan started importing them. Several years ago he closed

Daruma and opened O Chamé, a charming, peaceful tearoom with hand-crafted wooden furniture and a menu of noodles, soup, *bento* box lunches, and seasonal Japanese dishes. Many lunches are packaged to go and dispensed from an outdoor kiosk that also sells Pure T ice creams (see page 356).

Indoors, people order surprisingly hearty and tasty Japanese vegetarian stews of wheat gluten and root vegetables like burdock. I'm not kidding; they're really delicious and satisfying. At dinner you can make a meal of all sorts of little dishes served on a striking assortment of Japanese pottery. Start with a smoky miso broth with big cubes of kabocha squash, rings of leek, and shiitakes. Sashimi usually brings two kinds of pristine raw fish such as halibut and sea urchin roe with *shiso* leaves. If you like your fish cooked, try simmered white-fish dumplings in a clear broth with pale green winter melon, orange squash, and shiitakes, or grilled sea scallops split and filled with a slice of kiwi. One of my favorite dishes is a rich stew of tea-flavored hard-cooked eggs, velvety chicken livers, and diced tomatoes. Cold dishes bring a salad of fine organic greens in a rice wine vinegar dressing, and a traditional octopus and cucumber salad. Then, of course, there are many teahouse amenities to be savored after a meal or in the afternoon. Japanese teas are individually brewed in tiny brass pots. I find that the slightly bitter but nutty green teas finish off a Japanese meal like a cup of coffee, though fragrant jasmine tea or a full-bodied Daruma blend served with milk works well too. Hard, crunchy tea cakes full of peanuts go brilliantly with the teas, though O Chamé's chilled custard studded with pears poached in Zinfandel, or little dumplings made of mashed potatoes topped with plum sauce, also are fun. You never know what will turn up on Vardy's menus.

One of the meanings of O Chamé is "precious little girl." At the opening of the restaurant, Vardy's then one-year-old daughter, half Californian, half Japanese, charmed the room with her laughter. Though it was her mother who designed the lovely space, the little girl seemed to be the very incarnation of O Chamé's spirit.

dinner Monday through Thursday 5:30 to 9 p.m., Friday and Saturday until 9:30 p.m.
Price: Moderate
Credit cards: AE, DC, MC, V

OLIVETO

5655 College Avenue,
Oakland
Tel: 510-547-5356
Open for lunch Monday through Friday 11:30 a.m. to 2 p.m.; dinner Monday through Saturday 5:30 to 10 p.m., Sunday 5 to 9 p.m.
Price: Moderate
Credit cards: AE, MC, V

Paul Bertolli, a former downstairs chef at Chez Panisse, has taken the helm here as executive chef and the difference in the cooking is quite amazing. The food here was always good because the kitchen has always been committed to using fine ingredients, but now the cooking reflects Bertolli's unique style, which is traditionally Italian, intensely flavorful, but wonderfully light. The menus, though small, are dreamy. There are always two or three dishes that you can't decide between and simply no disappointments. Instead of raising prices, Oliveto has lowered them to cafe levels, and the result is a full house every night. It certainly has become my top choice in this part of the East Bay.

Some of the beautiful dishes I've had come as a result of Bertolli's intuitive ability to offer what people want to eat at the moment. One summer evening I had a pasta of tender homemade noodles bathed in tiny, crisp chanterelles, tons of fresh peas, and a little cream. It couldn't have been better. Shrimp poached in an aromatic court bouillon came on a salad dressed with Bertolli's signature cucumber vinaigrette, the very taste of summer. Even though it was a warm evening, a grilled quail salad in a warm pancetta vinaigrette couldn't have been more welcome. Sweet, juicy slices of leg of lamb came with an irresistible potato pancake; crisp-skinned chicken cooked under a brick was accompanied with a squash gratin and grilled tomatoes; juicy pan-fried skate wings in brown butter came nestled next to spinach and new potatoes. These compositions profoundly satisfied.

The airy upstairs dining room, painted in warm Mediterranean sienna, with the partially open kitchen in the middle of the room, has always been a welcoming environment. All the important details—good bread and olives to start, an imaginative wine list, knowledgeable service, graciousness—have always been in place. With Bertolli and a new, first-rate crew in the kitchen (from Stars and Campton Place) to execute from day to day, Oliveto is finally living up to its potential. It's almost as if a new restaurant had opened, though paradoxically, the changes have been relatively small.

PICANTE TAQUERIA

Jim Maser, the manager of Cafe Fanny, and Alice Waters's brother-in-law, bought this straight-ahead flatlands taqueria three years ago and has gradually introduced a new set of dishes and standards. Maser draws on his own experiences in Mexico, where he spent quite a bit of time traveling, eating, and taking classes from Diana Kennedy. When he opened Picante Taqueria, he consulted with Rick Bayless, the chef of the peerless Frontera Grill and Topolobambo in Chicago. Picante is now making tortillas to order from fresh *masa*; serving whole black beans slowly simmered with *epazote* and other Mexican herbs; and offering delicate little soft tacos laid flat on a plate and piled with beautiful fillings including house-made chorizo and potatoes with an avocado-tomatillo sauce; *rajas* (roasted pepper strips) topped with *queso fresco*; and moist, long-cooked pork *carnitas* topped with fresh tomato salsa among other things. The house-made tamales are light and tender, filled with zucchini, corn, poblano chilies, and *epazote,* or pork braised in ancho-chili sauce. The fresh tortillas and Picante's carefully made fillings give new vitality to the traditional taqueria menu. With lots of tasty vegetarian alternatives, house-baked rolls for Mexican sandwiches, avocado-rich guacamole, fried-to-order chips, and many other carefully rethought components of the basic menu, Picante takes the genre to new, interesting heights. Two long bars that serve lots of margaritas and Mexican beer, two large, gaily painted dining rooms, lots of room for families at booths and large tables, and inexpensive prices for high-quality food make Picante a true destination taqueria.

1328 Sixth Street, Berkeley
Tel: 510-525-3121
Open Sunday through Thursday 11 a.m. to 10 p.m., Friday and Saturday until 11 p.m.
Price: Inexpensive
Credit cards: MC, V

CAFES

CAFE AT OLIVETO

5655 College Avenue,
Oakland
Tel: 510-547-4382
Open for lunch Monday
through Friday 11:30 a.m.
to 2 p.m.; dinner Monday
through Saturday 5:30 to
10 p.m., Sunday 5 to 9 p.m.
Credit cards: AE, DC, MC, V

One reason this partially outdoor cafe is a popular spot is that people can get quick, savory little bites, such as a plate of braised fresh shell beans topped with shaved Parmesan, or croutons with roasted yellow peppers in anchovy vinaigrette with black olives. Warm toasts piled with marinated tomatoes look very appealing, as do pretty green salads. Wood oven pizzas and focaccia sandwiches provide more substantial sustenance along with the full upstairs menu, and of course there's coffee, wine, and Oliveto desserts. People sit at the bar or at tables by the open French doors, pretending they're in Italy.

CAFE 817

817 Washington Street,
Oakland
Tel: 510-271-7965
Open Monday through
Friday 7:30 a.m. to 5 p.m.,
Saturday 10 a.m. to 4 p.m.
No credit cards

In a narrow high-ceilinged storefront that adjoins G. B. Ratto, Oakland's great international foods store (see page 481), Sandro Rossi, a former electrical engineer from Northern Italy, and Teresa Sevilla, a Peruvian architect-designer, have created a resonant, art-filled, modern cafe that serves great coffee and miraculously inexpensive but authentic Italian cafe food. I was originally hooked by a small caffè latte made from Illy Espresso beans and served in a short tumbler, my idea of heaven. The coffee, aromatic and deep in flavor without bitterness, was smoothed with just the right amount of velvety steamed milk. Acme baguettes, *levain,* and focaccia are used for delicious sandwiches: combinations of ham, Fontina, and marinated artichokes; or warm grilled prosciutto, mozzarella, and tapanade, crisp and buttery, accompanied with a little green salad. The few hot dishes come straight from Rossi's home village and Northern Italian soul. You practically can taste the land in a Tuscan bean soup thick with cabbage and chard, and topped with grated real Parmesan. A bowl of soft, cheesy polenta is striped with mushroom ragout, sausage, and cherry tomatoes. Only Chiantis and Vernaccias are poured, and these light Italian wines taste terrific with the grilled sandwiches and soups. Medium-sized bottles of cold San Pellegrino come with just the right little glasses. In fact, all the carefully chosen plates, glassware, and cups, and the exquisitely designed room, make the food and drinks taste even better, one more proof that a great cafe can turn the act of drinking a cup of coffee into a religious experience.

CAFE FANNY

1603 San Pablo Avenue,
Berkeley
Tel: 510-524-5447
Open Monday through
Friday 7 a.m. to 3 p.m.,
Saturday 8 a.m. to 4 p.m.,
Sunday 9 a.m. to 3 p.m
Credit cards: MC, V

This is the third star in the triumvirate that lights up the Chez Panisse food universe. It's a charming little stand-up cafe in the tradition of French *tabacs* and Italian espresso bars, but the open-faced sandwiches, pizzas with bright Provençal toppings, house-baked pastries, and oven-fresh Acme breads are a cut above anything else of their kind. You get salads made of the tiniest lettuces topped with baked goat cheese; or a farm-egg salad sandwich moistened with house-made mayonnaise, topped with Italian sun-dried tomatoes and anchovies. The café au lait comes in bowls. The house-made granola has become so popular it has been packaged for customers to take home. You have to get to the cafe early to snag the lacy buckwheat crepes with fresh fruit conserves. They always run out. The crunchy millet muffins are some of the best I've ever tasted—a recipe I tried to get for this book, but manager Jim Maiser wouldn't let me have it. Even the orange juice is extraordinary, usually mixed with tangerine or blood orange juice and always freshly squeezed. Though there is only a stand-up bar, an indoor bench, and some outdoor tables that are always full during nice weather, the satisfaction you get from a quick, informal meal here lasts all day. Cafe Fanny's location between two other interesting shops, the Acme bread bakery and Kermit Lynch wine store, make a visit here all the more compelling.

CAFFÈ STRADA

**2300 College Avenue,
Berkeley
Tel: 510-843-5282
Open Monday through
Saturday 7 a.m.
to midnight,
Sunday 7:30 a.m.
to midnight
No credit cards**

In a choice location across the street from Boalt Hall, the architecture building, and the anthropology museum, Caffè Strada rises to the challenge of supplying thousands of students in this part of the U.C. campus with first-rate coffee, especially their fortifying *cappuccino doppio*, and surprisingly fine croissants baked on the premises. The croissants are buttery, flaky, and crisp, though I can't recommend any other baked goods here. With more outdoor seating than indoor, even on the coolest days the outdoor tables stay full. The large, constant flow of customers, morning, noon, and night, gives Caffè Strada the vitality of the great urban cafes in Europe.

BARS

BRENNAN'S RESTAURANT

See Restaurants, page 459.

KIMBALL'S EAST

**5800 Shellmound Street,
Emeryville
Tel: 510-658-2555
Open Wednesday through
Sunday 6:30 p.m.
to midnight
Credit cards: MC, V**

The supper club is alive and well at this spacious, comfortable, full-service venue owned by Kimball Allen, the man who started the San Francisco Real Food Company in some rental properties he owned. But his real passion is jazz, and Kimball's East provides a welcoming home for it by offering a small, decently priced menu of California-Caribbean dishes, a full wine list, a full bar, freshly squeezed fruit juices and espresso, and a well-trained, accommodating staff. The tiers of booths allow for an easy view of the stage no matter where you sit. By the time you've finished dinner, the lights dim and the music begins. The advantage of eating at the club is that you get the best seats, and besides, it's fun. You feel very grown up (even if you're pushing fifty), dining and drinking and then sitting back for the show. My parents used to go out for nights like this at the Chez Paree in Chicago in the fifties and early sixties, Mom in a cocktail dress, Dad with a cigarette between his fingers, always with a large group seated around a swanky table. The scene is more casual at Kimball's East—no tablecloths, no waiters in tuxes—but some of that grand old supper club spirit lives on. I've seen performances from the Kronos Quartet to Wayne Shorter here, and attending this club never feels like an ordeal. It's the one venue that is set up for the comfort of both the artists and the audience, and believe me, the civilized surroundings don't diminish the music one bit.

DELICATESSENS/TAKE-OUT

BLONDIE'S PIZZA

For other location, see page 149.

This original Blondie's location must sell more slices of hot, cheesy, saucy, bready pizza than any other place in the world. The line never stops, and the army of pizza makers barely keeps up with the demand. A fresh hot slice of this not-too-oily pizza is dirt cheap and fills you up for most of the day.

2340 Telegraph Avenue, Berkeley
Tel: 510-548-1129
Open Monday through Thursday 10:30 a.m. to 1 a.m., Friday and Saturday until 2 a.m., Sunday to midnight.
No credit cards

DOUG'S BAR-B-Q

I like Doug's. I'm not that much of a barbecue fan, but I like Doug's. I love the fresh green beans cooked with ham and sausage; the smoky baked beans that are whole, firm, but creamy; the potato salad in a pleasant, sweet-relish-studded mayonnaise with potatoes that still have texture. When it comes to the barbecue, the pork ribs are meaty and tender; the barbecue sauce balances hot, sweet, and sour with precision in all three degrees of hotness. I actually like the gigantic beef ribs, moist and meaty, better than the pork ribs, but I'm the exception. Doug's does not stick to the usual; they barbecue goat and turkey and deep-fry turkey as well, which gives

3600 San Pablo Avenue, Emeryville
Tel: 510-655-9048
Open Monday through Thursday 11 a.m. to 9 p.m., Friday and Saturday until midnight, Sunday 10 a.m. to 9 p.m.
Credit cards: MC, V

the meat a bit of an aftertaste although it stays juicier than the smoked. Both turkeys are immersed in sauce. Doug's calls itself a Texas-style barbecue and underscores the point by displaying several pairs of longhorns above the counter. The people working under them could not be nicer at this twenty-some-year-old smokehouse, and when I get the urge for barbecue I seriously consider coming all the way here.

MADE TO ORDER

1576 Hopkins Street,
Berkeley
Tel: 510-524-7552
Open Monday through
Saturday 9:30 a.m. to 6 p.m.
Credit cards: MC, V

Silvana La Rocca does an excellent job gathering all the necessities of the upscale East Bay pantry at her multifaceted food store. In addition to good olives in bulk, serrano ham from Spain, prosciutto from Parma, anchovies in salt, buffalo-milk mozzarella, high-quality Rustichella dried pasta, and house-made fresh pasta, La Rocca makes three types of Italian sausages; lots of bean, rice, and pasta salads; pesto sauce; and chicken stock for soups. During the season, Made to Order carries both black and white truffles and brings in a range of extra-virgin olive oils and balsamic vinegars, among other rarities. The store has everything from inexpensive wines to ceramic dishes, practically anything you might need to put together a good meal, either from scratch or with the help of some prepared foods. The staff is friendly and knowledgeable, and the displays are attractively arranged and the deli counter freshly stocked, making it one of the few vigorous, independent, full-scale delicatessens left in the world.

MARKET HALL PASTA SHOP

The busiest spot in a busy market hall by the College Avenue BART station in Rockridge, the Pasta Shop offers a huge variety of prepared and imported foods. Though it made its reputation on excellent fresh egg pasta used by many restaurants in the Bay Area, its ravioli and pasta sauces are a bit of a disappointment and the filled pastas really need some editing. I like the idea of being able to buy house-made mayonnaise for $2.95 a pound, which gives you a generous cup for $1.25. Olives in bulk from Liguria, Provence, Peru, California, and Morocco, among others; prosciutto, salami, Hobbs' pancetta, and a good-sized cheese department with lots of Italian cheeses and French goat cheeses just begin to scratch the surface of the large inventory here. A gigantic refrigerated counter with salads, highly seasoned house-made sausages, lasagne, meat loaf, grilled marinated half chickens, marinated artichokes, and whole roasted vegetables always has a crowd in front of it. Among the dry goods on shelves are Rustichella d'Abruzzo dried pastas, rare imported extra-virgin olive oils and vinegars, as well as more affordable ones, and small tins of my favorite Columbus anchovies packed in oil. Service is fast and efficient and your number comes up quickly. If you don't need anything from the deli counter you can pay without a number at the cheese counter, a humane system.

A huge new branch of the Pasta Shop has opened next to Cafe Rouge in Berkeley.

5655 College Avenue, Oakland
Tel: 510-547-4005
Open Monday through Friday 10 a.m. to 8 p.m., Saturday 9 a.m. to 7 p.m., Sunday 10 a.m. to 6 p.m.

1786 Fourth Street, Berkeley
Tel: 510-528-1786
Open daily 10 a.m. to 6:30 p.m.
Credit cards: MC, V

PHOENIX PASTAFICIO

This small shop makes its own extruded pasta; in other words, huge fresh tubes, shells, and wheels as well as spaghetti. In addition, it flavors them with dried porcini, saffron, chestnuts, or spinach. They have a fantastic texture, chewy yet tender, and they cook pretty fast, making them useful in restaurant kitchens, many of which use Phoenix pastas. The shop also makes sauces, breads, and sweet rolls in house, but the unique draw is the fresh noodle in fresh shapes.

1786 Shattuck Avenue, Berkeley
Tel: 510-883-0783
Open Tuesday through Saturday 8 a.m. to 7 p.m.
No credit cards

ULTRA LUCCA

3838 Telegraph Avenue,
Oakland
Tel: 510-654-9188
Open Monday through Friday 9 a.m. to 5 p.m.,
Saturday 10 a.m. to 4 p.m.

4001 Piedmont Avenue,
Oakland
Tel: 510-547-7222
Open Monday through Saturday 9 a.m. to 7 p.m.,
Sunday 9:30 a.m. to 6 p.m.

6119 La Salle Avenue,
Oakland
Tel: 510-339-9716
Open Monday through Saturday 9 a.m. to 7 p.m.,
Sunday 9 a.m. to 6 p.m.

2905 College Avenue,
Berkeley
Tel: 510-849-2701
Open Monday through Friday 10 a.m. to 7 p.m.,
Saturday 10 a.m. to 6 p.m., Sunday 10 a.m. to 5 p.m.
Credit cards: MC, V
See listing, page 515.

VIK'S KING OF CHAT

726 Alston Way (between Fourth and Fifth Streets)
Berkeley
No telephone
Open Saturday and Sunday only 11 a.m. to 7 p.m.
Cash only

Every weekend half the East Bay Indian community stands around this snack counter in the back of an Indian market, slurping down saucy, juicy vegetarian snacks, or *chat*, out of paper cartons. The lucky ones grab a folding chair at a card table. Others eat at a counter affixed to a wall. The rest just down their snacks out of hand, not worrying about dripping on the cement floor. A variety of snacks, each costing $2.50, are listed on a board. Some are based on crisp, deep-fried hollow spheres called *puri*, which are filled with potatoes, chilies, and onions and sauced with yogurt and tamarind chutney as in *batata puri*. Delicious *sev puri* are flat, crisp disks topped with potato, chickpeas, onions, chilies, tamarind, and mint-cilantro chutneys. *Dokla,* light, airy, steamed chickpea cakes sprinkled with coconut and fresh cilantro constitute another snack category; while *pakori chat* are soft, light balls of chickpea flour that are deep-fried, soaked in water, then squeezed dry and sauced with tamarind chutney and yogurt. A full range of Indian boiled-milk sweets and desserts are freshly prepared and OK, as Niloufer Ichaporia King, my ethnic-food expert, would say. I like the Indian ice cream called *kulfi kluge,* swathed in cream and clear wheat-starch noodles. The warm *gulab jamun,* fried milk balls soaked in scented syrup, are also nice. At Vik's, you get a little taste of what it's like to eat at snack shops in alleys in Varanasi or New Delhi—without the amoebas.

YUNG KEE

This small shop is regarded as the best place in Oakland's Chinatown for Chinese barbecued pork, ducks, and chickens. You can eat them with noodles and soup at Formica tables in the store, or take them home, chopped into neat pieces through the bone and packed in white cartons.

888 Webster Street,
Oakland
Tel: 510-839-2010
Open daily 9:30 a.m. to 2 a.m.
No credit cards

BAKERIES/PASTRIES

ACME BAKERY

When Steve Sullivan started baking bread at home and then at Chez Panisse, the long organic process overtook him. He became obsessional about bread making, and judging by the huge success of Acme Bakery, which he opened in 1983, a lot of people have become obsessional about buying his bread. Having the right loaf every day is important. I knew that Sullivan's loaves, especially a crusty whole-wheat sourdough round called *levain* and his baguettes, were right for me the moment I tasted them. They have tremendous character and

1601 San Pablo Avenue,
Berkeley
Tel: 510-524-1021
Open Monday through Friday 8 a.m. to 5 p.m.,
Saturday 9 a.m. to 5 p.m.
No credit cards

substance without being heavy, which can come only from that long and elusive bread-making process he worked on for so many years. Once you eat these breads you want to have them every day. I do buy other breads and enjoy them, but if I don't have a *levain* on my counter I get edgy, as if I don't really have food at home.

You can buy Acme loaves all over the Bay Area, but the ones you pick up at the bakery next to Cafe Fanny and Kermit Lynch Wines are always the freshest, the most fragrant, the best bread you will find in America. One of the finest qualities of Acme *levain* is that it lasts; it never gets moldy even when it stays in a bag for days. You can take this bread camping: I cart loaves of it to Maui and it lasts the whole vacation. I need my *levain* toast in the morning, and my little boy needs his garlic toast in the evening. As omnivorous as we all are in our family, Acme bread is the one food we all agree on.

BREAD WORKSHOP

1250 Addison Street No. 109, Berkeley
Tel: 510-649-9735
Open Monday through Friday 7:30 a.m. to 1:30 p.m.
No credit cards

The Bread Workshop's focaccia buns have provided a landing for some of the best hamburgers in the Bay Area. They're light and flavorful without being oily and make delicious sandwiches. Hundreds of East Bay mothers depend on the Bread Workshop's partially baked pizza dough rounds, which kids top themselves and finish baking. The multigrain bread is substantial and tasty without being tedious. Started by some ex-employees of Acme, the Bread Workshop supplied restaurants early on unlike Acme, which had a hard enough time meeting the needs of its retail customers and Chez Panisse. Bread Workshop now has a pleasant retail bakery-cafe in a redbrick building on meadowlike Strawberry Creek Park, with outdoor and indoor tables where you can drink coffee and eat freshly baked scones.

THE CHEESE BOARD

See Cheese, page 492.

KATRINA ROZELLE

A clean, modern little shop next door to a Dreyer's Ice Cream store, Katrina Rozelle shows particular strength in old-fashioned crumbly, buttery American-style cookies. Her shortbread rectangles are indeed "simple perfection," to lift the description on the bakery's brochure. Another standout, almond praline cookies, are full of chopped almonds and bits of praline. Their traditional chocolate chip, the Chocolust, one of the few good crisp chocolate cookies around despite the smarmy name; and the bright-flavored ginger cookies please both adults and children. This shop's reputation for cookies keeps the inventory turning over, which keeps the cookies fresh, the most important quality of any cookie.

5931 College Avenue, Oakland
Tel: 510- 655-3209
Open Monday through Saturday 9 a.m. to 6 p.m., Sunday 11 a.m. to 5 p.m.
Credit cards: MC, V

LA FARINE

This authentic French bakery started by Lili Le Coq has been passed on to two generations of new owners-bakers, but the quality of the buttery French tarts and cakes, croissants, *pain au chocolat,* and sweet rolls remains stellar. If there is one pastry associated with La Farine, it's the morning bun, a rich, cinnamony, sugared roll made with croissant dough, which no one can resist. Whenever I drive by this bakery, I have to stop in to buy one. Swiss twinkies, a flat, palm leaf–shaped sweet roll, have many fans, but not as many as the sublime morning bun. The breads here are soft and delicate; the egg bread makes superlative French toast, and this is also the place to buy brioches. The tarts topped with fresh fruit actually taste as appealing as they look. La Farine is one of the few great French pastry shops left in the Bay Area, and one hopes that the bakers will continue to pass on the secrets of the morning bun to succeeding generations.

6323 College Avenue, Oakland
Tel: 510- 654-0338
Open Tuesday through Saturday 8 a.m. to 6 p.m., Sunday 8 a.m. to 3 p.m.
No credit cards

SEMIFREDDI'S

372 Colusa Street,
Kensington
Tel: 510-596-9935
Open daily 7 a.m. to 7 p.m.
No credit cards

A bakery founded on a seeded baguette, Semifreddi's got its inspiration from breads baked at The Cheese Board, where Bob Wax taught many generations of bakers how to make them. Semifreddi's baguettes are on the hard side, very crusty with a meaty interior. The most popular are thickly coated with caraway, fennel, poppy, and sesame seeds, infusing each bite with a riot of flavors. I think the seeds take over the bread, making it conflict with other foods, but I'm in the minority here. A handsome wood-and-glass case displays other breads as well, including a whole-wheat walnut-raisin that has both flavor and unusual moistness. On the counter are wrapped slices of tasty fat-reduced lemon pound cake and whole roasted elephant garlics to squeeze onto bread instead of butter—if you're not going out on a date for twelve hours after you use it. The bakery also serves espresso.

ICE CREAM/CHOCOLATES

YOGURT PARK

2433-A Durant Avenue,
Berkeley
Tel: 510-549-0570
Open every day 10 a.m. to midnight
No credit cards

Gigantic cups of frozen yogurt topped with fresh fruit at the cheapest possible price means that the line never stops forming at Yogurt Park. The Honey Hill Farms yogurt pumped here used to be satisfying when it still had some fat in it. The nonfat mania has ruined most of it, but there's usually a vanilla low-fat option that doesn't taste like chemicals. I have an emotional attachment to this yogurt shop, one of the few remaining, because I used to eat quarts of it when I was pregnant thirteen years ago. My kid is pretty much made of frozen yogurt.

ETHNIC MARKETS

G. B. RATTO AND COMPANY

G. B. Ratto, the East Bay's premier international grocer, stocks hard-to-find items from all over the world, especially from the Middle East, but also from Brazil, the Caribbean, Africa, Portugal, France, and Italy. When you need pâté spice, Ratto's has it, along with hundreds of other specific cooking needs ranging from the most exotic spices in bulk, dried beans, flours, couscous, cooking oils, bottled syrups and pickles, and canned fruits and vegetables. In the deli cases are olives and hummus, Italian cured meats, an excellent imported salt cod from Italy, cheeses, yogurts, house-made vinegar in barrels, *harissa*, filo dough—the variety of foods sold here is astounding. Next door in a large corner space surrounded by windows, Ratto's does a well-attended cafeteria-style lunch every day with deli salads, hot soups, and Italian-style sandwiches. And on the weekends, Ratto's stages wildly popular communal spaghetti feeds with live opera singers. The food is cheap and the singing really good. G. B. Ratto has long been the best international foods store in the Bay Area and its reputation still stands. If you can't find it at Ratto's, it's probably not available in the United States.

821 Washington Street, Oakland
Tel: 510-832-6503
Open Monday through Friday 9:30 a.m. to 6 p.m., Saturday 9:30 a.m. to 5 p.m., Sunday 10:30 a.m. to 4 p.m.
Credit cards: MC, V

MILAN INTERNATIONAL

The smell of spices hits you long before you walk in the front door of this great Indian grocery with aisles and aisles of imported Indian foods, the longest bulk spice section you'll ever see, bulk flours, the best basmati rice being imported at the moment, and a rainbow of dried legumes. One whole wall is dedicated to shiny stainless steel plates, bowls, tiffin carriers and trays, woklike Indian cooking vessels, and utensils. Every sort of jarred chutney, pickle and spice paste, canned fruit, Darjeeling tea, *papadums* (lentil wafers that make the best snack imaginable, especially with martinis), and ever so much more, tempt you to spend hours here imagining how these things taste. Near the front counter on

990 University Avenue, Berkeley
Tel: 510-843-9600
Open Tuesday through Sunday 10 a.m. to 7:30 p.m.
Credit cards: AE, DC, MC, V;
$15 minimum

the floor are cartons of fresh items, such as ginger, fresh *kari* leaves, fresh turmeric (which looks like thumb-sized tubers), packaged *chapati* and *nan* (Indian breads), and once in awhile the most flavorful mangoes you'll ever taste in this country. Whoever buys them has flawless taste in this seductive fruit. You can also pick up Indian videos. If being around all the Indian ingredients makes you hungry, you can get a snack next door at Bombay Cuisine.

NEW SAIGON SUPERMARKET

**443 Ninth Street,
Oakland
Tel: 510-839-4149
Open daily 9 a.m. to 7 p.m.
No credit cards**

The Chinatown block of Ninth Street between Broadway and Franklin is lined with Asian grocery stores, their produce displays spilling out on the sidewalk, and shelves inside stacked to the rafters with products from all over the East. New Saigon is the largest and most densely packed of them all, with gorgeous fresh gourds, squashes, Chinese eggplants,

EATING IN OAKLAND'S CHINATOWN

Good small Vietnamese restaurants have been popping up in Oakland's Chinatown, and several are of note: VI'S VIETNAMESE CUISINE, 724 Webster Street, Oakland (510-835-8375), is a clean and modern dining room that serves excellent Vietnamese noodle salads in a deep bowl with shredded vegetables, pieces of grilled pork or chicken, a crisp, delectable deep-fried imperial roll, and a bowl of clear dressing to pour. I highly recommend any of the salads. VIEN HUONG, at 712 Franklin Street, Oakland (510-465-5938) is a popular *pho* restaurant, always packed, that specializes in Vietnamese soup and noodles. Other places of interest include NAN YANG, 301 Eighth Street, Oakland (510-465-6924), a Burmese restaurant where I recommend the incendiary sixteen-part ginger salad; and the ever popular JADE VILLA, 800 Broadway Street, Oakland (510-839-1688) for dim sum.

green papayas, mangoes, Asian greens, and seasonal delicacies in eye-catching piles. The large meat department is strong in fresh pork, meaty fresh bacon, piles of dewy ground pork, pristine pork liver and tongue, and every other imaginable part of the animal. French-style baguettes, dishware, tofu in bulk, noodles—all the southern Chinese and Southeast Asian cooking necessities are stocked. This is a destination for pork and Asian produce.

OAKLAND MARKET

Roomier and easier to negotiate than New Saigon, the Oakland Market is a modern pan-Asian grocery, with a large section of Asian kitchenware and dishes. You'll see shelves of inexpensive, clean-smelling Panther Peanut Oil in three-liter tins, excellent for deep-frying of all kinds, and more fragrant Lion and Globe peanut oil in plastic containers, good for salad dressings and cooking. There are refrigerated cases with wonton skins, tofu, and pickled greens. The grocery shelves have items like Japanese seaweed and wasabi, along with Thai, Vietnamese, and Philippine products. The selection of Asian goods is not deep, but it's diverse and comprehensive. Featured in the produce section one day in September were some beautiful-looking papayas for $1.39 each, a great price and probably a loss leader.

401 Ninth Street, Oakland
Tel: 510-835-4919
Open Monday through Saturday 9 a.m. to 6:30 p.m., Sunday 9 a.m. to 6 p.m.
No credit cards

SAM YICK

People love this resonant old-time Oakland Chinatown grocery store with tons of Chinese pottery, dried black mushrooms for good prices, packed and in bulk, and an extensive collection of Asian pantry items and dry goods, as well as a complement of necessary Western groceries like sugar, mustard, and sea salt.

362 Eighth Street, Oakland
Tel: 510-832-0662
Open Monday through Saturday 9:30 a.m. to 6:30 p.m., Sunday until 6 p.m.
No credit cards

PRODUCE

BERKELEY BOWL

2777 Shattuck Avenue,
Berkeley
Tel: 510-843-6929
Open Monday through
Friday 9:30 a.m.
to 7 p.m., Saturday
9 a.m. to 6 p.m.
Credit cards: MC, V

There are two destination produce stores in the Bay Area and the Berkeley Bowl is one of them. (Monterey Market across Berkeley is the other.) Your spirits will be lifted when you walk into this expansive former bowling alley turned market and see the amazing variety of healthy-looking produce available under one roof. The organic section alone would fill up most small produce stores and there is a large representation of Asian produce and tropical fruits. Organic Valencia juice oranges and fabulous organic grapefruits are dead center, and the rest radiates out in waves. Wild and cultivated mushrooms, lettuces, cooking greens, peppers, and chilies, and always lots of tropicals such as plantains, tomatillos, chayotes, pineapples, fresh coconuts, mangoes, papayas, *galangal*—all beckon at excellent prices. Also in the produce department are fresh breads, eggs, and dairy, plus a large Asian refrigerated section with noodles and tofu.

On one side of the building is a Japanese fish counter with fresh fish fillets marinated in *sake kasu* (the lees from sake fermentation) or miso, both yellowfin and white-fleshed *tombo* tuna, Pacific halibut, seaweed salad, and some shellfish. The meat and poultry counter isn't as strong. A grocery department takes up the other end of the building with beer and wine, Japanese products, grains, nuts, and spices in bulk, and chips. In essence, the Berkeley Bowl has become a supermarket that sells only fresh foods. If you live near the Oakland-Berkeley border, Berkeley Bowl should be your market of choice.

BERKELEY FARMERS' MARKET

Center Street at
Martin Luther King Jr. Way
Open Saturday
10 a.m. to 2 p.m.

With two great permanent produce markets in town, why shop at the farmers' markets? Because you can get produce that has been picked hours before, and you also might find some very local crops, grown in such small quantity that they could only be sold by the farmer directly. Produce bought directly from the people who grow it always tastes better, even if you can buy it more cheaply at Monterey Foods. I always make a detour for a farmers' market, if only for the pleasure of strolling down a street lined with fruits and vegetables.

Derby Street between Milvia and Martin Luther King Jr. Way
Tuesday in summer,
2 p.m. to 7 p.m.

Haste Street at
Telegraph Avenue
Sunday 11 a.m. to 3 p.m. May through November

MARKET HALL PRODUCE

A part of the Market Hall group of food stalls under one roof, this large, attractively arranged produce store offers a useful selection of organic and commercial produce at midrange prices. During a fall visit, fresh, dry, clean chanterelles at a good price of $7.99 a pound, organic apples, baby lettuces, and very pretty whole heads of organic oakleaf, red leaf, red butterleaf, and romaine lettuces caught my eye. Big bunches of arugula and lots of tomatoes cried out to be bought. The produce department also carries Straus Family Dairy organic milk and butter.

5655 College Avenue,
Oakland
Tel: 510-601-8208
Open Monday through Friday 9:30 a.m. to 8 p.m.,
Saturday 9 a.m. until 7 p.m.,
Sunday 9 a.m. until 6 p.m.
Credit cards: MC, V

MONTEREY FOODS

This stupendous produce market sets the standard for all others in price, variety, and completeness. There aren't many edible plants grown under the sun that don't show up on one of Monterey Foods' tables. Outside in the parking lot is a caged-in area with mountains of the best buys of the season, organic or not, but usually of excellent quality at phenomenal prices. You can't do better at farmers' markets or wholesale markets. Every cook I know periodically checks Monterey Foods to see what's available in the Bay Area and what they should be paying for it. Both big farmers and small producers have established long-term relationships with the two generations of the Fujimoto family who run this market. Bill Fujimoto knows everyone who grows in the northern part of the state and then some. Many farmers come to Monterey Market first

1550 Hopkins Street,
Berkeley
Tel: 510- 526-6042
Open Monday through Saturday
9 a.m. to 6 p.m.
No credit cards

because they might not have to go any farther to sell their harvest. Monterey makes its profits on volume, so they buy big and keep their markup tiny. When I started my first eight-table restaurant in Berkeley a million years ago, I shopped at Monterey Foods every single morning, and to tell you the truth, I've never done better on either price or quality since. The store also has a grocery department with fresh breads, pasta, and a dairy section.

OLD OAKLAND FARMERS' MARKET

**Ninth Street at Broadway,
Oakland
Friday 8 a.m. to 2 p.m.**

Next door to Oakland's Chinatown, the Old Oakland market features lots of fresh Asian produce, fresh nonorganic fruits and vegetables, and good prices on everything. Asian apple pears, dates, lots of oranges, and the whole spectrum of Asian greens, gourds, and root vegetables are usually represented. Anchored on one side by G. B. Ratto, the great international foods store, and Chinatown on the other, a trip to this part of the Bay Area on Friday could fulfill any number of food shopping goals. The composition of this market is similar to the Civic Center farmers' market in San Francisco.

MEAT AND POULTRY

ALAN'S MEATS

**Housewives' Market,
818 Jefferson Street,
Oakland
Tel: 510-893-9479
Open Monday through
Saturday 9 a.m. to 6 p.m.
Credit cards: MC, V**

What beautiful smoked and fresh pork this meat stand has! The piles of salt pork, fresh bacon, smoked bacon, ham hocks, smoked ham ends, and fresh, cured, and smoked ham of all sorts make you want to buy some red beans and get cooking. I bought some huge smoked ham hocks, which Alan's sliced, and I made the most delectable split pea soup with them. They were meaty with lots of marrow and gave the soup an honest, clean smoky flavor. When you visit the Housewives' Market, plan on picking up some bacon.

RED BEANS AND RICE

One of the most satisfying dishes in the world is red beans and rice. I first ate it in New Orleans, and now I prepare it for football playoffs on television. The best recipe comes from American Cooking: Creole and Acadian (*Time-Life Books, 1971*), the unsurpassed Time-Life Foods of the World cookbook series. The recipes in these books are so well researched and written that if you follow them carefully, you will always end up with something tasty. You can find these volumes in used-book stores.

The butchers at Alan's will slice their meaty ham hocks for you, which allows the marrow to enrich the beans. You can buy excellent dried beans at the Bean Bag stall in the Housewives' Market near Alan's.

Bring 6 cups of the water to a boil in a large saucepan. Add the beans and boil over high heat for 2 minutes. Turn off heat and let the beans soak 1 hour. Drain the beans, reserving the liquid, adding more water as needed to make 4 cups liquid.

Heat the butter or oil in a heavy 4- to 5-quart casserole over medium heat and cook 1/2 cup of the green onions, the onions and garlic until soft. Stir in the beans and their liquid. Add the ham hocks, salt, and pepper. Bring to a boil, then reduce heat to low and simmer gently, partially covered, until the beans are very soft, about 3 hours, periodically checking the pot for liquid and adding up to 1 cup of water little by little as necessary.

Remove the ham hocks. Cut the meat from bones and return it to the pot. Taste the beans for salt and pepper and adjust the seasonings as necessary. Put the rice in bowls, cover with beans, and top with the remaining 1/2 cup green onions.

Serves 4 to 6

---

6 cups water, plus more as needed
1 pound dried red beans
4 tablespoons butter or olive oil
1 cup green onions, finely chopped
1/2 cup finely chopped onion
1 teaspoon minced garlic
1 pound smoked ham hocks, sliced
1 teaspoon kosher salt
1/2 teaspoon freshly ground pepper or more to taste
6 to 8 cups freshly cooked long-grain rice

ENZO

**Market Hall,
5655 College Avenue,
Oakland
Tel: 510-547-5839
Open Monday through
Friday 10 a.m. to 8 p.m.,
Saturday until 7 p.m.,
Sunday until 6 p.m.
Credit cards: AE, MC, V**

This small high-quality butcher shop carries Harris beef, Petaluma Poultry Company chickens, house-made pork sausage, Grimaud rabbits, osso buco, and some nice-looking lamb from small animals. Enzo is an Italian butcher, so he cuts and grinds for Italian recipes. He also sells big Hebrew National Kosher hot dogs, which are very delicious. For an extra charge of $5 for ducks and $10 for turkeys, Enzo will cook them on the rotisserie for you, so you can pick them up hot and ready to serve.

MAGNANI'S POULTRY

**6317 College Avenue,
Oakland
Tel: 510-428-9496
Open Monday through
Friday 9 a.m. to 6:30 p.m.,
Saturday until 6 p.m.,
Sunday 11 a.m. to 5 p.m.**

**1586 Hopkins Street,
Berkeley
Tel: 510-528-6370
Open Monday through
Friday 9:30 a.m. to 6:30 p.m.,
Saturday until 6 p.m.
Credit cards: MC, V**

Chickens and chicken parts, ducks, turkeys, and other poultry are sold here, though at the College Avenue store the emphasis is on chickens and chicken parts. Of note are the rotisserie chickens, one marinated with Italian herbs, mostly lemon and rosemary, the other in a Japanese teriyaki marinade that is a knockout, especially at $5.75 for a moist, hot, flavorful chicken. The Hopkins Street store is now selling meat as well.

T & S MARKET

**323 Ninth Street,
Oakland
Tel: 510-268-1155
Open daily
8:30 a.m. to 6 p.m.
No credit cards**

This Chinatown poultry wholesaler also has a retail counter, though most of what they carry is kept in walk-in refrigerators in the warehouse. Just ask for what you need: ducks, chickens, chicken parts, poussins, large squab for $4 each, and exotics like black-skinned chickens. To restore a woman after giving birth, boil up a black-chicken broth with ginseng. The Chinese have been doing it for thousands of years. The results are good. So are the prices here.

TAYLOR'S SAUSAGES

In the course of doing research for this book, I've sampled many, many fresh sausages, but the ones I like the best come from this little stand in the old Housewives' Market. Their New Orleans–style *boudin blanc,* a mildly spicy white sausage with rice, is worth a special trip alone without even considering the perfectly seasoned and textured spicy Cajun chicken sausage, the Louisiana hot sausage, the garlic sausage, the Italian—every sausage these people make has balance; melded-together, deep, interesting flavor; and just the right amount of fat to lean to keep the sausages juicy and moist. The prices couldn't be better, the sausages fresher, or the variety more pleasing. No weird ingredients like fruit, curry, or sun-dried tomatoes ever ruin a Taylor sausage. Through several generations of owners, these have always been classic and great. Whoever runs this stand knows they have a good thing in these recipes.

Housewives' Market,
818 Jefferson Street,
Oakland
Tel: 510-832-6448
Open Monday through Saturday 9 a.m. to 6 p.m.
No credit cards

VER BRUGGE MEATS

This successful neighborhood butcher has a long counter filled with moderately priced fresh meat—especially good eastern pork and hams—and a handsome fresh-fish selection. They will cut to order and can get you anything you need if you call ahead.

6321 College Avenue,
Oakland
Tel: 510-658-6854
Open Monday through Friday 9 a.m. to 6:30 p.m.,
Saturday 9 a.m. to 6 p.m.,
Sunday 10 a.m. to 5 p.m.
Credit cards: AE, D, MC, V

FISH

BERKELEY BOWL FISH MARKET

See Produce, page 484.

MONTEREY FISH

1582 Hopkins Street,
Berkeley
Tel: 510-525-5600
Open Tuesday through
Saturday 10 a.m. to 6 p.m.
No credit cards

This is Paul Johnson and Tom Worthington's retail fish store and it is the best one in the Bay Area. You can't find a fish purveyor with higher standards or more integrity. Anything you buy from Monterey Fish will smell like the sea and stay fresh for several days at least, a tall order when it comes to seafood. The secret behind Monterey's quality is their buying. They seek out sources, cultivate them, and stick with them. If they can't get something in perfect condition, they don't carry it. A mitigating factor is that Monterey sells to a small number of picky restaurants from their wholesale location on the wharf in San Francisco, so they move what they have quickly and always have a fairly large variety of what they deem best at the moment. Monterey Fish is a source for fresh squid, carefully culled live lobsters and crabs in clean tanks, fresh shrimp, outstanding scallops and blue crab from a long-held source in Rhode Island, first-rate small shucked oysters from Washington State, and oysters in the shell from California on up to British Columbia.

Quality and freshness mean everything in seafood, because you don't even want to go near it if it isn't pristine. If you shop at Monterey Market you'll start cooking more and more fish at home and discover that it is the best convenience food you can buy. You don't have to do a thing to a fillet of king salmon, a slice of red-fleshed Hawaiian tuna, a slab of San Diego swordfish, or a piece of velvet-textured northern halibut except not to overcook it. And though some of this fish is expensive there's no waste, and you don't need a huge portion to satisfy. Fish is a clean, flavorful, elegant source of protein that goes with practically any vegetable and starch, so throwing a meal together with it is a snap. If you love fish, buy it at Monterey, and if you've been afraid to cook with it, come here too. You can't go wrong at this fish market; you can trust them. Paul Johnson sells only what he himself takes home to cook and his standards are high.

MOURA'S FISH MARKET

Next to Monterey Fish, I like this long, immaculate fish counter in the Housewives' Market the best. There are fish bargains to be found here, if you fancy catfish, gaspergoo, buffalofish, and gar. But some sparkling, bright-eyed wild Louisiana red snapper might be available, and if they are, buy one. They are some of the tastiest fish you can find. Moura's will clean it, scale it, and take out the gills, then you can roast it in salt (see recipe, page 59) or barbecue it whole. Its flesh is so juicy and flavorful, it doesn't require a bit of seasoning. If you like your seafood deep-fried, this is the place to find the fattier fish that lend themselves to this kind of cooking. There are also fresh whole sand dabs and rex sole in season, local rockfish and lingcod fillets, and shrimp of all sizes and grades. The people behind the counter know their fish and will be happy to discuss cooking methods with you. They are very nice.

Housewives' Market,
818 Jefferson Street,
Oakland
Tel: 510-832-6448
Open Monday through
Saturday 9 a.m. to 6 p.m.
No credit cards

NEW BASEMENT SEAFOOD MARKET

373 Eighth Street, Oakland
Tel: 510-763-8977
Open daily 9 a.m. to 6 p.m.
No credit cards

You walk down a flight of worn cement stairs to get to this Chinatown fish market full of ancient wood-framed tanks holding live lobster, crab, lingcod, striped bass, turtles, and more. On a table of crushed ice, clear-eyed local rockfish rest, along with whole sand dabs, rex sole, and whatever has been hauled in that day. As in every Chinatown fish store, you have to look for clear eyes, glistening skin, good smell—but the prices will be excellent and the whole fish will be cleaned and degilled for you. As in most Chinatown stores, most of the fish are whole because savvy buyers like to look a fish straight in the eye.

ROCKRIDGE FISH MARKET

Market Hall,
5655 College Avenue,
Oakland
Tel: 510-654-3474
Open Monday through
Friday 10 a.m. to 8 p.m.,
Saturday until 7 p.m.,
Sunday until 6 p.m.
Credit cards: MC, V

The small fish counter in this popular food shopping hall offers fillets of choice fish like mahi-mahi, swordfish, salmon, and tuna, along with fresh shrimp and live crab and lobsters from a tank. Some good-looking calamari salad, seaweed salad, and a few other fish preparations are also sold. The fish is nicely displayed and well cut. There are no bargains; the emphasis is on high-priced, easy-to-cook fish.

CHEESE

THE CHEESE BOARD

1504 Shattuck Avenue,
Berkeley
Tel: 510-549-3183
Open Monday through
Friday 10 a.m. to 6 p.m.,
Saturday until 5 p.m.;

In its third decade of operation, The Cheese Board not only stocks the largest collection of cheeses on the West Coast (or maybe in the United States), but a full-scale bread bakery and a to-go pizzeria a door away. Once merely a cheese store, The Cheese Board has become an important cultural institution. Over the years, this collectively owned shop has created a wide customer base that regularly makes the pilgrimage to Berkeley to buy cheese. Cheese Board customers have become sophisticated cheese buyers who will try new things.

This means that the store turns over enormous volume, not just of common cheeses, but of exotic ones, which in turn means that all the cheeses stay fresh and in perfect condition. The Cheese Board has cultivated this kind of response by requiring every customer to taste every cheese before they buy it. Every cheese is unwrapped in a split second and a taste is shaved off and handed over on waxed paper before you can protest. No one feels constrained to buy a cheese he or she doesn't like. One taste follows another until everyone is satisfied—customer and clerk—that the cheese is right. The cheese sellers taste along with the customers so they intimately know the inventory, which wheel of Brie is at a certain stage of ripeness, which aged Gouda is the nuttiest. They learn the characteristics of every new cheese, how to store, cut, order—and how to serve the customers, some of whom could try the patience of a saint. The clerks know which cheese to pull up for tasting when a customer gives some vague description. They can tell people what to buy for certain recipes; what to serve the day after tomorrow on a cheese tray; what to introduce kids to; what they personally love and the customer might like, too. The Cheese Board system is an amazing way to sell, unlike any other I've encountered. The end result is that people trust the store and are willing and eager to be turned onto an ever-expanding repertoire.

The smell of warm breads just out of the oven always wafts around the store, which only makes you want to buy more

pizzeria open Monday and Friday 4:30 to 7:30 p.m., Tuesday through Saturday 11:30 a.m. to 2 p.m.; coffee service open Monday through Friday 7 to 10 a.m. No credit cards cheese. My favorite is a round loaf called suburban bread, which has the most amazing crisp, thin, but chewy crust and a white, sweet, toothsome interior that's charmingly tender—a bread-baking triumph. Also, people go to The Cheese Board for fine olives in bulk at excellent prices. The pizza sold in a little shop that used to house Pig by the Tail charcuterie is sold slice by slice the minute it comes out of the oven. The bakers can barely keep up with the line. The slices are slapped onto a piece of paper and served on rattan plates. Customers sit or stand outside the store, eating and talking.

I have one bit of advice when visiting The Cheese Board. Take a playing card/number when you walk in and then look around at the breads and cheeses. Though the clerks are fast and efficient, and there are a lot of them, you never know how long the people in front of you will spend tasting, deciding, discussing. This exchange is the glory of the shop, and it has proven that education, generosity, and communal ownership can achieve the highest and best kind of success.

J. WIGGINS CHEESE

6309 College Avenue,
Oakland
Tel: 510-652-4171
Open daily 10 a.m. to 6:30 p.m., Sunday until 6 p.m.
Credit cards: MC, V

This tiny international cheese shop does such a good job of merchandising that a buyer can choose just by reading the little signs sprouting on all the cheeses. I was led to a fantastic super-aged *rocca* Parmesan—one of the best I've tasted in this country—and a hunk of Gruyère-like Comté from the French Alps, again one of the best I've encountered here. On a wooden cutting board in this densely packed store sat tastes of a goat milk Gouda and a flavorful Cantal, both so good I was tempted to buy those as well. Though the cheeses are prewrapped and tasting can be a bit of an ordeal here, my feeling is that the J. Wiggins people know what they are doing. Their cheeses are carefully selected, well stored and aged, and you can trust them. A deli counter with cured meats and hams, a large selection of olives, and a small selection of breads and crackers again are all carefully chosen.

COFFEE

PEET'S COFFEE AND TEA

See listing, page 199.

The perpetual crowd in front of the original Peet's never lets up and neither does the line inside the store. Per square inch, this coffee store must sell more beans and more cups of their intensely brewed coffee than any other, and deservedly so. Peet's has become such a social crossroads that a visit to this model for all the multitudinous coffee-store chains in the Bay Area is always an experience. You get a real whiff of old Berkeley milling outside, the maddening, wacky, passionate, political Berkeley that you can walk away from—or join—once you tame your cup of Peet's coffee with half-and-half and sugar.

2124 Vine Street,
Berkeley
Tel: 510-841-0564
Open Monday through Saturday 7 a.m. to 7 p.m., Sunday 8 a.m. to 6 p.m.
Credit cards: D, MC, V

WINES AND SPIRITS

KERMIT LYNCH WINES

Just as Berkeley has spawned Chez Panisse, The Cheese Board, Monterey Market, Monterey Fish, and Acme Bread, it has also nurtured Kermit Lynch, the groundbreaking wine merchant who brought the wines of Bandol from Domaine Tempier to the United States, along with many other wines from previously undiscovered (at least in the United States) wine-growing areas, which have now become icons of sophisticated eating and drinking. If you read Kermit Lynch's book *Adventures on the Wine Route: A Wine Buyer's Tour of France*, you'll get a firsthand account of what he was looking for: the quality of the land in the wine, the personality of the wine maker, direct purchasing from the people who make the wines (not *négociants*), and artisanal, not industrial, wine-making techniques.

1605 San Pablo Avenue,
Berkeley
Tel: 510-524-1524
Open Tuesday through Saturday 11 a.m. to 6 p.m.
Credit cards: MC, V

In his retail store, a cool redbrick room stacked with cases, you'll be able to buy the beautiful wines he made famous in this country, the Rhônes from Domaine Jean-Louis Chave in Hermitage and Auguste Clape in Cornas, plus many of what Richard Olney in his introduction to Lynch's book describes as "inexpensive, clean, refreshing and undemanding ideal daily aperitif and luncheon wines," such as Jean Berail-Lagarde's white Roque Lestière and Yves Laboucarie's *vin gris* Domaine de Fontsainte, both from the southwest Corbières apellation. All of Kermit Lynch's wines are imported, with particular strength in Burgundy, Alsace, Provence, and the Rhône, and most recently, a bunch of discoveries from the Loire and the Côte de Rousillon on the southeast coast of France. You won't like all the wines; some are very eccentric. But more often than not I've come around to appreciating them, the way you would a brilliant but slightly obnoxious person. When I first tasted the monumental Chablis from Raveneau, a rich, powerful wine aged in oak, a wine that is usually crisp and tart, I began to realize that every wine, even wines from the most traditional wine-growing areas, are as individual as their wine makers, and it is the wine maker's visions that captures Lynch's interest.

Shopping at the store is low-key and interesting. The friendly and extremely helpful clerks have tasted everything; they've traveled to the vineyards and eaten the foods that go with the wines. They are able to give good advice on food and wine matchups. Like the staff at The Cheese Board, they want to turn their customers on to new wines, hear what people think about them, and try to find wines that will please each palate—to be personal wine merchants.

Finally, though some of these wines are found at other stores, since Kermit Lynch is an importer and a wholesaler as well as retailer, you'll find the most complete collection at the best prices at the store on San Pablo.

NORTH BERKELEY WINE COMPANY

Rejuvenated by some ex-employees from Draper and Esquin, North Berkeley Wine Company meets everyday wine-drinking needs with their own-label Merlot, Zinfandel, and Cabernet, inexpensive and very decent, and with interesting imports like Portuguese reds, while also carefully selecting a range of pricier bottles. There are always good closeout specials, especially of Burgundies. The clerks know the wines and will be happy to gab about any of them; they hold special tastings and send out a chatty newsletter with special dinners and wine-tasting events. The East Bay supports a number of small independent wine stores, with years of experience behind their buying, that specialize in first-rate personal service. North Berkeley Wine Company is one of them.

1505 Shattuck Avenue, Berkeley
Tel: 510-848-8910
Open Monday through Saturday 11 a.m. to 7 p.m.
Credit cards: MC, V

ODD LOTS

The force behind this modest shop, Morgan Miller, has been in the wine trade for over twenty years. He has a great palate and tremendous knowledge, so he is able to pick up off-year vintages from excellent producers at bargain prices and pass them on to his customers. Wines in the store come from all over the world: Australia, Spain, Italy, small châteaux in Bordeaux. He understands the merits of a good neglected vintage in the middle of two greater ones, like 1987 Burgundies sandwiched between the great '85s and the excellent '88s. As he told me, he finds the wines that have fallen through the cracks of the wine market and offers them at small markups, especially wines wholesaled by Grape Expectations, who have represented and imported some of the best bottles from Europe over the years.

1025 San Pablo Avenue, Albany
Tel: 510-526-0522
Open Tuesday through Friday 11 a.m. to 7 p.m., Saturday 10 a.m. to 5 p.m.
Credit cards: MC, V

PAUL MARCUS WINES

Market Hall,
5655 College Avenue,
Oakland
Tel: 510-420-1005
Open Monday through
Friday 10 a.m. to 8 p.m.,
Saturday until 7 p.m.,
Sunday until 6 p.m.

1784 Fourth Street, Berkeley
Tel: 510-526-9093
open daily
10 a.m. to 6:30 p.m.
Credit cards: MC, V

Service is the thing at this small but very useful wine stall in the Market Hall, and now in the Pasta Shop on Fourth Street in Berkeley. The selection of wines here is personal and exciting, with a large section of wines well under $8 and a bunch of more expensive ones, particularly from small California producers and Italy. I spied tasty Rhônes from Château de Fonsalette and some swanky but not outrageous ports, Sauternes, and Champagnes. Lots of people walk out with cases. While you won't find the cheapest prices here, what you will find is enlightened selection, a bit of wine education, and a lot of friendly chitchat about what everyone is having for dinner. The vibes are great.

VINO

6319 College Avenue,
Oakland
Tel: 510-652-6317
Open Monday through
Saturday 10 a.m. to 7 p.m.,
Sunday 11 a.m. to 6 p.m.
Credit cards: MC, V

If you're looking for some outstanding buys on imported and California wines, check out Vino, a small store now owned by longtime wine importer Mike Temple. He knows how to choose the best bottles from the best small importers in the Bay Area. Recently the store boasted a deep collection of Oregon wines, the luscious pinot noirs and pinot blancs. As at Odd Lots, which Temple also owns, you can find tasty wines at closeout prices. With so much competition for the wine dollar these days, and such a mind-boggling collection of wines from all over the world, a small, expertly run, price-sensitive store like this can be a real boon.

COOKWARE AND BOOKS

BLACK OAK BOOKS

This independent bookstore has a large section of new and used cookbooks and an active program of visiting authors. Since it's practically next door to Chez Panisse, you can browse the shelves until it's time for your reservation. Its proximity to the destination food stores and restaurants nearby has raised its cookbook consciousness, so you will always be able to find many books by local authors as well as the classics.

1491 Shattuck Avenue, Berkeley
Tel: 510-486-0698
Open daily 10 a.m. to 10 p.m.
Credit cards: AE, MC, V

CODY'S

This may be one of the most complete bookstores in the world and one with the best service. If Cody's does not have the book you need on their shelves, they'll track it down for you. The clerks know an astounding amount about what is available on any subject. The cookbook section is one of the most complete and up to date because Cody's buyer loves and knows cookbooks. As in so many other areas of culinary interest, Berkeley has the stellar resource, and Cody's is it.

2454 Telegraph Avenue, Berkeley
Tel: 510-845-7852
Open daily 10 a.m. to 10 p.m.
Credit cards: MC, V

THE GARDENER

This enchanting store, constantly recreated by Alta Tingle, has the most unpredictable treasures for the house and garden. They might take the form of certain cookbooks, on rice perhaps; or sumptuous, brightly dyed cotton tablecloths from India, backed with material, trimmed and hand sewn; or market bags; or serving platters in the most arresting shapes and materials. You might find hand-forged iron candleholders or the perfect hand-painted dining room cabinet. There might be an outdoor picnic table and umbrella. The stock is ever changing and every item gives pause. Tingle has

1836 Fourth Street, Berkeley
Tel: 510-548-4545
Open Monday through Saturday 10 a.m. to 6 p.m., Thursday until 7 p.m., Sunday 11 a.m. to 6 p.m.
Credit cards: AE, MC, V

an infallible instinct for beautiful, down-to-earth objects that are always useful and well made. Whenever I'm in the neighborhood, having a bite at O Chamé next door, I stroll through the shop to see what I will be buying for the next year, for my friends and myself.

SUR LA TABLE

1806 Fourth Street,
Berkeley
Tel: 510-849-2252
Open Monday through Saturday 9 a.m. to 6 p.m.,
Thursday until 7 p.m., Sunday 9:30 a.m. to 6 p.m.
Credit cards: AE, D, MC, V
See listing, page 156.

Marin County

RESTAURANTS

BISTRO ALSACIENNE

Fritz Frankel, one of the most beloved maître d's in the city, has endowed a number of famous restaurants with European professionalism, elegance, and that warm smile of his. Most recently he opened his own place, Bistro Alsacienne, a cozy wood-paneled restaurant (that used to house Giramonti) with a view of Richardson Bay. Frankel decorated with lace curtains and knickknacks, and the bistro looks exactly like a country restaurant in Alsace. The menu offers some real regional dishes, such as the most divine schnitzel, a thin slice of pork or veal coated with bread crumbs and fried in butter to a breathtaking degree of buttery crispness. Served with long-simmered red cabbage and mashed potatoes, it may be one of my all-time favorite plates of comfort food anywhere. Also wonderful is L'Alsacienne's *choucroute,* long-braised sauerkraut full of flavor, topped with white sausages made by a German butcher in Santa Rosa, roast and smoked pork loin, and a few boiled potatoes. The combination of melting cabbage and smoky pork makes for pure pleasure, especially with a bottle of light, fruity German red wine called Ruppertsberger, perfect with the food and very reasonable in price. The house-made pâtés are also tasty.

655 Redwood Highway, Mill Valley
Tel: 389-0921
Open Tuesday through Sunday 5 to 9:30 p.m.
Price: Moderate
Credit cards: AE, MC, V

BUBBA'S

566 San Anselmo Avenue,
San Anselmo
Tel: 459-6862
Open Wednesday through
Monday 8 a.m. to 2 p.m.;
dinner nightly 5:30 to 9 p.m.,
Friday and Saturday
until 9:30 p.m.
Price: Inexpensive
Credit cards: AE, D, MC, V

Stephen Simmons, who worked with Brad Ogden for seven years, left the fold to take over a small authentic diner in sleepy downtown San Anselmo with his wife Elizabeth. He serves breakfast, lunch, and dinner; the menus for all three meals are listed on the paper place mats. Simmons has pared down his presentations radically, but that certainly hasn't diminished his Zenlike care and skill in the kitchen. There he is behind the counter, meticulously sautéing fresh green beans and corn, tasting a bean for doneness, while cooking pork chops smothered in vinegary cabbage, which he places on a plate next to sublime mashed potatoes. Next to him, his assistant takes apart heads of iceberg lettuce as if he were doing brain surgery, stacking the curled leaves in a pile and drizzling them with an exemplary Thousand Island dressing. A chopped salad turns out to be a colorful pile of grilled vegetables brushed with garlic oil and seasoned with a few drops of vinegar. Fried green tomato slices get a crunchy egg batter and a shot of vinegar for seasoning. It works. Real homemade chicken broth is loaded with diced celery, carrots, soft noodles, and chicken breast—a child's dream. I particularly like the hamburgers, thick and full of flavor, slathered with house-made mayonnaise and served on flavorful whole wheat buns. For dessert, have a slice of freshly baked apple pie with a slab of ice cream on top; the crust is a classic diner crumbly crust; the filling, long cooked.

This little place, with counter seats and some small booths, is the diner from heaven. The waitresses, in vintage bowling shirts, are as cheerful and efficient as any Happy Days walk-ons. Simmons and his assistant work carefully, keeping their kitchen immaculate and appetizing. With prices at true diner level, this authentic but unusually well-prepared American short-order food is certainly worth a special detour, and the lines are already forming at breakfast and lunch. Everything you ever wanted on a diner menu is offered, but without the usual complement of grease and canned food. This clean approach might be anathema for some die-hard greasy-spoon fans, but Bubba's certainly satisfied me.

FRANTOIO

At Frantoio, you can witness the sexiest culinary rite of passage in the Mediterranean world just across the bay in Mill Valley. At this large, bustling restaurant on the order of Il Fornaio, locally harvested green and black olives are transformed into precious extra-virgin olive oil by a state-of-the-art olive oil press located behind a window at one end of the dining room. During the day from late December through February, you can observe the whole process and taste the results.

Growers from all over Northern California bring olives they never bothered to harvest before—Manzanillo, Sevillano, Picholine, Mission—to see what kind of oil they will make. First, the crates of olives are poured into a machine that sprays them with water and shakes away the leaves. Then the olives are slowly fed into the grinder, two massive granite wheels that crush the fruit and pits into a rough paste, which is evenly spread by hand onto round mats and stacked on a spindle between steel plates. A water-driven hydraulic press gently squeezes out the oil and the water. You can see the liquid sensually dripping off the sides and being channeled into a centrifuge, which sends the pure oil into one bucket and the olive water into another. This is the moment to ask if you can have a taste from the golden stream of oil slowly dripping into a pail.

If the owner of the olives being pressed at the moment gives the nod, you will be able to taste a food that radiates raw energy, that dances on your tongue. Put your nose to the brand new oil and then sip it from a spoon, noisily drawing the oil through your teeth with air the way the experts do. Sensations will hit your mouth, starting with the fruitiness of the olives, then the subtle smell of perhaps almonds or apples, then the buttery, unctuous texture, and finally a hot and peppery jolt.

Compare this just-extracted oil to slightly older oils. Frantoio sets its tables with cruets of its own new-press olive oil (my favorite being their Sevillano). You'll learn firsthand that each oil has its own character, which like wine is due to geography, soil differences, the age and variety of the trees,

---

152 Shoreline Highway,
Mill Valley
Tel: 289-5777
Open for lunch Monday through Saturday 11:30 a.m. to 3 p.m.; dinner Monday through Saturday 5:30 to 10 p.m., Sunday 5 to 10 p.m.
Price: Moderate
Credit cards: AE, DC, D, MC, V

the blend of the olives that go into the press, and, of course, the method and cleanliness of the pressing. At Frantoio during the olive harvest, you will get to experience something afforded very few Americans, a taste of traditionally extracted, cold-pressed, locally grown, extra-virgin olive oil.

The restaurant is as professionally run as the olive oil press, with a crowd-pleasing Italian menu strong on pasta dishes and antipasti, and a first-rate, affordable Italian wine list. Prices are refreshingly moderate given the handsome modern dining room and a European level of service.

INSALATA'S

120 Sir Francis Drake Boulevard, San Anselmo
Tel: 457-7700
Open for lunch Monday through Saturday 11:30 a.m. to 2:30 p.m.; dinner Sunday through Thursday 5:30 to 9 p.m., Friday and Saturday until 10 p.m.; take-out Monday through Saturday 11 a.m. to 7 p.m., Sunday 11 a.m. to 5 p.m.; cafe open daily 7 a.m. to 3 p.m.
Price: Moderate
Credit cards: MC, V

When Heidi Insalata Krahling—a veteran of Square One, the chef at Perry Butler's former restaurant in Mill Valley, and one of the most generous contributors to community causes that I know—decided to open her own restaurant, the food mavens started buzzing. That the restaurant turned out to be in downtown San Anselmo caused some disappointment, but Insalata's location in Marin makes sense. The fact is that San Francisco is overrun with stylish, well-designed, professionally managed Mediterranean restaurants, while Marin County did not have one of the quality and vivacity of Insalata's. So from the moment it opened, this spacious, freestanding restaurant (surrounded by convenient parking) with high ceilings, an open kitchen, a take-out counter, an attractive little wine bar, tables on several levels, and an ebullient yellow paint job outside and in, was doing turn-away business. Most brand new restaurants falter under this kind of pressure, but Heidi Krahling and her experienced crew maintained control. As of this writing, I've had two absolutely marvelous meals there, and I'm eager to return for more of the Moroccan- and Tunisian-inspired dishes, in particular. Insalata's brings depth, integrity, and personality to a restaurant form that has become boilerplate in the Bay Area.

At Insalata's you can begin with *fattoush*, a Syrian salad of romaine tossed with feta, olives, and croutons of cracker bread in a lemon-mint vinaigrette, all of which melts together to form a creamy dressing. The different salads on the

Mediterranean platter—carrot, beet, rice, asparagus, mussel—sparkle. They taste bright, fresh, alive. I've had too many identical pasta dishes from one restaurant to the next, but Insalata's shell pasta bathed in a garlicky broccoli rabe "pesto" with white beans and Parmesan had an intriguing edge. It was a wonderful dish. I've eaten my way through buttery Catalan-style short ribs glazed in sherry, orange, and chocolate sauce on a bed of potato-celery root puree; a Tunisian Seven Vegetable *tagine* on couscous with *harissa*; a thick, moist pork chop with winter vegetables; and thin slices of rosy lamb sirloin on soft polenta with grilled vegetables and salsa verde. Prices are amazingly reasonable for these generous dishes—from $8.75 to $13. Even with wine and dessert, which isn't quite as stunning yet as the rest of the food, a meal rarely exceeds $35 a person.

At one point during my last visit, I noticed that we had collected on the table a delightful Cloudy Bay sauvignon blanc from New Zealand, a spectacular Chateau Musar from the Bekaa Valley in Lebanon, and Tunisian, Moroccan, Spanish, and Italian dishes. A world-beat assemblage had been created by this postmodern restaurant in San Anselmo across the street from a suburban shopping center, which puts Insalata's on the cutting edge of the Bay Area experience.

KASBAH

The Lahlou brothers, born in Casablanca and raised in Marrakech, cook and run the dining rooms of Kasbah, Marin County's (and arguably the Bay Area's) best Moroccan restaurant. They perform in an evocatively Moroccan-looking adobe building with two tented, carpeted dining rooms filled with low brass tables, banquettes, and soft lighting, immersing their diners in the North African experience. Having just returned from Morocco where I was practically submerged, I can attest to the fact that they are succeeding.

For a mere $21.50 a person you get an enticing Moroccan feast prepared with good ingredients (the kitchen is committed to using naturally raised chicken and lamb, organic rabbits, and organic vegetables whenever possible), which is not

200 Merrydale Road (North San Pedro exit from 101), San Rafael
Tel: 472-6666
Open for lunch Tuesday through Friday 11:30 a.m. to 2 p.m.; dinner Tuesday through Sunday 5:30 to 10 p.m.
Price: Inexpensive
Credit cards: AE, MC, V

overwhelming and tastes fresh and authentic. After hand washing (you hold your hands under a stream of water poured by the waiter into a brass basin) comes *harira*, a thin aromatic lentil soup served with lemon that prepares your palate for the spices to come. A hand-painted platter of Moroccan salads, always the most delicious part of the meal for me, must be devoured communally with fingers and pieces of house-baked Moroccan bread. A crisp and savory *b'stilla* (chicken pie wrapped in filo) comes next, another high point of a Moroccan meal, and then your choice of main course. I always opt for the rabbit *tagine* in a deep paprika-laced sauce; the honeyed lamb *tagine* with almonds; or the wonderful *tagine* of little meat balls called *kefta* topped with a poached egg. Dessert is simple, a plate of house-baked cookies with sweet mint tea.

A small wine list offers refreshingly inexpensive bottles—a Minervois from southeast France, a Vinho Verde from Portugal, the local McDowell Grenache Rosé—chosen specifically to match the food. The whole experience, whether you order a la carte or have the full course dinner, is a testament to the kitchen's sense of proportion and light touch. A meal at Kasbah sits comfortably in the stomach. In fact, you will want to return to order the dishes you had to pass up.

LARK CREEK INN

234 Magnolia Avenue,
Larkspur
Tel: 924-7766
Open for lunch Monday through Friday 11:30 a.m. to 1:45 p.m.; Sunday brunch 10 a.m. to 2 p.m.; dinner Monday through Thursday 5:30 to 9:15 p.m., Friday and Saturday 5 to 9:45 p.m., Sunday until 8:45 p.m.
Price: Expensive
Credit cards: AE, DC, MC, V

Lark Creek Inn used to be the only culinary reason for visiting Marin, as far as I was concerned, and it still ranks as a most compelling one. This great American restaurant started by Brad Ogden seven years ago, and now capably run day to day by talented young chef Todd Davies, aims high and delivers on all levels without being stuffy or formal, tones unacceptable to casual Marinites. In fact, visiting Lark Creek is pure fun. Everything that comes to the table, from the basket of warm house-baked breads and corn sticks to the big homey desserts, appeals to Americans' deepest appetites. People devour plates of vine-ripened tomatoes in creamy onion dressing; baskets of crisply fried calamari and clams with a peppery garlic mayonnaise; hearty Yankee pot roast with lots of gravy, airy onion dumplings, and an array of roasted root vegetables; deep bowls of tender braised pork shoulder with white beans and kale; juicy spit-roasted chicken with chive-flecked mashed potatoes and ears of white corn; and plate-sized grilled lamb steaks with fresh peas and irresistible scalloped potatoes and turnips. Even something as esoteric as ravioli stuffed with shredded ham hock in a roasted tomato broth has a down-home feel to it. For dessert, expect fresh fruit pies with house-made ice creams; fruit compotes with crème fraîche; shortcakes; butterscotch pudding; and spectacular versions of homemade pastries like a many-layered banana cake with mashed bananas and tons of frosting between the layers.

The cheerful yellow dining rooms, housed in a converted Victorian mansion set among towering redwood trees, are flooded with light from windows and skylights, and the service is both friendly and professional, a rare combination north of the Golden Gate Bridge. One of the nicest sights in the main dining room is the redbrick wood-burning oven out of which come aromatic stews, suckling pigs, and roast chickens. Other seating alternatives are an outdoor patio shaded by the gigantic trees, a natural form of air-conditioning necessary in this hot pocket of the bay, and a separate bar-cafe room where you can order from a bar menu or the regular one when you feel like dropping in at the spur of the moment.

All the details here ring true: the all–West Coast wine list with tons of interesting bottles from small producers (no bargains here, but lots of treats); thick, rustic pottery plates and serving dishes that suit the hearty food; thin, simple wineglasses that help you taste a wine; and lots of staff to make sure that everything runs smoothly. Ogden knows what really counts in a restaurant. He's a midwestern boy (raised in upper Michigan) who believes in substance. As a midwestern girl (suburban Chicago), I am 100 percent on the same wavelength. This is one of the few restaurants that both my mother and I agree on. I love it for its inventiveness and charm within an American context; she loves it for the pot roast.

LEFT BANK

507 Magnolia Avenue,
Larkspur
Tel: 927-3331
Open Monday 11:30 a.m. to
10 p.m., Tuesday through
Thursday 11:30 a.m. to
11 p.m., Friday and
Saturday until midnight,
Sunday 11:30 a.m. to 10 p.m.
Price: Moderate
Credit cards: AE, MC, V

Roland Passot, the genial chef-owner of the well regarded La Folie in the city, opened this vibrant bistro in a historic old hotel in downtown Larkspur, the Blue Rock Inn. To me, the classic, homey bistro fare he's serving here represents his true calling. The food at Left Bank is as straightforward and traditional as the cooking at La Folie is complicated and eclectic. I would be happy to eat every day at Left Bank, driving across the Golden Gate Bridge to sit outside on the covered veranda at a marble table at the center of Larkspur. I'd have a meal like the ones I get in Paris: tender leeks vinaigrette, a savory salad of frisée with lardoons of bacon topped with a poached egg; or a tomato salad in vinaigrette sprinkled with basil; then move on to a steak *frites;* superb coq au vin served in its own casserole; or *poulet grand-mère,* also in casserole, but braised with tons of julienned vegetables and finished with a little cream. Passot knows the technique behind these dishes inside and out; he can do them in his sleep, and the result is so rewarding, so satisfying, so completely there in flavor, texture, and appearance you want to cancel your flight to France. His portions are huge; his prices very reasonable. Customers get a bargain. Drink a bottle of California Rhône-style red from Qupé; have a warm *clafouti* or some *profiteroles* filled with ice cream in a pool of warm chocolate sauce for dessert; finish with an espresso. Have a cigarette. Just kidding. The whole meal is so French that I get carried away.

The airy interior of the restaurant, with a long bar and several rooms with banquettes and tables covered with white linen and butcher paper, has been cleanly remodeled, but the soul of Left Bank comes from its outdoor terraces. The weather is so clement in this particular part of Marin that you can sit outside on almost any sunny day of the year, especially when the heat lamps are switched on to take away the chill. The oversized French silverware, the little blue bowls of coarse salt on the table, the wicker chairs, the French mustard jars, those marvelous stone pillars supporting the red-tiled roof over the veranda, add immeasurably to the pleasure of eating anything, particularly right here in Marin County.

BRAISED LEEKS

This dish is easy to make in advance and is a good starter. Roland Passot's leek oil adds a glamorous touch.

Trim the ends of the green top of the leeks, then cut 2 inches off the green top and reserve. Slit the leeks lengthwise but leave the very ends attached. Cut off the root and soak the leeks in water for 10 minutes to remove sand. Put the leeks in a large saucepan and cover with the water, lemon juice, and flour. Bring to a boil and simmer until tender, 4 to 6 minutes depending on the width of the leeks. Drain and plunge the leeks into a bowl of ice water to stop the cooking. When cool, drain and dry.

Wash and dry the reserved green leek tops and coarsely chop them. Put 1/2 cup chopped leek greens in a food processor with 1/4 cup olive oil and puree. You should have a bright green liquid. Season with salt and pepper and set aside.

Make a vinaigrette by whisking together the mustard, sherry vinegar, and the remaining 3 tablespoons olive oil. Season with salt and pepper.

In a bowl, gently coat the leeks with the vinaigrette. Place the leeks on serving plates. Drizzle leek oil around the circumference and top the leeks with minced parsley.

Serves 4 as a first course

Note: Chef Passot cuts yellow and red cherry tomatoes of the same size in half and reassembles the tomatoes so they have two tones. He garnishes the plates with these.

12 to 16 small to medium leeks
4 cups water
Juice of 1 lemon
1 teaspoon flour
1/4 cup plus 3 tablespoons olive oil
Kosher salt and freshly ground pepper
   to taste
1 tablespoon Dijon mustard
1 tablespoon sherry vinegar
Minced fresh parsley for garnish

RICE TABLE

**1617 Fourth Street,
San Rafael
Tel: 456-1808
Open Wednesday through
Saturday 5:30 to 10 p.m.,
Sunday 5 to 9 p.m.
Price: Moderate
Credit cards: MC, V**

The Rice Table has been one of my favorite restaurants for years. The chef, the late Leonie Hool, personally cooked each of the myriad dishes that make up the lush Indonesian rice table with uncommon love and attention. One rarely gets to taste authentic home-cooked ethnic food, but at the Rice Table customers felt as if they had been invited to Ms. Hool's own dining room. The food had the freshness and integrity of family cooking.

Five years ago Leonie Hool died suddenly of a stroke. In shock, her family closed the restaurant, but about six months later her son and daughter-in-law reopened it with an inherited passion to prepare and serve genuine Indonesian food. In fact, they had worked with Ms. Hool for years, learning her recipes and assisting her in the kitchen. Recent visits have produced the same full-flavored, carefully prepared dishes that always have been the hallmark of this unique place. When a family believes in a tradition, they can carry it on. Ms. Hool's love of her native cuisine continues to be expressed in the cozy rattan-lined restaurant she started.

The menu is short and simple. There are only eleven dishes on it and you get all of them on the Rice Table Special, a bargain at $19.95 for a feast so large that it arrives in waves. The meal starts with three extraordinary *sambals*, or dipping sauces, with shrimp chips. The vitality of the *sambals* tells you right off that everything, including condiments and curries, will be made from scratch. One *sambal* is a creamy warm peanut sauce spiked with chilies and ginger. The second is a medium-hot, vinegary fresh green chili and onion salsa; the third, a searing-hot red chili paste, completes the hotness spectrum. Then, a bowl of soothing celery-scented dal-like split pea soup arrives. The deluge begins with crisp thumb-sized *lumpia*, or spring rolls; fabulous Indonesian coleslaw dressed with tiny threads of orange zest and fresh mint leaves; and a salad of crunchy bean sprouts with chopped peanuts.

Next come the satays: chicken in a complex teriyaki-like sauce; pork in a creamy peanut. Then the stir fries: shrimp with fruity tamarind seeds, an enchanting dish; whole button mushrooms stir fried with hot red chilies, a startlingly good dish. Then braises: a delicious beef stew called *semur* that seduces you with the sweet bouquet of cloves; a mild chicken curry with the subtle richness of fresh coconut milk. When you think the table can't hold any more, a crab and bean sprout pancake, kind of an Indonesian egg foo young in a perky sweet-and-sour sauce, is wedged in. Condiments—toasted coconut, pickled vegetables, cold deep-fried potato sticks coated in hot red chili paste—can be scattered on the curries, stews, and two kinds of fragrant rice: yellow saffron and nutty white basmati. The strategy is to mound a big pile of both rices in the middle of your plate and arrange little piles of the different foods around it. Finally, fried thin rice noodles, lushly sauced and studded with bits of pork and vegetables, banish any remaining hunger at the end of the meal. The problem is that the noodles are so tasty you could make a meal of them alone.

Dessert brings creamy deep-fried bananas sprinkled with powdered sugar; you order a second—even after all that food. Cinnamon-scented Indonesian coffee helps you rise from the table.

I feel almost giddy when I encounter a restaurant that is able to keep up its purity, energy, and spirit year after year, especially when the original chef's passion has been passed on from one generation to the next. Like all the Rice Table's longtime customers, I have been nourished, delighted, and embraced by the restaurant to such a degree that its success and well being feel like my own. As with all great restaurants, the Rice Table's best patrons have become part of an extended family.

CAFES

BOOK PASSAGE CAFE

See Cookware and Books, page 523.

PASTICCERIA RULLI

464 Magnolia Avenue,
Larkspur
Tel: 924-7478
Open Monday through
Friday 7 a.m. to 7 p.m.,
Saturday 7:30 a.m. to 7 p.m.,
Sunday 7:30 a.m. to 5 p.m.
No credit cards

This authentic, elegant Italian pastry shop and cafe is mentioned in many categories, because Pasticceria Rulli performs every part of Italian sweet and coffee service brilliantly. After a thoroughly French lunch at Left Bank, walk down the street to Rulli for a hit of Northern Italy. Have dessert and coffee at the marble tables, indoors or out, surrounded by hand-painted murals and beautiful dark wood paneling. Many informed clerks—efficient, helpful, smiling true professionals—work the counter, pulling out goodies from a sparkling glass case full of luscious cream cakes with names like Brasiliana (a chocolate sponge cake brushed with espresso liqueur, filled with whipped cream, and covered with chocolate shavings) and San Francesco (baked meringue filled with fresh fruit and pastry cream, topped with whipped cream and crumbled toasted meringue). The most elegant possible versions of *sacripantina* and St. Honore cakes, the staples of North Beach, are made here with all-butter puff pastry, the tenderest sponge cake soaked with fine wines and spirits, and freshly made custard. You can buy these dreamy cream cakes by the slice or whole. Above the cakes is a shelf of tiny cookies, fresh and crisp, like miniature *palmiers* (palm leaf–shaped cookies made of puff pastry glazed with sugar), amaretti, hazelnut balls, and meringues dipped in chocolate. You need to taste Pasticceria Rulli's version of Italian cookies to appreciate how unique they are, crumbly with bread crumbs or ground nuts, full of interesting flavors, often dense, but meltingly tender. You can choose a little sampler of them to eat with some of the cafe's superb coffee, among the best I've had here or in Italy. When you decide which cookies you adore, you can have the clerks pack an exquisite box of them to take home or give as a gift with a pound of Pasticceria Rulli's house-roasted coffee beans. For ice-cream lovers, house-made *sorbetti* and *gelati,* made with natural essences and fresh fruits, are scooped into tiny cones or glass dishes. Or, you might be tempted by Rulli's satiny hand-dipped chocolates. There's such an embarrassment of riches here you don't know which way to turn. This *pasticceria* was founded by the son of a famous Turin pastry maker, and why he settled in Larkspur, I can't imagine. The place belongs on a chic alley off Union Square. It's a completely first-class operation offering the world of Italian sweets at the highest level of quality. Marin doesn't deserve Rulli. I want them in the city!

BARS

GUAYMAS

5 Main Street,
Tiburon
Tel: 435-6300
Open Monday through
Saturday 11:30 a.m.
to 9:30 p.m.,
Sunday 10:30 a.m.
to 9:30 p.m.
Credit cards: AE, MC, V

There are far, far worse hours you can spend than those lounging on the sunny deck of Guaymas, right on the water, drinking fresh-lime margaritas and dunking chips into three appealing house-made salsas. This massive, airy restaurant, done in blonde wood, red tile, white adobe, and bright yellow furniture, reminds me of dining rooms in Mexican resorts during high season when everyone is on the American plan: three meals included in the price of a room and everyone eating at the same time. The place roars and the kitchen does its best to keep up. Still, the location of this Spectrum restaurant can't be beat, and Guaymas's long menu offers lots of tasty tidbits that go with drinks. If you bike over from the city, which isn't all that difficult, believe it or not, you can take the ferry back to Fisherman's Wharf. It loads on a dock right next to Guaymas.

SAM'S

27 Main Street,
Tiburon
Tel: 435-4527
Open Monday through
Thursday 11 a.m. to 10 p.m.,
Friday until 10:30 p.m.,
Saturday 10 a.m. to
10:30 p.m., Sunday
9:30 a.m. to 10 p.m.
Credit cards: AE, DC, D, MC, V

All the old salts dock their boats at Sam's and climb up the ramp onto the huge outdoor deck with a great view for a cold beer and a hamburger. The food is of absolutely no consequence here, but seats on the deck in this protected corner of the bay are much coveted and feel very good after beating into the wind to get there. After a few Bloody Marys, neither the trip nor the food seems so bad. Many sailors like me consider Sam's to be the high point of a typical day on the bay.

DELICATESSENS/TAKE-OUT

DAVID'S PRODUCE/DAVID'S TAQUERIA

See Produce, page 517.

"HAMBURGERS"

For those of you taking the ferry ride over to Sausalito from San Francisco, the preferred place to grab a bite is at the nameless hamburger joint with a round charcoal grill in the window and the line out the door. I don't know why or how, but these big, juicy, fire-licked burgers taste better than any others. Get some fries and lots of napkins and eat in the aquatic park across the street. These hamburgers rank with the best food you can find in this charming, if touristy, little village. You have to take them to go—there are maybe two unpleasant tables squeezed in the back of the room, but the weather in this protected part of the bay is usually mild.

737 Bridgeway,
Sausalito
Tel: 332-9471
Open daily 11 a.m. to 5 p.m.
No credit cards

ULTRA LUCCA

For other locations, see page 476.

This very complete and excitingly merchandised Italian delicatessen is one of five branches in the Bay Area, an empire started over forty years ago on 40th Street and Telegraph Avenue in Oakland. The Oakland mother ship makes all the salads, pastas, and sauces for the small chain, and I must say they do a rather good job. The fresh, small, cheese ravioli have pure white fillings of blended cheeses and are particularly tasty strewn with Ultra Lucca's well-made bolognese sauce. The cheese department always has some special, non-Italian selections, like a stunning aged Cheddar called Grafton Reserve, as sharp, nutty and buttery as any I've tasted. The real strength of Ultra Lucca is that they stock a full Italian pantry, starting with wines, waters, and Torani syrups; moving on to real imported buffalo-milk mozzarella balls; Reggiano Parmesan ($14.75/pound); Fontina Val d'Aosta ($13.99/pound), and manchego; tons of salads, house-made sausages, prosciutto from Parma ($19.99/ pound), and other

107 Corte Madera
Town Center,
Corte Madera
Tel: 927-4347
Open Monday through
Saturday 10 a.m. to 7 p.m.,
Sunday until 6 p.m.
Credit cards: MC, V

cured meats; olives; some first-rate Italian and Spanish olive oils (Lerida, L'Estornell), semolina flour, polenta, Arborio rice, fresh pasta, the highest-quality dried pasta from Rustichella d' Abruzzo (which is made on ancient machines with the hardest wheat flour), mascarpone, and fresh breads from all over the bay. This is one-stop Italian shopping and Ultra Lucca stocks the best. In the Corte Madera Town Center store, you can sit at a table by the front window with a made-to-order sandwich or plates of salads and antipasti.

The service is extraordinary. When your number comes up, which doesn't take long because the stores are so well staffed, a clerk will spend as much time as you need, patiently giving you tastes of cheeses, cutting the smallest amounts, fixing the most finicky sandwiches, carefully slicing each salami and ham. Though prices are high, you get exactly what you want in decent condition. As in most other cheese departments, their precut, prewrapped cheeses often take on the aroma of the refrigerator, but we don't live in a perfect world. Nonetheless, Ultra Lucca does make it a better one.

BAKERIES

PASTICCERIA RULLI

See Cafes, page 512.

ICE CREAM/CHOCOLATES

LYLA'S CHOCOLATES

Lyla's luscious handmade chocolates fall somewhere between See's and Godiva, and they earn extra marks for invention. The peanut butter swirls, rich milk chocolate with creamy peanut butter mixed in, or peanut butter frogs with centers of sweetened fresh peanut butter, will make Reese's Peanut Butter Cups pale by comparison. Lyla takes all sorts of American favorites—rocky road, honeycombs, caramels—and makes them with top-notch ingredients in small, rich, beautifully formed pieces, creating a unique line of elegant chocolates at their best. The store in Corte Madera sometimes puts two or three specially made tiny samples on the counter that will get you hooked. This candy shop is worth a special trip for the quality and interesting variety of its chocolates.

417 Miller Avenue,
Mill Valley
Tel: 383-8887
Open Monday through Friday 10 a.m. to 6 p.m., Saturday 10:30 a.m. to 5 p.m
Credit cards: MC, V

PASTICCERIA RULLI

See Cafes, page 512.

PRODUCE

DAVID'S PRODUCE/DAVID'S TAQUERIA

On one level, David Findlay's large produce market tries to emulate the great-granddaddy of them all, Monterey Produce in Berkeley, with outside tables and huge quantities of commercial and some organic fruits and vegetables, indoors and out. The variety doesn't approach what you can find in the East Bay, but David's features some good-quality produce at moderate prices. The bargains come prepackaged and marked "reduced."

Corte Madera
Town Center,
Corte Madera
Tel: 927-2431
Open daily 9 a.m. to 8 p.m.
No credit cards

What really sets David's apart are the products he makes out of produce, including a line of fresh juices that go far beyond tame orange and grapefruit to blends of fresh strawberry, apple and pineapple, pineapple and orange, and mango and orange, all pressed daily from fresh fruits. These come in three different sizes and are best drunk immediately to take advantage of their freshness. David's also makes some of the nicest Mexican salsas and guacamole around. Sold in half and whole pints, the guacamole tastes mostly of pure, ripe, creamy avocado seasoned with lime, cilantro, and onion, a simple formula that would make purists like Diana Kennedy happy—the only departure being the use of too much lime, which does keep the guacamole fresh and of good color. The tomato salsa is a classic too, just chopped tomato, lime, cilantro, onion, and chilies, and David makes an effort to get his hands on the flavorful tomatoes from local farmers when he can. A hot and a mild version of tomato salsa, a summer fruit salsa, and a sweet corn–tomato salsa are viable as building blocks of a meal. One reason the juices, salsas, and guacamole are so fresh is that they are kept really cold, buried in tables of crushed ice.

Finally, next door to the produce market, David's has opened a busy little taqueria that takes advantage of his salsa and guacamole factory. The integrity of the ingredients in a menu of take-out dishes such as soft tacos filled with grilled chicken, topped with shredded lettuce, salsa, and *queso fresco;* burritos; house-made tamales; and grilled half-chicken plates is high. However, the challenge of using a greater variety of the produce next door in some nonpredictable ways has yet to be taken.

MARIN COUNTY FARMERS' MARKET

Marin Civic Center, San Rafael
Thursdays and Sundays
8 a.m. to 1 p.m. year-round

This is one of the most vital farmers' markets in the Bay Area, much frequented by San Francisco cooks who live in the north end of the city until the Ferry Plaza Farmers' Market on the Embarcadero came along. A large market drawing many farmers of both organic and nonorganic produce in different price ranges, the Marin County market is known for its out-of-season, organic locally raised hothouse Wilgenburg tomatoes (people wait in line at the opening of the market to get them), dates, good medium-priced stone fruit in season, handicraft stalls, and lots of side events for kids. A strawberry farmer not only sells the fruit, but a refreshing strawberry cream sorbet made by his wife; an organic vegetable stand also sells natural wool, gathered from the sheep on the property. Each skein is a different color ranging from white to dark gray-brown; one could imagine a magical garment knitted from them. The Marin market has the luxury of space, so the stalls are spread out, and the variety and quality is large, concentrated mostly on produce with a little cheese, eggs, and some expensive, highly smoked salmon thrown into the mix.

CHEESE

THE CHEESE SHOP

This tiny, hidden-away shop is worth seeking out if you're a cheese lover. Owner Forrest Young has collected an eclectic group, which he keeps in top condition. A cheese expert, he knows how every cheese is made. He understands seasonality, the influence of locale, and the increased pleasure of eating cheeses when they are ripe and perfect. His attitude might seem prickly at first encounter, defensive somehow, as if he had had too many run-ins with customers who aren't serious about cheese, but once he sees you're a believer, the tastes are offered and the genealogies of the cheese explained. I came away with a Spanish cheese called Mahón, a nutty, buttery, slightly sharp cow's milk cheese made in the Balearic Islands (Minorca) and a wedge of tangy St.-André in perfect condition, both cut to specification. There's no prewrapping here, which keeps the cheese smelling more like cheese and less like plastic and refrigeration. Much information comes forth, if you're interested, with each cheese lovingly set on the

38 Miller Avenue,
Mill Valley
Tel: 383-7272
Open Tuesday through
Saturday 10 a.m. to 6 p.m.,
Sunday noon to 5 p.m.
Credit cards: D, MC, V

counter. Wines, baguettes from Bordenave's, and crackers fill up every inch of the wood-lined store all the way up to the ceiling. But cheese is the thing here, and Young's personal selections make the store interesting.

ULTRA LUCCA

See Delicatessens, page 515.

COFFEE

PASTICCERIA RULLI

See Cafes, page 512.

PEET'S COFFEE AND TEA

88 Throckmorton Avenue,
Mill Valley
Tel: 381-8227
Open Monday through Saturday 6 a.m. to 7 p.m.,
Sunday 7 a.m. to 6 p.m.
Credit cards: MC, V
See listing, page 199.

SPINELLI COFFEE COMPANY

Corte Madera Town Center,
Corte Madera
Tel: 927-0471
Open Monday through Friday 6:30 a.m. to 8 p.m.,
Saturday 7 a.m. to 7 p.m., Sunday 8 a.m. to 7 p.m.
Credit cards: MC, V
See listing, page 173.

WINES AND SPIRITS

MARIN WINE CELLAR

This large, air-conditioned wine warehouse behind a locked iron gate (you have to buzz to get in) is stacked floor to ceiling with cases of wine. A small desk with many phones and a wooden rack with some of the most amazing bottles you'll ever see are the only islands in the towering sea. At the back are wine lockers of private individuals. There must be $5 million worth of wine here, and it's traded mostly over the phone like a commodity (which it is, I guess). Harvey Buchbinder, the rotund, bearded, besandled partner of this operation calls wine collecting a rich man's sport. However, he says, certain classics are better investments than the stock market. I asked him if he knew the lineage of some of the blockbuster bottles I saw scattered around—where they came from, how they were cellared and shipped. He shrugged, and it made me wonder about the value of something like a 1918 Mouton Rothschild with an exquisite art deco label, listed at $1,395 (Visa, MasterCard, or American Express accepted). If you open it, what do you have? A dead liquid? A taste memory of the wine in whatever condition it happens to be, a period of anticipation, a trophy in the empty bottle? Displayed on the rack the day I was buzzed in were both 1935 and 1945 Lafites, the 1918 Mouton, and a 1955 Mouton with a beautiful Georges Braque label, a 1954 La Tâche, a bunch of magnums of 1989 Petrus—well, you get the idea. I asked Harvey who buys these wines. He told me that 98 percent of his business is done over the phone, all over the world. He has many private buyers in France, Switzerland, London, Mexico, and Hong Kong, and most sales involve single bottles—though he recently sent a case of '61 Latour ($8,400) to Barbra Streisand in Las Vegas. Harvey confided that he loves Vegas; that high rollers like big wines. He buys through auction and from private individuals and keeps a one-hundred-year back list for birthdays. When

2138 Fourth Street,
San Rafael
Tel: 459-3823
Open Tuesday through Friday 9 a.m. to 3 p.m. or by appointment
Credit cards: AE, MC, V

you visit the Marin Wine Cellar, if only to see millions of dollars of wine bottles piled up on top of each other, get a copy of the catalog, a fascinating document. You can price out a birth-year wine dinner, estimate the value of your own cellar, and actually find some affordable bottles from recent vintages. There's all sorts of fun to be had, but you take your chances here. To Harvey, every bottle is a crapshoot. You have to decide how much to lay down.

MILL VALLEY MARKET

12 Corte Madera Avenue,
Mill Valley
Tel: 388-3222
Open Monday through
Saturday 10 a.m. to
7:30 p.m., Sunday
9 a.m. to 7 p.m.
Credit cards: MC, V

An adjunct to the popular Mill Valley Market grocery store, this rustic wood-lined, red-tiled, air-conditioned wine cellar is stacked to the rafters with well-chosen California wines, often from such hard-to-find tiny producers as The Terraces and Sky Vineyard, both noteworthy for their Zinfandels, or Abreu Cabernet from Rick Forman. Top-of-the-line imports from Kermit Lynch, Diamond, and Italian wines from Estate are all present and accounted for. This is a Marin County outpost for the Bandols of Domaine Tempier. Finally, the shop has a good selection of specialty booze, lots of fancy tequilas, and Scotches.

COOKWARE AND BOOKS

A CLEAN WELL-LIGHTED PLACE FOR BOOKS

2417 Larkspur Landing Circle,
Larkspur
Tel: 461-0171
Open Sunday through Thursday 9 a.m. to 11 p.m.,
Friday and Saturday until midnight.
Credit cards: AE, MC, V
See listing, page 87.

BOOK PASSAGE

51 Tamal Vista Boulevard
(Market Place
Shopping Center),
Corte Madera
Tel: 927-0960
Open Sunday through
Thursday 10 a.m. to 10 p.m.,
Friday and Saturday
until 11 p.m.
Credit cards: AE, DC, D, MC, V

Anyone who travels should know about this excellent bookstore specializing in travel books and, hence, international restaurant and food guides. If you're going anywhere in the world, you will want to check out the guides, maps, and travel literature on your destination, if only to get an overview. You'll find hard-to-come-by restaurant guides like *Eating Out in Provence and the Côte d'Azur* by Edward Roch, Gaston Wijnen's *Discovering Paris Bistros,* and Faith Willinger's *Eating in Italy,* including restaurants, cafes, outdoor markets, wineries, bakeries, kitchenware shops, and picnic spots throughout Northern Italy. You can spend hours browsing the huge travel section, concocting trips and adventures you never even knew you wanted to take. When you tire of this, you can have a first-rate Illy Espresso espresso or cappuccino and a nice, light, health-foody, Marin County bite at the Book Passage Cafe in one corner of the bookstore near the magazine racks. The cafe gets special credit for using real plates, glasses, and silverware. Finally, Book Passage publishes a yearly catalog and newsletter, sixty-four pages long, with all sorts of information on which guides to buy for different parts of the world. If you're an omnivorous, international eater like me, you will find a trip to Book Passage essential before a trip out of town.

HOMECHEF

329 Corte Madera
Town Center,
Corte Madera
Tel: 927-3191
Open Monday through
Thursday 9:30 a.m. to
9 p.m., Friday and Saturday
9:30 a.m. until 7 p.m.,
Sunday 11 a.m. to 5 p.m.
Credit cards: AE, MC, V

See listing, page 331.

This branch has the advantage of having a large, airy shopping mall site so that the merchandise can be readily seen, examined, and plucked from attractive displays.

WILLIAMS-SONOMA

1802 Redwood Highway,
Corte Madera
Tel: 924-2940
Open weekdays 10 a.m. to 9 p.m.,
Saturday until 7:30 p.m., Sunday 11 a.m. to 6 p.m.
Credit cards: AE, MC, V
See listing, page 157.

The Wine Country of Napa & Sonoma

RESTAURANTS

ALL SEASONS CAFE AND WINE STORE

1400 Lincoln Avenue,
Calistoga
Tel: 707-942-9111
Open daily 9 a.m. to 10 p.m.;
lunch 11:30 a.m. to 3:30 p.m., dinner 5 to 10 p.m.
Price: Moderate
See Wine and Spirits, page 548.

BABETTE'S

464 First Street East,
Sonoma
Tel: 707-939-8921
Open Tuesday through Saturday 6:30 to 10 p.m.;
cafe open daily noon to 10 p.m.; call for winter hours.
Price: Wine bar/cafe: Inexpensive; Restaurant: Moderate to Expensive
Credit cards: MC, V

You're either charmed by Babette's, a passionate, personal statement from Chef Daniel Patterson and his partner Elizabeth Ramsey, or not. I happen to be wild about it. It reminds me of my first eight-table restaurant in a gerrymandered space in a residential building in Berkeley, equipped with a kitchen that most people wouldn't accept in the apartments upstairs. I cooked my heart out there. Babette's is much more sophisticated than my first venture, but it has that same organic, flea-market ambiance, and enough discipline behind it to transform the experience of dining there into a high pleasure. That an intimate, eccentric restaurant such as this even exists these days seems like a miracle.

Babette's is located down an alley next to the Sebastiani movie theater off the main square. The front part of the restaurant looks like a living room with couches, tables, and a small wine bar where people order light cafe fare and wines by the half and whole glass. In a separate room in the back, created by some artful draping of red upholstery fabric, people are presented with Babette's famous five-course prix-fixe meals available only on Thursday, Friday, and Saturday nights. You sit at white linen–covered tables on red hotel meeting room chairs. Everything on the table pleases—good silverware, glasses, simple white plates, wonderful soft/crusty rolls. Carefully chosen music plays in the background. The decor suggests comfort and luxury the way a cleverly designed Valencia Street cafe does. Though in the country, Babette's has recycled urban style.

Really, the ambiance becomes secondary when the beautiful food starts coming. You choose from three possibilities in each of five courses for $45. One night I began with a carpaccio of tissue-thin slices of scallop sprinkled with crunchy French sea salt, drops of new olive oil, and Meyer lemon—a brilliant dish. Then I wolfed down a delicious room-temperature marinated breast of quail on a salad of garden cress and quinoa in blood orange vinaigrette, followed by a crispy skate wing in brown butter sauce, followed by two delectable slices of duck breast rolled around a duck crepinette on a tiny pile of cabbage, bacon, and spiced apples. The $45 menu ended with Pico Picadine (creamy, aged goats' milk cheese) with a mâche salad. The portions were regulated so well that I easily polished off a divine coconut and banana napoleon with mango sauce; the pastry was so thin and crisp it melted in my mouth. With the meal we drank various glasses of wine: Etude Pinot Blanc; an Oregon *vin gris*; a wild, smoky Rhône from Alain Graillot; a Rhône-style cinsault from nearby Dry Creek. The meal showed such invention and good taste—such clarity of vision—that I now consider Babette's my destination restaurant in Sonoma. This place is a find, a treasure. Better get up there to eat now before naive Babette's turns into a high-concept version of Yountville's French Laundry.

BISTRO DON GIOVANNI

In a modern, barnlike space with tall windows that look out to a sea of vines and mountains in the distance, two expatriates from Piatti, Donna and Giovanni Scala, are cooking up a storm. Their winsome Italian fare includes thin-crusted wood-fired pizzas; fabulous deep-fried matchsticks of zucchini with Parmesan grated over them; and an antipasto of broccoli rabe sautéed with lots of garlic and Tuscan olive oil and draped with thin slices of fresh mozzarella. The pastas, such as thin, tender ravioli filled with ricotta in a delicate cream sauce flecked with lemon zest; or rustic handmade pappardelle in a juicy stew of braised rabbit, sage, and pancetta, are the high point of the menu. Focaccia sandwiches filled with grilled vegetables, slathered with lots of aïoli, and served with warm lattice potato chips are dreamy. Summery appetizers of large marinated shrimp grilled in the shell and served with a warm corn salad make for an appealing alfresco lunch on the broad wooden porch that rims the restaurant. Eating lunch outside near the herb garden is one of the pleasures of visiting the Napa Valley.

4110 St. Helena Highway (Highway 29), Napa
Tel: 707-224-3300
Open Sunday through Thursday 11:30 a.m. to 9:30 p.m., Friday and Saturday until 10 p.m.
Price: Moderate
Credit cards: AE, D, MC, V

BISTRO RALPH

Ralph Tingle, the chef-owner of this stunning-looking restaurant, happens to be the son of Alta Tingle, the creative genius behind The Gardener (see East Bay, page 499), who in turns happens to be a very good friend of conceptual artist David Ireland. (Ireland's seminal work was the stripping back of layers of paint and wallpaper in his turn-of-the-century Mission District house, treating the wadded-up peelings as art objects, then fixing the raw interior in varnish, making it look like a resonant, old Italian villa. Then he took the idea a step farther by using the stripped-away materials to make utilitarian objects like lamps.) Tingle enlisted Ireland's energy in designing her son's restaurant, and the result of their collaboration is one of the most compelling restaurant spaces in all of Northern California. Ireland's deconstructive inventiveness combined with Alta Tingle's intuitive understanding of materials created a room of surprising simplicity and beauty with completely unexpected

109 Plaza Street, Healdsburg
Tel: 707-433-1380
Open for lunch Monday through Friday 11:30 a.m. to 2:30 p.m., dinner nightly 5:30 to 10 p.m.
Price: Moderate
Credit cards: MC, V

forms, like a long, undulating wood and metal wine rack behind the counter and an entrance of raw concrete and steel. I like to be in this room at night when everything takes on a romantic Italian-villa glow, although it looks nothing like one.

The cooking can be uneven and quirky, but the whole-leaf Caesar is tasty and pretty, and I am fond of a spicy lamb burger made with local C. K. lamb and Downtown Bakery buns. Bistro Ralph is a destination, if only to experience the restaurant dining room as a work of art.

BROWN STREET GRILL

1300 Brown Street
(at Clinton),
Napa
Tel: 707-255-6395
Open for lunch Monday through Saturday 11:30 a.m. to 2:30 p.m.; dinner Monday through Thursday 5 to 9 p.m., Friday and Saturday until 9:30 p.m.
Price: Moderate
Credit cards: MC, V

My favorite spot in the town of Napa, the Brown Street Grill, turns home cooking into restaurant cuisine with a devotion not often found in either place. Formerly partners at the Diner in Yountville, the Brown Street husband-and-wife team of Nickie and Peter Zeller turns out thick, savory sandwiches of grilled ham and cheese or juicy roasted tomatoes with mozzarella. Their excellent roast chicken sets a standard, and the fresh, colorful, properly dressed salads sing. I have made a detour for the Gravenstein apple pie a la mode with its flaky, butter crust, followed by an excellent espresso. The friendly, low-key ambiance may not make this a glittering Valley destination, but if you crave lovely home-style food prepared by people who have high standards and good sense about what tastes right, you might want to seek this place out.

CATAHOULA RESTAURANT AND SALOON

1457 Lincoln Avenue,
Calistoga
Tel: 707-942-2275
Open weekdays (except Tuesdays) for lunch noon to 2:30 p.m., Saturday and Sunday noon to 3:30 p.m.; dinner Sunday through Thursday 5:30 to 10 p.m., Friday and Saturday until 10:30 p.m.
Price: Moderate to expensive

Calistoga, once a sleepy Napa Valley town best known for its hot springs and mud baths, has become the hot spot in the upper Valley. The latest evidence of Calistoga's transformation is Jan Birnbaum's Catahoula, a big-city restaurant with the latest in wood-burning ovens in the middle of the dining room, and a menu of updated American dishes that Birnbaum worked on when he was the chef at Campton Place in San Francisco. Catahoula is much more casual and fun than Campton Place, but the food is hardly homey. The plates, in many shapes, colors, and materials, are carefully arranged, and the combinations draw on the visual as much as the

GREEN ONION–CORN CAKES WITH SMOKED SALMON AND LEMON DILL SOUR CREAM

These corn cakes are a snap to mix up. The batter can be held in the refrigerator for 6 hours and then cooked. I top them with yogurt and eat about a dozen, but they are sublime topped with sour cream and smoked salmon, as they do at the Brown Street Grill.

Combine the cornmeal, salt, and boiling water in a medium bowl. Let stand for 10 minutes.

Melt 1 tablespoon of the butter. Beat the melted butter with the egg and milk, and add to the cornmeal mixture. Combine the flour and baking powder and stir into the cornmeal mixture until smooth. Do not overmix. Stir in green onions and corn.

Whisk together the sour cream, lemon juice, cream, dill, salt, and pepper.

In a large skillet over high heat, melt together the vegetable oil and the remaining 1 tablespoon butter. For each corn cake spoon about 2 tablespoons of batter into the pan and fry until the uncooked side starts to show bubbles. Turn. Cook until golden.

Drizzle with the sour cream mixture, top with a slice of smoked salmon, and serve at once.

Makes 8 cakes, serves 4 to 8 as a side dish

1/2 cup cornmeal
1/2 teaspoon kosher salt
1/2 cup boiling water
2 tablespoons butter
1 egg
1/2 cup milk
1/4 cup all-purpose flour
1 teaspoon baking powder
1/2 cup chopped green onions
1/4 cup sweet corn kernals
1 cup sour cream
2 tablespoons fresh lemon juice
1/4 cup heavy (whipping) cream
2 teaspoons minced fresh dill
Salt and pepper to taste
1 teaspoon vegetable oil
8 ounces good-quality smoked salmon, thinly sliced

---

flavorful. There might be a tasty duck *confit* salad with tangerines and blood oranges, or a tender-leafed green salad made with just-picked Forni-Brown greens in a mild Brazil nut vinaigrette. But sometimes the twists and turns taken to personalize the American menu work against the best interests of the food. Braised short ribs derive smokiness from the wood-burning oven, but they don't get tender enough; and sassafras and chipotle, just two of the flavors on the Sonoma lamb plate, have no real reason for being there. The best-looking thing to come out of the oven is a crusty herbed potato cake served with an oven-roasted free-range chicken.

A lively scene happens in the saloon across the lobby almost every evening, where people can order from a menu of "small plates": pizzas, crawfish tamales, salads, and richly topped flat breads. The informality here allows for real down-home food and Birnbaum's best efforts. You can sit at the bar or at counters, drink beer from small breweries, and taste local wines by the glass.

DOMAINE CHANDON

One California Drive,
Yountville
Tel: 707-944-2892
Open for lunch daily, May through October (closed Monday and Tuesday, November through April), 11:30 a.m. to 2:30 p.m.; dinner Wednesday through Sunday 6 to 9 p.m., Saturday until 9:30 p.m.
Price: Expensive
Credit cards: AE, DC, D, MC, V

Philippe Jeanty has been at the helm of this ambitious, very French dining room since it opened over eighteen years ago. As a California adjunct to the famous French Champagne house, Moctared Chandon, the intention was to bring a high-flying, rather formal French experience along with the prestigious name to the New World. The restaurant has achieved this. You can lunch outdoors on the terrace, sipping cold Domaine Chandon while you gaze at the vines, or dine indoors with sweeping views as well. The operation is large and multifaceted, and at its best, the food can evoke a meal taken in a one- or two-star restaurant in Burgundy. Provençal-accented fish and shellfish preparations go with white wines; sophisticated venison, lamb, and beef dishes with reds; and a barrage of sometimes lackluster desserts call for more Champagne. The food can be afflicted by a hotel-kitchen inconsistency, especially when wedding lunches are taking place, but the experience can be magical when everything is going right.

FRENCH LAUNDRY

Washington and Creek Streets,
Yountville
Tel: 707-944-2380
Open Tuesday through Sunday 5:30 to 10 p.m.
Price: Expensive
Credit cards: AE, CB, MC, V

Thomas Keller, a serious French-trained chef from New York, bought this venerable Napa Valley institution from the husband-and-wife team that ran it for years, and is turning it into the Valley's first high-concept destination restaurant. At Rakel, his restaurant in New York, Keller developed a poetic style based on tiny portions of composed dishes inspired by offbeat ingredients. At the French Laundry, the dishes have become even smaller as part of an inventive fixed-price five-course-plus meal that takes about four hours to be served. When you reserve you get a table for the evening, and Keller makes use of every minute of it. He starts sending out food, little bites that precede the five courses you've so carefully ordered. An oversized French tablespoon cradled in a linen napkin becomes the serving vessel for a tiny poached quail egg napped in beurre blanc and fragrant fresh herbs, one ethereal slurp. A martini glass filled with a clear "tomato water" appears with one grilled shrimp hooked onto its side. As you move into the meal you've actually selected, from a menu that offers four or more choices in each category plus a complete five-course vegetarian meal, the serving size hardly gets bigger than a few bites. A cold stew of tiny artichokes, a slice of monkfish in a verbena-scented tomato *coulis*, a round of veal breast layered with root vegetables, a potato-chip sandwich filled with peppery Brie next to a pile of miniature lettuces, and a warm individual chocolate cake that oozed in the middle made up my meal one night. You end up being entertained all evening by a parade of stylish dishes, amazingly unrepetitious when you consider how many ingredients are involved, without feeling stuffed. Keller has mastered the tasting menu by reducing it to edible scale. It's ingeniously put together like a jigsaw puzzle, so that no matter what you order it adds up to a pretty picture. Keller's cooking makes an intellectual as well as sensual statement, but he has advanced in his art to the point where the two support each other.

The setting is as much a part of the experience as the cooking. The French Laundry was always known as a prix-fixe, evening-long destination restaurant where people were encouraged to stroll mid-meal in the garden. The two-story stone building, like a French country house, has tables in two serene dining rooms with windows that look out to vines and greenery. Earlier in the evening before the chill sets in, you can eat outside on a beautifully manicured lawn enclosed by trees and flowers. The small kitchen, open to view both from the downstairs dining room and the garden, is an intrinsic part of the restaurant. You don't feel a separation between the front and back of the house here, because Keller so consciously molds your experience, from the wooden clothespin with the French Laundry logo holding your napkin at the beginning, to the laundry-list check at the end. Though the list does add up, you haven't been taken to the cleaners: the $59 per meal price does not seem stiff after what has been delivered.

THE GENERAL'S DAUGHTER

400 West Spain Street,
Sonoma
Tel: 707-938-4004
Open for lunch Monday
through Saturday 11:30 a.m.
to 2:30 p.m.; dinner Sunday
through Thursday 5:30 to
9 p.m., Friday and Saturday
until 10 p.m.; Sunday brunch
11 a.m. to 2:30 p.m.
Price: Moderate
Credit cards: MC, V

A cheerfully and imaginatively converted Sonoma mansion provides the setting for some satisfying country cooking. Portions at The General's Daughter are huge; ingredients top quality; preparations straightforward. This is a fine place to drink a bottle of Sonoma wine with meltingly crisp, deep-fried onion threads, juicy Caesar salads, and Sonoma lamb or rib-eye steaks with huge portions of roasted potatoes and two or three different vegetables. For dessert, there are fresh fruit crisps and hot fudge sundaes.

The large multiroomed restaurant feels like the fine country house it once was, with tall Victorian windows that look out onto porches and gardens, where tables are set up for warm weather eating. The walls are hung with eye-catching oil paintings of scenes you might see on the drive there. In keeping with the gracious American tone of the whole operation, service is exceptionally warm and friendly,

GREYSTONE RESTAURANT

2555 Main Street (Highway
29 just north of St. Helena),
St. Helena
Tel: 707-967-1010
Open for lunch
Wednesday through
Monday 11:30 a.m.
to 2:45 p.m.; dinner
5:30 to 9 p.m.
Price: Moderate
Credit cards: AE, CB, DC, MC, V

This glamorous tapas bar and restaurant with choice outdoor tables that overlook the Napa Valley is really part of a highly regarded continuing education facility for food and wine professionals run by the Culinary Institute of America in Hyde Park, New York. The cooking school moved into the majestic old stone Christian Brothers' winery and installed state-of-the-art kitchens and a dining room appointed with Christofle silverware, Villeroy and Boch china, and Reidel wineglasses. Though furnishings are top of the line, prices here are decidedly moderate.

My favorite way to visit Greystone, and I do practically every time I stay in the Valley, is to sit at the tapas bar where you can sample local wines and eat little plates of food. One hot afternoon, I slipped into the cool stone room to drink a glass of icy cold Cosentino Tenero Rosa, a crisp local rosé, with a Spanish-style potato, onion, and broccoli rabe omelet; miniature pork kabobs rubbed with hot, fragrant spices; excellent student-baked breads; bruschetta topped with wild and domestic mushrooms; house-made mozzarella with vine-ripe tomatoes; and three Middle Eastern dips with golden lavosh crackers. While you nibble, you get to watch the graduate chefs at work in the most elegant, up to the minute open kitchen I have ever seen, here or in France. The tapas format is a natural for the Napa Valley. It allows you to taste wines with just the right amount of food in a historic wine country building that exudes a sense of place.

MADRONA MANOR

The dining room of this stately Victorian mansion, built in 1881 and refurbished as an inn, trumpets a theme of wine country elegance with a lyrical menu based on locally raised ingredients. Chef Todd Muir takes advantage of the spacious grounds to cold-smoke his own fish, grow his own herbs and lettuces, and cellar an extensive collection of local wines. You can order a four- or five-course fixed-price menu or any dish a la carte. I have had his delicate smoked salmon on blini spread with sour cream, fabulous Bruce Campbell lamb, a pretty salad garnished with a round of warm breaded goat cheese, and a heavenly warm chocolate cake with dried-cherry ice cream for dessert. All of it tasted wonderful in a softly lit parlorlike dining room with Victorian fireplaces and tall French windows, served by a young, enthusiastic staff.

1001 Westside Road,
Healdsburg
Tel: 707-433-4231
Open nightly 6 to 9 p.m., closed Tuesday and Wednesday during the winter.
Price: Expensive
Credit cards: AE, CB, DC, MC, V

MUSTARDS

In some ways this first large-scale restaurant to open in the Napa Valley remains its most successful. Mustards is universally loved by local residents and tourists alike for its smoky, tender, spicy baby back ribs; cornmeal-coated fried green tomatoes; tasty Asian-marinated flank steak; Chinese chicken and noodle salad; and of course, Mustards' always-crisp tangle of deep-fried onion threads. The enduring vitality of this place perhaps comes from the fact that this was chef Cindy Pawlcyn's first endeavor and she put all of the dishes she loved on the menu: country dishes transformed by her sprightly offbeat style and sparkle.

Surrounded by a parking lot, the restaurant feels like the quintessential roadhouse with an airy, porchlike dining

7399 St. Helena Highway (one mile north of Yountville on Highway 29), Napa
Tel: 707-944-2424
Open daily
11:30 a.m. to 10 p.m.
Price: Moderate
Credit cards: DC, MC, V

room and constantly busy bar. The very mention of Mustards in the Valley conjures up fun. It's the place that launched the other Real Restaurants (Fog City Diner, Buckeye Roadhouse, et al.) and in some ways will always be the guiding light.

NAPA VALLEY WINE TRAIN

1275 McKinstry Street
(between First Street
and Soscol Avenue),
Napa
Tel: 707-253-2111
Departs daily
Credit cards: AE, DC, D, MC, V

Disdain may rain down on me from a certain group of exclusive Valley residents for touting the much-opposed wine train, but the slow-rolling, luxuriously appointed dining cars on this resurrected railway line offer lovely views of the valley and pretty decent food during its two-hour journey into the wine country. Wine makers are often in attendance, giving tastes and informal seminars on wine making, while the train staff coddles passengers from the moment they board. Meals begin informally in the wood-paneled club car with tasty pâtés and appetizers, and continue in the romantic dining car with straightforward preparations of salmon, chicken, or red meat. Remember, the food is not the main motivation for a tour, but a context for taking the train through a unique stretch of countryside. You can use your visiting relatives as an excuse to take the ride.

PIATTI

6480 Washington Street,
Yountville
Tel: 707-944-2070
Open Sunday through
Thursday 11:30 a.m. to
9 p.m., Friday and
Saturday until 10 p.m.
Price: Moderate
Credit cards: AE, MC, V

You can always find a good dish on the exuberant menu of this burgeoning Italian chain, which started here in Yountville in an airy wooden building with two outdoor patios and an open kitchen boasting a wood-fired rotisserie and a pizza oven. The menu concentrates on pizzas and pastas, some interesting appetizers, and chicken and rabbit cooked on the rotisserie. Though the noodle dishes have their ups and downs, look for the little ear-shaped pasta called *orrechietti* tossed with cabbage, pancetta, and Fontina; and the satiny, house-made ravioli. Not every dish gets the attention it needs, but a clever orderer can eat well. Ask your waiter for suggestions.

PINOT BLANC

Calling itself a "country bistro," this seventh restaurant of Southern California chef Joachim Splichal embraces contradiction. The pale stucco exterior baking in the Napa Valley sun belies a cool, dark, clubby interior with booths. And there's nothing "country" about the cooking except that it happens on Highway 29. The menu is a complicated, invented document with too many choices, oft-repeated ingredients, and supposedly witty descriptions, a Splichal trademark. The dishes tend to be rich, unevenly executed, but sometimes brilliant. Some favorites of mine have been roasted Sonoma foie gras with braised cherries and aged balsamic, a generous portion for a reasonable price; all the unctuous scallop dishes that gild the lily with buttery mashed potatoes as well as brown butter and truffle oil; and braised oxtail stew. Splichal does not shy away from underappreciated cuts of meat like beef cheeks, calf's tongue, sweetbreads, and marrow bones. This could be a plus if they were consistently prepared. The rumor is that Splichal is digging in for the long haul and plans to make Pinot Blanc succeed. I hope he does, because it would be nice to have a "grown-up" restaurant in the Napa Valley with a full-scale bar, large, bistro-ish menu, professional service, and luxurious appointments. The fact is that Pinot Blanc's high-concept Los Angeles cooking doesn't resonate in the conservative Napa Valley, but maybe the very presence of Pinot Blanc is a signal that times are a' changing.

641 Main Street (Highway 29 just south of St. Helena), St. Helena
Tel: 707-963-6191
Open daily 11:30 a.m. to 10 p.m.; closed Monday in the winter.
Price: Moderate
Credit cards: CB, DC, D, MC, V

RAVENOUS

For homey, satisfying, buoyant cooking inspired by seasonal ingredients, the locals head to Ravenous, a small, always-crowded cafe actually inside the Ravenous movie theater. People order from a small menu with daily specials written on a blackboard. Everything I've tried here sparkles, from grilled quail to chile verde over rice, pretty salads to housemade desserts. All prices are amazingly reasonable, including those for local wines.

117 North Street (1 block north of the main square), Healdsburg
Tel: 707-431-1770
Open for lunch Friday through Sunday 11:30 a.m. to 2:30 p.m.; dinner Wednesday through Sunday 5 to 9 p.m., Friday and Saturday until 9:30 p.m.
Price: Inexpensive
No credit cards

TERRA

**1345 Railroad Avenue,
St. Helena
Tel: 707-963-8931
Open Wednesday through
Monday 6 to 9 p.m., Friday
and Saturday until 10 p.m.
Price: Expensive
Credit cards: CB, DC, MC, V**

Terra is a ten-year-old restaurant located in a historic stone building (the registered Duckworth Foundry building built in 1884), trimmed with flower boxes overgrown with edible herbs and blossoms. To my mind it epitomizes the ideal wine country restaurant—impeccably appointed but still casual, with two uncluttered stone-walled dining rooms, terra-cotta tiled floors, massive rough beams across the ceiling, and low romantic lighting.

The chef-owners, Hiro Sone and Lissa Doumani, met in the kitchen of Spago in Los Angeles. Hiro grew up on a rice farm 300 miles north of Tokyo. He developed a passion for cooking as a child, attended a famous French cooking school in Japan, and ended up opening Spago in Tokyo for Wolfgang Puck. His cooking benefits from his flawless technique in French, Italian, and Japanese cookery, which allows his menu to deliver multicultural surprises. He likes to work with underused ingredients like tripe, sweetbreads, fish roe, and eel among others, and he prepares them so well that he has converted many a squeamish diner. His al dente spaghetti with tripe, white beans, and tomatoes has become a favorite on the menu, for me as well. He also cooks luscious beef fillet and osso buco, and some of the loveliest fish dishes I've ever encountered. His sake-glazed Chilean sea bass in a *shiso*-scented broth afloat with gossamer shrimp dumplings comes to mind. You'll find velvety terrine of foie gras and a fantastic rustic *sopa de ajo*, a garlic soup thickened with toasted bread, a poached egg in the center waiting to be swirled into the peppery red broth. Tiny fried oysters served in their shell; sweetbreads in a ragout of chanterelles, prosciutto, and white truffle oil; rosy-fleshed roast squab with pumpkin ravioli with shaved white truffles in season have delighted his diners over the years.

Lissa does the witty desserts (a tiramisù served in a deep pottery bowl, cannoli filled with orange-scented risotto), as well as running the dining room and managing the extensive, politically sensitive, wine list. Every local wine maker is represented and they all come in to order their own wine with the delicious food. I really love Terra. I feel close to the vineyards here, in tune with seasons, and always astonished by something I haven't tasted before on the menu.

TOMATINA

This order-at-the-counter pizza parlor, opened by the Tra Vigne people next door, brings a new type of eatery to the Valley. Big, informal, and quick, Tomatino is just the answer for adults eating with kids. People order thin-crusted, wood-oven baked pizzas and salads at a sleek wood-and-metal counter as they enter, and then find a seat at handsome tables set with metal pizza holders, silverware, and napkins. A small pizza Margarita (fresh mozzarella, tomato sauce, and basil) is not terribly satisfying for adults, but embellish it with shaved mushrooms and house-made pepperoni and you get a much livelier dish. To start, try a crunchy, lightly dressed chopped salad, a juicy dice of carrots, cucumber, romaine, radishes, iceberg, and croutons. Any of fifteen good local wines are available for $18 a bottle or $3.75 a glass.

1016 Main Street (Highway 29 just south of St. Helena), St. Helena
Tel: 707-967-9999
Open daily
11:30 a.m. to 10 p.m.
Price: Inexpensive
Credit cards: D, MC, V

TRA VIGNE

The tree-shaded courtyard and canopied terrace of this little piece of the Italian countryside in the Napa Valley transform the eating experience here. You can't stay grumpy in this marvelous setting, even if the service is sometimes amateurish or the smell of old garlic overtakes the olive oil set out to moisten crusty country bread. Although the stunning tiled floors have now been covered with utilitarian carpeting, and the marvelous faux stone walls have been softened with huge Milanese *aperitivo* posters from the thirties, the lofty, indoor dining room still represents classic eighties' Limn design: minimal, but opulent in materials.

1050 Charter Oak Avenue, St. Helena
Tel: 707-963-4444
Open daily
11:30 a.m. to 10 p.m.
Price: Moderate
Credit cards: DC, D, MC, V

The kitchen has always been maddeningly inconsistent, coming up with some real treats from an enticing menu but disappointments as well. Crunchy, perfectly fried calamari in an Arborio rice–flour batter were delicious one day, if you could fish them out of a pool of sweet mustard sauce, and some delicate Hobbs' prosciutto paired with strong pecorino and fresh cherries one early summer day didn't really taste all that good together. At that same summer lunch, the kitchen presented a wonderful bowl of tiny, tender spinach-and-ricotta-filled ravioli in a rich, buttery cheese sauce, while some overcooked curly strands of pasta suffered in a reduced rabbit and mushroom sauce with soapy-tasting pieces of rabbit. Interesting wines by the glass, like a new California wine made from Tuscan Sangiovese grapes, and some of the best restaurant espresso I've tasted, only make you wonder why the food often misses the mark. In the Napa Valley, however, Tra Vigne remains a destination for its ebullient sensibility and lyrical setting.

WAPPO BAR BISTRO

1226-B Washington Street, Calistoga
Tel: 707-942-4712
Open for lunch Wednesday through Monday 11:30 a.m. to 2:30 p.m.; dinner Wednesday through Monday 5:30 to 9:30 p.m.
Price: Moderate
Credit cards: AE, MC, V

The local secret in Calistoga is this small, stylish, homegrown cafe with a wonderful outdoor seating area in a brick courtyard shaded by trees and trellises. During lunch one hot day we stayed cool by ordering a leafy version of Greek salad flanked by tomatoes and tossed with sheep's milk feta, olives, and pine nuts, and a tasty Asian noodle salad topped with grilled chicken. A Mexican plate brought *masa* cakes topped with black beans, strips of sirloin, *queso fresco*, guacamole, and fresh salsa. For dessert during stone-fruit season, look for a pecan shortcake with fresh peaches and cream.

Indoors, the small copper bar offers a long list of beers and generally inexpensive, well-chosen local Italian and French wines. Also fun and refreshing are fresh fruit *liquados* (delicious mango and nectarine), mango *lassi*, citrus spritzers, and Javanese iced coffee.

CAFES

FLYING GOAT CAFE

For first-rate latte, cappucino, and freshly baked breakfast pastries, head for the Flying Goat, a handsome, modern, airy cafe right on the main square. The house-roasted coffee has depth of flavor without bitterness, and the milk is judiciously poured to create a proper balance. Any town would be happy to have a coffeehouse like the Flying Goat, and the locals show their appreciation by supporting it.

324 Center Street,
Healdsburg
Tel: 707-433-9081
Open Monday through Friday 7 a.m. to 7 p.m., weekends 8 a.m. to 7 p.m.
No credit cards

BARS

AUBERGE DU SOLEIL

The best way to take advantage of this tony wine country hotel is to have a bottle of Champagne at sunset on the outdoor terrace while you take in the sweeping view of the valley; or go there, perhaps, for Sunday brunch, and have a tasty Auberge Bloody Mary made with Absolut vodka and fresh horseradish.

180 Rutherford Hill Road,
Rutherford
Tel: 707-963-1211
Open daily 11 a.m. to midnight; restaurant open for breakfast, lunch, and dinner 7 a.m. to 9:30 p.m.
Credit cards: AE, D, MC, V

MARTIN'S JOHN AND ZEKE'S

Big sports TVs; two good pool tables; hot cashews and pistachios; big microwaved hot dogs with all the fixings; an excellent selection of local wines; a good liquor selection featuring high-end tequilas; tasty margaritas; keno; well-made drinks; friendly people on both sides of the bar; and it's clean and well kept. What more can I say?

111 Plaza Street,
Healdsburg
Tel: 707-433-3735
Open daily 10 a.m. to 2 a.m.
No credit cards

DELICATESSENS/TAKE-OUT

CANTINETTA AT TRA VIGNE

1050 Charter Oak Avenue,
St. Helena
Tel: 707-963-8888
Open Sunday through
Thursday 11:30 a.m. to
6 p.m., Friday and
Saturday until 6:30 p.m.
Credit cards: DC, D, MC, V

One of the most pleasant places to have a bite in the Napa Valley is under a shade tree in the courtyard of Tra Vigne. A glass of wine and a slice of pizza from the Cantinetta, a free-standing adjunct of the restaurant, can hit the spot on a warm Napa Valley afternoon. This delicatessen/wine bar sells prepared food, breads, and wine by the bottle and glass either to have outdoors here at the wrought-iron cafe tables under the plane trees, or to take home. The handsome breads from Pan-O-Rama bakery in Petaluma, an in-house operation that supplies all the bread needs of Real Restaurants, can be paired with chef Michael Chiarello's spicy, dry Calabrese sausage, delicious small oil-cured black olives, cold roast poussin, and green salad for a first-rate picnic. The long wine bar buzzes with activity as visitors to the Napa Valley taste the most interesting local wines. The Real Restaurants people seem to know instinctively what makes a food operation exciting. In the case of the Cantinetta, they cater to every visitor's desire to eat food that goes with wine outdoors in a beautiful setting, without paying restaurant prices for it. Once again, they've struck gold.

OAKVILLE GROCERY

7856 St. Helena Highway,
Oakville
Tel: 707-944-8802
Open daily 10 a.m. to 6 p.m.;
espresso bar opens at 8 a.m.
Credit cards: AE, MC, V

Early on, the Oakville Grocery knew that the Napa Valley couldn't live without prosciutto from Parma, six kinds of imported olives, goat cheese, aged Italian cheese, French triple-cream cheese, cheese from all over the world, Italian salami and cured meats, Passini baguettes, and a worldwide selection of mustards, jams, pastas, vinegars, and olive oils found in gourmet food departments in large cities. To go with these choice foodstuffs, the Oakville wine buyer (one of the partners is Joe Phelps, from Phelps winery) put together a distinguished group of Napa Valley and imported wines. Add a sprinkling of local and organic produce, particularly fruit, and you have one of the most important food resources in the area. Yes, you could find many of these things at stores and delicatessens in San Francisco, but their conjunction in a charming wood-floored store in the heart of the wine country gives everything a fresh context. The store is so well managed, the food so nicely displayed, the inventory of tempting things so creative, that the Oakville Grocery became a destination in its own right. When you rent a house in the Valley, the Oakville becomes a regular stop for essentials—the *New York Times,* coffee beans, Clover dairy products, and fresh baguettes. Once you are there, how can you pass up a piece of super-aged Reggiano Parmesan or a pint of that lusciouslooking potato salad? Prices were and still are astronomical, but the quality of everything is high. The cheeses are well cared for, the cured meats expertly sliced. Sometimes the produce looks sparse and a little tired, but greengrocer is not Oakville's identity. Its impetus cames from supplying the necessities of civilized life in the middle of the wine country, when no one else was doing it, and doing it better than anyone else, even today.

BAKERIES/PASTRIES

DOWNTOWN BAKERY AND CREAMERY

Kathleen Stewart continues to turn out the perfect desserts of Chez Panisse pastry chef Lindsey Shere, and then some, at this quintessential country bakery, a bakery everyone wishes they had next door. Every morning a seeming army of workers in the open kitchen turns out baskets of warm sticky buns and buttery almond-encrusted sweet rolls, hefty baguettes, and flavorful country breads. The fresh-fruit gallettes are dreamy: buttery dark-brown crusts folded over fillings of fresh plums, nectarines, and wild blackberries or rhubarb. They come in a variety of sizes; I eat a small one, still warm from the oven, for breakfast on a bench on the street. The fresh fruit tiramisù layered with berries and peaches has become a birthday classic. Dense, crumbly tea cakes are elegantly glazed with white icing

308-A Center Street, Healdsburg
Tel: 707-431-2719
Open weekdays 6 a.m. to 5:30 p.m., weekends 7 a.m. to 5:30 p.m.
No credit cards

and decorated with tiny tea roses. You can't go wrong with any of the beautiful-looking, simply decorated confections in the case. The main problem is deciding which to pick—and that goes for freshly baked cookies and biscotti and a few choice muffins like the sugar-topped "doughnut muffin." Several days a week the famous Como bread is baked, a rectangular loaf with the most delectable crumb and yeasty flavor, divine toasted and slathered with the bakery's jam. From the creamery department comes a seasonal selection of intensely flavored fruit sorbets and ice creams, which are scooped from a small ice cream freezer between the bakery cases. An espresso machine is constantly at work. In addition to being a pastry chef, Kathleen is notorious for the 600 rose bushes in her backyard. She brings in huge bouquets of the most exquisite antique varieties to decorate the bakery.

SCIAMBRA FRENCH BAKERY

685 South Freeway Drive, Napa
Tel: 707-252-3072
Open Monday through Saturday 7 a.m. to 5 p.m., Sunday 7 a.m. to 2 p.m.
No credit cards

I don't necessarily recommend that you visit this retail outlet store in Napa, but I highly recommend the bread, first baked by the Passini family in 1909. In 1972 Sciambra bought the operation, and the baguettes are still fantastic, chewy, sweet (or sour if you prefer), full of character, and denser than most. I discovered Passini baguettes at the Oakville Grocery, but they're distributed all over the Napa Valley, Sacramento, Palo Alto, and Vallejo. You can call the bakery to find out where their nearest retail outlet might be. When I visit the Valley, I look forward to making a picnic around them with some olives, cheese, and a bottle of local red wine. The bread makes the meal.

ICE CREAM/CHOCOLATES

DOWNTOWN BAKERY AND CREAMERY
See Bakeries/Pastries, page 541.

MARKETS

KELLER'S MARKET
See Meat and Poultry, page 547.

PALISADES MARKET
See Produce, page 544.

ETHNIC MARKETS

LA LUNA MARKET

All ethnic Mexican needs are supplied at this general store: tortillas, tomatillos, thinly sliced beef for *carne asada* at the butcher counter, white confirmation dresses, high black patent leather boots with pointy heels, piñatas, and videos in Spanish. Vineyard workers order their lunches of tacos and burritos in the morning and stop by at noon to pick them up, hot and ready to go. The house-made tamales, warm from the steamer in their corn husks, filled with spicy pork, taste mighty good with either cold beer or a bottle of soft Napa Valley red wine.

1153 Rutherford Road, Rutherford
Tel: 707-963-3211
Open Monday through Saturday 8 a.m. to 8 p.m., Sunday until 7 p.m.
No credit cards

PRODUCE

HEALDSBURG FARMERS' MARKET

Just west of the main plaza, Healdsburg
Saturday 9 a.m. to noon, Tuesday 4 to 6 p.m.
(Sometimes on Tuesdays evenings the market is on the Plaza.)

This is one of the sweetest little farmers' markets in Northern California, rife with beautiful, tender, mostly organic produce from a scattering of nearby farms. Before the ring of the opening bell, people line up in front of their chosen booth to grab the few baskets of *fraises des bois* or the limited supply of gold raspberries. Even if you miss the rarities, you'll find lovely things like Howard's Miracles, a large, juicy yellow-fleshed plum with a skin that makes it look like a nectarine, or old-fashioned fragrant strawberries, both from Malcolm Scott's Middleton Farm. He charges an arm and a leg for them, but they are worth it. However, at the Greenman stand next door, you can find equally wonderful Blue Lake beans for half the price of neighboring Malcolm's, exquisite lettuces, dewy watercress, and chard. Everything is very local—nothing much exotic or trucked in by farmers from outlying areas, but there's a certain charm to this. You eat what comes ripe and wait for it all year. You know that fragile apricots, vine-ripened tomatoes, and strawberries can't travel, making them all the more valued. If you're planning to visit the wine-growing areas around Healdsburg from May through December, try to take in this farmers' market, even if only to taste, and make a stop at the Downtown Bakery and Creamery for bread and pastries.

PALISADES MARKET

1506 Lincoln Avenue, Calistoga
Tel: 707-942-9549
Open daily 9 a.m. to 7 p.m.
Credit cards: AE, MC, V

This rustic wood-frame country store has become a Napa Valley destination for organic produce purchased directly from local farmers. You'll find tiny Forni-Brown Garden salad greens picked with roots intact and packed in green mesh cartons in water. These succulent greens appear in all the upscale Valley restaurants. Carefully labeled organic tomatoes, corn, beans, and other seasonal vegetables and lots of fruit, including melons, berries, and stone fruit, fill the long shelves. One time I found some really good English peas in the pod, small and sweet. The variety is amazingly large, and

UPSIDE-DOWN APRICOT OR PLUM TART

I have found small, fragrant Blenheim apricots here in the spring, and intensely flavored French sugar, or prune, plums at the end of the summer and early fall. This recipe from Anne Haskell puts either fruit to brilliant use in a rustic country tart. I am scared to death of pastry, but I followed this recipe exactly and made a wonderful tart. I know you can do it too.

To make the dough: Cut the butter into the flour until it is pea sized. I use my fingers, rubbing the butter into the flour and working quickly, but you can also use a wire pastry cutter. Stir in the water to form a dough. On a lightly floured board, form the dough into a disk. Wrap in plastic and chill for at least 1 hour.

Preheat the oven to 425°F. To make the filling: Melt the butter in a 12-inch cast-iron skillet over medium-high heat, and stir in the sugar until it dissolves. Turn off the heat.

Starting from the outer edge of the pan, lay the apricots or plums cut-side up around the pan. The fruit should fit snugly, with each circle slightly overlapping. Cut the remaining apricots or plums in quarters and scatter over the halved fruit.

Place the pan on the stove over low to medium heat. When the fruit starts to release some juice, raise the heat to medium-high and cook for about 25 minutes. The juices will get syrupy and eventually begin to caramelize.

While the apricots are cooking, roll out the tart dough slightly larger than the circumference of your skillet. The dough should be about 1/8 inch thick.

When the apricots are ready, remove the pan from the stove and cover with the dough. I just drape it over the pan and cut off the extra. The dough kind of falls down over the fruit by itself. Bake for 35 minutes. The crust will be nicely browned. Allow to rest 5 minutes.

Have a large flat plate ready. Place it over the tart. Wearing oven mitts and using both hands, flip the pan over so that the plate is on the bottom. If any fruit sticks to the pan, just use a spatula to place it on the tart.

The tart can be eaten warm, or within 3 to 4 hours of baking. The dough doesn't get soggy. Serve with sweetened whipped cream or vanilla ice cream.

Makes one 12-inch tart; serves 8

Dough
1 cup (2 sticks) cold butter
2 cups all-purpose flour
1/2 teaspoon kosher salt
7 tablespoons ice water

Filling
6 tablespoons unsalted butter
2/3 cup sugar
3 pounds firm apricots or prune plums, halved and pitted

surprises pop up since some of the produce is trucked up from brokers in the Bay Area. The store carries fresh breads and delicatessen items such as imported olives, prosciutto from Parma, and cheeses, while the grocery shelves are filled with such essentials as imported Italian pasta and olive oil. With the meat counter at Keller's in St. Helena, cooks in the upper Napa Valley can stay well supplied.

ST. HELENA FARMERS' MARKET

Railroad Avenue at Pine Street, St. Helena
Friday 7:30 to 11:30 a.m., May through November

This bustling, all-encompassing market not only offers local produce, but farm eggs, mushrooms, Bellweather Farm's sheep's milk cheeses and lamb, and put-up products like jams and vegetable sauces. At a typical late-June market you will find the first flavorful Early Girl tomatoes you've been hungering for all winter, tiny *haricots verts*, Santa Rosa plums, intensely flavored Blenheim apricots, some very nice lettuces, pickling cucumbers, blueberries, and fresh herbs. People know each other at this market, and I have spotted several chefs from Napa Valley restaurants talking up the growers.

MEAT AND POULTRY

BIG JOHN'S FOOD CENTER

1345 Healdsburg Avenue (at Dry Creek Road), Healdsburg
Tel: 707-433-7151
Open daily 8 a.m. to 8 p.m.
Credit cards: MC, V

The old-fashioned meat counter at this large, independently owned grocery store is manned by butchers who still cut to order. Featured here are treasures like Bruce Campbell's CK Ranch lamb, exceptionally sweet, tender, juicy and full of character without being muttony; excellent Petaluma Poultry Company chickens; and corn-fed pork.

KELLER'S MARKET

One of the attractions of this useful grocery store in downtown St. Helena is a small, but complete independently owned butcher counter that makes its own delicious mild and hot Italian sausages, as well as four or five other kinds. Besides the usual cuts of beef, you will find quick-cooking pork tenderloins wrapped in pancetta for the grill, Fulton Valley and Rocky chickens, and Sonoma lamb. The surrounding grocery gets fresh bread deliveries from Passini and others, and stocks imported pasta, olive oil, and other necessities of life.

1320 Main Street, St. Helena
Tel: 707-963-2114
Open daily 8 a.m. to 8 p.m., butcher shop open until 7 p.m.
Credit cards: MC, V

FOIE GRAS IN SONOMA

Sonoma Foie Gras
1905 Sperring Road, Sonoma
Tel: 707-938-1229

This is not a retail operation, but Junny and Guillermo Gonzales produce the highest-quality fresh duck foie gras in California, a product that certainly rivals the fine Hudson Valley foie gras from New York. You can call to find out how to get some (their foie gras is always available at Polarica in San Francisco, see page 241), or to make an appointment to visit the farm. The raw foie gras and ready-to-serve terrines (which will be made upon request) are vacuum packed and stay fresh for shipping. Raw foie gras actually is simple to prepare. Get a cast-iron frying pan really hot and sear slices of the foie gras for just a moment (15 seconds) on each side; any longer and the foie gras will melt like butter. Drape the warm slices on a very lightly dressed salad of haricots verts and baby lettuces in a sherry vinegar–shallot vinaigrette. Foie gras is expensive, but it's one of those ingredients that always seems worth it.

CHEESE

OAKVILLE GROCERY

See Delicatessens/Take-Out, page 540.

VELLA CHEESE COMPANY

315 Second Street East,
Sonoma
Tel: 707-938-3232
Open Monday through
Saturday 9 a.m. to 6 p.m.,
Sunday 10 a.m. to 5 p.m.
Credit cards: MC, V

Ig Vella and his staff of thirteen have been making Monterey jack and cheddar by hand since 1931 in this small plant with stone aging rooms a few blocks off Sonoma's central plaza. He is famous for his crumbly aged Monterey jack, which has won every cheese competition in the country. The two- to five-year-old wheels have a nutty, buttery flavor and can be shaved onto salads or pasta with a potato peeler. I eat it by the chunk. You can watch Ig and his crew making the cheese Monday through Thursday at 12:30 and 2:30 p.m. and get a tour of the aging rooms. You can taste cheese at the retail counter every day. A wheel or half wheel of Vella's Golden Bear, the longest-aged dry jack, makes for a lavish gift or souvenir of a trip to Sonoma.

WINE AND SPIRITS

ALL SEASONS CAFE AND WINE STORE

1400 Lincoln Avenue,
Calistoga
Tel: 707-942-6828
Open daily except
Wednesday,
11 a.m. to 7 p.m.
Credit cards: MC, V

This wineshop/cafe has put together a wonderful collection of both European and local wines at decent prices. You can buy French and California wines made with the same varietals to compare, or find tiny bottlings from small vineyards nearby to immerse yourself in Napa Valley wine making. One of the best ways to taste wine is with food, which the cafe end of the operation prepares with special attention to seasonal produce and artisanal ingredients. For a $7.50 corkage, you can pick out any bottle, pay the retail price for it (a big savings over wine list prices even with the corkage), and drink it with a charming country meal of one of the house-made pastas, sprightly salads, or well-prepared fish and meat dishes that go particularly well with wines. The desserts carry on the fresh seasonal commitment with the likes of summer berry pie with house-made vanilla ice cream; or consider the cheese plate, which makes perfect sense when you're eating in a room full of red wine waiting to be opened.

J. V. WAREHOUSE

Just as its name implies, wine, beer, and liquor are set out on shelves and you help yourself. The warehouse has lots of Napa Valley wines, including some old vintages. If you know what you want, like all the wine makers and growers in the Valley who shop here do, you can find some terrific bargains.

Vallergas Market
426 First Street,
Napa
Tel: 707-253-2624
Open daily 8 a.m. to 9 p.m.
Credit cards: AE, D, MC, V

OAKVILLE GROCERY

See Delicatessens/Take-Out, page 540.

The excellent wine department specializes in hard-to-find Napa Valley wines, which the store will ship. The staff is very helpful.

ST. HELENA WINE CENTER

Lots of local wines at good prices here, along with a few imports. Helpful and knowledgeable owner Fred Barringer can steer you to the right wines.

1321 Main Street,
St. Helena
Tel: 707-963-1313
Open Monday through Saturday 10 a.m. to 6 p.m., Sunday until 5 p.m.
Credit cards: AE, MC, V

VISITING WINERIES

Wine-tasting itineraries have become a conundrum because so many excellent wineries have opened tasting rooms over the last ten years. What used to be a fairly rare service to the public, mounted either by the biggest, most successful wineries able to afford staffing, or by very small wineries dependent on direct sales to visitors, is now de rigueur. So tasters have many, many options. Here are but a few, slightly offbeat, suggestions.

If you are new to the game, you might want to begin your wine-tasting career at ST. SUPERY (8440 St. Helena Highway, Rutherford, 707-944-9707) with its self-guiding wine education installation. The state-of-the-art interactive display includes an illuminating three-dimensional model of the Napa Valley; smell exhibits in which you put your nose into a mask and press a lever to get a whiff of aromas like grapefruit, black cherry, cedar, and wildflowers (typical components of various wines); and a series of photographs showing the natural factors that influence the flavor of a wine, such as fog, soil type, and elevation. The winery is owned by the Skalli family, the biggest sellers of pasta in Europe, and also owners of a large wine operation in the south of France near Languedoc. Their French wines cost under $10 here, a great bargain. The pricier California wines straddle the line between commercial and boutique, with competent bottlings in all major varietals. President Michaela Rodino hired a crack all-woman staff to run the winery, charm the public, and sell the wine.

Tiny CASA NUESTRA (3451 Silverado Trail, North, St. Helena, 707-963-4684) is one of those wineries that sells 90 percent of its production to visitors. The charming owner, an ex-lawyer (Harvard undergrad; Boalt Hall law school) turned grape grower, entertains and charms everyone he welcomes to his rustic piece of paradise, with its picnic tables by the river. He bottles a stunning light red called Cabernet Franc, reminiscent of Chinon from the Loire valley. He bottles some himself and sells the rest in barrels to more famous vineyards.

For the big winery experience, ROBERT MONDAVI WINERY (7801 St. Helena Highway (Highway 29), Oakville, 707-259-9463) offers tours, tastings, and retail sales of its consistently elegant European-style wines. For an art and wine-tasting experience, Donald Hess, the biggest marketer of bottled water in Switzerland, has installed a major modern art collection in an old Christian Brothers classroom-turned-gallery at the HESS COLLECTION (4411 Redwood Road, Napa, 707-255-1144). Along with curating, Hess makes a delicious reserve Cabernet.

In Sonoma County I like to base operations around Healdsburg, near the wineries on the Russian River. Driving down bucolic Westside Road, you'll pass many, but two right next to each other will give you an idea of the best wines from this area. ROCHIOLI (6192 Westside Road, Healdsburg, 707-433-2305) has achieved spectacular success from one vineyard, which for three years in a row produced the grapes that won the California State Fair Pinot Noir judging. In one of those years Rochioli made the wine, in others Gary Farrell and Williams Selyem made the award-winning Pinot Noirs. Rochioli has won the state twice with their gigantic, grassy Sauvignon Blanc, one year as the best overall wine in the state. This lovely little winery has a tasting room and picnic tables that overlook a vineyard planted with roses.

Next door is one of the most beautiful wineries, HOP KILN (6050 Westside Road, Healdsburg, 707-433-6491), with a historic hops-drying barn built in 1905, now preserved as part of the National Trust. Some of the wines come from ancient vineyards planted at the turn of the century by the once-large Italian-American enclave in the area (whose deposits, along with those of Italians on Fisherman's Wharf, started the Bank of America). Hop Kiln has identified many old grape varieties promiscuously planted in their vineyards and makes some monumental wines with them, like their Primitivo (what others call Zinfandel) characterized by a jammy, berryish flavor, and in old vintages, a spicy black-pepper edge. These wines are made in traditional California style as opposed to the more restrained French claret style, so they are big and chewy. Other interesting wines include a Petit Syrah and a wine called Marty Griffin's Big Red: a big, fruity blend of grapes from these old vines that sells for about $8.50 a bottle and beat out the Mondavi-Rothschild Opus One for the top award at the Orange County Fair one year.

Finally, if you like the idea of tasting wines and exploring the ever-expanding wine country in depth, get your hands on the *Wine Atlas of California* by James Halliday (Viking), an inclusive tome with color photographs, which won both the James Beard and Julia Child awards in 1993. It offers practical information on tasting rooms as well as the wineries.

ST. HELENA WINE MERCHANTS

699 St. Helena Highway (Highway 29), St. Helena
Tel: 707-963-7888
Open daily 10 a.m. to 6 p.m.
Credit cards: AE, D, MC, V

Formerly called Ernie's, this wine store has always stocked high-quality Napa Valley bottles. Now, a good selection from other areas in California coupled with wines from all over the world are included, making this a useful resource for Napa Valley wine growers in search of taste models. The prices are not terribly competitive, but the clerks are competent and enthusiastic. Savvy collectors used to be able to find quirky old vintages of European wines, but, alas, the buyers have caught up with the inventory.

TIP TOP

90 Dry Creek Road, Healdsburg
Tel: 707-431-0841
Open Sunday through Thursday 9 a.m. to 8 p.m., Friday and Saturday until 9 p.m.
Credit cards: MC, V

In an unlikely spot on the edge of Healdsburg, a funky, cool, cement-floored wine and liquor store offers a surprisingly diverse selection of spirits and wines—a selection that includes all the major growing areas of California and a commendable selection of wines from wine-growing regions all over the world.

Some examples: Cacchiano 1990 Chianti Classico for $12.50 a bottle, a good price; fine bottlings from Oregon, like Adelsheim Pinot Noir; an array of Ridge Vineyard wines; representative bottles of one of my favorite Bordeaux, Chateau La Lagune from the Haut Médoc, not to mention a good selection of other Bordeaux. Beware of prestigious labels from off vintages that catch your eye among the current offerings, like a 1986 Romanée St-Vivant from Romanée-Conti at $159, or some over-the-hill, fancy Italian white wines that probably would not be drinkable.

Restaurant Indexes

RESTAURANTS

Acquerello 339
Ajanta 457
Akasaka 312
Alain Rondelli 367
Alfred's Steak House 123
All Seasons Cafe
 and Wine Shop 525, **548**
Alta Plaza 305
Angkor Borei 209
Anjou 124
Antica Trattoria 340
Aqua 124
Armani Cafe 126
Babette's 525
Bacco 247
Bay Wolf 458
Beach Chalet 425
Betelnut 185
Bistro Aix 186
Bistro Alsacienne 501
Bistro Don Giovanni 527
Bistro Ralph 527
Bizou 397
Bombay Cuisine 459
Boulevard 93
Brennan's Restaurant 459
Bridges 460
Brown Street Grill 528
Bruno's 210
Bubba's 502
Burger Joint 211
Burma's House 127

Cafe at Chez Panisse 461
Café Claude 127
Cafe Jacqueline 267
Cafe Kati 306
Cafe Marimba 187
Cafe Rouge 462
Campton Place 128
Carta 67
Casa Orinda 463
Catahoula Restaurant and Saloon 528
Cha Cha Cha 163
Charles—Nob Hill 341
Chez Panisse 464
Cho-Cho 268
Citron 465
Cordon Bleu 342
Cypress Club 129
Dol Ho 35
Domaine Chandon 530
Dragon House 368
E'Angelo 189
Eagle Cafe 94
Ecco, Ristorante 405
El Balazito 211
Ella's 307
Enrico's Sidewalk Cafe 268
Eos 164
Esperpento 212
Fina Estampa 213
Firefly 248
Fleur de Lys 130
The Flying Saucer 214

Fly Trap 398
The Fog City Diner 95
Fountain Court 369
42 Degrees 399
Frantoio 503
French Laundry 530
Fringale 400
Ganges Vegetarian Restaurant 165
Gaylord of India 96
The General's Daughter 532
Gold Mountain 36
Golden Turtle 342
Greens 190
Greystone Restaurant 532
Hama-Ko 166
Hana 426
Happy Valley 97
Harbor Village 98
Harris' 343
Hawthorne Lane 401
Hayes Street Grill 69
Helmand 270
Hing Lung 37
Hong Kong East Ocean 466
Hong Kong Flower Lounge 369
Hong Kong Villa 370
House 271, 427
House of Nanking 38
House of Prime Rib 344
Ideale, Ristorante 278
Il Fornaio 99
Il Pollaio 271

Imperial Palace 40
Insalata's 504
Iroha 312
Isobune 312
Isuzu 308
J & J 41
Jackson Fillmore 308
Jakarta 371
Jeong Hyun Charcoal
  Barbecue House 427
Julius' Castle 272
Just Won Ton 429
Kabuto 372
Kasbah 505
Katia, A Russian Tea Room 373
Kui Shin Bo 312
Kyo-ya at the Sheraton
  Palace Hotel 402
Kyung Bok Palace 374
La Felce 272
La Folie 344
Laghi 374
La Movida 216
Lark Creek Inn 506
La Santaneca 216
La Taqueria 217
Le Central 131
Left Bank 508
Liberty Cafe 218
Lichee Garden 42
Little Joe's 273
Lo Coco's 274
Los Jarritos 218
L'Osteria del Forno 275
LuLu 404
MacArthur Park 131
Madrona Manor 533
Maki 309
Marcello, Ristorante 430
Marina Central 191
Masa's 132
Mayflower 375
Mecca 249

The Meetinghouse 310
Mifune 311
Millennium 70
Mo's 278
Mom Is Cooking 219
Moose's 276
Moxie Bar and Restaurant 405
Mustards 533
Napa Valley Wine Train 534
Nob Hill Grille 345
O Chamé 466
Old Krakow 429
Oliveto 468
One Market Restaurant 100
Oriental Pearl 44
Original Joe's 133
Oritalia 312
Osakaya 312
Pacific 134
Pacific Restaurant—
  Thai-Binh-Duong #2 72
Palio d'Asti 135
Pancho Villa Taqueria 220
Pane e Vino 191
Pastis 101
Pearl City 45
Piatti 534
Picante Taqueria 469
Pino Blanc 535
PlumpJack Cafe 192
Postrio 136
Pozole 250
R & G Lounge 45
Ravenous 535
Rice Table 510
Ristorante Ecco 405
Ristorante Ideale 278
Ristorante Marcello 430
Ritz-Carlton Dining Room 345
River Side Seafood Restaurant 431
Rose Pistola 279
Rosmarino 314
Rotunda at Neiman-Marcus 136

Rubicon 137
Rumpus 139
Sam's Grill 139
San Francisco Art Institute Cafe 280
San Tung & San Tung #2 432
Sanppo 314
Sanraku Four Seasons 140
Sapporo-Ya 312
Scala's Bistro 141
Sears Fine Foods 142
Slanted Door 221
Sol y Luna Restaurante 142
South Park Cafe 406
Splendido 102
Stars 74
Stoyanof 432
Straits Cafe 376
Suppenküche 75
Swan Oyster Depot 347, 361
Tadich Grill 143
Tai Chi 347
Taiwan 377
Taqueria El Balazo 167
Terra 536
Thep Phanom 167
Thirsty Bear 407
Ti Couz Crêperie 222
Timo's 222
Tokyo Sukiyaki 103
Tomatina 537
Tommaso's 281
Ton Kiang 378
Ton Kiang Cafe 379
Tra Vigne 537
Universal Cafe 407
Val 21 223
Vanessi's 348
Venticello 349
Vertigo 144
Vicolo Pizzeria 76
Vivande Ristorante 77
Wappo Bar Bistro 538
Win's 433

Woodward's Garden   224
Wu Kong   107
Ya, Halla from Nadia   168

Yank Sing   145
YaYa Cuisine   434
Zarzuela   350

Zax   282
Zinzino   193
Zuni Cafe   78

CUISINE

AFGHANI
Helmand   270

ALSATIAN
Bistro Alsacienne   501

AMERICAN
Beach Chalet   425
Brennan's Restaurant   459
Bubba's   502
Burger Joint   211
Casa Orinda   463
Catahoula Restaurant and Saloon   528
Eagle Cafe   94
Ella's   307
Fly Trap   398
The Fog City Diner   95
Lark Creek Inn   506
MacArthur Park   131
The Meetinghouse   310
Mo's   278
Mustards   533
Nob Hill Grille   345
One Market Restaurant   100
Original Joe's   133
Ravenous   535
San Francisco Art Institute Cafe   280
Sears Fine Foods   142

BURMESE
Burma's House   127

CALIFORNIA
All Seasons Cafe
   and Wine Shop   525, **548**
Alta Plaza   305

Bay Wolf   458
Bistro Ralph   527
Boulevard   93
Bridges   460
Brown Street Grill   528
Bruno's   210
Cafe Rouge   462
Campton Place   128
Charles—Nob Hill   341
Citron   465
Cypress Club   129
Enrico's Sidewalk Cafe   268
Firefly   248
The Flying Saucer   214
The General's Daughter   532
Greystone Restaurant   532
Hawthorne Lane   401
Julius' Castle   272
Liberty Cafe   218
Madrona Manor   533
Marina Central   191
Mecca   249
Moose's   276
Napa Valley Wine Train   534
Pacific   134
Pino Blanc   535
PlumpJack Cafe   192
Postrio   136
Rotunda at Neiman-Marcus   136
Rubicon   137
Rumpus   139
Stars   74
Terra   536
Val 21   223
Vertigo   144
Wappo Bar Bistro   538

Woodward's Garden   224
Zuni Cafe   78

CALIFORNIA/ASIAN
Cafe Kati   306
Eos   164
House   271, 427
Oritalia   312

CALIFORNIA/FRENCH
Babette's   525
Chez Panisse   464

CALIFORNIA/MEDITERRANEAN
Bizou   397
Cafe at Chez Panisse   461
Insalata's   504
42 Degrees   399
LuLu   404
Rosmarino   314
Splendido   102
Universal Cafe   407
Zax   282

CAMBODIAN
Angkor Borei   209

CARIBBEAN
Cha Cha Cha   163

CHICKEN
Il Pollaio   271

CHINESE
Dol Ho   35
Dragon House   368

Fountain Court 369
Gold Mountain 36
Harbor Village 98
Hing Lung 37
Hong Kong East Ocean 466
Hong Kong Flower Lounge 369
Hong Kong Villa 370
House of Nanking 38
Imperial Palace 40
J & J 41
Just Won Ton 429
Lichee Garden 42
Mayflower 375
Oriental Pearl 44
Pearl City 45
R & G Lounge 45
River Side Seafood Restaurant 431
San Tung & San Tung #2 432
Tai Chi 347
Taiwan 377
Ton Kiang 378
Ton Kiang Cafe 379
Win's 433
Wu Kong 107
Yank Sing 145, 151

CRÊPES
Ti Couz Crêperie 222

DIM SUM
Dol Ho 35
Gold Mountain 36
Harbor Village 98
Hong Kong East Ocean 466
Hong Kong Flower Lounge 369
J & J 41
Imperial Palace 40
Lichee Garden 42
Mayflower 375
Oriental Pearl 44
Pearl City 45

Ton Kiang Cafe 379
Wu Kong 107
Yank Sing 145, 151

FISH
Aqua 124
Hayes Street Grill 69
Sam's Grill 139
Swan Oyster Depot 347, 361
Tadich Grill 143

FRENCH
Alain Rondelli 367
Anjou 124
Bistro Aix 186
Café Claude 127
Domaine Chandon 530
Fleur de Lys 130
French Laundry 530
Fringale 400
La Folie 344
Le Central 131
Left Bank 508
Masa's 132
Pastis 101
Ritz-Carlton Dining Room 345
South Park Cafe 406

FRENCH/SOUFFLÉS
Cafe Jacqueline 267

GERMAN
Suppenküche 75

GREEK
Stoyanof 432

HAMBURGERS
Burger Joint 211
"Hamburgers" 515

Hamburger Mary's 412
Mo's 278

INDIAN
Ajanta 457
Bombay Cuisine 459
Gaylord of India 96

INDIAN/VEGETARIAN
Ganges Vegetarian Restaurant 165
Vik's King of Chat 476

INDONESIAN
Jakarta 371
Rice Table 510

INTERNATIONAL
Carta 67

ITALIAN
Acquerello 339
Antica Trattoria 340
Armani Cafe 126
Bacco 247
Bistro Don Giovanni 527
E'Angelo 189
Ristorante Ecco 405
Frantoio 503
Ristorante Ideale 278
Il Fornaio 99
Jackson Fillmore 308
La Felce 272
Laghi 374
Little Joe's 273
Lo Coco's 274
L'Osteria del Forno 275
Ristorante Marcello 430
Oliveto 468
Palio d'Asti 135
Pane e Vino 191
Piatti 534

Rose Pistola 279
Scala's Bistro 141
Tra Vigne 537
Vanessi's 348
Venticello 349
Vivande Ristorante 77
Zinzino 193

JAPANESE
Akasaka 312
Cho-Cho 268
Hana 426
Iroha 312
Isuzu 308
Kui Shin Bo 312
Maki 309
Mifune 311
O Chamé 466
Osakaya 312
Sanppo 314
Sanraku Four Seasons 140
Sapporo-Ya 312
Tokyo Sukiyaki 103

JAPANESE/SUSHI
Hama-Ko 166
Isobune 312
Kabuto 372
Kyo-ya at the Sheraton
   Palace Hotel 402

JEWISH
Moxie Bar and Restaurant 405

KOREAN
Jeong Hyun Charcoal
   Barbecue House 427
Kyung Bok Palace 374

MEXICAN
Cafe Marimba 187
El Balazito 211
La Taqueria 217
Los Jarritos 218
Mom Is Cooking 219
Pancho Villa Taqueria 220
Picante Taqueria 469
Pozole 250
Taqueria El Balazo 167

MIDDLE EASTERN
Ya, Halla from Nadia 168
YaYa Cuisine 434

MONGOLIAN
Happy Valley 97

MOROCCAN
Kasbah 505

PAN ASIAN
Betelnut 185

PERUVIAN
Fina Estampa 213

PIZZA
Blondie's Pizza **149**, 473
Lo Coco's 274
L'Osteria del Forno 275
North Beach Pizza 290
Tomatina 537
Tommaso's 281
Vicolo Pizzeria 76

POLISH
Old Krakow 429

RUSSIAN
Katia, A Russian Tea Room 373

SALVADORAN
La Santaneca 216

SINGAPOREAN
Straits Cafe 376

SPANISH
Esperpento 212
La Movida 216
Sol y Luna Restaurante 142
Thirsty Bear 407
Timo's 222
Zarzuela 350

STEAK HOUSE
Alfred's Steak House 123
Harris' 343
House of Prime Rib 344

THAI
Thep Phanom 167

VEGETARIAN
Greens 190
Millennium 70

VIETNAMESE
Cordon Bleu 342
Golden Turtle 342
Pacific Restaurant—
   Thai-Binh-Duong #2 72
Slanted Door 221

BY PRICE

INEXPENSIVE

Ajanta 457
Akasaka 312
Angkor Borei 209
Bombay Cuisine 459
Brennan's Restaurant 459
Bubba's 502
Burger Joint 211
Burma's House 127
Café Claude 127
Cha Cha Cha 163
Cordon Bleu 342
Dol Ho 35
Dragon House 368
Eagle Cafe 94
El Balazito 211
Ella's 307
Esperpento 212
Fina Estampa 213
Ganges Vegetarian Restaurant 165
Gold Mountain 36
Golden Turtle 342
Hana 426
Helmand 270
Hing Lung 37
House of Nanking 38
Il Pollaio 271
Imperial Palace 40
Iroha 312
Isobune 312
J & J 41
Jakarta 371
Jeong Hyun Charcoal Barbecue House 427
Just Won Ton 429
Katia, A Russian Tea Room 373
Kui Shin Bo 312
Kyung Bok Palace 374
La Felce 272
La Santaneca 216

La Taqueria 217
Lichee Garden 42
Little Joe's 273
Los Jarritos 218
L'Osteria del Forno 275
Mifune 311
Mo's 278
Mom Is Cooking 219
Moxie Bar and Restaurant 405
Nob Hill Grille 345
Old Krakow 429
Oriental Pearl 44
Original Joe's 133
Osakaya 312
Pacific Restaurant—
   Thai-Binh-Duong #2 72
Pancho Villa Taqueria 220
Pearl City 45
Picante Taqueria 469
Pozole 250
Ravenous 535
River Side Seafood Restaurant 431
San Francisco Art Institute Cafe 280
San Tung & San Tung #2 432
Sanppo 314
Sapporo-Ya 312
Sears Fine Foods 142
Slanted Door 221
Stoyanof 432
Suppenküche 75
Tai Chi 347
Taiwan 377
Taqueria El Balazo 167
Thep Phanom 167
Ti Couz Crêperie 222
Tomatina 537
Tommaso's 281
Ton Kiang 378
Ton Kiang Cafe 379
Universal Cafe 407

Vicolo Pizzeria 76
Win's 433
Ya, Halla from Nadia 168

INEXPENSIVE TO MODERATE

Fountain Court 369
Isuzu 308
Mayflower 375
Kasbah 505

MODERATE

All Seasons Cafe and Wine Shop 525, **548**
Alta Plaza 305
Anjou 124
Antica Trattoria 340
Armani Cafe 126
Bacco 247
Bay Wolf 458
Beach Chalet 425
Betelnut 185
Bistro Aix 186
Bistro Alsacienne 501
Bistro Don Giovanni 527
Bistro Ralph 527
Bizou 397
Bridges 460
Brown Street Grill 528
Bruno's 210
Cafe at Chez Panisse 461
Cafe Jacqueline 267
Cafe Kati 306
Cafe Marimba 187
Cafe Rouge 462
Carta 67
Casa Orinda 463
Le Central 131
Cho-Cho 268
Citron 465
E'Angelo 189

(Inexpensive: food $15 and under; Moderate: food $16 to $29; Expensive: food $30 and up)

Ristorante Ecco 405
Enrico's Sidewalk Cafe 268
Eos 164
Firefly 248
The Flying Saucer 214
Fly Trap 398
The Fog City Diner 95
42 Degrees 399
Frantoio 503
Fringale 400
Gaylord of India 96
The General's Daughter 532
Greens 190
Greystone Restaurant 532
Hama-Ko 166
Happy Valley 97
Harbor Village 98
Hayes Street Grill 69
Hong Kong East Ocean 466
Hong Kong Flower Lounge 369
Hong Kong Villa 370
House 271, 427
House of Prime Rib 344
Ristorante Ideale 278
Il Fornaio 99
Insalata's 504
Jackson Fillmore 308
Kabuto 372
Laghi 374
La Movida 216
Left Bank 508
Liberty Cafe 218
Lo Coco's 274
LuLu 404
MacArthur Park 131
Maki 309
Ristorante Marcello 430
Marina Central 191
Mecca 249
The Meetinghouse 310

Millennium 70
Moose's 276
Mustards 533
O Chamé 466
Oliveto 468
Oritalia 312
Pacific 134
Palio d'Asti 135
Pane e Vino 191
Pastis 101
Piatti 534
Pino Blanc 535
PlumpJack Cafe 192
R & G Lounge 45
Rice Table 510
Rose Pistola 279
Rosmarino 314
Rotunda at Neiman-Marcus 136
Rumpus 139
Sam's Grill 139
Sanraku Four Seasons 140
Scala's Bistro 141
Sol y Luna Restaurante 142
South Park Cafe 406
Splendido 102
Straits Cafe 376
Swan Oyster Depot 347, **361**
Tadich Grill 143
Thirsty Bear 407
Timo's 222
Tokyo Sukiyaki 103
Tra Vigne 537
Val 21 223
Vanessi's 348
Venticello 349
Vertigo 144
Wappo Bar Bistro 538
Woodward's Garden 224
Wu Kong 107
Yank Sing 145

YaYa Cuisine 434
Zarzuela 350
Zax 282
Zinzino 193
Zuni Cafe 78

MODERATE TO EXPENSIVE
Babette's 525
Catahoula Restaurant and Saloon 528

EXPENSIVE
Acquerello 339
Alain Rondelli 367
Alfred's Steak House 123
Aqua 124
Boulevard 93
Campton Place 128
Charles—Nob Hill 341
Chez Panisse 464
Cypress Club 129
Domaine Chandon 530
Fleur de Lys 130
French Laundry 530
Harris' 343
Hawthorne Lane 401
Julius' Castle 272
Kyo-ya at the Sheraton
 Palace Hotel 402
La Folie 344
Lark Creek Inn 506
Madrona Manor 533
Masa's 132
Napa Valley Wine Train 534
One Market Restaurant 100
Postrio 136
Ritz-Carlton Dining Room 345
Rubicon 137
Stars 74
Terra 536
Vivande Ristorante 77

FOOD SERVICE AT COUNTER OR BAR

Alfred's Steak House   123
All Seasons Cafe
  and Wine Shop   525, **548**
Alta Plaza   305
Aqua   124
Armani Cafe   126
Babette's   525
Betelnut   185
Bistro Aix   186
Bistro Don Giovanni   527
Bistro Ralph   527
Bizou   397
Boulevard   93
Brennan's Restaurant   459
Bridges   460
Brown Street Grill   528
Bruno's   210
Bubba's   502
Cafe Marimba   187
Cafe Rouge   462
Casa Orinda   463
Catahoula Restaurant and Saloon   528
Cha Cha Cha   163
Charles—Nob Hill   341
Cho-Cho   268
Citron   465
Cordon Bleu   342
Cypress Club   129
Eagle Cafe   94
Ristorante Ecco   405
El Balazito   211
Ella's   307
Enrico's Sidewalk Cafe   268
Eos   164
Firefly   248
Fly Trap   398
The Flying Saucer   214
The Fog City Diner   95
42 Degrees   399
Frantoio   503
Fringale   400

The General's Daughter   532
Greystone Restaurant   532
Hama-Ko   166
Hana   426
Harris'   343
Hawthorne Lane   401
Hayes Street Grill   69
Hong Kong East Ocean   466
House   427
House of Nanking   38
House of Prime Rib   344
Il Fornaio   99
Insalata's   504
Isuzu   308
Jackson Fillmore   308
Julius' Castle   272
Kabuto   372
Kyo-ya at the Sheraton
  Palace Hotel   402
La Felce   272
Laghi   374
La Movida   216
Lark Creek Inn   506
Le Central   131
Left Bank   508
Little Joe's   273
Los Jarritos   218
LuLu   404
MacArthur Park   131
Ristorante Marcello   430
Marina Central   191
Masa's   132
Mecca   249
Mo's   278
Moose's   276
Moxie Bar and Restaurant   405
Mustards   533
Nob Hill Grille   345
O Chamé   466
One Market Restaurant   100
Original Joe's   133

Oritalia   312
Palio d'Asti   135
Pastis   101
Piatti   534
Picante Taqueria   469
Pino Blanc   535
Postrio   136
Rose Pistola   279
Rosmarino   314
Rotunda at Neiman-Marcus   136
Rubicon   137
Rumpus   139
Sam's Grill   139
Sears Fine Foods   142
Sol y Luna Restaurante   142
South Park Cafe   406
Splendido   102
Stars   74
Straits Cafe   376
Suppenküche   75
Swan Oyster Depot   347, **361**
Tadich Grill   143
Tai Chi   347
Thirsty Bear   407
Ti Couz Crêperie   222
Timo's   222
Tokyo Sukiyaki   103
Tra Vigne   537
Universal Cafe   407
Val 21   223
Vanessi's   348
Venticello   349
Vertigo   144
Vicolo Pizzeria   76
Vivande Ristorante   77
Wappo Bar Bistro   538
Woodward's Garden   224
Wu Kong   107
Yank Sing   145
Zax   282
Zinzino   193

FOOD SERVICE AFTER 10 P.M.

Acquerello 339
Aqua 124
Beach Chalet 425
Betelnut 185
Boulevard 93
Bruno's 210
Burger Joint 211
Cafe at Chez Panisse 461
Cafe Jacqueline 267
Cafe Marimba 187
Cafe Rouge 462
Carta 67
Casa Orinda 463
Cha Cha Cha 163
Cypress Club 129
Dragon House 368
E'Angelo 189
Enrico's Sidewalk Cafe 268
Eos 164
The Flying Saucer 214
The Fog City Diner 95
42 Degrees 399
Fringale 400
Gaylord of India 96
Golden Turtle 342
Hing Lung 37
Ristorante Ideale 278
Il Fornaio 99
Jackson Fillmore 308
Jeong Hyun Charcoal
  Barbecue House 427
Kabuto 372
La Felce 272
La Folie 344
Le Central 131
Left Bank 508
Little Joe's 273
LuLu 404
Ristorante Marcello 430
Mecca 249
Mo's 278
Moose's 276
Original Joe's 133
Pancho Villa Taqueria 220
Pastis 101
PlumpJack Cafe 192
Postrio 136
Pozole 250
Rubicon 137
Scala's Bistro 141
Sol y Luna Restaurante 142
Splendido 102
Stars 74
Thep Phanom 167
Thirsty Bear 407
Ti Couz Crêperie 222
Timo's 222
Tokyo Sukiyaki 103
Tommaso's 281
Vicolo Pizzeria 76
Ya, Halla from Nadia 168
Zarzuela 350
Zax 282
Zuni Cafe 78

BREAKFAST OR WEEKEND BRUNCH

All Seasons Cafe
  and Wine Shop 525, **548**
Babette's 525
Bubba's 502
Cafe Marimba 187
Campton Place 128
Carta 67
Eagle Cafe 94
Ella's 307
Fountain Court 369
The General's Daughter 532
Gold Mountain 36
Greens 190
Hing Lung 37
Hong Kong East Ocean 466
Il Fornaio 99
Imperial Palace 40
Lark Creek Inn 506
Left Bank 508
Liberty Cafe 218
Lichee Garden 42
Los Jarritos 218
Madrona Manor 533
Mom Is Cooking 219
Moose's 276
Nob Hill Grille 345
Pacific 134
Pearl City 45
Postrio 136
Rosmarino 314
Rubicon 137
San Francisco Art Institute Cafe 280
Sears Fine Foods 142
South Park Cafe 406
Straits Cafe 376
Suppenküche 75
Ti Couz Crêperie 222
Ton Kiang Cafe 379
Universal Cafe 407
Val 21 223
Wu Kong 107
Yank Sing 145
Zuni Cafe 78

OUTDOOR SEATING

Armani Cafe   126
Babette's   525
Bay Wolf   458
Bistro Aix   186
Bistro Don Giovanni   527
Bistro Ralph   527
Bridges   460
Cafe Rouge   462
Carta   67
Catahoula Restaurant and Saloon   528
Citron   465
Domaine Chandon   530
El Balazito   211
Enrico's Sidewalk Cafe   268
42 Degrees   399
Frantoio   503
French Laundry   530
The General's Daughter   532
Greystone Restaurant   532
Il Fornaio   99
La Movida   216
Lark Creek Inn   506
Left Bank   508
MacArthur Park   131
Piatti   534
Rosmarino   314
San Francisco Art Institute Cafe   280
Splendido   102
Stoyanof   432
Tomatina   537
Tra Vigne   537
Wappo Bar Bistro   538
Zinzino   193
Zuni Cafe   78

CHILD-FRIENDLY

Ajanta   457
Brennan's Restaurant   459
Brown Street Grill   528
Bubba's   502
Burger Joint   211
Cafe at Chez Panisse   461
Casa Orinda   463
Dol Ho   35
E'Angelo   189
Eagle Cafe   94
El Balazito   211
Ella's   307
The Fog City Diner   95
Hong Kong Flower Lounge   369
House of Prime Rib   344
Il Fornaio   99
Il Pollaio   271
J & J   41
Just Won Ton   429
La Felce   272
La Movida   216
La Santaneca   216
La Taqueria   217
Liberty Cafe   218
Lichee Garden   42
Little Joe's   273
Los Jarritos   218
L'Osteria del Forno   275
MacArthur Park   131
Mifune   311
Mo's   278
Mom Is Cooking   219
Mustards   533
Nob Hill Grille   345
Pancho Villa Taqueria   220
Pearl City   45
Picante Taqueria   469
Ravenous   535
Rice Table   510
River Side Seafood Restaurant   431
San Francisco Art Institute Cafe   280
San Tung & San Tung #2   432
Scala's Bistro   141
Sears Fine Foods   142
Stoyanof   432
Taiwan   377
Taqueria El Balazo   167
Ti Couz Crêperie   222
Tomatina   537
Tommaso's   281
Ton Kiang   378
Ton Kiang Cafe   379
Vicolo Pizzeria   76
Win's   433
Yank Sing   145
Zinzino   193

BANQUET ROOM

Aqua 124
Babette's 525
Boulevard 93
Casa Orinda 463
Catahoula Restaurant and Saloon 528
Cho-Cho 268
Cypress Club 129
Domaine Chandon 530
E'Angelo 189
Fly Trap 398
Gaylord of India 96

The General's Daughter 532
Gold Mountain 36
Greens 190
Harbor Village 98
Harris' 343
MacArthur Park 131
Madrona Manor 533
Moose's 276
Napa Valley Wine Train 534
Oliveto 468
One Market Restaurant 100

Oriental Pearl 44
PlumpJack Cafe 192
R & G Lounge 45
Ritz-Carlton Dining Room 345
Splendido 102
Stars 74
Tokyo Sukiyaki 103
Vanessi's 348
Wu Kong 107

OF HISTORIC INTEREST

Beach Chalet 425
Boulevard 93
Casa Orinda 463
Chez Panisse 464
Eagle Cafe 94
Fly Trap 398
French Laundry 530

The General's Daughter 532
Harris' 343
Left Bank 508
Madrona Manor 533
Napa Valley Wine Train 534
Original Joe's 133
Sam's Grill 139

Sears Fine Foods 142
Swan Oyster Depot 347, 361
Tadich Grill 143
Terra 536
Tommaso's 281

Specialty Indexes

BAKERIES/PASTRIES

ABC Bakery Cafe   49
Acme Bakery   477
Ahern's   354
Alfred Schilling   83
Bagel King   92, 111
The Bagelry   354
Bakers of Paris   253, 439
Bob's Donuts   355
Boudin Sourdough
  Bakery and Cafe   111
Bread Workshop   478
The Cheese Board   492
Danilo   293
Downtown Bakery and Creamery   541

Eastern Bakery   51
House of Bagels   384
Il Fornaio   99
Just Desserts   175, 198
Katrina Rozelle   479
La Farine   479
La Nouvelle Pâtisserie   199
La Reyna Bakery and Coffee Shop   231
Le Chantilly   319
Liguria   294
Mee Heong Pastry Company   51
Mee Mee Bakery   52
Moscow and Tbilisi Bakery   384
Noe Valley Bakery   253

Panaderia La Mexicana   231
Pasticceria Rulli   512
Pâtisserie Delanghe   320
Schubert's   385
Sciambra French Bakery   542
Semifreddi's   480
Shaharazad Bakery and
  Filo Specialists   439
Stella   294
Sweet Inspiration   254
Victoria   295
Yamada Seika   321

BARS

Auberge du Soleil   539
Balboa Cafe   194
Bix   147
Brennan's Restaurant   459
Bus Stop   195
Caribbean Zone   411
Dalva   226
DeLuxe   170
Elbo Room   226
Eleven   412
Gino and Carlo's   287
Gordon Biersch
  Brewing Company   109
Guaymas   514
Hamburger Mary's   412

Harry Denton's   109
Harry Denton's Starlight Room   148
House of Shields   412
Infusion   413
Jack's   317
Johnny Love's   351
Julie's Supper Club   413
Kezar Bar & Restaurant   171
Kimball's East   472
Li-Po   48
Martin's John and Zeke's   539
New Orleans Room in the Fairmont
  Hotel   351
Noc Noc   171
The Paragon   195

Pat O'Shea's Mad Hatter   381
Perry's   195
Pier 23 Cafe   110
The Ramp   413
Red Room   148
The Saloon   287
Sam's   514
Savoy Tivoli   287
Specs'   287
Toronado   172
Tosca   288
Twenty Tank Brewery   414
Up and Down Club   414
Vesuvio   288

CAFES

Bean There   169
Book Passage Cafe   523
Brain Wash Cafe   409
Bugatti's Espresso Caffe   194
Cafe 817   470
Cafe at Oliveto   470
Café de la Presse   146
Cafe de Young   435
Cafe Fanny   471
Cafe Flore   251
Cafe Istanbul   225
Caffè Centro   409
Caffè Freddy's   283
Caffè Greco   204
Caffè Roma Coffee Roasting
 Company   285, 410
Caffè Strada   472
Caffè Trieste   285
Caffè Trinity   80
Flying Goat Cafe   539
Imperial Tea Court   47
Jammin' Java Coffee House   436
Java Beach Cafe   437
Mario's Bohemian Cigar Store   285
Momi Toby's Revolution Cafe   80
One World Cafe   170
Orbit Room Cafe   252
Palio Paninoteca   **146**, 410, 437
Pasticceria Rulli   512
Pier 40 Roastery   108
Radio Valencia   226
Sam and Henry's Cool Beans   380
Specialty's Cafe and Bakery   411
Spuntino   81
Tan Tan   316

CHEESE

California Street Creamery   329
Cheese Board   492
The Cheese Shop   519
Country Cheese   179
J. Wiggins Cheese   494
Leonard's 2001   361
Oakville Grocery   540
Say Cheese   179
Sixth Avenue Cheese Shop   391
24th Street Cheese Company   259
Ultra Lucca   476, **515**
Vella Cheese Company   548

COFFEE

Freed, Teller & Freed   357
Pasticceria Rulli   512
Peet's Coffee and Tea
 199, 322, 358, 442, 495, 520
Spinelli Coffee Company
 173, 256, 322, 358, 442, 520

COOKWARE AND BOOKS

A Clean Well-lighted Place
 for Books   **87**, 523
Biordi   298
Black Oak Books   499
Book Passage   523
Books, Inc.   330
Chong Imports   60
City Discount   362
Cliff's Hardware   261
Cody's   499
Columbus Cutlery   299
Cookin'   180
Cost Plus Imports   115
Crate and Barrel   154
Easy Money Discount Outlet   449
Echo   261
Economy Restautant Supply   420
Figoni Hardware   299
Fillamento   331
Forrest Jones   331
Fredericksen's Hardware   202
The Gardener   499
Ginn Wall   61
Green Apple Books   391
Homechef   331, 524
Kamei Household Wares   392
Kinokuniya Bookstore   332
Kitchen Friend   449
Lehr's German Specialties   262
Macy's Cellar   155
Mashiko Folkcraft   333
RH   333
Richard Hilkert, Bookseller   88
Sanko Cooking Supply   334
Soko Hardware   334
Sue Fisher-King   334
Sunset Bookstore   450
Sur La Table   **156**, 500
Tai Yick Trading Company   61
Williams-Sonoma
 117, **157**, 203, 450, 524

DELICATESSENS/TAKE-OUT

Arabi   110
Ba Le   82
Blondie's Pizza   **149**, 473
Brother-in-Law's BBQ   172
Bryan's Quality Meats   327
Cantinetta at Tra Vigne   540
David's Produce/David's Taqueria   517
Doug's Bar-B-Q   473
Florence Italian Deli and
   Ravioli Factory   289
Gastronom   382
Golden Boy   289
"Hamburgers"   515
Hungarian Sausage Factory   227
Janmae Guey   48
Just Like Home   437
La Palma Mexicatessen   227

Lucca   196
Lucca Ravioli Company   229
Macy's Cellar   149
Made To Order   474
Market Hall Pasta Shop   475
Maruya Sushi   318
Molinari   290
Neiman-Marcus Epicure   150
New Hai Ky   438
New Hong Kong Noodle Company   49
North Beach Pizza   290
Oakville Grocery   540
Odessa Deli   382
Palio Paninoteca   **146**, 410, 437
Panelli Brothers   292
Phoenix Pastaficio   475
Piccadilly Fish and Chips   352

Prudente & Company   292
Real Food Company
   173, **176**, 259, 358
Real Food Deli   352
Rosti   197
Saigon Sandwich Cafe   83
Shenson's   383
Specialty's Cafe and Bakery   **150**, 411
Sunrise Deli   438
Tip Toe Inn   383
Ultra Lucca   476, **515**
Vik's King of Chat   476
Vivande Porta Via   319
World Wrapps   197
Yank Sing   151
Yung Kee   477

ETHNIC MARKETS

Bangkok Grocery   387
Bombay Bazaar   234
Casa Lucas Market   235, **237**
G. B. Ratto and Company   481
Greek American Food Imports   235
Haig's Delicacies   387
Irving Seafood Market   446
La Luna Market   543

La Palma Mexicatessen   **227**, 236
Maruwa Foods Company   324
May Wah   444
May Wah Shopping Center   52
Metro   52
Milan International   481
New Chiu Fong Company   85
New May Wah Supermarket   388

New Saigon Supermarket   482
Oakland Market   483
Sam Yick   483
Samiramis Imports   236
Super Koyama   325
Twenty-Second and
   Irving Market   445
Uoki Market   326

FISH

Antonelli's Meat, Fish and
   Poultry in the Cal-Mart   326
Berkeley Bowl Fish Market   484
Bryan's Quality Meats   327
California Sunshine   418
Dragon Market   58
Irving Seafood Market   446

Maruwa Foods Company   324
Mission Market Fish and Poultry   240
Monterey Fish   490
Moura's Fish Market   491
New Basement Seafood Market   492
New Lee Sang Fish Market   59
Rockridge Fish Market   492

San Francisco Hong Kong Market   60
Seafood Center   390
Super Koyama   325
Swan Oyster Depot   361
Uoki Market   326
Yum Yum   447

ICE CREAM/CHOCOLATES

Candy Jar   152
Double Rainbow   **355**, 441
Downtown Bakery and Creamery   541
Gelato Classico   173, **295**, 386
Joe's Ice Cream   386
Joseph Schmidt Confections   255
Latin Freeze   232

Lyla's Chocolates   517
Mitchell's Ice Cream   233
Morrow's Nut House   152
Nuts About You   84
Pasticceria Rulli   512
Pure T   356
See's Candies   112, 153, 357, **386**, 441

St. Francis Fountain and
   Candy Store   233
Swenson's   357
Teuscher Chocolates
   of Switzerland   152
Yogurt Park   480

MARKETS

Andronico's   442
Ashbury Market   174
Big John's Food Center   546
Cal-Mart   322
Falletti's Finer Foods   175
Grand Central Market   324

Keller's Market   547
Marina Super   201
The Nature Stop   296
Palisades Market   544
Plaza Foods   175
Rainbow Grocery   415

Real Food Company
   173, **176**, 259, 358
Rossi Market   296
Tower Market   256
Trader Joe's   416
Whole Foods   359

MEAT AND POULTRY

Alan's Meats   486
Antonelli's Meat, Fish and
   Poultry in the Cal-Mart   326
Big John's Food Center   54
Bryan's Quality Meats   327
Enrico's   178
Enzo   488
Grand Central Market   324
Keller's Market   547
Kwong Jow Sausage Company   55
La Gallinita   239

Little City   297
The Lucky Pork Store   240
Magnani's Poultry   488
Man Sung   55
Ming Kee Game Birds   56
Mission Market Fish and Poultry   240
Mission Market
   Meat Department   240
New Hop Yick Meat   57
New On Sang and
   San Francisco Chicken   390

Polarica   241
Quilici's Meats in the Polk &
   Vallejo Market   360
Real Food Company
   173, **176**, 259, 358
T & S Market   488
Taylor's Sausages   489
United Fish and Poultry   178
Ver Brugge Meats   489
Viglizzo's Meats   256

PRODUCE

Alemany Farmers' Market   236
Barrasa Market   237
Berkeley Bowl   484
Berkeley Farmers' Market   484
Casa Lucas Market   237
Civic Center Farmers' Market   86
Clement Produce   388
David's Produce/David's Taqueria   51/
Ferry Plaza Farmers' Market   112
Harvest Ranch Market   258

Healdsburg Farmers' Market   544
Kum Luen   54
La Hacienda Market   238
Marin County Farmers' Market   518
Market Hall Produce   485
Mikeytom Market   258
Monterey Foods   485
New Chiu Fong Company   85
Old Oakland Farmers' Market   486
Palisades Market   544

Rainbow Grocery   415
Real Food Company
   173, **176**, 259, 358
St. Helena Farmers' Market   546
Sun Tong Lee Inc.   54
Sunny Food Mart   54
Twenty-Second and
   Irving Market   115
23rd and Mission Produce   239
Village Market   389

WINES AND SPIRITS

All Seasons Cafe and Wine Store 548
California Wine Merchant 202
Caruso's 260
Castro Village Wine Company 261
Coit Liquors 297
The Jug Shop 362
J.V. Warehouse 549
K & L Wines 419
Kermit Lynch Wines 495
London Wine Bar 154
Marin Wine Cellar 521
Mill Valley Market 522
Mr. Liquor 447
North Berkeley Wine Company 497
Oakville Grocery 540, 548
Odd Lots 497
Paul Marcus Wines 498
St. Helena Wine Center 549
St. Helena Wine Merchants 552
Tip Top 552
Vino 498
Wine House Limited 419
Wine Impression 330

RECIPES

Avocado Quesadillas 238
Braised Amaranth 53
Braised Leeks 509
Buttermilk Bread 353
Chicken-Vegetable Burger 403
Chocolate Sauce 321
Crab, Endive, and Radicchio Slaw 68
Escalivada 213
Filo-wrapped Apple Tart 440
Fresh Peas with Shallots 177
Green Onion Corn Cakes with Smoked Salmon and Lemon Dill Sour Cream 529
Insalata Rustica L'Osteria 277
Jardinière 114
Milk Chocolate Pecan Clusters 417
Niloufer's Turkey Kabobs 443
Pecan Tartlets 257
Quail Stuffed with Pancetta and Sage Leaves 116
Raised Waffles 158
Red Beans and Rice 487
Red Braised Whole Pork Shoulder 57
Scones with Dried Sour Cherries 71
Spaghettini with Pecorino Cheese 315
Stephano's Braised Rabbit, Italian Style 291
Upside-down Apricot or Plum Tart 545
Warm Berry Compote 323
Watermelon and Pineapple-Ginger Aguas Frescas 188
Whole Salt-Roasted Fish 59

SIDEBARS

A Coffee Tasting 200
A Small Japantown Detour 313
A Strategy for Visiting Fisherman's Wharf 106
Eating in Oakland's Chinatown 482
Eating on Pier 39 108
Foie Gras in Sonoma 547
Fresh Peas 176
Shopping in Chinatown 50
Specialty Restaurants in Japantown That Do a Good Job on a Single Type of Dish 312
Taking Advantage of the Bay 105
Tamales in the Mission, with a Mural Detour 228
Visiting Wineries 550

Alphabetical Index

A Clean Well-Lighted
  Place for Books **87**, 523
ABC Bakery Cafe 49
Acme Bakery 477
Acquerello 339
Ahern's 354
Ajanta 457
Akasaka 312
Alain Rondelli 367
Alan's Meats 486
Alemany Farmers' Market 236
Alfred Schilling 83
Alfred's Steak House 123
Alioto's 106
All Seasons Cafe and
  Wine Shop 525, **548**
Alta Plaza 305
Andronico's 442
Angkor Borei 209
Anjou 124
Antica Trattoria 340
Antonelli's Meat, Fish and Poultry
  in the Cal-Mart 326
Aqua 124
Arabi 110
Armani Cafe 126
Ashbury Market 174
Auberge du Soleil 539
Ba Le 82
Babette's 525
Bacco 247
Bagel King 92, **111**

The Bagelry 354
Bakers of Paris **253**, 439
Balboa Cafe 194
Bangkok Grocery 387
Barrasa Market 237
Bay Wolf 458
Beach Chalet 425
Bean There 169
Berkeley Bowl 484
Berkeley Farmers' Market 484
Betelnut 185
Big John's Food Center 546
Biordi 298
Bistro Aix 186
Bistro Alsacienne 501
Bistro Don Giovanni 527
Bistro Ralph 527
Bix 147
Bizou 397
Black Oak Books 499
Blondie's Pizza **149**, 473
Bob's Donuts 355
Bombay Bazaar 234
Bombay Cuisine 459
Book Passage 523
Books, Inc. 330
Boudin Sourdough
  Bakery and Cafe 111
Boulevard 93
Brain Wash Cafe 409
Bread Workshop 478
Brennan's Restaurant 459

Bridges 460
Brother-in-Law's BBQ 172
Brown Street Grill 528
Bruno's 210
Bryan's Quality Meats 327
Bubba's 502
Bugatti's Espresso Caffe 194
Burger Joint 211
Burma's House 127
Bus Stop 195
Cafe 817 470
Cafe at Chez Panisse 461
Cafe at Oliveto 470
Café Claude 127
Café de la Presse 146
Cafe de Young 435
Cafe Fanny 471
Cafe Flore 251
Cafe Istanbul 225
Cafe Jacqueline 267
Cafe Kati 306
Cafe Marimba 187
Cafe Rouge 462
Caffè Centro 409
Caffè Freddy's 283
Caffè Greco 284
Caffè Roma Coffee
  Roasting Company **285**, 410
Caffè Strada 472
Caffè Trieste 285
Caffè Trinity 80
Cal-Mart 322

California Street Creamery 329
California Sunshine 418
California Wine Merchant 202
Campton Place 128
Candy Jar 152
Cantinetta at Tra Vigne 540
Caribbean Zone 411
Carta 67
Caruso's 260
Casa Lucas Market 235, **237**
Casa Nuestra 550
Casa Orinda 463
Castro Village Wine Company 261
Catahoula Restaurant and Saloon 528
Cha Cha Cha 163
Charles—Nob Hill 341
Cheese Board 492
The Cheese Shop 519
Chez Panisse 464
Cho-Cho 268
Chong Imports 60
Citron 465
City Discount 362
Civic Center Farmers' Market 86
Clean Well Lighted
  Place for Books, A **87**, 523
Clement Produce 388
Cliff's Hardware 261
Cody's 499
Coit Liquors 297
Columbus Cutlery 299
Cookin' 180
Cordon Bleu 342
Cost Plus Imports 115
Country Cheese 179
Crate and Barrel 154
Cypress Club 129
Dalva 226
Danilo 293
David's Produce/David's Taqueria 517
DeLuxe 170
Dol Ho 35
Domaine Chandon 530

Double Rainbow **355**, 441
Doug's Bar-B-Q 473
Downtown Bakery and Creamery 541
Dragon House 368
Dragon Market 58
E'Angelo 189
Eagle Cafe 94
Eastern Bakery 51
Easy Money Discount Outlet 449
Ecco, Ristorante 405
Echo 261
Economy Restaurant Supply 420
El Balazito 211
Elbo Room 226
Eleven 412
Ella's 307
Enrico's 178
Enrico's Sidewalk Cafe 268
Enzo 488
Eos 164
Esperpento 212
Falletti's Finer Foods 175
Ferry Plaza Farmers' Market 112
Figoni Hardware 299
Fillamento 331
Fina Estampa 213
Firefly 248
Fleur de Lys 130
Florence Italian Deli and
  Ravioli Factory 289
Fly Trap 398
Flying Goat Cafe 539
The Flying Saucer 214
The Fog City Diner 95
Forrest Jones 331
Fountain Court 369
42 Degrees 399
Frantoio 503
Fredericksen's Hardware 202
Freed, Teller & Freed 357
French Laundry 530
Fringale 400
G. B. Ratto and Company 481

Ganges Vegetarian Restaurant 165
The Gardener 499
Gastronom 382
Gaylord of India 96
Gelato Classico 173, **295**, 386
The General's Daughter 532
Ginn Wall 61
Gino and Carlo's 287
Gold Mountain 36
Golden Boy 289
Golden Turtle 342
Gordon Biersch
  Brewing Company 109
Grand Central Market 324
Greek American Food Imports 235
Green Apple Books 391
Greens 190
Greystone Restaurant 532
Guaymas 514
Haig's Delicacies 387
Hama-Ko 166
Hamburger Mary's 412
"Hamburgers" 515
Hana 426
Happy Valley 97
Harbor Village 98
Harris' 343
Harry Denton's 109
Harry Denton's Starlight Room 148
Harvest Ranch Market 258
Hawthorne Lane 401
Hayes Street Grill 69
Healdsburg Farmers' Market 544
Helmand 270
Hess Collection 550
Hing Lung 37
Homechef **331**, 524
Hong Kong East Ocean 466
Hong Kong Flower Lounge 369
Hong Kong Villa 370
Hop Kiln 550
Hornblower Yachts 105
House 271, 427

House of Bagels   384
House of Nanking   38
House of Prime Rib   344
House of Shields   412
Hungarian Sausage Factory   227
Ideale, Ristorante   278
Il Fornaio   99
Il Pollaio   271
Imperial Palace   40
Imperial Tea Court   47
Infusion   413
Insalata's   504
Iroha   312
Irving Seafood Market   446
Isobune   312
Isuzu   308
J & J   41
J.V. Warehouse   549
J. Wiggins Cheese   494
Jack's   317
Jackson Fillmore   308
Jade Villa   482
Jakarta   371
Jammin' Java Coffee House   436
Janmae Guey   48
Java Beach Cafe   437
Jeong Hyun Charcoal
   Barbecue House   427
Joe's Ice Cream   386
Johnny Love's   351
Joseph Schmidt Confections   255
The Jug Shop   362
Julie's Supper Club   413
Julius' Castle   272
Just Desserts   175, **198**
Just Like Home   437
Just Won Ton   429
K & L Wines   419
Kabuto   372
Kamei Household Wares   392
Kasbah   505
Katia, A Russian Tea Room   373
Katrina Rozelle   479

Keller's Market   547
Kermit Lynch Wines   495
Kezar Bar & Restaurant   171
Kimball's East   472
Kinokuniya Bookstore   332
Kitchen Friend   449
Kui Shin Bo   312
Kum Luen   54
Kwong Jow Sausage Company   55
Kyo-ya at the Sheraton
   Palace Hotel   402
Kyung Bok Palace   374
La Farine   479
La Felce   272
La Folie   344
La Gallinita   239
Laghi   374
La Hacienda Market   238
La Luna Market   543
La Movida   216
La Nouvelle Pâtisserie   199
La Palma Mexicatessen   **227**, 236
La Reyna Bakery and Coffee Shop   231
Lark Creek Inn   506
La Santaneca   216
La Taqueria   217
Latin Freeze   232
Le Central   131
Le Chantilly   319
Left Bank   508
Lehr's German Specialties   262
Leonard's 2001   316
Li-Po   48
Liberty Cafe   218
Lichee Garden   42
Liguria   294
Little City   297
Little Joe's   273
Lo Coco's   274
London Wine Bar   154
Los Jarritos   218
l'Osteria del Forno   275
Lucca   196

Lucca Ravioli Company   299
The Lucky Pork Store   240
LuLu   404
Lyla's Chocolates   517
MacArthur Park   131
Macy's Cellar   149, 155
Made To Order   474
Madrona Manor   533
Magnani's Poultry   488
Maki   309
Man Sung   55
Marcello, Ristorante   430
Marin County Farmers' Market   518
Marin Wine Cellar   521
Marina Central   191
Marina Super   201
Mario's Bohemian Cigar Store   285
Market Hall Pasta Shop   475
Market Hall Produce   485
Martin's John and Zeke's   539
Maruwa Foods Company   324
Maruya Sushi   318
Masa's   132
Mashiko Folkcraft   333
May Wah   444
May Wah Shopping Center   52
Mayflower   375
Mecca   249
Mee Heong Pastry Company   51
Mee Mee Bakery   52
The Meetinghouse   310
Metro   52
Mifune   311
Mikeytom Market   258
Milan International   481
Mill Valley Market   522
Millennium   70
Ming Kee Game Birds   56
Mission Market Fish and Poultry   240
Mission Market
   Meat Department   240
Mitchell's Ice Cream   233
Mo's   278

Molinari   290
Mom Is Cooking   219
Momi Toby's Revolution Cafe   80
Monterey Fish   490
Monterey Foods   485
Moose's   276
Morrow's Nut House   152
Moscow and Tbilisi Bakery   384
Moura's Fish Market   491
Moxie Bar and Restaurant   405
Mr. Liquor   447
Mustards   533
Nan Yang   482
Napa Valley Wine Train   534
The Nature Stop   296
Neiman-Marcus Epicure   150
New Basement Seafood Market   492
New Chiu Fong Company   85
New Hai Ky   438
New Hong Kong Noodle Company   49
New Hop Yick Meat   57
New Lee Sang Fish Market   59
New May Wah Supermarket   388
New On Sang and
   San Francisco Chicken   390
New Orleans Room
   in the Fairmont Hotel   351
New Saigon Supermarket   482
Nick's   106
Nob Hill Grille   345
Noc Noc   171
Noe Valley Bakery   253
North Beach Pizza   290
North Berkeley Wine Company   497
Nuts About You   84
O Chamé   466
Oakland Market   483
Oakville Grocery   **540**, 549
Odd Lots   497
Odessa Deli   382
Old Krakow   429
Old Oakland Farmers' Market   486

Oliveto   468
One Market Restaurant   100
One World Cafe   170
Orbit Room Cafe   252
Oriental Pearl   44
Original Joe's   133
Oritalia   312
Osakaya   312
Pacific   134
Pacific Restaurant—
   Thai-Binh-Duong #2   72
Palio d'Asti   135
Palio Paninoteca   **146**, 410, 437
Palisades Market   544
Panaderia La Mexicana   231
Pancho Villa Taqueria   220
Pane e Vino   191
Panelli Brothers   292
The Paragon   195
Pasticceria Rulli   512
Pastis   101
Pat O'Shea's Mad Hatter   381
Pâtisserie Delanghe   320
Paul Marcus Wines   498
Pearl City   45
Peet's Coffee and Tea
   199, 322, 358, 442, 495, 520
Perry's   195
Phoenix Pastaficio   475
Piatti   534
Picante Taqueria   469
Piccadilly Fish and Chips   352
Pier 23 Cafe   110
Pier 40 Roastery   108
Pier Market and
   Seafood Restaurant   108
Pinot Blanc   535
Plaza Foods   171
PlumpJack Cafe   192
Polarica   241
Postrio   136
Pozole   250

Prudente & Company   292
Pure T   356
Quilici's Meats in the Polk
   & Vallejo Market   360
R & G Lounge   15
Radio Valencia   226
Rainbow Grocery   415
The Ramp   413
Ravenous   535
Real Food Company
   173, **176**, 259, 358
Real Food Deli   352
Red Room   148
RH   333
Rice Table   510
Richard Hilkert, Bookseller   88
Ristorante Ecco   405
Ristorante Ideale   278
Ristorante Marcello   430
Ritz-Carlton Dining Room   345
River Side Seafood Restaurant   431
Robert Mondavi Winery   550
Rochioli   550
Rockridge Fish Market   492
Rose Pistola   279
Rosmarino   314
Rossi Market   296
Rosti   197
Rotunda at Neiman-Marcus   136
Rubicon   137
Rumpus   139
Sabella & La Torre   106
Saigon Sandwich Cafe   83
The Saloon   287
Sam and Henry's Cool Beans   380
Sam Yick   483
Sam's   514
Sam's Grill   139
Samiramis Imports   236
San Francisco Art Institute Cafe   280
San Francisco Hong Kong Market   60
San Francisco Spirit   105

San Tung & San Tung #2   432
Sanko Cooking Supply   334
Sanppo   314
Sanraku Four Seasons   140
Sapporo-Ya   312
Savoy Tivoli   287
Say Cheese   179
Scala's Bistro   141
Schubert's   385
Sciambra French Bakery   542
Seafood Center   390
Sears Fine Foods   142
See's Candies   112, 153, 357, **386**, 441
Semifreddi's   480
Shaharazad Bakery and
   Filo Specialists   439
Shenson's   383
Sixth Avenue Cheese Shop   391
Slanted Door   221
Soko Hardware   334
Sol y Luna Restaurante   142
South Park Cafe   406
Specs'   287
Specialty's Cafe and Bakery   **150**, 411
Spinelli Coffee Company
   173, 256, 322, 358, 442, 520
Splendido   102
Spuntino   81
St. Francis Fountain
   and Candy Store   233
St. Helena Farmers' Market   546
St. Helena Wine Center   549
St. Helena Wine Merchants   552
Stars   74
Stella   294
Stoyanof   432
Straits Cafe   376
Sue Fisher-King   334
Sun Tong Lee Inc.   54
Sunny Food Mart   54
Sunrise Deli   438
Sunset Bookstore   450

Super Koyama   325
Suppenküche   75
Sur La Table   **156**, 500
Swan Oyster Depot   347, **361**
Sweet Inspiration   254
Swenson's   357
T & S Market   488
Tadich Grill   143
Tai Chi   347
Tai Yick Trading Company   61
Taiwan   377
Tan Tan   316
Taqueria El Balazo   167
Taylor's Sausages   489
Terra   536
Teuscher Chocolates
   of Switzerland   153
Thep Phanom   167
Thirsty Bear   407
Ti Couz Crêperie   222
Timo's   222
Tip Toe Inn   383
Tip Top   552
Tokyo Sukiyaki   103
Tomatina   537
Tommaso's   281
Ton Kiang   378
Ton Kiang Cafe   379
Toronado   172
Tosca   288
Tower Market   256
Tra Vigne   537
Trader Joe's   416
Twenty Tank Brewery   414
24th Street Cheese Company   259
Twenty-Second and
   Irving Market   445
23rd and Mission Produce   239
Ultra Lucca   476, **515**
United Fish and Poultry   178
Universal Cafe   407
Uoki Market   326

Up and Down Club   414
Val 21   223
Vanessi's   348
Vella Cheese Company   548
Venticello   349
Ver Brugge Meats   489
Vertigo   144
Vesuvio   288
Vi's Vietnamese Cuisine   482
Vicolo Pizzeria   76
Victoria   295
Vien Huong   482
Viglizzo's Meats (*See* Tower Market)
Vik's King of Chat   476
Village Market   389
Vino   498
Vivande Porte Via   319
Vivande Ristorante   77
Wappo Bar Bistro   538
Whole Foods   359
Williams-Sonoma
   117, **157**, 203, 450, 524
Win's   433
Wine House Limited   419
Wine Impression   330
Woodward's Garden   224
World Wrapps   197
Wu Kong   107
Ya, Halla from Nadia   168
Yamada Seika   321
Yank Sing   145, 151
YaYa Cuisine   434
Yogurt Park   480
Yum Yum   447
Yung Kee   477
Zarzuela   350
Zax   282
Zinzino   193
Zuni Cafe   78

INDEXES   **573**

UNTERMAN on FOOD

KEEP YOUR *FOOD LOVER'S GUIDE* **UP-TO-THE-MINUTE!**

A newsletter of contemporary eating in and around San Francisco, from restaurant critic and food writer Patricia Unterman

Reviews of new restaurants, old favorites, what to look forward to in the markets, recipes, and food travel

"Lively, comprehensive, indispensable for people who love good food."
—Alice Waters, owner, Chez Panisse

"I trust Unterman's palate. She loves the authentic…"
—Paula Wolfert, cookbook author

ES, send me a year of Unterman on Food *(six issues) and bill me $28.*

Name

Address

City   State   Zip

Mail to: PATRICIA UNTERMAN
320 Hayes Street
San Francisco, CA 94102